The Moral Commonwealth

The Moral Commonwealth

*Social Theory
and the Promise
of Community*

Philip Selznick

UNIVERSITY OF CALIFORNIA PRESS
Berkeley • *Los Angeles* • *London*

University of California Press
Berkeley and Los Angeles, California

University of California Press, Ltd.
London, England

© 1992 by
The Regents of the University of California

First Paperback Printing 1994

Library of Congress Cataloging-in-Publication Data

Selznick, Philip, 1919–
    The moral commonwealth : social theory and the promise of
community / Philip Selznick.
        p.   cm.
    "A Centennial book"—P.
    Includes bibliographical references and index.
    ISBN 0-520-08934-0
    1. Social ethics.   2. Ethics, Modern.   3. Community.   4. Community
life—Moral and ethical aspects.   5. Social institutions.
    I. Title.
HM216.S39   1992
170—dc20   91–47082
                                                             CIP

Printed in United States of America

9 8 7 6 5 4 3 2

Contents

Preface

In my late teens and early twenties I went through an intense, fruitful, and in some ways extraordinary experience. Like a number of my contemporaries who later became writers and scholars, I belonged for a time (1937-1940) to a Trotskyist youth organization. In those days the Trotskyists stood for militant anti-Stalinism as well as for revolutionary socialism. Beleaguered and despised in many quarters, the movement was nevertheless attractive to left-leaning intellectuals who were repelled by the tyranny and terror of the Soviet Union, the subservience and mendacity of American communists, and what they thought of as confusion and impotence among socialists and liberals.

At that time I was also an eager student of sociology and philosophy. The two parts of my life did not fit very well. I was soon aware that I could not accept the dialectical materialism of Marx and Engels. I could not be a Marxist and also respond as warmly as I did, during those same years, to the scientific humanism of Morris R. Cohen and, a bit later, to the pragmatism of John Dewey. For a time, like some of my elders, notably James Burnham, I suppressed the dissonance on the ground that practical aims were more important than philosophical differences. This attitude did not hold up for long. By 1940, shortly after a major controversy and split in the Trotskyist movement, I was pressing the larger issue. I even engaged in a formal debate in favor of the proposition "that Marxism should no longer be taught as the official doctrine" of the new political group. As that debate made clear, our

differences were irreconcilable, and I represented a tiny minority. Together with some others, I soon left the organization. We were convinced
that Stalinism was no aberration. Rather, the Leninist doctrine so faithfully preserved by Trotsky, and still adhered to by those who had recently rejected his leadership, was fully responsible for the dreadful outcome of the first Russian Revolution. We were, of course, only learning
for ourselves what had long been understood by others.

When I rejected Marxism/Leninism, and a few years later socialism
as well, I did not suppose I was abandoning the faith that reason, love,
and justice can be vital and transforming ingredients of human society.
This meant, for me, that the cause of American liberalism, with its recognition of the community's responsibility to secure justice for all its
members, is worthy of allegiance. Despite many shortcomings, liberalism is an alternative that can embrace moral, political, and economic realism without yielding to complacency. I therefore could not follow
those of my friends who became leading neoconservatives in the 1960s.
Indeed one of my (less important) reasons for writing this book was a
wish to respond to the neoconservative challenge. Many of its spokesmen shared my early experience, and we seemed to agree on many aspects of social and political theory. In my frequent conversations with
Martin Diamond, in the years before his early death, I was struck by the
extent of our agreement on such matters as the nature of human nature,
the relation between fact and value, and the limits of egalitarianism. Yet
we came to very different conclusions regarding issues of the day. Too
much had been left unsaid.

I recite this brief memoir because my youthful encounter with revolutionary socialism established a theme that influenced my work over
many years. I have in mind the fate of ideals in the course of social practice. Most of my specialized writings in the sociology of organizations
and sociology of law have been preoccupied with the conditions and
processes that frustrate ideals or, instead, give them life and hope. In my
study of a government agency, *TVA and the Grass Roots,* I traced the
conditions that produced a major flaw in its character and led to widespread dissatisfaction with what many people had hoped would be a
first-line conservation agency. *Leadership in Administration* was my attempt to show the relevance of character and integrity to the effective
functioning of large organizations. And *Law, Society, and Industrial Justice* sought to find, within the internal dynamics of industrial organization, conditions that encourage the rule of law. During the 1960s and
1970s, as I reflected on these and related efforts and as I deepened my in-

volvement with jurisprudence and moral philosophy, I began to formulate a more comprehensive perspective. This book is the outcome of those reflections.

Four main themes emerge:

Morality and community. I have found myself in sympathy with the communitarian turn in contemporary moral, social, and political theory. The philosophical writings of Alasdair MacIntyre, Charles Taylor, and Michael Sandel, among others, have renewed debate over the premises of liberalism, including the left or welfare liberalism of John Rawls and Ronald Dworkin. Liberal premises are thought to be overly individualistic and ahistorical; insufficiently sensitive to the social sources of selfhood and obligation; too much concerned with rights, too little concerned with duty and responsibility. These criticisms have brought the idea of community—a core idea in sociology—to center stage. In this book I have tried to show that a proper understanding of community, from a sociological point of view, presumes diversity and pluralism as well as social integration. The findings of sociology certainly emphasize human interdependence and the need for solidarity; they recall us to the specifics of culture and history. But those findings also bring home the compelling realities of personal and group autonomy; the heavy costs paid when autonomy is lost; and the emergence of broader perspectives within which a balance can be struck between the claims of piety and those of civility. The promise of community is, I suggest, a promise of justice and democracy—communitarian justice and communal democracy. The upshot is a point of view we may call "communitarian liberalism."

Subjectivism and relativism. A robust community, however pluralistic, must embrace the idea of a common good. Otherwise, it is incapable of justifying its moral choices, whether in educating children, supporting the arts, or protecting the public interest from private indifference and greed. Yet the idea of a common good, understood as based on objective criteria of personal and social well-being, runs up against the pervasive idea that moral judgment is inescapably subjective and relative; that beliefs about right and wrong are clues to personal history and upbringing but have no claim to being truths that should be accepted by all who are open to logic and evidence. This perspective reflects the corrosive, fragmenting experience of modernity—an experience that reveals the fragility of all structures, intellectual as well as social. I have therefore reviewed and criticized some of the main currents of thought that have produced modern subjectivism and relativism.

American pragmatism. This book may be read in part as a contribution to the revival of John Dewey's pragmatism. Signs are visible today of a rekindled appreciation for what was once considered a crowning achievement of American thought. Dewey was a great spokesman for communitarian liberalism. He combined a spirit of liberation and social reconstruction with a strong commitment to responsible participation in effective communities. On his view, communities are effective insofar as they encourage uncoerced communication and insofar as they can apply intelligence and experimentation to problems of collective life. For Dewey, morality itself is necessarily a communitarian idea, demanded by the requirements of social practice, transcending individuals, yet holding fast to ideals of personal growth and self-realization. Dewey's vision resonates with, and makes sense of, modern and postmodern sensibilities. Yet it does so without yielding to the nihilistic tendencies of a confused and distracted age.

Although references to Dewey abound in this volume, I have not sought to provide a full exegesis of his thought. With the exception of Chapter 1, and a few other passages such as the discussion of means and ends in Chapter 12, I have offered my own interpretations of moral experience. My analysis is deeply influenced by pragmatist premises and may perhaps be judged in the light of those premises. But Dewey would not have agreed with all of my conclusions; and other pragmatists may have their own differences. This is as it should be. Pragmatism is not a tight system, in which ideas are driven by an iron logic to inexorable conclusions. Such a claim would be foreign to its nature, which welcomes plurality and resists finality.

Moral and social theory. Although this work reflects my experience as a sociologist, I take an ecumenical view of that discipline. It makes little sense to restrict "sociology" to the work of people who are called sociologists. There is no fundamental difference between sociology and social or cultural anthropology or, in most respects, social psychology. A great deal of history and political science, especially in recent generations, is informed by sociological understanding and contributes substantially to it. In many other fields as well, including jurisprudence and moral philosophy, important sociological problems are addressed, frequently with an added measure of sophistication. All belong, in part at least, to the intellectual enterprise we call sociology. Therefore "social theory," as used in the subtitle here, includes political, legal, and moral theory.

Like Emile Durkheim, I believe sociology is preeminently a "moral science." Indeed, the main issues in political science, sociology, economics, anthropology, and social psychology are defined by the values at stake in social experience. Each subdiscipline is governed by implicit notions of personal or institutional well-being, which may take the form of economic rationality, administrative rationality, democratic government, cultural integrity, or effective socialization. Of course, many specific studies—many lines of inquiry—are mainly descriptive and explanatory. A study of changing sex ratios in ethnic populations, as affected by migration patterns, may have a bearing on values and policy, but the study itself need make no assessments. The closer we come, however, to what is central in the discipline, the more important is evaluation. For example, theories of socialization—the process by which human animals are transformed into social beings—cannot avoid assessment of psychic and institutional competence, psychic and institutional well-being. They are necessarily sensitive to the values at risk in child rearing, peer-group interaction, and formal schooling. Without appreciation of those values, the study of socialization is radically impoverished.

Hence the distinctive feature of a moral or humanist science is its commitment to normative theory, that is, to theories that evaluate as well as explain. In political science, constitutional theory is normative or evaluative, in that it speaks to the difference between superior and inferior constitutional systems, which may be strong or weak as ways of achieving the rule of law. Normative theory is value-centered. It identifies values, including latent or emergent values, and studies the conditions affecting their fulfillment or frustration. The values we study do not necessarily express our personal preferences. They are not selected for study because the sociologist or other analyst happens to be interested in them. Rather, we consider what is genuinely valuable—and affects the fate of values—in the social worlds we study, including our own, whether or not it conforms to our preferences.

At its best, normative theory is a fruitful union of philosophy and social science. On the one hand, philosophical acumen is necessary for understanding the complexity and subtlety of basic values and of value-related phenomena, such as autonomy, fairness, rationality, love, and law. Without sophisticated study of these interdependent variables—including how they have been understood in the history of thought—it is all too easy for values to be trivialized or shortchanged. On the other hand, philosophy alone, uninformed by social science, loses touch with empirical contingency and variation and with the insight to be gained from close study of actual experience. These dangers have been well understood by many writers, from Aristotle to Dewey. But a durable union of philosophy and social science is hard to sustain. I have tried, in my own way, to help save the marriage.

▼   ▲   ▼   ▲   ▼

The themes noted above appear as texts and subtexts throughout the book. Part One, "Morality and Modernity," deals directly with subjectivism, relativism, and the modern temper. After an introductory chapter on modernism and naturalistic ethics, I review three intellectual sources of moral disarray. My strategy contrasts modes of thought that are sound and beneficial with the less attractive correlates to which they give rise: reason and rationalism; authenticity and subjectivism; plurality and relativism. These chapters respect what is valuable in the Enlightenment project, and in its Romantic aftermath as well. At the same time, the enervating doctrines they encouraged, largely unwittingly, are examined and rejected.

Parts Two, Three, and Four continue the defense of objectivity in moral discourse, but the discussion becomes more substantive. I have made fairly extensive use of legal materials, especially in Parts Three and Four. In addition to discussion of particular cases, I have brought to bear some strands of thought in contemporary jurisprudence.

Three closely connected levels of moral experience are studied: persons, institutions, and communities. As we move toward Part Four the focus on community sharpens. Moral persons and institutions are "implicated selves" whose virtues depend on special forms of communal participation. A number of themes—particularity, integrity, the expansion of responsibility—connect the moral experience of persons and institutions with that of the community as a whole. The theory of institutions, as developed in Part Three, gives special attention to the strain toward community *within* special-purpose organizations. Part Four is a comprehensive discussion of the foundations of community, of its major antinomies—and of its promise.

Philip Selznick
January 1992

Acknowledgments

This book owes much to the collaboration of Kenneth I. Winston. From its earliest stages we had regular discussion of ideas as they developed, and he wrote extensive comments on every chapter. His philosophical learning and unflagging commitment to "getting it right" were invaluable. I am deeply grateful for his extraordinary help and warm friendship.

Charles H. Page, Leo Lowenthal, and Doris R. Fine were also dedicated readers of the whole manuscript. Parts were also read by Robert K. Merton, Sheldon L. Messinger, Robert C. Post, and Michael E. Smith. I thank them and also my other colleagues at Berkeley's School of Law (Boalt Hall), especially John E. Coons, Melvin A. Eisenberg, Sanford H. Kadish, Robert A. Kagan, David Lieberman, Philippe Nonet, Jerome H. Skolnick, and Jeremy Waldron.

I take this opportunity to extend thanks and greetings to Leonard Broom, with whom I worked for many years on a project that has had, I believe, a salutary effect on these pages; to Robert Bellah, Winfried Brugger, Jules L. Coleman, Jameson W. Doig, Edwin M. Epstein, Herbert Garfinkel, Joseph Grodin, Martin Krygier, Charles McCoy, Katherine Newman, Antonie A. G. Peters, Joseph Rees, Kahei Rokumoto, Robert E. Rosen, Paul van Seters, Gunther Teubner, and Ann Swidler; and to the John Simon Guggenheim Memorial Foundation.

The argument of this book was sketched in a valedictory lecture sponsored by the Department of Sociology at Berkeley in 1986. I benefited from discussions with colleagues and students at that time in

Berkeley as well as at the Hutchins Center for the Study of Democratic Institutions at Santa Barbara; and later at Yale University, Virginia Polytechnic Institute at Blacksburg, the University of Utrecht, the University of Tokyo, and the European University Institute at Florence.

I treasure the memory of Gertrude Jaeger, whose ideas are a living presence in this volume; and of my sister, May Brodbeck, who gave me welcome encouragement when the project began. My daughter, Delila (Margaret Jaeger) Ledwith, gladdened my heart by her response to what I was writing.

I wish to thank my publisher, James H. Clark, for a long period of patience and support; also Erika Büky, Eileen McWilliam, and Jane-Ellen Long, the last especially for her eagle eye and grammatical ardor; and Rod Watanabe for his gracious and unstinting help with many administrative chores.

Doris R. Fine shared these years of intellectual exploration. She gallantly accepted my preoccupation and the priorities it imposed. I am grateful for many hours of fruitful conversation, for much help in preparing the manuscript for publication, and for her sustaining love.

P. S.

PART ONE

Morality and Modernity

ONE

Nature, Ethics, and the Modern Mind

We are often told, and may readily agree, that modern society has produced many sources of moral disarray. These include the cult of the individual; the ascendance of the market; the temptations of technology; dependence on the welfare state; the decline of kinship; the erosion of parental, educational, and religious authority; and new forms of virulent ideology. Furthermore, in many quarters, our most sacred beliefs are thought to be inescapably contingent, relative, and subjective—without defensible foundations. A pervasive want of confidence in the possibility of moral truth limits our ability to seek the good and embrace the right. This spiritual affliction begins in a modest way, among intellectuals. The power of ideas is substantial, however, and in time major institutions and the population at large become uncertain, confused, and vulnerable.

These claims are frequently exaggerated. They often fail to take account of major advances in moral sensibility. Indeed, few, on sober reflection, would deny the moral achievements of modern civilization. Extremists aside, critics of modernity often take for granted—and forget to mention—the many contemporary institutions and beliefs that have great moral worth and are clearly preferable to those they replaced. Most would not give up the rule of law, democratic government, equality of opportunity, the rights of women, and any of a long list of other modern ideals. An ethic of impersonal judgment, for example, undercuts privilege, makes possible opportunity based on merit, and sustains equality before the law. At the same time, such an ethic robs the world of person-centered meaning and thereby breeds disenchantment and alienation. One may recognize the special virtues of modernity and yet believe that thereby the foundations of moral judgment and community are threatened, if not eroded.

Criticism of modernity need not look backward to a mythic past, need not ignore the miseries and brutalities that so often characterized earlier ages. Contemporary anxieties arise in part from raised expectations and from vulnerabilities born of success. Modern life offers a welcome if risky challenge to the moral order. As self-determination is enlarged, as awareness is sharpened, the complexity of moral choice increases. The responsibility of individuals and groups becomes in many ways more self-conscious and more demanding. More is asked of us, and we ask more of ourselves. The peril, therefore, need not be understood as a sign of pervasive decay. It may also be understood as a price paid for certain kinds of moral development. In what follows I take that latter understanding as a guide to diagnosis and assessment.

MODERNITY AND MODERNISMS

"Modernity" is not a synonym for the "contemporary" or "present-day." If that were so the idea would be trivial: any historical period would be "modern" in its day. In social analysis, "modernity" refers to the special features of the technologically advanced industrial, commercial, urban society that has taken shape in the West since the eighteenth century, anticipated, of course, by earlier trends and ideas. The most important element is the steady weakening of traditional social bonds and the concomitant creation of new unities based on more rational, more impersonal, more fragmented forms of thought and action.

This transformation has occurred in four main ways, which are well known and need only be mentioned here:

Separation of spheres. Activities, groups, institutions, and roles that once were unified or fused have become disentangled and specialized. Modernization is to a very large extent a process of "structural differentiation." Examples are the separation of production and consumption, household and work, church and state, religion and community, ownership and management, education and parenting, law and morality, private and public life.

Secularization. With the separation of spheres, religion loses its hold on practical affairs. Politics and economics are taken to be self-justifying, in no need of guidance from any source other than human purpose and utility. There is a waning of sacredness. Matters of faith are viewed as personal and private, not necessarily conditioned by deference to religious authority; holy days become holidays. Most important, there is a quest for secular foundations of morality, especially in the claims of reason. This, it turns out, is a shaky game. It makes the moral order more remote, more abstract, more dependent on the vagaries of the mind. Furthermore, secularization goes beyond the decline of religious participation. It is also manifested in the desiccation, the emptying out, of cultural symbols, which lose their hold on the deepest sources of commitment and belief.

Weakening of social ties. Many weighty terms have been used to describe this process: "individualization," "disaggregation," "atomization." Their main point is that modern life tends to loosen the intimate connections of shared experience and interdependence that characterized so much of premodern society. Localism, kinship, and the extended-family household created relatively isolated and largely self-sufficient communities. Modernization breaks up these unities, notably in the emergence of the detached nuclear family. The trend is toward a more fragmented social life; isolation of individuals replaces the isolation of communities. People participate segmentally, that is, on the basis of special interests and occasions rather than as whole persons, and they do so in groups that are themselves only weakly bound into the rest of society.

Rational coordination. The two modes of organization most characteristic of modern society are contract and bureaucracy. (In later chapters we shall have much to say about both.) Each coordinates activities, not persons. Each breeds fragmented experience even as it creates new forms of obligation and control. In the perspective of contract, voluntary agreement among rational and responsible individuals is the foundation of social order and the building block of larger structures. The social group is a composite of segmental ties and relationships; the person becomes an abstract individual. This perspective is carried over into the world of large-scale organization. It is an irony of modern history that the principle of contract, which celebrated freedom and did much to erode primordial ties of status, kinship, and community, has made possible new and in some ways more coercive forms of coordination and control.

These master trends are, of course, uneven and incomplete. They generate resistance and backlash, most notably in the case of secularization. However that may be, it is important to recognize that *each of the transitions can be a tonic to the moral order.* The separation of spheres has been a powerful engine for the release of energies, the achievement of excellence, and the protection of rights. The rule of law, for example, requires an independent judiciary; similar gains come from the autonomy of other institutions and professions. The transition from sacred to secular modes of thought enhances morality in that it tends to reduce narrow-mindedness and bigotry. Nor can the moral benefits of freedom be won without some loosening of social bonds. Rational coordination brings with it the virtues of efficiency and accountability we associate with professional administration of major institutions.

These benefits are purchased at the price of cultural attenuation. The symbolic experiences that create and sustain the organic unities of social life are steadily thinned and diminished. In almost every sphere of life there has been a movement away from densely textured structures of meaning to less concrete, more abstract forms of expression and relatedness. Churches, schools, colleges, neighborhoods, businesses, political parties, baseball teams, occupations, families—all have lost symbolic strength in the modern world. As institutions and roles become more utilitarian, more transitory, more interchangeable, more homogeneous, their symbolic significance weakens. They may contribute to civilization—to technical excellence and an impersonal morality—but not to the mainsprings of culture and identity.

The decay of expressive symbolism, and therefore of culture, is vividly portrayed in George Orwell's vision of Newspeak in *1984*. Orwell showed how language can be brutalizing and destructive of culture:

> The name of every organization, or body of people, or doctrine, or country, or institution, or public building, was invariably cut down into . . . a single easily pronounced word with the smallest number of syllables that would preserve the original derivation. . . . It was perceived that in thus abbreviating a name one narrowly and subtly altered its meaning, by cutting out most of the associations that would otherwise cling to it. The words *Communist International,* for instance, call up a composite picture of universal human brotherhood, red flags, barricades, Karl Marx, and the Paris Commune. The word *Comintern,* on the other hand, suggests merely a tightly knit organization and a well-defined body of doctrine. *Comintern* is a word that can be uttered almost without taking thought, whereas *Communist International* is a phrase over which one is obliged to linger at least momentarily. In the same way, the associations called up by a word like *Minitrue* are fewer and more controllable than those called up by *Ministry of Truth*.[1]

The transformation of connotative language, rich in associations, into narrowly denotative or referential language may be justified on technical

1. George Orwell, *1984* (New York: Harcourt Brace, 1949), 309f.

grounds. It is, however, a well-known breeder of linguistic barbarism. As Orwell suggests, the barbarism can be moral as well as aesthetic.

Culture is vulnerable whenever technology is free to follow its own logic, unrestrained by the human need for activities that are ends as well as means. A dramatic case is the shattering of indigenous cultures in the course of colonial and imperialist expansion. Traditional crafts, around which a large part of their symbolic order was built, could not survive competition with the technology of industrialized nations; and the authority of native institutions was undermined as they lost credibility. In such cases the key to cultural destruction is the loss of motivation that occurs when activities are robbed of symbolic meaning. Loss of motivation brings with it personal disorganization: the psychic inability to take care of oneself, relate to others, keep up a garden, hold a job, resist self-destructive gratifications. This loss explains the high incidence of apathy, alcoholism, and suicide among victims of cultural imperialism.

I mention these extreme situations—Orwell's fantasy; the destruction of indigenous ways of life—because they bring home the reality of cultural attenuation. They show that it can be irreversible and that the stakes are thus very high. The loss of a "genuine," intrinsically harmonious, culture is a loss of spiritual well-being, that is, the integration of personal, moral, communal, and aesthetic experience.[2] In some circumstances the destruction of this person-centered harmony is a threat to life itself.

To be sure, these *are* extreme situations and one should avoid a morbid preoccupation with them. Although the weakening of a received culture always has some human cost, it may be a necessary prelude to the emergence of better ways of life. We should not confound the pains of transition—among immigrants, for example—with a more profound and unredeemed disintegration. We cannot take for granted that cultural attenuation is morally undesirable:

> There may well be an empirical tension, though probably not a fatal one, between enlightened moral orders and the development of culture. To the extent that symbolization of persons and groups occurs, there is cultural enrichment. But symbolization can be demonic and go hand in hand with cruel and

2. "The genuine culture is not necessarily high or low; it is merely inherently harmonious, balanced, self-satisfactory. It is the experience of a richly varied and yet somehow unified and consistent attitude toward life. . . . It is, ideally speaking, a culture in which nothing is spiritually meaningless, in which no important part of the general functioning brings with it a sense of frustration, of misdirected or unsympathetic effort" (Edward Sapir, "Culture: Genuine and Spurious," *American Journal of Sociology* 29 [January 1924]: 402). Edward Sapir (1884–1939), an American anthropologist, was a specialist in Native American culture and a founder of descriptive linguistics.

inhuman moral systems. Moral enlightenment often depends upon the weakening of symbols, upon taking people for what they are and not for their
symbolic status and value. When we look at culture with a fascinated eye, it
is easy to forget that values realized through symbolic systems may inhibit
the realization of other values that depend upon more instrumental, more
rational, more disengaged behavior.[3]

On the other hand, we should not complacently assume that cultural attenuation is merely transitional. Any given setting may contain few resources for resilience and renewal.

The fundamental truth is that modernity weakens culture and frag-
ments experience. The gains of modernity are won, not easily and
smoothly, but at significant cost to the harmony and stability of human
experience. For most of human history, a received culture—embodied in
expressive symbolism, sustained by integrative institutions—has been
the main resource for moral confidence, steadiness, and discrimination.
A genuine culture is not a collection of abstract principles or precepts. It
is a web of person-centered meanings whose coherence makes possible a
world taken for granted, whose directives trump desire and chasten inclination. To say with Nietzsche that God is dead is to mourn in metaphor the atrophy of culture.

▼   ▲   ▼   ▲   ▼

There is a vital difference between the cultural *distress* we associate with
modernity and the cultural *destruction* described by Orwell or suffered by
indigenous people overwhelmed by a technologically advanced society.
The difference is that modernity, especially in its early stages, is marked
by an enlargement of individual autonomy, competence, and self-
assertion. In time, however, *a strong, resourceful self confronts a weakened
cultural context; still later, selfhood itself becomes problematic.* This central
tendency of modernity, from a psychological point of view, accounts
for many of the distinctive moral, intellectual, and aesthetic ironies of
our time.

Our concern is specifically with "the modern mind," not with modernity in general. The "mind" of an era is always elusive and protean, impossible to grasp with a simple formula. Nevertheless, some useful
things can be said. To make the effort, we must shift attention from modernity as a social condition to the ways of *thinking* that reflect the con-

3. Gertrude Jaeger and Philip Selznick, "A Normative Theory of Culture," *American
Sociological Review* 29 (October 1964): 666f.

dition, respond to it, and may change it. More precisely, we look to intellectual currents for clues to the moral atmosphere of a community or epoch. Whatever else we may say of them, writers and artists are highly sensitive to changes in the quality of life. They pick up the subtle effects of new styles and manners, new modes of communication, new forms of domination, new patterns of human relations, new aspirations for social reconstruction.

In tracing the trajectory of the modern mind it is helpful to distinguish three "moments" or stages. The first is most authentically modern, in that it expresses the spirit of a radically new, postmedieval world. This is the familiar age of reason and of confidence in progress. It takes as given a strong ego and a stable, if evolving, social world. Even bloody revolution does not shake that confidence. Within this stage a romantic reaction against rationalism occurs, but the sense of self, though altered, remains strong; the world is still coherent and understandable.[4]

The second stage, which has been called modernist, begins in the mid-nineteenth century with some strands of Marxist and Nietzschean thought. It grows in strength until it reaches apparent exhaustion in the mid-twentieth century. Here the sense of self is undiminished, even inflated, but the world is more disorderly. Modernism retains much of the "modern," but it also points, as we shall see, to ambiguous outcomes.

Finally, we can identify, more tentatively, a third, "postmodern" stage, which draws out and even celebrates a latent nihilism in the modernist outlook. Contemporary postmodernism may well reflect, with special acuity, today's moral and cultural distress. It is not necessarily the last word, however. Other, more hopeful forms may be lying in wait.

The ironies of modernity are best revealed in the second, modernist stage. Modernism is the response of nineteenth- and twentieth-century intellectuals and artists to the experience of modernity. The pattern is complex and unstable, yet it has a certain unity.[5] For our purposes five aspects are especially relevant.

Disintegration and dissonance. Modernism is in large part an effort to express the sensed incoherence of contemporary life. In its most distinctive products a disturbance of form and meaning is built into the work and becomes the hallmark of an artistic or intellectual style. The

4. Some relevant aspects of "modern" thought, thus understood, are discussed below, especially in Chapters 2 and 3.
5. See Irving Howe, ed., *The Idea of the Modern in Literature and the Arts* (New York: Horizon Press, 1967); Malcolm Bradbury and James MacFarlane, eds., *Modernism: 1890–1930* (Harmondsworth: Penguin Books, 1976); Daniel Bell, *The Cultural Contradictions of Capitalism* (New York: Basic Books, 1976).

fragmentation of experience is communicated by and reflected in a fracturing of aesthetic perception. A quest is made for new and very direct ways of conveying a sense of stress and crisis. The most striking feature of modern art and literature is not newness as such, or even radical discontinuity with the past. More basic is the effort to express a particular human predicament: the loss of stabilizing beliefs and perceptions; awareness that meanings—the symbolic sources of rootedness and continuity—have become elusive, transitory, self-constituted, and manipulable; in short, the sense of living at the edge of a moral and psychological abyss.

Modernism takes this predicament as a starting point. At its best it transforms existential anguish into exuberant creativity. In its symbolic expression of a disordered world, successful art generates new forms of coherence and sensibility. These new forms are precarious, subjective, and incomplete: wholeness, harmony, and stability are traded for compositions that are tension-laden, even clashing, yet aesthetically coherent. The great modernists in literature, painting, sculpture, and music have discovered and created many new—often dazzling—unities of form and feeling.

Revolt and reconstruction. A pervasive theme of modernism is the rejection of received realities. Whatever is given is suspect, for it is a potential obstacle to creative imagination. In art the modernist program called for a special kind of destruction, that of locating and disassembling constituent elements of emotion, perception, and form, to be followed by the creation of new realities through aesthetic manipulation. Abstraction, constructivism, and the bizarre dream-imagery of surrealism are characteristic vehicles of such an enterprise. They break down and reassemble ordinary experience, and they do so in a way that preserves a sense of inherent disarray.

The manipulative stance of the modernist—the impulse to break down and reconstruct—goes far beyond the world of art. It has become a dominant motif, not only in modern science, which has its own dynamic, but in architecture, planning, industrial organization, even family life. The modernist mode exhibits what Vilfredo Pareto called "the instinct for combinations," that is, a disposition to find new ways of recombining the familiar, and new elements for further combination.

Modernists as rebels and rearrangers are not truly comfortable figures. Displaying a nervous self-confidence, they perceive the world as infinitely malleable and exploitable; are astonished to find that received authority is so remarkably fragile; exult that art can probe for the universal and soar above the messy particularity of history and everyday experience. Yet all reality, they themselves declare, being self-constituted, is ultimately illusion; there is no escape from the transitory and insubstantial nature of human lives and achievements.

Order as emergent, contextual, fragile, and conflict-laden. The modernist is sometimes an enemy of order, an advocate of rage, destruction, and willful inarticulateness. That aspect cannot be ignored. But a more positive contribution of modernism is that it places at issue the *kind* of order we should seek in art, politics, or personal life. Its message is that a benign order must be compatible with—indeed, must sustain—the flourishing of freedom and vitality. To this end order is best when it is emergent rather than imposed; when it respects the context of which it is a part; when it finds principles of governance within that context; and when the disharmonies it holds in tension are plainly revealed. This theme is well exemplified in John Dewey's pragmatic naturalism, to which we return later in this chapter.

Immediacy, spontaneity, and the affirmation of impulse. Modernism teaches that the forms and conventions of everyday life—to say nothing of "academic" art and thought—get in the way of clear perception and genuine feeling. Hence the demand for direct, unmediated experience. Immediacy takes many forms in modern art, including such strategies as flattening perspective to bring visual directness, free use of primary colors, exploitation of shocking imagery. In order to see the world truly and possess it subjectively, it is necessary to break through perceptual barriers and overcome the repression of emotion. Psychoanalysis contributed to modernism in many ways, especially by encouraging awareness and affirmation of impulse. And while Freud was writing about the imperious Id, expressionist, dadaist, and surrealist painters were exploring the vigor and spontaneity of primitive art.

Perspectivism and unmasking. No idea is more characteristic of modernism than that of the multiplicity—and the alleged incommensurability—of human perspectives. Reality is elusive; point of view is all. Some benign forms of perspectivism are Gestalt psychology, cubist painting, and the concept of a pluralistic universe. More ambiguous, though in some ways more powerful, is the corollary that perspectives can be unmasked to reveal self-serving strategies and destructive impulses. The theme of unmasking and demystification has informed much of modernist thought, notably in the writings of Marx, Nietzsche, Freud, and the Vienna Circle. One face of modernism, then, is naive, open, and tolerant of difference; another, more grim, exposes and discredits.

THE POSTMODERN CHALLENGE

Some currents of modernism—abstract, rationalist, technocratic—have emphasized the free play of mind; others, such as surrealism, have released surges of feeling. In either case, the leitmotif is *subjectivity*. Individual human beings are the source and center of creative expression. And their world is full of options. In the modernist vision, artists can decide for themselves what creativity means and what direction it should take. In doing so, however, they assume a dire responsibility. Now they must make sense of a chaotic world without relying on external authority or a supportive tradition. The outcome is a demand for moral and intellectual self-sufficiency.

In this affirmation of selfhood, modernists were faithful to the spirit of the age. They belonged to the great humanist movement that began with the Renaissance; and they combined, in their own way, elements of the Enlightenment and Romantic imaginations. At the same time, *modernism exposed the latent contradictions of modernity*. The mirror held up was harsh and uncompromising. In its refracted image modernity could see where its own logic would lead. The quest for new forms of coherence—personal, social, aesthetic—was noticeably fragile and tainted by overreaching.

The most important source of this incoherence is the effort to maintain a strong sense of personal autonomy within a crumbling or disordered social framework. This project was bound to fail. Without supportive contexts of nurture and sustenance, and of inspiration as well, selfhood is at risk. When continuities of practice and judgment are discounted or abandoned, people become footloose, reactive, and, in David Riesman's phrase, "other-directed." To be truly independent, self-confident, and resourceful, people need *foundations*. Yet modernity, as expressed in modernism, offers "a life without fixity or conclusion," where dissonance and incongruity must reign.[6]

This latent challenge to coherence and stability becomes painfully explicit in contemporary postmodern thought.[7] Much of what is called

---

6. The quotation is from Howe, *Idea of the Modern*, 37.
7. For an overview see David Harvey, *The Condition of Postmodernity* (Oxford: Basil Blackwell, 1989); and Fredric Jameson, *Postmodernism* (Durham: Duke University Press, 1991).

postmodern in the arts, literary criticism, philosophy, and social theory is, above all, a challenge to coherence. Purported unities of self, community, culture, law, art, science, and organization are exposed as inescapably plural, conflict-filled, dissociated. Whatever unity we may find is imposed, not natural or organic. History is discarded as irrelevant; all is foreground, all surface, and multiple surfaces at that. Continuities of place and experience are lost forever in a world of homogeneous settings and replaceable modules. A ceaseless barrage of images and "sound bites" undercuts the capacity to make sense of public and private life. Consumerism reigns, and with it a transformation of things properly valued for themselves into fungible commodities.

In the postmodern perspective, all ideas are products of subjective interpretation, uncontrolled rhetoric, or political domination. They are radically contingent and without foundations. Human experience is best understood as "discourse" about "texts," which are patterns of life as well as words. Because texts have no intrinsic merit, no integrity of their own, they may be manipulated and deconstructed at will. Because the worlds we inhabit are products of human artifice, they are arbitrary "all the way down," that is, fundamentally and irredeemably. There is no appeal from the subjectivity of will, desire, creativity, and power.

Postmodernism is, to a large extent, the wayward child of modernism. Its central message carries "the logic of modernism to its farthest reaches."[8] It does so, however, without retaining the intellectual, moral, and aesthetic strengths of modernism; without the belief that there is genuine truth to be discerned; without confidence in the possibility of creating new and better ways of manifesting the human spirit; without tacit commitment to continuity as well as change. What there was of exuberant optimism has been displaced by cynicism and despair.[9] With some fidelity postmodern theorists reflect—and dramatize—the weakening of selfhood in late modernity.

This is not to deny all validity to postmodern perspectives. As did Michel Foucault, whom we discuss in a later chapter, postmoderns properly call attention to many insidious aspects of modern life, including hidden forms of power and manipulation. From the standpoint of diagnosis, they have much to say. But these insights often lead to grossly exaggerated claims, with little attention to variability or context. Every

8. Daniel Bell, *The Winding Passage: Essays and Sociological Journeys, 1960–1980* (New York: Basic Books, 1980), 288.

9. Tempered, to be sure, by some gleeful "trashing" and "demystification" of conventional or allegedly inauthentic ideas and practices. On postmodern thought, see the discussions below of Michel Foucault, pp. 250–54, and Erving Goffman, pp. 221–22.

disunity is a radical disunity; every evidence of superficiality and incoherence is accepted; every evidence to the contrary is ignored or discounted. Above all, a message is conveyed of recurrent crises and apocalyptic endings.

As I write, the term "postmodern" seems preempted by the bleak outlook just described. Other strands of thought with modernist roots, however, emphasize the more positive aspects of that legacy. I have in mind those gropings for cultural and institutional renewal that de-emphasize modern individualist values—achievement, discipline, independence, competition—in favor of more person-centered, more collaborative, more organic forms of life. Efforts to invent "postbureaucratic" forms of organization are postmodern in this sense, because they seek to transcend or at least moderate the modern commitment to systems of rational coordination. Another example is Jane Jacobs's argument for intricate and close-grained diversity to protect the vitality of spontaneous human relations in urban settings.[10] This is not anti-modern, not a plea for return to village life. Rather, it is a strategy for overcoming the egotism, monumentality, and impersonality, the indifference to human needs, that for many years characterized modern architecture and city planning. A postmodern architecture planned in this spirit does not focus on superficial efforts to decorate buildings with architectural quotations from the past. It looks for new ways of adapting structures of all kinds, large and small, to human needs and aspirations.

These are pragmatic and communitarian efforts to overcome the moral deficits of modernity. They reject unsituated rationalism, unmitigated individualism, and untempered claims to institutional autonomy. They accept openness, fluidity, and multiplicity as necessary and *welcome* parameters of modern life. In these and other respects they share the perspectives of many so-called postmodern critics, especially in social science, philosophy, and jurisprudence. They may, however, point the way to a more stable, more responsible, more affirmative vision than contemporary postmodernism suggests.

THE SOVEREIGNTY OF WILL

Modern, modernist, postmodern—all share a dream of *homo faber*, man the maker.[11] As the dream recurs the image shifts from fabrication of

10. Jane Jacobs, *The Death and Life of Great American Cities* (New York: Random House, 1961).

11. See Hannah Arendt, *The Human Condition* (Chicago: University of Chicago Press, 1958), 207ff., 305ff.

things—tools and objects—to fabrication of selves. "Man makes himself" becomes the motto of the age. This includes, most importantly, the choice of self-defining values. As a result, *morality is made, not discovered; personal, not social; self-imposed, not ordained.* With the ascendance of subjectivity—the human subject as its own legislator—even God becomes a human creation.

In an older vision, *homo faber* does not suggest unlimited horizons or unbounded choice. For the traditional craftsman, neither ends nor means can be freely chosen. The logic of craftsmanship transcends will and constrains choice. That is so because materials are respected as having their own nature—a nature that sets limits even as it opens possibilities. This way of thinking presumes a world of known materials and stable frameworks. When the frameworks themselves are challenged or when materials are not granted an integrity of their own, the ideal of *homo faber* loses its innocence. Man the maker readily becomes destructive and self-destructive.

The main temptation lies in a sensed sovereignty of will. If the world is made rather than received, it is plausible to suppose that there is no limit to human inventiveness. If moral judgments are leaps of faith or expressions of personal identity, we can and perhaps should make our own moralities. If law is nothing more than the will of a legislature or judge, it becomes a brute manifestation of power, available for any purpose, unconstrained by any inner morality. If democracy is the "will of the people," how is that will to be governed?

The achievements of modernity, which include achievements of awareness and self-awareness, are purchased at the price of moral disengagement. On matters of conscience there is no useful external guide. We fashion our own conceptions of the good; we rely on ourselves, ultimately alone; no safe harbor is to be found in biblical or other unquestioned authority. It was always tempting, in earlier times, to confound God's will with one's own. Now the very distinction fades. Who is to say, with conviction, where the difference lies? Sovereign will and freedom of choice are expressions of selfhood, and as such are self-justifying. Indeed, only *restrictions* on will and choice require justification.

This is the most telling criticism—and wrenching irony—of modern thought. The era begins with a quest for certainty, including moral certainty. "Unalienable rights" are bravely proclaimed, together with elegant arguments for morality based on reason. Today, however, the watchword is contingency, not certainty. In the contemporary idiom, moreover, "contingency" connotes *pervasive* doubt and *radical* uncertainty, not the variability and probabilism we recognize in empirical science.

This outcome may be traced to a fateful intellectual strategy. Beginning with the Reformation we see an effort to locate certainty in subjectivity, that is, in what we *cannot help* believing as conscious, rational, or spiritual beings. Assurance comes from within, that is, from Cartesian self-awareness, the Kantian structure of mind, or Protestant salvation through personal faith and witness. In time, however, as subjectivity is more fully explored, these inner sources of assurance are questioned. They are no longer considered convincing grounds for elementary, universal, or axiomatic truths. The subjectivity of mind and faith takes on new and quite different connotations: diversity, historicity, bias, deception, self-deception. Although the meaning of subjectivity changes, allegiance to it is not abandoned. On the contrary, there is an easy transition from the old to the new subjectivity. As a result, in late modernity more is given up than certainty born of untenable absolutes. The intellectual resources for recognizing human limits, and for grounding values in what we can learn from experience, are diluted or abandoned.

One of John Dewey's most influential books is *The Quest for Certainty*. There he criticized a long tradition of thought, going back to the Greeks, that sought certainty in the exercise of abstract reason, divorced from experience. The messy contingency of practical action could not, it was thought, yield genuine knowledge. Dewey's argument is seriously misunderstood, however, if it is taken as in any sense an invitation to radical skepticism, to say nothing of nihilism. In attacking the separation of theory and practice Dewey sought to ground knowledge, including moral knowledge, in the problem-solving experience of human communities. He favored "substituting search for security by practical means for quest of absolute certainty by cognitive means."[12] This "search for security" is not, indeed, a "quest for certainty." It recognizes that all knowledge is fallible and contingent, including knowledge of the good. But neither is it a plea for *un*certainty.[13]

12. John Dewey, *The Quest for Certainty* (1929; reprint, New York: G. P. Putnam's Sons, 1960), 24f.

13. Ernest Nagel makes this point and notes "a growing tendency among scientists as well as philosophers to argue from the fallibility of scientific inquiry to a denial that claims to knowledge are ever warranted, and to describe the enterprise of science as if it were a quest for uncertainty" ("The Quest for Uncertainty," in Paul Kurtz, ed., *Sidney Hook and the Contemporary World: Essays on the Pragmatic Intelligence* [New York: John Day, 1968], 408). Since that was written the tendency referred to has increased markedly. Subjectivism in science will be discussed in Chapter 3.

NATURALISM IN ETHICS

To reach beyond arbitrary will, beyond radical uncertainty, *and to do so in a way that retains what is best in modernity and modernism,* we need to re-affirm the central tenets of American pragmatism. In this naturalist philosophy, especially as developed by Dewey, the centrality of human purpose is underscored; the creativity of *homo faber* is recognized and appreciated; a spirit of liberation and reconstruction prevails. Yet all is constrained by the continuities of the natural world and the human. As the name suggests, ethical naturalism brings knowledge of a natural order to bear when questions of moral truth arise. This steadying framework presumes there is, in some significant sense, a message to be derived from nature.

The notion that there is such a message runs counter to much of modern thought. In a youthful prose poem Bertrand Russell wrote:

> Brief and powerless is Man's life; on him and all his race the slow sure doom falls pitiless and dark. Blind to good and evil, reckless of destruction, omnipotent matter rolls on its relentless way; for Man . . . it remains only to cherish, ere yet the blow falls, the lofty thoughts that ennoble his little day . . . to sustain alone, a weary but unyielding Atlas, the world his own ideals have fashioned despite the trampling march of unconscious power.[14]

These cadences did not please their author in later years, but the thought they express is wholly consistent with his lifelong dedication to positivism.[15] A radical disjunction of value and fact becomes, in the imagery of "A Free Man's Worship," opposition of moral person and amoral nature. Nature is "blind to good and evil," heedless of human purpose. To believe that "in some hidden manner, the world of fact is really harmonious with the world of ideals" is a remnant of primitive religious consciousness. For "the world of fact, after all is not good; and, in submitting our judgement to it, there is an element of slavishness from which our thoughts must be purged. For in all things it is well to

---

14. Bertrand Russell, "A Free Man's Worship," in *The Basic Writings of Bertrand Russell, 1903–1959*, ed. Robert E. Egner and Lester E. Dennon (New York: Simon and Schuster, 1961), 71.

15. In his eighties Russell referred to "A Free Man's Worship" as "a work of which I do not think well. At that time I was steeped in Milton's prose, and his rolling periods reverberated through the caverns of my mind" (*Basic Writings*, 64). However, ardent metaphors aside, Russell expressed precisely the same point of view many years later: "What we think good, what we should like, *has no bearing whatever* upon what is, which is the question for a philosophy of nature. . . . In the world of values, Nature in itself is neutral, neither good nor bad, deserving neither admiration nor censure. It is we who create value and our desires which confer value. In this realm we are kings, and we debase our kingship if we bow down to Nature" (ibid., 371, my emphasis).

exalt the dignity of Man, by freeing him as far as possible from the tyranny of non-human Power."[16]

A similar view was more coolly expressed, a generation earlier, by John Stuart Mill. Writing with great force and clarity, he sought to discredit for all time the use of "nature" as a term of "commendation, approval, and even moral obligation."[17] He thought it was folly to confuse the natural order, which includes *all* regularities, with human hopes and aspirations, which must choose some to make use of and others to resist:

> If the artificial is not better than the natural, to what end are all the arts of life?
> To dig, to build, to wear clothes are direct infringements of the injunction to
> follow nature. . . . . If, therefore, the useless precept to follow nature were
> changed into a precept to study nature—to know and take heed of the prop-
> erties of the things we have to deal with, so far as these properties are capable
> of forwarding or obstructing any given purpose—we should have arrived at
> the first principle of intelligent action, or rather at the definition of intelligent
> action itself.[18]

But this principle should not be talked of as conformity to nature or being guided by nature. For nature contains much that is, from a human point of view, destructive and indifferent.

Mill wrote in an era of confidence that progress consists in what was called the conquest of nature, that is, in subordinating the natural environment to human artifice and imagination. In late modernity we are more cautious, more sensitive to the values that inhere in a world we did not make. For us the word "artificial" carries a more negative connotation. We are more ready to find a latent wisdom in parts of the natural order.

Mill was surely right to say that humanity is in the business of *amending* nature, not of following it blindly. As he pointed out, the principle of conformity to nature is easy to accept if it means that intelligent action must take account of physical, organic, and social facts. That is no more than an invitation to realism. But Mill and Russell went too far in *counterposing* man and nature. On one side they saw human purpose and, in Russell's idiom, "our kingship"; on the other, the indifference and even hostility of nature.

We may readily agree that the workings of the cosmos—including natural selection in biology—are careless of moral outcomes; that morality is indeed an artifact of mind and spirit, a world our "own ideals

---

16. Ibid., 68.
17. John Stuart Mill, "Nature," in *Essential Works* (1874; reprint, New York: Bantam Books, 1961), 370.
18. Ibid., 376, 375.

have fashioned." But this fashioning does not take place in a vacuum; it is by no means wholly arbitrary or autonomous. Biological, psychological, and social conditions affect the reach, realism, and relevance of moral ideals. A morality that does not transcend nature may be unworthy of the name; but one that is out of touch with nature invites corruption, defeat, and opportunity forgone.

John Dewey rejected the opposition of humanity and nature. Not humanity *and* nature but humanity *in* nature should, he believed, be the guiding principle. In this view, morally defensible aspirations are not products of arbitrary choice. For him and others in the naturalist tradition, human values are rooted in the troubles and strivings of organic life, especially in the transition from immediate impulse to enduring satisfaction. They arise out of the continuities of social existence, including the need to nurture what is immature and unstable. An untended garden, a child given too much too soon, an arbitrary legal judgment: each exacts costs, each provides material for improved awareness of appropriate ends and effective means. We need not look beyond this experience to find the foundations of moral judgment.

Friendship, responsibility, leadership, love, and justice are not elements of an external ethic brought to the world like Promethean fire. They are generated by mundane needs, practical opportunities, and felt satisfactions. "The loftiest edifices," wrote George Santayana, "have the deepest foundations. Love would never take so high a flight unless it sprung from something profound and elementary. . . . In truth, all spiritual interests are supported by animal life."[19] These words reflect a long tradition of understanding that authentic human ideals have material foundations. They are rooted in existential needs and strivings. When a proposed ideal denies these roots it is to that extent a source of moral confusion and psychic malaise.

Thus the first principle of a naturalist ethic is that genuine values emerge from experience; they are discovered, not imposed. As Dewey said, "[N]aturalism finds the values in question, the worth and dignity of men and women, founded in human nature itself, in the connections, actual and potential, of human beings with one another in their natural social relationships."[20] Such discovery, he insisted, is the most important part of social learning.

19. George Santayana, *The Life of Reason* (1933; reprint, New York: Scribner's, 1954), 102.
20. John Dewey, "Anti-Naturalism in Extremis," *Partisan Review* 10 (January 1943): 32.

Values are not reducible to subjective preferences. Felt needs and immediate satisfactions are important *starting points* for "the construction of good." But that process must be faithful to the full range of relevant experience. It must take into account all that must be done to transform a situation initiated by subjective impulse into an objectively satisfactory state of affairs. Because this process requires knowledge, there must be a continuity of cognitive and moral experience.

The realm of spirit—of thought, sensibility, and aspiration—is as much a part of nature as is any other recurrent aspect of organic life. Naturalists are not materialists. In metaphysics they do not hold that matter is the only reality, all else epiphenomenon; in social theory they do not argue that economic forces or motives are the only or even the most fundamental determinants of social life. On the contrary, pragmatic naturalism recognizes no hierarchy of experience. If people form ideas and respond to them, that is a natural process like any other. Similarly, moral and aesthetic elaboration—and judgment—is a pervasive fact of human life. No explanation of why such elaboration occurs, or how it varies, can erase the experience itself. Naturalism does not reduce religion to fantasy, education to training, love to attachment, law to power. It respects the complexity, subtlety, and integrity of these phenomena even as it seeks their exigent conditions and material underpinnings.

Of Fact and Value

A basic message of Dewey's naturalism is that all *explanation* and all *justification* must rest on what we learn from experience; and useful learning must conform to the canons of scientific inquiry. Nothing was more alien to Dewey than a retreat from science, and he was especially vigorous in upholding a naturalist view of *moral* experience. This perspective excludes appeal to a realm beyond experience or to absolutes of any kind. Furthermore, all experience is seen as contextual; all conclusions are contingent and probabilistic.

Hence there are no moral absolutes. Moral propositions must be as open to inquiry as any other; and they are subject to revision in the light of logic and evidence. This does not mean that conclusions about morality are necessarily insecure or precarious. All science is subject to revision, but well-founded propositions—"warranted assertions," in Dewey's phrase—are routinely accepted as secure guides to action. It does mean that moral certainty is an impossible and even dangerous ideal; that debate about morality is a constant feature of civilized life; and that a scientific *spirit* must inform the discussion of moral issues. In clarifying our values, in adapting them to new circumstances, in determining the conditions of their fulfillment or distortion, we must be open to conclusions of social inquiry regarding the moral experience of human communities.

In many of his writings Dewey hammered away at what he took to be pernicious dualisms—between fact and value, ends and means, thought and observation, body and mind, knowing and doing, the ideal and the practical. These and other dualisms transform analytical or functional distinctions into ontological divisions, and the effect of the transformation is to frustrate inquiry and limit achievement. Analytical distinctions should not create walls of separation where the phenomena themselves are interactive and interdependent. The essential point, as Dewey would have said, is to avoid any dogma that blocks inquiry. Such a dogma is the view that fact and value, is and ought, belong to alien spheres.

▼   ▲   ▼   ▲   ▼

It is elementary good sense to distinguish what the world is like from what we would like it to be. Such a distinction is indispensable to clear thought; it cannot be abolished. Without it there could be no coherent criticism of existing states of affairs. Let us grant further that statements of fact differ, in form and function, from statements of preference and appraisal. From this distinction between *kinds of statements* it does not follow that fact and value, as *aspects of existence,* belong to wholly separate realms. It is one thing to derive sentences from other sentences as a matter of strict logic. It is something else to "derive" norms from facts, if by that we mean basing normative judgments on relevant empirical conditions. When human actors make moral judgments, especially collective judgments, they often attend to facts and are persuaded by facts. When factual circumstances make a difference for the choice of norms, as by limiting alternatives and fixing outcomes, it is reasonable to say that the norms are *to that extent* based on facts and even "derived" from facts. They may also, and at the same time, reflect quite arbitrary interests and inclinations.

The point is that arbitrariness in human judgment is a variable, not an all-or-nothing attribute. Beliefs about right and wrong are *more or less* subject to principled justification. They are differentially grounded in logic and evidence; in learning from experience as against simple conditioning; and in the contributions they make to personal and social well-being. A collective belief in the value of family life, one may suppose, is more firmly based on funded experience than, say, a belief in the intrinsic worth of higher education for everyone. Some values are more contingent than others, more transitory, more closely determined by unique historical experiences, including unreflective habit and tradition. Values are not *either* cognitive or emotive, *either* objective or subjective. They are variably one or the other and usually a mixture of both.

In John Dewey's naturalism the variability of arbitrariness is a central, if largely implicit, tenet associated with a functional approach to human psychology. For positivists, on the other hand, basic values are "gut" values. They are intrinsically arbitrary; and the conditioned response is seen as the paradigmatic arbitrary experience. Some kinds of conditioning are, however, less arbitrary than others. For example, operant conditioning may be adaptive and functional, as when pedestrians automatically watch for traffic coming from the left (in right-hand-driving countries) or when drivers automatically remove the ignition key after parking a car.

Furthermore, not all learning can be assimilated to conditioning. Much of learning must be understood as purposive and problem-solving, sustained by cognitive awareness and activity rather than by fixed neurological patterns. Dewey stressed this aspect of learning because he wanted to emphasize that the healthy, self-regulating organism is not a passive receptor of external stimuli but an active participant in testing and reconstructing the environment, testing and reconstructing the self. Hence he distinguished "behavior" from "action," the former largely governed by response to excitation, the latter a product of organization and purpose.

There is no question, of course, of rejecting conditioning as a mode of learning. Dewey could not be hostile to a process so natural and so useful. But in a normative theory of learning—which is what he was articulating—conditioning must be governed by the total situation of the organism as it seeks coherence, satisfaction, and fulfillment. Otherwise conditioning will be a process of discrete, unintegrated patterning; it will be mindless and arbitrary. Dewey's concept of "progressive education" therefore sought to limit the extent to which pedagogy relies on conditioning in order to make learning, including moral learning, less arbitrary.

Dewey was not imposing his own preferences. His model presumes that the human organism finds genuine satisfaction and enduring well-being in purposive, integrative, self-affirming conduct and suffers distraction and malaise when constrained, fragmented, and manipulated. These benefits and costs are aspects of the experienced world. They make themselves known in very practical ways, as when we try to mobilize effort or communicate effectively.

This normative approach to human and social experience is a key feature of Dewey's naturalism, and one that sets him off from proponents of positivism.[21] Dewey saw valuation as a natural process, a phase of the human quest for need-satisfaction; and he saw *what* is valued as warranted by its contribution to human well-being. It follows that the act of prizing is not an arbitrary, emotive response. It may have arbitrary elements and must be refined by the exercise of conscious intelligence, but it is founded in our conative and cognizing nature.

Even if we recognize an *ultimately* arbitrary element, inaccessible to rational appraisal, in human choice, this cannot justify the conclusion in any particular case that the irreducible element has been reached. Nor does it follow that we should fail to strive for the progressive reduction of arbitrariness in moral decision. The call for separation of fact and value is not without intellectual justification. As so often happens, it is the slogan, the polemical formulation, that has the greatest impact. Pressing a complex world into easy dichotomies, it induces a premature abandonment of wide areas of experience to a noncognitive realm in which "can't helps" and "fighting words" prevail.

Two Kinds of Naturalism

Dewey once said that "any theory of activity in social and moral matters, liberal or otherwise, which is not grounded in a comprehensive philosophy seems to me to be only a projection of arbitrary personal preference."[22] Pragmatic naturalism is such a philosophy. Dewey thought of it as providing a spacious *framework* for moral inquiry, including *grounds* for limiting the sovereignty of will. To say of him that he was "against foundations" requires the belief that only absolute or immutable premises count as foundational. This misreads Dewey's writings—and mocks his thought.

There is, however, some basis for the misunderstanding. It stems from the fact that much in Dewey's naturalism is modernist and therefore resonates, to some extent at least, with postmodern ideas. To appreciate

21. On the meaning of "positivism," see Chapter 2, "Rationalism and Positivism."
22. John Dewey, "Nature in Experience," *Philosophical Review* 49 (1940): 255.

this point, we need to distinguish two kinds of naturalism. One we may call "basic" or "generic" naturalism. This is the idea that every phenomenon, every aspect of experience, is appropriately studied by scientific method, broadly understood. Nothing can be explained or justified by reference to supernatural forces or untestable ideas. On this ground, the naturalist study of morality, religion, art—and inquiry itself, including logic—is vigorously defended:

> Thus, there is for naturalism no knowledge except that of the type ordinarily called "scientific." But such knowledge cannot be said to be restricted by its method to any limited field of subject matter—to the exclusion, let us say, of the processes called "history" and the "fine arts." For whether a question is about forces "within the atom," or about the distribution of galaxies, or about the qualities and patterns of sound called Beethoven's Second Razumovsky Quartet and the joy some men found in them—in any case there is no serious way to approach controlled hypotheses as to what the answers should be except by inspection of the relevant evidence and by inductive inference from it.[23]

Such study is normative as well as descriptive. Ideal or elaborated states are, as we have said, part of nature and conditioned by nature. To think otherwise "flies in the face of mountains of evidence concerning the place of man in nature, and leaves human values unanchored to any solid ground of experience."[24] These views *are* foundational. They define the boundaries of good sense and fruitfulness—not only in physics, biology, and engineering, but in moral and social inquiry as well. They are common ground for naturalists—Aristotle, Spinoza, Hume, Santayana, Dewey—who have differed, and will differ, on many specific issues.

Basic naturalism requires no special conception of nature. Whatever regularities we discover in the course of experimental inquiry—which includes practical experience—count as nature. Thus understood, naturalism speaks to limits as well as to opportunities; is neither pessimistic nor optimistic; is as open to a spirit of resignation as to a more abundant faith in what can be gained from cooperative study and collective action.

A more distinctive, more searching, more controversial aspect of Dewey's naturalism may be described as "pragmatic" or "humanist." Here we find a specific conception of nature; a philosophy of nature; even a metaphysics of nature. Although he ultimately renounced the use of the word, Dewey did engage in something like metaphysical

23. William R. Dennes, "The Categories of Naturalism," in Y. H. Krekorian, ed., *Naturalism and the Human Spirit* (New York: Columbia University Press, 1944), 289.

24. John Dewey, Sidney Hook, and Ernest Nagel, "Are Naturalists Materialists?" *Journal of Philosophy* 42 (September 1945): 400.

inquiry.[25] He believed philosophy could identify general characteristics of the natural world, what he called "generic traits of existence."[26] These traits are not deduced from abstract principles; they purport to be based on experience. However, they are more general than the traits that concern specific sciences.

For example, Dewey said that "every existence is an event."[27] This was his way of asserting that everything is ultimately contingent and temporal, at once stable and precarious. Other generic traits of nature are suggested by such ideas as "potentiality," "relation," "interaction," "transaction," and "emergence." Although nature assuredly contains forms and structures, these are not fixed or immutable. They cannot be understood if they are divorced from the processes that brought them into being, or from other (or the same) processes that may change or destroy them.

Dewey resisted the "common identification of reality with what is sure, regular and finished."[28] At the same time, he warned against "idealizing flux into a deity."[29] In a naturalist metaphysics "incompleteness and precariousness is a trait that must be given footing of the same rank as the finished and fixed."[30] The challenge is to see how structure and process involve each other, not only intellectually, as conceptual polarities, but as problematic and intertwined aspects of existence:

> We live in a world which is an impressive and irresistible mixture of sufficiencies, tight completenesses, order, recurrences which make possible prediction and control, and singularities, ambiguities, uncertain possibilities, processes going on to consequences as yet indeterminate. They are mixed

25. When he was ninety, Dewey wrote that he regretted having used the words "metaphysics" and "metaphysical," in that "it was exceedingly naive of me to suppose that it was possible to rescue the word from its deeply engrained traditional use. . . . And while I think the *words* used were most unfortunate, I still believe that that which they were used to name is genuine and important. This genuine subject matter is the fact that the natural world has *generic* as well as specific traits, and that in the one case as in the other[,] experience is such as to enable us to arrive at their identification" (John Dewey, "Experience and Existence: A Comment," *Philosophy and Phenomenological Research* [June 1949]: 712).

26. John Dewey, *Experience and Nature* (1929; reprint, New York: Dover, 1958), 51. For sympathetic reviews of Dewey's metaphysics, see Richard Bernstein, *John Dewey* (New York: Washington Square Press, 1967); James Gouinlock, *John Dewey's Philosophy of Value* (New York: Humanities Press, 1972); Raymond Boisvert, *Dewey's Metaphysics* (New York: Fordham University Press, 1988). For trenchant criticism, see Morris R. Cohen, "Some Difficulties in Dewey's Anthropocentric Naturalism," *Philosophical Review* 49 (1940): 196–228. A different view is expressed in Richard Rorty, *Consequences of Pragmatism* (Minneapolis: University of Minnesota Press, 1982), chap. 5.

27. Dewey, *Experience and Nature*, 71.

28. Ibid., 47.

29. Ibid., 71.

30. Ibid., 51.

not mechanically but vitally. . . . We may recognize them separately but
we cannot divide them, for unlike wheat and tares they grow from the
same root.[31]

A striking feature of Dewey's thought is the stress he gave to the *particularity* of the experienced world. Nature is concrete, not abstract. It is a
realm of unique entities, each, however, "pregnant with connections."[32]
"Everything that exists in so far as it is known and knowable is in interaction with other things. It is associated as well as solitary."[33] Dewey's purpose was to vindicate the primacy *in nature* of concreteness, individuality, and what he called "qualitative immediacy."[34]

This philosophy of nature is "naturalist" in a special sense that is reminiscent of the difference between theoretical science and what used to be
called "natural history." For modern theoretical scientists, nature is not
known directly and concretely but indirectly and selectively. Ideally embodied in mathematical propositions, nature becomes rarified and remote. In contrast, students of natural history—naturalists—are interested in the situated wholeness of objects and organisms. They perceive
a world of glaciered canyons, burnt prairies, migrating geese. Their interests may ultimately be no less abstract, as in refining theories of evolution, but their work encourages appreciation for the concreteness of
the environment, for its historical flux, and for the precarious integrity of
ecological systems. Dewey's philosophy of pragmatic naturalism is especially congenial to this second perspective. His conception of nature
exhibits the same preoccupation with particularity, the same sensitivity
to organic unities—the same love for the world.

Dewey's search for something beyond basic, uncommitted naturalism
led him to a human-centered account of "the generic traits of existence."
Although his aspiration was larger, in fact he was looking at the world
selectively, from the perspective of human need and intervention. He
preferred to treat "nature as it confronts and intercepts man in life."[35]

31. Ibid., 47.
32. John Dewey, "The Need for a Recovery of Philosophy," in *On Experience, Nature,
and Freedom* (1917; reprint, Indianapolis: Bobbs-Merrill, 1960), 23.
33. John Dewey, *Experience and Nature*, 175.
34. "In truth, the universal and stable are important because they are the instrumentalities, the efficacious conditions, of the occurrence of the unique, unstable and passing. . . . Standardizations, formulae, generalizations, principles, universals have their
place, but the place is that of being instrumental to better approximation to what is unique
and unrepeatable" (ibid., 116).
35. John Dewey, "A Philosophy of Scientific Method," in *The Later Works, 1925–
1953* (Carbondale: Southern Illinois University Press, 1985), 6:299. In this review of Morris R. Cohen's *Reason and Nature*, Dewey distinguished his own view, which holds that
"contingency is final because things in the universe have individuality, as well as having

"Nature as it exists at any particular time is a challenge rather than a completion; it provides possible starting points and opportunities rather than final ends."[36] These and many other comments account for Morris R. Cohen's complaint that Dewey was committed to an "anthropocentric naturalism."[37] It should be recognized, however, that the selectivity at issue here is not arbitrary or without justification. In trying to place humanity in nature, Dewey was attending to aspects of existence that have worth and relevance to us as animals and as human animals. This is not a celebration of subjectivity; on the contrary, it is an effort to connect human choice and aspiration to fundamental traits of an ambient world, a world on which we are dependent and with which we interact.

More specifically, pragmatism finds support in nature for secure and fruitful guides to moral reflection and prescription. This support is not a matter of strict logic. We cannot *deduce* a moral ontology from a philosophy of nature, if only because the terms of the latter are too vague. The philosophy can only establish a moral posture and lend it some antecedent credibility. There is no substitute for discovering what works, that is, for tracing the consequences of bringing to bear, within the sphere of morality, such purportedly generic traits and processes as "individuality," "potentiality," "development," "continuity," and "transaction."[38]

The moral vision is not far to seek. Context, growth, and interdependence; communication, intelligence, reconstruction, and consummation—these are pragmatist guideposts to moral judgment. Taken together, they carry a message of *controlled and responsible liberation*. This comes out most clearly, perhaps, in Dewey's emphasis on the idea of growth.[39] Growth is an inherent potential of interaction between organism and environment. When interaction is free and undistorted—when it

---

relations which are necessary, universal and invariant," from Cohen's view of nature as "distilled through the alembic of science and logic. . . . Except when he refers to the fact of contingency as a weapon of criticism of other theories, nature remains for him the character of things as determined in universal relations."

36. Dewey, *Quest for Certainty,* 100.
37. Cohen, "Some Difficulties," 198.
38. "In all Dewey's work the metaphysical basis is present and operative. . . . I do not contend that Dewey was thoroughly systematic in grounding his thinking in metaphysics. It is abundantly clear, however, that Dewey's work continually discloses, implicitly and explicitly, that his thinking about the moral life was throughout informed with his naturalistic metaphysics—as well as with his philosophy of nature" (Gouinlock, *Dewey's Philosophy of Value,* 57f.). Just what it means to be "informed with" such ideas, just how connections are made, for example, between Hegelian premises and Hegel's or Marx's moral and political conclusions, is a continuing puzzle in the history of ideas.
39. For an extended discussion, see Gouinlock, *Dewey's Philosophy of Value,* 237ff.

stimulates reflection and experiment—powers are enhanced, horizons expanded, connections deepened, meanings enriched. Growth depends on shared experience, which in turn requires genuine, open communication. Thus understood, growth is a normative idea—it must meet some standards; but it is rooted in and governed by the dynamics of interaction and the nature of the organism.

This philosophy establishes no fixed hierarchy of values, to be applied without regard to context. What is good depends on human (including institutional) needs in particular circumstances. On the other hand, it does provide ample resources for criticizing specific values, such as kinds of authority, recreation, work, or art. The criticism is necessarily contextual. It must consider the quality of experience in, say, listening to rock music or practicing a particular profession. Without knowing in detail what it means to be a *kind* of lawyer, teacher, or technician, no assessment can be made. Once the context is specified, however, we can bring to bear what we have learned about closely similar situations; and we can apply general standards, drawn from a moral ontology, such as the idea that situations that enhance growth are prima facie better than situations that constrain, stultify, or impoverish.[40] These are, of course, foundational notions for Dewey's theory of progressive education.

The principle of continuity has a special importance in Dewey's conception of nature, as well as in his moral and social theory. This is reflected in his criticism of various dualisms, as noted above. He thought it more fruitful for inquiry, and more faithful to what the world is like, to emphasize continuities—of science and common sense, individual and society, learning and doing, school and community, politics and economics, religion and natural piety, art and life—than to dwell on differences and disjunctions.[41] Dewey recognized the existence of distinctive forms, but he wanted to see them as emergent, fluid, and available for reconstruction. He could best serve the cause of openness and growth by focusing on the reality, and the frequent desirability, of blurred boundaries.

40. Even then, however, we do not engage in prejudgments. We leave room for the possibility that a particular situation may require (and justify) repressive rules, limited information, arm's-length communication. The theory does not exclude such possibilities, but it does suggest that they should be contained and offset.

41. For example, Dewey argued that the task of a philosophy of the arts "is to restore continuity between the refined and intensified forms of experience that are works of art and the everyday events, doings, and sufferings that are universally recognized to constitute experience." Aesthetic quality is "implicit in normal experience." A practical activity will have aesthetic quality "provided it is integrated and moves by its own urge to fulfillment" (Dewey, *Art as Experience* [1934; reprint, New York: Capricorn Books, 1958] 3, 39).

Here Dewey's thought converges with an important aspect of the sociological perspective. Sociological interpretation is not comfortable with clear lines drawn between one human activity and another, one social sphere and another. Sociological jurisprudence is uneasy with the separation of law and politics, law and economics, law and morality. The same may be said of any other social sphere, whether it be education, technology, science, business, or national security. Every practice and every institution is seen as "in society," fatefully conditioned by larger contexts of culture and social organization. Sociology looks to the continuities of life, to how things fit together and are interdependent, and it finds in those continuities the primordial sources of obligation and responsibility.[42]

Thus pragmatic naturalism strains toward a communitarian morality. Human beings are products of interaction; they are embedded in social contexts. This is a truism, but one that must be taken seriously. It is a challenge to recognize how much we depend on shared experience, including nurture, communication, stimulation, and support. People are prime examples of "individualities" "pregnant with connections," "associated as well as solitary." In pragmatist social theory the "social self" is a foundational idea, rich with implications for motivation, conduct, and moral development. The chief objects of moral concern are situated beings, not abstract individuals. Hence pragmatic naturalism is anti-individualist, as that term is commonly understood, yet wholly committed to the flourishing of persons.[43]

The pragmatic temper demands a *liberal* communitarianism, and that theme is developed in later chapters. A premise is that social contexts can be regenerative: appropriate environments bring forth and sustain "the better angels of our nature." There is basic confidence in what people *can be* if only the circumstances will be set right. Pragmatism knows little of pessimism, withdrawal, or alienation, for it is a philosophy of commitment and a philosophy of the present. The given world is accepted, even loved, as the indispensable arena of action and fulfillment. Yet that acceptance is neither supine nor self-effacing. Pragmatism presumes a posture of criticism and a strategy of reconstruction.

---

42. This does not deny the reality of conflict or the importance of autonomy for technical competence and for the moral integrity of specialized institutions. It does say that without attention to fundamental continuities, conflicts are exacerbated and autonomy degenerates into perverse and self-defeating isolation.

43. On "individual" and "person" see Chapter 8, "Integrity and Personhood."

▼   ▲   ▼   ▲   ▼

I suggested above that much in Dewey's naturalism reflects a modernist sensibility and therefore has some continuity with postmodern thought. This is in no way surprising: Dewey was keen to make philosophy relevant to the salient issues of our time—the most important being the need for a new foundation for morality.[44] In his view, a modern thinker must accept a world without absolutes; a world both made and discovered; a world of process, emergence, multiplicity, and historicity; a world instinct with solidarity, yet open to conflicting interests and divergent perspectives.

These themes help explain a renewed interest in pragmatism among contemporary postmodern writers, for whom incoherence and destabilization are central facts of modern existence; who are tempted to substitute deconstruction and demystification for more positive strategies of criticism and renewal; who look for refuge in personal sources of meaning and security; who have little confidence in redemptive knowledge and social reform.

It is suggested, for example, that "in the end, the pragmatists tell us, what matters is our loyalty to other human beings clinging together against the dark, not our hope of getting things right."[45] And that "in his [Dewey's] ideal society, culture is no longer dominated by the ideal of objective cognition but by that of aesthetic enhancement."[46] "We would see the social sciences not as awkward and unsuccessful attempts to imitate the physicists' elegance, certainty, and freedom from concern with 'value,' but as suggestions for making human lives into works of art."[47]

This highly selective interpretation of pragmatism builds on a disjunction Dewey could not accept. He did indeed prize aesthetic experience—as a potential consummation in everyday life—but he could not counterpose the cognitive and the aesthetic.[48] He might well agree that human lives should be in some sense works of art, but not as a rejection

44. "The problem of restoring integration and cooperation between man's beliefs about the world in which he lives and his beliefs about the values and purposes that should direct his conduct is the deepest problem of modern life. It is the problem of any philosophy that is not isolated from that life" (Dewey, *Quest for Certainty*, 255).

45. Rorty, *Consequences of Pragmatism*, 166.

46. Richard Rorty, *Philosophy and the Mirror of Nature* (Princeton: Princeton University Press, 1979), 13.

47. Rorty, *Consequences of Pragmatism*, 87.

48. See Dewey, *Art as Experience*, 15f., 37f., 46.

of scientific method. On the contrary, only on the basis of disciplined learning from experience can we presume to offer responsible "suggestions for making human lives into works of art."

The contemporary effort to subjectivize Dewey is not likely to survive sustained examination.[49] It is illuminating, however, in that it shows how pragmatism, like other modernist perspectives, is vulnerable to distortion in directions that reflect a loss of confidence and a failure of nerve.[50] In fact, Dewey retained a modernist commitment to the strong, resourceful ego, very much in the business of getting things right.[51] At the same time he shared a postmodern awareness of fragility and flux, contingency and diversity. His response, however, evokes strength, engagement, and faith in human nature. His vision of community calls for democratic, problem-solving interaction, not a desperate "clinging together against the dark."

I do not mean to suggest that Dewey's pragmatic naturalism, as distinguished from what I called generic naturalism, is wholly satisfactory. In one important respect he fails to meet the challenge of modernity, which requires a robust understanding of evil, especially evil encouraged by the sovereignty of will. The optimistic spirit of pragmatism looks to the solution of all human problems, so long as the ethos of science, which includes open communication, is honored and maintained. Human frailty and recalcitrance; the persistence of domination; genuinely tragic choices; the collusion of good and evil: these are theoretical orphans. They are by no means wholly overlooked, but they have no secure place in the pragmatist interpretation of moral experience. The need to modify pragmatism in this respect informs our discussion at a number of points in subsequent chapters.[52]

49. See James Campbell, "Rorty's Use of Dewey," Southern Journal of Philosophy 22 (1984): 175–87; Boisvert, Dewey's Metaphysics, 197ff.; Robert B. Westbrook, John Dewey and American Democracy (Ithaca: Cornell University Press, 1991), 539ff.

50. In 1943, Partisan Review ran a symposium in which Dewey, Hook, and Nagel assailed a "new failure of nerve," which they saw as displayed in a growing interest, at that time, in "anti-naturalist" theologies. Fifty years later much the same could be said of postmodern doctrines, including the pragmatism espoused by Rorty.

51. As Campbell points out, Rorty's statement about getting things right "is true only if we intend 'getting things right' to be an epistemological claim about the perfect mirroring of antecedent reality. But, for Dewey, we can do more than cling together in the dark because 'getting things right,' for Dewey, means effective social reconstruction to anticipate and deal with social problems" ("Rorty's Use of Dewey," 182).

52. See Chapter 6, "Recalcitrance and Frailty."

MORAL WELL-BEING

As befits a morality informed by the spirit of scientific inquiry, assessment of consequences is an indispensable phase of naturalism in ethics. In moral philosophy much is made of the distinction between "teleological" or "consequentialist" perspectives on one hand and "deontological" perspectives on the other. A deontological ethic is duty-centered or (in more recent discussion) rights-centered. The key to morality is conduct guided by unalterable precepts, received or divine, by a priori premises, or by an intuitive sense of the right. The motto of deontology is: follow the precept, whatever the consequences. A consequentialist ethics, on the other hand, treats all moral judgments as ultimately contingent and justified by their effects.[53] The motto is: morality is made for humans, not humans for morality.

There is no difficulty, of course, in assimilating to naturalism an operative or functional deontology. With respect to particular acts, roles, or institutions, it may well be desirable that judgment should conform to established precepts, especially in upholding duties and protecting rights; otherwise, rights and duties would be intolerably insecure. Given what we know of human nature and human society, it is easy to agree that "enough people, enough of the time . . . have to be prepared to stick at doing various things, whatever the consequences."[54] If we say torture should be excluded as a morally justifiable option in human affairs, the effect is to establish a deontological ethic. But the warrant of that ethic is a reasoned concern for processes and outcomes. It is justified by our understanding of what consequences ensue when torture is open to moral excuse.

Consequences for what? The easy answer is "human well-being" or "the general good." Morality does indeed enhance the common good, but so do health care, economic prosperity, fire protection, and education. Each of these has or can have a moral dimension, but the distinctively moral cannot be equated with whatever contributes to general utility.[55] Something special is at stake, a certain kind of well-being, perhaps best summarized as *the enhancement of fellowship*. Fellowship does

53. Because the analysis looks to outcomes or ends, it is sometimes called teleological, without, however, any necessary connotations of "immanent," "latent," or "unfolding" ends.

54. Bernard Williams, *Morality: An Introduction to Ethics* (New York: Harper Torchbooks, 1972), 105.

55. "[W]hat morality seems to need is not the gross notion of utility, but a notion more finely focused on the vital interests, the basic needs, the central human concerns, that create obligations" (James Griffin, *Well-Being* [Oxford: Clarendon Press, 1986], 40).

not entail the extinction of self-regard or the dissolution of self into collective life. There is a dual concern for the interests of others and for one's own integrity.

Much depends on how we understand "well-being." When well-being is taken to mean happiness, satisfaction, preference, or utility, we lose purchase on what is of genuine moral worth. It is not morally better to have more rather than less efficiency, more rather than less material goods, more rather than less fulfillment of desires, including "informed" desires. Either words like happiness and utility hide something more significant, or they refer to outcomes that do not warrant the kinds of self-sacrifice, deference to the interests of others, and assumption of responsibility we associate with morality. To gain a clearer focus, we need a conception of moral well-being.

Moral well-being has its roots in the mundane facts of dependency and connectedness, that is, in the inescapably social nature of human existence. Out of connectedness there develops, with considerable variability, what David Hume called "a tender sympathy with others and a generous concern for our kind and species."[56] Sympathy and fellow-feeling inspire benevolence; selfishness is condemned and guilt is evoked. These social and psychological facts explain the emergence, prevalence, and direction of moral sentiments. However, they do not quite capture the meaning of moral well-being.

It is one thing to be warm-hearted and benevolent; it is something else to appreciate the values at stake in our relations with others and in the construction of our selves. The first is worthy and beneficial, as is the care a mother gives her infant, but it is *pre-moral* in that it depends on an immediate context of mutual satisfaction. The second reaches a genuinely moral plane because it makes concern for well-being a governing standard or ideal, a claim upon the individual irrespective of immediate satisfaction.

Thus moral well-being is more than sympathy and concern. It refers to a kind of will, commitment, and *competence*. Moral competence is the capacity to be an effective moral actor. This requires reflection as well as feeling, responsibility as well as love. It demands an ability to distinguish "the enjoyed and the enjoyable, the desired and the desirable, the satis*fying* and the satis*factory*."[57] Moral competence is a variable attribute of persons, institutions, and communities.

56. David Hume, *An Inquiry Concerning the Principles of Morals* (1751; reprint, Indianapolis: Bobbs-Merrill, 1957), 10.
57. Dewey, *Quest for Certainty*, 260, Dewey's emphasis.

The ultimate point and object of morality is human betterment. But the betterment we have in mind is not that of improving material conditions or providing more pleasurable experiences. It is the realization of values that are genuinely good—for persons as psychic unities; for institutions as beneficial enterprises; for communities as frameworks for lives worth living. That is why reason, love, good faith, respect, and temperance are moral virtues. Other virtues—aesthetic sensibility, athletic skill, physical courage, business acumen—are justly prized, but their significance for morality may be small or even negative. Only distinctively moral virtues enhance the will to choose and the competence to pursue ideals of fellowship, that is, of mutual concern and respect.

A moral order is effective if it succeeds in creating widespread commitment to "desiring the desirable."[58] That commitment is an aspect of personality. Hence we look to virtue and character as the foundations of morality. To answer the question, Consequences for what? we look above all to *character-defining* or at least *character-impacting* choice. "Consequences include effects upon character, upon confirming and weakening habits, as well as tangibly obvious results."[59] This is a major theme in Dewey's moral theory.[60]

The creation of an integrated moral self, capable of exercising self-restraint, expressing love, shouldering responsibility, engaging in moral reflection, is the prime end or outcome that governs the assessment of consequences. At the same time, character and disposition are *causes* of consequences. We judge character by what it leads to and what we can rely on. "A holiness of character which is celebrated only on holy-days is unreal. A virtue of honesty, or chastity or benevolence which lives upon itself apart from definite results consumes itself and goes up in

58. This argument is developed in Raymond Jaffe, *The Pragmatic Conception of Justice* (Berkeley: University of California Publications in Philosophy no. 34, 1960), chap. 6.
59. John Dewey, *Human Nature and Conduct* (New York: Modern Library, 1930), 46.
60. See ibid., chap. 3, and his contribution to John Dewey and James H. Tufts, *Ethics* (New York: Holt, 1932), 176–88. Of course, Dewey is not alone in arguing for an ethics based on virtue and character. For contemporary treatments see Stanley Hauerwas, *Vision and Virtue* (Notre Dame: University of Notre Dame Press, 1981), chap. 3; Bernard Williams, "A Critique of Utilitarianism," in J. J. C. Smart and Bernard Williams, *Utilitarianism: For and Against* (Cambridge: Cambridge University Press, 1973); Alasdair MacIntyre, *After Virtue: A Study in Moral Theory*, 2d ed. (Notre Dame: University of Notre Dame Press, 1984); and Martha Nussbaum, *Love's Knowledge* (Oxford: Oxford University Press, 1990), chap. 2.

smoke."[61] Conduct is an expression of character; character is manifested in patterns of conduct.

Character is an attribute of institutions and communities as well as of persons.[62] At each level a configuration emerges that determines the contribution of character to moral competence. The configuration consists of morally relevant, variably integrated capacities and commitments. The latter include, for individuals, having appropriate feelings and mustering psychic resources; for institutions, the balance struck between special purposes and more comprehensive values; for communities, the capacity to integrate civility and piety. These matters are discussed at some length in later chapters.

Character is, to a large extent, a product of personal and social history. It is composed of habits, dependencies, interests, and values—all, for the most part, unconsciously developed and embraced. Nevertheless, character is also in some measure chosen. The task of moral awareness— and of leadership—is to replace uncontrolled, unreflective development with more controlled and deliberate ways of forming moral agents.

In this view, the moral worth of an act or rule is assessed by considering its consequences for character. This is a guide to making rules, and to applying them as well. The question is: What kind of person, institution, or community will result from following a particular course of conduct or from adopting a given rule or policy? This focuses attention on the *internal relevance* of what we do; and it allows the conclusion that consequences for character will have priority, in many important cases, over consequences for particular ends such as winning a game or managing an enterprise.

In an important sense, the perspective just outlined is very traditional. It makes the central problem of ethics the salvation of souls. We may take "soul" to be "the spiritual part of man considered in its moral aspect,"[63] without any connotation of disembodied being or afterlife. Soul is the moral unity and competence of a person, institution, or

61. Dewey, *Human Nature and Conduct*, 45. "[John Stuart Mill] brought utilitarianism in closer accord with the unbiased moral sense of mankind when he said that 'to do as you would be done by and to love your neighbor as yourself constitute the ideal perfection of utilitarian morality.' For such a statement puts disposition, character, first, and calculation of specific results second" (Dewey and Tufts, *Ethics,* 265).

62. See my *TVA and the Grass Roots* (1949; reprint, Berkeley: University of California Press, 1984), 181ff.; *The Organizational Weapon* (1952; reprint, Glencoe, Ill.: Free Press, 1960), 56ff.; *Leadership in Administration* (1957; reprint, Berkeley: University of California Press, 1984), 38ff. Also, see below, Chapter 12, "Ends, Means, and Integrity."

63. *Oxford English Dictionary,* s.v. "soul."

community. It is that elusive, fragile, but nonetheless real and valued phenomenon we call integrity.[64] To be in peril of one's soul is to place integrity at risk; to save one's soul is to establish or mend one's moral character. Considering how difficult this phenomenon is to identify, yet how important it is to human well-being, no wonder it has taken on richly symbolic vestments. Naturalists may wish to dismiss the symbolism as distracting and mystifying, but they need not ignore the underlying truth. Nor should we shrink from recognizing what the modern idiom owes to a religious heritage.

▼   ▲   ▼   ▲   ▼

A crucial component of moral competence is the capacity to engage in moral *inquiry*. For this something more is needed than mental ability: an array of psychological and institutional dispositions are required. These include the will to seek goods that are genuine and enduring rather than superficial, transitory, or ultimately self-destructive; critical distance from preconceptions and vested interests; stable feelings of sympathy, respect, and fellowship; toleration of ambiguity, diversity, and openness. This last is especially important under modern conditions. Flexibility and responsiveness are hallmarks of the modernist naturalism we have been describing. They are attributes appropriate to modern selves, institutions, and communities.

To determine the good requires an appreciation for particular circumstances, variable contexts, and competing values. What is genuinely good for a small child is not necessarily good for an older child or an adult. Children of the same age also differ among themselves, from a moral point of view, if only because some are more needy or vulnerable than others. And experience shows that many settings have roughly equivalent competing goods, such as alternative careers or life-styles. This plurality makes choice difficult, and sometimes tragic, especially when painful trade-offs are required.

Appreciation for diversity and particularity is no bar to drawing general conclusions about moral experience. On the contrary, it presupposes that possibility. If we recognize the claims of unique persons or artistic creations to be treated as such, and if we give them priority in moral or aesthetic judgment over the claims of rules or abstract principles, we are,

64. Integrity as a counter to utilitarian thinking is discussed in Williams, "Critique of Utilitarianism," 108ff.; and in Bernard Williams, *Moral Luck* (Cambridge: Cambridge University Press, 1981), chaps. 1, 3, 4.

in effect, generalizing about selected aspects of moral experience.[65] Thus we may say that "each friend is to be cherished for his or her own sake, not simply as an instantiation of the universal value, friendship."[66] This important moral truth is derived from implicit theories of personality and social process—theories constructed for the light they may shed on human well-being.

In a naturalist ethics we study the varieties, vicissitudes, and limits of moral experience. We do not necessarily assume that such experience is very orderly or determinate. *Insofar as* we can discern patterns, we try to use that knowledge to enhance our sensibilities and inform our judgments. This enterprise is neither a quest for algorithms nor an effort to identify, on analytical grounds, a "key" to morality or justice. Nor does it need a new beginning. A social science of moral ordering draws on a rich tradition of philosophical thought, from which it gains a steady focus on *the core values at stake* in moral experience, especially responsibility, autonomy, integrity, reason, fairness, equality; and on *recurrent perplexities and tensions,* for example, those affecting the determination of obligation and self-interest, formal and substantive justice, moral and social equality.

I do not mean to deprecate or deny the larger significance of moral philosophy for human self-awareness and the life of the mind. I suggest, however, that much of moral philosophy should be more fully assimilated to social theory and should be understood as setting an agenda for more incremental, more self-corrective, more empirical inquiry.

In the pragmatist conception, "experience" is active, purposive, problem-solving. People and institutions make choices, appreciate values, accept or withdraw from moral responsibility. What we *learn* from this experience guides the construction of a moral order. Much of this knowledge is tacit and "funded," that is, built up out of preconscious problem-solving by human communities.[67] Like principles of due process, which emerge out of recurrent encounters with the abuse of power, funded experience is grounded in felt need, suffering, and satisfaction. Thus understood, moral experience is fluid and variable, but it is also the crucible within which enduring values are established and institutional learning takes place.

65. See Chapter 7, "The Primacy of the Particular."
66. Nussbaum, *Love's Knowledge,* 82.
67. Here (and in pragmatist thought generally) "problem-solving" does not refer to explicit mental operations, as in solving a mathematical problem, but to finding ways of resolving "problematic situations."

Of all the subjects of that learning, none is more important than a balanced view of moral realism and moral idealism.[68] In later chapters of this book we more than once distinguish what we can *rely on* from what we can *aspire to;* moral realism looks to the former, moral idealism to the latter. Realism encourages sustained attention to the material foundations of morality, especially how self-interest generates incentives for moral restraint; and to the corruptions and frustrations that so often afflict the quest for fellowship. From the standpoint of moral realism, every virtue has a humbling vice.

A large part of naturalist ethics is the identification of reliable incentives and recurrent vulnerabilities. This leads readily to what we may call *baseline* morality—the idea that moral requirements should be closely tied to urgent problems, such as, in doing justice, protection of public order and basic rights; or, in the case of individual morality, the need for discipline of unruly passions. A baseline morality is often the most we can aspire to; and it is always a precondition for further development.

Nevertheless, we need not be content with limited aspirations. Once a baseline morality is secure, we can respond to opportunities for extending responsibility and enriching fellowship. The conditions of *survival* are easier to meet than those of *flourishing,* which are more complex and more fragile. It does not follow, however, that we should fail to treasure what is precarious or cease to strive for what is nobly conceived.

I do not doubt that the corruption of ideals is easier than their fulfillment and is, in that special sense, more natural. But a predisposition to growth and development is as natural, in organic life, as is a predisposition to decay. Good health and family bonding take work to sustain, but these conditions have biological worth and a biological foundation. It may be more difficult to hold on to a moral community than to let it fall apart, but the needs and impulses that sustain communities are no less natural than the forces of disintegration.[69]

68. As the context indicates, these terms do not refer to *epistemological* realism and idealism.

69. This Aristotelian perspective is shared by pragmatism. On Dewey and Aristotle, see John Herman Randall, Jr., "Dewey's Interpretation of the History of Philosophy," in Paul Arthur Schilpp, ed., *The Philosophy of John Dewey* (Evanston, Ill.: Northwestern University Press, 1939), 101f.

TWO

Reason and Rationalism

An ambiguous legacy of modernity, from the standpoint of morality, is the movement of thought we call rationalism. The Enlightenment thinkers disparaged the claims of faith and tradition. In the new age, they said, truth is to be found in the human capacity to know and evaluate, not in submission to received doctrine. When people are released from ignorance and superstition, the pure light of rational understanding will prevail. Therefore it is necessary to think anew about the foundations of that understanding. René Descartes set the tone in 1637 when he argued that valid knowledge requires sweeping away all prejudices that obstruct the formation of clear and distinct ideas. Individuals as truth-seekers, alone and self-sufficient, may begin with a clean slate.

Science and technology have gained immensely from this celebration of unfettered and rational thought. Their practitioners could look at the world with fresh eyes; experiment without worrying about sacred cows; construct models based wholly on scientific needs; promise new levels of health and prosperity. Moreover, the quest for intellectual clarity and self-sufficiency has done much to fortify and civilize the moral order— especially in demanding that reasons be given to justify power, policy, and custom.

But some forms of rationalism have undermined the community's capacity to grasp the full meaning of moral well-being. In doing so, they have impoverished the idea of reason. Many who have been skeptical of the claims of modernity have insisted on a contrast between "true," "substantive," or "comprehensive" reason and rationalist interpretations of value and conduct. A notable example is Edmund Burke (1729–1797), who strenuously opposed rationalist ideologies and policies, especially as reflected in the ideas of the revolutionary leaders in France. Against efforts to remake society in accordance with schemes devised by inevitably short-sighted individuals and groups, Burke recommended reliance on tradition and on the hard-won lessons of history. He was not hostile to reason.[1] But true reason is concrete, not abstract; it is bounded by and continuous with the common sense of mankind.

> The concrete reason, because it is not a wisdom merely of the intellect, is not a wisdom only of the few; it is latent and potential in all individuals of the community. The mass of Englishmen, who live according to traditional prejudices and habits, are safe, because customs are "the standing wisdom of the country."[2]

Concrete reason is not alien to critical thought, but "the science of constructing a commonwealth . . . is, like every other experimental science, not to be taught *a priori*. Nor is it a short experience that can instruct us in that practical science; because the real effects of moral causes are not always immediate; but that which in the first instance is prejudicial may be excellent in remoter operation. . . . The reverse also happens: and very plausible schemes, with very pleasing commencements, have often shameful and lamentable conclusions."[3]

Burke's reason is *anchored* rationality. When human needs and aspirations are at issue, only those ideas and programs make sense that are securely founded in the continuities of biological and social life. True reason is not counterposed to impulse or passion; rather, it builds upon them, is nourished by them, and leads them into constructive and self-enhancing paths. Ideas that ignore the persistent features of the human condition or seek to abolish them are to that extent offensive to reason.

From this perspective, it is unreasonable to decide concrete cases on the basis of an abstract morality. "Circumstances," wrote Burke, "give, in reality, to every political principle its distinguishing color and discriminating effect. The circumstances are what render every civil and political scheme beneficial or obnoxious to mankind."[4] Therefore anchored

---

1. "Burke's attack was not, as is often stated, a defense of history against reason. He was, perhaps above all else, a defender of reason. What he hated was rationalism, the derivation of a whole system of ideas from *a priori* or postulated grounds" (Louis I. Bredvold and Ralph G. Ross, eds., *The Philosophy of Edmund Burke* [Ann Arbor: University of Michigan Press, 1960], 5).

2. Charles Parkin, *The Moral Basis of Burke's Political Thought* (New York: Russell & Russell, 1956), 116.

3. Edmund Burke, *Reflections on the French Revolution* (1790; reprint, London: Dent, 1910), 58.

4. Ibid., 6.

rationality is self-limiting. Ideas footed in reality—the reality of present circumstance and past experience—lose their abstract quality and contain inherent principles of correction and restraint. This rejection of the pursuit of virtue "as the crow flies" has been a keystone of the conservative imagination.[5]

In Burke's view, genuine moral judgment is always concrete and always respectful of the person, institution, or social order whose ills are being considered. Genuine values are to be sought within those organic unities and not in some catalog of universal ideals. There are moral values in family life, and general statements about them can be made, but for purposes of judgment we must look to the experience at hand. We must consider the moral resources of a particular form of family in a particular historical setting. This is a far cry from imposing an ideal—say, of procreation as the aim of marriage—derived from abstract theological premises.

The critique of rationalism is no monopoly of conservatism. Max Horkheimer, founder of the Frankfurt School of critical theory, argued that in modern thought "objective reason" has given way to "subjective reason." Objective reason is the pre-Enlightenment conception that reason is "a structure inherent in reality."[6]

> This view asserted the existence of reason as a force not only in the individual mind but also in the objective world. . . . It aimed at evolving a comprehensive system, or hierarchy, of all beings, including man and his aims. . . . Its objective structure, and not just man and his purposes, was to be the measuring rod for individual thoughts and actions. This concept of reason never precluded subjective reason, but regarded the latter as only a partial, limited expression of a universal rationality from which criteria for all things and beings were derived. The emphasis was on ends rather than means.[7]

In that pre-Enlightenment tradition, reason is awareness and appreciation of a natural order. As part of that order, human beings find fulfillment in recognizing their place in the scheme of things, in cultivating virtues of dutiful participation, and in achieving appropriate standards of excellence. In the classic view, people make their own lives, but they do so within frameworks that transcend human choice. Again, morality is anchored, not freely constructed.

Subjective reason is the individual's capacity to classify and make inferences abstracted from specific content and essentially concerned with the articulation of means and ends. Thus subjective reason is

5. Michael Oakeshott, *Rationalism in Politics* (New York: Basic Books, 1962), 69.
6. *Eclipse of Reason* (New York: Oxford University Press, 1947), 11.
7. Ibid., 4f.

instrumental and technical. It does not find reason in the world but only in the individuals seeking the best way of attaining their ends, whatever they may be. As a result:

> Justice, equality, happiness, tolerance . . . [which] were in preceding centuries supposed to be inherent in or sanctioned by reason, have lost their intellectual roots. They are still aims or ends, but there is no rational agency authorized to appraise and link them to an objective reality. Endorsed by venerable historical documents they may still enjoy a certain prestige. . . . Nevertheless, they lack any confirmation by reason in its modern sense.[8]

As against modern subjective reason—another name for rationalism—Horkheimer preferred the objectivism of the past. In this respect, and in his attack on instrumental reason as a major source of alienation and domination, he agreed with many conservative critics of modern thought and culture.[9]

These yearnings for "genuine" reason reflect a pervasive discontent with detached, formal, or wholly instrumental modes of argument. The alternative is a quest for more substantive, more contextual, more experiential criteria of judgment. The latter cannot be derived from exercises of the mind, however subtle, that are divorced from history or that depend on simplified models of the springs of action or the foundations of decision.

RATIONALISM AND POSITIVISM

Two very different rationalist programs emerged during the seventeenth and eighteenth centuries. One we may call "axiomatic," the other "positivist." Each contributed to new ways of thinking about morality; each radically abridges the complexity of moral experience; each reduces reason to a more limited rationality.

Axiomatic Rationalism

Axiomatic rationalism may be traced in part to philosophical idealism, which asserts the primacy of mind in the quest for fundamental truth.[10]

8. Ibid., 23.
9. But this criticism took him and others of his school, such as Herbert Marcuse, in more radical and utopian directions. See Max Horkheimer, "Traditional and Critical Theory," in his *Critical Theory: Selected Essays* (New York: Herder and Herder, 1972), 188–243.
10. Here "idealism" refers to the foundations of knowledge, not to moral aspiration. The two meanings are connected when, for example, ideal forms are taken to represent especially pure or high expressions of knowledge, beauty, or the good.

Secure knowledge is made possible by the structured receptivity of the human intellect, which gives form to inchoate experience; or by an active process of interpretation, which grasps directly the logical structure of reality. This emphasis on mind lends a privileged status to *ideas*. The pure conception or abstract form is both the starting point and the outcome of serious inquiry. We begin with an intuition, or a set of axioms and theorems; we end by apprehending a completed system or full-blown theory of, say, morality, justice, or the common good.[11]

The ethos of idealism is rationalist in the great weight given to a priori conceptions and abstract reasoning. The result—not necessarily intended—is a postulational mode of thought. *Truth is arrived at by elaborating the logical consequences of a set of assumptions.* The empirical world sets conditions and imposes constraints, but its flux and variation are not the true source of understanding. In the idealist perspective we do not learn from experience. Rather, genuine knowledge flows from the play of intellect; it is deductive in spirit if not in strict logic.

The philosophers of the Enlightenment sought clear, simple, self-evident starting-points for reasoning about the nature of human understanding or about substantive issues of politics or morality. There were important differences in the premises they used—in political theory how the "state of nature" was conceived; in epistemology the givenness of innate ideas versus sense perceptions—but this did not change their postulational method.[12]

Axiomatic rationalism cuts across the once-conventional distinction between "rationalists" and "empiricists" among Enlightenment philosophers.[13] Thus John Locke (1632–1704) is classified as an empiricist because he argued forcefully against the concept of innate ideas, holding (with some important qualifications) that knowledge is ultimately derived from data of the senses. Moreover, he considered the mind a basically receptive organ, a tabula rasa on which is written the book of experience. In epistemology, therefore, Locke was not an idealist: he stressed neither the active nor the constitutive nature of mind. Nevertheless, like his older contemporary Thomas Hobbes (1588–1679), he

11. Even for Hegel, the idealist most concerned to show how ideas live and change in recurrent encounter with historical experience, history obeys an inner logic and is, in the end, the vehicle by which the immanent Idea is revealed and fulfilled.

12. For a recent argument to this effect, see Thomas A. Spragens, Jr., *The Irony of Liberal Reason* (Chicago: University of Chicago Press, 1981), chap. 2.

13. Now often questioned; see, for example, Hidē Ishiguro, "Pre-established Harmony Versus Constant Conjunction: A Reconsideration of the Distinction Between Rationalism and Empiricism," in Anthony Kenny, ed., *Rationalism, Empiricism, and Idealism* (Oxford: Clarendon Press, 1986), 61–85.

looked to mathematics as the paradigm of knowledge and did not hesitate to spin conclusions from abstract premises. This is clearly revealed
in their theory of the social contract, which begins with presuppositions
about self-preservation, self-interest, and reason in the state of nature and
then elaborates inferences about liberty, order, and prosperity. Much the
same can be said of Locke's theory of property. These exercises in me-
thodical reasoning from abstract premises were characteristic of the Enlightenment philosophers. In this respect they more closely reflected the
spirit of idealism than that of empiricism as we have come to know it.[14]

The foundational and constitutive nature of mind is the centerpiece of
that culminating philosophy of the Enlightenment, the idealism of Immanuel Kant (1724–1804). In his epistemology Kant upheld the validity
of Newtonian science—but he did so in his own way. According to
Kant, the knowledge we gain from observation of phenomena is
grounded in a priori intuitions and transcendental categories, notably
space, time, causality. Our minds are so formed that they cannot help
but apprehend sense data in accordance with orderly and systematic principles. To be sure, science is empirical: "percepts" are indispensable to
knowledge of the physical world. But the *foundation* of knowledge, what
gives us confidence that the findings are not wholly fleeting and contingent, is the structure of the human mind.

Kant drew a sharp line between physical science and moral reason.
The former is the realm of cognition and necessity; the latter is the realm
of will, action, and freedom. Kant thereby laid the basis for a wall of separation between the natural sciences and the human sciences. Natural science gives us reliable knowledge, but that knowledge, however secure,
speaks only to appearances; it does not tell us about the "noumenal"
world of "things-in-themselves." Behind the world of appearance lies a
deeper reality known only to God, but glimpsed by human persons in
their capacity as moral actors. As part of the larger realm of spirit, morality puts us in touch with a truth science cannot reach.[15]

14. Thus Ernst Cassirer notes that "even an empiricist like Locke had put the type of
relation dominant in moral truths on the same plane with the interconnection of geometric
judgments and theorems, and attributed to morality the selfsame demonstrative certainty as
in metaphysics" (*Kant's Life and Thought* [1918; reprint, New Haven: Yale University
Press, 1981], 232).
15. As an organism, a human being is subject to the same natural necessity as other objects; as a moral agent, however, endowed with free will, a person is "noumenon," not
"phenomenon." The noumenal self belongs to a realm beyond appearance, beyond nature,
and is therefore unknowable by the methods of science. See Immanuel Kant, *Critique of
Practical Reason* (1788; reprint, Indianapolis: Bobbs-Merrill, 1956), 98ff.; also Stephan Kör-
ner, *Kant* (New Haven: Yale University Press), chap. 7.

Nevertheless, a commitment to rationalism pervades Kant's thought, no less in ethics than in epistemology. Autonomous individuals, freely subordinating themselves to moral law, must ever attend to the rationality of their choices. And the supreme principle of rationality in moral affairs is the categorical imperative. One version reads: It would be inconsistent with your nature as a rational being to adopt a rule (a "maxim") for your own conduct that would not be applicable, as a law of nature, to all rational persons similarly situated. In ethics, as in science, there are formal principles derived from the structure and operation of intellect. They impose order upon moral experience by providing canons to which human action *must* conform, on pain of incoherence, and therefore of failure.

In this view, an ideal society is made up of rational actors whose reasonableness, from a moral point of view, consists in conforming conduct to a justified rule or principle. The rational justification of the rule in turn derives from *its* conformity to a meta-rule, the categorical imperative, which is the embodiment of practical reason. Thus *where basic principles are at issue* we need only understand what it means to be rational. We do not need to learn from experience: "For whereas, so far as nature is concerned, experience supplies the rules and is the source of truth, in respect of moral laws it is, alas, the mother of illusion! Nothing is more reprehensible than to derive the laws prescribing what *ought to be done* from what *is done,* or to impose upon them the limits by which the latter is circumscribed."[16]

Kant was surely right to stress that morality requires something more than inclination or emotion, however benevolent. Benevolent feelings may be *pre*-moral, that is, not governed by an understanding of what is *right* to do, regardless of immediate pain or satisfaction. We can also accept the idea that self-restraint—governance of the self—is a vital aspect of morality. Indeed, every theory of morality takes for granted the moral worth of self-restraint. Whatever else it may be, morality is a way of checking and transcending *raw* self-interest, *raw* passion, *raw* desire. Even the utilitarians, who associate morality with happiness or pleasure, understand that, to be moral, individuals have a duty to defer to aggregate well-being, that is, they must yield self-interest to the good of all.

16. Immanuel Kant, *Critique of Pure Reason,* 2d ed. (1787; reprint, London: Macmillan, 1929), 313. Kant cited Plato approvingly as one who held that "whoever would derive the concepts of virtue from experience . . . would make of virtue something which changes according to time and circumstance, an ambiguous monstrosity not admitting the formation of any rule" (ibid., 311).

But self-restraint is only one element of morality, one way of acting in the light of a standard or ideal. Another way is more positive—to accept responsibility, make commitments, foster appropriate feelings. All this may be done out of a sense of duty and thus meet Kant's criterion of moral worth, yet it need not involve, as a central matter, the repression of impulse or desire. Morality is not necessarily experienced as submission or constraint. Impulse and inclination may threaten morality, but they may instead nourish and support it.

In the austere vision of the Protestant moralists, of whom Kant was one, and in the Freudian canon as well, morality is achieved at the expense of more natural impulses. This gives to the idea of "governance" an import it need not have. Governance is always constraining, to some extent. But it can also summon and elaborate, form and develop, the impulses that sustain a moral order. Therefore we cannot be indifferent to the *variable* significance of passions and interests for moral well-being. Some pleasures, such as those that arise from the union of sex and love, and some interests, such as the benefits gained from reciprocity and cooperation, are reliable resources for moral development. Others, of course, are enemies of the good. We need to know which to foster and which to inhibit.[17] Hence morality must be informed by what we can learn from recurrent experience.

A serious consequence of losing touch with experience is intellectual hubris or pride, which often becomes a kind of arrogance. People who think that everything depends on the *premises* you select and that *argument* is the key to moral decision become easy prey to closed systems and impenetrable ideologies. Armed with what seems to be irrefutable logic— often heavily defended by an arcane vocabulary—the adherent accepts and justifies whatever conclusions the system generates. "Who says A," he cautions, "must say B."

An egregious example is the intellectual trap in which many Marxist-Leninists were caught, in the heyday of that doctrine. Those who accepted the system's axioms and theorems found it difficult to take account of relevant evidence regarding means and ends. They could not count the full costs of "revolutionary struggle," nor could they place that aim within an informing context of multiple, self-limiting ends.

In 1938 there occurred a revealing encounter between John Dewey and Leon Trotsky (1879–1940). The exiled, soon to be assassinated leader of the Russian Revolution had just published a polemic against

17. For a discussion of Kant's view "that all human interests and all human pleasures are on a par," see Spragens, *Irony of Liberal Reason,* 243.

liberal, socialist, and anarchist critics of "Bolshevik amoralism."[18] He ended his counterattack with a theoretical coda on the "dialectic interdependence of means and ends." Trotsky denied that the Marxist goal, "the liberation of mankind," justifies *any* means. Only those means are permissible

> which unite the revolutionary proletariat, fill their hearts with irreconcilable hostility to oppression, teach them contempt for official morality and its democratic echoers, imbue them with consciousness of their own historic mission, raise their courage and spirit of self-sacrifice in the struggle. Precisely from this it flows that *not* all means are permissible. When we say that the end justifies the means, then for us the conclusion follows that the great revolutionary end spurns those base means and ways which set one part of the working class against other parts, or attempt to make the masses happy without their participation; or lower the faith of the masses in themselves and their organization, replacing it by worship for the "leaders."[19]

All this, said Trotsky, flows from the perspective of dialectical materialism, which recognizes no dualism of means and ends.

Dewey was invited to respond.[20] He did so in part by calling attention to Trotsky's assertion that only such means are permissible as *really* lead to the liberation of mankind. That would be fine, said Dewey, if followed through. But in fact Trotsky has no procedure for assessing whether his more proximate end, proletarian revolution, is an appropriate means for human liberation.[21] On the contrary, the doctrine of class struggle, more specifically of proletarian revolution, and even more specifically of the leadership of a Marxist-Leninist "vanguard party," *is taken as given:*

> Since this end [the liberation of mankind] can be achieved only through revolution, the liberating morality of the proletariat of necessity is endowed with a revolutionary character. . . . It deduces a rule of conduct from the laws of the development of society, thus primarily from the class struggle, this law of all laws.[22]

But here Trotsky abandons the interdependence of means and ends. The means are not controlled by the end but are reached deductively on

18. Leon Trotsky, "Their Morals and Ours," *The New International* (June 1938): 163–73.
19. Ibid., 172.
20. At that time Dewey was chairman of a commission of inquiry into charges made against Trotsky at the Moscow Trials.
21. Of course this leaves unsettled the meaning of "liberation," but Dewey left that aside.
22. Trotsky, "Their Morals and Ours," 172.

the basis of a general theory of historical development. Since it is presumed to be the *only* road to human betterment, the class struggle, Dewey pointed out, "does not need to be critically examined with respect to its actual objective consequences." This is the basic flaw.

> It is as if a biologist or a physician were to assert that a certain law of biology which he accepts is so related to the end of health that the means of arriving at health—and the only means—can be deduced from it, so that no further examination of biological phenomena is needed. The whole case is prejudged.[23]

Trotsky did embrace, to some extent at least, a morality of class struggle. He argued that the integrity of the struggle places limits on the use of "base means" which, for example, "make the masses happy without their participation." This constraint has moral worth, just as good personnel policy has moral worth, but the connection between the technical means and the justifying end is at best loose and at worst self-defeating. A developed theory of class struggle may impose strategic and tactical limits, such as repudiation of terrorism, but the criterion remains *what serves the class struggle,* not what serves human well-being. The service of the former to the latter is guaranteed by the intellectual system, not by the study of revolutions and their aftermaths.

A very different example of the harmful effects of postulational thinking is to be found in Robert Nozick's theory of natural rights and the minimal state.[24] In a book widely appreciated as an elegant updating of John Locke's political theory, Nozick attempts to derive broad conclusions about the legitimacy of political authority from basic postulates about social participation. A major premise is that society consists of "distinct individuals" with "inviolable rights," most importantly rights in property. He concludes from "the fact of our separate existences" that "there is no justified sacrifice of some of us for others."[25] This conclusion in turn entails stringent limitations on the authority of government. Any effort to redistribute income by coercive taxation violates the rights of those whose income is taken for the benefit of others.[26] More gener-

23. John Dewey, "Means and Ends: Their Interdependence, and Leon Trotsky's 'Their Morals and Ours,' " *The New International* (August 1938): 233.

24. *Anarchy, State, and Utopia* (New York: Basic Books, 1974).

25. Ibid., 33.

26. One critic points to "an extraordinary but apparent consequence of this view that for a government to tax each of its able-bodied citizens five dollars a year to support cripples and orphans would violate the rights of the able-bodied, and would be morally impermissible, whereas to refrain from taxation even if it meant allowing the cripples and orphans to starve to death would be the morally required governmental policy" (Samuel Scheffler, "Natural Rights, Equality, and the Minimal State," in Jeffrey Paul, ed., *Reading Nozick* [Totowa, N.J.: Rowman & Littlefield, 1981], 151).

ally, the only legitimate function of government is to maintain essential services, especially protection of citizens from force and fraud. This is the so-called night-watchman state.

Although Nozick's argument is intricate, and some fresh ideas are presented, the main premises are not closely examined. We are asked to take as given, and intuitively clear, what it means to be a separate individual, and what follows from that meaning. In fact, however, there are kinds and degrees of separateness; and separateness is more important for some purposes than for others. Nor does it follow from the simple fact of distinctiveness that no sacrifice can be asked for the benefit of others, who may be dependent and needy as well as distinct. Some forms of coercion are more harmful than others; some are more readily borne; others cause much suffering and are indeed offensive to personal integrity. Although the Bill of Rights presumes the individuality of persons and their need for protection, no specific right derives from that presumption alone.

The postulational method is at best *pseudo*-naturalist.[27] It may invoke aspects of experience and may claim empirical support for various presuppositions, generalizations, and conclusions. But the postulates are not truly open to scrutiny, and the conclusions rest on chains of reasoning insulated from patient study of variables and contexts. A characteristic result of this rationalist strategy is failure to take into account the multiple values always at stake in the determination of rights and the design of institutions. The intellectual cost of this abridgment is high enough; the moral cost is even greater.

Positivist Rationalism

The second form of rationalism is positivist and utilitarian. Compared to axiomatic rationalism, positivism is a more radical departure from classical conceptions of objective reason. Idealism clings to the notion that reason is in some sense constitutive of the moral order. Whatever its limitations in overstressing the abstract and the a priori, idealism does try to establish an objective foundation for moral choice. The selection of particular ends may be left open, but rightful choice is always constrained by general principles, such as the categorical imperative, that identify a moral reality. Positivism, by contrast, rejects the doctrine of constitutive reason. Positivists derive morality from

27. For Dewey's critique of axiomatic rationalism, see his *Logic: The Theory of Inquiry* (New York: Holt, 1938), 503ff.

individual preferences and passions, constrained only by the technical requirements of adapting manipulable means to predetermined ends.

The most striking feature of the ethos of positivism is *a quest for determinacy*. Every variety of positivism—social, legal, logical—makes
much of the effort to eliminate vague notions and unanalyzed ideas. A
major strategy is the critique of blurred boundaries. The *precise* meaning, the *operational* indicator, the *definite* objective—these are watchwords
of a positivist program.

For example, legal positivists—Bentham, Austin, Kelsen, Hart—
want to make law clear and determinate.[28] They resist the idea of "incipient" or "emergent" law or any blurring of the boundaries between
law and custom, law and social practice, law and morality. Similarly, in
the theory of knowledge, logical positivism has struggled against ideas
that are not readily tested. The latter are dismissed as meaningless. And
positivism in social analysis seeks clarity of purpose and precision of
analysis in the service of engineering and reform.

In this way of thinking the "determinate" is a surrogate for the "certain." Positivists are quite comfortable with tentative and incomplete
conclusions. In exchange, however, they demand closely specified meanings and definite boundaries. They are quick to reject ideas that reflect,
in their indefiniteness, the subtlety or complexity of some phenomenon
or experience. The demand for determinacy has much in common with
what Dewey called the quest for certainty. Each seeks a comfortably ordered world, cleansed of disturbingly imprecise ideas; each tends to impoverish thought by premature or inappropriate demands for neat categories and quantified data; each overlooks important differences in the
stages of inquiry.

This central motif in positivist rationalism has, of course, much to
commend it. One can hardly oppose appropriate clarity or precision.
Nevertheless, among the costs of this passion for determinacy is a disposition to reduce complex unities or levels of experience to simpler,
more definite elements.[29] This reductionist impulse takes many forms,
the least harmful being the effort to make scientific findings more determinate (and theories more powerful) by reducing sociology to psychology, psychology to neurophysiology, biology to chemistry, chemistry
to physics. This program is salutary, and wholly consistent with scien-

28. See Chapter 15, "From Law to Justice."
29. Two other costs have special importance for moral and social theory. These are the
separation of fact and value, which was discussed in Chapter 1, "Naturalism in Ethics," and
the preference for external, "objective" phenomena over internal, "subjective" experience,
which we consider in Chapter 3, "Subjectivity and Social Reality."

tific progress, *insofar as it is disciplined* by careful regard for the logical conditions that must be met if a theory or regularity established in one field of inquiry is to be explained by (reduced to) a theory formulated in another science, one usually thought of as "more basic" or "primary." For example, the Boyle-Charles law (relating the temperature, pressure, and volume of ideal gases) can be derived from principles of mechanics "when these are supplemented by a hypothesis about the molecular constitution of a gas, a statistical assumption concerning the motions of the molecules, and a postulate connecting the (experimental) notion of temperature with the mean kinetic energy of the molecules."[30] A similar line of reasoning is required if specific biological phenomena are to be wholly accounted for by physico-chemical theories. These demanding conditions minimize the risk that, in moving from one level of explanation to another, important aspects of nature may be arbitrarily overlooked or, in some contexts, even degraded.

Positivism goes beyond what science requires when it insists that values must be understood as preferences or that social and economic phenomena can be wholly explained by the attributes and choices of individuals. These assertions stem from a general perspective—a nominalist ontology—not from the closely reasoned findings of focused inquiry. They reflect positivism's impatience with the more complex and elusive aspects of social and psychological reality. It is one thing to postulate *methodological* individualism, the view that ultimately collective phenomena must be *locatable* in the behavior and dispositions of individual human beings. It is quite another to argue that the collective phenomena—morale, bureaucracy, economic equilibrium, class conflict—have no distinctive attributes. Methodological individualism is a healthy safeguard against overly general and indefinite ideas, unanchored in behavior. But reduction based on a priori premises is more likely to impoverish understanding than to clarify it.

This impoverishment is especially acute when reductionism is applied to moral experience. In the ethos of positivism all the great moral ideals—love, justice, the common good—are remorselessly subjected to a nominalist solvent. No such idea has meaning, none has practical worth, save as it is reduced to some definite indicator. In positivist psychology love is "attachment behavior." In positivist legal theory justice is the impartial administration of a definite legal rule, whatever its moral content may be; at most it is a reflex of efficiency or equilibrium. In

---

30. Ernest Nagel, *The Structure of Science* (New York: Harcourt, Brace, 1961), 345.

positivist political theory the common good is whatever the majority says it is; the public interest is an idle dream, a "vague generality," or, at best, a vector sum of particular interests. In positivist moral theory happiness is pleasure and all pleasures have equal worth. In positivist social policy priority goes to whatever is of proximate benefit to individuals; more distant advantages have lesser claims.

The upshot is a disaggregated rationality whose moral correlative is preoccupation with the short run. Rationality is the disciplined pursuit of determinate goals by individual actors. The classic model is Jeremy Bentham's utilitarianism. Indeed, Bentham (1748–1832) is the beau ideal of positivism. A vigorous critic of moral abstractions, he sought to refine moral judgment by reducing it to a single straightforward, empirical principle. The criterion of a moral decision is utility, understood as whatever promotes the happiness of the greatest number of people. A key postulate is that each individual counts equally; and every satisfaction is of equal worth. The great aim of social policy in a moral community is to maximize pleasure and minimize pain.

Well-being is identified with happiness and happiness with pleasure. The subjective criterion makes the individual the sole judge of advantages and disadvantages. The aggregation of happiness, in the utilitarian calculus, presumes *dis*aggregated experience. In the end, what has moral worth is whatever a majority of rational, autonomous, self-interested persons say they want. There is no higher standard.

The Greatest Happiness Principle, taken literally, has few defenders. There is no way of implementing Bentham's "calculus of felicity," no way of aggregating diverse human preferences within the community as a whole. Nevertheless, the intellectual posture advocated by Bentham has greatly influenced the modern mind. If the *general* utility he envisioned cannot be calculated, it may yet be possible to aggregate *special* utilities, for example, in the management of forests or the allocation of housing. Although that procedure makes good sense for many purposes and cannot be forgone, it is vulnerable to the substitution of means for ends, narrow goals for broader objectives, and short-term for long-term criteria.

In the discussion of utilitarianism not enough weight is given to the ordinary meaning of "utility." A utility vehicle, apartment, or garment is wholly instrumental. It is a way of filling a need at minimal cost. Often it is an option available only at some sacrifice of comfort or adornment, or where such values are deemed irrelevant, as in the design of a mop or a military jeep. A utilitarian design is, ideally, wholly governed by engineering principles and quantitative reasoning. The focus is on sharply defined objectives and cost-effective means. This conception of utility is not logically necessary to utilitarian theory, which in principle might take account of *any* value. In practice, however, the utilitarian ethos is driven toward the common-sense meaning.

A reductionist strategy is the only way of saving Bentham's model of rational policy-making. In that model utility cannot be a synonym for well-being, still less for moral well-being. It cannot be, as John Stuart Mill preferred, "utility in the largest sense, grounded in the permanent interests of a man as a progressive being."[31] Rather, to make sense of Bentham, utility must be understood as a *proximate* good; it must be equated with a *determinate* end-state, not with a vague or speculative condition.

Hence objectives that are subtle and precarious find little support in utilitarian thinking. Whatever does not lend itself to precise formulation and ready manipulation is given short shrift. Where the ethos of utilitarianism prevails we are likely to find analysts who confound education with training, leadership with management, supervision with control, democracy with majority will. In this way the positivist quest for determinacy sustains and justifies narrowed values and foreshortened perspectives.

The Technocratic Mentality

The two forms of rationalism share a commitment to abstraction and simplification. Although positivists have rejected metaphysical abstraction, they have been drawn to their own forms of model-building and "abstracted empiricism."[32] The logical positivist (or empiricist) is, in truth, no great friend of concrete experience. Rigorous inquiry must have a definite starting point, which may be a theoretical construct or a standardized bit of data—something that can be processed, manipulated, and aggregated. The utilitarian theorist is comfortable with models of rationality that depend on artificial assumptions regarding human motivation and social contexts. In this version, rationalism *de*constructs experience as it prepares the way for manipulation and reconstruction.

This program reflects the positivist dimension of modern science. The natural world is broken down into elements as a prelude to physical

31. John Stuart Mill, *On Liberty* (1859), in *Utilitarianism, On Liberty, Considerations on Representative Government* (reprint, London: J. M. Dent, 1984), 79.
32. See C. Wright Mills, *The Sociological Imagination* (New York: Oxford, 1959), chap. 3.

or genetic recombination. Science puts nature "to the rack" not only, as Francis Bacon put it, "to compel her to answer our questions,"[33] but also to serve human needs. Knowledge is power, and the aim of science is control and manipulation. Nature has no worth or meaning save as an inventory of natural resources.

The result is an invitation to unbridled exploitation. As the capacity to make use of nature expands, the luxuries of yesterday become the necessities of today. The full use of resources becomes an end in itself, and the very word "exploitation" loses its negative connotation. Full use is seen as an aspect of progress; it appears wasteful to neglect an untapped potential.

Exploitation favors maximum productivity in the short term. Because nature is perceived as infinitely bountiful, the long run is left to take care of itself. The recuperative powers of nature, aided by an ever-advancing technology, will remedy any negative effects of human intervention. Furthermore, the environment is freely reconstructed and reconceived to fit human purposes. A stream is for damming as a source of hydroelectric power; a forest is a tree farm; the bottom of a shallow bay is potential real estate. These perceptions justify creating new lakes, rechanneling rivers, opening all lands to exploitation. Large engineering projects are perceived as heroic achievements rather than as potentially dangerous intrusions.

Although the intimate connection of modern science with technology has decisively influenced the mentality of exploitation, we should not forget that the duality of man and nature, and the rightness of human domination, were strongly supported by the Hebraic and Christian traditions. God fashioned man in his own image and appointed him lord of creation. "The earth is the Lord's and the fullness thereof," but man is God's delegate. All things, all other species, serve the purposes of him who shares in the divine glory and sovereignty.

Christianity rejected the idea of a chosen *people*, but accepted and reinforced the tenet that humankind was the Lord's chosen *species*. It made no challenge to the unique worth or the rightful domination of the human animal. When Saint Francis of Assisi "tried to depose man from his monarchy over creation and set up a democracy of all God's creatures,"[34] the church neatly deflected the challenge. It supported the expansion of

---

33. Quoted in William Barrett, *The Illusion of Technique* (New York: Anchor/Doubleday, 1978), 182.
34. Lynn White, Jr., "The Historical Roots of Our Ecologic Crisis," in Paul Shepard and Daniel McKinley, eds., *The Subversive Science* (Boston: Houghton Mifflin, 1969), 350.

a great Franciscan order but decisively rejected the heretical suggestion that all things created by God had something akin to a soul and were to be valued for their own sakes, not merely for their utility to man.

The technocratic mentality has two main ingredients. First is the *logic of domination,* as suggested above. In that perspective, the world is made up of objects, and no restraint is necessary when their manipulation is contemplated. Whatever is unique and self-determined—the employee as situated, responsive being, for example—interferes with rational control. It is noise in the system, to be eliminated as thoroughly as possible. The methodological postulate that some degree of order lies behind the variability and uniqueness of everyday life is transformed into a Procrustean bed to which the flux of experience must conform.

Second is the treatment of *ends as given or predefined.* For the technocrat, goals are set on nontechnical grounds by a client or constituency. They are, in principle, beyond rational questioning. Expertise has to do with means, not ends:

> Technique [in the idiom of Jacques Ellul] refers to any complex of standardized means for attaining a predetermined result. Thus, it converts spontaneous and unreflective behavior into behavior that is deliberate and rationalized. The Technical Man is fascinated by results . . . he is committed to the neverending search for "the one best way" to achieve any designated objective. . . . [A technical civilization] is a civilization committed to the quest for continually improved means to *carelessly examined* ends. Indeed, technique transforms ends into means. What was once prized in its own right now becomes worthwhile only if it helps achieve something else. And, conversely, technique turns means into ends. "Know-how" takes on an ultimate value.[35]

It would be wrong to equate this way of thinking with a scientific spirit or, indeed, with goal-directed conduct. Scientific method does *not* require that we treat ends as predetermined and unproblematic; nor is that posture a necessary condition of sound strategy or truly efficient enterprise. Rather, the preoccupation with technique is a special syndrome, a particular *way* of attending to means and ends.

An important part of that syndrome is what I have elsewhere called "the retreat to technology."[36] This occurs when moral and political responsibility is evaded under cover of apparently technical decision-making. An example is the frequent *misuse* of cost-benefit analysis in determining public objectives, such as whether a dam or highway should

35. Robert K. Merton, foreword to Jacques Ellul, *The Technological Society* (New York: Vintage/Random House, 1964), vi (my emphasis).
36. *Leadership in Administration* (1957; reprint, Berkeley: University of California Press, 1984), 74.

be built. A complex technical analysis may seem highly objective, yet it often obscures rather than clarifies the many assumptions that underlie apparently neutral estimates and choices. An independent study of decision-making in the Bureau of Reclamation, a government agency responsible for irrigation projects, concluded:

> As economists have sought to perfect the techniques of public policy analysis and introduce them into public decision-making process, they have only suc-ceeded in driving politics deeper into technical analysis, veiling the real choices from the public's eye. The public and its representatives in Congress who innocently believe that the single-number ratio represents economic truth are thereby excluded from the actual decision-making process. An agency, its beneficiaries, and a few congressmen continue to make policy largely as they please.[37]

In theory, and to a considerable extent in practice, cost-benefit analysis widens rationality by taking into account indirect as well as direct effects and by developing quantitative tools for choosing among policy alter-natives. But this procedure diminishes rationality when it obscures as-sumptions by burying them in technical analysis; when emphasis on quantifiable variables and quantitative reasoning leads to neglect of costs or benefits that are not readily quantifiable; and when technical analysis becomes a substitute for open and accountable political decision.[38]

Another sign of the technocratic mentality is the tyranny of means. One form of that tyranny is the pressure to turn *can* into *should*, that is, to let the capacities and requirements of technology dictate what ends will be pursued. Whatever is technically feasible—tactical nuclear weapons, a high dam at Aswan, testing a population for genetic de-fects—becomes an irresistible objective. When technology calls the tune, it threatens the integrity of moral, aesthetic, educational, and po-litical judgment. (We return to this topic in Chapter 12.)

The technocratic mentality embodies what is sometimes called in-strumental reason. Reason is instrumental when it abdicates responsibil-ity for determining ends and restricts itself to ways and means. In this view, unless ends are plainly means to other ends, they are fundamen-tally subjective. Since there are no objective grounds for determining in-

37. Steve H. Hanke and Richard A. Walker, "Benefit-Cost Analysis Reconsidered: An Evaluation of the Mid-State Project," *Water Resources Research* 10 (October 1974): 907.
38. See Steven Kelman, "Cost-Benefit Analysis: An Ethical Critique," *Regulation* (January 1981): 33–40; cf. Peter Self, *Econocrats and the Policy Process: The Politics and Phi-losophy of Cost-Benefit Analysis* (London: Macmillan, 1975).

trinsic worth, such choice is nonrational or irrational.[39] Objective inquiry can tell us *how* to get what we want; it cannot say what those wants should be.

FIVE PILLARS OF REASON

At the beginning of this chapter I sketched very briefly the concept of reason embraced by an eighteenth-century Whig, Edmund Burke, and a twentieth-century radical, Max Horkheimer. These very different thinkers, in very different times, shared a quest for "genuine" or "comprehensive" reason. This rich form of reason—substantive, historical, and objective—is anchored in a reality that transcends individual preference and will. Furthermore, its judgments cannot be derived from abstract models of motivation, cognition, or decision.

The idea of reason cannot be reduced to a single criterion or principle. No pithy formula will do. We can unpack the idea, however, by identifying some major themes that have, over many centuries, cast light on what it means to be reasonable. Our main concern is, of course, the relevance of reason for moral and social theory.

Five basic elements constitute—five pillars uphold—the ideal of reason. These are *order, principle, experience, prudence,* and *dialogue.* The following paragraphs indicate how they support reason and reject rationalism.

Order. The most familiar connotation of reason is orderly *thought.* To use reason, to be reasonable, is to accept criteria of sound argument, which include dispassionate consideration of evidence. The thoughtways of reason constitute an objective order, a source of discipline, a brake on emotion, rhetoric, and inclination. This order becomes part of the "anchored" rationality to which I have referred above, when it extends to the choice of ends as well as means. Positivist rationalism falls short in this respect because it treats ends as subjective manifestations of interest and desire, inaccessible to argument.[40]

---

39. "Nonrational" judgment may be the product of conditioning, as in habitual or customary practice; it may also be, and at the same time, adaptive and problem-solving, marked by preconscious trial and error, rather than by explicit choice of ends and means. "Irrational" judgment is inappropriate or otherwise self-defeating. The nonrational and the irrational are often conflated in positivist thought.

40. This claim may, of course, rest on an argument for the *limits* of reason. Such arguments are surely legitimate. However, positivists have treated these limits as postulates, not as conclusions based on evidence. The latter would reveal the *variability* of subjectivity and arbitrariness in judgments about ends.

The life of reason is also governed by the constraints and opportunities of an experienced world. People are "reasonable" and show "good sense" when they accommodate their goals to what the world is like. They seek change within a framework of limited alternatives and necessary trade-offs. This ambient order, properly understood, is not an alien system of domination. It is the world to which we belong, on which we depend, of which we are integral parts.

This perspective has great appeal today among environmentalists. Ecological awareness encourages respect for natural processes, especially the integrity, interdependence, and fragility of ecosystems. The rule is: handle with care. Beyond the rule is a profound appreciation for the integration of man with nature and for the importance of tailoring human aspirations to the requirements of organisms and systems whose well-being is intimately connected with our own. The presumption of mankind and the hard revenge of nature are nowhere more clearly revealed than in the rationalist effort to manipulate the environment without restraint.

There is a vast difference between the physicist who "accepts" $E=mc^2$ or the biologist who "accepts" the structure of DNA, and the ecologist's *deference* to organisms and their environments. The former take the laws of physics or molecular biology as technical constraints within which the release of energy or genetic recombination can go forward. The latter invests the world with value and thereby establishes a moral bond between scientist and subject matter. The ecological model brings a modern idiom to the classical understanding of how human beings should relate to the world of nature.

Perhaps the greatest significance of this perspective, from the standpoint of moral well-being, is that to maximize any *discrete* value, goal, or utility is prima facie offensive to the community of reason. There is a modern tendency to associate rationality with maximizing specific gains of one sort or another, whether they be profits, payloads, or Nielsen ratings. But anchored rationality has the effect of multiplying commitments. The pursuit of any given end is restrained by taking account of consequences for *other* ends whose fate we care about. The language of maximization is or should be an early warning that rationality, detached from reason, is out of control.[41]

41. This is not to deny that the technical logic of maximization or optimization may take account of multiple values or utilities and thus escape the judgment suggested here. I have in mind the world of practical decision-making, where bounded rationality prevails, not the formal theory of "utility functions" and rational choice. On bounded rationality and

We should think of order as a framework, not a blueprint. No one has supposed that deference to nature forecloses choice or preempts judgment. Rather, some choices work out well; others are frustrating or even destructive. This is partly due to luck and accident, but it also reflects how our choices fit or offend a natural order. To act in the light of reason is to recognize and *respect* persistent features of the human condition. Thus utopian doctrines are rationalist, not because they seek unattainable ideals or new forms of existence, but insofar as they fail to take into account limiting conditions and unintended effects.

Principle. The second pillar of reason is a commitment to "fundamental" principles and "ultimate" goals. Reason is end-centered: the fate of comprehensive or long-term objectives is always to be kept in mind, always open to intelligent assessment. When Aristotle speaks of reason in morality he emphasizes that the sagacious person reaches sound conclusions *for the good life as a whole* and not just for particular aspects of life, such as physical strength. Nor are ends fixed and predetermined, thus releasing the actor to concentrate on means to proximate ends without considering long-term effects.

The importance of principle in the life of reason is suggested in John Rawls's distinction between "the Reasonable and the Rational." The latter refers to the advantage each individual seeks and perceives; the former defines "the fair terms of cooperation."

> The Reasonable subordinates the Rational because its principles limit, and in a Kantian doctrine limit absolutely, the final ends that can be pursued. Thus, in the original position we view the Reasonable as expressed by the framework of constraints within which the deliberations of the parties (as rationally autonomous agents of construction) takes place. . . . Familiar principles of justice are examples of reasonable principles, and familiar principles of rational choice are examples of rational principles.[42]

Thus reason identifies the moral framework within which rational action takes place. Only if it is subordinate to such a framework can rationality have moral worth.

As commonly understood, a pragmatic outlook rejects theory and gives short shrift to principle; it deals with issues as they come up, in the

---

related matters, see Herbert A. Simon, *Reason in Human Affairs* (Stanford: Stanford University Press, 1983); on maximization, including "constrained" maximization, and the logic of cooperation, see David Gauthier, *Morals by Agreement* (Oxford: Clarendon Press, .1986), chap. 6.
42. John Rawls, "Kantian Constructivism in Moral Theory," *Journal of Philosophy* 77 (September 1980): 530.

light of available opportunities and short-run effects. But that is a parody of American pragmatism. William James and John Dewey had no use for mindless adaptation. They wanted all public policy, indeed all of life, to reflect informed awareness of what is worth having, doing, and being. Their pragmatism is not a flight from principle. On the contrary, it is an argument for discovering principles and for making them relevant to everyday life.

Experience. This element, which we have already considered, makes the clearest contrast between reason and rationalism. No deductive system, however elegant, can meet the requirements of reason if it is not responsive to and sustained by empirical evidence. Reason is a more comprehensive ideal than science, for it informs conduct as well as inquiry; but it shares the scientific commitment to learning from experience, including changes deliberately instituted. This focus on intervention, transformation, and outcomes places experiment at the center of experience. We act responsibly, in the light of reason, when we *test* ideas. One test is coherence—the fit with other, already tested ideas. Not less important, however, is what happens when we *use* ideas to solve problems and cope with difficulties.

Prudence. Reason cannot forgo abstraction; we cannot do without inevitably selective categories and theories. The rationalist flaw is not abstraction per se; it is excessive reliance on a conceptual apparatus, undisciplined by encounter with the flux and particularity of experience and judgment. The alternative is "practical wisdom" or prudence—what Aristotle called *phronesis*.[43] The Greeks and their Christian successors considered prudence a cardinal virtue. As such, it could not be a justification for expediency or opportunism or for a narrowly technical assessment of how to reach a given end. Rather, prudence is the making of appropriate moral judgments in concrete situations.

Such judgments require: (1) concurrent appreciation of universal and particular criteria of decision; and (2) recognition of the continuum of means and ends. A familiar example of the former is the ideal of doing justice, not by mechanical application of rules, but by sensitive awareness of the reasons behind the rules and the circumstances of the case at hand. By looking at the purpose of a rule, and its value premises, judges make good their commitment to principled decision; by examining particular circumstances they take account of the inescapable

43. Aristotle, *Nichomachean Ethics*, trans. Martin Ostwald (Indianapolis: Bobbs-Merrill, 1985), 1140a24–1140b30.

uniqueness of human situations. This is not a retreat from reason but a distinct mode of deliberation.

Although the continuity of means and ends is an idea we properly associate with John Dewey (see Chapter 12, "Ends, Means, and Integrity"), it is amply anticipated in the Aristotelian conception of prudence. No one can be prudent who is merely clever, said Aristotle. "Virtue makes us aim at the right target, and practical wisdom makes us use the right means."[44] A means cannot be right if it is not directed to the right end, and the ends we attain depend on the means we use. Thus prudence requires awareness of unintended effects, shortsightedness, and the contradictory impulses that afflict human judgment.

Dialogue. If reason is a quest for appropriate ends, then controversy over ends is a central concern. We recognize the plurality of values and interests even as we seek common goals and shared understandings. Here rationalist solutions are inappropriate. We cannot take ends as given or unproblematic; nor can we assume that means are narrowly instrumental or morally neutral. The alternative is a process of communicative inquiry whose central strategy is the exchange of views.

Dialogue cannot overcome all differences. It can, however, open minds, enlarge horizons, and overcome, in part at least, the inevitably parochial nature of human understanding. Nor should we expect or want finality. There can be no ultimate closure, because values reflect existential conditions, which are always subject to change. The great conversation about justice and the common good will continue, ideally, as long as civilized life persists. The lack of finality does not, however, preclude the deepening of understanding.[45]

The moral basis of dialogue is civility, which we discuss in Chapter 14. Civility is among the great principles of community, which it serves by protecting diversity while chastening conflict. It should not be supposed, however, that dialogue is necessarily sweet and uncontentious, eschewing all rhetoric, appealing only to the norms of argument. Dialogue can also be confrontational, as in the civil rights struggle led by Martin Luther King, Jr. A strategy of confrontation can reveal the creaky machinery of political and legal change, the torment and unrest behind a facade of social peace, the reservoir of support that may exist for new

44. Aristotle, *Nichomachean Ethics,* 1144a10.
45. For example, there is no finality in constitutional interpretation, but the history of equal protection of the laws shows increased sensitivity to the connection between moral and social equality. See Chapter 16, "Moral and Social Equality."

understandings and new policies. Although the risks are real, there is a place for the prophetic spirit, for passion and rhetoric, in communicative inquiry. Without confrontation, unspoken assumptions may never be truly exposed to criticism and debate. People may not really listen.

▼   ▲   ▼   ▲   ▼

These elements of reason—order, principle, experience, prudence, dialogue—are moral as well as intellectual. From Socrates to Freud, reason has been understood as a form of moral competence, a complex of virtues whose office is to discipline impulse and liberate thought. Reason takes into account the temptations and limitations of human conduct; therefore it is self-critical and self-limiting. This moderating outcome is also a source of *indeterminacy*. As we move from rationality to reason the ideal becomes more complex; we introduce more variables; more conditions must be met. As a result, our conclusions become less certain. Certainty is sacrificed on the altar of reason.

THREE

Authenticity and Subjectivism

An early signpost of the modern era is the Protestant emphasis on authenticity and autonomy in the realm of faith and morals. On that view, moral commitment is authentic only if it is sustained by genuine spiritual experience. That experience is personal, not social. Salvation depends on faith and resolve, not on outward signs of religious conformity. Although church and community demand participation and enforce obedience, everyone must take a lonely road to grace and forgiveness.

The Protestant heritage contributed significantly to modern ideals of independence and self-reliance. At the same time, the spiritual message of Luther and Calvin foreshadowed post-rationalist conceptions of choice and conduct. In the nineteenth and twentieth centuries, new ways of thinking would refuse to see moral actors as fully formed, unproblematic selves, making rational choices by following rules or by devising efficient means to clear-cut goals. Rather, *wholeness, inwardness,* and *self-formation* became keys to authenticity and moral competence.

This transition was aided by some tendencies within rationalism itself. The most influential forms of rationalism opened the door to winds of doctrine that were as alien as they were unforeseen.

FROM MIND TO SELF

In a famous passage Kant compared his own intellectual strategy to that of Copernicus:

Failing of satisfactory progress in explaining the movements of the heavenly bodies on the supposition that they all revolved round the spectator, he tried whether he might not have better success if he made the spectator revolve and the stars to remain at rest.[1]

Kant's "Copernican revolution" consisted in shifting the focus of attention from the world "out there" to the world as formed by the human mind. Secure knowledge depends on a priori concepts "to which all objects of experience necessarily conform."[2]

It was very far from Kant's intention to undermine the objectivity of physical science or moral judgment; nor would he wittingly have encouraged irrationality or self-indulgence of any sort. Nevertheless his philosophy, which quickly became very influential, did much to usher in a new era of subjectivism. This it did in three ways.

First, in Kant's theory of knowledge, as we have seen, mind is the foundation of necessity and order. Ideas are constitutive, objects derivative. Hence the knowing subject, equipped with a priori concepts, is the true hero of learning and enlightenment. It is not a big step from mind as objective reality to individual minds as agents of subjectivity. When that step is taken—when mind is understood as a product of personal history—we can readily suppose that individuals impose *their own* order on experience, in accordance with unique or historically conditioned predispositions.

Second, Kant stressed the limits of theoretical reason as the way to knowledge of things-in-themselves. In part the thing-in-itself must be understood as a metaphysical postulate introduced by Kant *to guard against an excess of subjectivism.* An "object" must have some form, and that form derives from the ideas and presuppositions we bring to our observations. Beyond "objects" or "facts," however, is a core reality without which there would be no empirical regularity. That core reality is hidden to science, which cannot do without preconceptions. But this shows only that cognition has limits; it does not deny that there is an external reality independent of our conceptions.[3]

In urging the doctrine that a "noumenal" reality lies beyond "phenomena" as they appear to our senses, Kant had still another axe to grind. His larger mission was to uphold the intellectual authority of

1. Immanuel Kant, *Critique of Pure Reason,* 2d ed. (1787; reprint, London: Macmillan, 1929), 22.
2. Ibid., 23.
3. All this is well and good, but the very idea of an unknowable reality—and its corollary, the sharp separation of appearance from reality—opens the door to subjectivism. If science deals *only* with appearances, then the "noumenal" world disappears as an operative constraint on our thoughts.

faith and morals. This led him to evoke the idea of *another realm* inaccessible to science, the special home of moral understanding. Such an idea was heady wine for those who believed that communion with "true" reality, with that elusive noumenal world, would be the highest and most worthy end of intellectual endeavor.

And, third, for Kant moral well-being presumes moral autonomy. Genuine morality is not based on deference to authority. That would be "heteronomy," not autonomy. Responsible persons choose duty over desire because it is rational to do so, and the commitment to rationality is nothing less than a commitment to life itself. For humans, to choose life is to choose rationality. It follows that there can be no morality without the freedom to formulate rules and make decisions in accordance with rational principles.

The logic of morality, as Kant understood it, combines objective and subjective truth. Moral choices are objective because rational judgment leads inexorably to conclusions that are independent of personal disposition or belief. On the other hand, moral choices are subjective in that they are freely made by duty-regarding persons who form their own judgments and make their own commitments. Kant had no doubt about the objective basis of moral rules, but his embrace of self-determination had the more decisive effect on nineteenth-century thought. For now it could be asked: What is *genuine* freedom of moral choice? Can rationality (or rationality alone) be the source of *authentic* moral commitment?

Authenticity is the experience of continuity and wholeness in thought, feeling, and moral choice. This ideal is threatened when human beings are seen as detached rational agents within an abstract moral order. Left out are the concreteness of existence, the sense of rootedness and embeddedness, the clash of incommensurables, the painful dilemmas of duty and commitment.

In their groping efforts to vindicate authenticity, post-rationalist intellectuals of the nineteenth and twentieth centuries—in philosophy, theology, history, psychology, and literature—made a transition from mind to self. This opening to the heart was already suggested in Kant's emphasis on "will" in ethics. "Good will," the disposition to do one's duty for its own sake and not merely out of external conformity, is the sine qua non of morality.[4] Therefore morality demands fidelity and commitment as well as rational judgment. In the next generations, however, and especially in the philosophy of G. W. F. Hegel (1770–1831), the passage from mind to self took on a larger significance. A new vocab-

4. Immanuel Kant, *Foundations of the Metaphysics of Morals*, trans. Lewis White Beck (1785; reprint, New York: Liberal Arts Press, 1959), 9.

ulary emerged: "consciousness," "meaning," "alienation," "realization." These ideas implicated the whole person in the quest for genuine
understanding. They made subjective experience—feeling, encounter,
interpretation, self-criticism—the route to knowledge and well-being.
Kant's *cognitive* subjectivism was pale by contrast.

The Genie of Consciousness

For Hegel, truth is drawn from the well of awareness. Transformations
of consciousness are the foundation of moral and intellectual development.[5] It is wrong, Hegel thought, to start from the premise that mind
is preexisting and preformed. Rather, we must see intellect and sensibility as *becoming* and not just as being. To simplify a very rich and complex argument, we may follow Hegel in identifying three stages in the
history of consciousness.[6]

First, human consciousness begins with naive acceptance of the external world, including external authority. At that stage we experience an
objectively given order, which we may dominate or which may dominate us. In either case, subject and object are separate; they deal with each
other at arm's length. From the standpoint of moral development, this is
a time of uncritical acceptance of parental authority or, as adults, of
whatever is demanded by conventional morality.

Next follows a time of *self*-consciousness, marked by critical awareness of how the external world impinges on our freedom and integrity.
In this period of "unhappy" or alienated consciousness, people are
aware of what they *could* be, from the standpoint of an ideal self. They
know social rules could be different and even better. However, because
of personal and historical limitations, the ideal cannot be reached.

Finally, reason is redeemed when overarching ideals of freedom and
community are fully realized within a particular human situation. When
the ideal is thus *historically embodied,* subject and object are reconciled.
Reflective persons make peace with their community, and give it new
vitality, by formulating and accepting the rational principles that underlie
a distinctive tradition. People can finally feel at home in a world from
which they had become estranged.[7]

---

5. Here consciousness has to do with deep structures of thought, perception, and
value, not with transitory ideas or beliefs.

6. G. W. F. Hegel, *Phenomenology of Spirit* (1807; reprint, Oxford: Oxford University
Press, 1977).

7. In overcoming alienation, what matters is "spirit," not mind alone. As in other aspects of his thought, Hegel is helped here by the special connotations of certain key words

These changes are accompanied by conflict, both between individual and society and within the individual as well. There are no smooth transitions. In this respect Hegel foreshadows Marx and Freud more than he does others who have had a roughly similar vision of moral development.[8]

At play in the evolution of consciousness as Hegel perceived it are three main values: freedom, reason, and authenticity. Their fates are inseparable. Freedom is realized only in the capacity to be one's true self; therefore it must be based on inner strength and self-awareness. At the same time, there can be no genuine self-determination without insight into objective necessity. The free person must rely on reason to discern what history demands and what opportunities it affords. And the highest exercise of reason is participation in a process by which consciousness is enlarged. Thus Hegel was not a moral subjectivist. He did not believe people choose ideals or decide for themselves what is right or wrong. Rather, the moral worth of an event, decision, or practice is known by the contribution it makes to an objective and immanent ideal, derived from human nature and the human condition, whose dimensions are revealed as history unfolds.

Once the genie of consciousness was out of the bottle, many efforts were made to explore its significance for philosophy and social theory. The preoccupation with consciousness is central to two closely related perspectives that played an important part in forming the modernist and postmodern outlooks we discussed in Chapter 1. These currents of thought, phenomenology and existentialism, have enriched our understanding of intellectual and moral experience. They have also led, in ways unintended, to a radical and unwarranted subjectivism.

In ordinary scientific usage, a "phenomenon" is simply a kind of fact, such as the rotation of the earth. Even in that context, however, the word "phenomenon" connotes description rather than explanation. To study something "phenomenologically" is to register and sort out observations without looking beneath the surface or constructing abstract models. This connotation of "surface" is echoed in the philosophical

---

in German. Thus *Geist* means "mind" but also "spirit," as when we speak of "the spirit of the age" or "the human spirit," or a person's "spiritual life." *Geist* suggests inwardness, self-awareness, sensitivity, refinement. It can also refer to the supernatural, as in "the Holy Spirit." On Hegel and "spirit" see J. N. Findlay, *Hegel: A Re-examination* (New York: Oxford University Press, 1958), chap. 2.

8. For example, despite the strong influence of Hegel, the focus on inner conflict drops out in John Dewey's thought. See also the discussion below (Chapter 6) of Piaget and Kohlberg.

meaning of "phenomenon," which at least since Kant has suggested what appears to the senses and is given form by the mind, as distinguished from the reality of things-in-themselves.

Hegel brought a decisive new turn by associating phenomenology with the study of consciousness. This lead was followed by what came to be known as "the phenomenological movement," a group of early twentieth-century philosophers who sought foundations of knowledge in the dynamics and forms of consciousness.[9] The movement encompassed a variety of views and shifting emphases. For our purposes, three themes are important.

First, genuine understanding requires that the phenomenal world be apprehended as directly as possible, without *unexamined* preconceptions. Every received category, everything presupposed in routine modes of seeing and evaluating, must be remorselessly subjected to critical analysis. Thus phenomenology is a philosophy of the "fresh look." It is a quest for liberated, purified consciousness.[10]

Second, consciousness gives form to experience, as when we recognize something as a "building," a "pasture," an "entrance," or an "obstacle." These and a multitude of other classifications are instruments of human purpose and meaning; they structure our perceptions; they create a world taken for granted. Hence consciousness is tacit as well as explicit, latent as well as manifest. To get at forms of consciousness, and to liberate our perceptions, we must look behind the flux of belief to identify persistent yet unacknowledged categories and assumptions. We cannot understand human conduct unless we locate it within that subjectively constituted structure of meanings. Therefore it is critical to know how people interpret and make sense of experience.

And, third, for human beings the paramount reality is everyday life. People are not abstract entities governed by abstract notions. On the contrary, everyone is part of a unique "lifeworld." This *Lebenswelt* is a very concrete, highly textured setting where all the empty boxes of social life are filled in. In the lifeworld real choices are made, such as how to act out the role of parent or friend; specific demands and opportunities are faced; other unique persons are encountered, whose world we share,

9. Major figures were Edmund Husserl (1859–1938), Max Scheler (1874–1928), Martin Heidegger (1889–1976), Jean-Paul Sartre (1905–1980), and, especially for social science, Alfred Schutz (1899–1959). See Alfred Schutz, *The Phenomenology of the Social World* (Evanston: Northwestern University Press, 1967); and, for historical background, Herbert Spiegelberg, *The Phenomenological Movement* (The Hague: Martinus Nijhoff, 1965).

10. Note the parallel to Zen Buddhism, discussed in Chapter 8, "Buddhist Self-regard."

but never completely; here the ambiguities of social rules are resolved or finessed. The urgency and immediacy of everyday life are wellsprings of our humanity. In the end, that is where we have our moorings; that is where we are accountable.

The phenomenological perspective in social science places the questing, problem-solving, responsive individual at the center of the life-world. Every act involves interpretation and is, therefore, inescapably symbolic. And routine action builds upon settled ways of knowing and perceiving. Through a never-ending process of classification or "typification," meaning and order are imposed on what would otherwise be an alien or chaotic environment. In this way the actor "constructs social reality" and is at home in the world.

A central message of phenomenology, as it bears on moral and spiritual life, is "the return to the concrete."[11] This means, above all, that attention is focused on the arena of action and practical choice. There persons, events, and situations are both unique and interdependent. Acceptance of uniqueness brings a realm of freedom—the freedom to be different and to be oneself. Interdependence, however, creates the enmeshed, embedded, implicated self. Without awareness of that condition, and responsibility for it, freedom is unguided and spiritually empty.

As a program for social science, the message of the "fresh look" is: give up your preconceived schemes and categories; take the point of view of the actor; observe the process by which meanings are created, sustained, and recreated; rework your concepts so as to minimize their distance from subjectively experienced reality; capture the concreteness and fullness of experience. As a program for humanity, the message is: overcome the false consciousness that derives from received ways of thinking and perceiving; do not yield to the "bad faith" that takes existing alternatives as fixed or exhaustive; approach the world with directness, openness, and authenticity.

Authentic Existence

These strands of phenomenological thought are closely interwoven with existentialist ideas.[12] In the idiom of existentialism, "existence" has two

11. See Hans Meyerhoff, "The Return to the Concrete," *Chicago Review* 13 (Summer 1959): 27–38.

12. The existentialist movement of thought, which began with the anti-rationalist eloquence of Søren Kierkegaard (1813–1855) and Friedrich Nietzsche (1844–1900), came to fruition in the writings of Martin Heidegger (1889–1976) and Jean-Paul Sartre

related meanings. First is the sense of concreteness, presentness, "thereness." This is a way of saying that abstraction of any kind is secondary and derivative, less "real," and potentially pernicious from a human standpoint. In Kierkegaard's phrase, "pure thought is a phantom" and existence is prior to essence.[13] The living, organic, socially situated person must be the starting point of analysis and the touchstone of value. Thus understood, existence as "thereness" has a normative connotation. One lives without really "existing" if vitality and commitment are lacking; if one is rootless; or if one becomes an object of technical or ideological manipulation.

A second meaning of "existence" retains the idea of concreteness but also suggests criteria of importance or fatefulness. When we speak of "existential choice" or "existential anxiety" we do not mean *any* choice or anxiety. Rather, an existential choice is self-revealing or character-defining, as when we make an irreversible commitment or decide between equally valid and demanding yet conflicting principles. Existential anxiety has to do with dread of self-extinction, which is not only physical death but loss of identity and encounter with emptiness; with the sense that moral choice is a construct of will, without moorings, adrift on a boundless sea.

In existentialism, authenticity is the key to psychic and moral well-being. The problem of authenticity arises because every person is a distinct biological and historical unity and is, at the same time, inescapably a part of animal and social life. Every person is ultimately alone, in choosing life, in facing death, in accepting some kinds of responsibility, and yet must depend on external and potentially alienating circumstances. This tension places at risk the highest and most difficult of all human achievements: genuine freedom. Freedom is spurious if it does not arise from, and if it does not sustain, the integrity of the person.

Existentialism reaffirms the Kantian ideal of moral autonomy. In doing so, however, it associates "autonomy" with a richer, more complex experience. To be truly autonomous is to act, not in the light of principle alone, even self-determined principle, but on the basis of concrete judgments regarding moral outcomes. There cannot be genuine freedom of moral decision when choices are predetermined by abstract rules.

(1905–1980). Religious existentialism is represented by Martin Buber (1878–1965) and Paul Tillich (1886–1965).

13. Søren Kierkegaard, *Concluding Unscientific Postscript* (1846; reprint, Princeton: Princeton University Press, 1944), 279, 281.

Authentic existence is the result of engagement as well as principle. Hence it cannot be wholly governed by any *doctrine,* however rational or even sublime.

A more radical autonomy is not, however, a prescription for isolation. Genuine freedom is not an absence of social relations. It is only through encounter and engagement that the authentic self is revealed, reconstructed, and made whole. "Nothing," it has been said, "reflects less than a mirror."[14] We cannot value ourselves—we cannot preserve our own integrity—if we do not value others. And to value others we must cut through the pretense and artificiality of everyday life. In Martin Buber's idiom, the immediacy of "I-Thou" (in contrast to "I-It") becomes the paradigm of authentic, self-affirming engagement. Here too is upheld a Kantian ideal, the principle of respect for all persons as ends in themselves, but with far more awareness of the struggle entailed and of the conditions that must be fulfilled.

Among these conditions is the creation of meaning. A key existentialist theme is that the self must contend with an inherently "absurd" or meaningless world. The need to overcome impersonality and invest the world with meaning is a basic part of the human condition.[15] The existentialists recognized, moreover, that the problem is exacerbated under conditions of modernity. They were acutely concerned with the threat of mass society and with the modern worship of technique.[16] They argued that humanity today cannot count on a received culture with its taken-for-granted structure of meaning. The modern person must create meaning afresh, and do so self-consciously, while fully recognizing that "you can't go home again."

Authenticity requires being open with oneself and others, not out of mindless candor, but in a spirit of caring and being cared for. At stake is the spontaneous expression of feeling and character. Whatever gets in the

14. A comment attributed to Jean Cocteau, *Times Literary Supplement* (9 March 1984): 226.

15. This investment of the world with meaning can be understood as the foundation of culture. "Culture is created when, in the struggle against alienation, man transforms the instrumental and the impersonal, the physical and the organic, into a realm of evocative, expressive, person-centered meanings. . . . The culture-creating act . . . is an effort to make the world rich with personal significance, to place the inner self upon the stage, to transform narrow instrumental roles into vehicles of psychic fulfillment. It implicates the self and strives to invest the environment with subjective relevance and meaning. In an older tradition we might have referred to this investment as 'the objectification of spirit' " (Gertrude Jaeger and Philip Selznick, "A Normative Theory of Culture," *American Sociological Review* 29 [October 1964]: 660, 659). That essay showed the strong influence of existentialist thought, whose continuity with American pragmatism we took for granted.

16. Karl Jaspers, *Man in the Modern Age* (New York: Anchor Books, 1957), 34ff.

way of such openness is an obstacle to moral and psychic well-being. In this respect, as in its theory of meaning and culture, existentialism is a restatement of basic sociological understanding. Sociologists have long recognized that the "primary relation," with its focus on intimacy, openness, and commitment, is a foundation of social life.[17] But they have treated it as a fact among other facts and not as a pivot of human existence. Moreover, in contrast to existentialism—and to Freudian theory—sociologists have understated the discontinuities between self and society.[18] For its part, existentialism emphasizes that openness and mutuality in human relations are always unstable outcomes of inner conflict and anguished self-scrutiny.

Authenticity is an ideal that is compromised as soon as its achievement is asserted. The very claim to be authentic is a mark of inauthenticity, for to make such a claim is to invoke an external standard and invite external approval. These moves are alien to interior dialogue and the examined life. It would be strange indeed if a philosophy of the concrete, rejecting abstractions, should recognize *any* general test or criterion. Authenticity is a highly personal matter, to be worked out in a spirit of communion between the historical self and whatever resources one has for self-transcendence. The appeal of religious existentialism, from Kierkegaard to Buber to Tillich, lies in this portrayal of a truly personal encounter with an ultimate source of value. The latter cannot be captured in a rule or formula, which can only get in the way of genuine self-knowledge.

The great paradox of authenticity is that it presumes a wholly personal moral life, yet also demands engagement with the world. To be authentic is to establish integral connections with other people, nature, work, and ideas, thus making the world really one's own. Love, truth, and justice are to be lived—internalized and acted out—not merely accepted as abstract goods. It follows that the focus must be on subjective experience, on how people perceive, feel, interpret, and respond.

These existentialist themes are a welcome counterpoint to the abstract, rule-centered moralities of rationalism. They highlight the dilemmas of choice, the fragility of personhood, the constraints of the human condition. They contain, however, a perilous flaw. The logic of existentialism makes the *content* of morality radically indeterminate. If values are

17. See Chapter 7, "Segmental and Core Participation."
18. Here we should distinguish theoretical statements, and many textbook formulations, from the empirical study of, say, the process of socialization. The latter necessarily considers differences and reveals discontinuities.

products of moral freedom and existential choice, facts have no bearing on means and ends. Genuine values come from within; there is no question of accepting the pragmatist view that values are discoverable by appropriate inquiry. Therefore the font of morality is subjective perception and will. No external standard can claim authority.[19]

At an extreme, this lack of objective standards becomes a license for any action that exhibits "existential" qualities of resolve, engagement, and self-determination. On that basis it becomes easy to justify, and even to celebrate, "authentic" acts of cruelty and terror. This is, of course, a shallow reading—indeed a parody—of existentialist doctrine. No one can be truly "engaged," for example, by embracing a *system* of any sort, including an ideological or political system. The authenticity of connectedness to particular others, and to the unity of one's own self, would then be in doubt. Furthermore, authenticity requires honesty, openness, and self-criticism—criteria not likely to be met by an "existential" killer or masochist.

Nevertheless, because existentialism emphasizes the qualitative aspects of moral conduct and leaves the content of morality to individual choice, it offers only limited guidance for the design of lives, institutions, and communities. Without an appreciation of content—the values and demands of parenthood or citizenship, for example—we lose purchase on the moral order. We may know what it means to be oneself, but not what it means to be a self worth having.[20]

SUBJECTIVITY AND SOCIAL REALITY

When Kant distinguished what is accessible to science from what is available to moral and aesthetic appreciation he did much to establish what later became a great divide in Western intellectual life. On one hand is natural science (*Naturwissenschaft*), which can deal effectively with sense data but cannot reach ultimate reality; on the other hand are the humanities and social sciences (*Geisteswissenschaften*), which must use

19. A related point is that "existentialism provides . . . no adequate means of elevating the individual's search for freedom to the status of a universal principle. It is not man as free being, in general, that existential philosophy can ask us to respect. It can demand only that each of us, solitary and unbefriended, seek his *own* freedom" (Marjorie Grene, *Dreadful Freedom* [Chicago: University of Chicago Press, 1948], 145).

20. Ironically, despite the emphasis on concreteness, existentialism becomes, in its own way, a procedural morality. We learn something about *how* to choose, not *what* to choose. In taking choice seriously, personal responsibility is enhanced. That project is undermined, however, by a want of faith in reason and by the radical subjectivism existentialism encourages.

more subjective methods, but are more searching and profound. This broad classification was not a pedantic exercise. It was an appeal for fidelity to distinctively human values, above all, the creative development of mind and spirit.

That the human sciences are special is an idea that has persisted despite vigorous criticism of much that has been written in the name of *Geist*. The second half of the nineteenth century saw a positivist reaction against the whole tradition of metaphysical speculation and "misty abstraction"; and in the first half of the twentieth century, as the philosophy of science came into its own, a consensus appeared to be emerging that favored unity in science: one basic ethos, one basic method. Nevertheless, support for the distinctiveness of social science (literature and the arts were not really in question) remained, and in recent years that support has experienced a considerable resurgence.

The appeal to a special ethos and a special method has usually been more negative than positive. It is a way of saying that science overlooks what matters most in the study of mankind. In Kant's idiom, science brings understanding (*Verstand*) but not reason (*Vernunft*). Reason transcends and criticizes the presuppositions of science in the light of all relevant values, including those of science itself. Thus Kant's philosophy already contains a strong hint that scientific truth, however valid, belongs to a lesser part of the human imagination. Hegel gave this distinction a larger import. He attacked *Verstand* as a limited form of rationality that leaves man alienated from nature and history, whereas *Vernunft* overcomes alienation by bringing about a dialectical integration of subject and object, mind and history. Hegel was saying, in his extravagant way, that a freer, more imaginative mode of thought than that of physical science is necessary if the world as reconstructed by the human mind is to be truly grasped.

Two themes were central to the nineteenth-century "romantic reaction" against what came to be known as positivism. First was the critique of *externality*. Positive science treats human experience, as it does any other phenomenon, by (a) observing behavior from outside and (b) imposing prior classifications based on its own necessities and utilities. This way of studying people and institutions neglects the interior life of psyche and mind; it cannot grasp, and tends to dismiss as superficial, the dynamics of consciousness, which include self-awareness, symbolism, and the formation of ideas. Second was the critique of *determinism*. The positivist model, it was thought, cannot do justice to the place of freedom and indeterminacy in personal and social life. These objections to externality and determinism have continued into the late twentieth century; they have sustained the idea that social science must have its own purposes and its own method.

The Centrality of Interpretation

The alternative to external analysis and observation is an interpretive method. At its core, interpretation pertains to the analysis of meanings. To interpret is to discern, explicate, and perhaps represent the meaning of a sign, a text, an event, or an idea. Interpretation is familiar ground to translators and actors, psychologists and historians. In the interpretation of texts the quest is for an "authentic" meaning; in the interpretation of dreams a latent or underlying meaning is to be discovered and laid bare. The study of interpretation—originally of sacred texts and, by extension, all similar intellectual operations—is called hermeneutics.

In the history of social science, as it bears on interpretation, the key word is *Verstehen* ("interpretive understanding") and the key figures are Wilhelm Dilthey (1833–1911) and Max Weber (1864–1920). Dilthey devoted a long and influential life to studying the foundations of the human sciences or *Geisteswissenschaften*. He rejected the grand theories propounded by Hegel in favor of a more empirical basis for historical reflection. At the same time, he did not want to give up the stress on ideas and ideals that had already played so large a part in German intellectual life and that seemed indispensable to a proper conception of what the human sciences should be. By attending to interpretation as a core activity of everyday life and by tracing the flow of meaning as it affects our understanding of comprehensive social unities, he hoped to bridge the gap between the concrete world of experience and the more abstract realm of thought and symbolism. Under Dilthey's influence, and because of his focus on the expressive and the meaningful, the human sciences came to be perceived as sciences of culture. Indeed, "cultural science" is a fairly common translation of *Geisteswissenschaft*.

For Dilthey, knowledge in the human sciences depends on interpretation at two levels. First, human conduct is interpretive. To comprehend what people do one must be able to reconstruct the process of interpretation. Here there is an implicit distinction between behavior and conduct (or action). Human beings "behave" when they respond directly to external stimuli. Conduct, however, is always mediated by the apprehension of meanings, that is, by what an idea, object, or event signifies for the individual.

Second, the analyst too must interpret, not only in reconstructing conduct—a task which may be quite trivial or commonplace—but even more in discerning structures or "complexes" of meaning as they emerge in social experience. Institutions, traditions, social orders, and historical epochs are precipitates of meaningful action. They are, as it were, congealed or "objectified" meaning. At the same time, they are vehicles for the *enlargement* of meaning. What a cultural form signifies historically depends on its context, and this is not necessarily discovered by studying the subjective interpretations of individuals. Thus the meaning of an architectural style may be the part it plays in the symbolism of power or in the celebration of rationality; the meaning of a revolution may be determined by its consequences and not by the intentions of its leaders or other participants.

Thus interpretation is not centrally concerned with causal analysis. Rather, it explores the relation between signs and significations, parts and wholes. To interpret an event is to seek an understanding of *how it fits into a pattern* of perception or motivation, history or culture. The focus is on an emergent unity or coherence—capitalism as a social order; modernism as a cultural phenomenon; a distinctive form of legal ordering—not on empirical regularities or causal connections. Of course, nothing hangs together in the absence of causes and effects. But in Dilthey's view the human sciences are mainly concerned with the study of symbolic and functional unities, especially those that produce values and realize ends.[21]

Dilthey wanted to uphold the humanist component of historical science without compromising ideals of rigor and objectivity. He thought of interpretation as a disciplined quest for orderly connections in an observable world—a way of doing science, not of escaping science. Yet he "often expressed the difference between the human and natural sciences by drawing a sharp distinction between understanding and explanation: 'We explain nature, we understand mind.' "[22] This way of thinking has been a source of sustained confusion. It suggests a radical difference in the foundation of knowledge instead of merely calling attention to a different mode of explanation or form of inquiry.

Some forms of interpretation do indeed center on meanings rather than causes, as when we interpret a poem or a painting in its own terms, apart from what the poet or artist intended. Other interpretations, how-

21. See Michael Ermath, *Wilhelm Dilthey: The Critique of Historical Reason* (Chicago: University of Chicago Press, 1978), 266.

22. Ibid., 246.

ever, try to make sense of conduct by identifying motives or intentions. The latter involve meanings, but they are more than meanings. Motives and intentions are states of mind and therefore are empirical phenomena that affect the making of choices and the mobilization of energies. Meanings per se are not necessarily causes, but the apprehension of meanings is characteristically part of causation in human affairs.

Of course it is important to bear in mind that human conduct is largely purposeful; what people do must be understood in the light of what they intend. But purposive action takes place within frameworks of constraint and opportunity, and it has outcomes that go well beyond subjective intentions. When organizations adapt to environments; when business cycles occur; when demographic changes take place, the pattern observed is necessarily *mediated* by the purposive actions of individuals. But that only guides, it does not negate, the quest for causal connections and general explanations. These may trace the unintended effects of many separate purposeful acts—for example, the effect on the economy or on population trends of decisions to buy a product or use a method of birth control.

When Max Weber studied the relation between the "Protestant ethic" and the "spirit" of capitalism, he was looking for a subjective link between religion and economic development.[23] He found that connection in what the Calvinist doctrine of predestination *meant psychologically* to the rising class of entrepreneurs. It was taken as a demand for individual and disciplined commitment to the service of God, a commitment that could be fulfilled by economic activity that was prudent, prayerful, systematic, and competitive. In Weber's view, this "meaning" of religion played an indispensable part in creating the distinctive ethos of Western capitalism. The claim that it was *the* cause of that ethos, or truly indispensable, is doubtful, but the intellectual worth of Weber's argument does not depend on that conclusion. Even as a partial truth his thesis is illuminating. And a larger lesson for the study of history remains: To make sense of ideological and institutional connections we must locate them in apprehended meanings, that is, in how people interpret doctrine and evaluate experience. Those interpretations lie within and not outside the causal order.

Weber lent immense authority to the centrality of interpretive understanding in social science by placing it at the center of his methodology. He took it as a postulate that the ultimate unit of analysis is the

23. Max Weber, *The Protestant Ethic and the Spirit of Capitalism* (1905; reprint, New York: Scribner's, 1958).

individual person, who is "the sole carrier of meaningful conduct," and
that it is the task of sociology to locate such global concepts as "state"
and "feudalism" in the actions of individuals. But Weber's own contributions to historical and analytical sociology had little to do with empathy or introspection, and he was no close student of the dynamics of
interpretation. His main concern, as his studies of politics, law, economics, religion, and bureaucracy show, was the analysis of ideas, interests, and institutions. He was, par excellence, a student of macro-
sociology, that is, of broad trends and large configurations.

The patterns he discerned were, nevertheless, "complexes of meaning." He saw in the rise of modern bureaucracy, for example, a transformation of what it "meant" to be an official and what it "meant" to have
a system of general rules. He does not forget the causes and vicissitudes
of bureaucracy, but at the center of attention is the emergence of new social forms and connections. In this way, Weber did much to fulfill
Dilthey's program.

A Moral Vision

The emphasis on subjectivity in history and social science is an echo of
the call to authenticity. For in this movement of thought something
more is at stake than scientific truth. Accurate description and powerful
explanation are only part of the story. More important is the moral vision
of the new hermeneutics.

The notion that interpretation is a *foundation* of the human sciences
would make little sense if it did no more than call attention to the
motivational and intentional aspects of human conduct. That would be,
at best, a modest methodological reminder. For Dilthey and others,
Verstehen had a larger significance. It was an appeal for fidelity to a special subject matter, the moral and spiritual core of personal choice and
relatedness. Such fidelity requires an internal point of view, that is, a perspective sensitive to the potential of all human beings for autonomy and
creativity in fashioning their own lives and social worlds. A corollary is
respect for human actors, who must be described and made intelligible in
terms that take seriously their perceptions, needs, and aspirations.

At the same time, interpretation is an inherently critical exercise.
When we take people seriously we assess what they do in the light of
their own goals and values, their own opportunities and circumstances;
and we bring to bear the moral awareness gained from precisely that enlargement of experience the process of interpretation affords.

Thus the moral import of the human sciences derives from a commitment to both sympathy and criticism. Interpretation demands sympathetic understanding of where people are and what they are about; but it also asks searching questions about frustration and achievement, impoverishment and fulfillment:

> A peculiar double ethic on the part of the interpreter is required: deep concern and interest, even "love," are necessary, but an impersonal attitude is also requisite. The interpreter must draw upon all the resources of his own experience and personality and yet not fall victim to a narrow subjectivism. Understanding depends on a double movement of immanence and transcendence, a going within and a going beyond: in short, what Dilthey called "immanent critique."[24]

Interpretation in social science need not confuse or conflate subjectivity and subjectivism. Indeed, objective standards of rationality, morality, and psychic well-being are essential for an adequate knowledge of subjective experience. We cannot make sense of purposive action without knowing the difference between fantasy and realism; we cannot understand the experience of loving if we are unable to distinguish superficial from genuine emotions; we cannot appreciate a psychic wound without an objectively confirmable theory of what makes for trauma and what constitutes defense.

The call for an interpretive and morally resonant social science is neither peculiarly German nor necessarily wedded to Dilthey's concept of *Verstehen*. In the United States the same basic point of view is represented by the American pragmatists. George Herbert Mead (1863–1931) had an especially important influence on contemporary sociology, where his perspective has been called "symbolic interactionism."[25] The pragmatists shared a Hegelian heritage and came in their own way to many of the phenomenological premises discussed above.[26] But in the writings of the pragmatists, especially James and Dewey, the German abstractions became less ponderous, more exuberant, more clearly relevant to practical affairs—in short, more American.

Pragmatists take as their starting point the active individual trying to make sense of and cope with problematic situations. To make sense of a situation is to interpret it and lend it meaning. (The act of interpretation gives interaction its symbolic character—hence "symbolic interaction.")

24. Ermath, *Wilhelm Dilthey*, 312.
25. See Herbert Blumer, *Symbolic Interactionism: Perspective and Method* (Englewood Cliffs, N.J.: Prentice-Hall, 1969).
26. See the references to Dewey in Alfred Schutz, *Collected Papers*. Volume 1: *The Problem of Social Reality* (The Hague: Martinus Nijhoff, 1962).

The meaning of a situation derives primarily from its relevance to human purposes. Therefore the conferral of meaning is need-centered, future-oriented, and selective. Thus it is that an inchoate, unstructured world is transformed into a more definite world of objects "constructed" by will and intention.

No one has taken meaning and subjectivity more seriously than the American pragmatists. They were no less serious about the immediacy and concreteness of the experienced world. At that level, in that context, the world is open and not fixed. Selves and situations are subject to reconstruction as people interact and realign, as they become aware of possibilities, shift meanings, change self-conceptions. The self is ineluctably social, but people responding to specific situations are not mere puppets or replicas of each other; they are not prisoners of abstract rules or roles; they act in the light of unique needs, wants, opportunities, and constraints. Individual action is situational; operative roles are emergent and not ordained by culture; collective action is best understood as a product of negotiation and mutual adjustment.

This perspective is in part a demand for psychological and sociological realism. The symbolic interactionists of contemporary sociology have mostly viewed it in that way. They have stressed the fragility of social structure, the impotence of rules, the remoteness of cultural values, the normality of deviance, strategies of interaction, and much else that reflects the concreteness and fluidity of social life. All this is fair enough. But in drawing from pragmatism a phenomenology of society they have muted and even overlooked the main point. In their psychological and sociological writings the pragmatists *were articulating a moral philosophy* as an integral part of the natural science of mind, self, and society, to which they all contributed. They did not expect the moral dimension to be neglected or forgotten.

Fundamental to the pragmatist argument is the view that social experience everywhere, if allowed to follow its natural course, will provide at least minimal opportunities for such positive goods as cooperation, reconciliation, personal autonomy, and enlargement of self. It would be fatuous to suppose that individuals always do or can achieve these benefits. Mostly they are frustrated or the outcome is distorted. That is why a moral theory is needed, one that builds upon and yet transcends the promise of ordinary experience.

The original pragmatist strategy was to identify the *potential for well-being* in certain universal features of social life. They were keenly aware of narrow-minded moralism, economic greed, and political domination.

They did not suppose we could do without a heightening of moral awareness and the sustained use of critical intelligence. But they saw in the inescapable concreteness of social existence—how people must interact and take account of each other—the true foundation of moral ordering.

SUBJECTIVITY AND SUBJECTIVISM

I have restated above, with considerable sympathy, the recurrent themes of authenticity and inwardness in modern thought. It is important to distinguish, however, the appreciation of subjectivity from the embrace of subjectivism. Subjectivity is an empirical reality: it is the world as experienced by conscious, striving, meaning-centered beings. Subjectivism, on the other hand, is a special perspective or belief. The most important subjectivist doctrine is moral skepticism—the view that there are no objective standards of moral worth or well-being; that good and evil, right and wrong, are expressions of personal preference; that values are "emotive" and have no independent validity as conclusions of reason or evidence.

The conflation of subjectivity and subjectivism is partly due to semantic and analytical confusion. When Kierkegaard said that "truth is subjectivity,"[27] he did not mean that in morality anything goes or preference is all. In existentialist thought there are objective goods, such as love, self-knowledge, and the psychic strength to cope with alienation, and there are objective evils, such as bad faith and complacency. To be sure, abstract truth is rejected as meaningless to the person struggling for spiritual redemption; authenticity requires that truth be lived and not just mouthed. But that does not deny the validity of conclusions made from the standpoint of one who seeks to learn from experience or, indeed, to offer instruction in the truths of existentialism. From that standpoint, some responses are healthy, others are pathological; some ways of overcoming alienation are self-enhancing, others are self-destructive. The two approaches to truth are simply different projects. One speaks to authenticity, the other to knowledge as generalization.

But the subjectivist impulse cannot be accounted for by simple errors of logic or language. Far more important is the sense of openness and instability engendered by modernity. That feeling is alien to any view of the world that suggests closure, finality, or a settled conception of what

27. Kierkegaard, *Concluding Unscientific Postscript*, 169.

is true, beautiful, or good. It is easy to understand the appeal of doctrines that speak to the experience of ambiguity, help make sense of it, and at the same time give it creative significance. The response evoked by modernist doctrines stems from the thrill of discovery that a potentially disabling condition can be, instead, a source of special insight, criticism, and intellectual power.

The modernist stress on subjectivity must be understood in this light. As we have seen, it is a way of breaking through imposed and abstract categories. Interpretive or hermeneutic inquiry justifies and reinforces the idea that what really matters is the openness, unpredictability, and fragility of experience, not the persistence of systems and routines. Even when routines are studied, as in the work of Erving Goffman, it is to show how vulnerable they are and how much they depend on sustained effort to create and hold fragile strands of meaning.[28]

Making Sense of Kuhn

In recent years the hermeneutic perspective has taken a new and more radical turn. Instead of being largely restricted to the human sciences, it is now applied to the physical sciences as well. A purportedly post-empiricist, post-positivist philosophy of science has emerged whose main thesis is that *all* science is irredeemably subjective. Moreover, the subjective component should be welcomed, not merely recognized and progressively erased. A somewhat reluctant leader of this movement has been Thomas S. Kuhn, whose work on scientific "revolutions" has touched a highly responsive chord in circles well beyond the history of science. It has been especially well received—and endlessly cited—among social scientists eager to be supported in their subjectivist inclinations.

Kuhn's argument takes as its starting point the social context of scientific inquiry. Science is, after all, a social institution; and it is best understood as carried on by communities made up of "practitioners of a scientific specialty."[29] The members of a scientific community are educated in much the same way, go through similar professional experiences, and teach each other how to be comfortable with one another and effective in their work. Scientific communities, like other cohesive social groups, rely heavily on in-depth communication of distinctive

28. On Goffman, see Chapter 8, "Integrity and Personhood."
29. Thomas S. Kuhn, *The Structure of Scientific Revolutions,* 2d ed. (Chicago: University of Chicago Press, 1970), 177.

norms, values, and perceptions. In time they become "producers and validators of scientific knowledge."[30]

All this is elementary and not controversial. But Kuhn takes sociology seriously. He brings to the history and philosophy of science what should be a familiar principle: the mind of the scientist is a social formation, and shared group experience has intellectual consequences. The practice of science cannot be explained by an abstract and idealized account of scientific method. Rather, what scientists do, including *how they think,* is decisively affected by their membership in a particular community at a particular time.

The vehicle of that influence is a scientific "paradigm" or, in a more cautious formulation, a "disciplinary matrix."[31] The notion of a paradigm suggests something more specific and more uniform than can really be justified, but what Kuhn had in mind was a set of "universally recognized scientific achievements that for a time provide model problems and solutions to a community of practitioners."[32] Enshrined in textbooks, they "define the legitimate problems and methods of a research field for succeeding generations of practitioners."[33] These models or premises include *basic theories* (e.g., as to the structure of atoms or the nature of light or heat or genetic inheritance), *modes of reasoning* (e.g., when and how to use differential equations), *key definitions* (e.g., "mass," "current," "recessive trait"), even *preferred metaphors* (e.g., "the molecules of a gas behave like tiny elastic billiard balls in random motion"),[34] as well as *scientific values* respecting degrees of accuracy, consistency, and simplicity. In short, "the disciplinary matrix contains all those shared elements which make for relative fullness of professional communication and unanimity of professional judgment."[35]

When there is an accepted paradigm, science is "normal," that is, routine and cumulative. The members of a particular specialty devote themselves to the problems set by the theories and methods they have been taught. They work within a framework, criticizing specific ideas and observations but not the framework itself. In time, however, anomalies accumulate and the discipline is ripe for a "paradigm shift," a new way of looking at the subject matter. This constitutes a scientific

30. Ibid., 178.
31. Ibid., 182ff.
32. Ibid., viii.
33. Ibid., 10.
34. Ibid., 184.
35. Thomas S. Kuhn, "Second Thoughts on Paradigms," in Frederick Suppe, ed., *The Structure of Scientific Theories* (Urbana: University of Illinois Press, 1974), 495.

revolution. Major examples are the Copernican, Darwinian, and Einsteinian revolutions, but many others occur as well, such as the breakthrough understanding of heat as kinetic energy or of the earth's crust as composed of tectonic plates.

No one doubts that dramatic changes have occurred in scientific theories and outlooks. The important question is: What do such changes say about subjectivity and objectivity in science? Kuhn stressed two aspects of subjectivity. (1) In normal science much work proceeds *from premises that are unexamined* so far as the individual scientist is concerned. Indeed, normal science depends on the viable, persistent, taken-for-granted thoughtways that constitute a large part of training in a particular specialty. (2) Important shifts in the disciplinary matrix entail *changes in perspective* that are resisted by mainstream scientists. A breakthrough must crack the crust of received doctrine; for that, persuasion and even "conversion" are needed; and scientific communication becomes in part a political process.

These views have been highly controversial because they seem to undermine the ideal of scientific objectivity. If social, psychological, and even political processes are at work, what happens to cool deliberation? What of logic and evidence? Despite some incautious language (later amended) and some overreaching to make a point, Kuhn's argument is not a rejection of scientific objectivity. Rather, it is an effort to enlarge our understanding of science as a human enterprise and especially to show that the dynamics of belief have a *constructive* part to play in science, as in other kinds of knowing. It is helpful if the scientist has internalized a way of thinking:

> Or else, like many of those who first encountered, say, relativity or quantum mechanics in their middle years, he finds himself fully persuaded of the new view but nevertheless unable to internalize it and be at home in the world it helps to shape. Intellectually such a man has made his choice, but the conversion required if it is to be effective eludes him. He may use the new theory nonetheless, but he will do so as a foreigner in a foreign environment, an alternative available to him only because there are natives already there. His work is parasitic on theirs, for he lacks the constellation of mental sets which future members of the community will acquire through education.[36]

And it may be helpful to science if a leap is made from one mode of thought to another:

> I do not doubt . . . that Newton's mechanics improve on Aristotle's and that Einstein's improve on Newton's as instruments for puzzle-solving. But I can

36. Kuhn, *Structure of Scientific Revolutions*, 204.

see in their succession no coherent direction of ontological development. On the contrary, in some important respects, though by no means in all, Einstein's general theory of relativity is closer to Aristotle's than either of them is to Newton's.[37]

This does not deny continuity in science with respect to what we find empirically under specified conditions; nor does it deny the importance of having good reasons for choosing a new perspective. But it does say that the furnished mind is creative, not only in solving particular problems, but in reorganizing perceptions and thereby pressing inquiry beyond the confines of the routine and the cumulative.

It might be supposed that these considerations are disposed of by the once-regnant distinction between a "context of discovery" and a "context of justification."[38] In the realm of discovery social and psychological factors have their place, as does whatever else may affect creativity and intellectual effort. Indeed, here anything goes: a brilliant physical theory may have a theological inspiration; a surreal dream may suggest a useful connection or pattern. Thus the context of discovery is the realm of subjectivity. Objectivity belongs to the context of justification, for it is there that rigorous standards of logic and evidence are applied.

But Reichenbach's distinction is no longer so easily accepted as conventional wisdom. It could not be sustained, because it created a vast residual category within which every aspect of "discovery" was included—the most random and subjective stimulus to thought together with frameworks and theories that are much more systematic and defensible. For example, theories of development or evolution arise in many fields of study. They are properly understood as more or less fruitful, more or less well founded empirically, more or less supported by rigorous logic. Such theories blur the boundary between discovery and justification. As proposed modes of thought they require justification; they must submit to reasoned argument. At the same time, their role in inquiry is to generate more specific hypotheses and more focused explanations; in that sense they belong to the context of discovery.[39]

37. Ibid., 206f.
38. Hans Reichenbach, *Experience and Prediction* (Chicago: University of Chicago Press, 1938), 6f.
39. Although the line between discovery and justification is less clear than was supposed, it does not follow that a corollary teaching of the logical empiricists, the difference between the *origin* of an idea and its *truth*, need be lost. We cannot conclusively judge an idea by inspecting its origins, which may be lost in mystery, or eccentric, or utterly misunderstood. Truth must be tested by a reconstructed logic whereby an argument is made plain for all to study, as well as by appropriate evidence.

Kuhn's perspective is best understood as a variant of pragmatism. Like Dewey, Kuhn finds in scientific *practice* a warrant for expanding objectivity, not for restricting it. The key point is that there is more than one road to objective judgment. Plurality and openness are vital ingredients of scientific practice, especially when a choice must be made between competing theories. But that is no challenge to objectivity, so long as impersonal standards are accepted and applied.

To help make this point Kuhn draws on a distinction between rules and values. A theory is not judged by applying a determinate criterion or algorithm, that is, a specific logical or computational procedure. Rather, scientists bring to bear more general criteria, such as accuracy, scope, consistency, fruitfulness, and social utility. This allows for openness, but it is not a plea for subjectivism:

> Two men deeply committed to the same values may nevertheless, in particular situations, make different choices as, in fact, they do. But that difference in outcome ought not to suggest that the values scientists share are less than critically important either to their decisions or to the development of the enterprise in which they participate. Values like accuracy, consistency, and scope may prove ambiguous in application, both individually and collectively; they may, that is, be an insufficient basis for a *shared* algorithm of choice. But they do specify a great deal: what each scientist must consider in reaching a decision, what he may and may not consider relevant, and what he can legitimately be required to report as the basis for the choice he has made.[40]

Scientific ideals are neither impotent, nor arbitrary, nor mere preferences. But they do allow for disagreement, and they must be balanced against one another when a choice of theories is to be made.

A striking parallel exists between this line of reasoning in the philosophy of science and the analysis of rules and principles in legal theory. Kuhn contrasts "rules, which determine choice," and "values, which influence it."[41] In the same way, as discussed below (Chapter 15, "From Law to Justice"), legal principles formulate recognized values rather than specific rules. "A principle like 'No man may profit from his own wrong' does not even purport to set out conditions that make its application necessary. Rather, it states a reason that argues in one direction, but does not necessitate a particular decision."[42] Principles are legal in-

40. Thomas S. Kuhn, *The Essential Tension* (Chicago: University of Chicago Press, 1977), 331.
41. Ibid.
42. Ronald Dworkin, *Taking Rights Seriously* (Cambridge: Harvard University Press, 1978), 26.

struments for devising rules and for criticizing them. New circumstances do not ordinarily alter principles, but they may and do require that new rules of law be formulated and old ones changed.

These convergent perspectives on science and law obey the same impulse and are governed by the same logic. Dworkin's theory is a defense of objectivity in legal judgment. At the same time, it allows for openness, indeterminacy, and plurality. By insisting on the authority of principles, and their effective role in decision-making, Dworkin upholds the place of reason in adjudication. By recognizing that principles leave room for situational judgment and offer opportunities for disagreement, he vindicates the place of criticism and debate in the legal process. In other words, he does not equate reasoned judgment with a mechanical procedure. This approach allows for subjectivity—including the constructive as well as the negative role of partisan advocacy—but it does not abandon the legal process to the subjectivism embraced by some "legal realists" of the 1930s or by the more recent proponents of critical legal studies.

Similarly, the main thrust of Kuhn's perspective is to preserve objectivity while legitimizing plurality:

> Because I insist that what scientists share is not sufficient to command uniform assent . . . I am occasionally accused of glorifying subjectivity and even irrationality. But that reaction ignores two characteristics displayed by value judgments in any field. First, shared values can be important determinants of group behavior even though the members of the group do not all apply them in the same way. . . . Men did not all paint alike during the periods when representation was a primary value, but the developmental pattern of the plastic arts changed drastically when that value was abandoned. . . . Second, individual variability in the application of shared values may serve functions essential to science. . . . If all members of a community responded to each anomaly as a source of crisis or embraced each new theory advanced by a colleague, science would cease. If, on the other hand, no one reacted to anomalies or to brand-new theories in high-risk ways, there would be few or no revolutions. In matters like these the resort to shared values rather than to shared rules governing individual choice may be the community's way of distributing the risk and assuring the long-term success of the enterprise.[43]

It may be that Kuhn overemphasizes the place of abstract values (accuracy, simplicity, consistency, etc.) in the scientific consensus brought to bear when new problems arise. Presumably a great deal more is taken for granted, including well-established empirical regularities and

43. Kuhn, *Structure of Scientific Revolutions*, 186.

well-tested ways of making observations and developing arguments. Nevertheless, values are critical to the issue at hand. They provide objective criteria of good work in science, yet allow for difference and controversy. Much the same may be said of adjudication. Judges must give reasons for their decisions—reasons that must fall within an acceptable range of credibility and legitimacy—but they may differ in their conclusions without loss of integrity or objectivity.

The larger issue is one of rationality itself. For inquiry or argument to be rational, must there be *determinate* criteria of choice, so that only one outcome is possible? Or must there be room—in the interests of rationality itself—for discretion and judgment within a framework of general guidelines rather than specific rules? When making a transition from the abstract to the concrete—from a theory to its application, a principle to a rule, a rule to a case—it is rational to rely on imagination, insight, and tacit knowledge. Therefore in many circumstances it is not only futile but counterproductive to press the search for an algorithm or for completely formalized reasoning.

Constructed Reality

To present a partial truth as the whole truth is so elementary an abuse of sound reasoning that one may hesitate to mention it. Yet that has been a persistent feature of subjectivism in philosophy and social science. Consider, for example, the idea that observation is "theory-laden." This is the view that all scientific observation involves preconceptions, especially prior classifications that make sense only in the light of some theory or perspective. It is indeed easy to show that any systematic observation is *to some extent* governed by an implicit or explicit theory. We cannot observe sunsets, storms, or rising tides, to say nothing of fleeting traces of subatomic particles, without some way of identifying each as a particular kind of phenomenon. The world must be sorted out, at least tentatively, prior to the observation. Theory and observation are intimately connected.[44]

But to say that a perception is "theory-laden" or "theory-impregnated" *suggests* more than it necessarily *asserts*. Such characterizations do not say precisely how far the process goes or just what takes

44. This is a central tenet of recent philosophy of science, which criticizes the sharp dichotomy hitherto made between theoretical and observational terms. Of course a functional *distinction* between theory and observation can be made without prejudice to their intimate *connection*. On this matter, see Frederick Suppe, "The Search for Philosophic Understanding of Scientific Theories," in Suppe, ed., *Structure of Scientific Theories*, 80ff.

place. In any inquiry some observations and classifications are more theory-dependent than others. If the theory is revised it may be necessary to alter our understanding of some but not all observation terms. For example, in the study of crowds we may "observe" emotional contagion and loss of self-control. These observations depend on the interpretation of specific bits of evidence regarding personal responses and patterns of behavior. Some such interpretations are likely to change if the theory is revised—for example, to take account of more rational aspects of crowd behavior. But it would still be necessary to identify observations that are neutral relative to the theory of crowds, for example, statements about the way people congregate, who says what, what leaders do. Otherwise, we could not test our theories:

> Though descriptive terms (such as "current" or "ampere") that are defined by way of some theory are often alleged to be observable phenomena, such use of terms is subject to important limitations. For example, suppose that some theory is being tested by obtaining certain experimental data. It would be clearly circular to interpret those data in such a way that they are described with the help of terms whose definitions presuppose the truth of the theory. . . . There must therefore be observation terms whose meanings are neutral with respect to the theory being tested, and indeed whose meanings are invariant under changes in accepted theories of a certain class.[45]

In other words, all observations are theory-laden, but some are more so than others, some more relevantly so than others. And that variation makes all the difference for how we assess our conclusions.

A similar caution applies to the enthusiasm with which it is asserted that "social reality" is "constructed" by the categories we invent. It is one thing to emphasize the social formation of "reality" as a way of cutting through taken-for-granted premises. We thereby encourage a wider, more generous view of human possibilities. It is something else to turn that partial truth into a radical denial of the objectivity of social circumstances, including the ways alternatives are limited by forces against which no change of perception can prevail.[46]

Social reality is indeed a web of meanings. No adequate understanding of human conduct is possible without taking into account how people perceive, intend, and appreciate. But conferred meanings are not the whole of social reality; in many contexts what they account for is limited

45. Ernest Nagel, "The Quest for Uncertainty," in Paul Kurtz, ed., *Sidney Hook and the Contemporary World: Essays on the Pragmatic Intelligence* (New York: John Day, 1968), 421f.

46. On the limits and hazards of subjectivism in sociology, see Robert K. Merton, *Social Research and the Practicing Professions* (Cambridge, Mass.: Abt Books, 1982), 239ff.

and marginal. Social reality includes such material, nonsymbolic conditions as the level of technology and the availability of natural resources. These realities are always meaning-laden to some degree—at times very heavily so, as when certain options are mistakenly perceived as closed or inescapable. But there is a hard core of nonsubjective reality beyond perception, beyond intention—such as the size and composition of a population or the effective distribution of talent, power, or resources. Poverty is indeed a social construct, but it is more plainly so when defined in a purely comparative way, as a statistical artifact, than when its definition is based on objective criteria of nourishment, morale, or employment opportunity. For those who live at the edge of desperation, or even in constrained circumstances, it is a cruel joke to be told that, to have their burdens eased, they have but to redefine their perceptions.

Conservatives worry about the social definition of poverty; radicals are more concerned about the social definition of crime. But if crime is a historically contingent construct, it is more plainly so when it refers to conduct that violates norms of decorum or of moral or religious sensibility than when it threatens the elementary conditions of public safety. Here again subjectivity is variable, not absolute. When that is overlooked, we lose our bearings. If everything is the product of conferred meaning, and meaning is a reflex of will and intention, then any reality can be changed. There is no check to fantasy.

The proper response to subjectivism is not to deny the significance of subjectivity in science, morality, and art. Subjectivity is indeed pervasive; its effects can be positive or negative, creative or subversive. But we must also be aware that subjectivity has limits *and those limits are defined by the outcomes of action*. We may entertain whatever ideas we like. There is no limit to the number of viewpoints from which we can approach the study of nature. But we cannot *do* whatever we like without attending to objective and often unintended effects. Reality is not in our heads. We learn what it is in the course of coping and responding, acting and adjusting. This is a central message of American pragmatism.

FOUR

Plurality and Relativism

An especially important aspect of modern subjectivism is the doctrine of cultural relativism. As part of the moral grammar of modernity, cultural relativism encourages appreciation for the plurality of social experience—the many different paths to group survival and to valued ways of life. This appreciation has tamed parochial passions, restrained group prejudice, and underpinned the ideal of mutual respect. At the same time, relativism has generated widespread and unjustified doubt regarding the objective worth of moral standards and has frustrated inquiry into the social foundations of moral achievement and deficiency. An alternative view, I shall argue, recognizes the plurality of moral experience, yet insists that justified plurality has limits. Diversity enlarges consciousness and teaches humility. It does not require equal regard for every culture or every lifestyle.

Cultural relativism has two main sources. First is the idea that every aspect of human experience, including the structure of mind itself, is decisively influenced by the historical context. The post-Kantian generations, as we have seen, traced transformations of consciousness, including ways of judging and evaluating, to historical circumstances. Even earlier, however, Giovanni Battista Vico (1668–1744) and Johann Gottfried Herder (1744–1803) sounded the call to relativism.[1] Herder studied under Kant in Königsberg, but he rejected the Kantian system as

---

1. See Isaiah Berlin, *Vico and Herder: Two Studies in the History of Ideas* (London: Hogarth, 1976); and Patrick Gardiner, "German Philosophy and the Rise of Relativism," *The Monist* 64 (1981): 138–54.

ahistorical and artificial. To understand how people behave and how they think, he insisted, one must approach a historical situation from within, entering into its distinctive thoughtways. Therefore no theory that classifies ideas or institutions by tearing them from their contexts can be valid; no evaluation is valid if it fails to take seriously the peculiar premises and perspectives of a time and place.

The second main source is contemporary social science, especially American cultural anthropology.[2] Franz Boas (1858–1942) did much to define the spirit and strategy of that discipline as it emerged in the early decades of the twentieth century.[3] Through his students, especially Ruth Benedict, Margaret Mead, and Melville Herskovits, Boas became the father of cultural relativism in America. Born and educated in Germany (he immigrated to the United States when he was twenty-nine), Boas was in a good position to act as a bridge between German thought, such as the ideas of Herder, and American enthusiasm for the uniqueness and intrinsic worth of preliterate cultures. In the 1930s and '40s Benedict and Mead brought the message to a large popular audience, including generations of responsive college students. Within a more limited scholarly circle, until his death in 1963 Herskovits championed a rather bald and uncompromising version of relativist doctrine.

For Herskovits the principle of cultural relativism is at bottom an empirical generalization: "Judgments are based on experience, and experience is interpreted by each individual in terms of his own enculturation."[4] Taken literally, and with due regard for its breadth and vagueness, this assertion is hardly controversial. Most people most of the time do make judgments in the light of cultural preconceptions; they do interpret in unconscious ways; what they perceive as real is real in its consequences. Therefore description and classification must be faithful to the perceptions of the people being studied; culture must be seen through their eyes as well as through the observer's. Furthermore, considering the profound influence of "enculturation," we are well advised to be careful in the judgments *we* make lest we commit the vulgar fallacy of treating our prejudices as objective critical judgments.

2. It was actually a conservative sociologist, William Graham Sumner, who introduced the idea of cultural relativity in America. See William Graham Sumner, *Folkways: A Study of the Sociological Importance of Usages, Manners, Customs, Mores, and Morals* (1906; reprint, New York: New American Library, 1960), 41, 438.

3. For background on Boas, including the limits of his relativism, see Carl N. Degler, *In Search of Human Nature* (New York: Oxford University Press, 1991), chap. 3.

4. Melville Herskovits, *Cultural Relativism* (New York: Random House, 1972), 15. In the original the sentence is italicized. "Enculturation" is the process by which an individual internalizes the practices and thoughtways of a particular culture.

These cautions, however, are a far cry from the radical relativism espoused by Herskovits and his co-thinkers. On that view, there is no way of transcending what is given and received; there is no objective standard an outside observer may properly use to evaluate a culture, or even a specific practice, as good or bad. If we judge another culture negatively, that is because our own culture has not taught us the values shared by the other culture; if we had the values of the other culture we would judge it positively. If we judge another culture positively, that is because at some point our cultural values converge with theirs. It is impossible to escape the closed circle of ethnocentrism. We are all culture-bound, and all equally so.

From about 1930 to 1960, perhaps a bit longer, this version of relativism attained a certain orthodoxy among American anthropologists, at least as evidenced by their popular writings and introductory textbooks. But it was by no means shared by all.[5] In the period after World War II dissent was expressed by a number of leading scholars, including Robert Redfield, Clyde Kluckhohn, and David Bidney.[6] They did not reject a moderate relativism, but they were decidedly uncomfortable with the more radical and popular position.

Redfield thought it was unrealistic and counterproductive to claim that no transcultural standard can be applied in making value judgments. In fact, anthropologists routinely apply such standards when they note the human worth of a stable and well integrated society (a "genuine culture," in Sapir's terms)[7] or when they regret the decline of folk arts and crafts. Confronting a primitive culture disorganized by its contact with Western society, "the anthropologist can hardly convince us—or himself—that so far as he is concerned a disorganized culture that fails to provide a desire to live is as valid as any other."[8] Furthermore, there is such a thing as improvement in moral understanding:

> The anthropologist impliedly recognizes a total trend of history which has given him an instrument for reaching truth that he regards as inherently better—not just better relative to the judgment impressed on him by his enculturated experience. . . . The moral order has been provided with measures of excellence unknown and unknowable in precivilized society. The

5. For a survey of this development, see Elvin Hatch, *Culture and Morality: The Relativity of Values in Anthropology* (New York: Columbia University Press, 1983), chap. 6.

6. Robert Redfield, *The Primitive World and Its Transformations* (Ithaca: Cornell University Press, 1953), chap. 6; Clyde Kluckhohn, *Culture and Behavior* (New York: Free Press, 1962), chaps. 16, 17; David Bidney, "Cultural Relativism," *International Encyclopedia of the Social Sciences* 3 (1968): 543–47.

7. See Chapter 1, note 2.

8. Redfield, *Primitive World,* 150.

anthropologist, insofar as his describing involves, as I think it does, some valuing, makes use of these new measures, and does not expect his subject matter, the preliterate people, to make use of them in valuing him.[9]

A similar note was struck by Bidney:

> The advocates of cultural relativism counsel us to suspend comparative judgment and to grant, in principle, the equality or equivalent value of all value systems. This assumed ability to doubt and suspend judgment . . . presupposes an inherent freedom of judgment that liberates the mind from its own prejudice and past cultural conditioning. Hence, the exercise of freedom of judgment and rational analysis is as much a fact of human behavior as is cultural determinism. Were it not for man's innate ability freely to evaluate and verify the truth of his ideas by subjecting them to empirical and critical tests, it would be impossible to overcome ethnocentric prejudices. . . . Man would be the prisoner and victim of his own cultural conditioning, and a science of anthropology would, in effect, be impossible.[10]

There is indeed a central paradox in cultural relativism. On the one hand, it is argued that every culture is unique and incommensurable; therefore we cannot evaluate beliefs and practices; it is not for us to second-guess another people's way of life. On the other hand, the main point of relativism is a moral lesson: *all people need and deserve respect* despite their diverse habits and customs. This teaching is not presented as a peculiar product of Western (or American) culture. On the contrary, it is a moral principle everyone should acknowledge.

It would be easy to dismiss this paradox as blatant self-contradiction, and some philosophers have done just that.[11] But it is better to understand what lies behind the apparent error of saying in one breath that all judgment is relative and in the next that respect for others is an objective moral truth. Cultural relativism is a doctrine of appreciative toleration, founded on a "postulate of humanity." The assumption is that all peoples seek their own welfare and in doing so tend to create ways of life that make sense to them and that, on the whole, serve them well. A corollary is the principle of self-determination. The paradox of relativism

9. Ibid., 158, 159.

10. Bidney, "Cultural Relativism," 546. George Murdock was more blunt. Speaking to a meeting of the American Sociological Association in 1960, he said: "[The idea] that all cultures must be accorded equal 'dignity' and equal 'validity' . . . seems to me to be not only nonsense but sentimental nonsense. It is one thing to respect the organization, integration, complexity and adaptiveness of cultural systems, but quite another to insist that all are equally admirable or even equally adaptive" (*Culture and Society* [Pittsburgh: University of Pittsburgh Press, 1965], 146).

11. See Bernard Williams, *Morality: An Introduction to Ethics* (New York: Harper Torchbooks, 1972), 20ff.

arises when the claims of self-determination are pressed so far that they undermine the principle of respect. At an extreme, self-determination would include the option to *reject* respect for others. The Italian Fascist leader Benito Mussolini, for example, proclaimed himself a moral relativist and happily inferred that "everybody has the right to create for himself his own ideology and to attempt to enforce it with all the energy of which he is capable."[12] Mussolini's doctrines did not include the principle of respect. In contrast, as envisioned by the students of Boas, cultural relativism contained, in the principle of respect, an implicit limitation on the reach of self-determination.

As is so often the case, the trouble comes from overreaching and not from egregious error. There are good reasons for holding to the prima facie truth that every distinct culture is the product of its own adaptation, must be understood in its own terms, and deserves to be respected as a valid rendering of human potentiality. *But these presumptions are rebuttable.* They derive from an underlying theory of what "normally" happens in the course of adaptation; and they must be read in the light of what we know, and come to know, about variable and contingent circumstances. Behind the moral commitment of the cultural relativists lies a conception of what it is like to live in a well-integrated community where there is a basic harmony of self and society. Many of the peoples they studied seemed to meet these conditions and to be living proof that human beings can survive and flourish with widely different beliefs and aspirations. But not enough attention was given to the conditions of human flourishing, as revealed in their own studies, with all that might mean for qualifying and even rejecting specific claims to respect and appreciation.

Perhaps it seemed sufficient to the day, from the standpoint of moral edification, to attack ethnocentrism by calling attention to diversity. This was, after all, a rich educational resource. From it much was gained in sympathetic understanding and a deeper sense of human community. But it was a disservice to social science to suggest that in human society anything goes.

DIVERSITY AND CONVERGENCE

The fact of diversity in moral codes has received dramatic demonstration from anthropological studies. But awareness of diversity is nothing new.

---

12. Quoted in Henry B. Veatch, *Rational Man: A Modern Interpretation of Aristotelian Ethics* (Bloomington: Indiana University Press, 1962), 41.

When the Greeks distinguished opinion from knowledge they understood that opinion is variable and strongly influenced by history and circumstance; and some used the fact of diversity to justify moral and even epistemological skepticism. In the governance of ancient empires the variability of custom was taken for granted, and it was common to allow local autonomy in the realm of faith and morals. In the seventeenth century Pascal pointed out, with no claim to originality, that "three degrees of latitude reverse all jurisprudence; a meridian decides the truth."[13]

Closely considered, however, diversity is not all it seems. As many students of culture have pointed out, a distinction must be drawn between specific rules or practices and more general values. A long list of "moral universals"[14] could be drawn up, including the fact of morality itself, which involves subordination of individual inclination to the perceived welfare of the group; the ideal of preserving human life; looking to the well-being of close relatives; prohibiting murder and theft; valuing affection and companionship; reciprocity in helping and being helped; and hospitality. There is considerable variation in what constitutes theft and how property is conceived; hospitality may involve wife-lending and other "strange" practices. But these different renderings of similar impulses cannot be used as evidence of *radical* discontinuity in human culture. On the contrary, the universals show that human societies are everywhere much the same in their appreciation of basic morality. At least, it is just as easy to be impressed by the uniformity as by the variation.

A proper relativism takes account of the fact that the same principle may yield quite different rules under different circumstances.[15] "Circumstances" include the state of knowledge as well as social constraints and opportunities. What people know about health, procreation, and technology will affect their moral insights and expectations. It is one thing to accept early death when no treatment is known, something else to withhold treatment when medicine is more advanced. So, too, infanticide is associated with the scarcity of food:

> In the West [infanticide] is a crime and sin. But in parts of the East and the South Seas it is regarded morally as no more than a painful necessity, as right

13. Blaise Pascal, *Pensées* (1670; reprint, London: Everyman's Library, 1904), 83 (no. 294).
14. For the term "moral universals," see Raymond Firth, *Elements of Social Organization* (London: Watts, 1951), 214.
15. See Morris Ginsberg, *On the Diversity of Morals* (New York: Macmillan, 1956), chap. 7.

to preserve the relation of family size to food resources. . . . In Tikopia it is practiced "proportioned to the food," as the people say. It is done by the midwife, who turns down the face of the newly born infant to smother, at a word from the father. It is done unwillingly, these people claim, with the limited family resources in mind; only after at least one child of each sex has been born is the act carried out.[16]

The killing of babies, when done to protect existing family members, including other children, deeply offends the Western conscience, and a more universal morality as well, but the clash of values is by no means beyond sympathetic understanding.

Like other cultural universals, such as division of labor, marriage, age-grading, and ritual, moral universals occur for good reasons. They can be accounted for in three main ways.

Human nature. Like other contemporary social scientists, anthropologists have been reluctant to speak of "human nature." But they do not doubt that all human beings are alike in being subject to conditioning; in having a similar range of emotions; in needing security, respect, and response; in the capacity to care for others; and in many other ways. When the same kind of organism responds to roughly similar circumstances, it is understandable that outcomes should be similar. Human nature does not determine specific rules of conduct, which must reflect history and circumstance. But it does provide the psychological foundations of moral experience, as in the capacity for self-transcendence; and it does make some moral principles, such as parental responsibility, more likely than others to form part of what is shared and mutually understood among many cultures.

Requirements of group life. Social life has functional necessities, that is, requirements that must be met if groups are to survive and flourish. These include leadership, communication, specialization, and symbolic affirmation of group identity. Many of these necessities, such as maintaining order, protecting property, and facilitating cooperation, generate moral obligations. For example, a norm of reciprocity ("people should help those who have helped them; people should not injure those who have helped them")[17] is, in one form or another, universally recognized. Such principles are not accidental developments. They are solutions to problems, rediscovered innumerable times as ways of dealing with ever-present demands of organization and solidarity.

16. Firth, *Elements,* 202.
17. Alvin Gouldner, "The Norm of Reciprocity: A Preliminary Statement," *American Sociological Review* 25 (1960): 171.

Limited alternatives. In the course of discussing convergence in culture, that is, the independent invention of similar ideas and practices, Goldenweiser formulated a "principle of limited possibilities." A boat or an oar could be made in any of a number of ways, but certain conditions must be met if the boat is to float or the oar to pull; if, in addition, the quest is for a *speedy* boat or the *most efficient* oar, the technical limitations are even more severe.

> If the situation allowed of only one solution, the object solving it would always be identical. This, of course, is a limiting case. The fewer the possibilities, at any rate, the more likely are similar solutions. As a general result of this principle it is to be expected that many objects or devices, independently invented in different parts of the world, and in different tribes, will in certain particulars be more or less similar.[18]

The principle of limited possibilities is most persuasive in explaining technological development, but it also helps explain widespread similarities in art, ritual, social organization, and morality. People have found many ways of choosing mates, extending hospitality, showing responsibility, demonstrating courage, being honest, propitiating the gods. But in practice these ways are not infinitely various. In all human settings customs must adapt to the resources available, including the structure of the human body, and to the problems and constraints of everyday life. Each society faces similar problems and solves those problems in its own way, but does so within a framework of limited alternatives.

▼   ▲   ▼   ▲   ▼

Neither diversity nor uniformity can, in itself, determine the moral worth of a cultural pattern. If every society subordinated women or countenanced rape, that would show something about human impulses and about the difficulty of controlling them, but it would not prove the moral rightness of male domination or sexual assault. Moral worth depends on a theory of the good, which must draw on general knowledge of human needs, dispositions, possibilities, and limits. But such a theory is not a simple empirical generalization. There is no question, no matter how widespread the practice or belief, of saying that whatever is, is good. On the contrary, we might well conclude that human beings everywhere, or the institutions they create, are even more unworthy, from a moral point of view, than we now consider them.

18. Alexander Goldenweiser, *Anthropology* (New York: Crofts, 1937), 125.

Much the same may be said of diversity. In itself, the fact of diversity does not settle any question of moral justification. It does not refute the idea that some ways of living may, by some objective and rational standard, be better than others. Even William Graham Sumner, famous for the slogan that "the mores can make anything right,"[19] stressed that customs can be well or ill adapted: " 'Good' mores are those which are well adapted to the situation. 'Bad' mores are those which are not so adapted."[20] Therefore we should not presume to judge a practice without taking the context into account; nevertheless, we can learn from other peoples' experience. Every community devises its own moral standards, which define what it is conventional to believe; therefore they "can make anything right." But when customs change they do so in response to felt needs and difficulties. A process of social learning takes place. Therefore in the process of adaptation we can discern implicit criteria of social well-being. These are not necessarily the same as criteria of *moral* well-being. But Sumner's logic, despite his reputation, takes us in the right direction.

The argument from diversity against absolute standards has three persuasive elements. First, as we have seen, rules are predictably different under different circumstances even when the foundations of morality are much the same. It follows, second, that we should not judge other people negatively *simply because they are different*. Third, diversity suggests that human culture, taken as a whole, is enriched by the variety of social forms, not only in bringing forth many potentialities but also in breaking down parochial, self-limiting perspectives. These are good arguments for a presumption of respect. But the presumption may be rebutted in a particular case by showing that the context does not excuse, the mere fact of difference is not at issue, and the practice is offensive to relevant standards of moral judgment.

THE IDEA OF HUMANITY

The American anthropologists celebrated diversity even as they stressed the psychic unity of mankind. This is an aspect of what I referred to above as the central paradox of cultural relativism. Respect for diversity went hand in hand with vigorous rejection of race differences as significant determinants of individual or group achievement. The point of relativism would be lost if diversity could be explained as biological

19. Sumner, *Folkways*, 438.
20. Ibid., 65.

differentiation. The anthropologists wanted to show that the human being, as *a single kind of animal*, in every important biological respect, is
open to transformation by cultural experience. Without a concept of
"mankind" or "humanity" there would be no lesson to be drawn from
the fact of diversity.

To fit the theory, the human animal had to be conceived as highly
malleable, that is, physiologically and psychologically adaptable to a
wide range of culture patterns. But plasticity had this implicit limit:
through all variations the essential humanity of the "enculturated" person would be sustained and recognizable. And this humanity would be
something more than the basic animal attributes distinctive of the human
species, such as the tissue tensions of hunger and sex, neurophysiological development, physical capacities, infantile dependency, survival
needs. Rather, to be counted as part of "humanity" is to show evidence
of participation in complex forms of social, moral, and aesthetic
experience.

"After Boas," it has been said, "it was impossible to view the artists
of primitive cultures as anything but conscious, functioning persons in
complex and rich societies." That is so because Boas "tried to look behind the surface of a culture to the thought that animated it, and he discovered in Northwest Coast art a complex system of symbolism."[21]
Boas concluded:

> the desire for artistic expression is universal. We may even say that the mass
> of the population in primitive society feels the need of beautifying their lives
> more keenly than civilized man. . . . It is the quality of their experience, not
> a difference in mental makeup, that determines the difference between mod-
> ern and primitive art production and art appreciation.[22]

It was this sort of similarity, of impulse and achievement, that gave
point to a doctrine of the psychic unity of mankind. Given the opportunity to survive—given, that is, a necessary minimum of physical and
social resources—human beings everywhere could be expected to be in-
ventive and expressive, cooperative and self-interested, caring and mean-
spirited, hopeful and resigned—in short, to have all the attributes we associate with the human person.

Among those attributes is the disposition to create and share a
moral order:

> Considering the exuberant variation of cultures in most respects, the circum-
> stance that in some particulars almost identical values prevail throughout

21. Douglas Newton, *The Art of Africa, the Pacific Islands, and the Americas* (New
York: Metropolitan Museum of Art, 1981), 7.
22. Quoted in ibid., 8.

mankind is most arresting. No culture tolerates indiscriminate lying, stealing, or violence within the in-group. The essential universality of the incest taboo is well-known. No culture places a value upon suffering as an end in itself: as a means to the ends of society (punishment, discipline, etc.), yes; as a means to the ends of the individual (purification, mystical exaltation, etc.), yes; but of and for itself, never. We know of no culture . . . where the fact of death is not ceremonialized. Yet the more superficial conception of cultural relativity would suggest that at least one culture would have adopted the simple expedient of disposing of corpses in the same way most cultures dispose of dead animals, i.e., just throwing the body out far enough from habitations so that the odor is not troubling.[23]

These are more than similarities of form. They speak to content and substance, that is, to the directions taken by human need, impulse, and sensibility. They tell us what kinds of experiences are likely to emerge in human communities, and they suggest the limits of variation.

There can be no effective social life without widespread commitment to responsible conduct, which requires virtues of truthfulness, courage, fidelity, and respect. These virtues are generic, that is, they refer to general attributes of a disposition or course of conduct and are therefore compatible with a wide range of specific behaviors. But they are not "merely formal" if by that is meant empty or without force. What constitutes honesty or fidelity may differ in different situations, but the generic virtue, properly formulated, can help us distinguish the true from the false, the genuine from the fake.

Thus the idea of "humanity" is both descriptive and normative: descriptive in that it is based on what we know of human capacities and inclinations; normative in that it stands for certain ideal states (or the striving for them) which are moral, spiritual, and aesthetic. When we speak of avoiding "dehumanization" or of exemplifying "the human spirit," we have in mind better ways of being human, especially as they are embodied in such personal virtues as fortitude, compassion, self-realization, and self-transcendence.

In his study of the Ik of Uganda, Turnbull documented the dehumanization of a people: a radical loss of relatedness, respect, meaning, hope. When the Ik were forced to give up their ancestral hunting lands and driven to an extreme of poverty, famine, and despair, all aspects of social life broke down. Individual survival became the only guide to conduct. In his effort to come to grips with this experience, Turnbull displayed a certain ambivalence about the idea of humanity:

23. A. L. Kroeber and Clyde Kluckhohn, *Culture: A Critical Review of Concepts and Definitions* (New York: Vintage Books, 1963), 349f. The specific example may not hold for a culture in extremis, as is indicated in Colin Turnbull, *The Mountain People* (New York: Simon and Schuster, 1972).

The Ik teach us that our much vaunted human values are not inherent in humanity at all, but are associated with a particular form of survival called society, and that all, even society itself, are luxuries that can be dispensed with. That does not make them any the less wonderful or desirable, and if man has any greatness it is surely in his ability to maintain these values, clinging to them to an often very bitter end, even shortening an already pitifully short life rather than sacrificing his humanity. But that too involves choice, and the Ik teach us that man can lose the will to make it. . . . The Ik have relinquished all luxury in the name of individual survival, and the result is that they live on as a people without life, without passion, beyond humanity.[24]

The experience of the Ik, as described by Turnbull, is not so very different from that of other people who, in extreme situations of fear or deprivation, have retreated to strategies of individual, short-run survival. This may well lead us to emphasize "how shallow is man's potential for goodness, and how deep-rooted his urge to survive."[25] It does not follow, however, that the impulse to sustain group life is just another survival technique, a matter of arbitrary choice or taste. Social life is indeed a way to survive, but it is a peculiarly effective way and it permits survival at higher levels of well-being and satisfaction. The Ik teach us that human values require certain material conditions, but that does not make the values any less "inherent in humanity."

It is one thing to say that moral virtues are fragile, variable, and not absolutely necessary to adult human life, at least in the short run. It is something else to deny that morality is functional—has practical worth—and that, therefore, a *strain* toward morality is a natural accompaniment of social development. When we say that certain values are "inherent" in humanity we mean (1) they are necessary elements of a certain level of existence, not of existence per se, and (2) they arise and are sustained in the normal course of human experience. That they can also be lost, at a cost that is known, or that they take work to maintain or that they require congenial conditions is no denial of their objective worth.

The idea of humanity necessarily speaks to what human beings have in common. But what they have in common *includes the particularity of cultural experience.* In discovering what it means to be human, we need not restrict ourselves to the "bloodless universals" complained of by Clifford Geertz:

> The notion that the essence of what it means to be human is most clearly revealed in those features of human culture that are universal rather than in those

24. Turnbull, *Mountain People*, 294f.
25. Ibid., 33.

that are distinctive to this people or that is a prejudice we are not necessarily obliged to share. Is it in grasping such general facts—that man has everywhere some sort of "religion"—or in grasping the richness of this religious phenomenon or that—Balinese trance or Indian ritualism, Aztec human sacrifice or Zuni raindancing—that we grasp him? . . . it may be in the cultural particularities of people—in their oddities—that some of the most instructive revelations of what it is to be generically human are to be found; and the main contribution of the science of anthropology to the construction—or reconstruction—of a concept of man may lie in showing us how to find them.[26]

It is certainly arguable, and wholly consistent with what was said above, that the human spirit is most directly revealed in, and most fully nourished by, *particular* forms of association and *particular* forms of expressive symbolism. People live and thrive in concrete settings. Abstract regularities and abstract principles are only pale reflections of human ingenuity, only weak indicators of the texture of social life. It is in and through the concreteness of social participation, especially moral, aesthetic, and religious experience, that much of what we call distinctively human emerges.

But it does not follow that general facts and abstract principles are irrelevant or pointless. For one thing, the experience of living in the light of abstractions—moral, technical, legal, philosophical—has its own human worth, which may undermine rather than support cultural particularity. Although much can be said on behalf of particularity, as in our discussion above (Chapter 3, "From Mind to Self") of existentialism and that below of universalism and particularism (Chapter 7, "The Primacy of the Particular"), we cannot impugn abstract thought or abstract ideals as alien to the human spirit. Instead, we should see the tension between the abstract and the concrete as a central feature of the human condition, a pervasive source of both self-doubt and creativity.

Furthermore, all cultural universals are not created equal. Some are more bloodless than others, more trivial than others. To know that all communities have division of labor, rules regulating violence, or even some form of religion does not take us very far beyond identifying the general features of human societies. But these are only starting points for the study of more focused but still general principles of organization, education, or symbolism, as they affect exercising authority, maintaining cohesion, and coping with uncertainty. The closer we get to the components of these phenomena, to their dynamics, and to

26. *The Interpretation of Cultures* (New York: Basic Books, 1973), 43.

understanding how they vary in different situations, the more likely we are to make sense of particular practices or beliefs, not by fitting them into preconceived patterns but by discerning what general problems they meet and what characteristic resources they use. *The regularities we find* in ritual, kinship, socialization, art, and politics—not the mere fact that these institutions are universal—are indispensable to the ethnographic imagination. Such regularities are often dimly perceived and far from explicit. But they insure that the interpretive mind is also a furnished mind.

Every human being is unique, as is every culture. But it is just as true that people and groups are the same in important respects. From the similarities we can draw general conclusions regarding the forms and limits of social life. From the study of uniqueness we can learn about the richness of cultural experience, and we can probe more sensitively the distinctive features of a way of life. It seems wrong and even perverse, at this stage in intellectual history, to renew the claim that we must choose between the "nomothetic" and the "idiographic," between a focus on generalization and a focus on particularity.[27] We can use either or both strategies, depending on what we want to learn in the inquiry at hand.

The lesson of historical and comparative study is that humans are both *one* and *many*—one in all that is implicit in the idea of humanity; many in diversity of forms and perspectives. As we noted above, "humanity" refers to certain higher-order dispositions, capabilities, and achievements. We have yet to draw the implications of that view for the basic challenge of relativism: the idea that moral judgments are inescapably arbitrary, subjective, and incommensurable.

PLURALITY AND OBJECTIVITY

Cognitive Relativism

In its most radical form, relativism is cognitive as well as moral. Cognitive relativism is the view that everything we purport to know—not just moral truth—is tainted by historical contingency. This is not a matter of personal bias or idiosyncrasy. Truth is said to be a social product

---

27. This distinction, stressed a century ago by Wilhelm Windelband as a key to the difference between the natural and the social sciences, has been revived in other language by advocates of the "new hermeneutics." Thus Geertz argues that analysis of culture is "not an experimental science of law but an interpretive one in search of meaning" (*Interpretation of Cultures*, 5).

whose very foundations are derived from the particular experiences of a culture or an epoch. Many writers since Hegel have stressed this historicity of mind and have then struggled to overcome radically relativist conclusions. For if the basic categories we use in interpreting experience are historically determined, it would *appear* that no objective standard is possible.

Here we encounter a familiar ambiguity and a correlative overreaching. To say that mind is "historically determined" or "context-dependent" is hardly controversial. But we should distinguish the assertion "all beliefs are alike in being context-bound" from "all beliefs are equally context-bound." Just as every observation is *to some extent* theory-laden, so too is there variation in the social determination of ideas. There is no reason to suppose that every belief, perception, or mode of thought is *equally* embedded in a distinctive cultural matrix, *equally* untranslatable, *equally* opaque to the outside observer. It is just as grievous a scientific fault to ignore the variability of historical determinism as it is to suppose that such determinism does not exist or is irrelevant.

We should always be ready to examine what makes a belief credible to the people who hold it:

> This means that regardless of whether the sociologist evaluates a belief as true or rational, or as false and irrational, he must search for the causes of its credibility. In all cases he will ask, for instance, if a belief is part of the routine cognitive and technical competences handed down from generation to generation. Is it enjoined by the authorities of the society? Is it transmitted by established institutions of socialization or supported by accepted agencies of social control? Is it bound up with patterns of vested interest? . . . All of these questions can, and should, be answered without regard to the status of the belief as it is judged and evaluated by the sociologist's own standards.[28]

This is the program of the sociology of knowledge, which examines "the contingent determinants of belief and reasoning without regard to whether the beliefs are true or the inferences rational."[29] We might go even further and say that the sociology of knowledge is especially interested in the *unconscious* premises and *nonrational* sources of belief. But this in no way bars us from recognizing the difference between what is rational and what nonrational. On the contrary, it presupposes that we can do so.

28. Barry Barnes and David Bloor, "Relativism, Rationalism and the Sociology of Knowledge," in Martin Hollis and Steven Lukes, eds., *Rationality and Relativism* (Cambridge: MIT Press, 1982), 23.

29. Ibid.

We can never entirely exclude the possibility that a preference or mode of thought contains an ultimate value premise or a distinctive perception of reality "that has only local credibility."[30] There is no such thing as a *purely* objective standard, except as an ideal; there are only more or less warranted assertions regarding matters of fact, including facts about human rationality and human well-being. It may well be that every system of thought contains a "local" element—some idea or perception that is wholly indigenous and idiosyncratic. But the real question is, what difference does it make? What reason have we to believe that the local element decisively affects the objectivity of judgment or makes a case against transcultural norms of rationality? These questions are open to inquiry; the answers to them may enlarge our understanding of objectivity and rationality; they should not be prejudged. The premise that we are all culture-bound does not bind us to any conclusion regarding *the extent to which* a particular belief or practice is warranted by objective standards of reasoning and evidence. If we are to criticize our own beliefs—for example, on the basis of what we have learned from studying other cultures—we must be able to discern and apply such standards.

The most important reason for supposing that there is an "epistemological unity of mankind"[31] is the overwhelming significance of practical judgment in the experience of all peoples everywhere. This should be too obvious to need mention, yet it is easily overlooked by intellectuals distracted by special theories, and by people whose perceptions are distorted by parochial and ethnocentric outlooks. In response to the latter, anthropologists have repeatedly stressed the practical rationality of the peoples they have studied—their commitment to dealing with the urgencies of everyday life in ways that are at least moderately successful. No community can survive and flourish without social learning. The core of that learning has to do with routines of feeding, shelter, nurture, mating, and public order. In the course of developing these routines, applying them in concrete situations, and modifying them as circumstances change, people do what is effective, or roughly so. They sharpen tools and space their plants; restrain their children in the face of danger; welcome assistance; establish enduring bonds; in short, they behave like sensible animals with human capacities.

The rationality of *practice* does not, of course, guarantee the rationality of *belief*. What people do may be quite different from what they

30. Ibid., 27.
31. Martin Hollis, "The Social Destruction of Reality," in Hollis and Lukes, *Rationality and Relativism,* 84.

say about what they do. In many settings expressive symbolism—metaphor, liturgy, myth, gesture, aesthetic design—is a more satisfying mode of thought and communication than is a logical account. There is no reason to assume that all people are equally capable of rational thought or equally comfortable with its strictures. On the contrary, careful reasoning and weighing of evidence is a hard-won, precarious, and selective achievement even among highly educated persons in Western society. It should not surprise us to discover wide variations in the extent to which accounts of practical activity are straightforward and objective or, instead, are heavily influenced by expressive symbolism.

We are all acquainted with the paradox that considerable insight and common sense can be displayed by people whose capacity for abstract thought is low and whose attraction to mythic thought is high. The rationality of their stated beliefs—a disease is the judgment of God or the effect of magic—may be low when taken literally. But practical understandings of how things work, shrewd perceptions of motivation and weakness, and the funded knowledge contained in customary routines are sure indicators of rationality in common sense.

The Rule of Saint Benedict, setting out the principles and regimen of monastic life, was deeply embedded in the symbolism of early Christianity. But the modern historian can readily reconstruct the common-sense basis of the Rule:

> The principal psychological dangers of such a life are neurotic depression and exaltation; and the answer to these, humanly speaking, is to maintain regularity and devotion. The regularity of the Rule is as inexorable as a doctor's prescription, and it has proved very effective.[32]

This analysis is confirmed by much else we know about the social psychology of devotional communities.[33] Those who have designed such communities may have lacked intellectual tools for making their assumptions explicit, but they usually knew what they were doing and could think logically about means and ends.

Objective knowledge is knowledge tested by practice. It is the truth people can rely on in making decisions and ordering their affairs. Therefore we should look to practice and to *tacit* understanding, not primarily to explicit statements, if we are to learn what people believe in the realm of practical judgment, and if we are to assess the rationality of those

32. Christopher Brooke, *Monasteries of the World: The Rise and Development of the Monastic Tradition* (New York: Crescent Books, 1982), 40.

33. See, for example, Benjamin Zablocki, *The Joyful Community* (Baltimore: Penguin Books, 1971).

beliefs. It may take some effort to draw back the heavy curtain of expressive symbolism. Where judgments are effective in solving problems, however, the core of common sense is usually revealed.

Belief and Rationality

The interpretation of belief is plagued by a persistent failure to recognize that people believe on many different levels and in many different ways. A discussion of this problem points out that "to decide whether some belief is rational we need to know not only its content but also in which sense it is 'believed.' "[34] Much of what we say is not meant to be taken literally. Most metaphors, most mythic images, are readily recognized as such. (When a biographer called Winston Churchill "the last lion," no one thought he had lost his mind or had regressed to a prelogical mentality.) Perhaps most important, many assertions are inherently ambiguous; they are capable of generating an outlook or perspective without commitment to a definite argument or empirical proposition.[35]

In the study of religion, myth, and art it has long been understood that one must look beyond literal and manifest meanings to figurative and latent meanings. The search for truth in expressive symbolism is endless, and perhaps always inconclusive, because the symbol demands participation in determining its meaning. It is a vehicle of *communion* and not of instrumental or linear communication. This does not justify dismissing such symbolism as noncognitive. Rather, in looking for the latent truth in a parable, legend, drama, painting, ritual, or sacrament, we presume that the "text" contains, with whatever indirection, a message that makes sense of some aspect of experience. Rarely is this message wholly tacit, and certainly the *thought* involved in creating the legend or the mythic imagery is relevant to its latent content.

The larger significance of this argument is, once again, to expand the idea of rationality. We cannot identify being rational with being logical. Rather, rationality is a variable attribute of purposive, adaptive, problem-solving *action*. The justifications people give for what they do may or may not meet present-day (Western) standards of reasoning and

34. Dan Sperber, "Apparently Irrational Beliefs," in Hollis and Lukes, *Rationality and Relativism*, 164.
35. See ibid., 166ff., for a discussion of "semi-propositional representations" whose reference is indefinite, e.g., "People of different cultures live in different worlds": "The speaker's or author's intention is not to convey a specific proposition. It is to provide a range of possible interpretations and to incite the hearer or reader to search that range for the interpretation most relevant to him" (ibid., 171).

evidence. However, when we recognize the ambiguity of the term "belief," and the uses of ambiguity in belief, we can more readily accept the claim of expressive symbolism to be taken seriously.

The anthropological evidence does not support a finding of radical diversity in the structure of mind. The most important deviation from that consensus was Levy-Bruhl's argument, in 1910, that the primitive mind is "pre-logical."[36] But he ultimately modified his theory to conform with mainstream opinion: "There is a mystical mentality which is more marked and more easily observable among 'primitive peoples' than in our own societies, but it is present in every human mind."[37] This echoes the views of the American anthropologist Alexander Goldenweiser, commenting on Levy-Bruhl's ideas:

> Is the mind of early man wholly submerged in pre-logical, irrational, collective ideas and attitudes? All who have come in contact with primitives, or have thought about them, without prejudice, know that this is by no means so. Thus Durkheim speaks of the profane periods of the life of the Australian which contrast so strikingly with the periodically recurring ceremonial frenzy. Now, the profane period, in primitive Australia as in modern society, is the abode of common sense, reason, logic. . . . In his multitudinous industrial activities—crude though they may be—the Australian shows common sense in abundance. Even though he may not count further than five, he can put two and two together very effectively. Nor does his wisdom extend only to the domain of material things, for evidence abounds of his shrewdness in matters human, and shrewdness is logic applied to psychology. . . . There is a streak of logic as well as irrationality in the make-up of the primitive mind; the same holds of the modern mind.[38]

And consider the following comments by Clyde Kluckhohn:

> In spite of loose talk (based upon an uncritical acceptance of an immature theory of cultural relativity) to the effect that the symptoms of mental disorder are completely relative to culture, the fact of the matter is that all cultures define as abnormal individuals who consistently fail to maintain some degree of self-control over their impulse life. Social life is impossible without communication, without some measure of order: the behavior of any "normal" individual must be predictable—within a certain range—by his fellows and interpretable by them.[39]

36. Lucien Levy-Bruhl, *How Natives Think* (1910; reprint, London: George Allen and Unwin, 1926), chap. 3.
37. Lucien Levy-Bruhl, *The Notebooks on Primitive Mentality* (1949; reprint, Oxford: Blackwell, 1975), 101.
38. Alexander Goldenweiser, *History, Psychology, and Culture* (New York: Alfred A. Knopf, 1933), 184f.
39. Kluckhohn, *Culture and Behavior,* 295.

In short, despite dramatic diversity in style and content, the human mind is everywhere the same in basic structure.

If humankind shares psychic and epistemological unity, no case can be made for a radical relativism of truth and rationality. If all humans must accept touchstones of reality; if they have in common essential features of the human condition, such as the formation and protection of personhood; if they have similar capacities for learning and relatedness, then what is rational can in principle be determined by objective criteria. These criteria are not arbitrary, nor are they random relative to the special circumstances or ethos of a people. Rather, they are founded in enduring parameters of human survival and well-being.

This conclusion is not a denial of social determinism. As George Herbert Mead made clear, the universal features of mind and self are, at the same time, part of our common humanity and emergent products of social interaction.[40] There is no contradiction between being basically similar and being socially formed.

Nor need we deny historical determinism or forget the sociology of knowledge. In question are the *reach* of history and the *claims* of relativism. The rich diversity of intellectual experience is eloquent testimony to historical determinism. That some ways of thinking are more congenial than others in particular circumstances, and more likely to thrive than others, means that a moderate form of cognitive relativism is indispensable. In affirming epistemological unity we are not called on to forget the attraction of German thought to holistic, configurational modes of analysis and of British thought to a more atomistic and empirical style. Each mind-set is historically determined; each has made distinctive contributions to philosophy and science; neither is self-justifying. However, the unquestioned worth of historical and relativist inquiry is no warrant for an assault on objectivity. Without objective standards we cannot know when we are doing proper history or offering an explanation within the framework of the sociology of knowledge.

Nor, finally, need we deny the reality of "primitive" thought or of cognitive development. Practical judgment is an ever-present anchor, but it may be more or less constrained, and more or less obscured, by prelogical thoughtways. An unanalytic mode of thought, dominated by person-centered imagery, is likely to develop "if environmental conditions are insufficiently demanding."[41] This thought is not "absurd or mistaken," but it is

40. *Mind, Self, and Society* (Chicago: University of Chicago Press, 1934).
41. C. R. Hallpike, *The Foundations of Primitive Thought* (Oxford: Clarendon Press, 1979), 59.

of limited generality and much more restricted to the phenomenal appearance of things than our own. Within these limits it is quite capable of solving the practical problems that are encountered in the circumstances of daily life . . . In particular, it is well adapted to the characteristics of *social* relations in small, face-to-face communities where experience is largely homogenous and unchanging, where values, affect, and participation in action are all-important, and where explicit verbal analysis and generalization have little relevance.[42]

Unsophisticated thinking is of course widely prevalent among adults in all societies, including our own technological society. If we are to identify the characteristics and assess the limits of this mode of thought, as theories of cognitive development suggest, the appeal must be to transcultural standards of mental achievement.

Responsible Relativism

The proper target of responsible relativism is *absolutism,* not objectivity. In its core meaning "absolute" refers to whatever is unconditioned, unqualified, or uncontingent—an idea, power, or rule that is not dependent on anything else and does not vary as circumstances vary. Hence we speak of "absolute truth" or "absolute power." Insofar as people suppose that a specific custom, standard, or interpretation has absolute merit (or demerit), regardless of context, the relativist critique is clearly appropriate. But in this respect relativism is simply an application of the scientific attitude, which treats all truth as contingent and corrigible. If that is so, and if it is accepted that science is in some clear sense objective, then responsible relativism cannot be an assault on objectivity.

Paradoxically, an absolutist view of moral law tends to breed a radical relativism. This is so because absolutist views are easily refuted, especially when held in popular and unsophisticated ways. The refutation is often experienced as traumatic, with an accompanying sense of lost moorings. The apparent alternative is a wholesale denial of objectivity. Morality is then perceived as a matter of arbitrary faith in one's own upbringing and identity. "Everything is subjective," say the bemused young scholars, perhaps distancing themselves from their upbringing. This is a classic response among those for whom education is unnerving.

The alternative to radical relativism on one hand and absolutism on the other is a pluralist view of truth and morality. The lesson of diversity

42. Ibid., 489.

is not that anything goes or that variation has no limits. "Plurality" refers to an indefinite number greater than one, but it is not a synonym for
"infinity" or "boundlessness." In the context of moral ordering, pluralism rejects the idea of one right answer but leaves open the question of
how many choices are valid or justified. Even when the context is closely
specified, the presumption is in favor of more than one acceptable
choice. This presumption reflects our understanding of the resilience and
adaptability of the human animal, the variety and complexity of environments, and the capacity of social learning to find alternative ways of
meeting similar problems. In the absence of particular facts, however,
nothing can be concluded as to which alternatives contribute in roughly
equal ways to survival or well-being.

Pluralism takes for granted that there are many worthy and even admirable forms of human life. This variety occurs because there is enough
leeway in adaptation to allow *trade-offs* among competing goods. Humans can flourish though they build their lives on different commitments and different excellences. The life of the small farmer is admirable, but so are the lives of skilled workers, lawyers, ministers, and
scholars. Each has worth, but not absolute or unqualified worth. Each
choice gives up some values in exchange for others.

Much the same may be said of cultures. The importance of trade-offs
is a major theme in Ruth Benedict's widely read *Patterns of Culture*. In
culture, she wrote, "selection is the prime necessity."[43] There can be no
cultural identity without selection from "the great arc" of potential interests and activities. But selection means emphasizing some things and
giving up others. Benedict was no admirer of Kwakiutl society; she particularly rejected its "notoriously wasteful" pattern of rivalry. But she
was quick to say:

> Nevertheless . . . the pursuit of victory can give vigor and zest to human ex-
> istence. Kwakiutl life is rich and forceful in its own terms. . . . Whatever the
> social orientation, a society which exemplifies it will develop certain virtues
> that are natural to the goals it has chosen, and it is most unlikely that even the
> best society will be able to stress in one social order all the virtues we prize
> in human life.[44]

Zuni culture, too, has "the defects of its virtues."

> It has no place, for instance, for dispositions we are accustomed to value
> highly, such as force of will or personal initiative or the disposition to take up

43. *Patterns of Culture* (1934; reprint, New York: Penguin Books, 1946), 21.
44. Ibid., 229.

arms against a sea of troubles. It is incorrigibly mild. . . . The freedom from
any forms of social exploitation or of social sadism appears on the other side
of the coin as endless ceremonialism not designed to serve major ends of human existence. It is the old inescapable fact that every upper has its lower, every right side its left.[45]

Packed in such phrases as "all the virtues we prize in human life" and
"major ends of human existence" are implicit criteria of well-being. A
viable and well-integrated society will meet at least some of those criteria. We who make our own trade-offs should not be quick to judge the
trade-offs of others. But this is no argument against the objectivity of
assessment, including self-assessment. Nor is it a bar to rejecting—even
abhorring—beliefs or practices that fail to meet or wantonly degrade the
elementary conditions of moral life.

Published in 1934, *Patterns of Culture* quickly became an icon of cultural relativism. It was an eloquent plea for tolerance, for recognizing
"the coexisting and equally valid patterns of life which mankind has created for itself from the raw materials of existence."[46] Benedict thereby
encouraged radical relativists, who read the book with passionate eyes.
Nevertheless, her basic message is really a plea for pluralism, not a justification for *every* form of social life.[47] There are many "equally valid"
ways of life, but they all involve trade-offs, and some, such as the
Dobuans, are hardly presented as admirable. Indeed, Benedict's work is
full of evaluations.[48] She had no qualms in describing Dobuans as
"lawless and treacherous" or as "consumed with jealousy and suspicion and resentment."[49] Nor did she hesitate to praise the Zuni for
peaceful modes of interaction, benign forms of socialization, and freedom from a sense of sin. Most important, perhaps, is her statement
that by raising consciousness about cultural determinism "we may
train ourselves to pass judgment upon the dominant traits of our own
civilization."[50] However, Benedict failed to draw the necessary conclusions for cultural relativism.

45. Ibid., 227.
46. Ibid., 257.
47. On the difference between pluralism and relativism, see also Isaiah Berlin, *The Crooked Timber of Humanity* (New York: Knopf, 1991), 78ff.
48. See Elgin Williams, "Anthropology for the Common Man," *American Anthropologist* 49 (1947): 84–90.
49. Benedict, *Patterns of Culture,* 121. Like Colin Turnbull's Ik, though apparently less desperately so, the Dobuans as described by Benedict (based on research by Reo Fortune) lived in a harsh environment: "rocky upcroppings that harbour only scanty pockets of soil and allow little fishing" (ibid., 155).
50. Ibid., 230.

▼   ▲   ▼   ▲   ▼

The logic of pluralism is familiar to students of "normative ethics," which is the quest for principles to guide moral conduct. Such principles range from familiar homilies—honesty is good, deceit is bad—to more subtle and unfamiliar ideas, such as "power is no argument in matters of justice" or "inequalities must be justified by benefits to the least advantaged." But no general formula can determine a specific rule of conduct. At best it is a hypothesis or a presumption, which may be qualified or rebutted when particular circumstances are considered. There may be a strong moral case for truth-telling, based on the utility of trust and communication in human affairs, but the presumption does not prevail when other values, such as concern for human suffering, are at stake.

Thus normative ethics cannot be absolutist. As a first step, it must yield to "objective relativism."[51] Moral rules and moral judgments are necessarily relative in that they must be framed in the light of specific circumstances. But what is good in the circumstances is objectively good, that is, it does in fact solve problems, provide satisfactions, enhance competence. "The proposition that one man's meat is another man's poison does not in the least impugn the objective validity of biochemistry but on the contrary presupposes it."[52] Or again: "[W]hether the shoe fits depends on who wears it, of course; but that fact didn't do Cinderella's sisters a bit of good—on the contrary, it is the fact which found them out."[53]

There is more to objectivity, however, than "what is good in the circumstances." To pursue Kaplan's example, the excellence of the *design* of the shoe, in the light of general knowledge, is as objective a judgment as is the *fit* of the shoe for a specific individual. The design is more indeterminate and must allow for an array of sizes, but its worth depends, among other things, on its capacity to generate sizes that fit. In other words, sound principles are vital ingredients of good engineering,

51. See Abraham Kaplan, *The Conduct of Inquiry* (San Francisco: Chandler, 1964), 392f. The phrase "objective relativism" is also used in a much broader, but related, sense to characterize the interaction between mind and nature. For an example see the discussion of George Herbert Mead in Charles Morris, *The Pragmatic Movement in American Philosophy* (New York: Braziller, 1970), 128ff.

52. Kaplan, *Conduct of Inquiry*, 392.

53. Abraham Kaplan, *New Worlds of Philosophy* (New York: Random House, 1961), 49.

whether of moral rules or anything else; and they hold true over a wide range of cases and contexts.

The chief difference between the pluralist and the relativist turns on how each perceives the objectivity of moral principles. The radical relativist does not admit any such objectivity: the particular circumstance or interest must be the ultimate judge of what is good. The pluralist takes a different tack. General principles should not be used to *prejudge* specific practices—polygamy may have its own virtue, infanticide or cannibalism its own excuse—but they can be used to criticize and assess a practice, so long as particular circumstances are taken into account. In the pluralist view no appeal to special circumstances or local interests is self-justifying. Such an appeal is the beginning of inquiry, not its end.

When we try to determine the real interests of particular persons, we have no difficulty in combining the universal and the particular, the objective and the subjective. We bring to bear general notions of what is good for *any* person, but we also consider what the particular individual is like. We agree that people should develop their own potentialities and follow their own inclinations, so far as they are *constructive*. We take account of how individuals view themselves and their worlds; but we do not shrink from criticizing those views insofar as they are impoverishing or self-destructive. The same logic applies in the assessment of cultures.

▼　▲　▼　▲　▼

Radical relativism is the enemy of reason, and therefore of communication and community. If values and beliefs are incommensurable, there is no basis for dialogue and mutual understanding. Such a perspective is wholly alien to the spirit of American pragmatism:

> Pluralism for the pragmatists never meant a self-enclosed relativism where we are forever doomed to be prisoners limited to our own conceptual schemes, frameworks, or horizons. Such a form of relativism is precisely what the pragmatists were always combating. Long before the current fascination (obsession?) with radical incommensurability, Dewey was aware of the danger of the type of degenerate pluralism that would block community and communication. He was perspicacious in seeing this not primarily as a theoretical problem but as a practical problem—a problem that demands working toward a type of society in which we can at once respect and even celebrate

differences and plurality but always strive to understand and *seek* a common ground with what is other and different.[54]

If the claims of radical relativism were valid, we would have to reconsider this pragmatist faith. As I have tried to show, however, the claims are overblown. They need not deter the quest for community.

54. Richard J. Bernstein, "The Varieties of Pluralism," John Dewey Lecture, *American Journal of Education* 94 (1987): 521.

PART TWO

The Moral Person

FIVE

Human Nature Revisited

The subject of human nature offers few difficulties when what we have in mind is the human biophysical organism. The more we learn about body chemistry and physiology, the more we can say about natural responses to the invasion of bacteria or viruses and to changes in temperature, stress, and nutrition. Similarly, some psychophysical phenomena, such as conditioning, seem to follow laws characteristic of the whole species. However, when we turn to human personality, and especially to *motivation,* the subject becomes more puzzling and controversial. This is the main focus of debate about "human nature." In intellectual history theories of human nature do not refer to *all* characteristics of the species. Such ideas are always selective. They have to do with the springs of action, with human capacities, needs, and dispositions as they affect the formation of motives and the direction of choice. Here we find the competing and complementary perspectives of Hobbes, Rousseau, Marx, Freud, and Dewey. They and others sought a conception of humanity that could be made the basis for social prescription, especially the design of institutions. They looked for salient attributes, including *reliable* motives and *critical* vulnerabilities.

There are and must be many "models of man." Economists, for example, expect material incentives to be effective (at least in contexts of production and consumption) and to follow the logic of marginal utility; political scientists invoke reliable patterns of deference to authority and of rising expectations to account for stability or change; students of culture and religion look to the search for continuity and meaning as a steady source of expressive symbolism and transcendental yearning.

But a theory of human nature cannot be content with this plurality of perspectives. Although each model may have explanatory power so long as appropriate conditions and contexts are specified, a deeper problem remains. The human personality is not a mere aggregate of diverse dispositions to maximize utility, seek affection, or find comfort in expressive symbolism. The person is an organic unity, and the well-being of that unity is at stake when particular dispositions are acted out. "Economic man," calculating proximate utilities and pursuing material gains, may undermine his integrity as a person; and the same may be said of one in quest of meaning if that quest gets in the way of practical judgment. There is potential distortion in any perspective that fails to take account of the whole person. Therefore the larger objective of the study of human nature is to discover what personal well-being consists of, what it depends on, and what undermines it.

That inquiry leads us to consider the moral relevance of human psychology. Without an understanding of human nature, we are hard put to criticize existing conditions, personal or social, from the standpoint of critical morality. We cannot do without a theory of what should be prized by human beings if they are to survive and flourish and if they are to attain moral well-being. We need not assume that people always *choose* the good, even though there may be, as many have supposed, a natural disposition to do so. Insofar as people seek to be moral, they can properly turn to psychology for guidance. The transition from "is" to "ought" is real enough, in moral experience as well as in logic. And there is no better springboard for it than sound knowledge of what the world is like, including what there is to like in the world.

As we pursue this theme, three cautions are in order. First, propositions about human nature usually purport to show that all people are alike in some relevant way. But that assumption may be too strong. The generalization may refer to attributes that are variable within a population. Not everyone has the same need for emotional support, the same capacity for self-transcendence, the same disposition to be greedy. To say with Lord Acton that "power tends to corrupt and absolute power corrupts absolutely"[1] is not to say that everyone, or even almost everyone, will be corrupted by power. But the aphorism does say that the corrupt-

1. See John E. E. D. Acton, *Essays on Freedom and Power* (Boston: Beacon Press, 1948), 364.

ing effect of power is sufficiently powerful and pervasive, as an attribute of *populations,* that every community should guard against it.

Second, human nature cannot be reduced to some small set of drives or impulses, such as pleasure, power, sex, altruism, rationality. Each of these has a part to play in human motivation—sometimes a vital part—but no small number can encompass the full range of morally relevant attributes. A great many dispositions, capacities, and vulnerabilities, including very ordinary features of rational choice as well as much that is irrational and nonrational, may affect the morality of conduct.

And, third, we cannot attribute to psychology alone the shortcomings or achievements of social life. A general disposition to defer to authority may exist;[2] and power may indeed tend to corrupt. But dispositions do not determine outcomes. Deference to authority may work for good or ill, and power may ennoble as well as corrupt. Human nature is best understood as setting limits and opening opportunities. What actually happens depends on proximate contexts and contingent circumstances. It is folly to ignore the dispositions, but it is just as wrong to suppose they are inexorable.

▼   ▲   ▼   ▲   ▼

The philosophers of the Enlightenment differed on what they took to be central to human nature, but they did not doubt the constancy and universality of basic capacities, passions, and interests. Even David Hume, the father of modern skepticism regarding the rational foundations of morality, was secure in the belief that an understanding of human nature must be the basis of "the experimental method of reasoning into moral subjects."[3]

In the mid-nineteenth century the idea of human nature began to lose its hold on the philosophical imagination. This disaffection was part of the romantic reaction against rationalist modes of thought, especially what were perceived to be the arid abstractions of the Enlightenment. The psychological axioms of Hobbes, Locke, and the Scottish moralists came to seem arbitrary, unrealistic, and, above all, uninformed by a sense of history. The new slogan was to be: "Man, in a word, has no nature; what he has is . . . history."[4]

2. As suggested in Stanley Milgram, *Obedience to Authority* (New York: Harper/Colophon, 1974).

3. This is the subtitle of Hume's *A Treatise on Human Nature* (1739–40).

4. José Ortega y Gasset, *History as System* (New York: W. W. Norton, 1941), 217, original sentence italicized, and with the ellipsis.

Here was a perspective in many ways congenial to the modern temper. It encouraged a mood of openness and transformation and could be read as offering an optimistic vision of human possibilities. If "man makes himself" and has no fixed nature, it is easy to believe in the creation of a "new man" by revolutionary reconstruction of the social order. At the same time, a pervasive skepticism was encouraged, filled with nagging doubts as to the constancy and universality of anything at all. These doctrines nicely expressed the ambivalence of modern thought. They created an intellectual environment that would, by the 1930s, bring "human nature" into disrepute. Indeed, by midcentury dispraise of the concept had become intellectual orthodoxy.[5]

Many efforts to describe human nature have foundered on the shoals of poor logic and parochial shortsightedness. In the late nineteenth and early twentieth centuries, it was popular to explain war by "pugnacity," capitalism by "acquisitiveness," and almost anything by "self-preservation." But such "instincts," taken alone, could never account for organized warfare or an economic system. Inadequate attention was given to the way motivational patterns, such as the will to achieve, are summoned and shaped by a culture and its institutions. Many of the interpretations crudely defended familiar ways of life as psychologically inevitable. All this discredited the concept of human nature.

Nevertheless the idea has persisted, amid considerable confusion and controversy. A resurgent interest in the evolutionary and biological foundations of human behavior has fueled the debate.[6] More important, perhaps, is the irrepressible recognition that social explanation ultimately requires psychological premises. It is hard to put down the belief that secure knowledge of human psychology is indispensable if sound

5. In *Human Nature and Conduct* (New York: Modern Library, 1930) John Dewey contributed mightily to that orthodoxy, in part because of his trenchant criticism of instinct psychology. And yet he could say, in a 1929 foreword: "When this volume was first produced, there was a tendency, especially among psychologists, to insist upon native human nature untouched by social influences and to explain social phenomena by reference to traits of original nature called 'instincts.' Since that date (1922), the pendulum has undoubtedly swung in the opposite direction. The importance of culture as a formative medium is more generally recognized. Perhaps the tendency today in many quarters is to overlook the basic identity of human nature amid its different manifestations. . . . [This book presents] an attempt to make clear that there are always intrinsic forces of a common human nature at work: forces which are sometimes stifled by the encompassing social medium but which also in the long course of history are always striving to liberate themselves and to make over social institutions so that the latter may form a freer, more transparent and more congenial medium for their operation."

6. Notably in recent writing on ethology and sociobiology. For a review of this development, see Carl N. Degler, *In Search of Human Nature* (New York: Oxford University Press, 1991).

inferences are to be made regarding people's intentions and actions.[7] The student of other societies and times must be alert to motives that are socially induced and historically contingent. But no one engaged in such inquiry has an obligation to invent a new psychology or to abandon hitherto reliable reasons for actions.

SOCIOLOGY AND HUMAN NATURE

In modern sociology, broadly understood, the discussion of human nature is both illuminated and obscured. It is illuminated above all by the insistence that humans are social animals. Thus George Herbert Mead, in his foundational lectures on social psychology, argued that the human individual is the *product* of society, not its creator. "The self . . . is essentially a social structure, and it arises in social experience . . . it is impossible to conceive of a self arising outside of social experience."[8] Mead disagreed sharply with the atomistic conception of man put forward in the seventeenth and eighteenth centuries. Hobbes, Locke, and Hume had placed man firmly in the natural order and appealed to experience as the basis of knowledge. Yet they and others had assumed that man is "naturally" endowed with reason and self-consciousness. Mead agreed that these are natural potentialities, but he insisted they could not be realized except in society. In the beginning is society, not the individual.

By examining closely the dynamics of socialization—communication, self-awareness, self-control, cooperation—Mead showed that mind and self are indivisible and that they are outcomes of interactions in which social others play a decisive role. The lesson is clear: everything we are, including whatever individuality we have, depends on the nurture and support of group life.

This sociological perspective is a denial of *pre-formed* personality, but it is far from a denial of persistent human attributes. To say that humans are social animals is to characterize them in decisive ways. Above all, it is to say that they depend on others for psychological sustenance, including the very constitution of the self, and that this dependency is the source of typical strengths, failings, and strivings. The formation of

7. This statement in no way denies that there are distinctively social attributes which are not attributes of individuals. For example, morale is a group attribute, as is cohesion, role differentiation, size, and much else. Organizations adapt to their environments, but that process is not the same as individual adaptation. In each case, however, the social attribute has individual correlates, and to understand it fully, which is not always necessary, the individual correlates should be specifiable.

8. *Mind, Self, and Society* (Chicago: University of Chicago Press, 1934), 140.

persons goes on in all human societies and everywhere follows the same basic patterns. Everywhere, for example, conscience is constructed largely by internalizing the attitudes of others.

The process of socialization reflects biological as well as social imperatives. To the sociologist there is nothing new or upsetting in the view that socialization has a biological basis—in particular, the capacity to learn and use language, a long period of physical dependency, and the absence of true instincts. Every human society is driven by biological necessities and makes use of biologically given opportunities. Each must provide for biological needs and must do so in ways that create socially effective individuals. Biology provides the materials to which society must fashion a response, and that response is not wholly free. It is governed by the social task at hand and by the nature of the materials, which includes the principle of limited possibilities.[9]

Mead's main concern was to spell out in detail why the self is inevitably a social product. He thereby shared in the larger effort of anthropologists and sociologists to downgrade biological factors and emphasize the influence of social learning. An important part of this strategy was to treat the person as socialized by definition. Everyone has a self, and no self is unformed by social life. To many sociologists (though not to Mead, as we note below) this seemed to allow no place for variation in the *quality* and *degree* of socialization. The process was thought to be unproblematic; only the content could vary significantly.

This polemical stance projected an image of socialization as a smooth continuum of adjustment. To make sure people understood the social nature of the self, most attention was given to the continuities of society and personality and to the many ways individuals are molded by families, peer groups, and other "transmission belts" for culture. This encouraged an overly optimistic view of the effectiveness of social learning. The troubles and pathologies of internalization had no central place in this emergent theory of society and the individual.

It was Sigmund Freud who first paid close attention to the pathologies of socialization and provided a theoretical framework for its study. In contrast to Mead (and to John Dewey as well) Freud emphasized that social life is no tranquil haven of nurture and support. Social experience is *necessary* to psychic well-being but does not *guarantee* it. On the contrary, the minimally or perversely socialized person may be wounded and brutalized, spiritually impoverished, socially incompetent. These findings remind us that socialization is a precarious venture, and a healing art.

9. See Chapter 4, "Diversity and Convergence."

Freud's ideas do not contradict the basic proposition that man is a social animal, incapable of surviving, to say nothing of flourishing, in the
absence of group life. But the human animal is still an *animal*, whose biological systems create drives and propensities that make a difference in
what socialization can achieve—and at what cost. Thus biology is not
merely a *basis* for socialization. It is an ever-present *source* of problems,
opportunities, and constraints.

Mead laid the groundwork for what Dennis Wrong once called the
"oversocialized conception of man" in modern sociology.[10] There is a
notable gap between the general tone of much sociological teaching and
the more empirical, more problem-centered world of sociological research. Studies of child development, mental disorder, and crime make
it abundantly clear that socialization can be radically defective and that
conformity is highly problematic. The true lesson of sociology is not
that people conform. Rather, it is that conformity is an important phenomenon which varies in degree and in kind. Part of that variation
stems from the group structure of society, for example, from competition among socializing agencies. But much is also due to the exigent demands of the human animal, within the framework of the life cycle, for
special kinds of nurture, freedom, and control.

Explaining Routine Delinquency

The idea that people are wholly determined by social experience is often
an obstacle to clear thought. An important example can be found in the
study of crime and delinquency. Much sociological writing has exaggerated the influence of culture and the effectiveness of socialization, even as
it attempts to explain deviance from social norms. As a result, necessary
premises about human nature are distorted or obscured, and the social reality of delinquency becomes tenuous and elusive.

Every human community takes for granted that delinquencies will
occur unless *work is done* to contain and redirect the impulses and
motivations that lead to wrongful conduct.[11] This work takes two main
forms: the formation of character and conscience, which we call socialization; and the maintenance of complex patterns of participation and

10. Dennis Wrong, "The Oversocialized Conception of Man in Modern Society,"
American Sociological Review 26 (1961): 183–93.
11. I use "delinquency" to denote any offense against a moral code or, in sociological
language, a violation of the *mores*. The offense may or may not be criminal or even illegal,
but it is more than simple deviance. Thus betrayal of a friend is a delinquency, though not
necessarily illegal; an eccentricity of dress or deportment is not.

control. The presumption is that any moral code will be broken if these disciplining forces are inadequate.

Behind this commonsense understanding is an implicit theory of society and human nature. To explain the persistence and universality of delinquency, we need only postulate that people are active, questing, and self-referring; that they are not puppets or automatons; that they continually make choices between one or another course of conduct, with a view to gaining immediate or long-run satisfactions. Furthermore, human choices are subject to many constraints and uncertainties, *and the community's moral code is only one constraint among others.* Conscience is by no means the only guide to action.

Thus no special theory of personality is needed to explain routine delinquency. (Other kinds are discussed in Chapter 6.) People act immorally in the course of pursuing quite ordinary and often legitimate objectives. Only a few have specific compulsions, such as kleptomania; a larger but still limited number flout the law because of hostility, alienation, or some other psychological distress. But most delinquency occurs because people want more money and more of what money can buy; because they want the esteem of their peers; or simply because they are in a hurry. These wants are not extraordinary or wicked in themselves. It is the willingness to use illegitimate *means* that sets delinquents apart. Insofar as that willingness is a temporary state of mind or a response to special circumstances, the difference between delinquents and nondelinquents, as kinds of persons, tends to fade. "There go I," one says, "but for the grace of God."

This emphasis on human autonomy and diversity is wholly compatible with sociological understanding. Although some writers project a vision of all-powerful society imposing its will on infinitely plastic human animals, the world of empirical and problem-centered sociology is less naive. Socialization and social control are *variably effective.* They are implemented by real people subject to many limitations, distractions, and temptations, who may or may not take their responsibilities seriously and may or may not be able to carry them out with the requisite skill and sensitivity.

There is nothing remarkable about these presuppositions. They do not require us to believe that people are naturally good or naturally wicked. But they do say that the wish to be moral must compete with other motivations, many of which elicit understanding, if not excuse and toleration. Therefore we must think of delinquency as a normal feature of social life, constrained in most settings by the claims of conscience and the strength of the social fabric. When either weakens, so does self-control. We can expect delinquency to be correlated with the prevalence of temptation and with conditions that produce low self-control.[12]

This perspective is at once tender-minded and tough-minded. It is tender-minded in that it insists on the continuity of delinquency with ordinary motivations and choices. It is governed by a "postulate of humanity." The presumption is that a person in a street gang or a prison, in a hospital or on welfare, is "one of us." No special psychological theory is needed to understand such persons' motives or conduct.[13] The perspective is tough-minded, however, in treating delinquency as inevitable and morality as precarious. It says that the moral order of every community has a prima facie claim to protection and that this task, like the protection of liberty, requires eternal vigilance.

An influential point of view in sociology takes a different tack, and is more consistently tender-minded in its treatment of delinquency. The root idea is that *culture, perception,* and *social learning* are the keys to understanding conduct and character. Some people go wrong, it is said, in the same way others go "straight," that is, by adopting the perspectives and thoughtways of the particular groups to which they belong and with whose members they identify. The master process is "differential association": "A person becomes delinquent because of an excess of definitions favorable to violation of law over definitions unfavorable to violations of law."[14] These "definitions" are established by the operative culture within which the person is absorbed. Delinquency is thus a reflex of culture and a product of social learning.

This is a quite different way of emphasizing the ordinariness of delinquency. The argument is that people who are offenders from the standpoint of a *putative* community are in fact conformists. They do what comes naturally—from their own perspectives and from the perspective of the more limited group that has won their adherence and taken them in hand. Two corollaries have been drawn that affect how delinquents are perceived and how moral responsibility is assessed.

12. This argument is developed, and distinguished from other theories of delinquency, in Michael R. Gottfredson and Travis Hirschi, *A General Theory of Crime* (Stanford: Stanford University Press, 1990).

13. More generally, the postulate of humanity holds that human actors are to be studied on their own terms, as authors of their own intentions, as active participants in constructing their selves and their social worlds. No sociological description is complete if it fails to include "the point of view of the actor." This does not necessarily assimilate all delinquent or deviant conduct to "normal" psychology; it does suggest that assimilation should be a first hypothesis, even in the case of mental illness.

14. Edwin H. Sutherland and Donald R. Cressey, *Criminology,* 9th ed. (Philadelphia: Lippincott, 1974), 75.

First is the proposition that delinquency is fundamentally a matter of culture conflict.[15] What we are observing, it is said, is social and cultural differentiation—the creation of *plural* communities—not a failure of socialization or a weakening of participation and control. Thus the coherence of a supposedly existing moral order is at issue, not the relation between individuals and "their" society. Indeed to speak of "the" moral order is taken as a sign of naiveté, insofar as it fails to see how dominant groups impose their own culture on other groups.

Closely related is the idea that delinquency (including criminality) is a matter of social definition. Every community decides for itself what will be called a moral or legal wrong. Therefore the meaning of delinquency must vary from one community to another, and within a community over time. The claim of a moral code to recognition and respect extends only to the boundaries set by culture and history.

These ideas are illuminating, and it may well be that much delinquency does involve some conflict over what rules to follow or what impulses to obey. But misconduct is not necessarily a challenge to the moral order. In the routine case it is a way of coping with competing motivations and demands and with mixed messages about right and wrong. Moreover, the justifications and excuses people offer for their offenses are usually drawn from within a *shared* framework of belief. It is wrong to suppose delinquency must be culture conflict by definition. Rather, the connection should be seen as variable, more likely to occur under some conditions than others. Sometimes crime *is* culture conflict and does indeed reflect deep divisions in the society; more often, culture conflict is a marginal phenomenon affecting a limited class of offenders, such as members of religious cults or other groups who have distinctive values but relatively little influence.

In the social learning perspective, as we may call it, the autonomy of the person plays no significant part; the cultural context is treated as decisive. In this view it makes no sense to examine the dynamics of choice, including the conditions that make for ambivalence, desperation, or limited options. And only the content of socialization varies, not its quality or effectiveness. The result is a highly unrealistic conception of what makes for delinquency—and what suffering it entails.

15. Sutherland's theory of differential association should not be held responsible for all of the conclusions other people have drawn. Nevertheless, a recent defense of Sutherland points out that "the theory assumes that, in two ways, crime is ultimately rooted in normative conflict." See Ross L. Matsueda, "The Current State of Differential Association Theory," *Crime and Delinquency* 34 (July 1988): 280ff.

It is certainly worth emphasizing that offenses are socially defined or constructed. People of all sorts, and not only the unsophisticated, are prone to treat received categories as absolutes. The world we take for granted often needs shaking up so that alternatives may be respected and perhaps chosen. *But social definitions are not necessarily arbitrary.* "Murder" and "theft," "deceit" and "betrayal," are indeed social constructs. (So is every other classification.) At the same time, such concepts are not formed out of thin air; they are not products of raw preference or unfooted imagination. They are outcomes of collective problem-solving; they belong to the funded experience of mankind as it bears on moral ordering; and they point to important truths regarding human nature and the requirements of group life.

The idea that "social groups create deviance by making the rules whose infraction constitutes deviance"[16] might be read as tautological. However, a substantive argument is intended—that such rules are often if not mostly arbitrary; and that the explanation of deviance must be found in the dynamics of group perception and group power, not in the characteristics of the offender. "From this point of view, deviance is *not* a quality of the act the person commits, but rather a consequence of the application by others of rules and sanctions to an 'offender.' "[17]

As a counterweight to oppressive demands for conformity, this doctrine has considerable moral worth. But it makes most sense where the harm at issue is speculative and where the conception of morality is contested. That is why most attention is given to peripheral, fluctuating, and debatable offenses.[18] The case is different, however, when we consider *core crimes,* which are wrongs that threaten the elementary conditions of personal safety and social order. Serious crimes against the person—willful homicide, forcible rape, aggravated assault, robbery—and against the household, especially burglary, are predatory offenses. They are central to the criminal law and, with minor variations, are recognized as crimes in every society.[19]

16. Howard S. Becker, *Outsiders: Studies in the Sociology of Deviance* (New York: Free Press, 1963), 9.

17. Ibid.

18. It is striking that the theory of crime as socially defined is applied most often to offenses of uncertain iniquity and controversial standing. The examples most often cited are gambling, drug abuse, vagrancy, prostitution, and obscenity.

19. "You can travel from country to country, comb through one penal code after another, and find little substantial variation in the basic crimes" (Leon Radzinowicz and Joan King, *The Growth of Crime: The International Experience* [New York: Basic Books, 1977], 105).

Obviously, human nature cannot by itself account for differences in *kinds* or *rates* of delinquency. The explanation of variability must be sought in social circumstances. It does not follow, however, that a conception of human nature has no part to play in explaining variability. If, on one hand, human nature is perceived as pliable, readily adaptable to any form of life, and naturally conformist, explanations based on social learning and cultural differentiation will be preferred. If, on the other hand, humans are perceived as active, self-referring, need-reducing, and potentially recalcitrant as well as cooperative, explanations that emphasize the strength or weakness of social control, especially the effectiveness of socialization and the viability of participation, will seem more plausible.[20]

Taking Biology Seriously

Human biology cannot account for specific ways of feeding, mating, competing, fighting, or helping. There is no genetic program for warfare, none for the complex realities of violence or love. It does not follow, however, that the emotions that cement or threaten social life have no hereditary basis. Since genes do govern the development of biochemical and neurophysiological systems, it is reasonable to suppose that some of them influence behavior, albeit indirectly and in special ways. Biology is not destiny, but it does help us know what there is in human temperament that eases the path to social objectives or, instead, takes work to overcome.

A biosocial perspective need not be identified with sociobiology, at least as the latter has been developed by Edward O. Wilson and his co-thinkers.[21] The two are related, but they are not the same. Sociobi-

20. For more extensive discussion of the issues raised here, see Ruth Kornhauser, *Social Sources of Delinquency* (Chicago: University of Chicago Press, 1978), and Gottfredson and Hirschi, *General Theory of Crime*.

21. Some initial claims of sociobiology seemed to challenge the importance of cultural and social explanations of why people fight, conform, cooperate, and care for others. Enthusiasm for a fresh approach and a new discipline is purchased at some cost to carefully qualified generalization. For example, Edward Wilson has talked loosely about an "upward-mobile gene" and has made such statements as "human beings are absurdly easy to indoctrinate—they *seek* it" and "men, it appears, would rather believe than know" (Edward O. Wilson, *Sociobiology: The New Synthesis* [Cambridge: Harvard University Press, 1975], 554, 562). Commenting on Mother Theresa's "altruism," he notes, "it should not be forgotten that she is secure in the service of Christ and the knowledge of her Church's immortality" (Edward O. Wilson, *On Human Nature* [New York: Bantam, 1978], 172f.). Although some of these statements would be defensible if more carefully formulated, they have raised many concerns about the care needed to apply to human society conclusions

ology has mainly emphasized *evolutionary* trends, that is, the effect of natural selection on behavior patterns, such as preference for kin or male jealousy. Applied to human society, sociobiology can easily become a game of finding a plausible biological, fitness-enhancing function to "explain" almost any social practice. Furthermore, caution is needed to guard against false or exaggerated conclusions regarding biological determinants of, say, intelligence, aggression, gender differences, or the limits of human potentiality for inclusive rather than bounded altruism.

Whatever the merits in this controversy, it should not distract us from taking biology seriously. The significance for social and moral life of being a human animal can be appreciated without invoking hypotheses about evolution. The evolutionary background, insofar as it is convincing, may enrich our understanding. It may lend confidence to empirical findings about biological influences on contemporary human behavior. But such findings must be based on directly relevant evidence. They cannot simply be deduced from the evolutionary theory.

The importance of biological processes is most plainly revealed in studies of the life cycle:

> [Biological processes] are critical in fetal development, at puberty, during pregnancy, but less potent during latency or early middle age. Thus, for example, there are quite high correlations between testosterone level and aggression among young men, but no significant correlations among older men, since the latter's greater social maturation permits higher levels of impulse control. . . . Think of the contrast in behavior of a 10-year-old and an 18-year-old male; one contributor to the different social behavior they show is androgens: the older boy will have on average an eight times higher level of androgen secretion than the younger, and a good deal of the behavior of the two males is affected by that difference.[22]

These and similar findings cannot explain specific patterns of adolescent conduct. Nevertheless, some general dispositions are identified, and these are important for social policy. A prima facie case can be made that male adolescents need outlets for hormonally induced excitement and that a special concern for discipline is indicated. This does not settle what form the outlets or discipline should take, but the special urgency of biology cannot be ignored.

---

drawn from ethology. For an extended criticism, see Philip Kitcher, *Vaulting Ambition: Sociobiology and the Quest for Human Nature* (Cambridge: MIT Press, 1985).

22. Alice S. Rossi, "Gender and Parenthood," *American Sociological Review* 49 (1984): 11f.

Similarly, biological differences between males and females have significance for the kind of parent each may be, and for special work that must be done to encourage male bonding to children and mates. These and other biologically based phenomena, such as the primordial preference for close relatives, may have to be countered—may take work to overcome—in the interests of morality. Still others, such as feelings of sympathy and consciousness of kind, may reinforce morality. All this presumes, of course, that the *capacity* to envision a moral order and to reach for it by transcending biological limitations is itself a product of human evolution.

Social science does no service to the study of man when it insists, as a matter of fundamental doctrine, that human animals are wholly malleable and, by implication, that *it makes no difference what culture does to them.* Social theory is distorted when inquiry is deflected from the human costs of socialization; and it is morally obtuse when the idea is promoted that every culture has the same worth, whatever its contribution to human flourishing or impoverishment.

A critic of sociobiology has argued that "the biological givens, such as human mating and other facts of life, come into play as instruments of the cultural project, not as its imperatives."[23] To counterpose "instruments" and "imperatives" is misleading. The means we use are seldom innocent or undemanding, and biological givens can be very demanding indeed, especially under conditions of deprivation and stress. To be sure, it is often helpful to think of cultures as wholly "constructed" symbolic systems. But humanity does not live by symbols alone. Culture provides guides to practical satisfaction and therefore must take into account a wide range of human wants and needs, not all of which are socially induced. Furthermore, biology is a *resource* for cultural symbolism, above all in the human propensity to elaborate meanings and find refuge from anxiety.

An affirmative view of the place of biology in human nature does not challenge social science. It does not require the belief that nature is more important than nurture. On the contrary, there is much agreement among biologists that this venerable antithesis is sterile and outmoded:

> The nature versus nurture controversy constitutes only a pseudo problem because . . . genes do not determine the characteristics by which we know a person; they merely govern the responses to experiences from which the personality is built. Recent discoveries are beginning to throw light on the

23. Marshall Sahlins, *The Use and Abuse of Biology* (Ann Arbor: University of Michigan Press, 1976), 63.

mechanisms through which environmental stimuli determine which parts of the genetic endowment are repressed and which parts are activated. . . . It can be assumed that gene activity is profoundly influenced by the composition of the cellular fluids and that various substances differ qualitatively and quantitatively in their activating or repressing effects.[24]

A chain of environmental influences is thoroughly implicated in how genetic programs work themselves out. Therefore the writ of nature does not run where nurture demurs.

We can readily accept the working postulate that "history rather than genetics must be the ground for our search to understand cultural diversity and change."[25] However, we cannot exclude the possibility that some cultural diversity may be explained, in part at least, by the distribution of genes. Insofar as there is a genetic basis for musical talent, we can conceive of genetic drift toward a concentration of such talent in a population, with some significant effect on a cultural preference. But such possibilities are marginal compared to the enormous influence of social experience and special histories; and we recognize that genetic differentiation, when it occurs, is likely to reflect the influence of culture on gene selection. In any case, as Wilson himself has said, "[H]uman social evolution is obviously more cultural than genetic."[26]

The study of human nature is not meant to account for diversity in specific behaviors or social structures. As we noted in another connection, however, human beings are drawn to particularity.[27] They respond well where life is person-centered; they thrive in settings that sustain the uniqueness of experience. Thus human nature is not only *compatible* with diversity, it is a *spur* to difference and distinctiveness.

▾   ▴   ▾   ▴   ▾

The idea that humans are social animals—not as insects are social but in and through self-awareness and symbolic communication—speaks to the ontology of human nature. It purports to identify what it means to be human and thereby to grasp the distinctive quality of human life. This ontological proposition has many implications for normative as well as descriptive theory. It is a starting point for the development of specific

24. René Dubos, *So Human an Animal* (New York: Scribner's, 1968), 97f.

25. Stephen Jay Gould, "Genes on the Brain," *New York Review of Books*, 30 June 1983, 8.

26. Wilson, *On Human Nature*, 160.

27. See Chapter 4, "The Idea of Humanity."

hypotheses about motivation, growth, integration, distress, adaptation, and much else that bears on moral well-being.

To many social scientists of the 1930s and beyond, "man is a social animal" meant that "no statement can be true of all men everywhere so long as cultural inheritance differs so profoundly."[28] It is the nature of human nature to be contingent and malleable, transformed as culture is transformed. In other words, *human nature has no content.* This perspective is powerfully supported by many studies of behavior and motivation. Modern social science has done much to make us aware of the way societies can induce people to do—and *want* to do—a wide variety of remarkable things. It is easy to understand why generations of sociologists and anthropologists should have wished to emphasize those findings. As in the case of cultural relativism, the excitement of the findings was reinforced by a sense of moral righteousness. Cultural determinism mitigates blame, sustains tolerance, and offers hope of reconstruction. But the truth in these ideas has obscured another truth no less important for morality and science. This is the sense in which human nature *does* have content, a content that transcends cultural differences and provides material for moral ordering.

MARX AND DURKHEIM

Marx as Humanist

Objection to the idea of human nature without content has been growing in recent years, and nowhere more remarkably than among students of Marxist thought.[29] Karl Marx lived during the heyday of historicism and was a vigorous advocate of its main principles. Following Hegel, he infused the study of consciousness with a sense of history, adding the idea that changes in consciousness are a reflex of changes in the "material foundations" of society. His revolutionary ardor was quickened by the prospect that a new social order might create a new humanity.

28. Ellsworth Faris, *The Nature of Human Nature* (New York: McGraw-Hill, 1937), 71.

29. See Erich Fromm, *Marx's Concept of Man* (New York: Friedrich Ungar, 1961); John McMurtry, *The Structure of Marx's World View* (Princeton: Princeton University Press, 1978), chap. 1; G. A. Cohen, *Karl Marx's Theory of History* (Princeton: Princeton University Press, 1978), 151ff.; Norman Geras, *Marx and Human Nature: Refutation of a Legend* (London: Verso, 1983); and Jon Elster, *Making Sense of Marx* (Cambridge: Cambridge University Press, 1985), 61ff.

"M. Proudhon does not know," said Marx in 1847, "that the whole of history is nothing but a continual transformation of human nature."[30] This passage is often cited, with much justification, as reflecting Marx's basic perspective. But the context is important. The sentence is a passing thrust at the view that economic competition is, in Pierre-Joseph Proudhon's words, "a decree of destiny, a necessity of the human mind."[31] Thus Marx was arguing against ascribing to human nature a specific pattern of social life.

Twenty years later, in another polemical aside, Marx wrote:

> To know what is useful for a dog, one must study dog-nature. This nature itself cannot be deduced from the principle of utility. Applying this to man, he that would criticise all human acts, movements, relations, etc., by the principle of utility, *must first deal with human nature in general, and then with human nature as modified in each historical epoch.* Bentham makes short work of it. With the driest naiveté he takes the modern shopkeeper, especially the English shopkeeper, as the normal man. Whatever is useful to this queer normal man, and to his world, is absolutely useful.[32]

Here Marx repeats his indictment of Proudhon: Don't confuse a historical type, "the modern shopkeeper," with "normal man." Now, however, he is more subtle and careful. By offering a distinction between "human nature in general" and "human nature as modified in each historical epoch," he opens the way to a better understanding of history and humanity.

This distinction has been interpreted as a "double conception of human nature,"[33] but Marx's own formulation (in the passage just quoted) is preferable. "Human nature in general" is all we should mean by "human nature," and the only question is what should be included in the concept. Human attributes "as modified in each historical epoch" should be characterized in some other way, not as "human nature."

It is easy to understand the impulse to speak of two models of human nature: on one hand, what is generic, original, and biologically given; on

30. Karl Marx, *The Poverty of Philosophy* (1847; reprint, London: Twentieth Century Press, 1900), 129.
31. As quoted by Marx, ibid., 130.
32. Karl Marx, *Capital: A Critique of Political Economy* (1867; reprint, New York: International Publishers, 1967), 1:609n., my emphasis. This was written in the course of a diatribe against Jeremy Bentham, "that insipid, pedantic, leather-tongued oracle of the ordinary bourgeois intelligence of the 19th century."
33. Daniel Bell, *The Winding Passage: Essays and Sociological Journeys, 1960–1980* (New York: Basic Books, 1980), 164. See also Isidor Walliman, *Estrangement: Marx's Conception of Human Nature and the Division of Labor* (Westport, Conn.: Greenwood Press, 1981), 11ff.; Geras, *Marx and Human Nature,* 24.

the other, the specific, historically formed "human nature" to which
Marx referred in his criticism of Proudhon. The latter has a *rhetorical* significance in that it points to the important transformations that can and
do take place in human perspectives, motivations, and practices. From
the standpoint of analysis, however, we should not have to postulate two
kinds of human nature. Rather, we want to understand how generic or
"true" human nature enters into the options open to cultures and epochs. The historical modifications to which Marx referred are better understood as transformations in "social character" or "modal personality."

Erich Fromm's concept of social character is a way of identifying "the
specific form in which human energy is shaped by the dynamic adaptations of human needs to the particular mode of existence of a given
society."[34] It is "the essential nucleus of the character structure of most
members of a group which has developed as the result of the basic experiences and mode of life common to that group."[35] Social character,
insofar as it exists, reaches deep layers of emotion and motivation and
gives them specific form, such as the ensemble of virtues Weber associated with the early capitalist entrepreneur. The change from one social
character to another can be profound, but it need not be conceived as a
change in human nature.

Marxist doctrine needs a theory of human nature because without it
there can be no secure basis for social criticism, especially radical criticism. Marxism does not offer itself as a limited, parochial standpoint
from which to attack and reconstruct a given society. On the contrary,
it purports to speak in the name of humankind. Therefore the idea of humanity must have meaningful content:

> Unless we have some notion of what it is to be a fully developed human be-
> ing, we have no ground whatever for condemning any social system or set of
> institutional arrangements: we cannot employ such notions as "alienation"
> or "exploitation"; we cannot recommend socialism as a "richer" or "higher"
> form of human existence. In short, unless we possess a normative criterion—
> a principle for distinguishing and grading the manifestations of human beings
> in the world—we are without a standard that would justify our political com-
> mitment to socialism.[36]

This may seem obvious to non-Marxists, but for many years it was "a
Marxist tradition to deny that there is an historically invariant human

---

34. Erich Fromm, *Escape from Freedom* (New York: Farrar & Rinehart, 1941), 278.
35. Ibid., 277.
36. Richard Lichtman, *The Production of Desire: The Integration of Psychoanalysis into
Marxist Theory* (New York: Free Press, 1982), 68.

nature."[37] In part the tradition reflected a reluctance to give up the rhetorical advantage of calling for radical transformation of self and society without worrying about limits or establishing safeguards against the corruption of ideals. There was also the belief that revolutionary criticism needs no warrant because socialism is not an ideal based on human choice and therefore requiring justification; rather, socialism is the inevitable outcome of the laws of history.

The foundation of Marx's criticism of capitalist society is, it turns out, fairly orthodox humanism. Marx postulates certain morally relevant attributes that distinguish homo sapiens from other animals. Most important is "free, conscious activity," which is "man's species-character."[38] This activity builds upon that vital human resource, the creative exercise of imagination, and results in the elaboration of moral, aesthetic, political, religious, and intellectual life. Such experience reflects and sustains, but also makes problematic, a basic human need for wholeness and integration as well as a life-enhancing capacity for growth and self-realization.

These ideas are hardly original or distinctively Marxist. They are broadly humanist, more specifically Rousseauist, and heavily indebted to German romanticism. But Marx made a significant contribution to humanist doctrine by emphasizing (1) the connection between work and human nature and (2) the special importance of alienation in the interplay of human nature and the moral order.

Work and human nature. In Marx's theory of historical materialism, production is the engine of change and the key to social organization. The main concern of the theory is to show how the mode of production defines the character of a social system, including its potentialities and "contradictions." But, for Marx, production had a deeper meaning as well. People are innately active and purposeful; therefore they cannot flourish without creative, self-fulfilling work. The good life for humans is not parasitic or self-absorbed; it requires productive participation in all aspects of social life.

At one point Marx took Adam Smith to task for thinking of labor as a kind of curse, a painful sacrifice of tranquillity, freedom, and happiness:

> "Tranquillity" appears as the adequate state, as identical with "freedom" and "happiness". It seems quite far from Smith's mind that the individual, "in his

---

37. Cohen, *Marx's Theory of History,* 151. See also Geras, *Marx and Human Nature,* 53.

38. Karl Marx, "Economic and Philosophical Manuscripts," in Loyd D. Easton and Kurt H. Guddat, eds., *Writings of the Young Marx on Philosophy and Society* (1844; reprint, New York: Anchor Books, 1967), 294.

normal state of health, strength, activity, skill, facility", also needs a normal portion of work, and of the suspension of tranquillity. . . . Smith has no inkling whatever that this overcoming of obstacles is in itself a liberating activity—and that, further, the external aims become stripped of the semblance of merely external natural urgencies, and become posited as aims which the individual himself posits—hence as self-realization, objectification of the subject, hence real freedom, whose action is, precisely, labour.[39]

Marx did not suppose a moral commonwealth could do without work, authority, or—a noncapitalist—division of labor. Rather, the whole of his argument, not only in the early "humanist" manuscripts but in his mature masterpiece, *Capital,* is suffused with outrage over the *kinds* of work and subordination demanded by capitalism. He thought these violated the integrity of the person, who is robbed of the opportunity for freedom and self-realization in and through productive activity. Marx considered capitalism a "progressive" system, paving the way for socialism. But this did not stop him from assailing it bitterly as a way of life alien to humanity. The implicit postulate is that *there are ends proper to man's nature.* This premise, which echoes the Aristotelian and Thomist traditions, lies at the heart of Marx's moral theory. It is this, not planning or economic rationality, which he thought would justify the politics of revolution and the blood of martyrs.

Hannah Arendt argued that "Marx's attitude toward labor . . . never ceased to be equivocal."[40] On one hand, labor belongs to that "realm of necessity" which will be eliminated when communism ushers in a "realm of freedom." On the other hand, the positive value of exertion and discipline in the service of production is central to Marx's thought. The apparent equivocation is fairly easily resolved. Marx wanted to eliminate *dehumanizing* effort, which he called "alienated labor." He did not mean to say that productive work had no place in the communist future. He could readily have accepted Arendt's distinction between "labor" and "work."[41]

Nevertheless, Arendt was right to sense a profound ambiguity in the ethos of Marxism. Despite his embrace of the humanist ideal—the well-rounded person engaging in multiple pursuits, with no clear boundary between work and leisure—Marx was committed to modern technol-

---

39. Karl Marx, *Grundrisse* (1857–58; reprint, London: Penguin Books, 1973), 611. I am indebted to McMurtry, *Structure of Marx's World View,* 32, for this reference.

40. *The Human Condition* (Chicago: University of Chicago Press, 1958), 104.

41. Ibid., chaps. 3, 4. In Arendt's scheme, labor is a biological necessity, characteristically painful, mechanical, coerced, and sterile, producing objects only incidentally, for consumption or exchange; work is creative and product-centered, producing lasting objects.

ogy and the abundance it might bring. He had no clear notion of how to attain and preserve humane productivity in such a context; he could only express the faith that collective ownership of the means of production, with some vague gestures toward democracy, would transform all social relations. As a result the humanist ideal slipped away and became irrelevant to Marx's heirs—at least those who came to power. As rulers they accepted the technocratic imperative without qualm or hesitation. Under actually existing socialism, as under capitalism, labor has been plentiful but work has been scarce.

Alienation. Marx's theory of human nature points to a fundamental pathology in selfhood and social participation. Like Hegel before him and Freud after, he realized that the encounter of self and society is not necessarily smooth, benign, or wholesome. Socialization cannot be *counted on* to form personalities that are at once autonomous and other-regarding. On the contrary, societies may survive and even prosper while they impoverish or suffocate the human spirit. People can be dehumanized, and a prime cause of that condition is "alienation."

The etymological root of "alienation" is the Latin *alius,* "other." To be or to be made "other" is the core meaning. Many derivatives are innocent enough from a metaphysical or psychological point of view, as when we distinguish aliens from citizens. A thicker meaning is suggested by the legal concept of alienation: transfer of title, especially property in land, from one person to another. Historically this meant that the individual parted from—made himself a stranger to—property that defined his status in society and therefore his personal identity. By extension, alienation refers to a condition of estrangement or discontinuity in the way individuals experience their own personalities and the world about them.

In Christian theology, the gravest feature of the human condition is spiritual alienation. To be separated from God is man's temptation and anguish; reconciliation with God is the spiritual imperative. This drama is reenacted in Hegel's thought, but there alienation is more a pathology of consciousness than of faith. At center stage is the relation between the aware subject and the external object. A condition of fundamental alienation exists when people see themselves as radically separated from a world in which they are implicated but which cannot command their full understanding and free allegiance. Reconciliation occurs when, by a progressive enlargement of consciousness and a final clarification of ideas, people manage to retain their identities and yet be at one with nature and the social world. The vehicle of reconciliation is not a leap of faith.

Rather, it is the power of reason and self-knowledge to overcome partial truths and limited perspectives. At that point, the person participates in an all-embracing and unqualified Idea. The world then becomes both meaningful and comprehensible.

This intellectual background helps explain why the idea of alienation was so important to Marx. He was a close student of Hegel's writings, as were many of his contemporaries, and like them he accepted the forms of Hegelian thought, and the emotional charge they carried, while modifying their content. It was natural for Marx to take for granted that the phenomenon of estrangement, including self-estrangement, was somehow fundamental. But he could not accept either the theological interpretation or Hegel's reconciliation at the level of consciousness. Rather, he placed the concept within the framework of social theory and thereby gave it a more concrete and empirical meaning. This could be done, he thought, while remaining faithful to a Hegelian vision of the self-creating, self-knowing person struggling to overcome an opaque and unresponsive external world.

For Marx the chief locus of alienation is industrial labor. Workers in modern society are estranged: (1) from *what they produce,* because the product of their labor belongs to someone else and has no direct relevance to their own needs as persons; (2) from *the way they have to work,* which "develops no free physical and mental energy but mortifies his flesh and ruins his mind;"[42] (3) from *other persons,* because they are forced to treat each other as means rather than as ends; and (4) from *humanity,* the sense of belonging to a part of nature that can transcend brute animal existence.

In this diagnosis the leading culprit is domination—a kind of domination that reaches the self. Something more than external oppression is at stake. Alienation distorts perceptions, abridges consciousness, and corrupts emotions. The obverse of alienation is the condition of being at home in the world and with oneself. The assumption is that human personality cannot flourish, and is likely to be radically degraded, in the absence of a certain continuity and wholeness. Serious dissociation within the self—between, say, impulse and satisfaction, past and present, knowing and feeling—threatens both moral and psychic well-being. And the integration of personality is in turn dependent on supportive, cooperative, person-centered connections with other persons and a community.

We can appreciate Marx's general theory, and the humanist agenda it implies, without endorsing his specific argument or his utopian vision.

42. Marx, "Economic and Philosophical Manuscripts," 292.

At this point we need only summarize by noting that Marx was necessarily committed to a theory of human nature, despite his strong historicist inclinations, and that this theory established what he took to be a moral imperative.

The basic feature of this imperative is that social conditions should sustain and encourage the full development of distinctively human sensibilities and powers. Marx shared the anarchist faith that a great flowering of creativity, spontaneity, and mutual aid would occur if institutions of domination were eliminated and new forms of cooperation established. Thus his theory of human nature is optimistic about the potential for moral, intellectual, and aesthetic development and includes the claim that the frustration of this potential brings about suffering and degradation. This is a theory of human flourishing and presumes perfectibility, but it does not necessarily entail a doctrine of original goodness and does not require Rousseau's premise that "man is born free; and everywhere he is in chains."[43] Man is not born free but *can be made free*. Primordial human nature motivates a striving for free, productive, other-regarding life, but it also carries the seeds of self-abasement. Only proper social conditions will bring out the humanity in man.

Durkheim as Moral Realist

The optimistic vision of the humanist Marx and his romantic forebears and successors may be contrasted with the more somber perspective of Emile Durkheim. A founding father of sociology, Durkheim helped establish its basic agenda: what holds human groups together and how they fall apart. He had much to say on both questions. Moreover, he thought sociology could be a science of morality.[44] His main strategy was to trace the influence of social organization on personal autonomy, psychic health, and moral commitment.

Durkheim and Marx had much in common. They agreed that humans are preeminently social animals, and they both resisted the idea of an abstract human nature. Although Durkheim was much influenced by Kant, he criticized Kant's notion of a nonempirical, "noumenal" self

43. Jean-Jacques Rousseau, *The Social Contract and Discourses,* trans. G. D. H. Cole (1762; reprint, London: J. M. Dent, 1973), 181.

44. Durkheim could not accept the idea that "good and evil do not exist for science," that science "can indeed illuminate the world, but it leaves darkness in our hearts; the heart must find its own light." In this view, he thought, "science loses all, or almost all, practical effectiveness and, consequently, its principal justification for existence" (Emile Durkheim, *The Rules of Sociological Method* [1895; reprint, Chicago: University of Chicago Press, 1938], 48).

whose rationality and moral freedom exist apart from and in opposition
to the sensual world of inclination, impulse, and social bonding. Morality, he believed, can only be realized in and through social experience.
Durkheim's work, like Marx's, contains an apparent paradox: human
nature is made manifest only in history and allows for considerable variation in character and personality; yet it has a persistent core of attributes
to which we must look when we consider how people fare under existing social conditions.

These and other continuities show that Marx and Durkheim were
wholeheartedly committed to a sociological framework. They both believed in a social self. Nevertheless, they presented strikingly different
images of the developed personality and of the relation between the individual and society. The contrasts are important, but they are not irreconcilable. They are best understood as complementary perspectives,
each emphasizing a different aspect of human nature, both necessary to
a proper understanding of moral experience.

In many ways Durkheim was what we might call today an establishment liberal or perhaps a relatively conservative social democrat. He favored improved conditions for industrial workers; would have been
comfortable with the modern welfare state; was optimistic about the
performance of a well-regulated and professional civil service; and was
sympathetic to guild socialism. Thus he too was critical of modern society. But he was no revolutionary; on the contrary, he thought social
reform would be counterproductive without gradualism and restraint.

In a classic study Durkheim explored the moral promise of modern
society. To do so he distinguished two types of social solidarity, "mechanical" and "organic," the latter a hallmark of modernity. Mechanical
solidarity is based on likeness and a sense of common identity. People
are bound together by the fact that they have been brought up to act
and think alike and to follow similar life routines. The main source of
cohesion is symbolic experience. This solidarity is "mechanical,"
Durkheim thought, because it resembles "the cohesion which unites the
elements of an inanimate body, as opposed to that which makes a unit
out of a living body."[45] Organic solidarity, by contrast, is based on differentiation; it is analogous to a complex living body with specialized
organs, each dependent on the others, the whole dependent on a functional integration of the parts. Mechanical solidarity presumes individuals are the same; organic solidarity presumes they are different. "The

45. Emile Durkheim, *The Division of Labor in Society,* trans. George Simpson (1893;
reprint, New York: Macmillan, 1933), 130.

first is possible only insofar as the individual personality is absorbed into the collective personality; the second is possible only if each one has a sphere of action which is peculiar to him; that is, a personality."[46]

In the stage of mechanical solidarity, social control through law is largely a matter of upholding the symbolic order. Group identity is reaffirmed by punishing deviants who violate what is sacred to the group. To reassert the common conscience, the community resorts to *punitive* law and *repressive* sanctions. With the development of organic solidarity, however, another type of law becomes predominant. This is *restitutive* law, which is the law of cooperation. Its purpose is to restore equilibrium by compensating people for losses they incur when other people fail to discharge their lawful obligations. The classic branch of restitutive law is the law of contracts. Contract is *"par excellence,* the juridical expression of cooperation."[47]

The division of labor and organic solidarity are not to be understood as economic phenomena. Durkheim was not celebrating the unseen hand of exchange and the market. Rather, he saw the great transformation—from status to contract, from *Gemeinschaft* to *Gesellschaft*—as the seedbed of moral development. Organic solidarity is not interdependence per se but consists of the new forms of association and new codes of conduct that arise from interdependence. The result is a new morality capable of serving social cohesion while supporting individual and group autonomy.[48]

Durkheim was keenly aware that social change may profoundly alter the foundations of authority and of human relations. He thought the division of labor in a modern economy would bring with it a new morality based on interdependent but autonomous transactions rather than on subordination, constraint, and conformity. Thus Durkheim was no friend to domination. Although it is fair to say that he had a conservative temperament, at bottom he was a child of the Enlightenment. He

46. Ibid., 131.
47. Ibid., 123.
48. Durkheim has been faulted for treating his social types (mechanical and organic solidarity) as evolutionary stages. See Steven Lukes, *Emile Durkheim: His Life and Works* (New York: Harper & Row, 1972), 159ff. Primitive societies are not necessarily more punitive than advanced societies; in settling disputes, they too rely on restitution and reconciliation. This is not to say that Durkheim's typology is false or unimportant. On the contrary, as a way of understanding normative ordering, it remains a powerful theory. We need to distinguish repressive from restitutive sanctions, prescriptive from facilitative rules, and to understand that behind these types of rules and sanctions lie profoundly different orientations toward social order. The chief significance of Durkheim's analysis lies not in his evolutionary hypothesis but in the connection he established between types of law and types of social solidarity.

recognized that society holds vast potential for oppression, and he looked to modernity as a liberating force.

Durkheim was first of all a sociologist, and he kept the faith by stressing the worth of social bonding. This recurrent theme comes out most clearly in his famous study of suicide.[49] In that work Durkheim offered a theory to explain why rates of suicide differ among social groups and categories. The core idea is that *suicide rates go up when social bonds are weak*.[50] The weakness may result from relative social isolation, which accounts for a higher suicide rate among people who are unmarried or otherwise weakly attached to groups or persons. When, for whatever individual reason, people have an impulse to commit suicide, they are not restrained by their social involvements and commitments.

Another form of weakness in social bonding is what Durkheim called "anomie," that is, normlessness or lack of rules. A well-integrated society provides individuals with a sense of security by limiting aspirations and establishing clear rules for moral conduct. Durkheim believed that an ever-present source of acute anxiety is unrestrained aspiration. When people live without attainable goals and defined alternatives, when there is "only empty space above them,"[51] they are subject to emotional distress. Here the problem is not a lack of involvement with others but inadequate self-discipline. The moral order allows too many options or fails to provide controlling standards.

In this and other ways Durkheim emphasized the importance *for the person* of being effectively integrated into group life and governed by social norms. This perspective led him to support some "conservative" principles. For example, he did not see discipline as the antithesis of freedom. Genuine freedom of choice is not possible if individuals are disorderly in their personal lives or incapable of connecting means and ends;[52] nor is it likely to be attained if the social world is chaotic. Freedom is incompatible with certain *kinds* of order, but it is wholly dependent on stabilities and continuities of many sorts.

For Marx, the experience of domination is the main source of dehumanization; for Durkheim, rootlessness is the grand malady. Despite

49. Emile Durkheim, *Suicide* (1897; reprint, Glencoe, Ill.: Free Press, 1951).
50. An important qualification: suicide rates may rise for individuals who are very tightly bound into a particular moral order. If the individual fails to meet group standards and has all his eggs in one basket, moral failure may encourage suicide; or suicide may be demanded by group norms. These Durkheim called "altruistic" suicide.
51. Ibid., 257.
52. "Liberty is the daughter of authority properly understood. For to be free is not to do what one pleases; it is to be master of oneself, it is to know how to act with reason and to do one's duty" (Emile Durkheim, *Education and Sociology* [1911; reprint, Glencoe, Ill.: Free Press, 1956], 89f.).

this difference in the theories, an important connection links alienation and anomie. Each speaks to separation, discontinuity, and estrangement. Anomic individuals are not at home in the world because sustaining frameworks of rules and objectives have weakened; they are self-estranged in that secure identities, which depend heavily on defined roles and statuses, are hard to come by. Thus anomie, an attribute of the normative order, is an important source of personal alienation. Both ideas presume that wholeness and continuity, in the organization of the self and in the relation between self and society, are vital to psychic health. Whatever destroys wholeness and disrupts continuity is a threat to freedom, rationality, and security.

I do not mean to blur or minimize the differences between the two theorists. Marx was more focused in his criticism of capitalism and more optimistic about the prospects for overcoming alienation in a world of "associated producers." His hopes for liberation, however, did not presume an absence of social bonds. On the contrary, the communist ideal is a cooperative commonwealth whose citizens freely accept responsibility for one another and for the community, without yielding their personal autonomy. It is hardly a world without frameworks or without socially defined objectives.

But Marx did not face up to the realities of cooperation. He well knew that revolution would not eliminate the need for social order, but he thought social discipline would be infused with an entirely new meaning. Through new forms of collective ownership, what was hitherto oppressive would be experienced as benign, demystified, and person-centered. Marx made no searching examination of what the new order would require and had little understanding of the evils it might contain. Here he fell back on the Hegelian faith that ultimately a transformation of consciousness would resolve all difficulties and bring an end to history. This strategy made it possible for him to believe that freedom, community, and advanced technology could exist in an environment unmarred by constraint. He could project an image of the liberated spirit led to fulfillment without pain or sacrifice.

Durkheim too was interested in the transformation of consciousness, as when he argued that the morality of constraint he associated with mechanical solidarity might be replaced by a morality of cooperation.[53] It is wrong to think of Durkheim as favoring constraint and regulation without regard to their quality or content. A science of morality, as he understood it, must cling to ideals—but not to illusions. Therefore he

---

53. "In reality, cooperation also has its intrinsic morality" (Durkheim, *Division of Labor*, 228).

emphasized objectives more limited than Marx's: authority based on reason rather than coercion; freedom buttressed by law and regulated by law; subordination mitigated by rational criticism, personal autonomy, and political pluralism.

In the theory of moral ordering, as I have noted before, we should identify both what we can aspire to and what we must guard against. Marx speaks to the former but is reckless of the latter. The ideal he helped frame has a certain claim to realism because it is rooted in human need and potentiality. But he does not specify how to achieve it or what the attendant costs and trade-offs may be. The true function of such an ideal is to serve as a judgment upon the more limited and more closely specified goals defined by those, like Durkheim, who tailor ideals to fit realities. For such as Durkheim to succeed, the activating ideal needs to be preserved, nurtured, and clarified. Without its guidance—without, say, a full understanding of freedom, positive as well as negative, psychic as well as political—we are deprived of a standard for evaluating what moral realists have to offer.

It has been said that Durkheim and Marx, in the moral conclusions they drew from their theories of human nature, represent "two quite opposite and incompatible ideals" and that to choose between them is to express an "ultimate and personal commitment."[54] No doubt it is often necessary for individuals to choose between prophetic idealism and moral realism. The choice may well reflect personal circumstance and temperament—for example, whether one is young or middle-aged, daring or cautious. But from the standpoint of theory and policy *there is no need to choose*. Rather, we should appreciate the different but complementary functions the two perform in moral judgment and institutional design.

Viewed in action rather than as abstract categories, the two moralities are not true opposites. They involve each other and need each other. One presses for ever-higher levels of achievement; demands experimentation; is reluctant to accept any frustration or limitation as final. The other preserves and stabilizes, but what it preserves is the same fundamental ideal of autonomy and wholeness, within a framework of interdependence and cooperation. In combination they contribute to moral harmony. One does so by unsettling complacency, the other by restraining fantasy.

54. Steven Lukes, "Alienation and Anomie," in Peter Laslett and W. G. Runciman, eds., *Philosophy, Politics and Society* (Oxford: Blackwell, 1967), 155.

▼   ▲   ▼   ▲   ▼

The perspectives of Marx and Durkheim have a special interest because of the commitment they shared to the historicity of motivation and character. Despite that commitment they had to accept, at least implicitly, fairly definite ideas about human nature. They are representative of the irrepressible effort to ground morality in basic attributes of the human animal; and they are paradigms of a recurrent counterpoint in moral theory between optimism and pessimism, fulfillment and restraint, aspiration and duty.

SIX

Moral Development

In the study of human nature, as it bears on morality, a key idea is development. The argument is that individuals are disposed to change—and under congenial conditions are likely to change—in directions that enhance moral outcomes.[1] The challenge is to show that moral competence is an objective condition and not an instance of reading into "nature" our own preferences or fears.

There is a striking congruence between contemporary theories of moral development and the classical view that a natural *telos* or end-state gives direction to our lives and is the source of our best-warranted ideals. Aristotle identifies this end-state as *eudaimonia,* meaning, roughly, the well-being that comes from a life of virtue, governed by reason. All animals seek satisfaction, but humans are peculiar in that they can *evaluate* their interests, *cultivate* their passions, and *choose* among options those that contribute to a desirable way of life. The good for humans—the natural good, the *telos*—is "an activity of the soul in conformity with excellence or virtue, and if there are several virtues, in

---

1. Moral development, like any development, "involves two essential components: the notion of a system possessing a definite structure and a definite set of preexisting capacities; and the notion of a sequential set of changes in the system, yielding relatively permanent but novel increments not only in structure but in its mode of operation as well" (Ernest Nagel, "Determinism and Development," in Dale B. Harris, ed., *The Concept of Development* [Minneapolis: University of Minnesota Press, 1957], 17). I would add "disposition" to capacities in the first part of Nagel's formulation. For our purposes the relevant "system" is the human personality or group, and the "novel increment" is the enhancement of moral competence.

conformity with the best and most complete."[2] *Eudaimonia* comes from a life of discrimination, intelligence, and commitment; a life guided by moral virtues such as generosity and courage; a life that makes possible long-range and comprehensive plans for achieving a satisfactory state of being. This *informed* pursuit of the good redeems the promise of what Aristotle considered most distinctive about the human animal. This is the capacity to use reason, not only for particular ends, but to order one's whole life and the life of a community.

This Aristotelian ideal, to which John Dewey subscribed, is discovered and clarified by self-conscious reflection. But it is not the product of reflection alone. What makes it a *telos* is the fact that it builds on the strivings and capacities of ordinary people living ordinary lives; on the experienced difference between being foolish or wise, shortsighted or prudent, self-destructive or constructive in the management of one's life. "It is distinctive of human beings that they care about the shape of their souls; they care about what values and characters they have, they care about how they should live."[3] These natural concerns and discriminations do not predetermine what is good in given circumstances. There is plenty of room for different life-plans. None can be chosen, however, without sober appraisal of costs and trade-offs.

The concept of *telos* is resisted by many contemporary philosophers,[4] mainly because the notion of a natural good is incompatible with the doctrine that value is a reflex of will and choice and that at bottom all serious moral choice is arbitrary. There is also concern that the notion of *telos* commits us to specific conclusions as to what ends are worth having or what lives are worth living. This would run counter to the evident plurality of reasonably defensible ways of life and would slight the significance for moral experience of conflict among competing goods.

However, a *telos* does not necessarily specify an outcome, nor need it deny that "it is through conflict and sometimes only through conflict

2. Aristotle, *Nichomachean Ethics*, trans. Martin Ostwald (Indianapolis: Bobbs-Merrill, 1985), 1098a16–18. Some readings of Aristotle's ethics emphasize the role of contemplative thought, *theoria*, as the highest good to which the life of virtue is subordinate and instrumental. But see J. L. Ackrill, "Aristotle on *Eudaimonia*," *Proceedings of the British Academy* 60 (1974): 339–59.

3. Jonathan Lear, *Love and Its Place in Nature: A Philosophical Interpretation of Freudian Psychoanalysis* (New York: Farrar, Straus & Giroux, 1990), 186.

4. But see Alasdair MacIntyre, *After Virtue: A Study in Moral Theory*, 2d ed. (Notre Dame: University of Notre Dame Press, 1984), especially chaps. 12 and 14; also Henry B. Veatch, *Aristotle: A Contemporary Appreciation* (Bloomington: Indiana University Press, 1974), chap. 4.

that we learn what our ends and purposes are."[5] The end-state may be *the integrity of a process,* as when we say law inclines toward the progressive reduction of arbitrariness in official conduct, or when we identify scientific ideals of free, rigorous, and self-corrective inquiry. The *telos* of friendship is mutual trust and care. This does not say, however, who should be friends; does not preclude different types of friendship; does not deny that friendship may conflict with other values and demand hard choices. The main point is to recognize that *ideal states may have natural foundations.* Where a *telos* can be identified, the ideal state is summoned and sustained by the dynamics of a system, that is, by energies generated in the course of routine efforts to make sense of a distinctive life or practice and to solve its recurrent problems.

Modern psychology has added depth and complexity to our understanding of how the human animal may reach beyond primal need and egocentric impulse. The psychological *telos* is not mysterious or ineffable. Like biological health, it is a potential state of well-being wherein needs are reduced and satisfactions are enhanced, a state toward which impulses are directed and in light of which they are transformed. Psychic health is in some respects more open-ended than physical health. More options are available. Nevertheless, beyond certain limits pathologies are likely, and certain psychic energies reach for security, autonomy, and creativity. As a result we can have a natural, if inexact, science of psychic and moral development.

No claim to necessity is required. Contingency and probability prevail. To be sure, we look to an "inner dynamic." A need, conflict, or other disposition sets problems for a system and presses it in directions that may strengthen one or more of its capacities. When these forces are described as if they lead by inescapable stages to preordained outcomes, considerable skepticism is in order. For this reason, critics of the idea of development are understandably wary of "systemic" or "inner" propensities and prefer to focus on external influences to explain the course of change. But such a response misses the mark. No inner dynamic is inexorable. Every impulse depends for fulfillment on congenial conditions. These are not always forthcoming, if only because countervailing conditions are always at work.

Theories of development commit us to sequence but not to definite stages. It is often convenient to delineate stages in describing, say, the individual life cycle or the transition from simple to more complex

---

5. MacIntyre, *After Virtue,* 164.

forms of organization, law, religion, or economic life. The convenience is that many empirical findings may be roughly sorted as belonging together at some level of development. This may lead to new insights in the evaluation or diagnosis of a case or to a theory regarding growth or adaptation. But it is the insight or theory that matters, not the way stages are described or milestones indicated. It is less important to know how to distinguish with precision a child from an adolescent, or an adolescent from an adult, than to know what processes are at work that affect the capacity to learn, work, or love.

Finally, and most important, although *enhancement of competence and sensibility* is central to moral development, we need not suppose that this outcome, or any other developmental outcome, is necessarily the most stable, the best adapted, the most efficient, or the most likely to survive. On the contrary, the emergent condition may be quite precarious. As George Santayana said, "[M]an, in becoming more complex, becomes less stably organized."[6] Complex ideals or states of well-being often depend on fragile networks of supporting circumstance. Without appropriate opportunities and supports, the quest for moral well-being may be confused, frustrated, and aborted; the *telos* may be experienced as dim and incoherent rather than clear and compelling. Therefore the injunction to follow nature must be sustained by a worked-out theory of what the natural end-state is and why it is worthy of our striving.

CONSCIENCE AND COMPETENCE

The natural process that bears most closely on morality is the formation of conscience, that is, the disposition to be governed by moral concerns. To be effective conscience depends on an array of psychic competencies, especially the capacity to defer gratification, experience guilt, make commitments, and fulfill obligations. These dispositions and capacities are not the whole of morality, which may require other competencies as well, such as the ability to be objective, expand horizons, and experience love. But without an elementary psychological underpinning, moral experience is hard to come by and even harder to sustain.

Thus the first stage of moral development is the formation of a self capable of making rational choices, exercising self-restraint, and

6. *The Life of Reason* (1933; reprint, New York: Scribner's, 1954), 94.

participating in social life.[7] Here the critical process is *socialization,* which has two main tasks: the transmission of a social heritage, which includes moral beliefs and prescriptions; and the transformation of newborn animals into effectively functioning persons. These objectives normally reinforce each other, but they are often in conflict and may even be self-defeating.

Socialization presumes what cannot be taken for granted: the stability of institutions and the steady efforts of a parent generation. How smooth the process is depends on many variables, including competition among socializing agencies (families, peer groups, schools), the homogeneity of populations, the adequacy of reinforcement, and the temperament of the child. The formation of personality is subject to many vicissitudes, which may impoverish or enrich, frustrate or enhance the capacity of the individual to be a moral person.

Closely observed, socialization is full of moral ambiguity. The transmission of culture has intrinsic worth, for without it there could be no morality and no personhood. Like friendship or knowledge, socialization is a prima facie "good thing." But how we should appraise it in specific circumstances depends on the content as well as the method of socialization, and especially on the extent to which techniques of domination or exploitation are employed.[8] Thus moral sophistication depends on how well we understand the structure of personality and the strategies of socialization.

Much of socialization is routine learning of language, skills, attitudes, and beliefs. Through conditioning and other mechanisms people inhibit some responses and adopt others as habitual. Without the disposition to form habits, including stereotyped ways of perceiving the world, social learning as we know it would be impossible. But the formation of conscience is more than habit, more also than cognitive awareness and problem-solving. Conscience is inner inclination, not external

7. This should be at least a partial answer to those who doubt that psychological growth is a meaningful idea. "When psychologists claim, then, to describe stages of personality growth and to measure levels of maturity, they are describing what must be at least to some extent a personal vision and are trying to measure a fiction" (Peggy Rosenthal, *Words and Values: Some Leading Words and Where They Lead Us* [Oxford: Oxford University Press, 1984], 77). It is difficult to know what weight to give the qualifying phrase "at least to some extent."

8. Among the great costs of social disadvantage, for example, is that it degrades the process of socialization. Disadvantaged groups have sometimes cooperated in their own subordination, as when children are taught not to aspire above their station in life. More important, socialization for disadvantage undermines psychic adequacy by denying the child a positive self-image. The disadvantaged may lack both a sense of mastery of the environment, and aspirations that expand the self rather than constrict it.

conformity. Although it arises in the course of social participation and derives much of its content from social learning, it is driven by and responsive to emotional needs, strivings, and conflicts.

To understand the emotional foundations of conscience we must turn to Freud's psychodynamic theory of self and society. This theory begins, logically as well as historically, by postulating that much of our mental and psychic life is unconscious. Moreover, the unconscious, as Freud understood it, is more than a passive reservoir of the discarded or the forgotten. The unconscious is potent and dynamic, the source of troubles, impulses, fears, and longings—all radically affecting the conscious choices we make as apparently self-determining beings.

Freud understood that a theory based on unconscious thoughts, feelings, and mechanisms would, if valid, greatly enlarge our capacity to explain belief and conduct. Such a theory does not take what people say at face value, as expressions of rational intent; it does not treat errors, dreams, and jokes as unexplainable detritus or "noise." Rather, Freud saw in the theory of the unconscious a resource for establishing "that even the apparently most obscure and arbitrary mental phenomena invariably have a meaning and a causation."[9] The psychology of mind, Freud reasoned, must look beyond awareness and beyond rationality. His study of the unconscious promised to reveal a natural order and thus to merit the name of science.[10]

As Freud developed his theory he moved from an earlier preoccupation with *mind* to a broader concern for the structure of the *self*. He did not lose his interest in "mental representations." On the contrary, ideas, symbols, images, and interpretations retained their importance, especially in psychoanalytic therapy. But Freud came to see that his real subject was not mind as such but the human personality understood as a constellation of passions and interests.

9. Sigmund Freud, "A Short History of Psychoanalysis" (1924), in vol. 19, *Standard Edition of the Complete Psychological Works,* trans. and ed. John Strachey in collaboration with Anna Freud (London: Hogarth Press, 1961), 197.

10. Freud's logic is reminiscent of (and helped stimulate) the sociological study of latent rather than manifest functions. In examining the determinants of decision-making, for example, it is not sociologically interesting to study accounting methods or other explicit forms of rational assessment and conduct. Rather, we look to premises and frameworks, often unstated, and to latent consequences for morale or institutional change. "There is some evidence that it is precisely at the point where the research attention of sociologists has shifted from the plane of manifest to the plane of latent functions that they have made their *distinctive* and major contributions" (Robert K. Merton, *Social Theory and Social Structure,* rev. ed. [New York: Free Press, 1968], 120). It does not follow, of course, that conscious choice has no causal efficacy of its own. We may understand that war has the latent function of sustaining an unstable regime without denying that people are killed and that territory is won and lost.

What emerged was the now-familiar conception of a triune self. According to this theory, three psychic systems dominate and organize our emotional lives, with important consequences for how we perceive, think, imagine, and judge. Each part of the self, id, ego, superego, has a distinctive function in the psychic economy of the person. How the parts relate to one another decisively affects the formation of conscience and character.

Id is a name for the biological core of the self, that is, for the urgencies inherent in our animal nature. These range from specific drives or tissue tensions, such as hunger and sex, to more general impulses, mainly libidinal and aggressive. Id is the realm of ungoverned freedom as well as compelled response. As the id presses for release and gratification, it obeys what Freud called the pleasure principle. Id is the part of the self society tries to control but never succeeds in thoroughly domesticating.

If the self is to survive and be coherent, gratification of id impulses must be restrained. The id is a threat to the self because its demands are often in conflict and may lead to self-destructive excesses. The controlling agency is the *ego,* a structure that emerges from the encounter of an impulse-dominated organism with a world of constraints and dangers. The ego mediates between the id and the external world and, in its beginnings at least, serves and represents the id by discovering how to gain instinctual gratification while avoiding pain, frustration, and worse. Its function is to take account of facts, avoid danger, and rechannel or postpone gratification. In short, it embodies a "reality principle." At the same time, the ego is in touch with the id, from which it draws energy and direction.[11]

The *superego* is the part of the self that internalizes the demands of society, especially prohibitions and punishments the strong can enforce. The child's dependency, emotional as well as physical, and openness to influence guarantee that social demands will be incorporated into the psychic organization of the developing person. This is done by reconstructing the ego. No longer a simple agent of the id, bent only on rational self-protection, the ego expands to include guilt and shame. Superego demands are more than external threats. They are charged with emotion; they share, as part of the ego, the energy of the id. This helps explain the deep and often irrational expressions of emotion triggered by violations of sex taboos and other rules of "superego morality."

11. For more on "ego" and "self" see Chapter 8, "Self-preservation."

This psychic configuration is characterized by *energy, conflict, adaptation*, and *development*. Freud's model is a dynamic theory of mind and self because it postulates forces at work and at odds generating problems that must be resolved in some way, and because it identifies distinctive modes of adaptation and reconstruction, notably mechanisms of defense against thoughts and feelings that provoke anxiety.[12]

As the logic of Freud's theory unfolded, it became clear that a key to psychic well-being is the development of the ego. The mature ego balances values of autonomous selfhood, emotional satisfaction, and social regulation. The ego is not the whole self; the latter includes everything that gives the biosocial organism a distinctive and continuous identity.[13] The ego is the *aspect* of the self that, in processing conflicting demands, determines how well a person deals with psychological stress or can gather strength for demanding efforts. In respect to these functions the self may be strong or weak, aggressive or submissive, dependent or autonomous.

The functions of the ego have mainly to do with psychic competence. A person with an adequate ego can tolerate frustration and deal with it rationally, perhaps by substituting another goal for one that is blocked; the inadequate ego responds to frustration by apathetic withdrawal or, perhaps, by a temper tantrum. The adequate ego sustains a person's capacity to resist group pressure; the inadequate ego is vulnerable to collective excitement and surrenders easily to group demands. The adequate ego can defer gratification, be realistic in expectations, correct mistakes, and call on inner controls when external supervision is withdrawn; the inadequate ego flees or attacks, interprets failure as worthlessness, and becomes anxious and disorganized when outside controls are relaxed. The adequate ego experiences feelings of love and hate without suffocating or denying them; the inadequate ego is overwhelmed by emotions and unable to establish constructive, self-preserving relationships.

These examples help specify the meaning of psychic competence. But the centrality of the ego in fashioning that competence should not be misunderstood. Freud did not mean to discount the significance of

12. Freud's theory may fairly be characterized as an instance of *dynamic functionalism*. It is functionalist because it posits a psychic system in quest of equilibrium; it is dynamic because the system is driven by inner demands and conflicts and is subject to reconstruction as it struggles to resolve its problems. Marx's theory of capitalist development is another important example of dynamic functionalism in modern social science.

13. See Daniel Yankelovich and William Barrett, *Ego and Instinct: The Psychological View of Human Nature . . . Revised* (New York: Random House), 23f.

superego and, especially, id. On the contrary, instinctual impulses and social pressures always set problems for an embattled ego. Still, the healthy, mature ego is not a constricting or punitive censor; rather, it is an agency of fulfillment tempered by realism.

This theory makes it easy to see the basic connection between psychic and moral competence. An inadequate ego cannot sustain concern for others or, indeed, for the integrity of the self. This theme pervades Freud's work. Although he was a physician who dealt mainly with mental and psychic disorders—although he founded a healing profession— his larger objective was a theory of human nature. This in turn led him to a major, if often implicit, preoccupation with the moral significance of psychodynamic processes.

A good example of this preoccupation is Freud's analysis of the relationship between sex and love, which he saw as a pervasive problem set by the conflicting demands of id, ego, and superego. The problem arises because a healthy personal and social life, especially within the nuclear family, requires the psychic competence to *divide* love and sex, that is, to repress sexuality while sustaining close ties of affection and intimacy. And there is as well a need to *combine* sex and love in adult, nonincestuous relationships. The combination is always precarious and sometimes perilous, but it is also full of promise for personal well-being in intimate settings.

In a famous paper on the debasement of love Freud argued that in the modern world, and especially among educated people, there is widespread incapacity to be sexually free and effective with the person one respects and loves:

> There are only a very few educated people in whom the two currents of affection and sensuality have become properly fused; the man almost always feels his respect for the woman acting as a restriction on his sexual activity, and only develops full potency when he is with a debased sexual object; and this in turn is partly caused by the entrance of perverse components into his sexual aims, which he does not venture to satisfy with a woman he respects. . . . It sounds not only disagreeable but also paradoxical, yet it must nevertheless be said that anyone who is to be really free and happy in love must have surmounted his respect for women and have come to terms with the idea of incest with his mother and sister.[14]

Here the theory of the Oedipus complex is drawn on to explain symptoms arising from the difficulty of fusing sex and love. Since even by

14. Sigmund Freud, "The Tendency to Debasement in Love" (1912), in vol. 11 of *The Standard Edition of the Complete Psychological Works,* trans. and ed. John Strachey in collaboration with Anna Freud (London: Hogarth Press, 1953), 185f.

Freud's account not everyone has these symptoms, at least not to an equal extent, it follows that their incidence and force must vary widely. The empirical generalization, like so many of Freud's, is doubtful, to say the least. Nevertheless, the theory led Freud to uncover a process that affects both mental health and morality. The inability to combine love and sex, when sexuality is appropriate, results in morally impoverished, exploitative, sometimes brutal encounters. The capacity to fuse sex and love (or to divide them while repressing and sublimating sexuality) is a psychological foundation of trust and of commitment to other persons as ends and not as means only.[15]

Thus the psychology of love is a message of nature in the sense that it points the way to moral achievement and to characteristic forms of moral regression. A theory of human need, conflict, and flourishing helps us distinguish good from evil. Indeed, psychological truth shades into moral truth as it attends to the integrity and well-being of the self. Psychological theories of responsible choice, healthy relatedness, self-reliance, and self-esteem, for example, broadly overlap the concerns and conclusions of moral inquiry.

The preoccupation with morality extends to much else in Freudian psychology. Most important, perhaps, are the related themes of *responsibility, liberation, reason,* and *self-knowledge.* Freud's theory of the ego adds an important dimension to our understanding of responsibility. In the formation of viable and effective selves, a major developmental task is the integration of id impulses—and other biological givens, such as being male or female—into an ordered personal life. This process can be understood as accepting responsibility for one's inner life—and for giving direction to it.[16]

Mental health requires release from the domination of unconscious fears and fantasies and of roles and relationships that reinforce dependency and impoverish the self. Liberation, however, must be governed by reason, which includes not only instrumental rationality—adaptation of means to predetermined ends—but a larger assessment of what ends make sense for the kind of person one is or can be. This requires self-knowledge, which is the aim of psychoanalytic therapy.

The morality embodied in Freud's vision is an exquisite combination of liberation and discipline. There is liberation in his insistence on the

15. On Freud's contributions to the psychology of love, and their implications for morality, see Philip Rieff, *Freud: The Mind of the Moralist* (New York: Viking Press, 1959), chap. 5.

16. See Hans W. Loewald, *Psychoanalysis and the History of the Individual* (New Haven: Yale University Press, 1978), 19, 47; cf. Lear, *Love and Its Place in Nature,* 65ff.

positive worth of id impulse and energy, therefore on the desirability of recognizing and accepting our animal nature, especially our sexuality; in his argument for seeing normal and abnormal psychology as a continuum, with all that implies in the way of humility, tolerance, and self-acceptance; in his radical reconstruction of the idea of self-knowledge as uncovering and releasing unconscious fears and desires; in his conception of a genital character capable of constructively channeling libidinal drives. These themes were developed in the course of dealing with neurosis. As tools of therapy, they speak only to the needs of the suffering person. They are not presented as moral prescriptions or even as moral principles. But they tell us what moral liberation means in psychological terms, how it is to be achieved, and what risks are entailed.

Like Marx, Freud sought emancipation from whatever crippled and alienated the human spirit. Unlike Marx, he was careful to reject the fantasy that a final liberation could be won by social transformation. In his understanding of the relation between the individual and society, and of the necessary demands of social life, Freud was closer to Durkheim than to Marx. Like Durkheim, he accepted the idea that discipline is a condition of effective freedom. Without discipline, especially internal discipline, the person is tormented by inner needs and incapable of coping with external demands. The unregulated life is not worth living, nor can it produce a culture worth having.

Therefore impulse must be restrained, social bonds respected, freedom of choice abridged. The result is no easy adaptation, no unbroken continuum of adjustment. Frustration breaks the continuum and guarantees an irrepressible conflict between self and society. The inevitable trade-offs may bring a sense of loss and even of despair. They also become a fresh challenge to psychic and moral development.

▾   ▴   ▾   ▴   ▾

Freud's theory of the superego seems to leave no room for critical or reflective morality. Formed in the crucible of impulse and dependency, the superego is above all an agency of conventional morality.[17] Social norms are more or less effectively internalized by processes, and especially the formation of guilt, that are mainly unconscious and nonrational.

In a larger sense, however, Freud was much concerned with critical morality. By showing how conventional morality may cripple and im-

17. See Chapter 14, "Critical and Conventional Morality."

poverish the self he encouraged people to appraise received precepts and expose their irrational bases. By exploring the dynamics of ego development he helped identify the psychological foundations of rationality and autonomy. Nevertheless, the Freudian theory of the self, rich as it is, cannot provide a full account of moral development. The concept of the superego is too closely tied to negative restraints, and the source of morality is too narrowly conceived as a response to inner conflict and external demands.

THE MORALITY OF COOPERATION

Freud's theory belongs to one of two competing perspectives that have dominated the study of moral development.[18] The first sees the basic process as the *internalization* of social norms, which are understood as predetermined. The mechanisms emphasized may be routine conditioning through positive or negative reinforcement, or they may be, as in Freudian theory, emotion-laden processes of identification and introjection.[19] Whatever the mechanism, the stress is on the power of conventional morality.

The second perspective sees moral development as an outgrowth of *discovery* and *reconstruction*. Thus understood, morality is not the offspring of authority, imposed from without by psychological mechanisms of conditioning and subordination. It is a product of autonomous experience, especially experience that leads to improved understanding or cognition. (Hence, in recent psychology, this approach is called "cognitive-developmental.") The decisive experience is social interaction, whose most important outcome is the enlargement of moral sensibility. In this process critical morality has a central place, not necessarily as a product of conscious moral will or of moral idealism, but as a natural, expectable, variable aspect of human socialization.

The two perspectives are often described as alternatives. In fact, however, they highlight different aspects of the psychology of morality.

18. For reviews of relevant psychological theory and research see Martin L. Hoffman, "Moral Development," in Paul H. Mussen, ed., *Carmichael's Manual of Child Psychology*, vol. 2 (New York: John Wiley, 1970); James R. Rest, "Morality," in Paul H. Mussen, ed., *Handbook of Child Psychology*, vol. 3 (New York: John Wiley, 1983); Elliot Turiel, *The Development of Social Knowledge: Morality and Convention* (Cambridge: Cambridge University Press, 1983).

19. Freud's model accounts, in important part, for the generation of motives that induce conformity. Since this conformity characteristically comes at some cost to psychic well-being, internalization is likely to be problematic.

Conditioning, identification, and "dynamic adaptation"[20] together have a major role in creating the dispositions and competencies we call character. In one form or another internalization goes on throughout life. That does not tell us much, however, about higher stages of moral development, about the psychology of moral sophistication and sensibility. Thus Freudian theory bears most closely on sources of irrationality, which may impair moral judgment, and on the need to overcome them. There is an implicit model of mental health, but only *baseline* competencies are identified; only modest aspirations are encouraged.

This limited moral achievement—the capacity to exercise self-control, experience empathy, feel appropriate guilt—is easy to think of as a natural process. The urgent need for minimum levels of moral competence stems from what the biosocial organism requires and from the elementary continuities of social life. When we look beyond this baseline, the case becomes more difficult. Yet this more complex issue is the main concern of much contemporary work in moral psychology. Moral development has come to be largely identified with *progressive enhancements* of moral awareness, discrimination, and reasoning. The large question is: Do more sophisticated forms of moral judgment have a natural foundation, or must they be understood as options defined by moral will and reasoning, having little to do with psychology or with objective criteria of personal maturity?

A moral ideal or achievement has a natural foundation if it is *latent* in human experience and is *viable* in the light of that experience. A latent ideal builds on dispositions and strivings that arise in the course of growth and interaction. It does not depend, for origin and vitality, on philosophical reflection or imagination. An ideal is viable if it is more than an abstract possibility or potential. It is not necessarily likely to be actualized, and certainly it is not inevitable. But it must be a live option, sustained and encouraged by dependable needs, wants, and energies; and it must hold promise of contributing to personal well-being.

---

20. "By static adaptation we mean such adaptation to patterns as leaves the whole character structure unchanged and implies only the adoption of a new habit. . . . By dynamic adaptation we refer to the kind of adaptation that occurs, for example, when a boy submits to the commands of his strict and threatening father—being too afraid of him to do otherwise—and becomes a 'good' boy. While he adapts to the necessities of the situation, something happens in him. He may develop an intense hostility against his father, which he represses. . . . This repressed hostility . . . is a dynamic factor in his character structure. It may create new anxiety and thus lead to still deeper submission; it may set up a vague defiance, directed against no one in particular but rather toward life in general" (Erich Fromm, *Escape from Freedom* [New York: Farrar & Rinehart, 1941], 15f.).

Mead and Reflective Morality

The idea that social interaction is the forcing-house of moral development is one of the main teachings of the American pragmatists, especially George Herbert Mead. (See Chapter 5, "Sociology and Human Nature.") Like Freud, Mead studied the psychology of mind and the interplay of mind and self. But he was more interested in the enlargement of consciousness than in mental or psychic disorders. In *Mind, Self, and Society*, one of the most influential books in modern social science, Mead located moral development in the transition from a regime of "significant others" to guidance by the "generalized other." Young children routinely internalize the attitudes and expectations of parents and others who dominate their lives. These "significant others" are experienced as powerful and demanding, and as speaking for a morality whose rightness cannot be questioned.

Gradually, however, children learn another way of participating in social life. They begin to grasp the meaning of cooperation and are able to govern their actions accordingly. In time they can be considerate of others, not by mechanically following an assigned course of conduct, but by recognizing why group rules are important and how they contribute to playing a game or achieving a goal. The "generalized other" is this perspective of cooperative group life.

Mead discerned moral development in the capacity for rational participation in rule-governed, organized social activity; in the growth of personal autonomy, mitigating the overdetermined, oversocialized self; and in the enlargement of the self as parochial perspectives are overcome and as individuals adopt the standpoint of ever-larger communities and universal values. The key to this process is the emergence of critical or reflective morality. This outcome depends on, is furthered by, and makes sense of three routine features of self and social interaction.

First, the self consists of an ego or "I," which is active, autonomous, and self-referring; and of a superego or what Mead called the "me." The "me" is the conventional or socially controlled part of the self. If group life is restrictive, the "me" dominates the "I" and individuality is minimized, though never eliminated. Under more congenial conditions the "I" influences and restructures social meanings, rules, roles, and relationships. Indeed, on some occasions the "me" legitimates and encourages the free expression of the "I," and these, Mead said, provide "some of the most exciting and gratifying experiences."[21]

21. George Herbert Mead, *Mind, Self, and Society* (Chicago: University of Chicago Press, 1934), 213.

Thus Mead did not equate the social self with the subordinate or heteronomous self. The "I" is as much a social product as the "me"; it can only develop through social interaction and by adopting the perspective of the generalized other. At the same time, the "I" is the agency of reflective morality. As such, it is not a sport or freak, nor is it something concocted by a psychologist turned moral philosopher. Like Freud's ego, Mead's "I" is a normal, if variable, aspect of human personality.

Second, significant social interaction implicates the self, enhances or distorts communication, and enlarges or cramps perspectives. Therefore *moral competence depends on the nature and quality of social participation.* A practical lesson is that morality is to be taught and encouraged, not by abstract precepts, but by enlarging opportunities for communication and responsibility.

Mead's theory of the self led him to emphasize the positive aspects of social life and the moral worth of cooperation. The self is not a passive recipient of fixed, external influences, nor is response a triggered release of preformed dispositions.[22] Rather, the self emerges and is *reconstructed* in the course of interaction; is impelled to take the point of view of the other; and is active, reflexive, interpretive, and purposive. Furthermore, genuine interaction is not mere inter-action; by deepening communication and blurring the boundaries of self and other, it creates new unities. Mead well understood that these outcomes require congenial conditions and are therefore often frustrated. He was pointing to an inner dynamic, an aspect of nature that serves well-being by stimulating the development of both criticism and commitment. With these ideas he shared (and helped form) the optimistic outlook of American pragmatism.

And, third, the psychology of moral development centers on cognition, not emotion.[23] In this respect Mead's theory of the self is radically different from Freud's. Mead was interested in the mental processes by which rationality is achieved. Here "mental" refers not to modes of *reasoning,* whether mathematical or discursive, but to modes of *consciousness.* The latter arise spontaneously as the human mind develops in the course of coping with the emergent self and the social environment. These

22. "Human society, we have insisted, does not merely stamp the pattern of its organized social behavior upon any one of its individual members, so that this pattern becomes likewise the pattern of the individual's self; it also, at the same time, gives him a mind, as the means or ability of consciously conversing with himself in terms of the social attitudes which constitute the structure of his self and which embody the pattern of human society's organized behavior as reflected in that structure" (ibid., 263n).

23. See David L. Miller, *George Herbert Mead: Self, Language, and the World* (Austin: University of Texas Press, 1973), 229ff.

"mental" or "cognitive" experiences generate and undergird modes of reasoning—which have, of course, their own integrity.

For Mead, the most relevant mental process, from the standpoint of rationality, is the taking of an objective, impersonal attitude toward the self. The rational self is reflexive, that is, treats itself as an object and not only as a subject. A person "becomes an object to himself only by taking the attitudes of other individuals toward himself" within a context of shared experience.[24] The relation between self and other, self and society, is one of testing and criticism, self-criticism and reconstruction. The process strains toward generalization, that is, toward ideas and attitudes that embrace ever-larger segments of experience. A relatively limited awareness is, for example, one that is oriented only to the present and cannot take account of past and future. Mead's language blends the normative and the descriptive. He speaks often of what the self "should" be or do if it is to be developed fully. But, like Dewey, he viewed rationality as implicit in the transactions of everyday life.[25]

These ideas suggest that reflective morality springs from basic human impulses and from the continuities of social interaction. Thus it is an ideal *derived* from nature, that is, from the dynamics of personal growth and socialization, and *warranted* by its contribution to the realization of vital interests common to mankind. Therefore reflective morality is not an exotic product of will and imagination; does not reflect arbitrary preference; is not based on a subjective view of the good. Furthermore, reflective morality is most credible and most vital when it remains in touch with *pre*-reflective conditions and problems. Reflective morality is not a roving commission to dream of possible worlds or to seek the good without consulting the sources of its own authority.

Because Mead saw reflective morality as part of moral development, he did not reduce conscience to superego constraint. In Freud's thought "conscience is furnished by social authority and remains, unreflectively,

24. Mead, *Mind, Self, and Society,* 138.
25. Compare Dewey's view that aesthetic quality is "implicit in every normal experience" (John Dewey, *Art as Experience,* [1934; reprint, New York: Capricorn Books, 1958], 12f.). When experience is meaningful and satisfying it takes on form and coherence, inner harmony and rhythm. "[A]ny practical activity will, provided that it is integrated and moves by its own urge to fulfillment, have esthetic quality" (ibid., 39). Like Mead in his treatment of rationality, Dewey specifies conditions that must be met if experience is to be authentic and have at least the rudiments of aesthetic quality. But these conditions *are* routinely met in much ordinary, practical activity. Note that Dewey blends the normative and the descriptive in the same way as Mead; neither is in any doubt as to the difference between what is and what ought to be. Their argument is that what ought to be, for example, authentic experience, is implicit in, but not guaranteed by, what is, that is, by ordinary experience.

at authority's disposal. . . . [F]reedom of conscience is a contradiction in terms; there are only alternative submissions."[26] Mead understood that at the level of moral development where the "me" predominates, conscience is based on feelings generated by external compulsion. But further moral development, in both society and the individual, frees the "I" to invoke a broader community of interests against the restrictions of the immediate and narrower community. Conscience has rational and cognitive foundations; it is not best understood as a product of emotional traumas and irrational guilt. A corollary is that the formation of conscience requires a social experience that enhances individuality even as it transmits social skills and ideals. Conscience requires self-transcendence but not subordination.[27]

Enter Piaget

As a philosopher and a social psychologist, Mead drew on ordinary experience rather than on systematic research. It was the Swiss psychologist Jean Piaget (1896–1980) who brought the study of moral sensibility into the mainstream of modern psychology. Piaget's lifelong interest was the psychology of mind, and he saw moral development as an aspect of mental development.

In an elegant and influential study, Piaget examined the responses of children to issues of punishment and fairness. He began with the premise that "all morality consists in a system of rules, and the essence of morality is to be sought for in the respect which the individual acquires for these rules."[28] As a result of this focus on rules, the theme of the study became the child's conception of justice.[29]

26. Rieff, *Freud*, 274. Although the Freudian concept of conscience is inadequate as a way of grasping the full meaning of the idea, it remains a powerful tool of analysis. Its focus is precisely on *when* and *how* conscience is reduced to superego constraint and becomes, to that extent, impoverished and potentially pathological.

27. "Hence social control, so far from tending to crush out the human individual or to obliterate his self-conscious individuality, is, on the contrary, actually constitutive of and inextricably associated with that individuality; for the individual is what he is, as a conscious and individual personality, just in so far as he is a member of society, involved in the social process of experience and activity, and thereby socially controlled in his conduct" (Mead, *Mind, Self and Society*, 255).

28. Jean Piaget, *The Moral Judgment of the Child*, trans. Marjorie Gabain (1932; reprint, New York: Free Press, 1965), 13.

29. This identification of rules with morality, and of morality with justice, is not wholly satisfactory, as we shall see. At this point, however, we are concerned only with showing that moral development has a psychological foundation. For a critical analysis of Piaget's argument, see Owen Flanagan, *Varieties of Moral Personality* (Cambridge: Harvard University Press, 1991), chap. 7.

Piaget distinguished two types of rules: coercive, and rational. The former are based on respect for authority, and compliance is won by punishment. Obedience to a coercive rule does not ordinarily depend on the child's understanding the purpose of the rule. The coercive rule is a received and external fact. Obedience to rational rules, by contrast, is founded on a sense of fairness, mutuality, and respect for the ends the rule is meant to serve. A regime of coercive rules is a "morality of constraint"; a regime of rational rules is a "morality of cooperation."[30]

The two types of morality are stages on life's way. A first period, lasting roughly until the age of eight, is characterized by submission to authority and externality of rules. It is a stage of "strict law," in which the bare fact of infraction, regardless of context or intent, warrants corrective punishment. In the second stage, ages nine to twelve, the preoccupation with retribution declines. There is greater awareness of reciprocity, equal treatment, and mutual respect among peers, as well as an increased capacity to distinguish a just rule from one that is merely authoritative.[31]

In Piaget's theory, moral evolution is marked by changes in personality and social relations. At the earlier stage children are "egocentric" rather than autonomous. Basically "loners," unable to engage in genuine cooperation, their play is characteristically mechanical and imitative. At the same time, they are dominated by adult wishes. At this stage children do not distinguish their own perspectives from the perspectives of others, and the psychological bases for criticism of authority have not been laid.

The transition to stage two brings a measure of release from adult constraint. The children look to peer groups for satisfaction and guidance. In the peer group an awareness of cooperation takes hold. Group participation encourages a more generalized, less egocentric approach to the world and, at the same time, helps the child discover the boundaries

---

30. Piaget, *Moral Judgment of the Child,* 335. Piaget's two stages correspond closely to Durkheim's: mechanical solidarity creates a morality of constraint; organic solidarity yields a morality of cooperation. Each posits a growth of rationality, social differentiation, and personal autonomy. But see Piaget's critique of Durkheim, ibid., 341ff.

31. "[The younger children] do not attempt to understand the psychological context; deeds and punishments are for them simply so much material to be brought into some kind of balance, and this kind of moral mechanics . . . makes them insensible to the human side of the problem. . . . In short, then, we may take it that children who put retributive justice above distributive are those who adopt the point of view of adult constraint, while those who put equality of treatment above punishment are those who, in their relations with other children, or more rarely in the relations between themselves and adults, have learnt better to understand psychological situations and to judge according to norms of a new moral type" (ibid., 267f.).

between self and other. As children grow in autonomy they gain respect for the autonomy of others. Thus for Piaget, as for Mead and the young Durkheim, the morality of cooperation is a morality of rational rules, interdependent activities, and autonomous persons.

These broad generalizations need to be qualified in several ways. In the first place, the process is much more complex and uncertain than Piaget's scenario suggests. Mental development, including moral judgment, is not a product of inexorable maturation. Ideas are not given or preformed.[32] They arise in the course of interaction and therefore depend on the nature and quality of social experience. Furthermore, there is evidence that even three- and four-year-olds are capable of distinguishing conventional rules, which depend on authority, from more distinctively moral questions of right and wrong such as the rules against hurting a playmate or taking someone's possessions.[33] Moreover, although many studies have confirmed Piaget's findings, others have cast doubt on their empirical validity.[34]

Piaget's two stages are indeed too general to withstand close scrutiny. His findings are best understood as a theoretical framework and a diagnostic tool. They illuminate certain important—perhaps crucial—aspects of experience. But the model should not be expected to describe with precision a complex and variable reality.[35] It cannot account for all the ways most children think about rules or fairness.

The important contribution of this research is that it helps identify, in psychological terms, the difference between conventional and critical morality. Like Freud, Piaget takes the former to be more primitive and less fully cognitive than the latter. And like Mead, Piaget went beyond Freudian theory to ask what are the specific components of reflective morality and what conditions sustain or undermine them. Such inquiry does not depend on a specific argument about stages. It does presume that the enlargement of moral competence has psychological correlates and can be understood as a process of growth to maturity.

32. Jean Piaget, *The Science of Education and the Psychology of the Child,* trans. Derek Coltman (New York: Orion Press, 1970), 704.

33. See Turiel, *Development of Social Knowledge,* chap. 3.

34. See Hoffman, "Moral Development," 265ff.; Rest, "Morality," 573; Turiel, *Development of Social Knowledge,* 145ff.

35. "Although Piaget referred to his two moralities as stages, he nevertheless disclaimed that they were tightly organized or clearly separated from each other. In light of subsequent research, Piaget's two moralities are best regarded as characterizations of the poles of development, that is, the two moralities are rough descriptions of the beginning and end points of the course of development rather than the successive transformations in cognitive systems over the course of development" (Rest, "Morality," 572).

Justice and Nurture

A vigorous effort to extend Piaget's conception of moral development was led by Lawrence Kohlberg (1927–1987). Using a research strategy similar to Piaget's (eliciting responses to hypothetical situations that pose issues of moral choice), Kohlberg and his colleagues studied children in the United States and other countries, including India, Turkey, and Israel. Following Piaget, Kohlberg took as his central concern the child's conception of what is just or fair and emphasized the importance of social participation. Kohlberg focused especially on the opportunity to broaden perspectives by taking the role of the other, including what Mead called the "generalized other."

The main assumptions of cognitive-developmental theory were summarized by Kohlberg as follows:

1. Moral development has a basic cognitive-structural or moral-judgmental component.

2. The basic motivation for morality is a generalized motivation for acceptance, competence, self-esteem, or self-realization, rather than for the meeting of biological needs or the reduction of anxiety or fear.

3. Major aspects of moral development are culturally universal, because all cultures have common sources of social interaction, role-taking, and social conflict which require moral integration.

4. Basic norms and principles are structures arising through experiences of social interaction rather than through internalization of rules that exist as external structures; moral stages are not defined by internalized rules but by structures of interaction between the self and others.

5. Environmental influences on moral development are defined by the general quality and extent of cognitive and social stimulation throughout the child's development, rather than by specific experiences of discipline, punishment, and reward.[36]

These postulates define an important perspective, but they do not require what was most emphasized by Kohlberg—a theory of invariant and universal stages. Nor are the postulates wholly incompatible with other perspectives, such as that of social learning or Freudian theory. To say that moral development has a basic cognitive component (point 1 above) does not deny the significance of other components, including identification, conditioning, and related mechanisms of "internalization." Similarly, if "major aspects of moral development are culturally universal," it may also be that other aspects, including styles of thought

---

36. Lawrence Kohlberg, *The Psychology of Moral Development* (San Francisco: Harper & Row, 1984), 196f.

and varieties of sensibility, are culturally contingent. As so often in these matters, the defense of a special perspective has led to exaggerated claims and futile polemics.

In presenting his findings, Kohlberg described six stages of moral development, grouped into three broad levels:

Preconventional morality is basically egocentric. Morality is a matter of avoiding punishment and accepting external authority (stage 1) or following rules because it is in the interest of cooperating individuals to do so (stage 2).

Conventional morality is a reflex of group membership. What matters is social approval, loyalty, and concern for the welfare of a particular group and its members. "The conventional individual subordinates the needs of the single individual to the viewpoint and needs of the group or the shared relationship."[37] In stage 3 the person is mainly concerned to live up to expectations. At stage 4 the individual adopts the point of view of the *system* of rules and roles and recognizes the duty to uphold the system.

Postconventional morality makes abstract principle rather than group affiliation the criterion of moral judgment. Here the point of view of the individual is regained, but not as a narrowly self-interested actor. Rather, morally autonomous individuals criticize social rules in the light of rational principles. They say it is wrong to steal because it violates someone's rights, not just because it is against the law. At stage 5 obligation is based on conceptions of social contract, social utility, and individual rights. Morality is still bound up with particular rules and prescriptions, but those rules are subject to criticism on "constitutional" grounds, such as what has been agreed to or what rights are fundamental. A stage 6—wherein morality consists of universal and self-chosen principles of justice, affirming "the equality of human rights and respect for the dignity of human beings as individual persons" was abandoned, at least tentatively.[38]

This account of moral development is based on studies that are at best suggestive. Much depends on the methods used to interpret and score

37. Ibid., 177.
38. Ibid., 215. A "soft" stage 7 was also considered, wherein a "response to ethical and religious problems is based on constructing a sense of identity or unity with being, with life, or with God." In this stage, suggested by some interviews, "postconventional principles of justice *and care* are perceived within what might be broadly termed a natural law framework" (ibid., 249f., my emphasis). Here, as elsewhere in this work, Kohlberg blandly accepts the criticisms by Carol Gilligan and others, noted below, while emphasizing that his own theory "is a pure theory of *justice reasoning.*" See ibid., 227ff., 211.

the responses.[39] We may well be skeptical about whether moral development follows so definite a path and whether moral maturity is so neatly congruent with (selected) Western ideals of principled conduct, equality of moral worth, and individual rights. It is one thing to assert, as Piaget did, that a developmental transition can be discerned from a morality of constraint to a morality of cooperation and that relevant psychological processes can be identified.[40] It is quite another to say that psychological maturity entails a commitment to specific ideals and concepts.

An alternative view of psychological maturity as it bears on moral competence has been proposed by Carol Gilligan.[41] On the basis of greater sensitivity to the experience of girls and women, Gilligan challenged the view that moral development necessarily culminates in awareness of universal principles of justice. Women are more sensitive to the continuity of relationships and are more disposed to associate "being moral" with help and nurture of those others in whose lives one's own is implicated. This way of thinking and feeling does not emerge as a high stage in Kohlberg's studies; it tends to be folded into a lower, less reflective stage of conventional morality. Yet the morality of *caring*, Gilligan argued, has at least an equal claim to be considered a form of moral maturity. Sensitivity to *needs* can be as important as sensitivity to *rights*. And such a morality cannot be denigrated as unreflective or unprincipled simply because it is anchored in the experience of attachment.

The focus on gender differences has been a source of some confusion. Gilligan claimed that Kohlberg's theory reflected a male bias, in part because he based his original findings on a longitudinal study of eighty-four *boys*. In fact, subsequent studies using Kohlberg's measures have not shown significant gender differences.[42] This suggests that Kohlberg, like Piaget, was guided by a selective theory of morality as justice, not by the special experience of boys. Gilligan was drawn to a different model of morality, and she was helped in doing so by what she gleaned from the experience of women:

39. See Rest, "Morality," 580ff.

40. Piaget's argument is stated with sufficient generality to allow for multiple outcomes: moralities of constraint and moralities of cooperation.

41. Carol Gilligan, *In a Different Voice: Psychological Theory and Women's Development* (Cambridge: Harvard University Press, 1982). See also Norma Haan et al., *On Moral Grounds: The Search for Practical Morality* (New York: New York University Press, 1985); Nel Noddings, *Caring: A Feminine Approach to Ethics and Moral Education* (Berkeley: University of California Press, 1984).

42. See Lawrence J. Walker, "Sex Differences in the Development of Moral Reasoning: A Critical Review," *Child Development* 55 (1984): 677–91.

The different voice I describe is characterized not by gender but by theme. Its
association with women is an empirical observation . . . but this association
is not absolute, and the contrasts between male and female voices are presented here to highlight a distinction between two modes of thought and to
focus a problem of interpretation rather than to represent a generalization
about either sex.[43]

Although the formal evidence is obscure and stereotypes abound, there
probably are important differences in the lives, and therefore in the orientations, of males and females. They are, of course, decisively influenced by history and culture; and they are more likely to be captured by
the experience of commitment to particular others than by a generalized
"altruism" or "empathy."[44] As Gilligan suggested, however, that is not
the main point. Even the stereotypes may suggest a "different voice."
The validity of that voice as an expression of moral principle must then
be evaluated.[45]

Piaget, Kohlberg, and, less clearly, Mead as well, emphasized the
importance of abstract rules and concepts for cooperative life, especially
in upholding fidelity to principle and purpose. In contrast, Gilligan
stressed the contribution of trust, nurturing, attachment, and interdependence. Each perspective brings into focus a different facet of the
morality of cooperation: one invokes the authority of a moral code,
which may be a code of high principle; the other calls for deference to
concrete needs and dependencies.[46]

There are echoes here of a long-standing concern for the interplay of
love and justice, as well as for the mitigation of general rules by taking
into account special needs and circumstances. In Christian thought, for
example, there is no question of reducing morality to justice. Love is the
higher ideal and one that must be drawn on to correct and improve justice by making it more sensitive to conscience. Love can be a principle
of action, not just a feeling, yet it strains toward concreteness, that is,
toward appreciating the uniqueness of persons and situations. We return
to that issue in Chapter 7.

43. Gilligan, In a Different Voice, 2.
44. Some of these matters are explored in Linda K. Kerber et al., "On In a Different
Voice: An Interdisciplinary Symposium," Signs: A Journal of Women in Culture and Society
11 (1986): 304–33.
45. For an assessment of the Gilligan thesis, see Flanagan, Varieties of Moral Personality,
chap. 9.
46. Ironically, the former can be considered a sublimated form of superego morality
and thus raise doubts, on this ground too, as to which is really more "primitive."

▼   ▲   ▼   ▲   ▼

It is always easier to identify pathologies and establish thresholds than it is to say objectively what is psychic health, maturity, or fulfillment. Therefore it is not surprising that modern research has thus far failed to establish wholly convincing psychological correlates of moral achievement.[47] Nevertheless, taken as a whole, this line of thought strongly suggests that moral competence and sensibility, which includes reflective morality, are aspects of a natural order. The capacities and needs of human animals, when combined with the dynamics of human association, produce characteristic outcomes, notably an awareness of justice and an acceptance of responsibility. These outcomes are variable and contingent; they necessarily reflect the experiences of different social groups and categories. At the same time they point to the latent promise of growth and interaction.

RECALCITRANCE AND FRAILTY

The natural history of moral development tells what we may *aspire to,* in the light of human capabilities and dispositions. It does not tell us what we should *guard against* or even what we can *rely upon.* To avoid undue optimism we need a complementary understanding of moral vulnerability, recalcitrance, and malevolence. Compared to moral development, the reality of these failings is much easier to discern and accept. No subtle argument is needed to show that immorality and moral weakness are pervasive aspects of human experience.

Yet the significance of recalcitrance and frailty, as pervasive human attributes and as irrepressible threats to moral well-being, has often been denied, or at least muted, in modern thought. In the eighteenth and nineteenth centuries a mood of optimism was widespread. Human will

47. Two mistaken strategies may have distracted the enterprise: (1) a focus on determinate stages; and (2) a preoccupation with expressed *beliefs* about right and wrong as against more general and more distinctively psychological indicators of moral competence, sensibility, and sophistication. A more qualitative assessment would ask, for example, whether the subject can appreciate the spirit as well as the letter of a rule; take account of multiple values; understand the interplay of ends and means; give consent without losing dignity and self-esteem. These and similar aspects of moral experience seem to have a more direct connection to psychic competence and maturity than the expression of beliefs. Furthermore, although such aspects are ingredients of reflective morality, they are compatible with many different values, sensibilities, and moral theories. It is not credible to suppose that a person who is indifferent to abstract principles but can judge wisely of human conflicts and follies should be rated "less developed."

and intelligence, freed of ignorance, superstition, and vested interest, would find a way to the eradication of evil. The power of science, including social science, was also its promise. The remaking of society according to rational principles was just another world to conquer; and that conquest might introduce a new humanity.

This optimistic vision was strongly held, as we have seen, by Karl Marx and his followers. But it has been equally evident, if more cautious and controlled, in the perspectives of liberal reformers. An important example is John Dewey's pragmatism. Dewey never fully integrated into his thought the darker side of human life. His perspective did not readily account for, or take seriously enough, the demonic and destructive aspects of personality and society. That is so because he was mainly concerned to show that the construction of *a culture based on the method and morality of science* should be the main objective of social reform. Such a culture is not rule by experts. On the contrary, it brings to ordinary people the sensibilities and thoughtways of the scientific community.[48]

For Dewey, democracy and science are intimately related:

> While it would be absurd to believe it desirable or possible for everyone to become a scientist when science is defined from the side of subject matter, the future of democracy is allied with the spread of the scientific attitude. It is the sole guarantee against wholesale misleading by propaganda. More important still, it is the only assurance of the possibility of a public opinion intelligent enough to meet present social problems. . . . A culture which permits science to destroy traditional values but which distrusts its power to create new ones is a culture which is destroying itself.[49]

This point of view is indeed attractive; it is the foundation of whatever confidence we have that, through dispassionate and comprehensive inquiry, institutions can be designed to serve the public interest. But in arguing for the ideal of community made whole by the ethos of science, Dewey gave short shrift to the deficiencies of human nature and the recalcitrance of institutions.[50] In this "philosophy of the once-born," as

48. These include "willingness to hold belief in suspense, ability to doubt until evidence is obtained; willingness to go where evidence points instead of putting first a personally preferred conclusion; ability to hold ideas in solution and use them as hypotheses to be tested instead of as dogmas to be asserted; and (possibly the most distinctive of all) enjoyment of new fields for inquiry and of new problems" (John Dewey, *Freedom and Culture* [New York: G. P. Putnam's, 1939], 145).

49. Ibid., 148f., 154.

50. But see Sidney Hook, *Pragmatism and the Tragic Sense of Life* (New York: Basic Books, 1974), chaps. 1, 2.

Gertrude Jaeger called it, "there is no political or social fact which is not ultimately transformable by the Great Community."[51]

Dewey's optimism derived from a belief that human nature is decisively affected by social conditions and is therefore open to reconstruction when those conditions are changed.[52] He dismissed as a "new failure of nerve" the pessimistic views that were gaining currency in the 1930s and early 1940s.[53] The social theories of Mosca, Michels, and Pareto; the psychology of Freud; the theology of Niebuhr—none of these persuaded Dewey that a new vision might be needed that would uphold liberal ideals while taking full account of unavoidable evil and the limits of intelligence.

Reinhold Niebuhr, himself an active socialist until 1940, took strong exception to the high hopes expressed by Dewey:

> Professor Dewey has a touching faith in the possibility of achieving the same results in the field of social relations which intelligence achieved in the mastery of nature. The fact that man constitutionally corrupts his purest visions of disinterested justice in his actual actions seems never to occur to him. . . . No one expresses modern man's uneasiness about his society and complacency about himself more perfectly than John Dewey. One half of his philosophy is devoted to an emphasis upon what, in Christian theology, is called the creatureliness of man, his involvement in biological and social process. The other half seeks a secure place for disinterested intelligence above the flux of process; and finds it in "organized co-operative inquiry." Not a suspicion dawns upon Professor Dewey that no possible "organized inquiry" can be as transcendent over the historical conflicts of interest as it ought to be to achieve the disinterested intelligence he attributes to it. . . . The worst injustices and conflicts of history arise from these very claims of impartiality. . . . The solution at which Professor Dewey arrives is therefore an incredibly naive answer to a much more ultimate and perplexing problem than he realizes.[54]

51. "Philosophy of the Once-Born," *Enquiry* 2 (April 1944): 14. This essay draws on a distinction between the once-born, who deny or ignore sin, and the twice-born, who take account of evil and for whom the world is a "double-storied mystery." See William James, *The Varieties of Religious Experience* (1902; reprint, New York: Mentor Books, 1958), 78, 140, 281.

52. "But the alleged unchangeableness of human nature cannot be admitted. For while certain needs in human nature are constant, the consequences they produce (because of the existing state of culture—of science, morals, religion, art, industry, legal rules) react back into the original components of human nature to shape them into new forms" (Dewey, *Art as Experience*, 112). But see also Chapter 5, note 5.

53. See John Dewey, "Anti-Naturalism in Extremis," *Partisan Review* 10 (January 1943): 24–39.

54. Reinhold Niebuhr, *The Nature and Destiny of Man* (1941; reprint, New York: Scribner's, 1949), 1:110–11.

In his plea for moral realism Niebuhr repeatedly attacked the naive optimism of liberal intellectuals. He asked them to face up to the limits of reason and the realities of power. "Since reason is always, to some degree, the servant of interest in a social situation, social injustice cannot be resolved by moral and rational suasion alone. . . . Conflict is inevitable, and in this conflict power must be challenged by power."[55] So long as hope is offered that evil can be eradicated rather than merely contained, naiveté remains and with it the easy conscience deplored by Niebuhr. This diagnosis has several implications for moral and social theory.

First, in public affairs we cannot *rely* upon goodwill, education, or moral sophistication. These achievements may be genuine enough; they may substantially mitigate self-interest and self-aggrandizement. But no important interest should be wholly dependent on benevolence or good intentions. In the end only power can check power—and the opportunity to do so must be a secure resource in every moral community. Dewey's conception of a scientific community includes, of course, commitment to openness, dialogue, and experimentation. Nothing was more alien to him than a closed society or an impenetrable ideology. But power and coercion have no place in the ethos of science. Niebuhr rightly saw that, just because American pragmatism places so much faith in science, it has no basis in its theory for accepting the moral worth of power and the legitimacy of coercion.

Second, moral realism puts the self on trial. Each time an act is performed in the name of good intentions, it must be scrutinized for the taint of subjectivity and the offense of overreaching. Dewey would be quick to respond that science relies on a principle of self-correction, not on a promise of perfection. But the evil to be feared goes beyond routine imperfection or subjectivity. It appears when we reach for an ideal but actually achieve, as a result of *over*reaching, a caricature of it. Because this potential is ever-present, no one can enjoy an easy conscience.

Third, the formation of the moral person is marked by conflict and challenge, not by a smooth process of adaptation and growth. Moral and psychic wholeness cannot be taken for granted. Dewey's stress on the adaptive, problem-solving, integrative nature of experience (as in his critique of learning as conditioned response) is in many contexts illuminating. But it supports his optimism and needs to be corrected by a Freudian understanding of inner conflict and the taming of unreason.

55. *Moral Man and Immoral Society* (1932; reprint, New York: Scribner's, 1960), xiv–xv.

Like Niebuhr, Freud takes human destructiveness seriously: moral development is a painful process by which self-control, self-knowledge, self-esteem, and the capacity for love and reason are only partially and precariously achieved.

In these perspectives evil is a sickness of soul. In its most serious forms it is a pathology brought on by forces at work *within* the human psyche and *within* groups and communities. The most important evils are those we generate ourselves, from ourselves, rather than those imposed upon us by external conditions. This is a lesson liberals and radicals have been slow to learn and loath to accept.

▼　▲　▼　▲　▼

Moral realism presumes a tough-minded conception of evil. It is not enough to recognize that corruption and oppression are pervasive. Nor is it enough to think of specific evils as problems to be solved or as obstacles to be overcome. Rather, the perspective of moral realism treats some transgressions as dynamic and inescapable. They can be depended on to arise, in one form or another, despite our best efforts to put them down.

When precious ideals are involved, this point of view may convey a mood of disenchantment or even of abandoned hope. But such a response is unnecessary and may indeed reflect moral weakness rather than strength. For realism is not pessimism. The familiar maxim "Eternal vigilance is the price of liberty" is not notably pessimistic in spirit. Yet it suggests that freedom is not self-sustaining but requires special support. Similarly, the United States Constitution, though it promises much, is full of sober premises about human nature and the uses of power. We do not suppose it thereby manifests a mood of tragic irony.

The Malignant Heart

We noted above that ordinary wrongdoing by ordinary people needs no special psychological explanation.[56] Varying opportunities, pressures, and constraints account for much of the difference between the straight and the crooked. Because everyone is potentially delinquent, there is an ever-present need for effective socialization and for a web of

56. See Chapter 5, "Sociology and Human Nature."

controls.[57] This everyday experience of temptation and restraint, appetite and channeling, is at best a precarious regulation of pervasive selfishness, harm, and disorder. Work must always be done if a moral order is to be maintained.

This way of thinking does not take us, however, to the evils that give human nature a really bad name. I have in mind crimes marked by cruelty, destructiveness, and extreme indifference to the feelings and interests of victims. Here the main locus of evil is the motivation and disposition of the offender. An "abandoned and malignant heart"[58] accounts for the character of the crime and requires special psychological explanation.

Everyone has lapses of conscience, but for some people conscience is so attenuated as to be virtually inoperative, at least with respect to a range of morally relevant activities and relationships. These people are the so-called psychopaths, sociopaths, or antisocial personalities. The most important underlying condition is *lack of guilt,* the psychic capacity to injure others without remorse. Such individuals may be effectively socialized in respect to language, skills, and personal aspirations. But they have failed to develop appropriate superego controls, to say nothing of nobler aspects of conscience.

Psychopathic personality is a troublesome idea because diagnosis depends so much on assessing the propriety of conduct, thus undermining the apparent objectivity of medical judgment. Equally frustrating to the psychiatrist is the fact that the offender's psychic structure is otherwise intact. Indeed, one clinical profile points to the psychopath's "superficial charm and intelligence," "absence of 'nervousness' or psychoneurotic manifestations," and "absence of delusions and other signs of irrational thinking."[59]

A striking variant of this phenomenon is described by Hannah Arendt in her study of Adolf Eichmann. One of the chief organizers of the Holocaust, Eichmann fled to Argentina several years after the defeat

57. There are of course other reasons socialization and social control are important: they form, sustain, and enrich people's lives. In some circumstances, however, they may also deform, destabilize, and impoverish.

58. This phrase echoes an old concept in Anglo-American law respecting the degree of recklessness and indifference to human life that warrants a charge of murder when the killing is unintentional. Section 188 of the California Penal Code reads in part: "[Malice aforethought] is implicit, when no considerable provocation appears, or when the circumstances attending the killing show an abandoned and malignant heart."

59. Hervey M. Cleckley, *The Mask of Sanity,* 4th ed. (St. Louis: C. V. Mosby Co., 1964), 362f.

of Hitler's Germany. In 1960 he was seized by the Israelis and brought to Jerusalem for trial. Found guilty of crimes "against the Jewish people" and "against humanity," he was executed in 1962.

In oral testimony and written memoirs, Eichmann presented himself as less a Nazi than a Nazi *official*. To be a super-efficient and super-loyal official was his highest aspiration. He was, he thought, preeminently a man of duty. By this he meant not only obeying orders but doing so willingly and zealously. Thus it was that, in a bizarre but revealing comment, he could say "he had lived his whole life according to Kant's moral precepts, and especially according to a Kantian definition of duty."[60]

> This was outrageous, on the face of it . . . since Kant's moral philosophy is so closely bound up with man's faculty of judgment, which rules out blind obedience. [On being questioned, however,] Eichmann came up with an approximately correct definition of the categorical imperative: "I meant by my remark about Kant that the principle of my will must always be such that it can become the principle of general laws." . . . He then proceeded to explain that from the moment he was charged with carrying out the Final Solution he had ceased to live according to Kantian principles. . . . What he failed to point out in court was that in this "period of crimes legalized by the state," as he himself now called it, he had not simply dismissed the Kantian formula as no longer applicable, he had distorted it to read: Act as if the principle of your actions were the same as that of the legislator or of the law of the land—or, in Hans Frank's formulation of "the categorical imperative in the Third Reich," which Eichmann might have known: "Act in such a way that the Führer, if he knew your action, would approve it."[61]

Eichmann was a psychopath of a special sort. He was not entirely lacking in conscience, but his was a pathologically distorted conscience. An elaborate system of rationalizations, made available to him by the culture he inherited, allowed him to participate in brutality and genocide on a massive scale. Eichmann's conception of duty neutralized the immorality of what was being done and distanced him from the experience of his victims. This parody of conscience became part of his character. The capacity to justify any conduct, however evil, so long as it carried the stamp of authority was sustained by psychological dispositions as well as by deeply held convictions. The effect was to

60. Hannah Arendt, *Eichmann in Jerusalem: A Report on the Banality of Evil* (New York: Viking Press, 1963), 120.
61. Ibid., 120f.

insulate him from guilt and thus to permit him to achieve the classic "competence" of the psychopath.[62]

It seems perverse, therefore, to treat Eichmann as representing the "banality of evil." By this phrase Arendt intended to emphasize that the Eichmanns of this world are not driven by hatred, aggression, or a lust to annihilate. She wanted to show that evil people can have commonplace emotions and conventional responses. In this she was amply justified. But there is nothing commonplace, trite, or drearily predictable about Eichmann's psychology or beliefs. The horror was not in the banality of his thought and expression. It lay in his capacity to do great harm without experiencing guilt or remorse.

Because his conscience was grotesquely distorted, it is right to think of Eichmann as a monster. Nevertheless, it should be remembered that his character was in large part shaped by a distinctive cultural, political, military, and bureaucratic milieu. That milieu may not be entirely unique. Consider, for example, the planner and executor of mass destruction in modern warfare. Behind a screen of technical language the fates of thousands, and perhaps millions, are coolly manipulated. For "freedom" or "motherland" no risk is too great, no human cost too high. There is a continuity impossible to ignore between this grim pattern and the Eichmann syndrome. In the right circumstances, where similar justifications and distancing mechanisms are available, almost anyone's conscience can be twisted and deformed. This is the basic truth in Arendt's conception of evil as banal.

▼   ▲   ▼   ▲   ▼

In describing crimes of malevolence we should distinguish pathologies of conscience from pathologies of aggression. A weak or distorted conscience allows self-interest (or a single-minded goal) to be pursued, unfettered by any restraints save self-preservation, narrowly understood. In contrast, emotion-driven efforts to hurt or destroy have independent force and may override an otherwise effective conscience. In either case, the integrity of personality is breached.

The psychopath suffers from a defective conscience; the vicious or violent person is driven by rage, jealousy, desire for vengeance, or sadistic

---

62. Erich Fromm suggests that Heinrich Himmler, a Nazi leader, had similar traits of "inhuman bureaucratic conscientiousness and methodicalness . . . not [those] of a hater or . . . of a monster as the latter is usually conceived, but of an extremely dehumanized bureaucrat" (Erich Fromm, *The Anatomy of Human Destructiveness* [New York: Holt, Rinehart & Winston, 1973], 299).

and masochistic impulses. Both are "antisocial" or "sociopathic." The most virulent evil occurs when the two pathologies are combined, when destructiveness and cruelty are set free and enhanced by lack of guilt or concern for others. But the psychopath is not necessarily vicious or violent. He may be a liar, a swindler, a confidence man. Furthermore, malignant aggression may be accompanied by guilt and followed by remorse. It does not necessarily depend on the absence of conscience or the destruction of conscience. Hence the two pathologies differ in moral significance as well as in psychodynamics. In the case of the psychopath, there is little basis for empathy and excuse, because the attack is on morality itself; without conscience there can be no moral actor. The malignant aggressor, on the other hand, if he is not also psychopathic, is more readily understood and even forgiven.

The Vulnerable Will

The most subtle and insidious form of moral weakness is the disposition to justify evil in the name of the good. The desire for self-justification shows the pull of morality. But the same impulse leads to a profusion of lies, rationalizations, and self-delusions. Tainted as they are, these justifications blur the distinction between what is objectively good and what is merely the claim of passion and interest. Therefore the temptation to take the name of the good in vain has long been considered a grave weakness of the human spirit. In its worst form it is *idolatry,* which breeds both arrogance and self-abasement.

Idolatry is the worship of something contingent and limited—a person, an office, a party, an idea, the self—as if it possessed absolute truth, power, or perfection. In Christian doctrine as interpreted by Niebuhr, idolatry is a pathological response to the tension between freedom and finiteness. Humans are free to choose, within a framework of limits. But because they can discern the possibility of transcending those limits, the stage is set for restless striving, anxious self-scrutiny, and destructive overreaching.

The temptation to escape anxiety has a decisive effect on moral well-being:

> Anxiety, as a permanent concomitant of freedom, is thus both the source of creativity and a temptation to sin. . . . When anxiety has conceived it brings forth both pride and sensuality. Man falls into pride, when he seeks to raise his contingent existence to unconditioned significance; he falls into sensuality, when he seeks to escape from his unlimited possibilities of freedom,

from the perils and responsibilities of self-determination, by immersing himself in a "mutable good," by losing himself in some natural vitality.[63]

Thus the closely connected sins of pride and sensuality can be understood in naturalist, psychological terms. They are, in Freudian language, mechanisms of defense against ego weakness and anxiety. These mechanisms exploit widely present opportunities to yield freedom or to seek absolute dominion.

A theological idiom of temptation and sin is not much appreciated in modern social science. However, the underlying reality does not escape our notice. We have no trouble recognizing a widespread disposition to flee responsibility and embrace absolutes. The most familiar example is unquestioning acceptance of parochial attitudes and perceptions. Not everyone is ethnocentric, or equally so, but it is plausible to postulate that most people most of the time live in a world taken for granted. They do not readily perceive alternative frameworks of belief and action; moreover, they actively resist ideas that, if accepted, would upset the even tenor of their lives.

This servitude of the mind needs no special explanation. It is the natural correlate of routine socialization. To counter it, work must be done in the form of education or the enlargement of experience. The following comment from a study of anti-Semitism in the United States makes the point:

> In common with many other studies, *The Authoritarian Personality* was led astray by asking: Why do people *accept* anti-Semitic beliefs? In a culture that embodies anti-Semitism, no recondite or elaborate theory is required: individuals acquire anti-Semitism through the normal processes of socialization. The more pertinent question is why in such a society some people *reject* anti-Semitic beliefs. Once the question is posed in this way, instead of looking for inner pressures that impel people toward prejudice, one looks for countervailing forces that lead people to renounce it.[64]

In other words, parochial attitudes are held in place by a latent, self-activating energy, the "natural vitality" of group life, which includes all the psychological benefits of participating in a culture and adopting its thoughtways. To lose oneself in that vitality is a constant temptation. Overcoming the temptation requires sustained effort. It may also require at least some sacrifice of social cohesion and personal security.

---

63. Niebuhr, *Nature and Destiny of Man*, 185f.
64. Gertrude (Jaeger) Selznick and Stephen Steinberg, *The Tenacity of Prejudice: Anti-Semitism in Contemporary America* (New York: Harper & Row, 1969), 169; T. W. Adorno et al., *The Authoritarian Personality* (New York: Harper & Brothers, 1950).

Routine socialization inevitably establishes a cultural hegemony. This can be, as we know, benign as well as harmful.[65] A less routine source of overconformity is collective excitement and group pressure. (Emotional contagion in panics, riots, and demonstrations has been widely documented, if not fully understood.) More revealing, perhaps, is the way group pressure can undo the moral competence of highly intelligent and educated people, including leaders and policymakers.

The psychological vulnerability of leaders shows up dramatically in many accounts of policy failures. Stimulated by the Bay of Pigs disaster,[66] Irving L. Janis analyzed this and several other situations in which a high-level advisory group was required to deal with a foreign policy crisis. In a number of cases the process was deeply flawed. The trouble could be traced to subtle pressures and temptations that arise in the course of group participation. The members of these task groups were under pressure to accept a premature definition of the situation; to limit the exploration of alternatives; to go along with a selective reading of the facts; and to yield to the authority of presumed experts. These and other influences diminished their independence and critical objectivity, thereby limiting the competence and rationality of the group:

> Over and beyond all the familiar sources of human error is a powerful source of defective judgment that arises in cohesive groups—the concurrence-seeking tendency, which fosters overoptimism, lack of vigilance, and sloganistic thinking about the weakness and immorality of outgroups. This tendency can take its toll even when the decision-makers are conscientious statesmen trying to make the best possible decisions for their country and for all mankind.[67]

The result is "groupthink"—the "deterioration of mental efficiency, reality testing, and moral judgment that results from in-group pressures."[68]

The lesson is that everyone is potentially vulnerable to the perils of overconformity. Education and high office are not wholly reliable as measures of prevention. They must be supplemented by institutions and practices that take account of the temptation to escape responsibility. To worship the group, or what stands for the group, or what makes for

65. Received frameworks are benign insofar as they provide indispensable starting points for thought. But they are limiting as well; in their own way they too create servitudes of the mind.

66. In April 1961, early in President John F. Kennedy's term, a Central Intelligence Agency project sought to land a brigade of anti-Castro exiles on the southern coast of Cuba.

67. *Victims of Groupthink: A Psychological Study of Foreign Policy Decisions and Fiascos* (Boston: Houghton Mifflin, 1972), 13.

68. Ibid., 9.

group solidarity, is the most common form of idolatry. It is the handiest way of justifying evil in the name of the good.

▼   ▲   ▼   ▲   ▼

The human potential for iniquity is, I have suggested, stronger than the potential for moral achievement. It is easier to yield to temptation and come to ruin than to summon oneself for demanding tasks. And moral development presumes a complex, well-balanced, inherently precarious state of affairs. Therefore in many aspects of personal and social life the initial presumption must be that good intentions will be distracted, diffused, or subverted. It is the business of critical morality to overcome that presumption.

This cursory review of human frailty has explored what may be called an original-sin model, that is, a conception of human nature as morally recalcitrant and potentially demonic.[69] I have sought to make clear that moral *development* finds an inescapable, unwelcome, but challenging counterpoint in moral *regression*. Both belong to human nature, the one as a genuine possibility, the other as a limiting reality. Unless we take both into account, recognizing how they involve each other, we become easy victims of careless optimism or enervating pessimism.

69. This statement should be read in the light of the caution noted above, p. 120f., to avoid attributing to individuals characteristics belonging to populations.

SEVEN

Virtue and Commitment

A recurrent theme in this book has been the intimate connection between moral well-being and social participation. The weaknesses and strengths we attribute to human nature are decisively affected by ways of relating and belonging. Without appropriate social support, moral development is frustrated or distorted; and moral recalcitrance is fostered in some social settings, restrained in others. Therefore the most important aspects of the human condition, viewed in the light of moral experience, are the nature and quality of social participation.[1]

In this chapter and the next, we explore the connection between virtue and relatedness. The underlying issue is: What does it require to be genuinely other-regarding and, at the same time, genuinely self-preserving? A partial answer, I shall argue, is that both ideals are attenuated when virtue is perceived as abstract or rule-bound; they are

---

1. The distinction between "human nature" and the "human condition" is often blurred but is worth retaining. "Human nature" refers to the needs, vulnerabilities, and aspirations that characterize all human populations. The "human condition" is the *setting* within which those characteristics develop or are frustrated. The general features of the human condition, as they interact with human nature, account for the universal or near-universal aspects of group life, including culture and moral ordering.

Of course the *operative* human condition is always specific, always to some extent unique and variable. What kind of moral order will arise in a given context—the level of moral achievement; the prevalence of moral regression—necessarily depends on local circumstances and historical developments. Nevertheless, when we want to *diagnose* that setting and make sense of what has happened, we need to bring to bear what we know about the more general features of human nature and the human condition. These include the exigencies, limits, and opportunities of social participation.

strengthened insofar as organic ties to persons, history, deeds, and nature are created and sustained.

To make this case we first review, very briefly, some relevant ideas in the sociology of participation. These ideas lend support to a subsequent argument for the primacy of particularity in moral experience. The related concepts of integrity and personhood are examined in Chapter 8.

SEGMENTAL AND CORE PARTICIPATION

In sociological analysis, and in moral theory as well, we return again and again to two ways of participating in society and the moral order. The first reflects a need for intimacy and, more fundamentally, for connections that are central to a person's life experience and identity. This we may call *core* participation.

The second principle is based on expediency and takes its name from the human capacity to cooperate with others while maintaining psychological and moral distance. Here participation is *segmental:* only a part or segment of the person's life—and not the core part—is brought to bear. Thus segmental participation is limited, peripheral, and instrumental.[2]

Each mode of participation has something to offer from the standpoint of personality and morality; each has costs. Core participation is a mainstay of psychological strength and a key to moral competence. But it may also limit our horizons, place too great a burden on our emotional resources, and strain our capacity for obligation. Segmental participation eases these burdens and greatly facilitates cooperation with strangers. At the same time it often introduces unwelcome confusion, frustration, and distorted commitment. The two methods of participation, as they compete and interact, give rise to urgent issues of personal satisfaction and moral well-being.

In its most familiar forms, segmental participation presumes *limited obligation*. The clearest example is the modern commercial contract. Ideally, the terms of a contract are specific rather than vague; determinate, not open-ended. What the parties agree to fixes their responsibilities. That is why contract as a legal device is so well adapted to the market economy. Business people know what they are getting into and can calculate their costs. They can preserve the freedom to make flexible decisions in the light of changing economic conditions.

2. See my *The Organizational Weapon* (1952; reprint, Glencoe, Ill.: Free Press, 1960), 286ff. The term "core participation" was suggested by Paul Kecskemeti.

This modern contract of limited commitment may be compared with the "status contract," which had its heyday in feudal times:

> By means of such a contract a person was to become somebody's child, father, wife, brother, master, slave, kin, comrade-in-arms, protector, client, follower, vassal, subject, friend, or, quite generally, comrade. [This was not an agreement for some specific object. Rather, the contract] meant that the person would "become" something different in quality (or status) from the quality he possessed before.[3]

Here what is agreed to is the establishment of a continuing relationship that affects the total legal situation of the individual. The status contract is voluntary at its inception, but once the act of adherence occurs the relationship is governed by preexisting rules or by the authority of a dominant partner. For each participant a status is generated or confirmed; and the status, not the terms of the agreement, defines their obligations. Furthermore, the contemplated relationship commits the parties as persons, in respect to their salient identities, not as suppliers of specific resources or activities.

The best-known example of a status contract is the exchange of marriage vows. In Western societies marriage is based on mutual and voluntary consent, but after the ceremony law and tradition determine a broad range of rights and duties. In recent years easy divorce, an egalitarian ethos, and a greater variety of family arrangements have made it plausible to conceive of marriage as a contract definite in its terms.[4] But the importance of trust and intimacy as well as the hope for continuity through changing circumstances create an ineradicable tension between the idea of marriage and the idea of contract in its modern form.

A similar tension occurs in the experience of group membership. People belong to organizations in very different ways. At one extreme are members who give almost no attention or energy to the group's affairs. They may have little invested beyond the cost of a subscription, a donation, or a few shares of stock. This narrowly segmental participation makes possible the "Michels effect" (discussed in Chapter 9), including self-perpetuating management in large corporations. The limited commitment (and limited liability, in the case of shareholders) of such members makes them passive participants in a formally democratic association. They lack incentive for effective choice, monitoring, and

---

3. Max Weber, *Max Weber on Law in Economy and Society*, trans. Edward Shils and Max Rheinstein (Cambridge: Harvard University Press, 1954), 106.
4. See Lenore J. Weitzman, *The Marriage Contract* (New York: Free Press, 1981).

replacement of management. When things go wrong the most convenient and most sensible option for such participants is usually to withdraw rather than fight, to choose "exit" rather than "voice."[5]

This state of affairs is not necessarily troublesome if the association is simply a marketing device. The product may include the services of a headquarters staff (hence the apparent need for an imagery of association) such as that of an automobile club, an association of retired persons, or a special-issue political cause; or it may be the opportunity to earn dividends and increase capital. Self-perpetuating management does not matter much if the member/consumers can easily vote with their feet, whether because they do not really need the product or because they have alternative ways of getting it. The staff is in effect an entrepreneurial group bidding for a market share.

Difficulties arise, however, when the member, client, or employee depends on the organization, or when the enterprise is best served by continuity of participation, strong commitment, and concern for its well-being. When there is full freedom of movement from one organization to another, the cost to the individual may not be great. But freedom of choice and movement can hardly be taken for granted. Many, if not most, people have strong ties to their jobs; and so-called voluntary associations may control access to employment and other opportunities. Members of a trade union may dislike attending meetings or taking responsibility for union affairs, but they have a substantial stake in what the leadership does, and their opportunity to "exit" is very limited.

From the standpoint of the group or enterprise, limited commitment is costly when members are valued as human resources. There is constant tension between maintaining a posture of limited commitment—being able to dismiss an employee "at will," for example—and doing what is necessary to gain high levels of initiative, discipline, competence, and energy. The cost is also plain when, in response to a hostile takeover bid, shareholders gladly sell their stock to a high bidder, with little concern for the fate of the enterprise.[6]

Segmental participation does have moral worth, especially in protecting people against inappropriate or premature commitments.[7] A

5. Albert O. Hirschman, *Exit, Voice, and Loyalty: Responses to Decline in Firms, Organization, and States* (Cambridge: Harvard University Press, 1970).

6. The costs of "exit," and especially the way "the exit alternative can . . . *atrophy the development of the art of voice*" are discussed in Hirschman, *Exit, Voice, and Loyalty*, 43ff.

7. A poignant example of premature commitment is familiar to many who in their youth embraced sectarian political or religious doctrines. There is tragedy in the story of

popular book of the 1950s made much of the greedy organization—greedy, that is, for wholehearted involvement and loyalty.[8] It was argued that individuals should avoid giving too much of themselves to the large organization, and especially to the benevolent, soul-suffocating business enterprise. People can preserve their freedom only through a measure of alienation:

> He must *fight* The Organization. Not stupidly, or selfishly, for the defects of individual self-regard are no more to be venerated than the defects of cooperation. But fight he must, for the demands for his surrender are constant and powerful, and the more he has come to like the life of organization the more difficult does he find it to resist these demands, or even to recognize them.[9]

Similarly, Clark Kerr, then president of the University of California, argued that associations of limited function, correspondingly restrained in the demands they make upon the individual, are most congenial to a free society. "The organization which seeks to encompass the totality of the life of the individual can subject him to its control as no limited-function organization can. An organization with limited functions and limited rules can require only limited commitments from its participants."[10] The point—up to a point—remains well taken.

These words in praise of limited commitment are based on a presumption of available wholeness and autonomy. It is taken for granted that well-socialized persons, sustained by their nuclear families and by networks of kinship and friendship, do not need to find psychological sustenance in less intimate, more impersonal settings. So long as person-centered experience is intact and available—and so long as expectations are held in check—the "real world" of system, rationality, and power need not be experienced as alienating or oppressive. The prescription is: look for nurture in a proper place.

---

young persons in their late teens who make sincere, naive, and full commitments, but not long after, having learned a bit more, must break away. In many cases the break cannot be a simple withdrawal or change of affiliation. Because identity, loyalty, and self-regard are at stake, the break is often heavily burdened by reproaches (including self-reproaches) of "apostasy," "betrayal," and "turncoat." Much the same may be said, of course, regarding a premature marriage.

8. William H. Whyte, Jr., *The Organization Man* (New York: Simon & Schuster, 1956). See also Lewis A. Coser, *Greedy Institutions: Patterns of Undivided Commitment* (New York: Free Press, 1974).

9. Whyte, *The Organization Man*, 404.

10. Clark Kerr, "Individual Rights in an 'Organizational Society,'" address to the Los Angeles Bar Association, 28 May 1959. Mimeographed.

Some clues to understanding the psychology of segmental participation can be found in the theory of "mass society."[11] A major theme of that theory is the way social participation is transformed by (1) the attenuation of primordial human bonds, especially ties of kinship, locality, occupation, ethnicity, and religion; and (2) the vast proliferation and commanding presence of impersonal settings. These master trends are driven by urbanization, industrialization, and technological development.

Thus mass society brings with it hierarchy as well as leveling, control as well as loosening. The same master trends that have unraveled the social fabric and destabilized human relations have also produced centralized power and bureaucratic organization. Mass society builds as it destroys, but it builds on a new basis and with new materials. It succeeds because it can harness human energies through formal systems of mobilization and coordination. These new systems are wholly compatible with segmental participation and with the undoing of more spontaneous, more person-centered, more communitarian relationships.[12]

The distinguishing feature of mass society is not the size or density of a population but the quality of participation. Where a dense population is accompanied by a corresponding density of social texture and relatedness, as in traditional India and China, the concept of mass society has limited relevance. "Mass" connotes a loosely bound aggregate of relatively homogeneous units. The texture of human relations is thinned as more and more people become rootless, detached, mobile. Connections to other persons, to sustaining ideas, and to clear self-conceptions weaken and fluctuate. And modern society has a homogenizing effect; diversity tends to be superficial, transitory, and faddish. The outcome is that people in a mass society are, relatively speaking, and from a psychological point of view, *uncommitted*.

In such a setting, where the quality of human relatedness is at stake, limited commitment loses its innocence. It cannot be understood as a ra-

11. For an overview see William Kornhauser, "Mass Society," *International Encyclopedia of the Social Sciences* 10 (1968): 58–64.
12. Which are, of course, unlikely to be egalitarian. A similar paradox sometimes obscures the distinction between specialization and social differentiation. Mass society tends to make people alike; for example, by erasing traditional way-of-life differences among occupations, localities, and ethnic groups. Where these differences persist they become anachronisms, or trivial, or reflect special employment circumstances, as in police work or mining. At the same time, specialization proceeds apace, as is reflected in the vastly increased number of occupational titles within every industry and profession. But specialization is not the same as social differentiation proper, which creates and sustains subcultures, that is, distinctive styles, outlooks, expectations, and destinies. Modern society weakens social differentiation even as it increases specialization.

tional strategy for allocating scarce energies and resources or as a way of protecting personal coherence and well-being. When it takes the form of psychic distance or disengaged emotion and, at the same time, invades the precincts of person-centered experience, limited commitment gives rise to inauthentic feelings which impoverish or distort relationships. A familiar, if extreme, example is the psychic cost of sexual promiscuity, gamesmanship, and exploitation. Because personal commitment is weak or absent, emotions—one's own as well as another's—can be manipulated.

Indeed, manipulation is a hallmark of segmental participation in its psychological aspect. When people relate to one another on a wholly symbolic level, perhaps as followers of a leader, or as a mass audience, or as participants in a crowd, they do not bring to bear the restraints implicit in concrete personalities and life-situations. As interaction becomes one-dimensional, psychological immune systems break down. Emotions, perceptions, beliefs, and understandings are detached from social frameworks of meaning and experience. Packaged and stereotyped, they become available as commodities and as devices for mass manipulation. People become vulnerable to the play of uncritical judgment and are readily swayed by fantasy and illusion, managed communication, and collective excitement.

There is a subtle connection between being selectively committed psychologically and being available for "total" mobilization and involvement. Anyone driven by a single passion—anger, lust, envy, pride, greed—may well be drawn into a total, though self-destructive, commitment. People caught up in collective excitement, who are responding only on the basis of selected emotions, may nonetheless be wholly absorbed by the situation. Much the same may be said of those who embrace a tight ideology and respond with unlimited commitment to the appeal of abstract ideas or slogans. Thus in the psychology of collective behavior, including social movements, "total" and "segmental" participation are not necessarily antithetical. On the contrary, one is often a reflex of the other.

▼   ▲   ▼   ▲   ▼

The perspective just outlined leads to the conclusion that segmental participation, whether contractual or psychological, is more likely to undermine moral competence than to enrich it. In both forms it *weakens personal responsibility*. A contractual relationship (including narrowly defined group membership) may leave individual rationality and self-control untouched, but it abridges obligation and insulates large areas of human activity from moral concern.[13] In its emotional form, of course, the potential of segmental participation for ungoverned conduct is more direct and more apparent.

The alternative is not total involvement or commitment, for that may be a sign of compulsive, impulse-driven, manipulated behavior. Rather, *core* participation is the social and psychological foundation of moral competence. The name may be unfamiliar, but the idea is well grounded in the findings of sociology, especially in the theory of primary relations. The latter does not capture the full meaning and significance of core participation, but it bears closely on what I have in mind and is worth reviewing briefly.

In the language of sociology, primary groups are intimate associations that do the main work of socialization and from which, throughout life, we derive nurture and support. Families are the chief example, but other groups have similar functions. Some are enduring, others are transitory. All vary considerably in how *closely* they approximate the ideal; all build upon and draw upon the resources of intimate association.

The most important features of the primary relation, as they bear on moral well-being, may be summarized as follows.[14]

Response is to whole persons rather than to segments. The participants interact as unique and integrated persons. The closer we come to the primary-relations model, the more attention we give to the special characteristics of each person. Wholeness means (1) that one takes account of many aspects of another's personality, background, and behavior; and (2) that one responds spontaneously and freely, as a unified self, permitting feelings to color judgment.[15] Thus the primary relation is a paradigm of person-centered experience and is most fully realized in love and friendship.

Each participant is perceived as having intrinsic worth. This worth derives from the particularity of selfhood and relatedness. It is fundamentally

13. This is not to deny the important contributions of contract law and practice to the release of social energies—by facilitating transactions and combinations of all sorts—and to furthering values of freedom, equality, and self-government. Nevertheless, the principle of limited commitment is a poor foundation for moral ordering.
14. The comments that follow recast the discussion in Leonard Broom and Philip Selznick, *Sociology: A Text with Adapted Readings,* 5th ed. (New York: Harper & Row, 1973), 132ff.
15. Note that judicial or administrative decisions that try to be individuated, that is, to take account of special circumstances and the person's particular needs or characteristics fulfill criterion (1) but not (2).

ascriptive. What counts is who you are, where you belong, and what you are as a unique person, not what you can do or accomplish or what you are generically, say, as a rational being. Ideally, people feel accepted and wanted for themselves. They do not need to be on guard, or prove themselves, or appeal to their "rights."

Communication is open and founded on trust. Without a free flow of thoughts and emotions—without relatively full disclosure—spontaneous, whole-person interaction founders. The main obstacle is lack of trust. Being trustful means being open to influence, and influence in depth. When that occurs, interaction is enriched and solidarity is reinforced.

Obligation is mutual, diffuse, and open-ended. A norm of limited commitment is alien to the spirit of the primary relation. Obligation adheres to the person and to the relationship, not to the terms of an agreement. If the needs of the individuals are paramount, the responsibility each has for the other cannot be neatly bounded or closely specified. This principle shows that the primary relation cannot be identified with *every* intimate association and person-to-person interaction. The presence or absence of commitment must always be considered. Hence "encounter groups" often make a poor substitute for genuine primary relations.

There is a sense of belonging together and sharing a common identity. As Charles Horton Cooley put it:

> The result of intimate association, psychologically, is a certain fusion of individualities in a common whole, so that one's very self, for many purposes at least, is the common life and purpose of the group. Perhaps the simplest way of describing this wholeness is by saying that it is a "we"; it involves the sort of sympathy and mutual identification for which "we" is the natural expression.[16]

This emphasis on "weness" and solidarity must be qualified. Primary relations usually entail a positive valuing of the group, but it does not follow that affection and cordiality invariably prevail. The primary relation can be a cauldron within which resentments simmer and hostilities erupt.

Personal development, security, and satisfaction are paramount. Primary relations within a household, business, or military organization may be effective instruments for enhancing cohesion and morale.[17] This occurs,

---

16. *Social Organization* (New York: Scribner's, 1909), 23.
17. This presumes effective articulation of primary-group interests with the larger organization or community. When that is lacking, the effect may be to undermine rather than support cohesion.

however, only insofar as personal needs are served. Because of what the primary group can do, it is the characteristic agency of socialization. Wherever there is an effort to influence persons deeply, at whatever age, in whatever setting, primary relations are encouraged and exploited. The price of such influence, through such means, is a corresponding commitment to the person.

▼   ▲   ▼   ▲   ▼

The sociological model summarized above is both descriptive and normative. It is descriptive in that it identifies a set of empirical generalizations—varying patterns of response, need, satisfaction, perception, communication, and obligation—that are readily observable and everywhere characterize primary-group experience. At the same time, each element of the model describes *a strain toward* an ideal pattern of interaction, obligation, or belonging. When we examine the strains or immanent tendencies we can see that a condition of healthy relatedness is the end-state or *telos* toward which those impulses are directed; that person-centered participation is an implicit moral ideal; and that the ideal must be reasonably closely approximated if the promise of the primary relation, as a path to personal and social well-being, is to be fulfilled.

Thus the model should be understood as a diagnostic tool. The ideals it brings to bear are discovered by studying the adaptive, problem-solving experience of the participants; they are not, or should not be, the imposed or arbitrary preferences of the analyst. And of course diagnosis presumes variation, incompleteness, and disorder. In real life primary relations are subject to many conflicting pressures and temptations; they are vulnerable to the destructive effects of openly expressed feelings and emotional demands; and much in the dynamics of interaction may inhibit communication, stunt growth, and impoverish obligation. There is no question of idealizing primary relations *as we find them*. The point is, rather, to understand, from the standpoint of the participants, what benefits are at stake and what conditions will foster or frustrate their achievement.

Primary relations temper and mediate participation in the larger society. The primary group is both a bridge and a refuge. In all societies, families and peer groups are the main agencies of socialization and the main avenues to participation in a wider world of education, work, religion, and community. At the same time, bonds of kin and friendship buffer the demands and mitigate the indifference of strangers. The primary group serves society by inculcating and sustaining motivations and disciplines. As it does so, however, it takes into account the person's special needs and intrinsic worth.

This tempering and mediating function is the key to core participation. When impersonal activities are divorced from the basic satisfactions, meanings, and commitments established in primary relations, they are experienced as fragile and frustrating. By contrast, when such activities are sustained by ties of affection and mutual responsibility, the integrity of persons is more easily preserved. People are then less readily available for exploitation, or for self-destructive mobilization and manipulation.

In today's mass society, core participation in its classic form is bound to weaken. People are absorbed directly, as mobile, separated, interchangeable individuals, into a world of symbols dominated by mass communication; and into the large organizations that manage work, politics, education, and leisure. Segmental participation is the order of the day—a price many millions pay for the material benefits of modern life.

Nevertheless, the ideal of core participation remains hardy and relevant. The family-based form may fade empirically, but it remains a paradigm of moral competence and self-preserving participation. As such, it is a guide to the proper organization of more distant, more impersonal, more task-oriented settings. The sociological lesson is not that the clock must be turned back. It is, rather, that we must now more frequently acquire by sensitive design what once could be taken for granted.

THE PRIMACY OF THE PARTICULAR

The concept of core participation speaks to the need for a stabilizing center in human life. For such a center to exist, there must be psychic autonomy *within a framework of bonding* to other persons and to person-centered activities, and all this must form part of an integral self. Such a self is not free-floating: it emerges from and is sustained by specific personal relationships. Only in and through such bonds will the center hold.

This rich but parochial bonding—this particularity of association and symbolism—is a striking feature of the human condition. But what is its moral worth? The question brings us to a persistent ambivalence in both moral theory and moral experience. This is revealed in the competition between two basic forms of altruism: particularism and universalism.

Particularism is *bounded* altruism. It is an ethic of commitment to individuals who matter because of the special connections they have, not because of their general characteristics, whether as humans, children, voters, or consumers. The "other" to be regarded, for whom self-sacrifice is appropriate, belongs to one's own family or community. A classic expression of particularism is nepotism—hiring or doing business with relatives, friends, or other in-group members in preference to outsiders. A religion is particularist insofar as it is committed to maintaining the distinctive identity of a sacred community or "chosen" people.

Universalism is *inclusive* altruism. In defining objects of moral concern, the special interests of persons and groups are set aside. An impersonal standpoint becomes a prime virtue. People are classified according to such objective criteria as age, need, talent, or achievement, in the light of general policies or purposes, without considering the special claims of kinship or group affiliation. This is the morality of fairness, the familiar logic of the "rule of law."

Bounded and inclusive altruism are both responses to biosocial imperatives and opportunities. Neither is, in its beginnings, a product of self-conscious choice. People do what is satisfying and convenient in their circumstances. As a result, over many generations, each form of altruism contributes to the evolution of moral ordering.

Of the two, particularism is the more secure and the more primordial. Parents often abuse, abandon, and even kill their children, to say nothing of how they treat their siblings or more distant relatives. Nevertheless, the biological bond, in humans as in other mammals, is a dependable source of motivation. (Just who will be considered a close relative, or ignored as kin altogether, is a matter of social definition; but all kinship systems are keyed to biological affinity.) However, particularism does not *require* biological bonding. Identification with an in-group is a powerful impulse readily accounted for by the psychic sustenance it offers and the social power it yields. It may be said, indeed, that particularism is overdetermined, the product of many parallel and convergent causes, any one of which might be sufficient to sustain a fairly high level of commitment to kin, locality, and primordial community.

Universalism is more precarious—and more distinctively human. The impersonal standpoint is an outgrowth of (l) the capacity to reason and (2) the experience of cooperation and reciprocity. The ability to reason creates demands (from oneself as well as from others) for consistency and justification.[18] These demands become salient features of human interaction. As a result, moral argument pervades everyday life. It is everywhere an important part of the symbolic order we call culture.

When people are pressed to justify a claim and cannot close the discussion by resort to violence or by terminating the relationship, they are likely to appeal to comprehensive interests and shared expectations:

> When they are wronged, people suddenly understand objective reasons, for they require such concepts to press their resentment. That is why the primary form of moral argument is a request to imagine oneself in the situation of another person.[19]

Little is really known about the natural history of justification, but we know enough to say that, in the normal course of interaction, people very often feel compelled to offer reasons that transcend their private interests.

Particularism and universalism are usefully understood as polar contrasts, that is, as very disparate and even incompatible ways of relating to oneself and to others.[20] They define different moralities and perhaps different ways of life. Universalism fits well with achievement-centered values and with instrumental rather than expressive modes of thought and action. Particularism is the characteristic ethos of a traditional society: what counts is who you are, not what you can do or what purpose you serve.

Nevertheless, the two moralities coexist as well as compete. That is so in part because universalism is a natural accompaniment to the formation of communities. As opportunities for cooperation are enlarged and their benefits perceived, the application of altruism is no longer limited to a small band of close relatives. Particularism is diluted as the community expands. More and more people are recognized, first as fellow-creatures and then as colleagues or members of the same in-group. In the modern nation-state the particularist connotations of "citizen," though far from lost, are greatly attenuated. The experience of

18. See Peter Singer, *The Expanding Circle: Ethics and Sociobiology* (New York: Farrar, Straus, & Giroux, 1981), chap. 4.

19. Thomas Nagel, *The Possibility of Altruism* (Princeton: Princeton University Press, 1970), 145.

20. Universalism/particularism is one of the "pattern variables" introduced by Parsons and Shils (Talcott Parsons and Edward A. Shils, eds., *Toward a General Theory of Action: Theoretical Foundations for the Social Sciences* [New York: Harper Torchbooks, 1951], 76–91) and Parsons (Talcott Parsons, *The Social System* [Glencoe, Ill.: Free Press, 1951], 45–67). Others include ascription/achievement, instrumental/expressive, specificity/diffuseness. These contrasts have long been familiar in sociology, as implicit in the theory of *Gemeinschaft* and *Gesellschaft*. (See Chapter 13, "The Sociology of Community.")

citizenship encourages larger perspectives and undercuts primordial ties of family, tribe, religion, and locality. Patriotism and nationalism remain, however, as benign and virulent expressions of the particularist impulse.

A mix of both perspectives is guaranteed by the ordinary demands of group life. The ethos of particularism may be paramount in the family and in many communal groups, but it can never wholly satisfy the psychic needs of members or the requirements of effective social organization. In the division of labor and allocation of resources, conceptions of fairness are bound to arise even where primary bonding is strong; criteria of merit and achievement are too useful to be dispensed with altogether; rules and principles are framed because people expect consistency and demand justifications.

The moral worth of universalism has long been appreciated. The transition from kinship to *polis,* from the "significant other" to the "generalized other," from the "we" of affinity to the "we" of humanity—all are expressions of a quest for community *that looks outward rather than inward.* A crucial step is the embrace of strangers. When strangers are treated with the respect due members of an enlarged community, a moral watershed is reached. Every source of estrangement, of being divided from another part of humanity, is alien to the outward-looking aspect of community.

Furthermore, universalism is indispensable to critical or reflective morality. To assess a received morality, objective criteria of judgment are required. Without an ethic that transcends the personal and the parochial—without detachment, without a regime of rules—even conventional morality cannot justly be applied to competing claims and special circumstances. Insofar as justice matters, an impersonal standpoint must prevail.

There is indeed a splendid array of distinctively universalist virtues. These include fidelity to principle; intellectual honesty; impartiality; tolerance; having the courage of one's convictions. The job of a judge obviously demands universalism, and many other roles at least intermittently include responsibility for general precepts, purposes, and ideals. When the task at hand is to protect, elaborate, or implement standards or other guides to conduct, rather than to achieve concrete ends, a special moral competence is required. It is one thing to uphold high standards in industry, law, or education; it is something else to turn out a product, win a case, or raise a child.

And yet, despite these strong claims, the impersonal standpoint is not and cannot be embraced wholeheartedly. Judgment in the light of rule and principle has serious limitations from a moral point of view. That is so, fundamentally, because rule-centered judgment does not adequately appreciate the place of concreteness and particularity in moral experience. This criticism has existentialist overtones, as we have seen, but many who are not existentialists have had the same insight.

"There is no general doctrine," wrote George Eliot in *Middlemarch*, "which is not capable of eating out our morality if unchecked by the deep-seated habit of direct fellow-feeling with individual fellow-men."[21] This comment was stimulated by the author's account of one man's effort to find, in the cunning of Providence, a godly justification for his worldly transgressions. The lesson is that impersonal precepts must be tempered and assessed in the light of very specific human outcomes.

A contemporary moral and legal philosopher makes a similar point:

> [I]t is plain that those most likely to abandon their moral beliefs when these are shown to have a subjective source are those whose moral sentiments have been formulated apart from concrete situations and kinds of conduct, and have become focused on general principles and theories or on the divine will or on whatever is taken to be a general authoritative source of all moral right and wrong. . . . Conversely, those whose moral education or self-education has not led them into this mode of moral thinking and who find their moral reasons at the ground-floor level of particular concrete situations are least likely to be disturbed by the revelation that their moral practices, and the feeling of constraint and necessity that accompanies them, are reflections of concerns which lie deep in their character.[22]

Here again an empirical argument—an appeal to experience—purports to show that morality anchored in concrete situations and in character has greater depth and durability than one that looks to general principles and theories. A morality based on abstract ideals, and on the arguments that support them, is vulnerable to the challenge of fresh insights, new arguments, and revised convictions. If there are no surer touchstones for belief and conduct, morality easily becomes a sometime thing, superficial and transitory, and may readily be used, in systematic ways, to justify evil in the name of the good.

Even in a system of justice, rules and principles are not ends in themselves; they do not have intrinsic worth. They are judged according to the contribution they make to *substantive* justice, which is the ultimate

21. George Eliot, *Middlemarch: A Study of Provincial Life* (1872; reprint, New York: New American Library, 1964), 601.

22. H. L. A. Hart, "Who Can Tell Right from Wrong?" *New York Review of Books*, 17 July 1986, 52.

criterion. Substantive justice is concrete, not abstract. It is fairness made good for particular litigants, taking all their circumstances into account. It is the just *outcome,* not the fair procedure.

In legal reasoning the search for a principle—reaching beyond a specific rule to some more general formula—is not an academic exercise or even mainly a quest for consistency. It has the practical aim of cutting through the rigidity of rules *the better to take account of particularity and concreteness.* We discover principles, in the first instance, by looking for the reason behind a rule. When we know the purposes or policies the rule is meant to serve—when we know why, for example, students are required to take a certain number of courses in science and the humanities; or why a building permit is required for a remodeling project—we have a basis for making rational adjustments and exceptions.[23]

A well-known paradox calls attention to the fact that as a community we may care more about the suffering of a few persons whose fate we confront directly than about many thousands for whom we may be more distantly responsible:

> People who would be horrified by the idea of stealing an elderly neighbor's welfare check have no qualms about cheating on their income tax; men who would never punch a child in the face can drop bombs on hundreds of children; our government—with our support—is more likely to spend millions of dollars attempting to rescue a trapped miner than it is to use the same amount to install traffic signals which would, over the years, save many more lives. Even Mother Teresa, whose work for the destitute of Calcutta seems to exemplify so universal a love for all, has described her love for others as love for each of a succession of individuals, rather than "love of mankind, merely as such."[24]

If rationality is understood as a sharply focused calculus of costs and benefits or of equally regarded preferences, then the most rational approach would be, as Peter Singer suggests, "to save as many lives as possible, irrespective of whether we do it by reducing the road toll or by saving specific, identifiable lives; and we would be no readier to kill children from great heights than face to face."[25]

But morality based on reason need not accept this rationalist premise. A different criterion is the effect of our choices on the construction of moral character, individual as well as social. From that standpoint it makes sense to hold on to the concreteness of persons and "direct fellow-feeling" rather than risk attenuating that feeling by transforming

23. On legal rules and principles, see Chapter 15, "From Law to Justice."
24. Singer, *Expanding Circle,* 157.
25. Ibid.

everyone into abstract individuals. An important moral distinction must be drawn between an impersonal crime, such as some forms of embezzlement, and the more personal assaults and intrusions of burglary and robbery, even though the former may have greater consequences for the lives of the people affected. Similarly, there is an important moral difference between a government's failure to install traffic signals, which might decrease injuries and deaths, and its failure to respond when specific people are in distress. The consequences of the policy decision may be remote, contingent, and in part bound up with the responsibility of individuals for their own safety; there may be justifiable trade-offs in the use of resources. But palpable distress is a direct challenge to commitment and character.[26]

It is tempting to say that universalism has the greater claim to moral worth (1) because it is so closely bound up with human rationality, which is the receptacle of so many hopes for betterment; and (2) because in principle it may draw the boundaries of moral equality wide enough to include all humans and potentially other animals as well. But universalism need not go beyond *baseline* protection of all who are included as objects of moral consideration. Taken alone, therefore, it may serve only as an ethical minimum, much as "equal protection of the laws," itself an expression of universalism, defines minimal constitutional safeguards.[27]

Being impartial has undoubted worth if only because it shows respect for interests not our own. But respect is not the whole of morality. As Ronald Dworkin and others have emphasized, there is also *concern* or *caring*, which presumes a desire to further the interests of others, to make them whole if need be—not merely to give them the consideration they deserve as moral equals. An impersonal standpoint may lead to moral probity but not necessarily to moral enrichment. Only a context of commitment, in which the unique person really matters,[28] generates full concern for the well-being of others. The idea of morality is impoverished when it is reduced to disinterestedness.

The alternative is to recognize the moral primacy of love over justice; over rationality; over any other abstract or judgmental way of deciding

26. Therefore our aim should be to reduce the psychic distance between those who inflict harm, for whatever reason, and their victims. See Charles Fried, *Right and Wrong* (Cambridge: Harvard University Press, 1978), chap. 2.
27. See Chapter 16, "Moral and Social Equality."
28. This does not mean that only what is unique to that person matters, rather than what is shared with other persons. But in the process of attending to someone's needs, which may be similar to other people's needs, the person is treated as a distinctive bearer of intrinsic worth. See Lawrence A. Blum, *Friendship, Altruism and Morality* (London: Routledge & Kegan Paul, 1980), 95.

and relating. In love the claims of particularity are paramount. One does not truly love others without caring for specific persons for their own sake. That is so not only in ordinary human relations but in the more subtle and demanding ideal of "neighborly love":

> Christian love does not mean discovering the essentially human underneath differences; it means detecting the neighbor underneath friendliness or hostility or any other qualities in which the agent takes special interest. The full particularity of neighborly love . . . should not be reduced to universal brotherhood or the cosmopolitan spirit. This is stoicism, not Christianity. . . . Love for men in general often means merely a bifocal "self-regarding concern for others," a selfish sociability, while love for neighbor *for his own sake* insists upon a single-minded orientation . . . toward *this* individual neighbor with all his concrete needs. Christian love . . . begins by loving "the neighbor," not mankind or manhood.[29]

Thus understood, neighborly love cuts through abstractions, well-intended or otherwise, to discover and embrace the person as a vividly realized organic unity. A poignant example is George Orwell's encounter with a Fascist soldier during the Spanish Civil War:

> Early one morning another man and I had gone out to snipe at the Fascists in the trenches outside Huesca. . . . At this moment, a man . . . jumped out of the trench and ran along the top of the parapet in full view. He was half-dressed and was holding up his trousers with both hands as he ran. I refrained from shooting him. It is true that I am a poor shot and also that I was thinking chiefly about getting back to our trench. . . . Still, I did not shoot him partly because of that detail about the trousers. I had come here to shoot at "Fascists"; but a man who is holding up his trousers isn't a "Fascist," he is visibly a fellow-creature, similar to yourself, and you don't feel like shooting at him.[30]

This anecdote, said the author, proves "nothing very much, because it is the kind of thing that happens all the time in all wars."[31] On the contrary, George Orwell's stayed hand is the stuff of which legends are made. It is testimony to his own humanity and to the resilience of neighborly love even under conditions of deprivation, hostility, and stress.

The primacy of the particular, from a moral point of view, derives from what it means to be—and what it takes to be—genuinely other-regarding. If the other is an abstraction, a unit within a category, as must

---

29. Paul Ramsey, "Love and Law," in Charles W. Kegley and Robert W. Bretall, eds., *Reinhold Niebuhr: His Religious, Social, and Political Thought* (New York: Macmillan, 1956), 94f.
30. *Homage to Catalonia* (1938; reprint, London: Penguin Books, 1974), 230f.
31. Ibid., 231.

be true for many purposes, other-regarding conduct loses direction, strength, and clarity. In welfare programs for the poor, in education, in schemes for protection of the environment, in medicine, in the administration of justice, the more impersonal the program or procedure the more chance there is that the true object of moral concern may be poorly served or even lost from view. To be effectively other-regarding we must, at some crucial point, where the fate of persons is decided, directly perceive and appreciate them. Only where love plays a part can justice, administration, and professionalism attain their highest potential as moral activities.[32]

The ideal of "particularity"—so important in neighborly love and its institutional offspring, substantive justice—should not be equated with the ethos of "particularism," explained above. If prosecutors, judges, and juries are to provide substantive justice, they must take account of concrete persons and circumstances. No continuing relationship is presumed, however, and none is formed. The officials do not have personal ties to the defendants nor, for the most part, are they responsible for them beyond the disposition of the case.

So too with the ideal of neighborly love. The individual human being, not the mass of humanity, is the preferred object of moral concern. But a particularist connection, on the model of family or friendship, is not necessarily contemplated. The ideal is to love *every* human *as a neighbor,* not to differentiate or discriminate among them. Therefore the claims of particularism, though they overlap with those of particularity, must be examined on their merits.[33]

THE IMPLICATED SELF

Consider the case of Mrs. Jellyby, a notorious character in Charles Dickens' novel *Bleak House.* Mrs. Jellyby practiced what Dickens called "telescopic philanthropy." She was indifferent to the chaos in her household and to the welfare of her husband and children. All her philan-

32. That universalism is a weaker form of morality than particularity is shown by the criticisms that can be made of decisions that sacrifice persons to the needs of a process or system of rules. See John T. Noonan, Jr., *Persons and Masks of the Law* (New York: Farrar, Straus & Giroux, 1976), xii, 18, 167.

33. The distinction between particularity and particularism is similar to a distinction that may be drawn between universality and universalizability on the one hand and universalism on the other. The ethos of universalism, or inclusive altruism, pushes outward the bounds of community, expands obligation, and celebrates the impersonal standpoint. How widespread or universal that ethos is and whether it is universalizable in a Kantian sense are questions that may be raised about the ethos. The same questions may be put to the ethos of particularism.

thropic energies were directed to furthering the prosperity of an African people who lived on the left bank of the Niger. Mrs. Jellyby is described as "a pretty, very diminutive, plump woman . . . with handsome eyes, though they had a curious habit of seeming to look a long way off. As if . . . they could see nothing nearer than Africa."[34]

Telescopic philanthropy is still philanthropy, which is much better than nothing from a moral point of view, and can often be justified. But charity begins at home. As a general rule we doubt the authenticity of sentiments that slight the interests of those in whom one's own life is directly involved. Mrs. Jellyby is a comic figure in the novel, an object of skepticism and scorn. That would not be the case if she were devoted to her family's health and comfort at the cost of neglecting her African friends. She seems to have her priorities wrong.

If there are special obligations of the kind we might attribute to Mrs. Jellyby, what is their source and justification? According to David Hume, "we are naturally very limited in our kindness and affection."[35]

> Now it appears, that in the original frame of our mind, our strongest attention is confin'd to ourselves; our next is extended to our relations and acquaintance; and 'tis only the weakest which reaches to strangers and indifferent persons. . . . From all which it follows, that our natural uncultivated ideas of morality, instead of providing a remedy for the partiality of our affections, do rather conform themselves to that partiality, and give it an additional force and influence.[36]

Our "natural uncultivated ideas of morality" are entitled to respect. But they are not self-justifying. For one thing, it is clear, as Hume observed, that even our "common judgements" will "blame a person who either centers all his affections in his family, or is so regardless of them . . . as to give the preference to a stranger, or mere chance acquaintance."[37] Thus uncultivated, unreflective morality is itself a resource for restraining partiality and extending affection to strangers. In striking the balance we implicitly recognize that particularism's claim to represent "natural virtue" must be scrutinized and assessed.

Robert E. Goodin has argued that "the most coherent theory available to explain our special responsibilities to family, friends, and so on also implies that we must give far more consideration than particularists

34. Charles Dickens, *Bleak House* (1853; reprint, Harmondsworth: Penguin Books, 1971), 85.

35. *A Treatise of Human Nature,* ed. L. A. Selby-Bigge (1740; reprint, Oxford: Clarendon Press, 1955), 519.

36. Ibid., 488f.

37. Ibid.

allow to at least certain classes of strangers."[38] In other words, revealing the true grounds of special obligation will lead to a more generous view of what they entail.

According to Goodin, special obligations are both explained and justified by the vulnerabilities and dependencies we create:

> What is crucial, in my view, is that others are depending upon us. They are particularly vulnerable to our actions and choices. That, I argue, is the true source of all the standard special responsibilities that we so readily acknowledge. The same considerations of vulnerability that make our obligations to our families, friends, clients, and compatriots especially strong can also give rise to similar responsibilities toward a much larger group of people who stand in none of the standard special relationships to us.[39]

With the added assumption that reference to "our" actions and choices means responsibility is collective as well as individual, a case can be made for the welfare state, foreign aid, and concern for future generations, as well as, perhaps, animals and natural environments. In sum, "we should protect *all* those who are particularly vulnerable to our actions and choices, rather than restricting our attention to the narrowly defined subset enshrined in conventional morality."[40]

The vulnerability and dependency of others account for many moral duties. These extend not only to our children and dependent relatives but also to people who have relied on our promises or whom we have injured as a result of intentional or negligent conduct. Thus the realm of special obligation extends well beyond particularist bonds of kinship. Special obligations arise whenever the choices we make, as individuals or as group members, impinge on the lives of others in ways that cause them *to rely on us* for restraint or benevolence. The "others" are not all of humanity, but they need not be limited to relatives, spouses, or friends.

This line of reasoning is compelling, but it has important limitations. As a critique of particularism it is unsatisfactory because, in choosing among competing claims, "whom we should favor depends, according to this analysis, upon the relative vulnerability of each party to us."[41] This calculus is no help when vulnerabilities are roughly equal, as they are in many emergencies, or when they are indeterminate, as they are in many situations, and yet one must decide between helping a close relative or a stranger. Nor does the thesis adequately account for obligations

---

38. *Protecting the Vulnerable: A Reanalysis of Our Social Responsibilities* (Chicago: University of Chicago Press, 1985), 9.
39. Ibid., 11.
40. Ibid., 206.
41. Ibid., 119.

that arise from relationships that encompass much more than vulnerability. The morality of the "significant other" extends beyond damage control. It looks to the *flourishing* of children, spouses, friends, and community; it is not mainly a morality of reparation.

The fundamental source of moral obligation is our own sense of identity and relatedness, not the vulnerability of others. To be sure, many specific obligations are triggered and defined by vulnerability and dependency. What children need, and to whom they must turn, tells us what parents must do if they are to fulfill their responsibilities. But the *ground* of these obligations lies in the parental role, not in the child's needs. It is their commitment to relevant roles that governs how people should respond to the dependencies they create or accept.[42]

Many marital obligations, such as caring for one another during illness, fidelity in times of trouble, and appropriate settlement in case of divorce, are triggered by vulnerability. But it is the institution of marriage that confirms and undergirds these obligations. It is the institution that transforms a discretionary act of benevolence into a binding duty.

As the examples of marriage, employment, and naturalized citizenship make clear, the obligations of a "status contract" may indeed be self-assumed. What is remarkable about such contracts, however, is that once the relationship has been established, *prior consent wanes* as a governing principle. Negotiation and bargaining continue (in marriage and employment, though not in naturalization), but typically as responses to problems that cannot be solved by reference to the initial agreement, but must be dealt with within the framework of new circumstances and emergent obligations. In redefining the relationship, the changing parameters of a marriage (especially the claims of children) or the present needs of an enterprise play a central part.

Two meanings of "self-assumed" should be distinguished. In one meaning, self-assumed obligations are narrowly contractual acts of promising, whereby the promisers know definitely just what their commitments are. Here "commitment" connotes a deliberate exercise of will and choice. It is an explicit decision to be bound, one often expressed in a form of words, as a speech act.

---

42. To perform a role is to act in the light of governing norms. Therefore to some extent this ground of obligation introduces an element of universalism. The immediacy of the relation reinforces the obligation but is not its ground. Furthermore, as the role is generalized—fellow-citizen, fellow-human, fellow-creature—responsibility for particular others is attenuated.

Another meaning of "self-assumed" looks to the construction of the self. Here the formation of identity, character, and conscience is what matters, not the making of specific engagements. Obligations are assumed, but not necessarily as a result of conscious deliberation, and always within a demanding social context. Out of the meshing of lives and activities there emerges an implicated self whose obligations are neither wholly voluntary nor wholly imposed.[43]

Obligations based on affinity are self-assumed in this second sense. They arise from the continuities of socialization, selfhood, and shared experience. They are faithful to and nourished by the sustaining particularities of emotion, interaction, and interdependence. This accounts for the depth and salience of such obligations, as well as for their paradoxically open-ended yet bounded altruism.

In the morality of the significant other, commitment is selective, but it is not segmental in the sense discussed above. The bond is between one living unity and another, rather than being a coordination of specialized activities or interests. Obligation runs to definite persons, groups, and situations, not to abstract ideals or defined utilities. Since needs and interests are notoriously subject to change and redefinition, such a commitment calls for fidelity despite new and unforeseen demands. An ethos of diffuse, open-ended obligation prevails.

This open-endedness points to the moral worth of particularism, and therefore to its justification. For only thus can we make good "a deep caring and identification with the good of the other from whom one knows oneself clearly to be other."[44] In other words, only open-ended commitment, made by an integral, self-constituted being, is thoroughly and genuinely other-regarding. We cannot be other-regarding when we are concerned only with selected attributes of the other, such as a child's achievements, or when we are willing to give only a part of ourselves to the relationship.

There is no denying, of course, that particularism often shows the darker as well as the brighter face of human association. Bounded altruism can be a source of moral blindness. We know well that parochial attitudes breed willful ignorance, intolerance, group egotism, and worse. These evils must be disciplined by a universalist ethic. Nevertheless, the

43. In his critique of liberal theory Michael J. Sandel employs the related idea of a self "encumbered" by "constitutive attachments." See Sandel, "The Procedural Republic and the Unencumbered Self," *Political Theory* 12 (February 1984): 81–95.
44. Blum, *Friendship*, 70.

virtues and obligations we associate with particularism are, in their pure form, the fullest expression of other-regarding conduct.

The conventional forms of particularism—bonds of family, friendship, ethnicity, and locality—need not be perceived as its only province. The same ethos may be applied, with due respect for context, to wider worlds of work, education, and government. Virtues of caring, fidelity, and reverence—for persons, not abstractions—may flourish in many settings. And these virtues bring to those settings their greatest moral competence and worth.

EIGHT

The Responsible Self

We noted in Chapter 1 that morality entails the enhancement of fellowship and that fellowship requires a dual concern for the interests of others and for one's own integrity. Having considered the foundations of *other-regarding* conduct, especially the implicated self and the primacy of the particular, we turn to the place of *self-regard* in moral experience.

SELF-PRESERVATION

A long tradition of thought takes as given that a primordial ego—bound to the physical body, driven by irresistible appetites, threatened by external dangers—is unceasingly engaged in a struggle for survival. In the stark imagery of Thomas Hobbes, the human being is at bottom selfish and amoral, engaged in "a perpetuall and restlesse desire of Power after power, that ceaseth onely in Death."[1] This condition is redeemed in part by the natural prudence of the organism, that is, by the disposition to defer or limit gratification in the interests of survival. Narrowly conceived self-interest, disciplined by a primitive rationality, thus becomes the mainspring of moral ordering.

It is often thought that the Hobbesian view of human nature is wholly repudiated by our modern understanding of the self as a social product, but that is a mistake. Socialization is variably effective in both reach and depth. In any society some people are more thoroughly socialized than others; and for any person, under the press of circumstance,

---

1. *Leviathan* (1651; reprint, London: Pelican Books, 1968), 161.

socialization may prove an ineffectual barrier to amoral conduct. No one can survive without being socialized to some extent; every self is indeed a social self. But that does not settle what kind of person one is or what course of conduct one will choose.

The concept of a primordial ego speaks to a biological and social reality. Whatever our connections to other people, however much our individuality owes to social origins and social support, we remain ultimately separate organisms. Under ordinary circumstances in a healthy social environment this separateness is mitigated and even obscured. But it is seldom, if ever, wholly overcome, even where identification is very strong, as in the love of parents for children. That agonizing choices are sometimes made and heights of self-sacrifice occasionally reached does not alter the fundamental truth that self-preservation *in its narrowest sense* is an ever-present, if often hidden, item on almost everyone's agenda. Furthermore, as the character of social life deteriorates—as we enter, for example, the world of the drug-addict hustler, or prison life—the struggle for elementary survival is open and brutal.

The Hobbesian model is best understood as a summons to realism. It is far from the whole truth about motivation, morality, and political order. But it does identify important aspects of the human condition— above all, the propensity to equate self-preservation with maximizing individual short-run benefits. This propensity is a steady source of moral regression, especially under conditions of deprivation and stress, where survival is at issue or thought to be at issue, and where options are limited or perceived as limited. These empirical contingencies necessarily *qualify* the Hobbesian argument—they say in what ways, for what ends, and under what conditions his postulates make a difference—but they do not *refute* them.

In the design of human institutions Hobbes must be taken seriously. He showed what in human nature we must guard against; and he found in rational self-preservation a reliable, if limited, source of moral ordering. For the most part, it is self-interest, not virtue, that underpins reciprocity, compromise, and fidelity to obligation.

The premises of Hobbesian moral realism do not tell us, however, what it means to be a moral person or what it takes to have a flourishing moral order. Narrow self-interest and coercive authority account for the starting mechanisms of morality and for the core motivations that sustain it at minimal and precarious levels. Beyond lies the prospect of a moral experience enriched by more sensitive ways of thinking, feeling, and relating. To the extent this is achieved, survival in the narrow sense recedes as an operative goal; its meaning is enlarged to include more stringent criteria of moral well-being. Among these is a different understanding of what self-preservation entails.

This larger conception requires, in the first instance, a broader view of what it means to be *rationally* self-preserving. For Hobbes, rationality is a matter of deferring or limiting gratifications, calculating trade-offs, and forming contracts. In this scenario the actors are fully competent individuals; their nature is given and unproblematic; no reconstruction of the self is contemplated.

A quite different point of view harks back to Aristotle and the Stoics and is strongly reflected in the writings of Hobbes's younger contemporary, Benedict Spinoza (1632–1677). Spinoza made much of the postulate that all men seek their own preservation and, as a corollary, extension of their powers of self-maintenance. "No virtue can be conceived," he wrote, "as prior to this virtue of endeavouring to preserve oneself."[2] But "this virtue" is a gift of enlightenment:

> Since reason postulates nothing against nature, it postulates, therefore, that each man should love himself, and seek what is useful to him—I mean what is truly useful to him—and desire whatever leads man truly to a greater state of perfection. . . . Nothing, I say, can be desired by men more excellent for their self-preservation than that all with all should so agree that they compose the minds of all into one mind, and the bodies of all into one body, and all endeavour at the same time as much as possible to preserve their being, and all seek at the same time what is useful to them all as a body. From which it follows that men who are governed by reason . . . desire nothing for themselves which they do not also desire for the rest of mankind, and therefore they are just, faithful, and honourable.[3]

Here rationality requires everyone to discover what is "truly useful" for that "greater state of perfection" which is the goal and criterion of self-preservation. The voice of reason, as heard by Spinoza, calls for composing "the minds of all into one mind" to the end that the common good may be known and served. At the same time, all are to "preserve their being," that is, their own integrity. Unity, not separation; concord, not arm's-length accommodation: these are the conditions of genuine self-preservation.[4]

2. *Ethics* (1677; reprint, London: Dent, 1910), 157 (book 4, prop. 22).
3. Ibid., 154f. (book 4, prop. 18n).
4. "To Hobbes, the self which man's first impulse endeavors to preserve is of a purely egotistic nature and excludes other beings; to Spinoza the self of self-preservation is an expanded self of which the needs of the society of others is a constituent part" (Harry Wolfson, *The Philosophy of Spinoza* [1934; reprint, New York: Meridian, 1958], 2:247).

In more recent Western thought the path to moral understanding, and through it to genuine self-preservation, has taken a psychological turn. As we saw in Chapter 3, the transition from mind to self was a major theme in the nineteenth-century romantic reaction against rationalist philosophies. The emphasis shifted from intellect to will, from thought to action, from abstract to existential choice. Enlightenment is superficial and arid when abstract knowledge is the only guide to action. Having the right ideas counts for much less than having the right psyche, soul, or self.

A concept of the self as problematic, open to reconstruction, the key to salvation, is a major if ambiguous legacy of Western romanticism. For some it has meant a *repudiation* of reason: what counts is purity of spirit, emotional bonding to "blood and soil," or a leap of faith to what is beyond understanding and even absurd. These are facets of modern subjectivism, including much in existentialism. But for many who have shared the legacy of romanticism, among whom we may count Freud and the American pragmatists, the quest is for a more powerful *union* of thought, action, and self. Reason and enlightenment are not rejected; on the contrary, they are ardently sought. But their achievement depends on emotional as well as intellectual liberation.

For William James, George Herbert Mead, and John Dewey, morality is at bottom a work of self-formation. In this respect they adhered, more or less unconsciously, to the teachings of their Protestant milieu. As did the religious doctrines they otherwise rejected, these pragmatists extended the reach of moral responsibility by insisting on the fateful significance of moral choice for the actor. The process of choosing among conflicting goals or values is never wholly innocent:

> Now every such choice . . . reveals the existing self and . . . forms the future self. . . . This fact is especially marked at critical junctures, but . . . every choice . . . shuts off certain opportunities and opens others. In committing oneself to a particular course, a person gives a lasting set to his own being. Consequently, . . . in choosing this object rather than that, one is in reality choosing what kind of person or self one is going to be.[5]

Insofar as acts and their consequences are morally significant, they have an internal as well as an external relevance. They reflexively inform selfhood and character.

A corollary is that "intelligence"—Dewey's synonym for "reason"—is something more than the articulation of means to ends. "The self is not a *mere* means to producing consequences because the consequences,

5. John Dewey and James H. Tufts, *Ethics* (New York: Holt, 1932), 317.

when of a moral kind, enter into the formation of the self and the self enters into them."[6] In the perspective of pragmatism, the quality of moral choice is decisively enhanced when the fate of the self, as a moral and psychological unity, is at the forefront of our concern.

Freud shed a special light on this transition from a narrow to a broad view of self-preservation. In his basic model, as we have seen (Chapter 6, "Conscience and Competence"), "ego" is not a synonym for "self." The ego is a specialized agency of control and adaptation, "an intermediary between the id and the external world" whose task is narrow "self-preservation."[7] But this does not mean Freud was unconcerned about the human psyche or soul, more broadly conceived, or did not see it as viable and coherent.[8] On the contrary, the point of his theory is to make sense of the whole self, which is the tension-laden *unity* of id, ego, and superego. In the achievement of that unity, always understood in historical perspective, the ego plays a decisive part. It then becomes something more than a specialized psychobiological agency. The relation of ego (in Freud's special meaning) and self (in its larger meaning, as psyche or soul) is variable and problematic. That is why Freud could say of psychoanalysis that "its intention is, indeed, to strengthen the ego, to make it more independent of the super-ego, to widen its field of perception and enlarge its organization, so that it can appropriate fresh portions of the id. Where id was, there shall ego be."[9] As the ego is strengthened the self is reconstructed.

It has been said that Freud "oscillated between treating [the ego] as a self and then again as a control system which was only a part of the whole person."[10] That may be so, but the more important truth is that Freud held on to his basic model, including the mediating, controlling, reality-testing ego, because he remained convinced that the biological substratum of personality must not be forgotten or trivialized. Freud shared the Hobbesian view of a primordial, narrowly self-interested ego and

6. Ibid., 316.

7. Sigmund Freud, *An Outline of Psycho-Analysis* (1938), in vol. 23, *Standard Edition of the Complete Psychological Works,* trans. John Strachey in collaboration with Anna Freud (London: Hogarth Press, 1964), 145. At another point in this late work Freud writes: "Just as the id is directed exclusively to obtaining pleasure, so the ego is governed by considerations of safety. The ego has set itself the task of self-preservation, which the id appears to neglect" (ibid., 199).

8. On Freud's use of *Seele* (soul) and its mistranslation as "mind," see Bruno Bettelheim, *Freud and Man's Soul* (New York: Alfred A. Knopf, 1983), 70ff.

9. Sigmund Freud, *New Introductory Lectures on Psycho-Analysis* (1932) in vol. 22 of the *Standard Edition,* 80.

10. Harry Guntrip, *Psychoanalytic Theory, Therapy, and the Self* (New York: Harper Torchbooks, 1973), 12. "The ego is not really the I, the core of selfhood in the person. Freud takes the whole self for granted and nowhere discusses it specifically as the one psychic phenomenon that matters most of all" (ibid., 74).

of survival as an almost inescapable human imperative. Like Hobbes, he wrote in a spirit of unflinching realism about human motives and limitations.

Freud differed from Hobbes, however, in that he had a far more sophisticated theory of human nature and therefore could account for a richer, more complex experience. He could envision the possibility of transforming the self by education in depth, that is, by the reconstruction of *emotions* and not only of *minds*. Freud well knew that more is at stake in self-preservation than minimal psychobiological survival. As the self is enlarged, the meaning of survival changes. So too do the import and the moral worth of self-regarding conduct.

INTEGRITY AND PERSONHOOD

"I am the last person," wrote John Stuart Mill, "to undervalue the self-regarding virtues; they are only second in importance, if even second, to the social. It is equally the business of education to cultivate both."[11] Here Mill postulates an ultimate harmony of self-interest and virtue.[12] For him "self-regarding virtue" is not an oxymoron. Morality is not an enemy of the self; on the contrary, it is a kind of self-enhancement. This follows from the close connection we have emphasized between psychic competence and moral competence.[13] As people mature psychologically—for example, in the emotional capacity to experience trust and make commitments—they also grow in moral competence and well-being. The most important self-regarding virtues are those that help form a mature, well-tempered, and effective personality.

The Virtues of Integrity

Self-regarding virtue makes integrity the centerpiece of morality and the main concern of the moral actor. In ordinary language "integrity" suggests both honesty and coherence. For integrity is not just any coherence of self, group, or society, nor can it be reduced to consistency of thought or conduct.[14] We do not speak of the integrity of a psychotic personality,

11. John Stuart Mill, *On Liberty* (1859), in *Utilitarianism, On Liberty, Considerations on Representative Government* (reprint, London: J. M. Dent, 1984), 144.

12. See Henry Sidgwick, *The Methods of Ethics*, 7th ed., chap. 9, "Self-Regarding Virtues" (1907; reprint, Indianapolis: Hackett, 1981), 327.

13. See Chapter 6, "Conscience and Competence."

14. In the course of modifying a view he had expressed earlier that "one should perhaps say integrity is not a *virtue* at all," Bernard Williams rejects the assimilation of integrity to "mere consistency." Rather, integrity presumes that "the person in question has,

however consistent or integrated the symptoms; or of the integrity of Nazi Germany or Stalinist Russia, even though, in each case, we may be able to identify a principle of organization. Integrity properly denotes *both wholeness and soundness*. To have integrity is to be unmarred by distortion, deception, or other forms of disharmony and inauthenticity.

John Rawls identifies the "virtues of integrity" as "truthfulness and sincerity, lucidity and commitment, or, as some say, authenticity." Nevertheless, he suggests, integrity "allows for most any content: a tyrant might display these attributes to a high degree." Therefore "it is impossible to construct a moral view from these virtues alone; being virtues of form they are in a sense secondary."[15]

No doubt integrity is mainly a virtue of form rather than content. It has to do with ways of thinking, feeling, and acting, not with specific choices or judgments. To act with integrity is to *have* values and *take them seriously*, but the values themselves may be very diverse. It is important to recognize, however, that form and content cannot be radically separated. Form has implications for content. A tyrant who acts with "truthfulness and sincerity," who examines his own qualities as a person and, therefore, his relations with others, is likely to show some self-restraint.

Integrity is easier to come by in some circumstances than in others. Under conditions of stress and anxiety, and in the absence of an adequate ego, psychological coherence and competence are hard to maintain. In a business where fraud and deception are run-of-the-mill, or where clients and markets exert heavy pressure, personal integrity is not easily protected. Some occupations, by contrast, are welcome refuges from demands that subvert integrity. These variations should remind us that integrity is a hard-won achievement and that it is often manifested in rudimentary, partial, and groping ways. Therefore we should not say that every persistent pattern of motivation or conduct, just because it is

---

as seriously as possible, tried to think about the standards or the fundamental projects which are sustaining him or her. If he has done that and if, in the light of the thought he has displayed there, he comes out and does say, this is what I do most fundamentally believe in, and this is what I am going to do, then that person is displaying integrity, even though you do not agree with whatever it is that is sustaining him" ("The Uses of Philosophy: An Interview with Bernard Williams," *The Center Magazine* [November 1983]: 49). We may presume that the norm of "thinking seriously" about one's identity and commitments is meant to encourage moral awareness, not insensitivity. Much depends on what it means to have a value or to be principled.

15. John Rawls, *A Theory of Justice* (Cambridge: Harvard University Press, 1971), 519.

a pattern, has the virtue of integrity. To do so ignores the interplay of form and content—and the personal struggle entailed in that interplay.

The virtues of integrity cannot guarantee morally right outcomes, any more than due process of law can guarantee substantive justice. The same might be said of the virtues of reason. These qualities of persons and systems are necessarily detached from content, because their office is precisely to *assess* the content of particular choices and patterns of conduct. Nevertheless, to the extent that people strive for integrity, moral competence is likely to be enhanced; to the extent that ideals of due process are made good, substantive justice is more likely to be done.

It is helpful to distinguish *moral* integrity from, say, *aesthetic* integrity. Dedicated artists respect the integrity of their work, but as persons they may be distracted and distorted, confused and self-deceptive. Moral integrity depends on how well the whole personality, including those aspects that impinge on the interests of others, is integrated and governed. It is the integrity of the self, not of a specific activity, that matters most for moral experience.

The meaning of moral integrity is explored in Shirley Letwin's study of "the gentleman" in Trollope's novels. Integrity is the "moral excellence that defines a gentleman."[16] It is the wholeness that makes up a person's character, and this wholeness is protected by a pattern of awareness, restraint, and commitment. "A gentleman's self-awareness is . . . a delicate sense of responsibility for the coherence of all his thoughts, words, and actions."[17] In the service of that coherence, the gentleman is disinterested, thoughtful, diffident, prudent, realistic, and courageous—and all this is readily discernible.

In Trollope's vision, moral virtue is a subtle blend of idealism and realism. The true gentleman—more properly, the competent moral actor—has mastered the complex art of holding in tension self-regard and humility, prudence and courage, engagement and distance. We need not be parochial in our conception of the gentleman. Trollope would agree, perhaps with some hesitation, that the true gentleman may be a woman and may be found, with variable frequency, in any class, epoch, or culture.[18] The idiom would be different, the character the same.

16. *The Gentleman in Trollope: Individuality and Moral Conduct* (Cambridge: Harvard University Press, 1982), 65.
17. Ibid.
18. "I do not know that she was at all points a lady, but *had Fate so willed it* she would have been a thorough gentleman" (Anthony Trollope, *Can You Forgive Her?* [1864–65; reprint, Harmondsworth: Penguin Books, 1972], 523f. [my emphasis]). I owe this reference to Jane-Ellen Long.

The idea of integrity shifts attention from conduct to structure. Our main concern is not acts or even rules but effective *organization* of person, institution, or community. Organization for moral well-being establishes basic values, and it also mobilizes resources and nurtures relationships. The moral integrity of a family, for example, depends on values of kinship and intimacy; it also requires appropriate forms of communication and patterns of mutual support.

As a moral standard, integrity is a union of the abstract and the concrete. The system whose integrity is at issue must be understood in its own terms as a unique entity or at least as a certain *kind* of person, practice, institution, community, or culture. The abstract ideal provides guidance, but the operative meaning of integrity must be determined in the light of historically situated capacities, constraints, and opportunities. It is not a question of adapting rules to particular circumstances. The *standard itself* cannot be known apart from a theory of what constitutes wholeness and soundness in the context at hand. We must know what makes for the integrity of a parent, a teacher, an architectural style, or a legal process.[19]

Individuals as Persons

The concept of integrity goes to the heart of what is meant by "person" and "personhood." In Western philosophy, theology, and social theory "person" used as a term of art has reappeared perennially since ancient times.[20] Although frustratingly vague and elusive, the idea persists because it contains a core of meaning that seems indispensable to moral thought and judgment.

Many analysts of Western thought have found it helpful to distinguish between "individual" and "person."[21] That is so because, in the doctrines of modernity, individuals tend to lose their distinctiveness. They become interchangeable, ahistorical units within a political, legal, or economic scheme of things. The driving ideals of liberal capitalism— national unity, the rule of law, political democracy, free enterprise—all

19. For further discussion of the concept of integrity, with special reference to *institutional* integrity, see Chapter 12, "Ends, Means, and Integrity."

20. For a history of "person" see Adolf Trendelenburg, "A Contribution to the History of the Word Person," *The Monist* 20 (1910): 336–63.

21. See Jacques Maritain, *The Person and the Common Good* (New York: Scribner's, 1947); Steven Lukes, *Individualism* (Oxford: Blackwell, 1973), chap. 20; J. S. La Fontaine, "Person and Individual: Some Anthropological Reflections," in Michael Corrithers, Steven Collins, and Steven Lukes, eds., *The Category of the Person: Anthropology, Philosophy, History* (Cambridge: Cambridge University Press, 1985), 123–40.

have the effect of identifying people by *general categories* rather than by
the concreteness of selfhood, connection, and context. As the category
is abstract, so too is the individual; hence the phrase "abstract individual." This abstraction is one of the more barren and dehumanizing leg-
acies of modern rationalism.

Such an outcome was certainly not intended. The architects of the
Enlightenment wanted to enhance and vindicate, not diminish, the
moral worth of the individual person. They therefore stressed the importance of moral autonomy and freedom, including freedom from unchosen obligation and from the fetters of the past. In this process it was natural to celebrate *detached* individuals, responsible for their own fates,
authors of their own opinions, finding their own ways to association,
prosperity, and God. Rationalists took for granted much in traditional
society, especially the continuities of family and rural life. They did not
foresee the moral and cultural attenuation that would stem from an ethos
of individualism set loose in a world of industrial and urban expansion.

To many observers, conservative as well as progressive, "individual"
and "individualism" have taken on connotations that are deeply offensive from a moral point of view. The image of a self-distancing individual is hardly a convincing or attractive picture of what participation in a
moral order should entail. When the human being is abstracted from history and context we lose purchase on what it means to be a multi-
dimensional moral actor and a fully realized object of moral concern. In
short, the texture of moral ordering is lost.

The concept of "person" is an effort to retrieve that texture. The individual *as person* is discovered, protected, and fulfilled only in a specific
historical setting. This particularity resists and mitigates abstraction. Yet
the point of the exercise is to vindicate a general idea: human dignity and
worth. Although the value at stake is necessarily abstract, it is realized
through concreteness. This union of the general and the particular distinguishes the person from the abstract individual.

In etymology and social theory "person" suggests particularity, coherence, and responsibility. The Latin and Greek terms (*persona, proso-
pon*) refer to the masks used in classical drama and, by extension, the part
or character represented by the actor. This identification of "person"
with "role" takes on ethical meaning in the Stoic tradition. It is the duty
of moral persons to "play well" the roles they are assigned:

> The well written part, furthermore, *particularizes the universal* in accordance
> with the nature peculiar to each individual and grounds it in a rational mean.
> In this way the aim of the Stoics is realized. . . . For everything is as it should

be and the course of life is beautiful when the will of the universal disposer and the *daemon* of the individual are in harmony. Inasmuch as the role is subordinated to the drama as a whole, but has its being nevertheless in the particular part, it is an artistic way of stating the Stoic doctrine.[22]

The Stoic ideal presumes a moral order largely founded on assigned roles and fixed statuses. In such a society, role and person are closely congruent; indeed, roles are constitutive of personal identities. To meet the expectations one's received identity generates is the main criterion of social responsibility. Thus to be a person is to be defined by one's place in the moral order.

These overtones of hierarchy and discipline are reflected in what used to be called the "law of persons." Historically this branch of Anglo-American law dealt with all those relations that could be said to create a legal identity: slave, serf, master, servant, ward, infant, husband, wife, cleric, king. All these were statuses recognized by law. Each clothed the individual in salient, identity-fixing privileges or disabilities. Thus the law of persons was the law of status. It was rooted in a society where everyone was presumed to belong somewhere, and the great parameters of belonging were kinship, locality, religion, and social rank. In all aspects of experience, including spiritual communion, subordination to legitimate authority was thought to be a natural, inevitable, and welcome avenue to moral grace and practical virtue.

By the middle of the nineteenth century it was clear that the law of persons would soon become an anachronism. The knell was tolled by Henry Sumner Maine in his famous "law of progress." "The movement of the progressive societies," he wrote, "has hitherto been a movement *from Status to Contract.*"[23] Maine perceived that contract was the preferred form of legal relation in modern society. The effect of the change was to diminish the perceived reality of both persons and groups. Persons are reduced to individual units of investment, labor, or consumption. Their special identities are lost in the egalitarian, free-market imagery of "economic man." The group becomes an aggregate or, at best, a composite of freely chosen individual arrangements.

This transition brings home the fact that the historical reality of personhood is closely associated with status and subordination. With that in mind it is easy to appreciate how great was the appeal of the new

22. Trendelenburg, "Contribution to the History of the Word Person," 345, my emphasis.
23. *Ancient Law* (1861; reprint, Boston: Beacon Press, 1963), 165. On the limits of Maine's formula, see my *Law, Society and Industrial Justice* (New York: Russell Sage, 1969), 61f.

individualism and the contract model. As it developed in the nineteenth century, the law of contract embodied values of freedom, equality, and self-government. Contract law was liberating and facilitative; a channel for the release of energies through economic cooperation; a powerful device for defining rights and enforcing accountability. All this weighed heavily against the received morality of role and status.

The lesson to be derived is that our understanding of personhood should give full weight to *self-affirming* participation in a moral order. Respect for individuals as persons requires "that we regard and act towards [them] in their concrete specificity, that we take full account of their specific aims and purposes and of their own definitions of their [social] situations."[24] In other words, the person as an object of moral concern can never be an abstraction, never be wholly subordinated to social needs, never be dissolved into a group or process. Here again the primacy of the particular is reaffirmed.

The moral unity of the person is a counterweight to demands for sacrifice to the common good. As Bernard Williams has argued, "[T]here can come a point at which it is quite unreasonable for a man to give up, in the name of the impartial good ordering of the world of moral agents, something which is a condition of his having any interest in being around in that world at all."[25] This something is what Williams calls a "ground project," that is, a set of activities and commitments that, taken together, construct a moral identity and give meaning to a life. Such identities are ever-present sources of conflict among persons, including friends and relatives, and between the individual and society. The implicated self is also a particular self, with its own claims to individuality and autonomy.

But this is the autonomy of selfhood, not of unfettered or ungoverned choice. An unspoken condition of moral individuality is that "ground projects" must meet a threshold standard of moral justification. Each project or way of life is unique, but this does not mean that all are acceptable. It is not moral autonomy to do as I please, heedless of outcomes for my own character and integrity. Rather, self-determination is the freedom to find one's proper place within a moral order, not outside it. In doing so one takes account of the qualities of that order—its legitimacy and the propriety of its demands, for example—as well as one's own nature and experience.

24. Lukes, *Individualism*, 148.
25. *Moral Luck* (Cambridge: Cambridge University Press, 1981), 14.

This argument takes seriously the idea that persons are at once socially constituted and self-determining. To be socially constituted is
not, in itself, to be imprisoned or oppressed; it does not require that people be puppets or act out prescribed roles in excruciating detail. Nor is
self-determination properly understood as gratification of impulse,
compulsive dependency, or opportunistic decision. Insofar as it has
moral import, the theory of the social self makes plain that a morally
competent self must be a product of affirmative social participation and
of responsible emotion, belief, and conduct.

FROM JAMES TO GOFFMAN

Much in contemporary social reality and in the postmodern consciousness it creates is an offense to personhood and a parody of self-
determination. The meaning of "self" in self-determination becomes
intellectually cloudy and morally destructive when autonomy is equated
with unrestrained and arbitrary choice; when people are impulse-driven
or helplessly adrift on a sea of change; when psychic manipulation—of
self and of other—is the order of the day.

I suggested in Chapter 1 that a central fact of modernity is the confrontation between a strong sense of self and a weakened culture. Therefore Yeats was not wholly correct, for his time at least, when he said that
"Things fall apart; the centre cannot hold."[26] In the late twentieth century, however, we have come much closer to the condition he described,
so far as intellectual, aesthetic, and moral life is concerned:

> And where we are now is the no man's land that more and more begins to in-
> herit the name Postmodern—atomized, leveled, thoroughly democratic turf
> where anything goes, everything counts, significance is what I say it is. . . .
> Whether in painting or in literary theory, there is the glee of plenitude and pro-
> liferation along these Postmodern boulevards, and a dogged pluralism, and
> individualism splintering off into idiosyncratic fits of unconventionality des-
> perate to pass for original. With so much originality at hand (originality with-
> out origin), and no center (or any number of centers, one to a customer),
> what's left to be eccentric?[27]

26. William Butler Yeats, "The Second Coming," in *The Collected Poems of W. B.
Yeats* (1933; reprint, Macmillan, 1966), 184. As Cynthia Ozick points out, "[O]ne center
did hold, one pledge stuck. This was the artist's pledge to the self. Joyce, Mann, Eliot,
Proust, Conrad (even with his furies): they *knew*. And what they knew was that—though
things fall apart—the artist is whole, consummate" (Cynthia Ozick, "The Muse, Postmodern and Homeless," *New York Times Book Review*, 19 January 1987, 9).
27. Ibid.

Postmodernism thus understood reveals a weak sense of self in an even
more attenuated culture. This poses a new problem for integrity and
personhood. Whereas earlier we had to distinguish person from *individual,* now it is a question of rescuing the person from a fractured sense
of *self.*

In this century many writers have called attention to the psychic costs
of depersonalization, mobility, homogenization, privatization, consumerism, rootlessness, and the fragmentation of experience. These changes
are by no means the whole of social reality; continuity, as well as discontinuity, can be discerned.[28] But the changes are important enough to
bring about a transformation of consciousness, including the introduction of new and pervasive discontents. The distracted culture of late modernity becomes known by fluidity of self, not by the abstractly conceived, narrowly defined, yet coherent individual; by expense of spirit,
not robust self-assertion; by moral confusion, not moral indifference.

The intellectual corollary is a theory of the self as multiple, situational, mutable, even empty. This was anticipated by William James in
his discussion of "The Consciousness of Self":

> Properly speaking, *a man has as many social selves as there are individuals who
> recognize him* and carry an image of him in their mind. . . . But as the indi-
> viduals who carry the images fall naturally into classes, we may . . . say that
> he has as many different social selves as there are distinct *groups* of persons
> about whose opinion he cares. . . . From this there results . . . a division of
> the man into several selves; and this may be a discordant splitting, as where
> one is afraid to let one set of his acquaintances know him as he is elsewhere;
> or it may be a perfectly harmonious division of labor, as where one tender to
> his children is stern to the soldiers or prisoners under his command.[29]

For James, the plurality of selves is not tragic or pathological. It is potentially an expression of openness and competence. In the optimistic
vision of American pragmatism, there is no great advantage in fixed
identity. Under modern conditions a fixed identity may reflect poverty
of experience, limited opportunity, maladjustment, and unhappiness.
Furthermore, in a democratic society individuals should be flexible and
resilient enough to perform a variety of social roles, ranging from
household tasks to community leadership, without damage to their
self-conceptions.

28. When we speak of the decline of kinship, for example, we do not suppose that
family ties have been completely lost, for obviously that is not so. But kinship has de-
clined as a source of occupational continuity and security, as an extended-family context of
everyday life, and in many other ways.
29. *The Principles of Psychology* (1890; reprint, Dover, 1950), 294, James's emphasis.

The fluidity of self has a different and more chilling aspect in the writings of Erving Goffman (1922–1982). In *The Presentation of Self in Everyday Life,* and in a number of other essays, Goffman explored the rituals of interaction and the management of impressions. Using the metaphor of drama (hence a "dramaturgic" perspective), he vividly described the imperatives of performance in social situations. In the world portrayed by Goffman, people protect their fragile selves by a wide variety of defensive maneuvers and face-saving gambits. These same tactics, he insisted, sustain the fabric of day-to-day interaction; they are the stuff of which social order is made—an order that is episodic and precarious.

What is this self defended so urgently, so resourcefully—sometimes, so comically?

> Each moral career, and behind this, each self, occurs within the confines of an institutional system, whether a social establishment such as a mental hospital or a complex of personal and professional relationships. . . . The self in this sense *is not a property of the person to whom it is attributed,* but dwells rather in the pattern of social control that is exerted in connection with the person by himself and those around him. This special kind of institutional arrangement does not so much support the self as constitute it.[30]

Here the self is minimal, defensive, and elusive, reflecting shifting interests and transitory interaction. That is why Goffman advocated a "sociology of occasions" where "social organization is the central theme, but what is organized is the co-mingling of persons" in "temporary interactional enterprises" which are "necessarily evanescent, created by arrivals and killed by departures."[31] Selfhood, integrity, and self-determination are, at best, pathetic illusions.

These ideas have struck a responsive chord, partly because it is fun to expose the games people play as they strive to make points and avoid embarrassment. More important, however, is that Goffman grasped and revealed a pervasive feature of modern life: the insubstantial self in an insubstantial world, a world that is, nevertheless, opaque and oppressive.

30. Erving Goffman, *Asylums* (New York: Anchor Books, 1961), 168, my emphasis.
31. Erving Goffman, *Interaction Ritual* (New York: Anchor Books, 1967), 2. Goffman could be taken as merely focusing attention on a neglected aspect of social psychology—interaction and the micro-order. Thus understood, his contribution could easily be assimilated to conventional social science, But that would be to miss the wider appeal and relevance of Goffman's work. A critical essay makes the point that "the dramaturgic approach is applicable to the analysis of moral conduct in any age. We agree . . . however, that the growing amorality of urban individuals may help account for the emergence of the dramaturgic perspective" (Sheldon L. Messinger, "Life as Theater: Some Notes on the Dramaturgic Approach to Social Reality," *Sociometry* 25 [March 1961]: 105n).

Goffman was heir to the "symbolic interaction" perspective we associate with George Herbert Mead.[32] Like Mead, he took seriously the vital role of gesture and interpretation in human interaction. But he gave that perspective a wrenching twist. What for Mead was health, growth, openness, and empowerment became, in the new interactionism, anguish, fragility, manipulation, and impoverishment. There is nothing healthy-minded in Goffman's vision, and this marks a radical departure from the pragmatist tradition.

There is truth in Goffman's sociology—and distortion as well. His own writings can be read as richly documenting the human aspiration to sustain coherence and resist fragmentation. In the stories he tells, strategies of control are met by counter-pressures which, in prisons for example, "provide the inmate with important evidence that he is still his own man, with some control of his environment" and especially of his identity.[33]

The fragile self revealed by Goffman—defensive, cynical, manipulative, constricted—makes problematic what the pragmatists took for granted. The management of impressions is indeed pervasive in social life, but it is often quite superficial compared to other ways of responding and belonging. In the moral psychology of American pragmatism, the "open" self is a welcome promise of flexibility, growth, and generosity of spirit. At bottom the pragmatists believed that mental health and moral competence require integration, resilience, continuity, and strength of character and that a weak sense of self brings psychic disarray. They well understood that integrity and personhood must thicken the self and make it more determinate. They were at war with the rigidities of their Protestant heritage, but they had no thought of abandoning a basic faith in the Western ideal of autonomy, purposefulness, resolve, and self-realization.

32. See Chapter 3, "Subjectivity and Social Reality."
33. Goffman, *Asylums*, 55. See also his discussion of "role distance," where the tension between role performance and identity is explored. Role distance refers to "actions which effectively convey some disdainful detachment of the performer from a role he is performing" (Erving Goffman, *Encounters* [Indianapolis: Bobbs-Merrill, 1961], 110). At stake is the person's self-image or "virtual self." "Some of the most appealing data on role distance come from situations where a subordinate must . . . go along with the situation as defined by superordinates. At such times, we often find that although the subordinate is careful not to threaten those who are . . . in charge of the situation, he may be just as careful to inject some expression to show . . . that he is not capitulating completely to the work arrangement. . . . Sullenness, muttering, irony, joking, and sarcasm may all allow one to show that something of oneself lies outside the constraints of the moment and outside the role within whose jurisdiction the moment occurs" (ibid., 114). Note that Goffman could not really sustain his concept of the self as stringently institutional and derivative, "not a property of the person."

BUDDHIST SELF-REGARD

A powerful intellectual and moral tradition casts doubt on this Western view. Buddhism seems a clear and challenging alternative to the moral psychology of the West. It resonates at many points with contemporary ideas about the fluidity of self, and this may account for much of its attraction as a vehicle of counterculture. In theory at least Buddhism departs from the Western conception of the moral person in two significant ways. First, *selfhood is denied*, its trappings vigorously repudiated. Second, *nonattachment* is the preferred way to moral and spiritual well-being.

Over twenty-five centuries Buddhism has taken many forms and spawned numerous sects. There is broad agreement, however, that "the fundamental dogma of Buddhism," "the cornerstone of Buddhist thinking," is "the assertion that there is no 'self.' "[34] What we think of as the self is but an illusion. It is a preconception we impose on the flux and plurality of experience. In words attributed to the historical Buddha:

> Consider your "self"; think of its transiency; how can you fall into delusion about it and cherish pride and selfishness, knowing that they must all end in inevitable suffering? Consider all substances; can you find among them any enduring "self"? Are they not all aggregates that sooner or later will break apart and be scattered?[35]

Much the same conclusion was drawn by David Hume in his *Treatise on Human Nature*. People, he wrote, "are nothing but a bundle or collection of different perceptions, which succeed each other with an inconceivable rapidity, and are in perpetual flux and movement." Yet for practical purposes we tend "to confound identity with relation," as when we say "an oak, that grows from a small plant to a large tree, is still the same oak; tho' there be not one particle of matter, or figure of its parts the same. . . . All the disputes concerning the identity of connected objects are merely verbal, except so far as the relation of parts gives rise to some fiction or imaginary principle of union."[36]

Of course our David was no closet Buddhist. As a thoroughgoing empiricist he was eager to deflate such abstractions as "the self," but he had no religious agenda. In Buddhism, on the other hand, denial of self

---

34. Edward Conze, *Buddhist Scriptures* (London: Penguin Books, 1959), 190.

35. Bukkyō Dendō Kyōkai, *The Teaching of Buddha*, 93d rev. ed., (Tokyo: Kosaido, 1979), 20.

36. David Hume, *A Treatise of Human Nature*, ed. L. A. Selby-Bigge (1740; reprint, Oxford: Clarendon Press, 1955), 252, 254, 257, 262. For a discussion of Hume and Buddhism see Nolan Pliny Jacobson, *Understanding Buddhism* (Carbondale: Southern Illinois University Press, 1966), chap. 8.

is an aspect of moral psychology. The self is seen as more than an illusion, more also than a philosophical mistake. It is a *pernicious* illusion and the chief source of human suffering. The illusory self is the seat of desire, and desire is the root of evil. "But whoever in this world overcomes his selfish cravings, his sorrows fall away from him, like drops of water from a lotus flower."[37]

The Buddhist vision is neither a simple rejection of selfishness nor a plea for the control of passions. The demand is more radical: destruction of ego and transcendence of self. The great aim of Buddhist practice is release from the bondage of fantasy and craving, especially the craving for individual existence. The idea that one has a determinate self, to be defended and aggrandized, is, therefore, the master illusion.

And yet there is an inescapable paradox. The selflessness of Buddhism is profoundly self-regarding. This is most clearly manifest in the vital role of will and discipline. At least in Zen, there is no easy way to the "awakening," "perfection," "light," and "love" that constitute Buddhahood. Nor is it mainly an intellectual exercise, a gift of reason. Nirvana is to be sought in strenuous spiritual struggle carried on by an active center of some sort, call it what you will. *Some* psychological agency must be the locus of that "mindful and disciplined attitude to the body [which] is the very basis of Buddhist training."[38]

The path to enlightenment must pass through a strait gate: the experience of self-mastery. This is not to be understood as submission to God or even to nature. As the Buddhist *Dhammapada* says, "Self is the lord of self, who else could be the lord?"[39] And "[L]et no one forget his own good for the sake of another's, however great; let a man, after he has discerned what this good is, be ever intent upon it."[40] The lesson is clear: my first duty is to my own integrity.

Another self-regarding theme is the irrepressible search for a "true" self to be realized in the course of spiritual emancipation. Everyone is presumed to have a "Buddha-nature," which is a potential for purity, spontaneity, creativity, benevolence, openness, and concreteness. "Behind the desires and worldly passions which the mind entertains, there abides, clear and undefiled, the fundamental and true essence of

37. *The Dhammapada: Path of Perfection,* 336, trans. Juan Mascaró (Harmondsworth: Penguin Books, 1973), 83.
38. Conze, *Buddhist Scriptures,* 97.
39. *The Dhammapada,* 160, trans. Irving Babbitt (1936; reprint, New York: New Directions, 1965), 26. Another translation from the Pali is: "Only a man can be the master of himself: who else from outside can be his master?" (*The Dhammapada,* trans. Mascaró, 58).
40. *The Dhammapada,* 166, trans. Babbitt, 27.

mind. . . . However buried in the defilement of flesh, or concealed at the root of worldly desires and forgotten it may be, the human affinity for Buddhahood is never completely extinguished."[41] Thus Buddhism is a philosophy of liberated consciousness. As such, it has much in common with the phenomenological perspective discussed in Chapter 3, "From Mind to Self." Reconstruction and renewal, not extinction; energy and strength, not passivity; sharpened awareness, not want of form: these are the true goals of self-transcendence.

One student of Zen points to an "ego-less ego" as the wished-for product (though the wish is always suspect) of a reconstructed consciousness. The aim is to expunge the "I" in its separateness by overcoming the split between subject and object. This is not a negative state. It is a positive intensification of consciousness such that self and object are in total harmony. The ideal is exemplified in master craftsmanship, especially in the fine arts:

> The painter sits in quiet contemplation, intensely concentrating his mind upon the ideal image of the bamboo. He begins to feel in himself the rhythmic pulsebeat of the life-energy which keeps the bamboo alive and which makes the bamboo a bamboo. . . . And finally there comes a moment of complete unification, at which there remains no distinction whatsoever between the life-energy of the painter and the life-energy of the bamboo. Then there is no longer any trace in the consciousness of the painter of himself as an individual self-subsistent person. . . . At that very moment the painter takes up the brush. The brush moves, as it were, of its own accord, in conformity with the pulsation of the life-rhythm which is actualized in the bamboo. In terms of the traditional Far Eastern theory of the pictorial art, it is then not the man who draws the picture of the bamboo; rather, the bamboo draws its own picture on the paper. The movement of the brush is the movement of the inner life of the bamboo.[42]

The capacity to lose oneself in what Dewey called "the moving unity of experience" is hardly a sign of psychological dissolution.[43] On the contrary, it presumes inner harmony, control, and integration. That is true in part because the experience in question—craft, dance, composition,

41. Bukkyō, *The Teaching of Buddha*, 138, 144. "The Buddha-nature is ever-present, not something to be attained or awaited, but only to be realized" (Edward Conze, *Buddhism: Its Essence and Development* [New York: Harper Torchbooks, 1959], 99).

42. Toshihiko Izutsu, *Toward a Philosophy of Zen Buddhism* (Boulder: Prajna Press, 1982), 80. Lest this ideal be considered unique to the East, note the following: "A piano player who had perfect mastery of his instrument would have no occasion to distinguish between his contribution and that of the piano. In well-formed, smooth-running functions of any sort,—skating, conversing, hearing music, enjoying a landscape,—there is no consciousness of separation of method of the person or of the subject matter" (John Dewey, *Democracy and Education* [1916; reprint; New York: Free Press, 1966], 166).

43. Dewey, *Democracy and Education*, 167.

an excellence of any kind—has a worth, structure, and integrity of its own. To be at one with its demands and rhythms is to lose the *separateness* of self but not the *coherence* of self. Neither Zen Buddhism nor pragmatism contemplates a loss of self in disordered ecstasy or sacrifice of will.

A major form of self-regard is the Buddhist imperative of *nonattachment*. To be self-less is to be unattached to the idea of one's own continuity, permanence, and substantiality. Salvation lies in a loosening of bonds, and moral responsibility is uniquely personal, not to be shunted off or shared:

> In Chinese Buddhism the most important practice, therefore, was to purify one's own mind so that one would need to depend exclusively upon oneself, and not rely upon any other power, not even the power of Buddha. In this connection, Hu-hai (A.D. 550–606) said: "You should realize the fact that man saves himself, and the Buddha cannot redeem man. . . . It is set forth in the sutra: 'Therefore, those who look for the true *dharma* should not rely upon Buddha.' "[44]

What, then, of altruism? Buddhism is a deeply compassionate faith, but Buddhist compassion derives from a premise of selflessness, not from a morality of commitment. For the "selfless person" the line between self and other is indistinct if not extinguished.[45] The duality of self and other is an alien idea, if only because every human experience is thought to be an integral part of a larger, all-embracing unity.

Therefore nonattachment derives from a deeper principle of continuity. As we overcome the bondage of existential attachment we experience a shared fate or karma and accept our place in a universal, timeless, open-ended process of change and interaction. In Buddhism the foundation of benevolence is this openness of self, not the natural sympathy of person-to-person experience or the abstract, rational morality of Western universalism. Nonattachment is not *de*tachment in the sense of impersonal or self-distancing judgment. Rather, Buddhism holds in tension moral strategies of insularity and openness. Self-preservative nonattachment goes hand in hand with wholehearted embrace of a world in which one is deeply implicated. Whatever we may think of this paradoxical doctrine, the ideal is a vigorous assertion of inner strength and harmony. As one kind of selfhood is denied, another is affirmed.

44. Hajime Nakamura, *Ways of Thinking of Eastern Peoples: India-China-Tibet-Japan*, trans. and ed. Philip P. Wiener (Honolulu: University of Hawaii Press, 1964), 253f.

45. Steven Collins, *Selfless Persons: Imagery and Thought in Theravada Buddhism* (Cambridge: Cambridge University Press, 1982).

Although some strands of Buddhist thought resemble late-modern conceptions of the fluidity of self, it is doubtful that this is a family resemblance. Nonattachment and openness are resources of strength, not weakness; of guarded optimism, not despair; of engagement, not alienation. And they presume a context of order. For the Buddhist there is no question of deciding for oneself what morality entails. To be sure, precepts of right conduct are best understood as moral insights we ourselves reach and experience concretely, in the course of our struggle for enlightenment. But what we discover is not uniquely our own. There is endless rediscovery of what the Buddha learned and taught his disciples.

CONCLUSION

As empirical phenomena, human selves are variable and contingent. They may be strong or weak, well-integrated or disorganized, tightly defensive or open and flexible. There is every reason to explore this variability by studying how social and cultural changes affect the experience of selfhood. From the standpoint of psychological and moral well-being, however, it is impossible to make sense of that experience without a normative theory of the self such as that to which Part Two has been devoted.

A pervasive theme in these chapters has been the quest for moral competence. The argument has led us to a fairly close inspection of what it means to be both genuinely other-regarding and constructively self-regarding. This difficult union may be thought of as the creation of a *responsible self,* which is manifested in three main ways: character-defining choice, self-affirming participation, and personal statesmanship.

Character-defining choice. The primary responsibility of moral persons is to look to their own salvation, that is, to form selves capable of making moral choices. This consciousness of character—of structured selfhood—gives center stage to integrity. When a person's integrity is at stake, there is responsibility *for* the self (what I have become), *to* the self (sustaining and strengthening my moral character), and *of* the self (accepting as my own the consequences of my existence and my acts).

The formation of character encompasses responsibility for one's own history, biological as well as social, including much that one did not choose and could not control. Insofar as strength and vitality are drawn from a distinctive personal heritage, this constraint is positive and even liberating. But responsibility for self is not mindless deference to an encumbered past. To *form* the self by making choices that define and fix a moral character is to treat oneself as an object—but one to be examined and refashioned, not manipulated. The examined life is a life open to reconstruction in a spirit of critical affirmation, within a framework of order, not in anguished flight, defense, desire, or aggrandizement.

Self-affirming participation. Integrity, personhood, and character gain substance from the experience of belonging to a specific moral community. In core participation, responsibility runs three ways: to the particular others in whose lives one's own is implicated; to the moral order as a common mooring that establishes the shared premises of selfhood and thereby transcends individuality; and to personal integrity and moral autonomy.

Responsible participation is not supine obedience; neither is it unreflective acting-out of prescribed roles. The perspective of critical affirmation applies to moral rules no less than to the self. It entails, at least, looking not only to the letter but the spirit of a rule, and assuming personal responsibility for exercising judgment to fill gaps in the normative order and reconcile its conflicting messages.

Personal statesmanship. Moral competence and well-being are something more than the control of passions or the achievement of blissful harmony. The former is too narrow an objective, the latter too fleeting or of doubtful relevance to everyday life. More pertinent is the task of recognizing and managing the recurrent antinomies of moral experience. These include some we have discussed, such as the tension between universalism and particularism, justice and love, narrow and broad self-interest. Many others might also be considered—duty versus aspiration, rights versus utility, roles versus integrity—which, taken together, constitute the substance of moral theory. The antinomies make choice difficult, and sometimes tragic, because they put integrity at risk.

Personal statesmanship is governance of the self in the light of moral *ideals* and not only in conformity to moral *rules*. Its great aim is to find a healing balance between nonattachment and attachment, alienation and reconciliation. Moral commitment, whether other-regarding or self-regarding, cannot be made without reserve or limit. If we go too far in one direction we suffer loss of self; in the other direction we slight the claims of others. Virtue and commitment are inescapably in tension; therefore irony and distance are essential ingredients of moral experience. Ultimately the moral person must be, as Walt Whitman wrote in Stanza 4 of *Song of Myself,* "both in and out of the game and watching and wondering at it."

The Moral Institution

NINE

Theory of Institutions

In Part Three we examine the moral experience of large, special-purpose organizations.[1] These "bureaucratic structures" or "corporate groups" dominate the social landscape. They are the representative institutions of government, business, politics, communications, education, philanthropy, medicine, and religion. Largely self-governing, they often command huge resources, have multiple constituencies, and decisively affect the fate of persons and the quality of community. To see these organizations as moral agents—as participants in the moral order; as potential objects of moral concern—we may draw some insight from the sociology of institutions. A strategic focus is the transformation of organizations into institutions and into agencies of community.

ORGANIZATION → INSTITUTION → COMMUNITY

In sociology two leading ideas have clear but often unacknowledged moral significance: socialization and institutionalization. We have touched on the former at a number of points. Socialization has to do mainly with

---

1. In this chapter and other sections of Part 3, I draw upon and recast some relevant material from earlier writings, especially *Leadership in Administration* (1957; reprint, Berkeley: University of California Press, 1984); *Law, Society and Industrial Justice* (New York: Russell Sage, 1969); and *TVA and the Grass Roots* (1949; reprint, Berkeley: University of California Press, 1984).

the transformation of human animals into human persons.[2] The moral relevance of institutionalization is less apparent but becomes clear when we recall that institutions are intimately associated with the realization of values. It may be said, indeed, that institutionalization and socialization have parallel functions. One lends shape to individuals; the other forms groups and practices.

As an abstract idea, shorn of normative connotations, institutionalization is the emergence of orderly, stable, *socially integrating* patterns out of unstable, loosely organized, or narrowly technical activities.[3] The underlying reality—the basic source of stability and integration—is the creation of social entanglements or commitments. Most of what we do in everyday life is mercifully free and reversible. But when actions touch important interests and salient values or when they are embedded in networks of interdependence, options are more limited. Institutionalization constrains conduct in two main ways: by bringing it within a normative order, and by making it hostage to its own history.

Institutions, it has been said, "fix processes that are essentially dynamic."[4] This fixing legitimizes and thereby establishes social groupings. The starting mechanism is often a formal act, such as the adoption of a rule or statute. To be effective, however, the enactment must build upon preexisting resources of regularity and legitimacy and must lead to a new history of consistent conduct and supportive belief. Institutions are established, not by decree alone, but as a result of being bound into the fabric of social life. Even so weighty an enactment as the United States Constitution cannot be understood apart from the legal and political history that preceded it, the interpretive gloss given it by the courts, and the role it has played in American history and consciousness. The formal acts of adoption and ratification were only part of a more complex, more open-ended process of institution-building.

The term "institution" may refer to a group or a social practice, to the Catholic Church or the ritual of communion. This ambiguity is easy to live with, for the basic phenomenon is the same. The group itself may

2. In addition to this central function, socialization also refers to the process by which people who are "unformed" from the standpoint of a particular group or organization come to internalize appropriate habits and norms. The logic is the same, however: movement from a relatively open and unformed state to a more developed and determinate condition.

3. Leonard Broom and Philip Selznick, *Sociology: A Text with Adapted Readings*, 5th ed. (New York: Harper & Row, 1973), 232. See also Mary Douglas, *How Institutions Think* (Syracuse: Syracuse University Press, 1986), 46: "What is excluded from the idea of institution in these pages is any purely instrumental or provisional practical arrangement that is recognized as such." For recent work on the sociology of institutions, see Lynne G. Zucker, ed., *Institutional Patterns and Organizations* (Cambridge, Mass.: Ballinger, 1988).

4. Douglas, *How Institutions Think*, 92.

represent an institutionalized way of carrying out a social function. Whether it is a group or a practice or both, a social form becomes institutionalized as, through growth and adaptation, it takes on a distinctive character or function, becomes a receptacle of vested interests, or is charged with meaning as a vehicle of personal satisfaction or aspiration. A developed institution is not readily limited to narrowly defined goals. It is valued for the special place it holds in a larger social system. Institutions endure because persons, groups, or communities have a stake in their continued existence.

That existence is inescapably relative and a matter of degree. Groups and practices are more or less institutionalized, more or less immersed in social frameworks, more or less preoccupied with maintaining their special functions or identities. Institutionalization is relative in that, for example, a government agency may be a locus of commitment and value for its staff or for a special constituency, yet may be conceived and handled in quite narrowly instrumental terms by the larger system of which it is a part. A local business may be an integral part of a community or neighborhood, but that may not matter to its more distant shareholders.

A "pure" organization is a special-purpose tool, a rational instrument engineered to do a job, a lean, no-nonsense system of consciously coordinated activities. An institution, on the other hand, is better understood as a product of social adaptation, largely unplanned, often a result of converging interests. A given enterprise need not be solely either one or the other. On the contrary, most are complex mixtures of designed and adaptive problem-solving. The more settled the practice, the more firmly vested the interests, the more values at stake, the more sense it makes to speak of "an institution."[5]

I once suggested that the most significant meaning of "to institutionalize" is "to *infuse with value* beyond the technical requirements of the task at hand."[6] A familiar example of this process is the way individuals invest their churches, schools, firms, and military units with high levels of loyalty and commitment. Similarly, a community may find its well-being bound up with the fate of a local school, baseball team, or

5. In addition, the greater the need for institution-building (even in contexts that are mainly rational and instrumental), the more justified we are in treating the organization as an institution, or as a potential institution. For example, the more concerned we are about the assimilation of banking to ordinary business, with a loss of distinctive commitments to "savers" (as distinguished from "customers" or "investors"), the more relevant will be a focus on institution-building.

6. Selznick, *Leadership in Administration*, 17.

enterprise. The test is *expendability*, that is, the readiness with which the association or practice is given up or refashioned in response to practical or instrumental demands.

"Infusion with value" can be misleading, however, if it is thought of in psychological terms alone. It takes place in other ways as well: for example, by selective recruiting of members or personnel; by establishing strong ties or alliances; by creating a special language; and by the many commitments to persons and groups made in the course of implementing a policy or protecting a going concern.

From a moral point of view, institutionalization may be positive or negative. Much depends on *what* is institutionalized. There may be built-in deficits, as when a rule or practice becomes rigid or outmoded or a firm or agency becomes abuse-prone and unresponsive. We cannot determine the moral worth of an institution without knowing its character and what ends it serves. Nevertheless, the embodiment of values in organizations has a central place in the theory of institutions. Wherever that process matters to a community or culture, it is because some value is at stake or at risk. The trouble is that some aspects of institutionalization nourish the value, while others undermine it. Characteristically, to the dismay of all concerned, both outcomes occur.[7]

▼   ▲   ▼   ▲   ▼

In the transformation of organizations into institutions we may discern a two-step process. The first is foundational and formal. The act of association is itself a quest for "institutional" solutions to problems of economy and coordination. Instead of relying on spontaneous interaction or on markets and contracts, a need (or advantage) is perceived for authority and discipline. The formal structure of the organization is a long first step toward institutionalization. Explicit goals and rules; a chain of command; channels of communication: these *designed* modes of social integration overcome the looseness, instability, and limited rationality of ad hoc or contractual arrangements.[8]

7. Similarly, people may be socialized to accept disadvantage, or for criminal conduct. Nevertheless, both socialization and institutionalization can tap natural tendencies toward moral outcomes, tendencies that must be nurtured and directed. The child's need for governance, including self-governance, is a moral resource; so too is the institutional tendency to deepen commitments and broaden perspectives.

8. Some economists and sociologists have tried to identify the basic benefits gained from (hence the explanation for) association rather than contract or spontaneous interaction. See especially Oliver E. Williamson, *Markets and Hierarchies* (New York: Free Press, 1975); also James S. Coleman, *Foundations of Social Theory* (Cambridge: Harvard University Press, 1990), part 3.

But this is only a beginning. Beyond lies what we may call "thick" institutionalization. Formal systems act only through people. A social reality must be created, and that reality, which has its own dynamic and its own imperatives, lends texture to the organization. The official design is always supplemented by an informal structure, which is composed of attitudes, relationships, and practices that arise in the course of social interaction—as individuals and groups bring into play their own personalities, values, and interests. The underlying truth is that no organization can easily confine behavior to formally defined roles. The effort to do so takes work and vigilance and usually meets with uneven success.

Nor is it necessarily a good idea to restrain this spillover effect. When an organization (or part of it) becomes a social group, a unity of persons rather than technicians is formed. *New energies are generated*, which may or may not be constructive from the point of view of the organization. The unity of persons breaks through the neat confines of rational organization, producing individual struggles for place and preferment, rivalry among units, and commitment to ingrained, self-protective conduct. However, with proper guidance the informal structure may *uphold* the formal system by enhancing cohesion, initiative, and morale.[9]

The inevitability of informal patterns and practices does not mean the formal system is unimportant. In special-purpose groups the operative reality is always a combination of the formal and the informal, the designed and the organic. The formal system is effective to the extent work is done to maintain it and insofar as it is supported by an adequate array of incentives, including motives that drive the informal structure. Rules and purposes must be effectively part of and made good by a social matrix. This *operative system*, not the formal system alone, is the focus of institution-building.

Thick institutionalization takes place in many different ways. Familiar examples are: by sanctifying or otherwise hardening rules and procedures; by establishing strongly differentiated organizational units, which then develop vested interests and become centers of power; by creating administrative rituals, symbols, and ideologies; by intensifying "purposiveness," that is, commitment to unifying objectives; and by embedding the organization in a social environment. On the one hand, these and other institutionalizing forces tend to stabilize expectations, conduct, and belief. They create a distinctive, more or less integrated social reality. On the other hand, each is a potential source of distraction and

9. The informal structure is a kind of "social capital." See Coleman, *Foundations of Social Theory*, chap. 12.

incoherence. Even an elementary act of delegation carries the risk that authority will be attenuated and goals displaced. Furthermore, the institution is an arena within which multiple interests arise and contend. These include organizational divisions, employee groups, and constituencies of various kinds. Hence a measure of disunity must be expected. A living enterprise is likely to be at best somewhat disjointed, at worst barely capable of surviving. Hence there is no escaping the need for institutional self-awareness and self-criticism. If purposes are to be achieved, and values realized, the course of institutionalization must be monitored and controlled; and this must be done in institutionalized ways.

Students of organization have done much to deflate claims of purposefulness, system, and discipline. As against the "rational model" of tight organization, they have described "loose coupling" and even "organized anarchy."[10] Although organizations purport to be goal-driven, in fact many of their stated goals are too vague and abstract to be capable of determining policy choices. We must infer operative goals from actual practice. In this view, the typical large organization is better understood as a coalition, and as governed by multiple rationalities and negotiated authority, than as a unified system of coordination. These coalitions are marked by fluid and permeable boundaries, and by complex transactions with the environments they depend on and which they may control.[11]

This emphasis on open systems undercuts the idea that organizations are mainly devices for achieving specific objectives. At an extreme, organizational goals are considered irrelevant, indefinable, or concocted after the fact. The alternative is to see "the emergence of organizations, their structure of roles, division of labor, and distribution of power, as well as their maintenance, change, and dissolution . . . as outcomes of the complex exchanges between individuals pursuing a diversity of goals."[12] They are marketplaces in which individuals exchange a variety of incentives.

10. Michael D. Cohen, James G. March, and Johan P. Olsen, "A Garbage Can Model of Organizational Choice," *Administrative Science Quarterly* 17 (March 1972): 1–25. The authors note that "these properties of organized anarchy . . . are characteristic of any organization in part—part of the time. They are particularly conspicuous in public, educational, and illegitimate organizations. A theory of organized anarchy will describe a portion of almost any organization's activities, but will not describe all of them" (ibid., 1).

11. Viewed as an open system, "an organization is a coalition of shifting interest groups that develop goals by negotiation; the structure of the coalition, its activities, and its outcomes are strongly influenced by environmental factors" (W. Richard Scott, *Organizations: Rational, Natural, and Open Systems* [Englewood Cliffs, N.J.: Prentice-Hall, 1981], 22f.).

12. Petro Georgiou, "The Goal Paradigm and Notes Toward a Counter Paradigm," *Administrative Science Quarterly* 18 (1973): 308.

There is much to be said for this way of thinking, which focuses attention on the work that must be done to create a viable organization and maintain it in a steady state. There is no necessary contradiction, however, between the goal and the market paradigm. If social life is to go forward, adequate incentives and lively reciprocity are always needed. The life of special-purpose organizations is no exception. Indeed, what makes institutional design effective is the creation and maintenance of *appropriate* incentives and *appropriate* controls. To interpret organizations as open systems and as natural systems—as products of social adaptation and tacit learning—is as important for leadership as it is for analysis.

These ideas have a special relevance as a prelude to discussion of the morality of institutions. They point to a movement from organization to institution to *community*. An ideal of community, or at least a strain toward community, is implicit in both institution-building and openness. This is revealed both internally and externally.

Internally, as the organization takes on a distinctive identity the source of integration shifts from goals to values, from specific objectives to ways of thinking and deciding. In short, a corporate culture is created. The culture is sustained by a sense of community, that is, in the context of organization, by person-centered sharing in a common enterprise. To sustain the enterprise at high levels of initiative and commitment, something more is needed than rational coordination of clearly defined activities. Attention must be paid to fragile incentives, multiple interests, and the dynamics of cooperation and conflict. This requires a transition from *managing* organizations to *governing* communities—a theme we will explore in Chapter 11.

Externally, the institutionalized organization is a locus of value and a center of power. The surrounding community has a stake in its existence and in the proper conduct of its affairs. There is pressure from without to make the organization an integral part of the larger community, and to do so in part by recognizing its claims to moral autonomy. For an open system with permeable boundaries, no transaction with the environment is more important than negotiating its place in the moral order, that is, dealing with demands that it be responsible and responsive.[13]

This elaboration of organizational experience is obviously subject to considerable variation. A sense of institutional identity and an ideal of

---

13. These demands may be countered by showing that autonomy or even insularity best serves the cause of moral integration. In many contexts we recognize that professional, artistic, or academic autonomy may be needed to protect and nourish relevant ideals—ideals in which the community has a stake. See Chapter 12, "Autonomy and Responsiveness."

community are most likely to develop where values are more central than goals or at least are equally important, and where goals are multiplied in order to accommodate a broad range of interests. The formula "organization→institution→community" applies most clearly (but also variably) to schools, universities, hospitals, churches, professional associations, advocacy groups, political parties, and government agencies. The narrower and more instrumental the animating purpose, the more resistance there will be to thick institutionalization and the claims of community.

Nevertheless, the model is useful for diagnosing *any* large and enduring organization. The latter is, inevitably, a creature of its own history, responsible to numerous constituencies, and not easily confined to specific goals. No such organization can be wholly indifferent to self-defining values. From the standpoint of the larger community, moreover, the very size of the organization matters; and the institutionalized *practice* it represents—the way it carries on economic or governmental functions—may be in need of examination and reform.[14]

RATIONAL SYSTEMS AND MORAL AGENCY

The themes sketched above bear closely on the problem of moral agency. They suggest ways of thinking about corporate groups as responsible participants in a moral order. At the same time, the reality of incoherence and openness raises questions about what sense it makes to treat the association as a locus of responsibility and a bearer of rights. Here sociology touches a special branch of moral theory: how collective and individual responsibility are distinguished and related. Only people, it is often said, can be virtuous or vicious; only persons, not groups, have moral obligations; accountability runs to individuals, not systems.

"Agency" connotes competence, intentionality, and accountability. To be an agent is to act purposively, and to do so on behalf of a principal or in the service of a goal or policy. To be a *moral* agent, something more is required. There must be values in play beyond technical excellence, efficiency, or effectiveness. In its usual meaning, moral agency presumes

14. "We cannot solve the problems of corporate life simply by improving individual organizations; we have to reform the institution itself. If we confuse organizations and institutions, then when we believe we are being treated unfairly we may retreat into private life or flee from one organization to another—a different company or a new marriage—hoping that the next one will treat us better. But changes in how organizations are conceived, changes in the norms by which they operate—institutional changes—are the only way to get at the source of our difficulties" (Robert Bellah et al., *The Good Society* [New York: Alfred A. Knopf, 1991], 11; see also 289ff.).

a capacity to appreciate and reason from principles that speak (in the context at hand) to fellowship and integrity. Whether the agent does this well or poorly is a separate question.

However, moral agency need not presuppose moral competence. An object of moral concern may be a *locus* of values and may have moral *effect*, yet not be capable of autonomous action or moral reasoning. Young children have agency in this sense. They are receptacles and vehicles for ideals of caring, commitment, and nurture; they may be efficacious in binding the family unit; but they have not attained rationality, to say nothing of moral competence. Much the same may be said of a social practice, such as a religious or family ritual, or the institutions of constitutional government.

Applied to organizations, the concept of moral agency should embrace both meanings, intentionality as well as embodiment. When we view an organization "as an institution," we may mainly be concerned with the values it embodies, from the standpoint of the people whose lives it touches as well as that of the larger community. Insofar as it is "infused with value," the organization is likely to claim and be granted respect and concern. At the same time, to be an effective participant in the moral order, it must be competent, intentional, and accountable.

Moral agency may be weak or strong, positive or negative. In the case of organizations, much depends on the extent and direction of institutionalization. (In the case of individuals, the content and quality of socialization make the difference.) As the organization takes on a specific culture or character, its moral agency becomes clearer, more definite, more fully developed. This is likely to be positive, in some respects at least, insofar as it is the product of social learning and adaptation. It may also be evil or amoral, embodying vices rather than virtues, or may combine instrumental virtue, such as courage or resolve, with morally regressive ends. In any case, we must be able to characterize the system as morally good or bad, responsible or irresponsible. And this presumes both moral relevance and institutional coherence.

It has been argued that formal organizations are so constrained by their special purposes and by technical rationality that they cannot be moral actors:

> We cannot and must not expect formal organizations, or their representatives acting in their official capacities, to be honest, courageous, considerate, sympathetic, or to have any kind of moral integrity. . . . Actions that are wrong by ordinary standards are not so for organizations; indeed, they may often be required. Secrecy, espionage, and deception do not make organizational

action wrong; rather, they are right, proper and, indeed, *rational,* if they serve the objectives of the organization. They are no more or less wrong than, say, bluffing is in poker. From the point of view of organizational decision-making they are "ethically neutral." . . . [O]rganizations are like machines, and it would be a category mistake to expect a machine to comply with the principles of morality. By the same token, an official or agent of a formal organization is simply violating the basic rule of organizational activity if he allows his moral scruples rather than the objectives of the organization to determine his decision.[15]

This point of view takes too seriously an abstract conception of formal organization. It is, we might say, an exercise in reification. Viewed concretely, as operative systems, organizations are not so single-minded. They can and do take account of multiple values; accept limits on the ends they may pursue and the means they may use; devise procedures for controlling conduct in the light of moral concerns. They are in principle capable, through organizational measures, of recognizing moral issues, exercising self-restraint, and improving moral competence. They can, in short, be responsible participants in a moral order.

Instrumental rationality is no bar to moral agency. If it were, we would have trouble treating *individuals* as moral agents. People are often committed to projects that demand fidelity to purpose or to selected values. Artists, scientists, and lawyers often protect their professional identities by resisting extraneous influences, including the demands of morality. But they are also persons, and as such have moral capacities and responsibilities, which intrude as necessary into the realm of work, refashioning means and ends. As operative systems, organizations must accept similar limitations on the single-minded pursuit of efficiency or effectiveness.

To be sure, organizational imperatives often lead to immoral outcomes—deception, corruption, exploitation, domination—and these are considered at some length below. But such outcomes are variable. Some organizations are under greater pressure than others or are engaged in activities that invite abuse. The variability shows that rational systems need not be amoral. Under congenial conditions an organization may choose, and is likely to choose, acceptable ways of doing business. The mere fact that something *might* be advantageous—selling shoddy goods, for example—does not necessarily make it the rational way to go. From the standpoint of organizational interests, there may be good reasons to limit the choice of means. In other words, the demands of rationality can-

15. John Ladd, "Morality and the Ideal of Rationality in Formal Organizations," *The Monist* 54 (1970): 499f.

not be met if the full interplay of means and ends is neglected. A narrow view of rationality, uninformed by the continuum of means-ends, is the chief flaw in the view that organizations are necessarily amoral.

It must be admitted that some elliptical (and perhaps careless) formulations in organization theory have encouraged this perspective. For example, from Herbert A. Simon: "Decisions in private management, like decisions in public management, must take as their ethical premises the objectives that have been set for the organization."[16] This can be read as denying a connection between organizational decisions and principles of morality.[17]

But Simon also wrote, at about the same time:

> No knowledge of administrative techniques, then, can relieve the administrator from the task of moral choice—choice as to organization goals and methods and choice as to his treatment of the other human beings in his organization. His code of ethics is as significant a part of his equipment as an administrator as is his knowledge of administrative behavior, and no amount of study of the "science" of administration will provide him with this code.[18]

The point of the discussion (in both texts) was to uphold a positivist science of administration, which requires, Simon and his co-authors thought, a sharp separation of fact from value. However, "this emphasis on the factual does not mean that we discount the importance of values. It simply reflects our belief that the competent administrator reaches his desired ends—whatever they may be—through a mastery of the phenomena he is dealing with and a clear, objective understanding of their behavior."[19] Here values are assimilated to ends; the constraint of means is neglected. But the neglect is an oversight, as the context makes clear. In Simon's view, values are inaccessible to science. They are, however, drawn from morality, and they are vital aspects of administrative decision-making.

A necessary tension exists between the claims of specialized activity and the claims of morality. The former strains toward single-mindedness, the latter toward recognition of multiple values and commitments. Although this tension occurs in individual life as well, it is especially important in the moral experience of special-purpose groups. Better to explore the tension, and learn from it, than to dismiss it as a "category mistake."

16. Herbert A. Simon, *Administrative Behavior* (New York: Macmillan, 1958), 52.
17. As in Ladd, "Morality and the Ideal of Rationality," 499.
18. Herbert A. Simon, Donald W. Smithburg, and Victor A. Thompson, *Public Administration* (New York: Alfred A. Knopf, 1950), 24.
19. Ibid., 20.

▼   ▲   ▼   ▲   ▼

The moral premises and dilemmas of administration are corporate and collective, not merely individual. Hence there is corporate accountability, and there are corporate rights. Organizations have attributes that cannot be reduced to individual motivation and conduct. These include a decision-making structure, a system of coordinated roles, and a history of policy and practice. An organizational decision is likely to involve many participants, each contributing in different ways to a composite outcome. We may be able to fix individual responsibility for a final decision or for initiating and implementing a policy.[20] Nevertheless, the pattern of decision-making is an organizational phenomenon, and for many purposes the organization must be held accountable for the way individual decisions are made. Studies of decision-making, established practice, and corporate culture are the stock-in-trade of management consultants and government regulators. A postulate of such studies is that the *system* determines individual behavior. Motives are structurally induced or frustrated. Hence the structure must be assessed, and changed as necessary.[21]

There is no contradiction between the reality of structure and "methodological individualism." According to the latter, "the ultimate constituents of the social world are individual people who act more or less appropriately in the light of their dispositions and understanding of their situation."[22] Indeed, every statement about the structure of an organization, or about an organizational process, should ideally be anchored in evidence about individual decisions and responses. In principle, we must be able to *locate* the collective phenomenon in what individuals want, do, and perceive. It does not follow, however, that the behavior of individuals is self-defined or that organizational characteristics are nothing more than the characteristics of individuals. If social cohesion exists,

20. We need not choose between individual and collective accountability. Both may be appropriate. A·railroad may be liable for its negligence, and individual employees may be punished as well.

21. For discussions of organizational structure as it bears on collective responsibility, see Peter A. French, *Collective and Corporate Responsibility* (New York: Columbia University Press, 1984); Larry May, *The Morality of Groups* (Notre Dame: University of Notre Dame Press, 1987); and Meir Dan-Cohen, *Rights, Persons, and Organizations* (Berkeley: University of California Press, 1986).

22. J. W. N. Watkins, "Methodological Individualism and Social Tendencies," in May Brodbeck, ed., *Readings in the Philosophy of the Social Sciences* (New York: Macmillan, 1968), 270.

there must be an objective correlate in individual feelings, perceptions and conduct, but that does not change the collective nature of the phenomenon.[23]

Nor need we say that institutions are "persons." The metaphor is sometimes useful, but the distinctive attributes of human beings as natural persons should not be obscured. Persons have moral and ontological *primacy*. They are ultimate objects of moral concern, whereas institutions must be judged by the contributions they make to personal and social well-being. Institutions may be highly prized, but they are always more or less utilitarian, more or less expendable.

Many religious, educational, legal, and political institutions are valued for their general functions and long-range benefits. They are vehicles for meaningful, self-affirming participation in the life of the community; and they may properly ask for personal sacrifice, the more readily as they become symbols of group identity or otherwise serve the general welfare. On these grounds, institutions may be said to have intrinsic worth. On close inspection, however, we see that the worth they are assigned is based on consequentialist reasoning and presumes more fundamental values. Institutions are made for people, not people for institutions.

As organizations can be more or less institutionalized, so they can be more or less utilitarian or instrumental. Some have greater moral worth than others, hence a greater claim to be treated as objects of moral concern. This proposition bears closely on the matter of organizational *rights*, especially rights normally assigned to natural persons. If we think of organizations as merely furthering individual purposes, it may seem persuasive to say that the rights of organizations should be narrowly conceived, or derivative from the rights of individuals.[24] If we grant institutions legal autonomy, it is only because doing so protects the autonomy of the members of the institution or serves the proximate interests of the community. Therefore, if the members can be protected in other ways, the community is free to treat the organization as wholly subject to regulation—naked, as it were, before legislative will and executive discretion.

This model works fairly well in the case of the "pure" organization created to pursue narrowly defined ends with maximum efficiency and effectiveness. The model weakens, however, as wider values are

23. See May Brodbeck, "Methodological Individualism: Definition and Reduction," 269–303 in Brodbeck, ed., *Readings in the Philosophy of the Social Sciences*.
24. See Dan-Cohen, *Rights, Persons, and Organizations*, 55ff.

implicated—from the standpoint of participants as well as the community. The rights of the association become more secure as it comes to serve larger interests. Thus the historic claims to autonomy of churches and universities do not derive solely from ideals of *individual* religious or academic freedom. Rather, the *institution* is thought to serve public ends and to do so best when insulated from political intrusion.[25]

The moral logic we apply to institutions is in important respects the same as that we apply to persons. As will appear in more detail later on, the idiom of Part Two—moral development and recalcitrance, the implicated self, constructive self-regard—is useful for the diagnosis of institutions. That is so not by grace of reasoning by analogy from persons to institutions but because the concept of moral actor is more general than that of person. The logic of moral action governs all moral actors, collectivities and persons alike.[26]

THE MICHELS EFFECT

Institutions embody values, but they can do so only as operative systems or going concerns. The trouble is that what is good for the operative system does not necessarily serve the standards or ideals the institution is supposed to uphold. Therefore institutional values are always at risk. Insofar as organizational, technological, and short-run imperatives dominate decision-making, goals and standards are vulnerable. They are subject to displacement, attenuation, and corruption.

Some ideals are especially precarious, either because they are subtle and require sensitive awareness or because they compete directly with more urgent or more seductive alternatives. For example, democracy, education, scholarship, and love need sustained nurture and vigilant protection. Moral failure largely stems from this competition between indefinite, elusive, but possibly higher goods and more definite or more immediate satisfactions. A major function of the moral order is to pre-

25. Similarly, the right of business firms to freedom of speech is bolstered when the interest of the community in listening to all viewpoints is considered. However, as Dan-Cohen points out, restrictions on corporate speech may be justified if it can be shown that excessive spending for political advertising may dominate the public forum. See ibid., 109. For a critique, along lines similar to mine, of Dan-Cohen's general argument, see Richard B. Stewart, "Organizational Jurisprudence," *Harvard Law Review* 101 (November 1987): 371–90.

26. It does not follow, of course, that collectivities and persons have the same moral worth or the same obligations. Because collectivities are ultimately instrumental, they have lesser moral worth than persons. But that does not mean they have no moral worth or cannot be moral actors.

serve inherently precarious values against ruinous competition from the cheap, the easy, the cost-effective, and the urgent.

The pernicious effect of organizational imperatives was explored in a famous study by the German political sociologist Robert Michels (1876–1936).[27] Michels's examination of the experience of European socialist parties and trade unions before World War I led him to the conclusion that democracy and socialism are unattainable ideals. "The socialists might conquer, but not socialism, which would perish in the moment of its adherents' triumph."[28] That was so, he argued, because leadership in democratic organizations is readily and fatefully self-perpetuating. Where collective action is contemplated, delegation of tasks and powers to leaders is indispensable. The unintended result is a concentration of political skills and prerogatives, including control over staff and channels of communication. Furthermore, the position of the leaders is strengthened by the members' political indifference and by the sense of obligation they have to those who guide them and do the main work. In the ordinary case the rank and file submit willingly rather than reluctantly to the widening power of officials. This usually occurs, not for any arcane psychological reason, such as self-abasement, but because as persons the members have more interesting and more compelling things to do than attend meetings and monitor officials. This lack of supervision and participation by the members frees leaders to subvert the aims of the association, whether in their own interests or in the interests of others.

Michels had the idea that leaders try to stay in office and exploit their privileges because it is inherent in human nature to seek power and retain it. "The desire to dominate, for good or evil, is universal."[29] This proposition is not really necessary to his argument. He need only have postulated ordinary human desire for security, comfort, and status. These motivations, which are sufficiently powerful, and the recurrent phenomena to which Michels called attention—especially the prerogatives of office and the nature of rank-and-file participation—adequately explain the drift to oligarchy.

This "Michels effect" should not be confused with the simple necessity for leadership and hierarchy. The delegation of tasks and powers to officials is not in itself undemocratic, so long as leaders are held accountable and can readily be removed and replaced by democratic methods.

27. *Political Parties: A Sociological Study of the Oligarchical Tendencies of Modern Democracy* (1915; reprint, Glencoe: Free Press, 1962). For a discussion of Michels's background and influence see the introduction by S. M. Lipset.

28. Ibid., 391.

29. Ibid., 206.

The Michels effect speaks to *self-perpetuating* leadership, which is oligarchical in that leaders can replace themselves by co-optation and can go
their own way on matters of policy. When Michels wrote of the limits of
democracy he had in mind something more than delegation of authority.
Delegation is the starting mechanism that, under appropriate conditions, brings domination and subversion.[30]

Michels thought he had discovered an "iron law." "Who says organization," he wrote, "says oligarchy."[31] It is obvious, however, that in
many organizations democracy does survive and even flourish. In fact we
can only say there is a predisposition to oligarchy among certain kinds of
organizations. We learn what will happen in the absence of countervailing forces or definite social checks. There is, of course, no "iron law."
Nevertheless, the Michels effect identifies a fundamental social process.
It can account for a great deal of organizational experience, especially
where special-purpose associations, formally democratic, are committed
to collective action and therefore to administrative staffs.[32]

Ironically, despite his apocalyptic rhetoric Michels himself called attention to countervailing forces. At least at the time he published his
study, he thought democracy could be "if not a cure, at least a palliative,
for the disease of oligarchy."[33] He identified two regulative principles
which restrain the drift to oligarchy and mitigate its effects.

First, democracy tends to "stimulate and strengthen in the individual
the intellectual aptitudes for criticism and control."

> Now this predisposition towards free inquiry, in which we cannot fail to rec-
> ognize one of the most precious factors of civilization, will gradually increase
> in proportion as the economic status of the masses undergoes improvement

30. Because he studied social reform movements, Michels was especially interested in
the apparent subversion of ideals that comes from the conservatism of an oligarchic leadership that places stability and security for the organization (and for the leaders) above all
other aims. To assure stability, action is slow and cautious, risks are minimized, powerful
enemies are placated, and aims are modified.

31. Ibid., 365. Part 5, chap. 2, is entitled "Democracy and the Iron Law of
Oligarchy."

32. A strikingly similar argument is found in Adolph A. Berle, Jr., and Gardiner C.
Means, *The Modern Corporation and Private Property* (New York: Macmillan, 1933), the famous study of managerial control in large corporations characterized by widely dispersed
stock ownership. The separation of ownership and control is based on mechanisms very
like those discussed by Michels. The moral significance is different, of course, because in
the corporate context the value of democracy is less salient. It should be noted, however,
that even in the political and public-issue realm the Michels effect is not always morally offensive. Many voluntary associations are democratic in form but create little or no expec-
tation that the members should exercise "voice" rather than "exit." In effect they volun-
tarily pay a tax to support the staff, which carries on the work of the organization. If they
don't like what is done they withdraw support.

33. Michels, *Political Parties*, 369.

and becomes more stable, and in proportion as they are admitted more effectively to the advantages of civilization. A wider education involves an increasing capacity for exercising control. . . . It is, consequently, the great task of social education to raise the intellectual level of the masses, so that they may be enabled, within the limits of what is possible, to counteract the oligarchical tendencies of the working-class movement.[34]

The second regulative principle is "the *effective* counter-tendency of democracy towards the creation of parties ever more complex and more differentiated—parties, that is to say, which are increasingly based upon the competence of the few."[35] In other words, oligarchy can be limited when power is available to check power, a process which, to be sustained, depends on the energy and activity of elites. The proliferation of elites is an aspect of democracy.[36]

Although Michels recognized these countervailing conditions, he gave at most one muted cheer for democracy. Like Winston Churchill, he wrote that if we compare it to other systems, such as aristocracy, "we must choose democracy as the least of evils." And "nothing but a serene and frank examination of the oligarchical dangers of democracy will enable us to minimize these dangers, even though they can never be entirely avoided."[37]

The Michels thesis has been troublesome to Marxists and to others who have hoped that humanist and democratic ideals might be fulfilled without taking personal and institutional recalcitrance into account. If there is recalcitrance, and if pressure to undo ideals is inevitable, then

34. Ibid.
35. Ibid., 370, Michels's emphasis.
36. The social sources of pluralist democracy in a major trade union are explored in Seymour Martin Lipset, Martin A. Trow, and James S. Coleman, *Union Democracy: The Internal Politics of the International Typographical Union* (Glencoe, Ill.: Free Press, 1956). As Paul Jacobs noted in reviewing the book, this case also shows that union democracy does not necessarily coincide with serving the public good. See his *The State of the Unions* (New York: Atheneum, 1963), 138ff.
37. Michels, *Political Parties,* 370. This is the way Michels concluded the German edition of his book, published in 1911. For the Italian edition published in 1915, from which the English translation was made, he ended on a more somber note: "The democratic currents of history resemble successive waves. They break ever on the same shoal. They are ever renewed. This enduring spectacle is simultaneously encouraging and depressing. When democracies have gained a certain stage of development, they undergo a gradual transformation, adopting the aristocratic spirit, and in many cases also the aristocratic forms, against which at the outset they struggled so fiercely. Now new accusers arise to denounce the traitors; after an era of glorious combats and inglorious power, they end by fusing with the old dominant class; whereupon once more they are in their turn attacked by fresh opponents who appeal to the name of democracy. It is probable that this cruel game will continue without end" (ibid., 371). The author's darkening mood, apparently affected by the onset of World War I, has no bearing, of course, on the logic or validity of his argument.

appropriate safeguards must be kept in place. For the prophets among us, this constraint is an irritation and a stumbling block. The vision of a perfect commonwealth is necessarily and permanently dimmed. There can be no appeal to millennial yearnings, no promise of a kingdom come. Above all, no movement or party can be trusted to impose its will in the name of "the people" or "history" without effective protection against abuse of power.

▼   ▲   ▼   ▲   ▼

Although Michels's study speaks directly to socialists and trade unionists,[38] it contains a lesson for all institutions: *Ideals go quickly by the board when the compelling realities of organizational life are permitted to run their natural course.* The imperatives of organization are sometimes ennobling, as we shall see, but they can also corrupt and demoralize. This ill effect occurs, for example, when the organization as such, or some proximate objective, becomes the prime locus of loyalty and commitment. What is good for the party, the agency, or the company becomes the operative criterion of moral worth, to which all other goods are subordinated. Or profit as a goal is offered in excuse of flagrant immorality, such as the marketing of clearly harmful products. These may be extreme cases, but they point to a process at work wherever administrative and economic necessities—budget, personnel, productivity, cost, competition—override concern for personal and institutional integrity.

Organizations of many kinds are notoriously prone to turn moral persons into immoral agents. Many forms of corruption, especially deception, are relied upon routinely to defend the reputation of the organization, protect it against competitors, and market its products. These practices are often thought of as necessary and defensible ways of getting a job done, not only in obvious cases, such as espionage or the making of television commercials, but in the gray areas of almost any business or occupation.

A good supply sergeant understands reconnaissance in his own way. He knows where the generator desperately needed by his unit lies idle and might be "scrounged." The road from that experience to black-market trading may not be difficult to negotiate. An organizational culture of deceit, theft, cynicism, and opportunism does not make for a moral in-

---

38. The full import of his argument was brought home to socialists after the Russian Revolution, and especially after the totalitarian character of the communist regime became apparent.

stitution, even if its ends are justifiable and even if it leaves the moral character of the person largely unblemished.

The irrelevance of individual motive and intent is apparent in institutional racism or sexism. When such charges are made, the claim is that invidious discrimination is not necessarily a product of conscious bias or deliberate choice. The system is indicted, not the individual prosecutor, personnel manager, lawyer, physician, or faculty member. Institutional racism and sexism are products of history and culture, that is, of largely unconscious dispositions and preferences. Being unconscious, they are insulated from critical scrutiny. Furthermore, they are sustained by practical routines and vested interests, including well-established lines of communication and cooperation. These contexts of everyday life define what is convenient and "sensible." Because the practices and the discriminatory outcomes are systemic, a sociological diagnosis is needed—which is not a quest for something ineffable or disembodied. Institutional racism must be located in what individuals do and how they react. But to identify institutional bias does not require that we prove willful or purposive misconduct.

The most pervasive cause of institutional debasement is *opportunism,* understood as the pursuit of short-run advantage without effective restraint by principle and ultimate consequence.[39] All human life contains an element of opportunism, because moral codes and distant objectives are never fully effective as guides to conduct. In many special contexts, however, opportunism is endemic and dominates decision-making. A marginally profitable enterprise may have little choice but to be opportunistic, so long as the need to survive is taken for granted. But opportunism can also be encouraged and even celebrated. This occurs, for example, when short-term "bottom-line" results are made the measure of executive success.

Among the ironies of moral sociology is the intimate association of opportunism and utopianism. As Michels and others understood, words like "democracy" and "socialism" are effective as calls to action and as cementers of solidarity, but they are not useful guides to decision-making. Insofar as they fail to specify how and at what cost ideals are to be fulfilled, they are utopian "unanalyzed abstractions," and they invite opportunism because they readily serve as protective covers behind

39. Opportunism has been more narrowly defined as "self-interest seeking with guile" and "more generally" as "the incomplete or distorted disclosure of information, especially calculated efforts to mislead, distort, disguise, obfuscate, or otherwise confuse" (Oliver E. Williamson, *The Economic Institutions of Capitalism* [New York: Free Press, 1985], 47).

which wholly self-interested decisions can be made. Utopians avoid hard choices by a flight to abstraction; they pay a heavy price, however, when events spin out of control.

Wherever purpose is overgeneralized, endemic opportunism is likely to appear. Goals such as "to make a profit," "education," "rehabilitation," and "equality" are too vague to serve as guides to responsible decision-making. When purposes are abstract, yet decisions must be made, more realistic but *uncontrolled* criteria will govern. Thus do the polarities of opportunism and utopianism meet and embrace.

THE CRITIQUE OF DOMINATION

The writings of Jacques Ellul, Ivan Illich, and Michel Foucault, among many others, indict modern institutions as irredeemably oppressive. The critics differ on many points, but all of them speak to a fundamental conflict between rational organization on the one hand and more spontaneous, more organic forms of life on the other. They share a concern about the human costs of technology, including, above all, technologies of social control.

We have encountered this theme before, in reference to rationalism, instrumental reason, and the technocratic mentality (see Chapter 2). There we discussed the "logic of domination" as revealed in the exploitation of natural resources. The same concerns arise when *human* resources are at stake. People become objects; they are means rather than ends; they are subordinated to the requirements of rational systems. Karl Marx's theory of alienation spoke to this issue, but Marx did not see that the afflictions of technique and system would reach beyond capitalism to affect socialism as well. Later writers have extended his diagnosis and deepened his criticism.[40]

The Subtleties of Power

One of the most perceptive and radical of these theorists was Michel Foucault (1926–1984). In a series of provocative works on insanity, penology, medicine, and sexuality, Foucault professed to reveal hitherto unrecognized forms of domination, especially forms obscured or justified by the myths and pretensions of liberalism and rationalism. In Foucault's vision a matrix of power envelops and pervades everyday life:

40. On Marx and alienation, see Chapter 5, "Marx and Durkheim."

I would suggest . . . (i) that power is co-extensive with the social body; there are no spaces of primal liberty between the meshes of its network; (ii) that relations of power are interwoven with other kinds of relations (production, kinship, family, sexuality) . . . ; (iii) that these relations don't take the sole form of prohibition and punishment, but are of multiple forms; (iv) that their interconnections delineate *general conditions of domination,* and this domination is organized into a more-or-less coherent and unitary strategic form; that dispersed, heteromorphous, localised procedures of power are adapted, reinforced and transformed by these global strategies . . . ; (v) that power relations do indeed "serve," but not at all because they are "in the service of" an economic interest taken as primary, rather because they are capable of being utilized as strategies; (vi) that *there are no relations of power without resistances;* the latter are all the more real and effective because they are formed right at the point where relations of power are exercised; resistance to power does not have to come from elsewhere to be real, nor is it inexorably frustrated through being the compatriot of power. It exists all the more by being in the same place as power; hence, like power, resistance is multiple and can be integrated in global strategies.[41]

The play of power invades our intimate social worlds and is deeply constitutive of our personalities; it is a process in which we are all implicated and from which we cannot escape. Networks of power, strategies of control, and acts of resistance are fundamental attributes of the human condition.

Foucault moves easily from these generalizations to the study of very specific "technologies of power."[42] *Discipline and Punish,* for example, traces the emergence of the prison, with its sustaining ideologies, as a representative institution of our epoch. During the eighteenth and nineteenth centuries a major transition took place in the forms and justifications of punishment. Public flogging, branding, maiming, and execution gave way to forced detention and correction. Instruments of terror and punishment as "political ritual" were replaced by more rational systems of isolation, deterrence, and rehabilitation.[43] The latter were hailed as reforms, but they were in their own way no less oppressive.

The prison as an institution arose as part of a broader response to a key problem of that era: how to overcome the outlooks and habits of a peasant society. New ways of summoning and directing human

41. *Power/Knowledge: Selected Interviews and Other Writings, 1972–1977,* ed. Colin Gordon (New York: Pantheon Books, 1980), 142, my emphasis.
42. Michel Foucault, *Discipline and Punish: The Birth of the Prison,* trans. Alan Sheridan (New York: Vintage Books, 1979), 23, 30.
43. Ibid., 47ff.

resources were being sought, and the keynotes were efficiency and discipline. A new "political technology of the body" was vividly apparent in military training and organization:[44]

> By the late eighteenth century, the soldier has become something that can be made; out of a formless clay . . . the machine required can be constructed; posture is gradually corrected; a calculated constraint runs slowly through each part of the body, mastering it, making it pliable, ready at all times, turning silently into the automatism of habit; in short, one has "got rid of the peasant" and given him "the air of a soldier."[45]

A similar process was spreading to schools and the larger workshops. The foundation was being laid for an array of "disciplines" or "general formulas of domination."[46]

The "disciplines" are techniques of meticulous regulation and close supervision. They are ways of imposing order on what would otherwise be a motley collection of soldiers, prisoners, students, or workers. In this "political anatomy of detail,"[47] people are *segregated* physically in cell blocks, barracks, classrooms, shops, and offices; *supervised* by guards, sergeants, foremen, and teachers; *routinized* by prescribed timetables, exercises, and body movements; *corrected* or "normalized" whenever deviations from a rule occur; and *inspected* at all times and by easy access.

"The perfect disciplinary apparatus would make it possible for a single gaze to see everything constantly."[48] This "disciplinary gaze" is much enhanced when buildings

> are no longer built simply to be seen (as with the ostentation of palaces), or to observe the external space (cf. the geometry of fortresses), but . . . to render visible those who are inside it; . . . an architecture that would operate to transform individuals: to act on those it shelters, to provide a hold on their conduct, to carry the effects of power right to them, to make it possible to know them, to alter them. Stones can make people docile and knowable.[49]

"Stones" are material—as are many other devices for controlling conduct—but the true target is the human spirit. By acquiescing in the disciplines, by absorbing their message, people become instruments of their own subjugation.

44. Ibid., 26, 30.
45. Ibid., 135.
46. Ibid., 137.
47. Ibid., 139.
48. Ibid., 173.
49. Ibid., 172.

The prison is not a marginal, isolated, or specialized institution. For Foucault it is the very face of modernity. Because technologies of control are so useful and so effective, they have brought into being the "disciplinary society." A "carceral archipelago" spreads the technology of imprisonment to "the entire social body."[50]

The emphasis on method and system brings home the role of knowledge in social control. Indeed, the true villains of this drama are the purveyors of social knowledge. The "human sciences" have much to answer for. These dubious enterprises have, willy-nilly, forged the chains of domination. "The Enlightenment, which discovered the liberties, also invented the disciplines."[51] Knowledge, once welcomed as liberating, has become the handmaiden of power.

The intimate bonding of knowledge and power is, for Foucault, a fundamental postulate. It is not only that some people deliberately use knowledge to advance their influence and dominate others. The connection is more profound. Knowledge and power "directly imply one another . . . there is no power relation without the correlative constitution of a field of knowledge, nor any knowledge that does not presuppose and constitute at the same time power relations."[52] Knowledge takes for granted the power to classify events as well as persons, and to do so *authoritatively*. Nor is this an innocent technical exercise. Knowledge creates a common currency in the distinctions we take for granted as we perceive and interpret the world. Received classifications govern and therefore limit our ways of thinking. The categories we use are not our own; we are all victims of the politics of language.

"My objective . . . has been to create a history of the different modes by which, in our culture, human beings are made subjects."[53] To be made a subject is to experience the subjugation of mind, self, and body. This subjugation begins with the ordinary process of growing up in a particular society. It is a result of the many ways language, thought, and practice form minds and selves. As identities of gender, role, and social class are fixed, persons are objectified and made amenable to systems of

---

50. Ibid., 216, 298. Foucault's "carceral archipelago" echoes *The Gulag Archipelago,* "made up of the enormous network of penal institutions and all the rest of the web of machinery for police oppression and terror imposed throughout the author's period of reference on all Soviet life. Gulag is the acronym for the Chief Administration of Corrective Labor Camps which supervised the larger part of this system" (Aleksandr F. Solzhenitzyn, *The Gulag Archipelago: 1918–1956* [New York: Harper & Row, 1973], 616).

51. Foucault, *Discipline and Punish*, 222.

52. Ibid., 27.

53. Michel Foucault, *Beyond Structuralism and Hermeneutics*, 2d ed. (Chicago: University of Chicago Press, 1983), 208.

control. At bottom, therefore, every culture knows sin, and original sin at that. It is the sin of domination.

Foucault's remedy of choice for this subjugation of the mind is culture shock. History is deployed to bring home the lesson that today's premises are neither necessary nor immutable; they have not been with us always. On the contrary, every aspect of life is contingent and arbitrary. Foucault's popularity in the 1970s and 1980s was in part a more sardonic, more sophisticated, more exotic replay of the radical cultural relativism whose heyday was the 1930s.[54] Foucault added a new slant, however. The earlier relativists saw truth as a reflex of culture, but they thought of culture as essentially benign. Foucault saw truth (at least *social* knowledge) as an instrument of domination—inherently subjective and mainly a sham.

This cynicism is only superficial, however. Unflagging in his criticism of things as they are and were, Foucault nevertheless displayed an irrepressible yearning and latent hope for true liberation. The very idea of domination suggests that there is a spirit struggling to be free: hence his emphasis on inevitable resistance to systems of control. Although that resistance must itself adopt strategies of power, there is an underlying goodness to be realized--if only social life were properly reconstructed, if only we might be free to "create ourselves as works of art."[55]

System and Lifeworld

The themes of domination and liberation are pursued in more responsible, if less arresting, ways by the German philosopher and social theorist Jürgen Habermas. Heir to the Frankfurt School's critique of instrumental reason, Habermas has offered his own diagnosis of our time. There is a fundamental conflict, he argues, between the rationality of "systems" and the rationality of the "lifeworld" or *Lebenswelt*. On the one hand, "systems" are technologies of all sorts and as such are "instrumental," "functional," and "purposive."[56] They are governed by ends that have their own logic and that are divorced from the direct expression of human needs and concerns. The realm of system is preeminently—though not exclusively—the realm of rational special-purpose organization.

54. See above, Chapter 4.
55. Foucault, *Beyond Structuralism*, 237.
56. Jürgen Habermas, *The Theory of Communicative Action*, trans. Thomas McCarthy (Boston: Beacon Press, 1984), 2:chap. 6; also 332ff.

The lifeworld, on the other hand, is the scene of unprogrammed, adaptive, self-implicating conduct. It is a world experienced concretely by persons who interact as organic unities, not as abstract or segmental role-players. In the context of organization, the "lifeworld" is roughly what sociologists have called "informal structure." More generally, the lifeworld is the realm of distinctively social and cultural experience, which can never be equated with formal systems of any sort. The heart of social life is more adaptive than purposive, more attuned to the integration of persons than to the coordination of activities.

In the lifeworld, as in culture, communication is person-centered and symbolism is expressive. In culture the fundamental quest is for integrative meanings, not technical knowledge. The abstractions of language are filled in through everyday practice and interpretation. Only then do they become part of a world that makes sense to situated beings. This concreteness is indispensable to genuine communication—and therefore to community.

The fate of communication is Habermas's main concern. The waning of traditional authority, he argues, has made the modern lifeworld more rational. New ways of thinking and of participating in the culture of everyday life have contributed to a more critical, less tradition-bound spirit. A "culture of reflection"[57] makes problematic what was once unquestioned. In public life it transforms expectations regarding the quality of consent and the legitimation of authority.

The rationality of the lifeworld is oriented toward mutual understanding (*Verständigung*), not success. Human interaction becomes more rational as people come to know each other's premises; as they properly interpret meanings and motivations; as they use the resources of a shared language for criticism, dialogue, and agreement. The rationality that looks to success or goal-seeking employs other resources and a different logic. Instead of relying on human communication and natural language, which are inherently disorderly, fuzzy, and connotative, rationality is sought in artificial languages. These include the abstractions of money and command, which reduce persons to manipulable units of cost, energy, and obedience. In engineered and programmed systems, the processes of *Verständigung*, of working toward mutual understanding and rational consensus, are swept out as unwelcome distractions.

The problem is that, in practice, system and lifeworld are largely interdependent. Under modern conditions at least, technical systems are

57. Ibid., 1:341.

indispensable for security and prosperity. Yet they tend to "colonize" the lifeworld. They impose an instrumental or impersonal logic on spheres of life that should be, from the standpoint of interaction and communication, freer and more organic. (This sort of imposition is seen, according to Habermas and others, in the excessive legalism of the welfare state and in its tendency to bureaucratize human relations.)[58] Furthermore, the logic of success, with its rejection of communication as a goal, is generally self-defeating. Much efficiency is lost when rational organizations are unable to sustain viable lifeworlds within them, and when they do not maintain effective connection with the lifeworlds about them.

The tension between lifeworld and system has long been a master theme in sociology.[59] The contrast between culture and civilization, and many similar dichotomies, have implicitly given a central place to *the human encounter with impersonality.*[60] It may be said, indeed, that the foundation of culture, the primordial culture-creating act, is the transformation of impersonal settings into personal ones.[61] This transformation begins when people encounter an indifferent and threatening natural environment, and it continues as they construct impersonal technologies, including economic and political systems. To preserve settings within which people can feel at home and unalienated; to infuse technical systems with the vitality of informal, life-affirming, communication-easing interaction: these are essential functions to which much of sociology has been addressed.

To a large extent, therefore, Habermas has restated and renamed a well-known aspect of the sociological perspective. But he has added a fresh emphasis on the importance of communicative rationality in modern culture. Like Foucault, Habermas locates the fundamental source of domination in oppressive forms of discourse. The alternative is wholly emancipated communication, unburdened by coercion of any sort, in-

58. Ibid., 2:362.
59. "The invasion of the community by the new and relatively impersonal and mechanical modes of combined human behavior is the outstanding fact of modern life" (John Dewey, *The Public and Its Problems* [New York: Holt, 1927], 98).
60. The contrast between civilization and culture is almost forgotten in contemporary thought, but a humanist social science should renew acquaintance with it. As is discussed in Robert M. MacIver and Charles H. Page, *Society: An Introductory Analysis* (New York: Rinehart, 1949), 498ff., civilization is the utilitarian order, the apparatus of living, the realm of technique and sophistication. Culture is the realm of activities valued for themselves. The two great branches of human achievement differ in decisive ways. Progress in civilization is readily perceived, and because technique has an impersonal and universal logic it is fairly easily transferred. Culture, by contrast, is bound up with the particularity and concreteness of social life; it is less readily assessed and less easily transferred.
61. Gertrude Jaeger and Philip Selznick, "A Normative Theory of Culture," *American Sociological Review* 29 (October 1964): 658.

cluding that of uncritically received beliefs and perspectives. Through discourse free from domination the unfulfilled ideals of the Enlightenment may be redeemed.

INDIFFERENCE TO VARIATION

Habermas does not share Foucault's passion for unmasking or his rejection of the Enlightenment dream that human conduct should be guided by rational principles. He does not accept Foucault's view that *any* claim to truth is an illusion and a stratagem in the great game of power. On the contrary, Habermas insists that criteria for assessing the quality of arguments are in principle accessible to human judgment. They become available in practice under conditions of robust, unfettered, and responsible criticism. The flourishing of such criticism within a framework of shared understandings makes genuine knowledge possible and keeps domination at bay.

This perspective is incompatible with Foucault's refusal to recognize *empirical variation* in the pervasiveness of domination. If all is subjugation, and if society is inherently coercive, it becomes impossible to make sense of relative freedom, authenticity, and individuality. As Habermas points out, Foucault shows little appreciation for the positive role of law, including criminal law, in protecting the interests of citizens.[62] Nor does Foucault draw a distinction between truly repressive socialization and socialization that forms, more or less effectively, competent and autonomous persons.[63]

Indifference to variation is a persistent failing among critics of domination. A notable offender was Karl Marx, who argued that a whole array of institutions, including democracy and law, belong to the superstructure of capitalism and are therefore irredeemably bourgeois. The virtues of free speech and election can be ignored or denied; they count for nothing when weighed against the basic fact of class domination. Ironically, this sweeping indictment is itself a strategy of domination. As

62. Jürgen Habermas, *The Philosophical Discourse of Modernity* (Cambridge: MIT Press, 1987), 290.
63. As Habermas says, "If one admits only the model of empowerment, the socialization of succeeding generations can also be presented only in the image of wily confrontation. Then, however, the socialization of subjects capable of speech and action cannot be simultaneously conceived as individuation, but only as the progressive subsumption of bodies and of all vital substrata under technologies of power. The increasingly individualizing formative processes that penetrate ever broader social strata in societies with traditions that have become reflective . . . have to be artificially reinterpreted to make up for the categorical poverty of the empowerment model" (ibid., 287).

a weapon of revolutionary struggle, Marxist doctrine became a cold-blooded exercise in labeling and stigma. Institutions were attainted, not analyzed; discriminating judgment was discouraged.[64] This ideological style pervades much of the discussion of domination, even where Marxism proper is modified or even rejected.

Foucault has a similar strategy. He makes full use of vivid metaphors and tendentious categories. "The disciplines"—his own term of art, artfully employed—associates *all* discipline with special techniques of close supervision. As a result he cannot distinguish discipline that gives coherence to life and sustains autonomous projects from techniques of control that regiment, denude, and degrade.

Dispraise of Structure

The same indifference to variation is evident among radical critics of organization theory. Here again, domination is the keynote and liberal reformers are the main enemy. An instructive illustration is a contemporary critique of "the ideology of bureaucracy" in American law.[65] In this essay the main strands of doctrine in corporation law and administrative law, that is, in the law of bureaucracy, private and public, are attacked and repudiated. They are presented as insidious efforts "to assuage the long-standing fear that bureaucracy is a form of human domination."[66] The legal ideas, and the theories of organization that support them, are at bottom "defenses of bureaucratic power." These defenses "are no more than variations on a single story about the acceptability of bureaucratic organization," which, "far from building a convincing case for bureaucracy, is a mechanism of deception." The deception must be exposed, thus revealing "the inadequacy of the ideology that helps perpetuate currently entrenched nondemocratic forms of human association."[67]

According to this argument, bureaucracy is legitimated by the very legal doctrines that purport to control it.[68] Even when, by instituting

64. Of course, when properly understood as corrigible and as offering limited insights and generalizations, Marxist theories have significant intellectual worth.
65. Gerald E. Frug, "The Ideology of Bureaucracy in American Law," *Harvard Law Review* 97 (April 1984): 1276–1389. This wide-ranging analysis is a product of the "critical legal studies" movement whose main base in the 1980s was the Harvard Law School.
66. Ibid., 1277f.
67. Ibid., 1278.
68. For example, the judicial review model assumes that bureaucracies cannot be entirely self-policing. People should be able to appeal to the courts for redress of their grievances against administrative agencies, and the courts should formulate rules to check and guide official conduct. In American law, however, judicial intervention is supposed to be minimally intrusive. Judges do not have license to substitute their own views on the substance of a matter for those of officials who know the circumstances and who have special

judicial review and by enlarging opportunities for private citizens to participate in rule-making by government agencies, the law recognizes that bureaucracies need policing, it nevertheless treats bureaucracy as a necessary aspect of modern life. The law may say in various ways that bureaucratic power is dangerous if uncontrolled, but *complete* control is not contemplated, because it is thought to be neither possible nor desirable. Each legal theory leaves plenty of room for administrative discretion and thus for arbitrary, self-serving conduct. Indeed, it is argued, the controlling doctrines are so vague, and *must be* so vague, that no meaningful line can be drawn "between arbitrariness and proper discretion and between excessive restraint and needed restraint."[69]

This pessimistic conclusion has as its complement a radical optimism. "New forms of human association" must be designed to take the place of bureaucracy, and these can be achieved only "when people jointly recognize that *no structure can protect us from each other,* given the variable, intersubjective, interdependent nature of human relationships."[70] Furthermore, the models of bureaucracy implicit in legal doctrine "are attempts to escape from the problems of face-to-face human relationships; all of them promise us that human relationships—even relationships built on hierarchy and separation—can be made unthreatening through some organizational arrangement."[71] Therefore we should reject all structural arrangements for checking power and demanding accountability.

In the 1960s the New Left had similar ideas. Forms and structures of all sorts were disparaged; they were to be replaced by spontaneous association and interaction. Law and bureaucracy were favorite targets, and participatory democracy was the ideal. Twenty years later, in what might appear an unlikely forum, the *Harvard Law Review,* the same banner was raised:

> [True participatory democracy refers] to the process by which people create for themselves the form of organized existence within which they live. . . . Moreover, unless people do so *themselves,* the artificial structures through which they operate will threaten to function beyond their control. In this view, the term "participatory democracy" does not describe a fixed series of limited possibilities of human organization but the ideal under which the possibilities of joint transformation of social life are collected.[72]

---

responsibility for getting a job done. Therefore courts tend to rely on procedural requirements, such as notice and hearing, or the preparation of environmental impact reports.

69. Ibid., 1324.
70. Ibid., 1295f., my emphasis.
71. Ibid., 1382.
72. Ibid., 1296.

Much is valid and appealing in the call for participatory democracy. The ideal makes sense, however, only *within,* not outside of, appropriate rules and procedures. To say "No structure can protect us from each other" is to misread the most important lessons of institutional history. The rejection of structure is a rejection of ordered liberty and constitutional government. Forms and procedures are not effective by themselves—they need support in belief and action—but as routine restraints on the abuse of power they do indeed protect us from each other.[73]

In the American political system, separation of powers is by no means complete, nor should it be. It is largely effective, however; it protects, for example, the independence of the judiciary. To be sure, independence speaks to a baseline morality rather than to higher aspirations. An *excellent* judge must be more than independent. Wisdom, courage, and compassion are wanted, to say nothing of legal sophistication. But we would not wish to give up the fundamental virtues of honesty and integrity that we associate with judicial independence.

A morality of aspiration is not easily captured or readily cabined by rules and systems.[74] Parents are required by law to care for their children, but beyond a minimum the level and quality of care are unspecified. A political constitution must state clearly how long a government may remain in office and how its successors are to be chosen, but its larger ideals may well be stated only as abstract concepts, such as equal protection of the laws, or as necessarily vague connotations that point, for example, to an implicit constitutional right of privacy. But the constitution would be hopelessly ineffective if it failed to specify, or could not sustain in practice, the elementary conditions of stability and legitimacy.

▼   ▲   ▼   ▲   ▼

In the critique of domination the very idea of purposive organization is sometimes called into question. One writer rejects, as "a rational model," the "postulation of a goal or purpose" and suggests, as an alternative understanding of organizational life, "one which places the individual rather than the productive process at the center of our analysis, and which seeks its justification . . . in personal growth and develop-

73. They are also important for the release of energies, for example, by limiting the liability of shareholders for corporate debts or that of newspapers for causing embarrassment to public figures.

74. On "the moralities of duty and aspiration," see Lon L. Fuller, *The Morality of Law* (New Haven: Yale University Press, 1969), chap. 1.

ment." In this perspective a realm of freedom or "interaction," wherein "we may arrive at fundamental decisions about the direction of our lives and our societies," is counterposed to "the realm of discipline and order, of rigor and efficiency, of regulation."[75]

This line of thought is more than a plea for responsive, participatory, humanized administration. It is a general indictment of all organization that takes for granted the need for authority, direction, discipline, and training. "Organization theory and management practice conspire to limit our options to those consistent with the accomplishment of the organization's goals."[76] This is the crux of the criticism, for the premise is that limiting options limits our humanity.

It is true enough that students of organization have sometimes projected an unattractive image of "administrative man." In analyzing authority, for example, Chester I. Barnard and Herbert A. Simon pointed to the "zone of indifference" or "area of acceptance" within which subordinates willingly defer to the decisions of superiors.[77] There is nothing wrong with this concept; it helps to clarify the operational meaning of authority. Taken out of context, however, the idea evokes an image of passivity; it appears to encourage a spirit of subordination.[78]

Similarly, organization theorists of many stripes, even if they do not accept a rigorously rational model, are likely to emphasize the importance

75. Robert R. Denhardt, *In the Shadow of Organization* (Lawrence, Kansas: Regents Press of Kansas, 1981), 20, 14, 72.

76. Ibid., 73.

77. "The phrase 'zone of indifference' may be explained as follows: If all . . . [directives] be arranged in the order of their acceptability to the person affected, it may be conceived that there are a number which are clearly unacceptable, that is, which certainly will not be obeyed; there is another group somewhat more or less on the neutral line . . . and a third group unquestionably acceptable. This last group lies within the 'zone of indifference.' The person affected will accept orders lying within this zone and is relatively indifferent as to what the order is. . . . The zone of indifference will be wider or narrower depending upon the degree to which the inducements exceed the burdens and sacrifices which determine the individual's adhesion to the organization. It follows that the range of orders that will be accepted will be very limited among those who are barely induced to contribute to the system" (Chester I. Barnard, *The Functions of the Executive* [Cambridge: Harvard University Press, 1947], 169). See also Simon, *Administrative Behavior*, 133f. Simon's phrase "zone of acceptance" is preferable because the intended meaning is only that various alternatives are equally acceptable from the standpoint of obedience, not necessarily that people do not care about the process or the substance of the matter.

78. This interpretation is not really justified by what Barnard and Simon wrote. Both emphasize that the zone of indifference or acceptance may be highly problematic. As Barnard says, "[T]here is no principle of executive conduct better established in good organizations than that orders will not be issued that cannot or will not be obeyed" (*Functions*, 167). And Simon points out that authority thus defined "can operate 'upward' and 'sidewise' as well as 'downward' in the organization. If an executive delegates to his secretary a decision about file cabinets and accepts her recommendation without reexamination of its merits, he is accepting her authority" (*Administrative Behavior*, 12).

of training within organizations, including training that inculcates a shared vision of appropriate means and ends. Here again, an image is projected of initiative at the top and acceptance below. And again, such a conclusion is by no means necessary. Socialization may be helpful and empowering; it need not be restrictive or stultifying, even when a particular competence, loyalty, or dedication is sought. Nevertheless, it is understandable that a strong emphasis on the utility of socialization, from the organization's point of view, may create an unfavorable impression among those who would like to see the ethos of democracy more warmly accepted and more firmly implanted.

That unfavorable impression, however, is still a far cry from the claim that "the rational model of organization provides the same justification for action as that presented at the Nuremberg trials, that the efficient execution of one's orders is the proper task of the organizational member."[79] The lesson of Nuremberg is *not* that people in organizations should follow their own inclinations or rely exclusively on their own moral judgments. Nuremberg did not eliminate the zone of indifference. Rather, the judges spoke to the *content* of the zone—specifically, that it should not include patently illegal or immoral decisions. One may hope that the Nuremberg trials changed some attitudes toward authority. Soldiers (especially officers) can less readily excuse heinous crimes by claiming they were only obeying orders. Responsibility is more widely shared and, in matters of obedience, more critical judgment is expected. But these moral advances, important as they are, hardly deny the legitimacy of command or the propriety of subordination.

Nor does it make sense to say that rational organization is wedded to the status quo because it "partakes of a particular version of social reality, bound to existing social arrangements and existing distributions of power."[80] A moment's reflection reminds us that organizations of all kinds, including revolutionary parties and New Model armies, cannot do without authority. New forms may be fashioned and a new spirit may emerge, for good or ill. But each must accept the logic of hierarchy and the sovereignty of purpose.[81]

We cannot do without authority, nor can we forgo rationality in the management of resources. But authority and rationality are highly problematic ideas, and no particular way of doing things can be considered

79. Denhardt, *In the Shadow of Organization*, 29.
80. Ibid., 32.
81. Failure to grasp this necessity, and consequent failure to make provision for its mitigation, have doomed revolutionary governments to ape the oppressive regimes they have replaced.

inevitable or beyond question. Therefore we should ask: What *kinds* of purposive organization are justified by the nature of the institution? what *kinds* of authority? what *kinds* of subordination?

What is domination in one context may be wholesome discipline in another. The stringent rules of barracks life or of a religious commune might be intolerable in ordinary civilian life; controls suitable for young children are not appropriate for adolescents. In each case we must consider how people experience and interpret their subordination;[82] otherwise we may be too quick to identify "total" control in a prison with, say, "total" control in a military academy. The just claims of authority and the practical urgencies of subordination are very different in armies, schools, business firms, and monasteries. And they are different for different units and ranks within each institution.

▼   ▲   ▼   ▲   ▼

Whatever its failings, the critique of domination properly insists on the moral promise of human association. We should not be content with any system that reduces persons to abstractions or that denies the human need for respect, communication, and concern. Nor should we cease to explore the contribution organized group life may make to personal security, satisfaction, and growth. Thus understood, many utopian criticisms are well taken. They call attention to ideals that have genuine relevance but are easily ignored or routinely shortchanged. Furthermore, we are indebted to those critics for the light they have shed on the more subtle and insidious forms of domination, which include the many ways power is extended and subjugation is reinforced.[83]

A note of caution is in order, however. In our preoccupation with subtle forms of oppression and with high aspirations for fairness and well-being, we may forget that resistance to domination must begin with the obvious and the unsubtle. Arbitrary power is all too often blunt and crude; the pain it inflicts is readily apparent; there is no need for a guide to suffering, no need for consciousness-raising. Rather, we require elementary constraints on the abuse of power. When these are

82. This is not to say that domination is a wholly subjective phenomenon. Some techniques of physical and psychological control are so degrading—in the way they erode or destroy self-respect, for example—that they may be said to be wholly or intrinsically incompatible with autonomy and dignity. Other forms of control are only suspect, for example, those that create and sustain personal dependencies.

83. For example, by classifying people in arbitrary or tendentious ways, often under a cloak of neutrality; by controlling agendas of discussion or action; by legitimizing some viewpoints and delegitimizing others.

discounted—as "mere structures" or as "liberal legalism"—people are left unprotected where protection is most urgent. This posture often signals a failure to appreciate the gains other generations have won and that are now taken for granted. We may lose sight of the need to build on those foundations as we reach for more sensitive and demanding standards.

TEN

Authority and Bureaucracy

The moral character of an institution is largely determined by the kind of authority it sustains and how that authority is used. Ideologies of authority are a prime resource for justifying evil in the name of the good. When institutions mobilize human energies, the temptation is ever-present to treat persons as manipulable resources. Their humanity is subordinated to the needs of the institution as perceived by those who control it.

For many purposes, however, authority is both indispensable and wholesome. Deference to authority—whether to a dictionary, a physician, a supervisor, or a rule—often has great practical worth. By deferring to others, people are freed to do what they do best and to pursue concerns that are, for them, truly relevant and problematic. Moreover, the experience of belonging to an authoritative order is a reliable source of security and empowerment; it may also be enriching and ennobling.

In this chapter and the next, we consider how this moral tension may be understood and resolved, recognizing that every institution must deal with it in its own way. For guidance we turn to the theory of authority as it bears on the governance of large, special-purpose institutions.

▼   ▲   ▼   ▲   ▼

Authority may be defined as a rightful claim to deference or obedience. Although this definition is spacious and undemanding,[1] it contains the threshold idea of rightfulness. We cannot make sense of authority if we do not distinguish it from naked power. Authority generates a *kind* of power—the power to win assent, deference, obedience—but its distinctive basis is a recognized claim of right. The claim to deference must be accepted as rightful by a relevant class of persons. *This acceptance need not come from those who are expected to defer or obey.* Parents, teachers, police, and many other institutional officers derive their authority from the community, not from the children, students, offenders, or inmates over whom the authority is exercised. As a result, those most nearly *subject* to authority do not necessarily experience it as rightful.

In other words, the existence of authority does not settle *whose* consent is necessary or desirable. Nor does it say how much consent there need be. A claim to rightful rule may rest on a broad base of assent, may be deeply rooted in law, custom, and institutional practice, or it may be recognized by only a small group of adherents or officials.[2] Even when authority appears secure and seems to have worked fairly well over a long period, it may nevertheless be eroded swiftly. "There is nothing more surprising to the holders of power, or perhaps to its subjects, than the frailty of their commands in certain types of crises."[3]

When we define authority as a rightful claim to obedience, we mean only that it is *accepted* as such. Whether the claim is justified—whether people ought to defer or obey—is a separate question. The latter belongs to the theory of authority and to its applications, not to a definition. The theory includes standards of critical morality, which in turn depend on what we can know about the limits and dynamics of authority. As a baseline criterion, the consent that generates authority is unexamined—a brute given. We then consider how effective the authority is and what its

1. That is, it is appropriately "weak." In this formulation, authority embraces advice and instruction as well as command, and it contemplates many different kinds and sources, as well as wide variation in the extent and quality, of deference and obedience. Because the concept of authority (like law, community, culture, and many other key ideas in social science) points to phenomena intimately connected with the realization of values, there is a temptation to pack into a definition what should be developed in a theory.

2. As analyzed by H. L. A. Hart, a legal system requires different obligations from citizens and officials. Officials, such as judges, have a special obligation to be guided by "secondary" rules that determine which "primary" rules must be obeyed by citizens. Hence the fidelity of relatively small groups may be of crucial importance to the stability of the system. See Hart's *The Concept of Law* (Oxford: Clarendon Press, 1961), 113.

3. Charles E. Merriam, *Political Power, Its Composition and Incidence,* in H. D. Lasswell and T. V. Smith, *A Study of Power* (1934; reprint, New York: Free Press, 1950), 156. The most vivid contemporary example is the swift erosion of communist authority in Eastern Europe and the former Soviet Union.

moral worth may be. We can judge the effectiveness of authority by how widely and deeply it is accepted; we can judge its moral worth by how it affects the values at stake in personal and institutional life. In some contexts at least, as we shall see, the conditions that make for effective authority also contribute to moral well-being.

LEGITIMACY: THE QUALITY OF CONSENT

Authority presumes consent. The crucial question is, however: What *kind* of consent yields what *kind* of authority? Consent is not the same as compliance or acquiescence. One may comply with the orders of a gunman, or acquiesce in the settlement of a dispute, without recognizing a rightful claim to obedience or agreement. Furthermore, consent may be unconscious or self-aware; absolute or contingent; rational, nonrational, or irrational.

The moral ambiguities of authority and consent are evident in the fundamental social process we call socialization. Without effective authority the transmission of culture is impossible. But an inherent tension exists between that great aim and the no less important function of producing effective and fully realized persons. At a root level the conflict is irreducible, but some varieties of socialization are more capable than others of reconciling authority and autonomy.

Consider, for example, a distinction we may draw between *repressive* and *participatory* socialization.[4] Both strive for conformity, but the kinds of conformity are different, as are the mechanisms by which they are produced. Repressive socialization emphasizes punishment, obedience, and respect based on external controls. Parents rely mainly on shame, ridicule, and corporal punishment. Communication is a one-way process—downward. Gesture and nonverbal communication are conspicuous. The child must learn to assess how serious is the command to "shut up" by taking account of tone of voice, facial expression, and the apparent readiness to grab or hit.

Participatory socialization is child-centered rather than parent-centered. Adults assume responsibility for discerning the child's needs rather than expect the child to discern the parents' needs. Supervision is permissive in that it gives children freedom to try things out for themselves, explore the world on their own terms, and make known their

---

4. This discussion draws on Leonard Broom and Philip Selznick, *Sociology: A Text with Adapted Readings,* 6th ed. (New York: Harper & Row, 1977), 95f.

needs and desires. It is not necessarily neglectful, however. Parents may exhibit a great deal of concern and attention, but supervision is general, not detailed or intrusive. Rather than conformity as such, the requirements of cooperative activity are emphasized, as are the benefits of trust and fellowship. Thus repressive and participatory *socialization* entail, respectively, repressive and participatory *authority*.[5]

The two forms persist and recur, now as necessity, now as temptation. At times, repressive authority is in truth the only means of establishing order or accomplishing a morally worthy task; in the circumstances the alternative may well be utopian and self-defeating. But it is more often tempting to *claim* there is no other way and to rely on repression as a first rather than as a last resort. For its part, participatory authority requires very congenial conditions and may readily degenerate into weakness, negligence, and undue permissiveness. Yet it holds the greater promise, not only for moral development but for high levels of personal achievement.

The contrast we have drawn holds good when we move from family and child-rearing to political and institutional authority. In schools, business firms, and churches, and in the political community itself, the same "problem of authority" arises: how to balance coherence and initiative. The paradigms of repressive and participatory authority frame debate at every level. This can be seen if we review, very briefly, a few of the basic ideas that have informed the discussion of institutional authority.

Principles of Legitimacy

In contemporary social science the connection between authority and consent is captured in the idea of legitimacy. Some rule, it is said, and others obey, because they share certain beliefs called principles of legitimacy. Power justified by such beliefs is political authority. Many principles of legitimacy are familiar, and they are clues to the ethos of a culture or an epoch: divine will, democratic election, hereditary succession, private property, legislative supremacy, seniority, special competence,

5. These varieties of socialization and authority bring to mind G. H. Mead's distinction between "significant others" and "the generalized other." (See Chapter 6, "The Morality of Cooperation.") When obedience is the keynote, socialization tends to remain at the level of the significant other. Children take their cues from particular persons, mainly parents, who dominate their social and psychological environment. When cooperation for shared goals is emphasized, a more general standpoint is adopted. Conduct is governed by the requirements of group life, including family life, not by imitation of or deference to parents, teachers, or older siblings. The understanding of means and ends is stressed rather than the performance of prescribed roles.

among many others. Contests over power and interest are commonly expressed as conflicts over principles of legitimacy. "I am God's anointed," said Charles I; "I run this company because I own it"; "I fought in the Resistance."

Although these "political formulae," as Gaetano Mosca called them, justify systems of power, they are not "mere quackeries aptly invented to trick the masses into obedience. . . . The truth is that they answer a real need in man's social nature . . . of governing *and knowing that one is governed* not on the basis of mere material and intellectual force, but on the basis of a moral principle."[6]

"Even the tyrant must sleep," wrote one who knew the hazards of power. Dictators as well as democrats strive for legitimacy. In exchange, some trade-offs or limits are accepted. Legitimate power tends to be *restrained* power. Principles of legitimacy encourage at least a rudimentary rule of law that stands above the rulers, to which they are responsible, and in the light of which they govern.

Max Weber (1864–1920) made legitimacy the linchpin of his theory of authority. His analysis is suggestive, both for what it includes and for what it leaves out. Above all, it reveals how close may be the connection between authority and domination.

Weber distinguished three kinds of authority.[7] *Traditional* authority invokes immemorial custom and unquestioned social practice. The memory of man, it is said, runneth not to the contrary. In the usual case, obedience is a matter of personal loyalty to a parent, elder, or other chief within the framework of customary obligation. *Rational* authority rests on a belief that rules and commands are binding elements of an impersonal order. Obedience runs to the system, not to particular persons. *Charismatic* authority is the claim of prophets or heroes to be followed and obeyed. Perceived as extraordinary individuals, "endowed with grace," they reaffirm or reconstruct the values of a community. They evoke a felt *duty* "of those subject to charismatic authority to recognize its genuineness and to act accordingly."[8] Charismatic leaders may occupy traditional roles or legally constituted offices, as did Moses, Napoleon, and General Douglas MacArthur. But their special authority derives from personal qualities and achievements, not from social position.

6. *The Ruling Class,* trans. Hannah D. Kahn (1896; reprint, New York: McGraw-Hill, 1939), 71, my emphasis.
7. *Economy and Society: An Outline of Interpretive Sociology,* ed. Guenther Roth and Claus Wittich (New York: Bedminster Press, 1968), 1:212–45.
8. Ibid., 242. This is a crucial way Weber's concept differs from currently popular, somewhat debased usage.

This threefold classification must be understood as part of a broader theory of modernity. In that theory the key to pervasive change in economics, politics, law, and cultural life is the rational reconstruction of social institutions. A fundamental disenchantment, Weber argued, has loosened the bonds and denatured the symbols of the premodern world. In the new age, old unities are sundered, fragmented, and rearranged to serve definite objectives and rational principles.

As clues to this master trend, "traditional" and "rational" authority are the most important categories. Yet Weber saw the importance of charismatic leaders who remind us that the course of history is neither smooth nor inexorable. Major social change is subject to, and may depend on, creative or demonic forces that mobilize energies and give direction to emotions.

Behind this admittedly rough classification lies a rich appreciation of how each kind of authority is justified and what sort of consent it presumes. Traditional authority is communal and person-centered. The more traditionalist it is, the more it is hemmed in by restraints based on custom, reciprocity, and the continuities of life. Consent to political or religious authority is summoned and sustained by those continuities, especially the integration of family, work, religion, and locality.

Rational authority has a quite different foundation. Instead of immemorial custom, whose origins are lost in mystery, some form of *enactment* is the font of legitimacy. Rationality calls for explicitness, coherence, predictability, and impersonality. The strain is toward a legal model of rule-making and decision. Hence Weber's idiom slips imperceptibly from "rational" to "rational-*legal*" authority. Law thus understood does not appeal to the whole person, that is, to social identity and particularist obligation. Rather, "right," "duty," and "rule" become ideas more abstract and universal than in the traditionalist model. To participate in the legal order is to be faithful to a consistent system of abstract rules. The ideals of legality become independent sources of loyalty and obligation. Consent runs to the rightness of the rules and of the formal system, not to the sanctity of a social order.

Each kind of authority evokes characteristic principles of legitimacy; each gives a different meaning to autonomy and consent. In charismatic authority, for example, legitimacy derives from heroic deeds or from the making of miracles, not from contract or custom; consent is emotion-driven, unmediated, directly focused on the leader; it is not filtered through the texture of social life or regulated and refined by procedural rules.

These comments suggest that Weber's categories speak to differences in the quality of consent. Nevertheless, there is much truth in the criticism that his conception of authority and legitimation gives too much importance to systems of *belief.*[9] Weber wanted to give the idea of legitimacy a clear empirical meaning and, in keeping with his general views on fact and value, he sought to avoid confusing the fact of legitimacy with its moral justification. The easiest way to accomplish these aims was to associate legitimacy with doctrines of one sort or another, without looking behind the doctrines to assess their claims. In other words, Weber thought of legitimation as a fundamentally nonrational expression of group or cultural values. Even rational authority, despite the Kantian overtones, is a historically determined belief in a certain kind of order.

Furthermore, in Weber's analysis authority is a form of domination. His key word is *Herrschaft,* which carries strong connotations of power, command, and prerogative. *Legitime Herrschaft* is translated as "legitimate domination" or, with some hesitation, as "authority."[10] In the Weberian perspective, which was strongly influenced by German language and history, people who accept a regime as legitimate do so in a spirit of submission.

Weber cannot properly be faulted for offering a weak definition of authority or for choosing as a starting point the bare fact of acceptance based on belief. This is a strategy I have defended at a number of points. But such a choice loses its innocence if it is not presented as an integral part of a stronger *theory* that speaks to the dynamics of authority, and particularly to the transition from primitive to more elaborated forms. Because Weber was not aware of this logic, or not interested in it, he helped to foster a rather crude understanding of what authority entails.[11]

9. Carl J. Friedrich, "Authority, Reason, and Discretion," in Carl J. Friedrich, ed., *Authority* (Cambridge: Harvard University Press, 1958), 28–48; see also Jürgen Habermas, *Legitimation Crisis,* trans. Thomas McCarthy (Boston: Beacon Press, 1975), 97ff., and Jürgen Habermas, *The Theory of Communicative Action,* trans. Thomas McCarthy (Boston: Beacon Press, 1984), 1:262.

10. See the editors' comments in Weber, *Economy and Society,* 1:61f.; Reinhard Bendix, *Max Weber: An Intellectual Portrait* (New York: Doubleday & Co., 1960), 296.

11. The analytical shortcoming may reflect Weber's more substantive ideas about democracy. In 1919 he is reported to have said, "In a democracy the people choose a leader whom they trust. Then the chosen man says 'Now shut your mouths and obey me.' The people and the parties are no longer free to interfere in the leader's business" (Marianne Weber, *Max Weber: A Biography* [New York: John Wiley, 1975], 653). In Tom Bottomore's phrase, "Vote, Shut Up, and Obey" (*Times Literary Supplement* [19 April 1985]: 429).

One of Weber's strongest critics, Carl J. Friedrich, sought to give critical judgment its proper place in the concept of authority:

> [W]hen I speak of authority, I wish to say that the communications of a person possessing it exhibit a very particular kind of relationship to reason and reasoning. [Such communications] . . . possess the *potentiality of reasoned elaboration*—they are "worthy of acceptance."[12]

Friedrich was reluctant to insist that "the potentiality of reasoned elaboration" must be part of the *definition* of authority, that is, of its baseline or threshold meaning. But he perceived, more clearly than did Weber, that legitimacy generates demands for its justification. This "reasoned elaboration" may be only an appeal to tradition, but even that appeal requires interpretation, which may be contested, and which opens the door to dialogue.

Legitimation is indeed often crude, rudimentary, and inchoate. It may be based on little more than a belief that someone is thought to have communication with the gods or special magical powers, or a recognition that the person belongs to a noble family. There need be no awareness of the habit of thought involved, nor any self-conscious choice of principle or doctrine.

Many regimes properly classified as legitimate, in the sense that they are well-founded in consent, retain a very large amount of arbitrary rule. A legitimate ruler may be a tyrant, whose claim to rule rests on principles that encourage uncritical acquiescence on the part of subjects and supine obedience on the part of officials. But legitimacy carries the lively seed of legality, or the rule of law, implanted by the principle that reasons must be given to defend official acts. For reasons invite evaluation, and evaluation encourages a quest for objective standards of accountability. At the same time, implicit in the fundamental norm that reasons should be given is the conclusion that where reasons are defective, authority is to that extent weakened and may even be destroyed.

Legitimacy is primitive when it speaks only to the *gross* justification of a claim to authority. Only the right to hold office is in question; the evil addressed is usurpation. Once the right to rule is established, the mouths of critics are stopped. Their duty is to submit to what they themselves have accepted; they have but to "vote, shut up, and obey." This Hobbesian premise carries a promise of things to come, but it falls short of a developed rule of law. The latter gains strength and focus when criteria of legitimacy are relied on to query *particular* acts and pol-

12. Friedrich, "Authority, Reason, and Discretion," 35.

icies. The restraining force of legitimation increases as we move from gross legitimation to legitimation *in depth*. The transition is from a blanket certification of the source of authority to a sustained justification of its use.

The fundamental fact is that some principles of legitimacy are more competent than others to sustain a posture of criticism.[13] If power is justified on the basis of hereditary succession, for example, it is difficult to find leverage for calling officials to account. The same may be said of any principle of legitimacy that amounts to a laying on of hands, whereby an act of investiture conveys plenary or unfettered authority. The "democratic" conferral of unlimited powers by a plebiscite is a case in point. That is why "majority rule" is an impoverished and self-defeating interpretation of democracy.[14]

THE MORAL WORTH OF BUREAUCRACY

An obvious obstacle to reconstructing authority in the direction of effective criticism and participation is the apparent inevitability of bureaucratic organization. Here deference is pervasive and domination persists. Bureaucracy has been a major preoccupation of modern social science, but the moral issues often fade from view, overshadowed by concern for efficiency and effectiveness. In what follows we consider, first, the contested meaning of bureaucracy, and then its moral worth and deficits.

Since it first came into use in the eighteenth century,[15] and as it is still very commonly understood, "bureaucracy" has had strong negative connotations. Among its definitions of the term, *Webster's Third International Dictionary* (1971) describes bureaucracy as "a system of administration marked by constant striving for increased functions and power, by lack of initiative and flexibility, by indifference to human needs or public opinion, and by a tendency to defer decisions to superiors or to impede action with red tape." The focus is on *pathologies,* especially rigidity, insensitivity, and overreaching.

Contemporary students of organization usually define bureaucracy in a more neutral way: a bureaucrat is simply an official, or a certain kind of official. They leave to the theory of bureaucracy any conclusions that

---

13. See Antonie A. G. Peters, "Law as Critical Discussion," in Gunther Teubner, ed., *Dilemmas of Law in the Welfare State* (Berlin: de Gruyter, 1986), 250–79.

14. See Chapter 16, "Communal Democracy."

15. See Martin Albrow, *Bureaucracy* (London: Pall Mall Press, 1970), chap. 1; Eugene Kamenka and Martin Krygier, eds., *Bureaucracy: The Career of a Concept* (London: Edward Arnold, 1979).

should be drawn about characteristic pathologies. An advantage is that pathologies are not considered inevitable. They may well be significant, and even highly probable in some circumstances, but their attributes— which specific pathologies occur, how often, how seriously, and with what effect—are considered to be variable and potentially subject to control. Furthermore, bureaucracy understood neutrally as "administration of a government chiefly through bureaus staffed with nonelective officials" has positive worth,[16] and that worth is obscured when the pejorative meaning prevails.

Bureaucracy is not a synonym for "formal organization" or even for "rational coordination." Ordinary employees are not bureaucrats, nor are students, teachers, or soldiers, though they belong to formal organizations and are subject to rational coordination. Nor does bureaucracy include the political leaders of a government or, in many cases, the directors of a corporation, at least not in their capacity as directors. Bureaucracy is a *kind* of organization and usually only *part* of a formal structure. As such it has special importance for authority and domination.

Max Weber's model is still the most useful starting point for understanding the nature of bureaucracy. He recognized its virtues and accepted its historical necessity, yet he was deeply distrustful of what he came to call a "house of bondage." He saw in bureaucracy a quintessentially modern form of domination, one that was inescapable just because it was, "from a purely technical point of view, . . . the most rational known means of exercising authority over human beings. It is superior to any other form in precision, in stability, in the stringency of its discipline, and in its reliability."[17]

To make sense of this statement, and others like it, we should recall that "rationality" has a special significance in Weber's thought. The modern Western rationality he tried so hard to understand is not the same as ordinary problem-solving or the common-sense articulation of means and ends. Weber was interested in a special *style* of thought, action, and organization. This style is characterized by active clarification of goals; a preference for well-defined objectives; disciplined mobilization of energies; precise allocation of resources; a willingness to defer gratification; and a perception of the world as freely manipulable.

16. This is the first-mentioned meaning of bureaucracy in the *American Heritage Dictionary* (1981), and it perhaps reflects the social science preference for a neutral definition. Two pejorative meanings are included, however, and a note adds that "in American usage, *bureaucrat* is almost invariably derogatory unless the context establishes otherwise."

17. Weber, *Economy and Society*, 1:223.

The concept of disciplined rationality is a major theme in Weber's most famous work, *The Protestant Ethic and the Spirit of Capitalism.* There he explored the historical foundations of *personal* rationality. Calvinism and its offshoots freed the individual from traditional restraints and fostered a life-style based on strenuous effort, abhorrence of waste, and deferred gratification.

Weber's other work is mainly concerned with institutional rather than personal experience. He thereby shifts attention to modern bureaucracy, free enterprise, and law. These forms are, necessarily, historically contingent renderings of rationality as an abstract ideal. Weber was fascinated by the tendency of modern society to objectify the abstract concept, to make the word flesh by embodying it in enduring activities and agencies. In studying this trend he was not imposing a "rational model" on human affairs. He saw the coming of rationality as a historical process, largely unplanned, always problematic, always dependent on congenial circumstances, always bearing with it unintended and unwanted effects.

It is also important to distinguish, as Weber did, between "formal" and "substantive" rationality. A system is *substantively* rational when it effectively serves human purposes. It is *formally* rational when institutionalized criteria of efficiency or logic, including a legal or theological logic, govern what means are chosen and how they are used. When such a logic prevails, substantive purposes tend to lose their power to control decisions. Thus cost accounting and budgeting may contribute to the formal rationality of business or government, but they do not guarantee that marketable products will be made or that the public health will be protected. Similarly, legal decisions may be rigorously controlled by internal criteria of validity, such as adherence to precedent, yet substantive justice may be wanting.

It was formal rationality that caught and held Weber's attention and he had that in mind when he described bureaucracy as the "most rational" form of organization. We should not make too much of Weber's judgment. The opinion he expressed is colored by his special interest in comparing premodern and modern institutions. And we need not labor to show that bureaucracy is less fully rational, from the standpoint of purpose, than Weber thought. Rather, *we should stress and deepen his insight into the organizational embodiment of values.* His contribution is best understood as a close analysis of bureaucracy as a form of organization oriented to a norm of rationality and committed to values of system and legality.

▼   ▲   ▼   ▲   ▼

The bureaucratic phenomenon par excellence is the defined jurisdiction or sphere of competence. The "bureau" is constituted by delegation to it of continuing responsibilities; authoritative channels of communication and control are presumed. In a bureaucracy one goes "through channels"; "back channels" are anathema. Bureaucratic hierarchy is, therefore, more than a formal chain of command. It is an arrangement of parts that have an integrity and continuity of their own. Every large enterprise has subunits and is, therefore, "an organization of organizations." But it is not necessarily bureaucratic. It becomes a bureaucracy as the units attain a measure of autonomy based on special responsibilities and corresponding authority.

The alternative to bureaucratic hierarchy is a more ad hoc form of organization. Assignments of work and authority do not crystallize as fixed spheres of competence. The person holding the office may be more important than the office itself, which can be reshaped to fit the incumbent's needs and inclinations. Prebureaucratic leaders insist that their administrative staffs be personally dependent upon them. They sense the tension between effective personal command and the creation of legally competent officials. As a result, assignments are made on the basis of personal qualities; authority is not formally delegated to subordinate offices but merely invested in individuals, to be held at the pleasure of the chief. In postbureaucratic organization, as is suggested below, the same flexibility is sought, but by other means.

Weber stressed that administration according to "calculable rules" is "of paramount importance for modern bureaucracy."[18] The bureaucrat's main commitment is to an impersonal order, a system of rules that limit discretion and must be applied in an evenhanded way. In speaking of "calculable" rules, Weber was emphasizing that modern administration seeks to make decisions as objective as possible, eliminating whatever is subjective and irrational. A calculable rule is, first, a dependable rule. But it is also "intellectually analyzable," based on rational assessment of aims and resources. A self-serving rule, however dependable, would not meet the test.

Theoretically, a definite purpose is a necessary ingredient of formal organization, which is the genus of which bureaucracy is a species. Indeed, it is the purposive character of the group that most clearly marks

18. Weber, *Economy and Society,* 3:975.

it as "a system of consciously coordinated activities."[19] Conscious co-ordination has to be aimed at some goal. Furthermore, the more explicit the purpose, the better it can serve as a premise of decision and as an instrument of control. An explicit purpose helps hold officials accountable and provides guidelines for the improvement of administration.[20]

In his study of bureaucracy, however, Weber hardly mentions the place of purpose. He simply takes it for granted that bureaucratic organization is a rational instrument subordinate to given ends. This neglect of purpose is not wholly innocent. In Weber's model, bureaucracy is not a dynamic institution committed to solving problems and attaining objectives. He saw it, rather, as a relatively passive and conservative force preoccupied with the detailed implementation of previously established policies. In such a setting, purpose lacks creative significance; it is not in the foreground of bureaucratic awareness. The focus shifts to *values,* and especially to values associated with correct procedure and fidelity to rules.

From the point of view of moral theory, the most striking feature of bureaucracy is this stress on objectivity and impersonality. Ideally, bureaucratic administration is the antithesis of arbitrary rule. Bureaucracy formalizes every facet of decision-making and, *up to a point,* embraces a norm of limited discretion. People who act in an official capacity are not free to hire relatives, act out their prejudices, or pursue their own policy agendas. They are called on to resist every choice that is, from the standpoint of the system, an arbitrary intrusion of alien standards or interests.

This strain toward controlled, nonarbitrary decisions is the underlying phenomenon that justifies Weber's conception of bureaucratic authority as "legal-rational." As is suggested below (p. 445), the ideal of legality stimulates a quest for progressive reduction of arbitrariness in rule-making and administration. This reduction proceeds as the rational component of law is enlarged. Bureaucratic administration, as Weber saw it, has a similar logic.

"Bureaucratic rule was not and is not the only variety of legal authority, but it is the purest."[21] In thus stressing the close association of legality and bureaucracy, Weber was making two points. First, as an instrument of *public* law, bureaucracy is the vehicle by which that law

19. Chester I. Barnard, *The Functions of the Executive* (Cambridge: Harvard University Press, 1947), 73.
20. See Philippe Nonet, "The Legitimation of Purposive Decisions," *California Law Review* 68 (March 1980): 263–300.
21. Max Weber, *From Max Weber,* ed. H. H. Gerth and C. Wright Mills (New York: Oxford University Press, 1968), 299.

becomes increasingly objective and rational, therefore more closely ap-
proximating what Weber thought of as the pure type of legal authority.
The modern *Rechtsstaat,* he would have said, finds its genius in bureaucratic administration.

Second, Weber glimpsed a more general connection between bureaucracy and law. It was clear to him that bureaucracy could be private as
well as public. "Bureaucracy, thus understood, is fully developed in political and ecclesiastical communities only in the modern state, and, in the
private economy, only in the most advanced institutions of capitalism. . . . It does not matter for the character of bureaucracy whether its
authority is called 'private' or 'public.' "[22]

Thus the legality of bureaucratic authority does not require that it be
part of public law or government. Rather, legality derives from the internal life and order of the association. Bureaucratic authority is "legal"
because (1) its legitimacy is of a special kind—warranted by rational
principles, justified by its contribution to the organization; and (2) it is
committed to rule-governed decision-making, with all that entails for
the quality of the rules themselves, for the nature of delegation, for objective recruitment and assignment, for equal treatment of like cases, for
the visibility of norms, for appeal to authority as a paradigm of official
conduct, for the elaboration of principles of criticism. The source of
these attributes is internal, and it is the dynamic they create that calls
forth the ideals of legality.[23]

If bureaucratic authority is *legal*-rational, it should not be looked to
for maximum *purposive* rationality. The very joining of "legal" and "rational" indicates rationality of a particular kind. In Weber's vision, law-
minded bureaucrats are rational in that they strike down the arbitrary intrusions of nepotism, social status, and personal exploitation of official
position. They come upon the scene to champion the free and rational
manipulation of resources, including human resources. Yet their commitment to legality *as the preferred means to that end* must fetter managerial decision-making. Thus Weber was describing an organizational setting in which certain moral commitments are more important than, or at
least must be weighed against, the attainment of practical objectives.

22. Ibid.
23. Although the essentials of bureaucracy as a legal order are stated by Weber, we
should bear in mind that he shared a continental and even Roman perspective on law and
authority. In that view, authority takes on a heavy, somber note; law is fundamentally a
system of command. If "correctness" is a keynote, so too is obedience. The whole is
stuffy, pompous, and uninviting. Weber's image of law does not reflect the critical, searching, dynamic character a legal ethos can have.

Legality and rationality are to some extent conflicting ideals, for the former is, at least in part, a stabilizing principle. Under its aegis rights are vested; flexible management is limited. Seniority and other tenure rights are quite compatible with a bureaucratic-legal model of administration. But the rigidities they introduce compromise purposive rationality when, for example, new circumstances call such entitlements into question.[24]

The true lesson of Weber's theory is this: bureaucratic organization is most useful when *values*, as distinct from *purposes*, are of uppermost concern.[25] Weber was preoccupied with values, not purposes, when he argued that modern administration institutionalizes the Protestant ethic by building thrift and system into its representative forms and methods. Thus bureaucracy is value-centered. The range of values it may foster is, however, by no means limited to the rational forms and procedures Weber had in mind. The fate of other, *more substantive* values may also depend on bureaucratic organization and commitment.

Consider, for example, how the American constitutional system enshrines a bureaucratic principle. The great branches of government—legislative, executive, judicial—are legally defined spheres of competence. Each branch is jealous of its prerogatives, which are distinct but overlap. The stage is set for conflict and accommodation. Administrative rationality is not the main objective, for democracy and liberty are at stake. The constitutional arrangement is a check on institutional arrogance and abuse of power.

Here, again, the bureaucratic principle limits efficiency and effectiveness. From the standpoint of purposive rationality the separation of powers is a burden and a stumbling block. That was intentional. As Thomas Jefferson wrote:

> [F]ree government is founded in jealousy, and not in confidence; it is jealousy, not confidence, which prescribes limited constitutions, to bind down those whom we are obliged to trust with power; . . . in questions of power, then,

---

24. A source of confusion is that, as Talcott Parsons and others have noted, Weber was not careful to distinguish legal competence from technical competence (Max Weber, *The Theory of Social and Economic Organization*, trans. A. M. Henderson and Talcott Parsons [New York: Oxford University Press, 1947], 58–60). Legal competence as traditionally understood is a defined sphere of authority; officials act "competently" insofar as they act on proper authority. Technical competence is a matter of skill and expertise. As against earlier systems, Weber saw in bureaucracy the possibility of uniting authority and expertise, but he did not study how these principles conflict and interact.

25. I do not mean to suggest that Weber was clear about this, nor do I mean to deny that his model can be read as a vision of monocratic, authoritarian administration.

let no more be heard of confidence in man, but bind him down from mischief by the chains of the Constitution.[26]

American government is forever trying to overcome, and at the same time to sustain, the costs imposed by an imperfect separation of powers. The system must infuse public policy with unified commitment and direction, yet this must be done without yielding the principle of checks and balances.

A well-tempered bureaucracy is driven by the same impulse and faces the same dilemma. Power is diffused, consultation is demanded, but coordination is problematic. It is normal and usually proper for established divisions to uphold their prerogatives and resist encroachments. By doing so they defend the structure and competence of the enterprise. If the system is properly designed, the conflicts that ensue will bring much-needed information to the top of the hierarchy.

Struggles over bureaucratic turf are often unconscionable, but they often may be justified as responsible conduct. That is so because, in any large institution, various constituent units are expected to act as guardians of particular policies, programs, or procedures. Each such division is thought of—and perceives itself—as a positive source of moral energy. Each has a special obligation to preserve and nurture the values entrusted to it. This value-centered division of labor is one of the most important ingredients of institutional life, because policy needs a social base within the enterprise. Without such a base, the institution may persist but its vitality and commitment will wither.

Lessons of Watergate

The virtues of bureaucracy are (1) *fidelity* to assigned responsibilities; (2) *accountability* to the institution and its sponsors; (3) *consultation* as a corollary of the diffusion of authority; and (4) *mitigation of arbitrariness* through self-restrained, rule-governed decision. These are "process values," but they protect and enhance substantive interests.

These virtues were brought home by the Watergate crisis of 1972–74, which led to the resignation of President Richard M. Nixon, and by the Iran-Contra scandal of 1986–87, which badly wounded the Reagan administration. The details were different in the two cases, but the main theme was much the same: abuse of power by the president's staff, by

26. Quoted from E. D. Warfield, *The Kentucky Resolutions of 1798* (New York: G. P. Putnam's, 1887), 157f.

the president himself, and by others in the administration. Accountability was evaded by illegitimate secrecy, deception, and cover-up; the powers of government were used for purposes that could not be acknowledged publicly; departments responsible for orderly government were misused or bypassed.

In each case subversion of process was driven by political expediency and sustained by unprincipled loyalty. It was thought that the president's interests must be protected, and his aims prevail, at all costs. In Watergate the reelection of the president was of paramount concern; in Iran-Contra it was frustration regarding American hostages held in Lebanon, especially with a congressional election imminent, and the reluctance of Congress to support the president's policy in Central America. Behind these concerns, moreover, lay a set of unspoken assumptions as to how the government should be run. The operational code of the Nixon White House included the following premises:

- The President's constitutional powers, including his inherent powers, may be delegated and may be legitimately exercised by his principal assistants acting in his name. . . .
- Department and agency heads must obey orders from White House staff even in those areas where statutory powers are vested in them, and they are legally accountable for the actions taken.
- Agency heads should understand that when a request comes from the White House, they must accomplish it without questioning the merits. Even suggestions from the President's principal assistants are to be construed as orders coming directly from the Oval Office.
- The bureaucracy is engaged in a kind of guerrilla warfare against the President. The lack of key Republican bureaucrats or "RN supporters" at high levels precludes the initiation of policies which would be proper and politically advantageous.
- The President is both the nation's Chief Executive and the leader of his political party. Members of the White House staff are properly assigned "political duties" and are expected to supply the President with the information he needs and wants about issues, supporters, opponents, and every other political subject known to man.[27]

In this perspective, government officials are the president's soldiers, to be deployed and monitored from a command post in the White House. A "responsive" bureaucracy is one that jumps when the White House speaks. Leaving aside the political opportunism revealed, this is an ideal

27. Frederick C. Mosher et al., *Watergate: Implications for Responsible Government* (New York: Basic Books, 1974), 30. This was the report of a panel of the National Academy of Public Administration, prepared at the request of the Senate Select Committee on Presidential Campaign Activities, Senator Sam J. Ervin Jr., Chair, which conducted the Watergate hearings.

of monocratic or authoritarian administration. All initiative comes from above and all the levers of control are in the hands of top management. At best it is a form of Leninist "democratic centralism," which allows prior debate but demands full obedience once a decision is made. The underlying assumption is that bureaucracy is solely an instrument of purposive rationality, with no reason for being beyond its utility in advancing the leader's goals.

All this is offensive to American political institutions. It also runs counter to the ethos of bureaucracy. In response to Watergate, the constitutional tradition was summarized as follows:

> • The President is recognized to have general authority and responsibility over the agencies of the Executive Branch, subject to restrictions on such authority in law, and over the nature and direction of public policy within the framework of law;
> • Virtually all the executive agencies were established by law, duly passed by the Congress subject to Presidential veto, or by Reorganization Plan, initiated by the President, subject to Congressional veto; with a few exceptions, all received their powers and responsibilities in the same ways, not by delegation; and, for the most part, their ability to operate is annually renewed through appropriations passed by Congress, subject to Presidential veto;
> • The top leaders in almost all the agencies are appointed by the President, subject to confirmation by the Senate;
> • The heads of the agencies are therefore responsible, in different ways, to both the President and the Congress.[28]

Thus bureaucratic officials must obey congressional mandates as well as presidential directives. Their obligations run to legally defined purposes and values, and it is dereliction of duty to be supinely responsive to pressure, whether from self-interested clienteles or from a president's staff. It was a major lesson of Watergate that bureaucratic prerogatives and restraints are, in important respects, wholesome and even indispensable. They cannot be dismissed as inherently evil or as undesirable obstacles to rational administration. That the lesson is one not easily learned was vividly demonstrated in the subsequent Iran-Contra scandals.

▼   ▲   ▼   ▲   ▼

These experiences have vindicated Weber's conception of bureaucracy— not as the whole truth, or quite as he saw it, but as a still vital guide to responsible conduct. Furthermore, the scandals remind us that a neo-Weberian model calls for subtle understanding of both "hierarchy" and "fidelity."

28. Ibid., 47.

Bureaucratic hierarchy is not *any* system of ranking within an organization. The array of echelons in a line infantry division, from squad leader to commanding general, is not a good example of bureaucracy. The military units are fully deployable and expendable, wholly subordinate to the exigencies of command. In contrast, many staff units at headquarters (legal, intelligence, logistical, planning) form a bureaucracy, as do some specialized operational units. The army, air force, navy, and marines are, of course, bureaucratic units within the Department of Defense. The key is responsibility for a defined sphere of competence, which carries with it a duty to uphold the integrity of the office and not merely to obey commands from above.

As the Executive Office of the President has expanded, the connection between hierarchy and accountability has often been forgotten. The title "presidential assistant" blurs the distinction between "assistants *to* the president" and "assistant presidents." The former are accountable to the president alone, who in turn is directly responsible for them. Assistant presidents, on the other hand, would be officers in their own right to whom special functions and authority have been delegated, for the proper exercise of which they would be accountable. The distinction between intimate advisers, who are outside the hierarchy, and executive officers or administrators, who belong to it, is crucial for accountability. Hence it was that, when the Executive Office of the President was created, President Franklin D. Roosevelt promised that his staff members would not "become in any sense Assistant Presidents, nor are they to have any authority over anybody in any department or agency."[29] This was not the White House of later Presidents.[30]

In a (rational-legal) bureaucracy, fidelity runs to the institution, not to the leader.[31] Indeed it is useful to distinguish "fidelity" from "loyalty." Fidelity suggests a broad context of ideals and responsibilities; loyalty is

---

29. Ibid., 29. The report adds the following comment, which turned out to be quite prescient in the light of the Iran-Contra affair: "A President does not protect himself against special pleaders in the Executive Branch by transferring them to his own household. Staff with specific operating or investigatory responsibilities and intent on covering up their mistakes are not likely to provide the confidential, independent, objective advice and assistance which any President requires. Furthermore, the President cannot disavow acts by White House aides even when acting on their own. All of the mistakes become the President's mistakes" (ibid., 35).

30. See Arthur M. Schlesinger, Jr., *The Imperial Presidency* (Boston: Houghton Mifflin, 1973), 220ff.

31. To be sure, the principle of fealty is far from dead in modern organizations. A personal staff loyal to the boss is highly prized and not uncommon. When executives move from one organization to another they frequently take along key assistants who have accepted what amounts to a bond of fealty. These "premodern" relationships are at home in modern bureaucracy, so long as their character is well understood and so long as they

a more narrowly focused allegiance. The two ideas converge when loyalty moves from mindless to principled particularism, that is, from uncritical support of a group or leader to appreciation of the moral premises that justify or reinforce allegiance.

By the same token, fidelity to law must be distinguished from submission to authority. Fidelity to law is a commitment to *valid* rules, *restrained* authority, and *legitimated* criticism. Submission to authority is less discriminating. It is more appropriate in a military setting, which emphasizes unhesitating obedience to authoritative commands, than in civilian life. Although this view of military obedience has been modified somewhat since the Nuremberg trials and the excesses of the Vietnam war, military organization is hardly a model of the rule of law or of the best that bureaucracy can offer.

The norm of institutional fidelity governs the place of disobedience in official conduct. Directives from above are properly resisted if they offend the morality of the institution, and every bureaucratic official has *some* responsibility for interpreting that morality. It does not follow, however, that disobedience is justified by a personal policy agenda. Fidelity has to do with the premises of official conduct, not with parochial interests or individual preferences.[32]

▼   ▲   ▼   ▲   ▼

These reflections on the moral worth of bureaucracy in no way deny that it can also be morally regressive. The darker side is notorious, to say the least, and in many respects its features are better understood. Therefore we need not dwell on the many modes of domination, or on the evasions of responsibility, that have brought bureaucracy into bad repute.

The critique of bureaucracy comes from two sources, one technocratic, the other moral. The technocratic criticisms have to do with the way bureaucracy interferes with the rational pursuit of administrative goals. Weberian rationality, as we have seen, has to do with form and process, not purpose. The preoccupation with formal rationality reduces flexibility and inhibits consultation. Therefore, as Michel Crozier has

---

operate with respect for legitimate channels and procedures. It is offensive to accountability, however, to demand of the hierarchy proper that it act as a personal following and acknowledge a principle of fealty.

32. On the relation between institutional purpose and "justified rule departures by officials," see Mortimer Kadish and Sanford H. Kadish, *Discretion to Disobey: A Study of Lawful Departures from Legal Rules* (Stanford: Stanford University Press, 1973), chap. 2.

said, with some exaggeration, a bureaucratic organization "cannot correct its behavior by learning from its errors."[33] This cost is imposed by
the *stabilizing* aspects of bureaucracy, especially the hierarchy of defined
jurisdictions and the commitment to rule-governed administration.

More generally, formal rationality overstresses means and neglects
ends. The virtues of process are real enough, but they are readily transformed into the vices of formalism and legalism. Nurturing the system
takes precedence over solving problems; husbanding authority is more
important than taking risks and exercising initiative. Genuine matters of
policy, which may require debate, are treated as issues to be resolved by
the application of preexisting rules.[34]

The *dynamic* aspects of bureaucracy—the energies released by the
vested interests it creates—also threaten purposive rationality. To delegate authority, especially in a fixed or institutionalized way, is to create
a vehicle of group egoism. In many respects this egoism is benign. It
may generate wholesome rivalry and high levels of initiative and morale.
But it will also impose heavy costs, as the history of service rivalry in
the American military establishment has shown.

The distinctively moral criticism centers on bureaucracy as domination. Systems matter more than persons, procedures more than outcomes, stability more than risk. Weber's bleak assessment—bureaucracy
as an "iron cage," a "parcelling-out of the soul"[35]—has been shared by
many other writers. Among them was Weber's friend Michels, who saw
in bureaucracy a mortal threat to freedom and democracy. In fact, bureaucracy is not wholly alien to democracy, for it makes possible vastly

33. *The Bureaucratic Phenomenon* (Chicago: University of Chicago Press, 1964), 187.
Crozier's phrasing suggests that he intends to offer this as a definition of bureaucracy, but
that is not necessary to his argument.

34. "The fundamental tendency of all bureaucratic thought is to turn all problems of
politics into problems of administration. . . . Bureaucratic thought does not deny the
possibility of a science of politics, but regards it as identical with the science of administration. Thus irrational factors are overlooked, and when these nevertheless force themselves to the fore, they are treated as 'routine matters of state' " (Karl Mannheim, *Ideology
and Utopia: An Introduction to the Sociology of Knowledge* [New York: Harcourt Brace,
1936], 105f.).

35. "This passion for bureaucracy, as we have heard it expressed here, is enough to
drive one to despair. It is as if in politics the spectre of timidity . . . were to stand alone at
the helm; as if we were deliberately to become men who need 'order' and nothing but order, who become nervous and cowardly if for one moment this order wavers, and helpless
if they are torn away from their total incorporation in it. . . . [T]he great question is therefore not how we can promote and hasten it, but what we can oppose to this machinery in
order to keep a portion of mankind free from this parcelling-out of the soul, from this supreme mastery of the bureaucratic way of life" (Quoted in J. P. Mayer, *Max Weber and German Politics* [London: Faber & Faber, 1943], 127f.); see also Arthur Mitzman, *The Iron
Cage: An Historical Interpretation of Max Weber* (New York: Grosset & Dunlap, 1969), 260f.

increased participation in political, cultural, and economic institutions. But it also concentrates power and extends control.

The irony is that bureaucratic domination stems in large part from some of the very features that encourage self-restraint. The ethos of system, and of governance by rules, professionalizes administration and limits corruption. At the same time, it produces a people-processing culture in which persons are treated as administrative objects and their special needs and circumstances are ignored. Among ordinary clients and subjects, this is mainly what domination is about.

Ideally, bureaucracy limits discretion, that is, the right of officials to make decisions solely in the light of their own judgments about means and ends. Compared to wanton irregularity, unpredictability, nepotism, and corruption, bureaucratic systems do indeed promote regularity and restraint. But in most institutions some discretion is inevitable—and desirable as well. At bottom this is so because rules and categories are abstract, able to deal only with aspects of the world; whereas actions, situations, and persons are concrete, demanding attention on their own terms. Classifications are always to some extent arbitrary and incomplete. That is where the potential for domination begins. A purportedly neutral classification, supposedly based on technical criteria and expertise, may hide important policy choices. The rule may have a subtext as to who is deserving or undeserving. Furthermore, when the rule is applied someone must determine which classification is appropriate; whether a new one is required; whether an exception should be made. In framing rules, as well as in implementing them, the many unconscious assumptions of a world taken for granted are brought into play.

BEYOND DOMINATION

The limits of bureaucracy, moral as well as practical, have encouraged a quest for new postbureaucratic forms of organization. In contrast to the Weberian model, with its emphasis on defined spheres of competence and on governance by rules, the new model is more fully purposive, more flexible, more responsive, more susceptible to leadership, more congenial to initiative at all levels. Communication is less firmly channeled; authority is more diffuse; consultation and participation are more strongly encouraged. The system is open and fluid in many ways, as the following comment suggests:

> The social structure of organizations of the future will have some unique characteristics. The key word will be "temporary." There will be adaptive,

rapidly changing *temporary* systems. These will be task forces organized around problems to be solved by groups of relative strangers with diverse professional skills. The group will evolve . . . in response to a problem rather than to programmed role expectations. The executive thus becomes a coordinator or "linking pin" between various task forces. . . . Organizational charts will consist of project groups rather than stratified functional groups.[36]

Here institutionalization is contained and even reversed. A postmodern spirit of openness, adaptation, participation, and problem-solving prevails. The idea of top-down, authoritarian administration is rejected.

This development was anticipated in some early writings on authority and domination. Perhaps the sharpest contrast to Weber's perspective is found in what Durkheim and Piaget called a "morality of cooperation," which they distinguished from a "morality of constraint." A morality of cooperation does not contemplate submissive acceptance of received beliefs, even beliefs that are rational in Weber's sense. Rather, the emphasis is on group process and on the understanding that comes from effective and self-affirming participation.

Some early students of formal organization, strongly influenced by American pragmatism, were highly sensitive to the morality of cooperation. In the writings of Mary Parker Follett and Chester I. Barnard, for example, the efficient and effective organization must be a "cooperative system." In such systems authority is not self-justifying, nor does it rest on received beliefs. It is founded on practical necessity, subject to criticism and reconstruction, and disciplined by the "authority of the situation." This pragmatic authority has no place in Weber's scheme.

Follett once wrote that administrative wisdom lies in depersonalizing the giving of orders, thus separating authority from domination:

> One *person* should not give orders to another *person,* but both should agree to take their orders from the situation. . . . Our job is not how to get people to obey orders, but how to devise methods by which we can best *discover* the order integral to a particular situation. When that is found, the employee can issue it to the employer, as well as the employer to the employee. This often happens easily and naturally. My cook or my stenographer points out the law of the situation, and I, if I recognize it as such, accept it, even although it may reverse some "order" I have given.[37]

36. Warren G. Bennis, "Beyond Bureaucracy," in Warren G. Bennis and Philip E. Slater, *The Temporary Society* (New York: Harper & Row, 1968), 73f.

37. Henry C. Metcalf and L. Urwick, eds., *Dynamic Administration: The Collected Papers of Mary Parker Follett* (New York: Harper & Row, 1942), 59. Barnard's theory has a similar logic, but is less dynamic and is less sensitive to the creative needs and potentials of lower participants.

In the morality of cooperation, authority is situational, problematic, and responsive.

For Piaget, for the American pragmatists, and for these students of organization as well, individuals are not submissive, reactive participants in a regime of mechanical solidarity. They make their own assessments, transcend egocentric boundaries, and criticize authority. In short, they are responsible and rational actors.

In this perspective, rationality and legitimacy are most securely based and most fully achieved if they emerge from below instead of being imposed from above, whether by coercive measures or by repressive socialization. In the morality of constraint, norms are received, preordained, and prescriptive; codes of conduct are transmitted by authority figures who claim unqualified deference. The morality of cooperation, by contrast, looks to norms that arise in the course of group experience. It is a morality of participation and a philosophy of the present. The outcome of group learning may be a rediscovery of truths long since understood, but the moral effect is to make each generation its own master.

The upshot is a principled rejection of authority as domination. Consent is founded on practical requirements, including personal needs and satisfactions. This foundation makes authority more precarious, more open to negotiation, more dependent on offering inducements, more supportive of personal autonomy, and more adaptive to an institution's special needs and aspirations.

▼   ▲   ▼   ▲   ▼

The alternative to domination just described is full of promise, but it has risks as well. Enthusiasm for openness, negotiation, and self-affirming consent invites excessive optimism; and the virtues we associate with form and discipline are easily misunderstood and too readily disparaged. It is not likely that bureaucracy can be wholly transcended. Management will continue to depend on professionalism and will be required to offer security of employment; authority will have to be delegated, thus creating spheres of competence; and rules of some sort will remain indispensable. If there is a postbureaucratic world, it will not be one in which bureaucracy is eliminated. As we have seen, the positive functions and moral worth of bureaucracy cannot be ignored. Rather, the new, nonbureaucratic forms will be essential leaven in the bureaucratic dough.

ELEVEN

Management and Governance

As we have seen, a specter of oppression haunts the discussion of authority and bureaucracy. Legitimacy tends to restrain authority and holds it accountable, yet is compatible with uninformed consent and largely unbridled power. Bureaucracy encourages fidelity to institutional values, but it is also the "iron cage" Weber deplored. We have noted some alternatives, especially "legitimacy in depth" and the "morality of cooperation." But we have as yet only hinted at the most important way repressive authority can be countered. This is the appeal to principles of governance and the rule of law.

Here the connection we drew in Chapter 9 between organization and community comes into play. The taming of repression in large organizations builds on the funded experience of the political community. In bringing that experience to bear, we consider how far the special-purpose organization, if it is to be a moral institution, must take the community as a model, and do so without undermining the organization's distinctive responsibilities. We must bear in mind that such institutions are, after all, mainly devices for mobilizing energies and achieving purposes.

In taking community as a model, we must make a distinction between management and governance.[1] "Management" suggests rational, efficiency-minded, goal-driven organization. This is the realm of

1. I first drew this distinction in *Law, Society, and Industrial Justice* (New York: Russell Sage, 1969), chap. 3, but did not then grasp its significance for the connection between organization and community.

administrative rather than political decisions. Ends are characteristically taken as given, and every act is justified by the contribution it makes to those ends. All else is a distraction. Authority depends on what Barnard called the "zone of indifference." Employees, students, and soldiers—to say nothing of visitors to Disneyland—are expected to defer to legitimate authority, having agreed beforehand to subordinate their own preferences and suspend their own judgments, within more or less well-defined limits. So long as those limits are respected, the managers can take obedience for granted.

This well-ordered world of expertise and rationality, of deference and limited commitment, is not easily maintained. An alien political element intrudes at many levels and in many ways. Thought must be given to ends as well as means, to principles as well as rules, and to trade-offs among competing goals and values. The life of the organization generates groups of various kinds, including both internal and external constituencies. Negotiation and compromise, interest-balancing and dispute resolution are activities intrinsic to the institution. The organization-in-being is in many respects an open system with uncertain and ever-changing boundaries. The members are not only members but persons as well; they have strong connections to families and other groups; they are embedded in the community as a whole. All these factors give a political cast to the operations of even a moderately complex special-purpose institution.

To govern is to accept responsibility for *the whole life* of the institution. This is a burden quite different from the rational coordination of specialized activities. Governance takes account of all the interests that affect the viability, competence, and moral character of an enterprise. The strategies of governance are basically political. They have to do with forming public opinion, accommodating interests, and determining what ends should be chosen and by what means those ends should be pursued. Therefore governance cannot take obedience for granted. Rather, governance comes into play at the margin of harmony and in the shadow of dissensus; it begins where the zone of indifference ends.

A vital aspect of governance is that it *has the care* of a community or quasi-community. People subject to managerial direction may be thought of as interchangeable, deployable, expendable units, to be used or discarded as efficiency may require. They are not objects of care or of moral concern. In government, on the contrary, leaders (or systems) have a basic commitment to the participants *as persons* and to groups as vehicles of legitimate interests. Such a commitment is diffuse and open-ended, not narrowly defined. It need not presume altruism, however. In its beginnings it may reflect nothing more than an elementary need for cooperation. A victorious army, for example, when it becomes an army of occupation, must accept basic responsibility for the care and protection of the conquered population—or suffer very high costs. A claim to sovereignty, with its special privileges and immunities, is coupled with this assumption of comprehensive responsibility.

The place of governance in special-purpose organizations can never be eliminated, so long as real people and practices are involved. But it is highly variable. The imperatives may be marginal or central, modest or substantial. *The broader the organization's goals, the more leeway it has in defining its mission, the more requirements there are for winning cooperation, the more fully the lives of participants are lived within it, the more important does governance become.* Each of those conditions brings the organization closer to the model of community and therefore makes that model more useful as a guide to policy.

This perspective suggests that the transition from management to governance, like that from organization to institution to community, is best understood as a continuum rather than as one marked by clean breaks. The two functions, management and governance, coexist and interact. An organization that *tries* to be instrumentally single-minded, guided wholly by norms of purposive rationality, nonetheless finds itself faced with more comprehensive obligations. Insofar as that is so, governance cannot be avoided.

The idea of a continuum does not preclude classification, however. It cannot be a bar to judgment. For practical purposes it may be useful to classify some decisions and activities as *mainly* managerial, others as *mainly* governmental. In particular contexts this will help in deciding what expectations are legitimate and what standards should apply. The continuities remain, however, and are always troublesome.

SPEECH AND COMMUNITY

The Public Forum

The significance of the distinction between management and governance is brought home by its relevance for some important issues in American constitutional law. Among these is the regulation of speech by agencies of government.[2] Controversy arises in two ways. People *within* the agency—students or teachers in a public high school, for example, or employees of the post office, or soldiers—may claim rights of expression, as members or as citizens, that are denied by the agency or restricted by its rules. And people *outside* the agency may seek to use its premises or facilities for, say, distributing leaflets or conducting meetings. The question is how far, if at all, the special mission of the agency justifies its restriction of the freedom of speech guaranteed to all persons by the First Amendment.

In dealing with this issue the Supreme Court has relied on the idea of a "public forum." This concept reflects the Court's awareness that *some* facilities subject to government regulation have a special place in the life of the community. These are, most clearly, streets and other spaces to which people have routine access as part of everyday life and within which free communication has long been expected and practiced. Thus in *Hague v. CIO* (1939) Justice Owen J. Roberts wrote that "wherever the title may rest, streets and parks have immemorially been held in trust for the use of the public and, time out of mind, have been used for purposes of assembly, communicating thoughts between citizens, and discussing public questions."[3] In that landmark case it was held that Jersey City, New Jersey, could *regulate* the use of streets and parks but could not claim the power to *exclude* citizens from using them as sites for political gatherings.

The *Hague* case bears directly on speech and community. Activities of the general public are at issue, not those of a specialized staff, membership, or clientele. In streets and parks, people interact as persons rather than according to narrowly defined roles. The sights and sounds of normal community activity—commercial, recreational, familial, religious, political—are expected, tolerated, even appreciated. Bids for attention, offers of information, expressions of controversy must all be regulated from the standpoint of governance, not management. Especially in a free society, governance protects and enhances opportunities for public discussion and debate.

The cases are harder, however, when the government agency can plausibly claim that its facilities should be insulated from the distractions of free speech. Here the Court has relied on a theory of property rights.

2. This discussion is indebted to Robert C. Post, "Between Governance and Management: The History and Theory of the Public Forum," *UCLA Law Review* 34 (1987): 1713–1835.

3. Hague v. CIO, 307 U.S. 496, 515 (1939).

Whether or not a public forum exists is made to turn on a distinction be-tween *kinds of property*. Some facilities are not really government prop-erty, or are proprietal in a weak sense, because they have been open, and are meant to be open, to public access and use. They belong to the com-mons, as it were. Government property is truly proprietal only when it is dedicated to a specific purpose. A government agency responsible for educating children, training soldiers, confining prisoners, collecting taxes, or regulating business can treat its facilities as a species of private property, or on the analogy of private property. So long as minimal standards of reasonable and evenhanded administration are met, the ad-ministrators can determine how the property should be used. They may abridge freedom of speech within the agency; and they may forbid pub-lic use of its facilities for purposes they consider extraneous.[4]

The speech of employees, members, and clients is, of course, rou-tinely restricted in special-purpose organizations. People are very often told what to say and how to say it—for example, when they write pub-licity handouts or advertising copy, and even when they prepare policy memoranda or newspaper articles. Courts may bar certain testimony as unreliable, privileged, or irrelevant. Thus there is nothing unusual about the management of speech: it is readily justified by the need for orderly and effective administration. The question is, in many cases, whether management has overstepped its bounds and entered the realm of governance. To the extent that it has done so, different principles must be invoked.

To reach those principles, as Robert Post has argued, we need to look to kinds of *authority*, not kinds of *property*. When the Supreme Court upheld a military regulation prohibiting political activity on the grounds of Fort Dix—despite much public access and many nonpolitical meetings—it was speaking to the perceived requirements of military

4. There are, of course, many borderline cases, which may raise important questions of principle. Thus in 1990 the Supreme Court upheld a regulation forbidding solicitation of contributions (but not other free-speech activities) on a sidewalk "constructed solely to assist postal patrons to negotiate the space between the parking lot and the front door of the post office, not to facilitate the daily commerce and life of the neighborhood or city" (U.S. v. Kokinda, 110 S. Ct. 3115, 3120.) Justice O'Connor's plurality opinion accepted the government's claim that "solicitation is inherently disruptive of the postal service's busi-ness." A dissent by Justice Brennan argued that "no particular inquiry into the precise na-ture of a specific street is necessary; all public streets are held in the public trust and are properly considered traditional public fora." Although Brennan agreed that "the Govern-ment has an interest in preventing the obstruction of post offices' entrances and the dis-ruption of postal functions, there is no indication that respondents interfered with postal business in any way." The regulation "sweeps an entire category of expressive activity off a public forum solely in the interest of administrative convenience."

discipline, not to property rights. Similarly, when the Court sustained the convictions of students who demonstrated against segregation on the premises of a county jail, it was upholding the authority of the jail officials to protect the security of the installation. These, not rights of property, were the real concerns.

The focus on authority rather than property is important for two reasons. First, the idea of property offers no guidance when we need to distinguish one situation from another. A claim of necessary authority, on the other hand, is open to evaluation in light of the agency's purposes and circumstances. Second, property connotes *dominion,* that is, full power to do as one likes with one's own, including the exclusion of strangers. "The owner," wrote Oliver Wendell Holmes Jr., "is allowed to exclude all, and is accountable to no one."[5] Although the law may set limits, the spirit of property rights is one of exclusive and unlimited control. To classify something as proprietal is to prejudge precisely what is open to question, that is, how much control is justified.

When issues of governance arise, the courts withhold deference to managerial authority. The post office is granted considerable discretion with respect to managing customer service inside the post office, but efforts to control what goes on in large lobbies or in adjacent streets are likely to receive closer scrutiny. Similarly, the courts will defer to academic administrators on class size, scheduling, and many other matters, but not on regulations regarding political speech. Such regulations must be more than "reasonable." They must be narrowly drawn to serve a compelling interest. Thus the vision of governance generates very different rules and expectations from that of management.

Schools as Communities

The tension between governance and management, as it bears on freedom of speech, is especially acute in schools and colleges. Here the special purpose of the institution aggravates the tension. Much of what goes on in school requires disciplined learning, systematic teaching, and efficient coordination of many complex activities. Skillful management is needed, and it is very helpful if the attitudes of teachers and students contain a generous zone of indifference with respect to room assignments, registration procedures, and many other aspects of administration. Similarly, in most courses students readily defer to their instruc-

5. *The Common Law* (Boston: Little, Brown, 1881), 246.

tors' decisions regarding assigned readings, testing procedures, and the like. Most important, the maintenance of an atmosphere conducive to undistracted teaching and learning is a proper objective of management.

The importance of schools for students as persons, however, goes well beyond formal learning. A school is a setting for interaction, communication, and growth—a center of life as well as learning. The school does best, as Dewey argued, when it becomes "a genuine form of active community life, instead of a place set apart in which to learn lessons."[6] In most contexts it is neither practical nor desirable to treat students as segmental participants in a narrowly defined system of work and discipline. They come to school as whole persons, and the authority exercised by teachers and administrators must be tailored to that reality.

Moreover, education itself requires a genuine concern for freedom as well as discipline. It is a commonplace that many subjects cannot be taught effectively to passive students or by rote learning. Thinking is too closely bound up with questioning, and the life of the mind, even for the very young, cannot flourish when it is wholly programmed. Thus the very purpose of the institution demands that management be tempered by governance.

In a well-known case, *Tinker v. Des Moines School District,* decided in 1969, a divided Supreme Court refused to sustain the suspension of three young students who wore black armbands at school in protest against the war in Vietnam. The District Court had said that the students' freedom of expression could properly be abridged if the educators feared that the tranquillity of the schools would be disturbed by the students' demonstrative speech. But the Supreme Court majority saw "no evidence whatever of petitioners' interference, actual or nascent, with the schools' work or of collision with the rights of other students to be secure and to be let alone. . . . [I]n our system, undifferentiated fear or apprehension of disturbance is not enough to overcome the right to freedom of expression. . . . It can hardly be argued that either students or teachers shed their constitutional rights to freedom of speech or expression at the schoolhouse gate."[7]

The *Tinker* opinion eloquently upheld the rights of students to invoke the protection of the First Amendment. Even the very young, not eligible to vote, can have their say on school grounds so long as they do not interfere with, or seriously threaten, the normal work of the school. The Court strongly affirmed the place of freedom in public

6. John Dewey, *The School and Society* (Chicago: University of Chicago Press), 27.
7. Tinker v. Des Moines School District, 393 U.S. 503, 508, 506 (1969).

education: "In our system, state-operated schools may not be enclaves of totalitarianism. School officials do not possess absolute authority over their students. . . . [S]tudents may not be regarded as closed-circuit recipients of only that which the State chooses to communicate. They may not be confined to the expression of those sentiments that are officially approved." And the "personal intercommunication" among students that takes place outside the classroom but within the context of the school "is also an important part of the educational process."[8]

In this case the Court did not have to do more—and as a matter of precedent did not do more—than say that for students (not the general public) the school is a public forum. In that forum they have, as it were, "soapbox rights." They can speak out as persons whose everyday life happens to include going to school. But those rights are different, and must be differently regulated, from rights of free speech in the class-room, in student government, or as student journalists. The Court had yet to deal with the *academic* freedom of pre-college students.

In 1988 such a case did arise, and the outcome revealed a different perspective. A divided (and more conservative) Court upheld the au-thority of a high school principal who censored a student newspaper. The paper was written and edited by a journalism class and therefore was part of the school curriculum. The instructor of the course served as faculty adviser, and proofs were routinely submitted to the principal for review prior to publication. In this incident, the principal reluctantly de-leted two articles (on pregnancy and divorce) whose content he consid-ered inappropriate.

When the student editors sought vindication of their First Amend-ment rights, the district court said they had no case. A court of appeals thought otherwise, holding that the newspaper should have been con-sidered a public forum *as well as* a part of the school curriculum. There-fore the school officials could only censor the content of the paper if they had reason to expect substantial interference with school work and dis-cipline or with the rights of others. But there was "no evidence in the record that the principal could have reasonably forecast that the censored articles . . . would have materially disrupted classwork or given rise to substantial disorder in the school."[9]

The Supreme Court majority took a harder line. They did not over-rule *Tinker.* Rather, they distinguished the school's right to "silence a student's personal expression that happens to occur on school prem-

8. Ibid., 511.
9. Hazelwood School District v. Kuhlmeier, 795 F.2d 1368, 1375 (1988).

ises"—the situation in *Tinker*—from "the educators' authority over school-sponsored publications, theatrical productions, and other expressive activities that students, parents, and members of the public might reasonably perceive to bear the imprimatur of the school." The majority went on to argue:

> Educators are entitled to exercise greater control over this second form of student expression to assure that participants learn whatever lessons the activity is designed to teach, that readers or listeners are not exposed to material that may be inappropriate for their level of maturity, and that the views of the individual speaker are not erroneously attributed to the school. . . . A school must be able to set high standards for the student speech that is disseminated under its auspices—standards that may be higher than those demanded by some newspaper publishers or theatrical producers in the "real" world. . . . Accordingly, we conclude that the standard articulated in *Tinker* for determining when a school may punish student expression need not also be the standard for determining when a school may refuse to lend its name and resources to the dissemination of student expression. Instead, we hold that educators do not offend the First Amendment by exercising editorial control over the style and content of student speech in school-sponsored expressive activities so long as their actions are reasonably related to legitimate pedagogical concerns.[10]

The opinion was arguably right to distinguish the claims of *persons who happen to be students* from the claims of *students as students,* that is, as disciplined participants in a process of learning and teaching. In respect to the latter, educators have a great deal of authority. But is their authority limited only by the criterion that it must be "reasonably related to legitimate pedagogical concerns"? Missing here is a robust theory of the institution—of its mission, character, and distinctive methods. Nothing is said about the place of freedom in effective learning, and in that respect the spirit of *Tinker* is lost even as the rule is sustained.

Student writers and editors in this country ought to be learning how to take a responsible part in American journalism. To do that effectively they need a *free* press, not a *managed* press. (Presumably they are not being trained to publish propaganda sheets or house organs.) At the same time, and in addition to their own needs as students, they have duties to the student body as a whole, for which a free press should be an aspect of community life. Thus student journalists, though subject to academic discipline, have a proper claim to academic freedom.

Much the same may be said of other courses of instruction, especially where controversial topics are discussed. Here speech is not properly

10. Hazelwood School District v. Kuhlmeier, 484 U.S. 260, 271–73 (1988).

managed merely for administrative convenience, nor may it be manipulated to attain conformity of opinion. Rather, education for responsible freedom looks to the integrity of the process, which includes high standards of communication, logic, and civility. As it does so, an ethos of governance, not management, must prevail.

These cases show us that institutional governance must recognize (1) the continuities of life within and outside the organization and (2) the special claims of members. In allowing students to wear provocative armbands, the Court's majority in *Tinker* recognized the school's distinct but permeable boundaries. Self-expression on legitimate topics of general concern ought not to be very different, let alone suffocated, when young people enter school grounds. For them, the school is an extension of community, not an abridgment of it.[11]

▼   ▲   ▼   ▲   ▼

The school cases discussed above concern the connection between freedom of speech and institutional competence. Schools are not alone, however, as institutions whose lives are bound up with freedom of information and communication. An obvious example is a legislature. Still another context was pointed up in *Rust v. Sullivan*, a highly controversial decision which had to do with government policy on abortion. In 1988 new regulations were promulgated by the Department of Health and Human Services with respect to family planning projects funded by the federal government. The regulations prohibited such projects from *counseling* or *advocating* abortion as a method of family planning. By a vote of 5–4, the Court upheld the regulations as reflecting a defensible "value judgment favoring childbirth over abortion." The majority argued that the government had no obligation to fund advice favoring or condoning abortion and that the regulations "did not significantly impinge upon the doctor-patient relationship." The dissent by Justice Harry A. Blackmun held, on the contrary, that the doctor-patient relationship was severely compromised by regulations that said a project must "refer for prenatal care each woman diagnosed as pregnant, irrespective of the woman's expressed desire to continue or terminate her

11. The same claims cannot be made in respect to every institution, for some are necessarily less person-centered and have more narrowly defined aims. But all institutions have at least this moral bridge to the larger community, that their members are also persons who belong to that community and who therefore can invoke its baseline standards of respect and care.

pregnancy. If a client asks directly about abortion, a Title X [federally funded] physician or counselor is required to say, in essence, that the project does not consider abortion to be an appropriate method of family planning."[12]

These views contrast a managerial perspective with one that takes account of multiple values, including the professional autonomy of physicians and the right of patients to be fully informed of their medical options. As we move in the latter direction, the exercise of authority includes respect for professional judgment and for patients as whole persons. Managerial imperatives are not lost from view, but they are broadened to include the responsibilities of governance. Among these is the integrity of the program, which in this case involves the obligations of physicians toward their patients. The government directives constituted a flagrant effort to impose an anti-abortion policy without regard for the internal life of the projects, which includes the kind of care they could give to their—mostly poor—clientele.

Constitutional issues of free speech were raised because federally funded staff members were prohibited from providing, and their patients were barred from receiving, information about the benefits or availability of abortion as a personal alternative. This allowed the dissent to say that the government had imposed an "unconstitutional condition" on receipt of a public benefit. The more distinctive issue of the case, however, has to do with the nature of medical practice. Operating a medical facility staffed by professionals requires a free flow of relevant information. When that process is blocked or distorted by intrusive governmental regulation or by insensitive management, an appeal to institutional rights is in order. Just as academic freedom has received constitutional protection, so free speech in medical practice, especially now that much of it takes place in organizational settings, requires legal attention and concern.[13] Even if the *constitutional* status of such rights is doubtful, the courts can still apply the principle when, as in this case,

12. Rust v. Sullivan, 59 *U.S. Law Week* 4451 (1991).

13. The majority opinion in *Rust* notes: "[W]e have recognized that the university is a traditional sphere of free expression so fundamental to the functioning of our society that the Government's ability to control speech within that sphere by means of conditions attached to the expenditure of Government funds is restricted by the vagueness and overbreadth doctrines of the First Amendment. It could be argued by analogy that traditional relationships such as that between doctor and patient should enjoy protection under the First Amendment from government regulation, even when subsidized by the Government. We need not solve that question here, however, because the Title X program regulations do not significantly impinge upon the doctor-patient relationship" (ibid., 4459).

the interpretation of a statute is in question. The protection runs to the institution and to the conditions that enhance its service to the community, not merely to the individual rights of patients and doctors.

It is not too much to ask that judges in a modern legal system should be reasonably sophisticated in their understanding of major institutions. The claims and limits of authority in military, medical, police, educational, journalist, religious, and industrial organizations are surely as worthy of study—and of discriminating judgment—as are many arcane issues lawyers have addressed. Judges cannot do this job alone, if only because, to protect their legitimacy, they must exercise restraint in moving beyond received categories and doctrines. They need help from legislators, who can more readily establish new policies and new points of departure for legal reasoning. But judges are in a good position to take advantage of whatever sound thought modern scholarship may offer.

PRIVATE GOVERNMENT

The "public forum" cases discussed above deal with *public* government, that is, with city, county, state, or federal agencies, including local school boards, irrigation districts, and the like. As units of government these agencies are clearly subject to provisions of the United States Constitution as interpreted by the courts. The idea of governance, however, has a more general significance. Governance is found (and is appropriate) in many institutions we usually think of as private. As such they are, to a large extent, beyond the reach of the Constitution. They are subject to regulation by statute or by common-law rules and principles, but these do not easily address the special problems of governance. And yet, wherever institutional authority is exercised—wherever there is bureaucracy—people need protection from arbitrary rule. Just governance is a moral necessity, in private as well as in public institutions.

As Max Weber understood, law, authority, and bureaucracy are not uniquely associated with the state. Law is endemic in all institutions that rely for social control on formal authority and rule-making. This idea is captured in Lon Fuller's characterization of law as "the enterprise of subjecting human conduct to the governance of rules."[14] He further argued that law should not be equated with public government.[15] Indeed, to equate law with the state impoverishes both sociological and legal

14. Lon L. Fuller, *The Morality of Law* (New Haven: Yale University Press, 1969), 106.
15. Ibid., 129.

analysis. When we fail to see the place of law in "private" institutions we withhold from that setting the experience of the political community in matters of governance.

▼   ▲   ▼   ▲   ▼

In 1875 Congress passed a Civil Rights Act, prohibiting racial discrimination by "any person" in places of public accommodation and amusement. A few years later, however, the Supreme Court declared these provisions unconstitutional, insisting that the Fourteenth Amendment's guarantee of civil rights could be asserted only against *public* government.[16] "It is State action of a particular character that is prohibited. Individual invasion of individual rights is not the subject-matter of the amendment."[17] Sixty-five years later, a controversial opinion greatly expanded the meaning of "state action" by including the role of the courts in enforcing private agreements.[18] At the same time the Court reaffirmed that "since the decision of this Court in the *Civil Rights* cases . . . the principle has become firmly embedded in our constitutional law that the action inhibited by the first section of the Fourteenth Amendment is only such action as may fairly be said to be that of the States. That Amendment erects no shield against merely private conduct, however discriminatory or wrongful."

When a clear public responsibility is at stake, as in the administration of elections, the modern Court has pierced the shield of seemingly private action. In 1935 the Court upheld a procedure by which the Democratic party of Texas, purporting to be a private organization with inherent power to determine its own membership, excluded blacks from participation in the party's primary election.[19] Nine years later the Court changed its mind,[20] arguing that the Democratic party's activities were too intimate a part of the election process to be other than a public function, even though no direct action by the legislature or public officials was involved.

16. The relevant passage of the Fourteenth Amendment reads: "No State shall . . . deprive any person of life, liberty, or property, without due process of law; nor deny to any person within its jurisdiction the equal protection of the laws."
17. Civil Rights Cases, 109 U.S. 3, 11 (1883).
18. Shelley v. Kraemer, 334 U.S. 1 (1948), holding that racially restrictive private agreements do not violate the Fourteenth Amendment, but their enforcement by the courts constitutes impermissible "state action."
19. Grovey v. Townsend, 295 U.S. 45 (1935).
20. Smith v. Allwright, 321 U.S. 649 (1944).

Other decisions have struck at private action when the government is in some way implicated.[21] In these cases, the Court's main purpose has been to hold *public* government to its constitutional responsibilities; those responsibilities cannot be diluted by the use or intervention of private agencies. In *Marsh v. Alabama,* however, the phenomenon of private government was brought into sharper focus. A member of Jehovah's Witnesses, who had distributed literature without a license, was prosecuted and convicted for criminal trespass. The Gulf Shipbuilding Corporation, which owned the town and rented stores on a "business block," had posted a notice forbidding vending or solicitation without written permission. This privately established rule was applied to bar the Witness from distributing religious literature on the company-owned sidewalk.

The Supreme Court held that the state's criminal trespass statute could not be applied in these circumstances without violating the First and Fourteenth amendments. This finding of unconstitutional *state* action, the enforcement of laws against trespass on private property, was not the heart of the matter. The nature of the *private* conduct was at issue. The majority opinion was clear that the corporation was being permitted "to govern a community of citizens." The justices reasoned that residents of the town were entitled to uncensored information on the same terms as residents of other towns. Therefore the town managers should be held to the same standards as other municipal officials. The latter may not "completely bar the distribution of literature containing religious or political ideas on its streets, sidewalks and public places or make the right to distribute dependent on a . . . permit to be issued by an official who could deny it at will."[22]

A company town, said the Court, is still a town. People who govern towns must do so responsibly, and responsibility flows from function. To apply the Constitution might require a finding of state action, such as the state's "permitting" the corporation to govern, but the underlying social and legal reality is the process of governing by a private group.

21. For example, if a state agency provides a public facility, such as a parking garage, a private operator of the facility will be held to Fourteenth Amendment standards. If a pattern of private violation of individual rights involves state officials, including the courts, as abettors, the amendment may be brought into play. "In a variety of situations the Court has found state action of a nature sufficient to create rights under the Equal Protection Clause even though the participation of the State was peripheral, or its action was only one of several co-operative forces leading to the contitutional violation" (U.S. v. Herbert Guest et al., 383 U.S. 745, 756 [1966]).

22. Marsh v. Alabama, 326 U.S. 501, 504 (1946).

The *Marsh* doctrine has been narrowly construed to apply only where the private property has *"all* the attributes of a town, i.e., 'residential buildings, streets, a system of sewers, a sewage disposal plant and a "business block" on which business places are situated.' "[23] This stringent criterion may be necessary to trigger application of *all* First Amendment rights. But in a later case, Justice Thurgood Marshall offered a more flexible reading:

> The underlying concern in *Marsh* was that traditional public channels of communication remain free, regardless of the incidence of ownership. Given that concern, the crucial fact in *Marsh* was that the company owned the traditional forums necessary for effective communication; it was immaterial that the company also owned a sewer system and that its property in other respects resembled a town. . . . The roadways, parking lots, and walkways of the modern shopping center may be as essential for effective speech as the streets and sidewalks in the municipal or company-owned town. . . . In *Marsh,* the private entity displaced the "state." . . . The shopping center owner, on the other hand, controls only a portion of such places, leaving other traditional public forums available to the citizen. But the shopping center owner may nevertheless control all places essential for the effective undertaking of some speech-related activities—namely, those related to the activities of the shopping center. As for those activities, then, the First Amendment ought to have application under the reasoning of *Marsh.*[24]

This perspective upholds the free-speech values vindicated in *Marsh* without creating a rigid rule, and without abandoning respect for the special purposes of a privately owned facility.

▾   ▴   ▾   ▴   ▾

The *Marsh* case showed that principles of governance may be applied to private settings. However, the focus was on the rights of *citizens* to pursue constitutionally protected activities in places that are functionally public though privately owned. What of the rights of *members,* from whom disciplined conduct is expected? We have touched on this matter above, in connection with the First Amendment rights of students. Those examples are only part of a broader movement toward legal scrutiny of how authority is exercised in special-purpose institutions. A

23. Amalgamated Food Employees Union v. Logan Valley Plaza, 391 U.S. 308, 331 (1968). The quotation is from a dissent by Justice Hugo Black, who wrote the Court's opinion in Marsh v. Alabama.

24. Hudgens v. National Labor Relations Board, 424 U.S. 507, 539ff. (1976), dissenting opinion. This case held that members of a union picketing a store in a shopping center were not protected by the First Amendment.

different and in some ways more important phase of that movement is the demand for due process in schools and colleges.

For many years, on the theory that being a student is a privilege and that rights may be waived by contract, the courts upheld wide administrative discretion in both public and private institutions. Schools were thought to be in loco parentis and thus endowed with largely unfettered authority in matters of discipline as well as academic judgment. In 1961, however, a new departure was heralded by *Dixon v. Alabama Board of Education,* a case that involved the expulsion of demonstrating students. A U.S. court of appeals answered yes to the question "whether due process requires notice and some opportunity for hearing before students at a tax-supported college are expelled for misconduct." The court held that "the State cannot condition the granting of even a privilege upon the renunciation of the constitutional right to procedural due process."[25]

The rights of students attending *private* institutions have been less easily recognized, but the trend has been the same.[26] At first the courts fell back on the prerogatives of private ownership and stressed the importance of autonomy for institutions of higher education. Thus in 1967, in *Greene v. Howard University,* a U.S. district court upheld the dismissal without notice or hearing of disruptive students at Howard University.[27] The court explicitly denied that the rule in *Dixon v. Alabama* was applicable, on the ground that Howard University is a private corporation and therefore beyond the reach of the Bill of Rights. It refused to find state action in the fact that a large part of the university budget came from the federal government:

> It would be a dangerous doctrine to permit the Government to interpose any degree of control over an institution of higher learning, merely because it extends financial assistance to it. . . . Surely it should not be held that any institution by entering into a contract with the United States . . . has placed its head in a noose and subjected itself to some degree of control by the Federal Government. Such a result would be intolerable, for it would tend to hinder

25. 294 F.2d 150, 156 (1961). This doctrine was upheld by the Supreme Court in Goss v. Lopez, 419 U.S. 565 (1975), which found that high school students briefly suspended for misconduct were entitled to some form of notice and hearing.

26. Today a court can say: "The requirements imposed by the common law on private universities parallel those imposed by the due process clause on public universities" (Abbariao v. Hamline University Law School, 258 N.W.2d 108, 113 [Minn. 1977]). "Courts have analyzed the relationship between a student and a private university under several legal theories, including the law of contracts and the law of associations. . . . Neither theory fits perfectly and, therefore, should not be rigidly applied. . . . It is clear, however, that a private university may not expel a student arbitrarily, unreasonably, or in bad faith" (Harvey v. Palmer College of Chiropractic, 363 N.W.2d 443, 444 [Iowa App. 1984]).

27. Greene v. Howard University, 271 F. Supp. 609 (1967).

and control the progress of higher learning and scientific research. Higher education can flourish only in an atmosphere of freedom, untrammeled by Governmental influence in any degree. The courts may not interject themselves into the midst of matters of school discipline. Such discipline cannot be administered successfully in the same manner as governs the trial of a criminal case or a hearing before an administrative agency.[28]

It is by no means clear either that education in public institutions has a lesser need for an "atmosphere of freedom" or that judicially imposed standards of due process are necessarily an intolerable interference with institutional autonomy. The decisions affecting public schools and colleges have been careful to specify only minimum standards, leaving a great deal of room for variation to take account of the academic context. Thus in *Dixon* the court held that a "hearing" should provide "an opportunity to hear both sides in considerable detail," but this "is not to imply that a full-dress judicial hearing, with the right to cross-examine witnesses, is required. Such a hearing, with the attending publicity and disturbance of college activities, might be detrimental to the college's educational atmosphere and impractical to carry out. Nevertheless, *the rudiments of an adversary proceeding* may be preserved without encroaching upon the interests of the college."[29]

The main weakness of the opinion in *Greene* lies in the comment that Howard University "is not a public institution nor does it partake of any governmental character."[30] It is one thing to say that the autonomy of religious, educational, or economic institutions may be more easily protected if they are not classified as "public," with all that might mean for the assertion of authority by agencies of public government. It is something else to deny the sociological phenomenon itself, that is, the sense in which private authority "partakes" of a "governmental character."

The idea of private government need not "constitutionalize" the issues. That is, it does not require that the Constitution be invoked wherever governance is found. The alternative is to view the Constitution as a *resource* for the development of standards to be applied in the course of nonconstitutional adjudication. The effect is to call for a legal doctrine, as part of developing common law, that would apply to any school that is functionally a government. This might be supplemented by appropriate statutes, but the point is to know that governance is at stake and to fashion remedies accordingly. These would *draw on* constitutional

28. Ibid., 613.
29. Dixon v. Alabama, 159 (1961), my emphasis.
30. Greene v. Howard University, 612f. (1967).

experience without necessarily *invoking,* or being bound by, specific rules of due process applied by the Supreme Court to public government.[31] For many purposes, including that of freedom to experiment with rules of governance and to adapt them to special purposes and perspectives, the distinction between public and private institutions would be preserved.

THE LAW OF EMPLOYMENT

Perhaps the most important private arena within which a law of governance has developed is the unionized firm. The labor legislation of the New Deal made it an unfair labor practice for an employer to refuse to bargain with employee representatives. This gave great weight to the ensuing agreement, but for some years it was not clear what sort of contract this was and therefore what principles should govern its interpretation by the parties and the courts.

The collective agreement does not fit easily into the premises of contract law. Under its terms, new and continuing institutions are created, such as the bargaining unit and grievance machinery; the terms apply not only to the contracting parties but to an indeterminate number of present and future employees; and the needs of a going concern require that rules be elaborated over time, in response to changing circumstances. In effect, an arrangement is made for governing an enterprise.

The governmental analogy has been adopted by many commentators, including the Supreme Court:

> A collective bargaining agreement is an effort to erect a system of industrial self-government. . . . It is more than a contract; it is a generalized code to govern a myriad of cases which the draftsmen cannot wholly anticipate. . . . The collective agreement covers the whole employment relationship. It calls into being a new common law—the common law of a particular industry or of a particular plant.[32]

The widespread establishment of grievance and arbitration procedures under the collective bargaining agreement lends much support to the governmental analogy, for the adoption of these procedures is a response to the need for lawfulness in the day-to-day administration of a large enterprise. The grievance procedure provides a forum for criticizing man-

31. See also "Private Government on the Campus—Judicial Review of University Expulsions," *Yale Law Journal* 72 (1963): 1362–1410, and "Common Law Rights for Private University Students: Beyond the State Action Principle," *Yale Law Journal* 84 (1974): 120–50.

32. Steelworkers v. Warrior & Gulf, 363 U.S. 575, 578–79 (1960).

agerial decisions and holding management accountable to prior commitments and policies, as well as to principles of fairness. It offers a
machinery for case-by-case review. As a result the collective contract becomes a system of order rather than an aggregate of discrete, bargained-
out provisions. As specific cases are adjudicated the meaning of general
clauses, such as "employees shall not be discharged except for just
cause," can be spelled out and developed.

From the point of view of institutional morality, the main contribution of collective bargaining is the domestication of managerial authority. The agreement provides a framework within which legitimacy may
be tested in depth. And limits are set, not only by the agreement's specific terms, but by implicit principles of good order. The employer has
general supervisory authority, but that authority is limited, not absolute.
Most important, the existence of the collective contract creates an inherent bar to arbitrary action by the employer.[33]

Many *nonunion* employees have gained indirectly from the existence
of trade unions, and specifically from the popularity of grievance and arbitration systems. Nonunion companies have frequently responded to
union pressure by establishing some form of grievance procedure. But
in the absence of collective bargaining and the power-sharing institutions it creates, such systems are usually less complete and less effective.
In most cases the company, not an arbitrator, makes the final decision.
"This is not to say that no nonunion firm will have a viable grievance
system, for some do, but rather that it is exceedingly difficult to institute
an effective system in the absence of a union."[34]

In the United States, nonunion employees—who are the overwhelming majority—have had, until recently, little general protection from
the arbitrary power of management.[35] This condition has its roots in the
resolutely contractual theory of employment that won acceptance in the
nineteenth century. The old law of "master and servant" had stressed
mutual obligation, but now limited commitment became the reigning
doctrine. In line with this thinking a fateful presumption emerged: the
employment contract is *terminable at will*. The employer can dismiss
an employee at any time, for indefensible reasons or for no reason at all;
and employees have a corresponding right to quit when they wish.

33. This principle is not unquestioned and was by no means obvious at first. See my
Law, Society and Industrial Justice, 164ff.
34. Richard B. Medoff and James L. Medoff, *What Do Unions Do?* (New York: Basic
Books, 1984), 109.
35. See Clyde W. Summers, "Industrial Protection Against Unjust Dismissal: Time
for a Statute," *Virginia Law Review* 62 (1976): 508ff.

The "contract at will" is not much of a contract. No continuing relationship is established or even contemplated, and one cannot readily sue for breach of an agreement that may be terminated without notice. The idea of contract is so attenuated here that, it could be said, "the labor contract is not a contract, it is a continuing renewal of a contract at every successive moment, implied simply from the fact that the laborer keeps at work and the employer accepts his product."[36]

The at-will doctrine lent much support to the practice of unfettered managerial discretion. If the contract is at will, no limits are set on the employers' authority. They are free to hire and fire, unrestrained by the need to show good cause for rescinding a contract still in force. Moreover, the contract at will is not a device for framing agreed-upon conditions to govern ongoing activities. Since the contract has no definite duration, its terms are not binding for the future. Employers may change them at their convenience.

In one crucial respect, however, the courts did find substance in the contract at will. This was the distinctive right of one party *to exercise authority* over another. Once the contract was defined as an *employment* contract, the master-servant model was brought into play. The employer is "master," the employee is his "servant." In effect, the law imported into the employment contract a set of implied terms reserving full powers of direction and control to the employer. The "natural and inevitable" authority of the master—which had already been established as a defining characteristic of the master-servant relation—could then be invoked. This imagery lent decisive legal support to managerial prerogative. Thus was perpetuated, in the heyday of contract, a traditional law of subordination.

But the old master-servant model was only partially incorporated into the new law of employment. The traditional association of "master" and "authority" was welcomed, but in its modern dress authority was stripped of the sense of personal duty, commitment, and responsibility that had once accompanied it, at least in theory. Although many employers in fact felt such obligations, the new legal doctrine showed little interest in managerial benevolence. It presumed that the parties would provide for their own interests in a freely bargained agreement. The limited moral commitment of the employer justified any arrangement he could impose. And of course most workers, powerless as individuals, had no choice but to accept the terms they were offered.

36. John R. Commons, *Legal Foundations of Capitalism* (1924; reprint, Madison: University of Wisconsin Press, 1959), 285.

The capstone of this edifice was set in place when the Supreme Court elevated managerial authority to a constitutional right. It did so in 1915, by striking down a Kansas statute that prohibited "yellow dog" contracts.[37] The Court held that, because it infringed on the employer's right to hire, such legislation violated the due process clause of the Fourteenth Amendment. Process could not be "due," it was then believed, if it interfered with liberty of contract and other rights of property.

The structure began to crumble in the 1930s when, for example, the Supreme Court upheld a provision of the National Labor Relations Act that prohibited dismissal for union activity. This was an important breach in the wall of doctrine that had defended full managerial authority. In ensuing decades the breach widened considerably. Exceptions multiplied as statutes were adopted forbidding discrimination on the basis of race, sex, age, handicap, and the like. Nevertheless, these remained *exceptions* to the general rule that, in the absence of a collective agreement or an individual contract of definite duration, employers could dismiss their employees at will.

In more recent years, since about 1970, the doctrine of employment-at-will has lost much of its authority. It has come under increasing attack and to some extent has been eroded in the courts.[38] In a well-known case, a California court of appeals found an implied promise by the employer that "it would not act arbitrarily in dealing with its employees." The court took seriously the idea that employment-at-will is at best a *presumption,* "subject, like any presumption, to contrary evidence." The promise was inferred from "the duration of appellant's employment, the commendations and promotions he received, the apparent lack of any direct criticism of his work, the assurances he was given, and the employer's acknowledged policies."[39]

In these cases the employment contract has been reconceived to give it, from the employees' point of view, more texture and more bite. The increased protection for employees stems from the law of contracts,

---

37. These were agreements in which employees promised, as a condition of their employment, not to join a union. The case was Coppage v. Kansas, 236 U.S. 1 (1915).

38. By 1987 it could be said that "a clear trend has developed in various legislatures, the scholarly press, and particularly in the courts which has resulted in the doctrine of employment-at-will being riddled with exceptions and exemptions depending on the jurisdiction and the focus of each individual case. A recent survey, in fact, notes that more than two-thirds of American jurisdictions have abandoned an absolute employment-at-will rule" (Andrew D. Hill, *"Wrongful Discharge" and the Derogation of the At-Will Employment Doctrine* [Philadelphia: University of Pennsylvania Press, 1987], 13f.). See also Henry Perritt, *Employment Dismissal Law and Practices* (New York: John Wiley, 1987), 16ff.

39. Pugh v. See's Candies, Inc., 116 Cal.App.3d, 311, 324, 329 (1981).

which can readily find "implied terms" in the nature of a relationship and in the conduct of the parties. Other courts look to "public policy," as when they grant relief to a worker who was dismissed for refusing to commit an unlawful act, such as perjury, or for whistle-blowing. These conclusions do not challenge the basic authority of employers to dismiss or lay off *for good cause*, including defensible economic and administrative objectives. The thrust is against arbitrary, discriminatory, or otherwise wrongful decisions.

The recent changes in employment law owe much to the American experience with collective agreements. The operation of grievance and arbitration systems has demonstrated the governmental nature of private associations; and it has shown that business firms can readily accept, as a practical matter, significant limitations on arbitrary power.

At the same time, the arbitrators, most of them lawyers, have brought to the private sector many of the concepts we associate with due process in public government. They have been sensitive to the integrity of adjudication, fairness in rule-making, the propriety of punishments, and maintenance of appropriate standards of accusation and proof. Without invoking either the Constitution or statutes and decisions framed for public agencies, arbitrators have developed rules and principles that bring at least partial justice to the workplace. The lesson is: where there is governance, we may look to the ethos of due process for inspiration and guidance.

THE POLITICS OF HUMAN RELATIONS

In the reconstruction of managerial authority something more is at stake than fairness in hiring, discipline, and dismissal. Even "legitimacy in depth" may leave many problems unresolved. The exercise of authority touches the whole round of life in organizations; as it does so it may stifle or encourage personal autonomy, self-esteem, security, and growth. At bottom, therefore, what counts is how people experience the everyday life of the institution.

Widespread agreement exists among students of modern management that good "human relations" serves the interests of efficiency and effectiveness. Employees and clients should be treated with respect, with concern for their needs, and with sensitive awareness of who they are as whole persons. Furthermore, it is understood that the "human contribution" cannot be equated with energy expended. Its most important aspect is the acceptance of personal responsibility.[40] Therefore the administrative ideal is self-generated commitment, and a premise is that people do their best when they are persuaded and supported, not when driven and constrained.[41]

Of course, none of this applies with equal force to all organizations or at all stages of organizational development. Sometimes it is convenient to settle for a less stable, less efficient, and less costly work force. But the representative large enterprise, where training is important and where labor turnover is costly, stands to gain by striving for each individual's maximum contribution.

The most important conclusion we may draw from the study and practice of human relations (mainly in industry, but elsewhere as well) is that managerial absolutism has no place in an organization attuned to human needs. But this moral and legal potential of good management has not always been appreciated. Indeed in some quarters the concept of human relations has had a rather bad reputation. Since the 1940s its doctrines have been widely complained of as serving rather than mitigating domination—as a way of winning the assent of subordinates by manipulating their ideas and feelings.[42]

The criticisms had considerable validity. Much of the human-relations literature seemed to sidestep important issues of organization, especially the distribution and uses of power. The most prominent research has been mainly concerned instead with attitudes, beliefs, and emotions, or with status systems and the behavior of small groups. Elton Mayo, the father of industrial human relations, indeed vigorously refuted the idea that management can deal with workers as atomized individuals rather than as social beings. But his vision of the group was foreshortened, focused mainly on the "informal" relations that lend psychic and social coherence to the factory floor.

The theory of human relations celebrated harmony and denigrated conflict. Relatively little attention was given to negotiation and bargaining. This seemed naive, and subservient to management's anti-union strategy. The critics stressed that the clash of competing interests

40. See Peter F. Drucker, *Management: Tasks, Responsibilities, Practices* (New York: Harper & Row, 1974), chap. 21.

41. This is the "principle of supportive relationships" formulated by Rensis Likert in *New Patterns of Management* (New York: McGraw-Hill, 1961), 103.

42. For reviews of this literature see Paul Blumberg, *Industrial Democracy: The Sociology of Participation* (New York: Schocken, 1968); Charles Perrow, *Complex Organizations: A Critical Essay*, 2d ed. (Glenview, Ill.: Scott, Foresman, 1979), chap. 3; Nicos P. Mouzelis, *Organization and Bureaucracy* (London: Routledge & Kegan Paul, 1975).

cannot and should not be avoided. Human relations seemed to offer a utopian and enfeebling ideal of worker-management collaboration, to be achieved by resolving tensions and sublimating aggressions. The alternative was to see labor-management relations as essentially and properly political.[43]

But what is a "political" perspective? Much of the discussion, often influenced by Marxism, has equated participation with conflict and politics with power. This is a healthy counterpoint to the social philosophy of Elton Mayo, but it does not speak to the true promise of participation, nor does it appreciate the larger significance of politics and governance in institutional life.

Toward Civic Competence

In human-relations theory, participation has indeed had a psychic, interpersonal, and private cast. The important thing is to "clue people in," make them feel wanted and appreciated, perhaps allay their fears. These efforts may be humane and gratifying. They may mitigate authoritarian administration. But they do not necessarily presume that individuals can make up their own minds to pursue their rightful ends through a public process. They do not treat employees as competent participants in a civic order.

One might treat slaves humanely, with due regard for good human relations. Personal and emotional needs would be considered, if only as a price paid for reliable, dedicated, and creative service. But this would still leave them dependent "unpersons," incapable of asserting their own will save privately and by indirection. The political perspective asks that this basic dependency be transformed, and it blends into a legal perspective as the transition is made to orderly process for invoking rights and redressing grievances.

Properly understood, therefore, the form of participation sought in a political model of industrial order is not conflict and struggle as such, but legitimate self-assertion. The assumption is that dignity and self-respect

---

43. These criticisms were not entirely fair. Certainly F. J. Roethlisberger and W. J. Dickson, in *Management and the Worker* (Cambridge: Harvard University Press, 1939), did not shrink from recognition of conflicting aims and unfulfilled aspirations. One of their main findings could be read as the location of incipient unionism in the social structure of the plant. (See Clinton Golden and Harold J. Ruttenberg, *Dynamics of Industrial Democracy* [New York: Harper & Row, 1942], 182; Henry A. Landsberger, *Hawthorne Revisited* [Ithaca: Cornell University Press, 1958], 64.) Nevertheless, the critics were basically correct. A political perspective did not inform the diagnosis or guide the therapy.

cannot rest on the favor or good will of a master. The institutional order must provide some basis for a claim of right.

As a condition of civic competence, employees need group support. Effective civic participation is founded on latent power. The membership or citizenry cannot be an aggregate of atomized units confronting a single dominating center—the command structure of the firm. Rather, the employee's participation in the enterprise is mediated by membership in relatively autonomous subgroups and parallel organizations, such as trade unions, which can act as independent centers of support and influence.

Human-relations specialists have been sensitive to some aspects of the group structure of the enterprise, but the emphasis has been apolitical. When group conflict has been recognized, it has been taken to be a symptom of ineffective management; it has not been perceived as an appropriate means of clarifying and resolving policy issues. Elton Mayo asked, "How can mankind's capacity for spontaneous collaboration be restored?"[44] He was right to ask the question. But the movement he helped to create looked mainly to psychological mechanisms of integration: internalization of values, norms, and disciplines, and overcoming barriers to consensus and mutual understanding.

Consensus is not alien to politics, but as a political phenomenon it differs from human relations in two ways. First, political consensus is something more than the like-mindedness that springs from interpersonal cohesion or solidarity. It is agreement on publicly acknowledged principles and goals. Second, in political consensus contending interests are recognized, not submerged. Demands for full compliance or subordination, for eradication of "special interests," or for psychic union with a charismatic figure are incompatible with genuine politics. Politics is subverted when it is transformed into administration or when it is diffused into cultural or pseudo-cultural symbolism. True civic participation affirms the worth of constituent individuals and groups; it does not absorb and extinguish them.

The lesson is that accommodation—the mutual adjustment of groups in ways that preserve their distinctive identities and interests—is the only road to harmony consistent with a political model of institutional life. That model is neither a derogation of harmony nor an affirmation of conflict. It does not deny the role of common values and shared experience in creating strong commitments and unified perspectives. But it

44. Quoted in Roethlisberger and Dickson, *Management and the Worker*, xiv.

does say that personal and group integrity are touchstones of health in a political community.

Thus understood, the political model enriches and supplements, it does not supplant, the perspective of human relations. Political experience cannot be divorced from modes of perception, response, and relatedness. How people perceive and treat one another and, above all, how they allocate respect, including self-respect, is vital to the formation of political reality. Without a concern for human relations, including precisely the values stressed in industrial studies, politics is reduced to a naked contest for power. It is to that extent impoverished and debased.

Participation and Empowerment

In terms of the perspective just outlined, participation is meaningful if it makes a difference for personal autonomy and empowerment. Two roads to that end are of special importance. The first is *legal:* participation as a process of offering proofs and arguments to restrain authority and vindicate rights. Within a legitimate and accessible procedure people can appeal from specific decisions to rules, and from rules to principles. The second is *situational:* participation as significant control over the immediate conditions of living and working. Here people can exercise judgment, assume responsibility, and experience accomplishment. A critical factor is freedom from excessively close or burdensome supervision.

The values to be gained from these ways of participating are clear and unproblematic. They speak to elementary conditions of dignity and well-being. The matter is less clear, however, when participation is equated with *democracy.* Beyond legal and situational empowerment lies the larger horizon of "participatory democracy." In this view, workers and clients—not investors, not the state, not the general public—should control the institutions to which they give so much of their lives, on which they depend, and which threaten them with domination and exploitation. The premise is that democratic forms of institutional decision-making reduce alienation and educate people for effective and responsible participation in civic life. The members benefit directly from their involvement in the process, and the community gains a welcome increment of socialization and commitment.

Advocates of participatory democracy have mainly been concerned with the role of citizens in the larger political community. They reject the theory that widespread participation destabilizes political systems and that, therefore, democracy is best understood as a competition among political elites for the support of basically passive voters. On the contrary, democracy is impoverished when citizens can do no more than "vote, obey, and shut up." The people should have more say, more often, on more topics; they should be able to determine the political agenda as well as who should be political candidates; they should play an active part in formulating and implementing policy.

A corollary is the call for maximum participation in all institutions. The claim is that workers' control in industry would make political democracy more robust and more secure. There is modest evidence (and a modestly persuasive argument) to support this hypothesis.[45] Indeed, it is reasonable to expect that experience gained from workplace democracy would raise the level of civic participation, at least in the long run.

The case for institutional participation does not depend, however, on these rather speculative connections. It can rest more securely on the experience of collective bargaining and on the theory and practice of human relations in industry. These have shown that participation has psychological, moral, and practical worth. Contemporary theorists of participatory democracy have embraced these findings.[46]

If we look in that direction, however, it is difficult to justify more than a general principle that participation should be encouraged *wherever it is feasible and appropriate*. There is, one may say, a presumption in favor of participation— but it is only a presumption. Furthermore, there is no warrant for the conclusion that full-blown democracy in special-purpose institutions is the logical end point of a participatory strategy. Even if the evidence were stronger that enterprise democracy reduces alienation and brings other benefits, that would hardly suffice to justify a basic decision as to who should control business firms, government agencies, and colleges. In each case much more is at stake than psychological benefits or gains in civic competence. In economic enterprise, prosperity is at issue; in education, learning; in a government agency, fidelity to legislative purpose. Whether democratic forms are appropriate cannot be decided by consulting only the interests of employees or clients.[47]

45. See Carole Pateman, *Participation and Democratic Theory* (Cambridge: Cambridge University Press, 1970), chap. 3; Ronald Mason, *Participation and Workplace Democracy* (Carbondale: Southern Illinois University Press, 1982), chap. 4; Edward S. Greenberg, *Workplace Democracy: The Political Effects of Participation* (Ithaca: Cornell University Press, 1986), chap. 5.
46. See Blumberg, *Industrial Democracy,* chaps. 2, 3; Pateman, *Participation,* 62ff.
47. This may be said without prejudice to the desirability, within a mixed economy and an open society, of new forms of enterprise, including employee ownership, worker cooperatives, and many other "alternative" institutions.

Participatory democracy is not best understood as a specific program. It is a moral ideal *and a road to community;* it should not be a demand for exuberant exercise of majority will. "The theory of participatory democracy," it has been said, "is built round the central assertion that individuals and their institutions cannot be considered in isolation from one another."[48] This premise looks to the integrative function of social, institutional, and political participation. The opportunity to vote on general issues, or for general control, is only one of many forms of participation. Although vital in some contexts, in others it may be of little relevance or importance. What matters most is effective belonging, which means, among other things, being taken seriously as a person and as a member. This requires, at a minimum, legal and situational participation. The larger objective is the creation of viable communities so far as may be possible within the framework of purposive institutions.

The Israeli kibbutz is often cited as a successful example of participatory democracy. But kibbutzim have a special character. The enterprises they operate are not autonomous systems divorced from family, child care, education, ritual, and ideology. On the contrary, a salient feature of kibbutzim is the continuity of enterprise and community.[49] Participation in enterprise decision-making is nurtured by the experience of living in a tightly knit community whose members share a vital stake in its fate and its affairs. This institution may be, in some respects, "a forerunner of more general trends toward participatory democracy, nonbureaucratic organization and improved quality of working life."[50] Even in Israel, however, kibbutzim account for only 6 percent of industrial production, and they are subject to many strains, such as the use of hired labor, that undermine the cooperative ideal. It is hardly plausible that this model could sustain, in any major way, the life of a large and complex industrial society. If nothing else, we must acknowledge that the close integration of natural community and economic enterprise is not likely to be a reliable source of institutional well-being. That

---

48. Pateman, *Participation,* 42.

49. "The kibbutz is not only an economic organization, such as a producer cooperative. The kibbutz branches belong to and are an integral part of the community. This community integration creates conditions of social cohesion and solidarity that facilitate informal and everyday participation. The high social visibility in the rather small communities offers safeguards against deviation" (Menachem Rosner, "Theories of Cooperative Degeneration and the Experience of the Kibbutz," Institute for Research and Study of the Kibbutz and the Cooperative Idea [University of Haifa, 1985], report no. 63, 15). See also Menachem Rosner, *Democracy, Equality and Change: The Kibbutz and Social Theory* (Darby, Penn.: Norwood Editions, 1982), chaps. 4, 5.

50. Rosner, "Theories of Cooperative Degeneration," 17.

strategy is fundamentally premodern and therefore requires special circumstances or improbable effort.

In modern special-purpose institutions the great need is cooperation, not democracy as such. Appropriate forms of democracy may well enhance cooperation, however, and are sometimes indispensable to it. The most important form is *shared governance,* not employee or workers' control. In major universities, for example, faculties have a great deal of authority over appointments and curriculum, but much power is reserved to the administration and the governing board. The German system of *Mitbestimmung,*[51] which calls for works councils at the shop level and worker representation at the enterprise level, is an even more explicit and formalized case of shared governance. The system has strengthened the position of trade unions and, at the same time, has "fostered accommodation and cooperation."[52]

The communitarian face of participatory democracy has been obscured at times by the radical politics of its proponents. In the 1960s and 1970s the doctrine was associated with confrontational tactics and with perspectives, such as the rejection of all structure, that were more a parody of democracy than a fulfillment of it. Properly understood, however, participatory democracy carries a latent message of loyalty and commitment. It is a way of saying, "We belong; we want to build, not destroy; we want to make this institution a better place in which to work, study, or pray." The logic of this position is, inescapably, a corporatist logic. It presumes that the enterprise can be a locus of value and a vehicle of meaningful participation. A sincere demand for participation is incompatible with an alienated, class-struggle, or nakedly adversarial orientation.

The dilemma of American trade unionism is a case in point. On the one hand is the long-standing view, born of bitter experience, that a union can best protect its members by maintaining an arm's-length relationship with the employer; a corollary is that the union should resist company-sponsored forms of worker participation. On the other hand is the recognition that unions are fundamentally *derivative* institutions whose members' prosperity is tied to the prosperity of the firm; that if

---

51. Usually translated as "co-determination," but "shared governance" would be better.
52. Wolfgang Streeck, "Co-determination: The Fourth Decade," in B. Wilpert and A. Sorge, eds., *International Yearbook of Organizational Democracy* (London: John Wiley, 1984), 2:397. The system "has had a deep and lasting impact on the German political economy and has significantly changed the relations between capital and labour in German society" (ibid., 411).

the quality of working life is to be improved workers and managers must cooperate in the design and governance of the workplace.[53]

The objective is not harmony based on powerlessness. It is the creation of a civic order, guided by ideals of community, within which the terms of cooperation can be negotiated and decisions can be monitored, criticized, and changed.

53. See Thomas A. Kochan, Henry C. Katz, and Nancy R. Mower, *Worker Participation and American Unions: Threat or Opportunity* (Cambridge: MIT/Upjohn Institute for Employment Research, 1984).

TWELVE

Integrity and Responsibility

The union of management and governance, which we explored at some length in the preceding chapter, is a variation on a theme by Kant: "Act so that you treat humanity, whether in your own person or that of another, always as an end and never as a means only."[1] The claims of purpose and efficiency are strong, but they cannot justify practices that reduce human beings to "means only." Such practices make them victims of domination. Therefore the first requirement of a moral institution is systematic self-restraint in the exercise of authority. As we have seen, this calls for appropriate forms of the rule of law and shared governance.

But legitimacy and justice are only parts of institutional morality. We must also consider the character of the enterprise and its role in the community. In this chapter we explore the concepts of integrity and responsibility as they bear on the study of institutions and as they reflect the interplay of means and ends. A fundamental question is how to reconcile a morality that is merely *useful* from the institution's point of view, and a morality that meets a broader test from the standpoint of critical judgment.

This concern has strong resonance in moral theory. What makes a "virtue" truly virtuous? Many traits of character and disposition—loyalty, dedication, self-discipline, courage—are called virtues because they usefully serve a wide range of projects. From the standpoint of those projects, such traits are indeed helpful and virtuous. Moreover, from a

1. Immanuel Kant, *Foundations of the Metaphysics of Morals*, trans. Lewis White Beck (1785; reprint, New York: Liberal Arts Press, 1959), 47.

broader standpoint, many instrumental virtues have *presumptive* moral worth. In ordinary situations, where the continuities of life are upheld, they are *likely* to enhance moral competence and well-being. But a thief may be courageous and intrepid; an assassin may show exemplary discipline, dedication, and self-sacrifice. The presumption is rebuttable, and the question remains: How can we assure, or what will enhance, the virtue of the virtues?[2]

Much depends on how fully the virtue in question is realized. Intelligence and prudence *narrowly conceived* may well be mainly instrumental; they may be self-serving and manipulative. But if together they ripen into wisdom—if they bring self-knowledge, self-enlargement, and insight into the multiple dimensions of thought and action—the moral quality of substantive ends is likely to be improved. Much the same may be said of other virtues, including courage, love, and justice. Each has limited and spiritually impoverished forms. More fully realized, each lends moral substance to character and choice.

ENDS, MEANS, AND INTEGRITY

The study of administration and leadership is largely dominated by instrumental perspectives. Efficiency and effectiveness are the main concerns. Some analysts use the idiom of Machiavelli's *The Prince,* others the language of cost / benefit ratios; still others speak of organizational "culture" and "excellence." All share an implicit postulate: the *aims* of the organization are not in question. It is the business of the analyst to consider ways and means, not ends. And the problems of the organization are usually viewed from the standpoint of a governing elite.

This way of thinking makes considerable sense. A great many problems may be studied without questioning the organization's purposes, without worrying about institutional morality, and with confidence that management's viewpoint is appropriate and legitimate. Even the morally self-aware institution must bracket those issues at some point and get on with its business.

2. See Amélie O. Rorty, *Mind in Action: Essays in the Philosophy of Mind* (Boston: Beacon Press, 1988), chap. 16. In the Western philosophical tradition there is an answer of sorts. A *moral* virtue must be self-regulating; it may be inherently so, as in the case of temperance, or it may be balanced and perhaps checked by commitment to other virtues, including such "master virtues" as wisdom, prudence, justice, and goodwill. Thus the moral worth of a particular virtue is a function of the way it fits into a larger moral whole, taking into account the range of values to which it is sensitive. Plato, Aristotle, Kant, and Dewey offered different versions of this basic strategy. Each wed virtue to reason; each found in reason a self-limiting principle.

Nevertheless, a fundamental tension exists between instrumental rationality and moral reason. The former depends on definite purposes and clear criteria of cost and achievement, with a natural preference for specialization and for the autonomy of professional or craft decisions. This way of thinking tends to narrow perspectives and limit responsibilities. Moral reason, by contrast, makes goals problematic and broadens responsibility. It asks: Are the postulated ends worth pursuing, in the light of the means they seem to require? Are the institution's values, as presently formulated, worthy of realization? What costs are imposed on *other* ends and *other* values?

We cannot forgo purposiveness, nor need we deny the imperatives of technical judgment. What we can do is enlarge horizons and extend accountability. An important step is taken in that direction when the leaders and members of an association express concern about its *identity* and *character*. In doing so they may simply seek a deeper commitment—"a renewed dedication"—to goals and strategies that have been only superficially understood or nominally accepted, with no genuine questioning of means and ends. That is often the case when a special "organizational culture" is designed and fostered. From a moral point of view such a strategy is a way of raising consciousness about the group's values and about the consequences of its acts and beliefs.

As applied to institutions, "character" is a broader idea than "culture." Culture is the symbolic expression of shared perception, valuation, and belief. Therefore the idea of "organizational culture" properly emphasizes the creation of common understandings regarding purpose and policy. The character of an organization includes its culture, but something more as well. A pattern of dependency—for example, on a specific labor force, a market, or particular suppliers—may have little to do with symbolism or belief. The character of a company or a trade union owes much to the structure of the industry, the skills of employees or members, the alliances that can be fashioned, and many other practical limits and opportunities. Attitudes and beliefs account for only part of an organization's distinctive character.

The hallmarks of character are special competence and disability. "Character" refers to the commitments that help to determine the kinds of tasks an organization takes on, the opportunities it creates or closes off, the priorities it sets, and the abuses to which it is prone. Some of these outcomes are planned; others are contingent and unintended. We cannot presume that every organization has a definite character. When one does, however, we can usually identify premises that fix, for substantial periods, the association's operative goals and characteristic methods. The latter are not always explicitly stated or clearly understood. It is not easy to know just what we are about or "the business we are in."[3]

An organization with a weak or superficial culture is not likely to be of much use to itself or others. But an organization that is taut and well defined can be morally obtuse or evil. This ambiguity appears in our ordinary language. "Character" and "culture" have positive connotations, but we know that character can be pathological and culture can be demonic. Hence a neutral definition may be preferred: for example, that character is "the combination of qualities or features that distinguishes one person, group, or thing from another."[4] This avoids a verbal ambiguity, but the underlying question—the moral worth of character—is not so easily finessed.

A test of moral character is the ideal of *integrity*.[5] This ideal brings morality to bear in a way that respects the autonomy and plurality of persons and institutions. The chief virtue of integrity is fidelity to self-defining principles. To strive for integrity is to ask: What is our direction? What are our unifying principles? And how do these square with the claims of morality?

Integrity counts as a virtue even where considerable doubt exists as to the moral quality of the person or institution being judged. A person who makes wrong and damaging choices, or an institution devoted to morally dubious strategies, may still have a measure of integrity.[6] This leniency has its limits, however. We do not easily speak of the integrity of administration in a Nazi death camp or in a highly oppressive or exploitative enterprise. Nor does it ring true to say of a piece of writing we judge to be trash that it has integrity. This suggests that the idea of integrity presumes at least a core of morally justifiable commitments. For that reason, as I have suggested earlier, integrity involves both wholeness and soundness. It is something we associate with moral coherence, not with coherence of every sort.

3. "Nothing may seem simpler or more obvious than to know what a company's business is. . . . Actually, 'What is our business?' is almost always a difficult question and the right answer is usually anything but obvious" (Peter F. Drucker, *Management: Tasks, Responsibilities, Practices* [New York: Harper & Row, 1974], 77).

4. *American Heritage Dictionary*, s.v. "character."

5. See Chapter 8, "Integrity and Personhood." On institutional integrity, see also my *Leadership in Administration* (1957; reprint, Berkeley: University of California Press, 1984), 63, 119, 138f.

6. My study of communist organization (*The Organizational Weapon* [1952; reprint, Glencoe, Ill: Free Press, 1960]) gave considerable attention to problems of integrity, from the standpoint of Leninist principles. But there integrity was limited because Leninism could not ask hard questions about means and ends.

Integrity has to do with principles, and therefore with principled conduct. Not every belief is a principle, nor may every action in the name of belief be considered principled conduct. A political, administrative, or judicial decision is principled if it is guided by a coherent conception of institutional morality, that is, of appropriate ends and means. A principle is not an idée fixe; not an instrument of ideological thinking; not a prejudice; not a rule to be applied mechanically. It belongs to a larger whole, which includes textured meanings and concrete understandings as well as abstract ideas. Only if that whole is implicated can there be genuinely principled judgment. In this way the idea of integrity lends substance to the idea of principle.

We sometimes identify integrity with consistency—doing the same thing in apparently similar cases, sticking to accepted rules, practices, or categories. This can be misleading. Consistency thus understood asks both too much and too little. It asks too little if it does not require judgment based on the integration of purpose, policy, and implementation; it asks too much because integrity is not sacrificed merely because decisions are highly circumstantial, selective, or for other reasons do not follow a definite pattern.

Prosecutors who enforce the criminal law selectively violate the integrity of their office—but only if their reasons for selective enforcement are wrong. Such a policy may be justified by scarcity of resources and the needs of public safety.[7] The bare fact of consistency or inconsistency tells us little. Similarly, if a legislature provides benefits for some while denying them to others, it may do so with an easy conscience:

> If the legislature provides subsidies for farmers who grow wheat, for example, in order to ensure an adequate crop, or pays farmers not to plant because there is too much corn, it does not recognize any right of the farmers to these payments. A blind form of consistency would require the legislature to offer subsidies or payments for not planting to all farmers, or at least to all farmers whose crops were essential or who produced crops now in oversupply. But there might be sound reasons of policy—perhaps of a very different sort— why the legislature should not generalize these policies in that way. Integrity is not violated just by accepting these reasons and refusing to make the policy of subsidy more general.[8]

The integrity of a legislature depends on its fidelity to its own unifying principles. These are embodied in procedures that (1) give effect to

---

7. Of course, official integrity is enhanced when the reasons for a policy of selective enforcement are publicly stated, defended, and accessible to criticism.

8. Ronald Dworkin, *Law's Empire* (Cambridge: Harvard University Press, 1986), 221f.

political (usually majority) will, while (2) protecting fundamental rights and (3) encouraging rational pursuit of the public interest. Within that framework, many follies may be committed, many differential burdens imposed, and many shifts in policy accepted, all without violating integrity.

As this example shows, we cannot know what integrity requires unless we have *a theory of the institution*. What counts as integrity and what affects integrity will be different for a research university and a liberal arts college; for a constitutional court and a lower court; for a regulatory agency and a highway department. Each institution, or each type of institution, has special functions and values; each has a distinctive set of unifying principles. When an institution is charged with lack of integrity, the charge always contains an implicit conception of what the institution is or should be.

Lon L. Fuller's theory of "internal morality" speaks to this point.[9] Fuller was mainly concerned with the integrity of law, but his ideas have much broader relevance. An internal morality is the set of standards that must be honored if the distinctive mission of an institution or a practice is to be realized. Thus the internal morality of *legislation* requires generality, publicity, intelligibility, and constancy. The internal morality of *adjudication* includes impartiality and the opportunity of the parties to offer proofs and arguments. The internal morality of *family life* includes trust and shared commitment. In each case the standards identify an appropriate excellence—an excellence that is, of course, only variably achieved.

An internal morality does not specify or assess particular ends or outcomes. The morality of legislation leaves unrestricted the subject matter of legislation, at least within broad limits. The morality of scholarship, publishing, or carpentry does not tell us what should be studied, published, or constructed. It asks fidelity to standards that define and uphold a special competence.

Of course, some competencies are more distinctive—and correspondingly more demanding—than others. Carpentry is a rougher skill than cabinetmaking; therefore cabinetmakers faithful to their trade are likely to be more selective than are carpenters about what they make and how they make it. Similarly, the internal morality of adjudication is more complex and more constraining than the internal morality of mediation,

9. *The Morality of Law* (New Haven: Yale University Press, 1969). See also Fuller, "The Implicit Laws of Lawmaking," in Fuller, *The Principles of Social Order*, ed. Kenneth I. Winston (Durham, N.C.: Duke University Press, 1981), 158ff.

as is that of a university press compared to a commercial publisher or of an art museum compared to an art gallery.

In one sense every developed craft has its own morality, which consists of the virtues that must be cultivated if standards of craftsmanship are to be met. The master virtue is commitment to excellence, and subsidiary virtues include self-discipline, respect for tools and materials, and concern for the user or consumer. But a craft morality is at best rudimentary if it is not connected to and governed by a more general ethic.

The inner morality of law cannot be fully accounted for by technical criteria of effective rule-making, such as those described by Fuller. Rather, we must look to the special connection between those principles and the fate of persons, for whom law is always both threat and opportunity. The norms of legal craftsmanship are not merely technical. They restrain arbitrary power, and this efficacy is central to their moral worth. It is the combination of values at stake and technical requirements fulfilled that truly defines the inner morality of law. This was recognized by Fuller when he said, for example, that "every departure from the principles of the law's inner morality is an affront to man's dignity as a responsible agent."[10]

Lionel Trilling once remarked that in the nineteenth century the English naval officer held a special place in the moral imagination of his countrymen:

> The sailing officer was admired as the exemplar of a professional code which prescribed an uncompromising commitment to duty, a continuous concentration of the personal energies upon some impersonal end, the subordination of the self to some general good. It was the officer's response to the imperatives of this code that made for the singleness of mind and the openness of soul imputed to him.[11]

In this moral type, with its "openness of soul" and "subordination of the self to some general good," we see something more than commitment to technical aims or obligations. Nevertheless, the claims of technique make their own contribution to moral development. In special-purpose institutions, and in many more informal contexts as well, the quest for excellence and a sense of responsibility for technical standards are important sources of moral discipline and energy:

> The reality of the moral factor in much work commonly regarded as merely technical . . . may be illustrated by the following case. A manufacturer was

10. Fuller, *Morality of Law,* 162.
11. *Sincerity and Authenticity* (Cambridge: Harvard University Press, 1971), 111.

engaged in producing a certain type of vehicle of very high quality, using the best materials and a high grade of precision workmanship. . . . It was decided to produce the same type of vehicle by mass production methods, using materials of lower quality and less precision in mechanical work. The manufacturer attempted to do this in the same plant, merely lowering standards and using some new machines, but with the same organization. The attempt was a failure. The old organization simply could not produce effectively with lower standards, so that finally a new plant in a distant city with a new organization was set up to produce the cheaper product. Note that this was not a case where new skills had to be learned. In general, less skill and less time were required. The acceptance of lower standards was morally repugnant.[12]

The lesson is that standards of craftsmanship can help to generate a morality and give it a distinctive focus.[13]

But we know that technical skill can serve odious ends. The practice of murder, however expert, lies outside the pale of morality. To be judged as moral, the craft in question must be at least minimally acceptable as a legitimate aspect of social life. This baseline or threshold does not tell us how much or what kind of morality there is. It is only a starting point for more searching inquiry.[14]

Once the threshold criterion has been met, as it is in most ordinary situations, we can explore the *variable connection* between morality and technical excellence. In one major class of cases, which includes word-processing, marksmanship, and many other skills, technique is wholly or largely autonomous. It follows a logic of its own and may serve many different ends. In these cases technical excellence makes little, if any, independent contribution to the integration of means and ends. The more rigorously or narrowly technical the activity, the greater is its autonomy and the weaker its potential as a moral resource. Here technique—as technology—is morally neutral; but it is also a potential "loose cannon." Insofar as this is so, we must rely on *external* controls

12. Chester I. Barnard, "Elementary Conditions of Business Morals," *California Management Review* 1 (Fall 1958): 9. For a comparable instance—let us hope not the very same case!—see my *Leadership in Administration*, 53f.

13. As a result there are many different moralities, each associated with an occupation or practice. But these moralities are not equally coherent, not equally sensitive to personal integrity, not equally other-regarding. Some are more rudimentary than others, more ill-defined, more distant from the most important objects of moral concern. Thus we can easily appreciate (though we may have trouble articulating) the inner moralities of law, medicine, and family life, whereas we may have to strain to see the inner morality of business or bureaucracy.

14. This postulate of legitimacy is implicitly accepted by most writers, from Aristotle to Dewey, who have found in craftsmanship a moral resource.

to insure, as best we can, that the technology is directed by appropriate and legitimate ends.

Another large class of cases reveals a more dynamic connection between means and ends. Marksmanship may be morally neutral, but a police department's choice of uniforms, weapons, and methods of patrol will seriously influence (or reflect) its internal morality and its relation to the community. In child-rearing, education, health care, business, and government, including foreign policy and military operations, the line between technical and moral decisions often blurs. The claim to a purely military judgment weakens as we ascend to the echelons where major choices of strategy and policy are made. Similarly, methods of medical care become increasingly problematic as issues of cost, professional organization, accountability, bioethics, and prevention are raised.

In these cases technique is not autonomous. What constitutes a method of education, for example, depends crucially on what we take education to be. The more closely an end is implicated in determining what "method" includes, the less likely is it that the latter will be narrowly technical. Whenever we go beyond simple or modular activities, the definition expands to include strategies that reflect a distinctive conception of what we are about. As the meaning of "method" is enlarged, so too is the continuity of ends with means.

As methods lose their autonomy they become more like art than technology. They require *a pervasive exercise of judgment* rather than the application of a recipe or rule. An artist's tools and materials have their own imperatives, to be sure, but they must yield at every point to an informing vision. The craft of surgery requires great skill and much apparatus, but ideally the craft is not merely a technology. Insofar as it becomes that alone, the integrity of medical practice is undermined.

If an organization has a well-developed internal morality—driven by the quest for excellence, sustained by the interplay of means and ends— the community's strategy may well shift from *external* to *internal control*. Instead of demanding conformity to standards imposed by legislation and regulation, we may place greater reliance on moral development. In this way, the internal morality of an institution becomes a resource for public policy. Paradoxically, an inherently autonomous technology calls for intervention and constraint, whereas if a practice or institution has an effective internal morality we may grant it, and its efficacy may require, broad powers of self-regulation.

The Continuum of Means and Ends

The argument made above takes its point of departure from John Dewey's theory of "the continuum of means-ends."[15] His central insight is that ends and means involve each other. Three corollaries are:

Ends as well as means are instrumental. The ends we have in mind—Dewey calls them "ends-in-view"—are "hypothetical and directive" means for guiding action.[16] They are indispensable for making rational choices. If our desire is to have a good time at a picnic, the end-in-view must be specific enough to be helpful in deciding where to go, what time to arrive, what clothes to wear, and what food to bring. It follows that ends-in-view must be subject to evaluation as more or less effective guides to action.

This point shows that Dewey's "instrumentalism" should not be confused with what we now often call instrumental reason or rationality. The latter takes purpose as given, not subject to evaluation or reconstruction, not tested and informed by the experience of implementation. In that idiom only means are instruments. Dewey's more thoroughgoing instrumentalism pervades the whole process of judgment, including how ends are conceived and how they are chosen.[17]

Means as well as ends are valued for themselves. Insofar as they bring direct satisfaction, means partake of the end; they anticipate the rewards of success; they are not merely instrumental. Thus work may be experienced as good in itself and not merely as an onerous way of getting a paycheck. Dewey understood the virtues of discipline, but he was no great friend of deferred gratification. To him, experience on the road to an unfulfilled end should have its own warrant in immediate satisfaction. Indeed, the most complete union of means and ends occurs when, as in love, friendship, play, and art, process and outcome are indistinguishable. Together they are vehicles of what Dewey called "consummatory" experience.

Ends cannot be determined properly apart from how they are to be achieved and what they cost. Otherwise we have "an idle fantasy, a futile wish,"[18] not a genuine objective. To make his point Dewey invoked Charles Lamb's "Dissertation on a Roast Pig":

15. *Theory of Valuation* (Chicago: University of Chicago Press, 1939), 40ff.
16. John Dewey, *Logic: The Theory of Inquiry* (New York: Holt, 1938), 496.
17. On "naive" and "sophisticated" instrumentalism see Kenneth I. Winston, "Is/Ought Redux: The Pragmatist Context of Lon Fuller's Conception of Law," *Oxford Journal of Legal Studies* 8 (1988): 348.
18. Dewey, *Theory of Valuation*, 35.

The story, it will be remembered, is that roast pork was first enjoyed when a house in which pigs were confined was accidentally burned down. While searching in the ruins, the owners touched the pigs that had been roasted in the fire and scorched their fingers. Impulsively bringing their fingers to their mouths to cool them, they experienced a new taste. Enjoying the taste, they henceforth set themselves to building houses, inclosing pigs in them, and then burning houses down. Now, if ends-in-view are what they are entirely apart from means . . . there is nothing absurd, nothing ridiculous, in this procedure, for the end attained, the *de facto* termination, *was* eating and enjoying roast pork, and that was just the end desired. Only when the end attained is estimated in terms of the means employed . . . is there anything absurd or unreasonable about the method employed.[19]

The moral should be obvious: we cannot know whether an end is desirable without knowing what means are entailed.

From the standpoint of practical judgment, the most important application of Dewey's perspective is the criticism it suggests of the troublesome maxim "The end justifies the means." If the maxim is interpreted as saying that the means we choose must be warranted by a contemplated end and assessed in the light of probable outcomes, no objection can be made. But in practice *one* contemplated end is often made to justify *any* effective means, without taking account of the full range of empirical consequences. When that happens, the outcome may be very unsatisfactory, not only with respect to a particular objective but also with respect to other ends whose fate has been ignored in the process.

The maxim is fallacious, said Dewey, insofar as it presumes a conception of ends-in-themselves:

One [such conception] is that only the specially selected "end" held in view will actually be brought into existence by the means used, something miraculously intervening to prevent the means employed from having their other usual effects; the other (and more probable) view is that, as compared with the importance of the selected and uniquely prized end, other consequences may be completely ignored and brushed aside no matter how intrinsically obnoxious they are. This arbitrary selection of some one part of the attained consequences as *the* end and hence as the warrant of the means used (no matter how objectionable are their *other* consequences) . . . is inherent in *every* view that assumes that "ends" can be valued apart from appraisal of the things used as means in attaining them.[20]

In much ordinary life this logic is intuitively understood. It does not take long for people to realize that pigs can be roasted without burning

19. Ibid., 40f.
20. Ibid., 42. See also Dewey, *Logic: The Theory of Inquiry*, 496.

down houses. But Dewey sensed that human institutions are highly vulnerable to the divorce of means and ends. He sought to display the folly of that divorce, and he offered a framework for studying how it generates persistent pathologies of moral choice.[21]

From Procedure to Process

Social science provides ample support for the idea that many frustrations of purposive action stem from the divorce of means and ends. The "Michels effect," discussed in Chapter 9, is a well-known illustration, from the study of organizations, of the widespread tendency in social life for means to displace ends. This goal-displacement occurs when instruments are prized for themselves, either as vehicles of satisfaction or as embodiments of vested interests, and when the continuity between instrument and purpose is attenuated or lost. The combination of the two conditions is necessary for goal-displacement; as Dewey emphasized, there is nothing wrong with valuing a means for its own sake. The experience of cooperation, for example, has intrinsic worth, yet it does not usually lead to a divorce of means and ends. Subversion of integrity is more likely to result from narrowly centered interests and self-serving strategies than from high valuation of means.

Goal-displacement is a product of what we may call the tyranny of means. Means tyrannize when they demand inappropriate allegiance. A familiar example is the single-minded devotion expected in some political and religious groups. The ideal or cause—the original reason for belonging—becomes dim and unreal, indistinguishable from commitment to the organization as such. Goals and policies come to reflect the organization's needs for survival and security. The means swallow the end.

A variant is the decay of *legality* to *legalism*. "Legality" refers to appropriate norms of legitimacy, regularity, and fairness. "Legalism" is mechanical or mindless following of rules and procedures, without regard for purposes and effects, so that the substantive aims of justice and

21. Although Dewey's *concerns* were substantive, his *strategy* was analytical. He wanted to show that means and ends involve each other intrinsically, functionally, even logically. If that is demonstrated, it follows that *any* purposive enterprise can be assessed for its fidelity to the continuum of means-ends. Although this approach has great merit, it does not take account of empirical variation in the separation of means and ends; nor does it consider that, in some contexts, because of the autonomy of technology, separation-in-fact may be irresistible or a forgone conclusion.

public policy are lost to view. Legal technique turns inward and takes on a life of its own. The result is often costly and oppressive.

Unless form unites with substance, procedure becomes arid and self-defeating. To sustain that union—to avoid the degradation of legality to legalism—we must recognize the importance of "process values." These are the values at stake in procedure, not specific rules or forms. The process values of law include eliminating bias, providing opportunities for reasoned argument, assuring accurate and reliable determination of facts, and upholding legal stability. The focus is on method—a way of making judgments—not on particular results; but method is broadly conceived and is efficacious only insofar as it leads to the achievement of substantive justice.[22]

Indeed, the idea of process is richer than that of procedure. It contains the whole matrix of values, purposes, and sensibilities that should inform a course of conduct. The integrity of process, thus understood, cannot be protected unless we appreciate those values, purposes, and sensibilities. Therefore process requires the integration of means and ends.

Nor can process be reduced to a specific set of forms or rules. Consider, for example, the problem of determining what "process" is "due" when people confront the exercise of authority. According to the Constitution, no agency of government can deprive a person of life, liberty, or property without affording due process of law. But the courts have resisted a rigid or complete definition of what due process entails. One element of due process, it is said, is "a fundamental principle of liberty and justice which inheres in the very idea of free government."[23] According to Justice Felix Frankfurter, the meaning of due process "unfolds," presumably as history offers new possibilities, or makes new demands, for the application of legal ideals.[24] Due process is "not a stagnant formulation of what has been achieved in the past but a standard for judgment in the progressive evolution of the institutions of a free society."[25]

22. Some values that impinge on procedure do not necessarily improve the quality of specific judgments—for example, a judgment of guilt or innocence. They may, however, contribute to substantive justice. For one example, a norm against self-incrimination limits truth-finding in the interests of upholding a certain conception of personhood. For another, rules excluding illegally acquired evidence, or testimony by a spouse, have independent policy grounds, such as restraining police misconduct or protecting the integrity of family life. They reflect values implicated in the legal process—derived from a broader context of sensibility and responsibility—but they do not necessarily make for justice in a particular case.

23. Twining v. State of New Jersey, 211 U.S. 78, 106 (1908).

24. Joint Anti-Fascist Defense Committee v. McGrath, 341 U.S. 123, 162–63 (1951).

25. Malinsky v. New York, 324 U.S. 401, 414 (1945).

Due process is a governing ideal. No set of rules can exhaust its meaning, for no one can be sure what protections a new situation may require. Therefore rules of due process must be fashioned—and refashioned—by applying general principles to factual circumstances. This exercise calls for an ever-present interplay of procedure and substance.

To determine whether a set of procedures fulfills the requirements of due process, two questions must first be answered: What rights are placed in jeopardy here? How much protection do they need or merit? If the rules of due process vary from one setting to another, as is generally granted today, this is in part because the *weight* we give to a substantive right determines *how much* procedural nicety is required. This weighting depends in part on the right's intrinsic merit, in part on how gravely at risk we believe it to be, and in part on the competing social interests to be served.[26]

Thus the morality of process is not rule-bound. Meticulous concern for definite rules and clearly specified rights is surely justified in some contexts, and especially in the legal system. But even there, greater flexibility is required as issues become more person-centered or more complex. For example, decisions about child custody must give priority to substantive outcomes—the well-being of children and parents—not to forms, rules, or even rights.

The need for flexibility is strongest when a process is meant to sustain long-term relationships, subtle practices, and fragile forms of institutional life. Friends and family members do not ignore their own and others' rights, but they accept, as necessary and desirable, uneven reciprocity and rough justice. If the relationship is important, trust will emerge as a salient value; if there is trust there must also be forbearance, adaptation, and sacrifice. Obligations are open-ended, not fixed and predetermined.

Similarly, the educational process cannot be reduced to particular methods or content. The end to be achieved is too subtle, variable, and concrete. Learning to read, for example, involves much more than distinguishing and memorizing phonemes. Good teaching encourages children to apprehend meanings by participating, so far as they are able, in

26. Thus the right to a jury trial is more important in criminal cases than in civil suits, and a number of other procedural safeguards, such as the exclusion of illegally obtained evidence and protection against self-incrimination, are especially valuable when imprisonment or worse may be in store for the defendant. If the harm that may be done is more tolerable—imposing a traffic fine, for example—a greater risk of unfairness may be acceptable.

a richly textured symbolic experience. Reading is a way of living imag-
inatively, and as such it depends on the capacity of the text, and of the
learning environment, to evoke images, suggest connections, and generate excitement. The process is subverted when teaching is equated
with a particular technique or is indifferent to the quality of what is read,
or when teachers are mainly in the business of preparing their pupils for
set examinations.

Every institution has process values, embodied in policies and procedures that reflect the institution's distinctive character and mission. Every institution is vulnerable to the degradation of those values. Any enterprise can do better, and be better morally as well, if its process values
are made explicit. And it can benefit from recognizing that the most
prevalent form of degradation is the reduction of process to procedure.
When that occurs, letter prevails and spirit decays.

The spirit of a practice or institution is intrinsically elusive; it can
seldom, if ever, be easily specified. But it is not ineffable or mystical.
What constitutes the spirit of a law, a policy, or even a musical composition cannot be wholly explicit and predetermined. It is not prior to or
independent of perception, interpretation, and interaction.[27] Hence the
need for sustained and intimate experience. We are reluctant to appoint
business leaders as college presidents just because the spirit of collegi-
ality in higher education is difficult to communicate abstractly. Much the
same may be said of other professions that depend on intensive socialization. What it means to "do" science, to "think like a lawyer," or to
absorb the special perspectives of any other discipline or enterprise must
be learned in the course of practice. That makes spirit vulnerable, but
hardly unreal.

The vulnerability of spirit is most apparent where values and purposes are fragile or precarious. To be sure, institutional values are always at risk, always subject to displacement, attenuation, and corruption. But some ideals are especially vulnerable. The more complex and
subtle the value, the more readily it is reduced to an impoverished
form. Democracy is equated with majority rule; education with training; justice with procedural fairness; love with dependency; socialism
with nationalization of industry. Hence there is a never-ending quest for
a genuine rendering of the ideal. What makes it genuine is its capacity
to capture the full meaning of the ideal, and thus its spirit.

27. Musicians know the difference between playing perfectly, from the standpoint of
technique, and capturing the spirit of the music. The latter requires subtle variation, even
a certain imperfection, to convey the emotional power of the music.

AUTONOMY AND RESPONSIVENESS

In defending institutional integrity two basic strategies have long been followed. One focuses on a jealous regard for *autonomy;* the other, a wary quest for *integration.* Autonomy safeguards values and competencies by entrusting them to their most committed agents and by insulating them from alien pressures and temptations. Integration, for its part, widens support for the institution and provides opportunities for growth and adaptation.

The community has a stake in both strategies. Autonomous institutions lend density, texture, and strength to the moral order. They are viable centers of energy and discipline; within them internal moralities may flourish. But interdependence, reciprocity, and obligation necessarily blur institutional boundaries.. With integration, power is restrained, responsibility is enhanced, and the connection between internal and external moralities is sustained and reinforced. Without attention to the important continuities among institutions, autonomy can degenerate into perverse and self-defeating isolation. At that point insulation becomes insularity.

Perhaps the best-known affirmation of institutional autonomy is the constitutional doctrine of "separation of powers." In designing the new American government, James Madison stressed the virtues of separation, rather than integration, as a way of taming power and regulating self-interest. Three independent branches of government—legislative, executive, judicial—and a bicameral Congress would "by their mutual relations, be the means of keeping each other in their proper places."

> Ambition must be made to counteract ambition. . . . This policy of supplying, by opposite and rival interests, the defect of better motives, might be traced through the whole system of human affairs, private as well as public. We see it particularly displayed in all the subordinate distributions of power, where the constant aim is to divide and arrange the several offices in such a manner as that each may be a check on the other—that the private interest of every individual may be a sentinel over the public rights.[28]

If institutions are properly arranged, group egoism can be made to serve larger loyalties and aspirations. Nevertheless, we cannot rely on the idealism or goodwill of institutional leaders. Their power must be checked by power.

28. Alexander Hamilton, James Madison, and John Jay, *The Federalist* (1787; reprint, New York: Bantam Books, 1982), no. 51, 262.

As Madison made clear, however, no wall of separation divides the branches of government.[29] Their boundaries are indistinct at many points. By interpreting statutes, including the Constitution itself, and by creating common-law rules and doctrines, judges have a hand in "the legislative power." The president nominates judges; and executive officers of many kinds participate in the interpretation of law. Congress controls appropriations and has power to reorganize the executive through legislation, subject to the president's approval. The branches are interdependent as well as independent. To get anything done, they need each other. They must build bridges and avoid the sharpest confrontations.

In constitutional law, separation of powers applies to the institutions of government. The principle has much broader relevance, however. It is a policy that "might be traced through the whole system of human affairs, private as well as public." Autonomy in the service of countervailing power is essential wherever freedom is at stake—in the structure of society as well as of government. Madison might have added that countervailing power is not the only virtue of institutional autonomy. Another is the development of internal morality, such as the morality of judging, teaching, or scientific inquiry. Autonomy is necessary, not only for freedom, but for the protection of other fragile or vulnerable values; and often for efficiency and effectiveness as well. Therefore every major institution can claim—and usually does claim—that its autonomy serves the common good.

The merits and limits of this claim are, of course, enormously variable and contingent. One recurrent pattern is worth noting, because it can often be properly used as a basis for diagnosis and prescription. For many institutions, a large measure of autonomy is especially important in its *formative* stages. When policies and perspectives must be nurtured—given a chance to become established and secure; in a word, institutionalized—they need the protection autonomy can give. Once the system or policy is secure, that need becomes less compelling. Then more precision is required as to *what kind of* autonomy and *how much* is required or desirable.

In Western law the centerpiece of institutional autonomy is an independent judiciary. If courts are not independent, their impartiality is suspect. Furthermore, judges are responsible to a legal tradition that includes a mode of reasoning and a body of doctrine. Fidelity to that

29. Ibid., no. 47, 245ff.

tradition requires insulation from extraneous pressures. Therefore the legitimacy of the courts depends on effective (and perceived) autonomy.

This strategy is by no means unique to law. The separation of law and politics has parallels in the separation of education and politics, business and politics, military strategy and politics, religion and politics. In each case, the practitioners, vulnerable to political intrusion, find safety and legitimacy in a distinctive function. They claim the right to resist intrusion and follow the logic of their specialties. From their point of view, separation of spheres is the foundation of good order.

Government agencies, professions, schools, business firms, foundations, and many other institutions need protection from external pressure and manipulation. But they cannot fulfill their responsibilities if they lose touch with reality; if they act as though they live in a static environment; if they fail to understand the true part they play in the life of the community. The claim to autonomy has a hollow ring when it is, in effect, a flight from responsibility.

The Meaning of Responsiveness

The alternative to irresponsible autonomy is the creation of *responsive* institutions.[30] The challenge is to maintain institutional integrity while taking into account new problems, new forces in the environment, new demands and expectations. A responsive institution avoids insularity without embracing opportunism. Thus understood, "responsiveness" belongs to our moral vocabulary.

Responsiveness is often wrongly identified with uncontrolled adaptation and capitulation to pressure. But that confuses responsiveness with drift or opportunism. Few would argue that isolation and inflexibility are, apart from some special cases, necessary conditions of institutional integrity. The need for *controlled* adaptation is widely appreciated. If an institution is too weak (or too inept) to defend its integrity, we should call it opportunistic rather than responsive.

Even institutions that have a special commitment to openness must remain aware of the difference between responsiveness and opportunism. As devices for registering majority will, democratic legislatures may seem to be wholly open institutions. But legislatures offend their own moral principles when they yield supinely to public pressure or execu-

---

30. See Amitai Etzioni, *The Active Society* (New York: Free Press, 1968), chap. 18, and Philippe Nonet and Philip Selznick, *Law and Society in Transition: Toward Responsive Law* (New York: Harper/Colophon, 1978), chap. 4.

tive will. A panoply of procedures are available to safeguard the *deliberative* character of legislation. When that is compromised, law-making is likely to be crude and even self-defeating. The need, therefore, is for response, not merely reaction.

A business enterprise is, ideally, highly sensitive to information derived from the market. According to economic models, the business should be ready to adapt as quickly as possible. But well-established companies—as distinguished from marginal, fly-by-night ventures—have many commitments that interfere with openness and flexibility. Some commitments are "noise" to be suppressed or eliminated, but many are benign. They arise from the continuities of technology, skill, employment, customer relations, supply, and, above all, a conception of "the business we are in."

In the years since World War II, colleges and universities in the United States have opened their doors to vast numbers of students, and not only to the best and brightest. This extension of opportunity—this "democratization of higher education"[31]—could not help but raise serious questions about the maintenance of academic standards. Many new policies and practices had to be put in place. Among these was a strategy of *differentiation*. In California, for example, a master plan called for three tiers or "sectors": the University of California, with nine campuses; a separate system of state colleges and universities; and many junior or community colleges. The university admits only a small fraction of high school graduates—a selectivity that depends on the existence of the other, less selective sectors. Without the latter, the pressure from citizens to admit their children to higher education would make it impossible for the university to maintain its moderately elitist policy. In the same way, the state colleges benefit from the buffer provided by the junior colleges.[32]

This strategy of institutional diversity could not save the University of California from the need to take account of major changes in demography and consciousness. In the 1970s and 1980s "diversity" came to mean that the university should be responsive to the just claims of minorities and women. The institution could no longer remain a bastion of white male privilege. Doors had to be opened at all levels, to affect students, faculty, and staff. Many established practices in personnel hiring

31. Martin Trow, "The Democratization of Higher Education in America," *Archives Européennes de Sociologie* 3 (1962): 231–62.
32. The solution is by no means perfect. To some extent it has sacrificed one set of institutions to preserve the integrity of others. The community colleges, especially, have been shortchanged in the distribution of resources.

and promotion, curriculum, and student life had to be reexamined. The challenge was to make these necessary changes without seriously compromising the university's commitment to excellence in research and scholarship and without neglecting its special needs as a world-class center of learning. The challenge has been met, with uneven success, in part by relying on internal differentiation; for example, by maintaining the strength of research units and creating separate departments for ethnic studies and women's studies; by providing special resources to help students meet university standards; and by resisting the equation of responsiveness with proportional representation.

In short, to be responsive is a way of being *responsible*. Responsibility runs to an institutional self or identity; to those upon whom the institution depends; and to the community whose well-being it affects. Thus responsiveness entails reconstruction of the self as well as outreach to others. Established structures, rules, methods, and policies are all open to revision, but revision takes place in a principled way, that is, while holding fast to values and purposes. This we might call self-regarding or reflexive responsibility.

Every institution needs a supportive environment, if only to protect access to resources and opportunities. Therefore institutional outreach is necessary. The initial impulse to make this move is pre-moral: outreach begins as narrow self-regard. Nevertheless, it is the foundation of moral sensibility, and genuine responsiveness is the fruit of that sensibility. Under its aegis the inevitably selective nature of outreach is clarified, criticized, and justified. The criterion is the contribution of outreach to comprehensive values and institutional integrity.

The Perils of Responsiveness

A strategy of responsiveness entails a burden of choice. There is always a need to decide who shall be the privileged beneficiaries of help or forbearance. *Selectivity is, indeed, the Achilles' heel of responsiveness.* Because of selectivity, what appears to be responsiveness may turn out to be a hidden form of domination or a screen for covert, opportunistic adaptation.

The perils of responsiveness appeared early in the history of a much-analyzed government agency, the Tennessee Valley Authority.[33] The

33. This discussion is based on my *TVA and the Grass Roots,* and on R. G. Tugwell and E. C. Banfield, "Grass-Roots Democracy: Myth or Reality," *Public Administration Review* 10 (Winter 1950); Erwin C. Hargrove and Paul K. Conkin, *TVA: Fifty Years of Grass-*

TVA was established in 1933 as a major effort by the New Deal to test the efficacy—and the social value—of public enterprise. President Franklin D. Roosevelt envisioned a regional agency, neither national nor statewide in scope, centered on the drainage basin of the Tennessee River, which includes portions of seven states. The agency was to build multipurpose dams on the river and its tributaries to improve navigation and flood control and to produce electric power. Its mission was conceived in much broader terms, however, extending to "national planning for a complete river watershed involving many States and the future lives of millions." To carry out this conception the president recommended "legislation to create . . . a corporation clothed with the power of government but possessed of the flexibility and initiative of private enterprise. It should be charged with the broadest duty of planning for the proper use, conservation, and development of the natural resources of the Tennessee river drainage basin and its adjoining territory for the general social and economic welfare of the Nation."[34]

The coming of the TVA was a major event for the people and institutions of the valley. The new agency would bring money, jobs, and the promise of cheap electric power—all very welcome in the Depression years. At the same time, the TVA represented a potential threat of domination. Here was a new way of bringing the power of Washington to bear on southern and border states. The TVA would not be accountable at the local level, and it would be largely autonomous within the federal government. Furthermore, the agency's mandate for planning and social change would not necessarily prove congenial to the region, which was conservative in outlook and politics.

The TVA sought to allay these fears by adopting a posture of responsiveness. This took the form of a well-developed doctrine, that of "grass roots" administration, and a set of correlative policies. The doctrine defended the TVA's managerial autonomy both as in itself a desirable form of administrative decentralization and as a necessary condition if the TVA was to maximize the participation of the people themselves. The TVA would be shaped by intimate association with long-established institutions, thereby drawing vitality from below. An imposed federal program, it was argued, would be alien, unwanted, and

Roots Bureaucracy (Chicago: University of Illinois Press, 1983); and William U. Chandler, *The Myth of TVA: Conservation and Development in the Tennessee Valley, 1933–1983* (Cambridge, Mass.: Ballinger, 1984).
    34. U.S. Congress, *House Document 15*, 73d Cong., 1st sess., 1933.

ultimately accomplish little, unless it brought together at the grass roots
all the agencies concerned with development of a region's resources: local communities, state government, universities and colleges, private
associations, cooperating federal agencies. Such a partnership would be
grass roots democracy at work.

There was no real question of local control (or consultation, for that
matter) with respect to the authority's core activities: building dams and
electric power facilities. The focus was on more peripheral programs, especially in agriculture. Here "grass roots democracy" came to mean that
the TVA would channel its services through a privileged instrument, the
land-grant colleges. In effect the Agricultural Extension Services of the
colleges became a close collaborator—virtually an operating arm—of
the TVA in the agricultural field. The agency thereby accepted a number
of commitments that reflected the character of the extension services in
those days, most prominent among which were an intimate relation
with the American Farm Bureau Federation, a disposition to deal mainly
with relatively prosperous elements of the local farm population, and a
tendency to reflect dominant attitudes toward blacks and farm tenants.
In practice, therefore, the "grass roots" doctrine masked a selective strategy of responsiveness.

Furthermore, the alliance created a group *inside* the TVA that vigorously defended the interests and perspectives of the extension services and
exerted pressure on other TVA programs affecting forestry, recreation,
and conservation. For example, the TVA agriculturists successfully opposed an early policy of maintaining in public ownership a protective
strip of land around the reservoirs. Economic development inside the
strip was to be regulated in the interests of conservative land-use and
other public benefits. In contrast, the agriculturists argued that a policy
of *minimal* land acquisition "would provide the opportunity for private
enterprise to exercise its initiative in the development of the waterfront
free from the stifling effects of public ownership and control and in accord with the public demand."[35]

The TVA gained a considerable advantage from this arrangement. It
won the support of important local interests, the land-grant colleges, and
a powerful national lobby, the American Farm Bureau Federation. These
supporters came to the defense of the TVA when it was threatened by the
political power of the private electric utilities it was displacing. By modifying its agricultural program and retreating from certain broad social

35. Selznick, *TVA and the Grass Roots*, 181.

policies the authority was able to ward off possible dismemberment and win time for the successful development of what it came to take as its key activity, the expansion of electric power facilities.

This political bargain had a peculiar aspect. It was implemented by permitting a part of the TVA, its Department of Agricultural Relations, to become the direct agent of an external constituency. The group became a dynamic force within the authority, able to influence programs that were marginal to its agricultural responsibilities but significant for conservation and rural life. As a result, the authority was not able to retain control of the basic compromise. Concessions were demanded and won that might have been turned aside had there been fundamental unity within the agency. Something more than simple compromise was involved: there was also a kind of organizational surrender.

Thus in the first decade of its history, despite high hopes and broad national support, the character of the authority as a committed conservation agency was placed in doubt. At this early period the foundations were laid for a weakness that was to affect its policies for many years. After World War II, the TVA engaged in extensive strip-mining of coal, with consequent erosion of hillsides and pollution of streams; resisted environmental controls; and for a considerable period was unresponsive to criticism. By 1983, after fifty years of operation, the authority's reputation as a moral institution stood in great need of rehabilitation.

A root cause of the difficulties was the persistence of a technocratic perspective in the TVA. The authority was founded on the implicit premise that expertise would govern its decisions. For a time this vision seemed easy to accept. As the high multipurpose dams were built; as TVA officials reached out to serve local communities; as they preached the virtues of soil conservation; as it became apparent that the agency was staffed by highly competent, idealistic, and honest people, many commentators sang its praises.

Indeed, in its first decade the TVA's technocratic outlook was to some extent mitigated by the apparent scope of its responsibilities, justified by the need to move forward quickly, and vindicated by the brilliant engineering and sensitive administration of its dam-building projects. But the era of good feeling could not last, especially after the authority began to narrow its mission, becoming a giant public utility company with very limited perspectives beyond the production and distribution of cheap electricity. A shadow hung over the agency: the lack of effective procedures for accountability and responsiveness.

The TVA was given—and vigorously defended—a large measure of autonomy so that it could pursue a "technical" program free from distraction by the political process. A premise was that a sharp separation could be drawn between technical and political decisions. As one official said, "[W]hether you build a steam plant is an economic question. It isn't a political question."[36] This way of thinking undercuts responsiveness in two ways: it denies the legitimacy of nontechnical criticism, which brings to bear values, interests, and perspectives beyond those of engineering and economic analysis; and it sacrifices the integrity of the institution by constraining its mission and narrowing its responsibilities.

Low Politics and High Politics

The conflicting demands of autonomy and responsiveness are present to some degree in every enterprise. They are especially important, however, in public "authorities" such as the TVA. These authorities have proliferated in recent decades, especially at the local level.[37] They are characteristically enterprise-centered; for example, they build and operate bridges, housing developments, or water systems. A defining characteristic of such institutions is financial autonomy based on tolls, fees, and other revenues generated by the enterprise. With those revenues in hand and in prospect, additional money can be raised in capital markets. The agencies have broad discretion to use their resources as they see fit; they are not subject to the constraints of annual budgeting and appropriation by legislative bodies; and (unlike local school districts, for example) they do not depend directly on taxpayer support.

Such autonomy undoubtedly enhances the competence of government, especially in the operation of complex but coherent projects such as marine terminals, airports, or urban transit. The directors can engage in long-range planning, spend or save money as required, and encourage innovation and initiative in management. The effort to be self-supporting is an incentive to reduce costs and improve operations in

36. Remark attributed to Charles McCarthy, former chief counsel, TVA, in Chandler, *Myth of TVA*, 177.

37. See Annmarie H. Walsh, *The Public's Business: The Politics and Practices of Government Corporations* (Cambridge: MIT Press, 1978); Ira Sharkansky, *Wither the State? Politics and Public Enterprise in Three Countries* (Chatham, N.J.: Chatham House, 1979).

response to consumer demand. And if the agencies are properly organized they can resist undesirable political intrusion.[38]

The problem is that there is more to politics than the play of influence
and power. Public corporations can be "nonpolitical" only to the extent
that they are insulated from direct involvement in partisan conflict and
from the short-term demands of political officeholders. But they are
deeply implicated in "high politics," that is, in the determination of public policy:

> While authorities are designed in part to take their operations "out of poli-
> tics," the nature of this insulation must not be misunderstood. Nor must it be
> thought that the creation of an authority puts an end to political discussions or
> transmutes matters of political and social policy into pure matters of fact sol-
> uble in engineering and business terms. . . . The vital political problems
> which arise in government are not the questions of patronage. They are the
> questions of basic social and economic policy. . . . For example, a port au-
> thority has the power to determine whether a community as a whole will ex-
> pand as a raw material center or as a manufacturing center by the priorities
> which it gives to port facilities, loading and unloading equipment, wharfage
> rates, and rail and road connections. Toll rates on bridges will determine the
> rapidity of suburban development. . . . The location of inland terminals, the
> creation of central bus facilities, the elimination of grade crossings, the ar-
> rangement of tunnel entrances and exits will determine the immediate and ul-
> timate fate of entire neighborhoods. . . . Because these decisions cannot be
> made without weighing the needs of the people and their effects upon the dis-
> tribution of wealth and welfare, they are *political* decisions of the most fun-
> damental sort.[39]

A well-founded fear of "low politics" justifies the autonomy of public
corporations. But the special form this autonomy takes—commitment
to a self-sustaining operation, to the financial markets that make it possible, and to a technological mission—has its own heavy cost. These
conditions create a significant risk that the agency will shortchange the
public interest by narrowing its perspectives:

> Because of their insulation, they [public corporations] overemphasize finan-
> cial returns and reflect or accept the viewpoints of banking and busi-
> ness participants. They bias government investment in favor of physical in-
> frastructures for short-term economic return. Ideologies of laissez-faire,

38. If the enterprise is brought within the jurisdiction of the general government, it becomes vulnerable to excusable pressures, for example, to yield its revenues for general purposes and thus mitigate the need to raise taxes, or to conform to otherwise justifiable but
inappropriate or unnecessarily rigid administrative procedures. Stronger intrusion takes
the form of blatant patronage or log-rolling.

39. Luther Gulick, " 'Authorities' and How to Use Them," *Tax Review* 8 (1947): 50f.

localism, autonomy, and limited politics converge . . . to preserve the power of groups with narrow and specialized aims, and to relieve the enterprises themselves of obligations to respond to broader interests.[40]

The challenge is to enlarge accountability without giving up the main benefit of autonomy: long-range, flexible, purposive, "nonpolitical" management.

In our quest for solutions to this dilemma we should take seriously the difference between responsiveness and majoritarian democracy. A formally democratic solution would reinstate the power of elected executives, such as mayors and governors, to substitute their own priorities for those of the corporate directors; or it would subordinate directors, in their specific decisions, to the will of legislative majorities.[41] Responsiveness, however, is not a majoritarian principle. The responsive institution is open and outreaching, but the paths of openness and the forms of outreach are cut to the cloth of institutional integrity.

An appropriate strategy combines external constraint with moral development.[42] This is done by establishing general standards to which a public corporation must adhere and for which it can be held accountable by legislatures and courts. Principles governing the definition of mission, personnel policy, contract negotiation, fiscal responsibility, fiduciary obligation, and visibility of decisions become part of the corporate charter. Such a charter also requires regular procedures for determining what interests are affected by the corporation's major decisions; sustained consultation with constituencies and critics; and periodic review by competent independent auditors. Within this normative framework the agency makes its own decisions regarding specific objectives, internal organization, and allocation of resources.

For institutions, as for persons, self-regulation does not mean freedom to do as one pleases. Rather, it implies the exercise of options that will strengthen the enterprise, release its energies, and enhance its integ-

40. Walsh, *The Public's Business*, 6.
41. When the New York/New Jersey port authority wanted to finance several projects by raising the fares on its rail system, the governor of New Jersey "evidenced little interest in these broader financial and economic-development issues. . . . But he showed great interest in possible criticism by New Jersey commuters (and voters) . . . and blocked the increase for several years." Also, in San Francisco and Los Angeles, subordination of port agencies to municipal authorities "severely weakened" leadership and management effectiveness (Jameson W. Doig, "Public Authorities: Tensions Between Entrepreneurship and Accountability," paper delivered at the Annual Meeting of the American Political Science Association, 31 August 1985, 18f.).
42. Ibid., 22f. See also Jameson W. Doig and Jerry Mitchell, "Expertise, Democracy, and the Public Authority Model: Groping Toward Accommodation," in Jerry Mitchell, ed., *Public Authorities and Public Policy,* forthcoming.

rity. All this takes place within a moral order, not in opposition to it or in disregard of its claims. The great task of institutional design is to build moral competence into the structure of the enterprise. This is the key to corporate responsibility—private as well as public.

THE RESPONSIBLE ENTERPRISE

Responsibility is something more than accountability. To be accountable is to be subject to judgment or, as we sometimes say, to be *held* responsible. The focus is on conformity to an external standard. This requires only minimum conditions of moral agency, such as the capacity to distinguish right from wrong. We need not ask whether the person or organization *wants* to act responsibly. But a responsible enterprise, like a responsible person, must have an *inner* commitment to moral restraint and aspiration.

Institutional responsibility is perhaps best explored where it is most troublesome—in the modern business enterprise. According to classical free market doctrine, no more should be expected of a business, even a large business, than that it operate within the law, and the law should protect the autonomy and rationality of the enterprise. After all, it is argued, a firm is the very model of instrumental rationality. However, the social costs of moral indifference—distorted priorities, defrauded consumers, degraded environments, deformed babies—have created an irrepressible demand for enhanced accountability, more external regulation, *and* a stronger sense of social responsibility. In response to this call for a corporate conscience, theories of the corporation have taken an institutional turn, that is, the enterprise has come to be perceived as infused with value and thickened by commitment.

This development has not come easily, and it is still precarious and highly controversial. A significant stumbling block has been the economists' view of the firm as thoroughly instrumental and disposable, a way of thinking that is strongly reinforced by the legal concept of the corporation. In 1819 Chief Justice Marshall set the stage when he called the corporation "an artificial being, invisible, intangible, existing only in contemplation of law. Being the mere creature of law, it possesses only those properties which the charter of its creation confers upon it either expressly or as incidental to its existence."[43]

The legal concept has much justification. It reserves to government the power to decide what groups under what conditions should be

43. Dartmouth College v. Woodward, 4 Wheaton 518, 627 (1819).

granted the special benefits of incorporation, which include limitation of liability, collective acquisition of property, and the capacity to sue and be sued by members and outsiders. As a dominant imagery, however, the doctrine slights the significance of the operative system, which is anything but invisible or intangible.[44]

A related obstacle to taking institutions seriously is the still-dominant view that the business corporation is essentially a voluntary association of investors. Here, again, legal doctrine has offered a compelling but distorting imagery. Incorporation does make it easy to pool the resources of many individuals. It does not follow, however, that we should say that the corporation is "a verbal symbol, a mathematical expression . . . quite unnecessary for those patient people who feel that they would rather, in any given case, enumerate the several million stockholders of the American Telephone and Telegraph Co. than say briefly and concisely, 'Tel. and Tel.' "[45]

Ironically, this apparent realism—an attempt to demystify the abstract collectivity by specifying its "true" components—has lent support to a highly unrealistic view of the enterprise. It radically limits who is to count as a *member*. Who belongs? Whose interests matter? Are the shareholders the only true members?

> A concept of the corporation which draws the boundary of "membership" thus narrowly is seriously inadequate. It perpetuates . . . the superficial analogy of the seventeenth century between contributors to a joint stock and members of a guild or citizens of a borough. The error has more than theoretical importance because the line between those who are "inside" and those who are "outside" the corporation is a line between those whom we recognize as entitled to a regularized share in its processes of decision and those who are not. A more spacious conception of "membership," and one closer to the facts of corporate life, would include all those having a relation of sufficient intimacy with the corporation or subject to its power in a sufficiently specialized way.[46]

A more spacious conception of membership can make sense only if we reject the moral and legal primacy of the shareholder.

In corporation law, and in common understanding as well, the shareholders are *owners*. This conception brings to bear a long history of un-

44. "The enterprise, not the incorporation papers, is the true entity" (A. A. Berle, Jr., "The Theory of Enterprise Entity," *Columbia Law Review* 47 [April 1947]: 358).

45. Max Radin, "The Endless Problem of Corporate Personality," *Columbia Law Review* 32 (1932): 658.

46. Abram Chayes, "The Modern Corporation and the Rule of Law," in Edward S. Mason, ed., *The Corporation in Modern Society* (Cambridge: Harvard University Press, 1959), 41.

examined beliefs regarding the meaning of the idea of property, and especially the association of property with exclusive rights and absolute control. When applied to the corporation, this doctrine obscures the realities of power, authority, and subordination. It dims the legal perception of how corporate, collective property is organized and what human values are at stake. A doctrine rooted in another age—John Locke's image of lonely, resolute, pioneering man appropriating material objects through toil and binding self to possessions—is carried into a world of complex organization and fragmented investment.

Perhaps most important, the primacy of the shareholder has had a pernicious effect on what we take to be corporate rationality. If the corporate "bottom line" is return to the investor, in dividends or in increased share value, it is easy to suppose that rationality consists in maximizing shareholder returns. Presumably that is what individual investors would like. Their interests extend no farther, however. They want safety for themselves, within a framework of accepted risk, but they need not accept, and for the most part do not accept, responsibility for the enterprise as a going concern. When a takeover bid is made, they consult their own advantage, and they do so with an easy conscience. What is rational for them is, however, not necessarily rational for the enterprise, which may be burdened with debt as a result of the takeover, broken up, even looted.

Furthermore, the integrity of the enterprise as a rational system is undermined when *maximizing* financial gain, without regard to source, becomes the operative goal. This attitude detaches profit-making (or activities, such as buying and selling corporations) from substantive decisions. The provision of particular goods and services takes a back seat to financial manipulation. When this occurs, the mission of the enterprise is likely to be disoriented and subverted. Quality suffers, including the quality of transactions in banks and other financial institutions.

Enhancing vs. Maximizing Profits

The limits of single-minded maximization as a guiding principle for corporate conduct are recognized in a "tentative draft" prepared by the American Law Institute for the guidance of judges and lawyers:[47]

47. On single-minded maximization see Chapter 2, p. 58, "Five Pillars of Reason."
The American Law Institute is a private agency whose members include senior judges, law school deans, law professors, and practitioners. The institute is dedicated to improving legal rules and principles while building upon received doctrine. Thus from time to time

§2.01   The Objective and Conduct of the Business Corporation

A business corporation should have as its objective the conduct of its business activities with a view to enhancing corporate profit and shareholder gain, except that, whether or not corporate profit and shareholder gain are thereby enhanced, the corporation, in the conduct of its business
    (a) is obliged, to the same extent as a natural person, to act within the boundaries set by law,
    (b) may take into account ethical considerations that are reasonably regarded as appropriate to the responsible conduct of business, and
    (c) may devote a reasonable amount of resources to public welfare, humanitarian, educational, and philanthropic purposes.[48]

Subsections (a)–(c) "reflect a recognition that the corporation is a social as well as an economic institution, and accordingly that its pursuit of the economic objective must be constrained by social imperatives and may be qualified by social needs."[49]

Once we grant that the business corporation is "a social as well as an economic institution" the line between economic and political rationality is blurred, as is the line between economics and ethics. If directors are to function as monitors of corporate managers,[50] if they are to be responsible for general oversight, *including adherence to ethical principles,* they must be something more than economic actors, or at least "economic" must be interpreted very broadly. The directors cannot escape concern for constituencies, nor can they be single-minded in defining "the objective" of the corporation. They must balance "corporate profit and shareholder gain," which are not necessarily the same. They must consider what *level* of profitability is reasonable and compatible with a spectrum of responsibilities that includes appropriate concern for human and environmental impacts. They must weigh short-run opportunities against long-run effects. These judgments require, in variable amounts, political sensitivity and moral awareness. Errors of judgment constitute failures of leadership, and they cannot be excused on the ground that only purely economic criteria are relevant.

---

it issues "restatements of the law." The tentative report on corporate governance, however, does not purport to be only a restatement of existing law; it is subtitled "analysis and recommendations." Section 2.01 was drafted by Professor Melvin A. Eisenberg, Chief Reporter for the ALI on issues of corporate governance.
    48. American Law Institute, *Principles of Corporate Governance: Analysis and Recommendations* (Philadelphia: American Law Institute, 1984), draft no. 2, 25.
    49. Ibid., 28.
    50. See ibid., 66, where it is recommended that the board of directors should "oversee the conduct of the corporation's business with a view to evaluating, on an ongoing basis, whether the corporation's resources are being managed in a manner consistent with the principles of §2.01 (Objective and Conduct of the Business Corporation)."

Significantly, the ALI draft speaks of *enhancing* profits, not of maximizing them. Although the Reporter's commentary suggests that "the first clause of §2.01 may be thought of as a broad injunction to maximize economic returns," it is also said that "certain kinds of conduct must or may be pursued whether or not they enhance such returns (that is, even if the conduct either yields no economic return or entails a net economic loss)." Furthermore, "a corporate manager is not less morally obliged than any other citizen to take ethical considerations into account, and it would be unwise social policy to preclude him from doing so."[51] Given these strictures, it makes sense that the codification in §2.01 has shrunk from the language of maximization.

There is a good deal to be said for the idea that a statesmanlike concern for the long run may resolve the conflict between economic single-mindedness and moral responsibility. The report we have been following emphasizes that enhancing profit

> does not mean that the objective of the corporation must be to realize profit in the short run. . . . [T]he economic objective does not imply that the corporation must extract the last penny of profit out of every transaction. . . . Activity that entails a short-run cost to achieve an appropriately greater long-run profit is therefore not a departure from the economic objective, and an orientation toward lawful, ethical, and public-spirited activity will normally fall within that description.[52]

Much depends, however, on what is meant by "long-run." A rather blunt and hardheaded interpretation is that

> [r]ational enterprise managers judge the yield of outlays for social purposes by their long-run effect upon profits. They measure the return on the "investment" in each social program. Each outlay is tested by a cost / benefit analysis. Among the benefits may be a reduction in the costs of defending the firm's actions before the legislative or executive agencies of government, an avoidance of onerous governmental regulation, or a reduction in property damage at the hands of activists. Social pressures generate costs, the amount of which can be minimized by appropriate corporate outlays. When viewed in the perspective of our model, there is no conflict between profit maximization and corporate social activity. The popular notion that a company which pursues profit must eschew a social role, or that social involvement means a sacrifice of profit, is unfounded. On the contrary, *the contemporary corporation must become socially involved in order to maximize its profits.*[53]

Here the emphasis is on response to pressures and impending costs. But concern for the long run may also be understood as focusing attention on

51. Ibid., 28, 36.
52. Ibid., 28f.
53. Neil H. Jacoby, *Corporate Power and Social Responsibility: A Blueprint for the Future* (New York: Macmillan, 1973), 196f., Jacoby's emphasis.

the enterprise as an institution rather than upon specific transactions, including political maneuvers. The going concern, with all it needs to survive and to flourish, including what it needs to survive as a certain kind of business, becomes the focus of policy and strategy. In the large complex corporation, what constitutes such a long-run benefit is not likely to be obvious. It requires an assessment more akin to defining the public interest than to any tight managerial logic.

▼   ▲   ▼   ▲   ▼

The discussion of corporate responsibility has been overly preoccupied with whether a business may properly "devote a reasonable amount of resources to public welfare, humanitarian, educational, and philanthropic purposes."[54] The emphasis is understandable, given the ambiguities of corporate practice and the need for legal clarification. But the high visibility of this issue deflects attention from more fundamental concerns.

The moral responsibility of the enterprise, like that of the natural person, runs primarily to the control *of its own conduct* (1) in the light of how its activities affect the community, especially the persons, institutions, and values in which it is directly implicated, and (2) in the light of its internal morality, that is, of the ends and means to which it is committed. It is vastly more important for a corporation to avoid corruption, control pollution, and treat employees fairly than for it to contribute to education or the arts. Philanthropy is morally proper and legally permissible, but it is not at the center of moral responsibility.

Corporate directors have fiduciary duties, that is, obligations of fidelity, good faith, and fair dealing. Historically, the primary beneficiaries of fiduciary duty have been the shareholders, on whose behalf the directors are supposed to act. Since the 1930s, however, many critics of corporation law have argued, with modest success, for widening the circle of beneficiaries to include employees, customers, and the general public. The strategy is to extend the reach of responsibility by enlarging the number of constituencies whose interests the directors must consider.

The emphasis on constituencies suggests a political model of corporate organization.[55] The argument is that the business corporation is es-

54. See the American Law Institute formulation, quoted above.
55. Described but not endorsed in Melvin A. Eisenberg, "Corporate Legitimacy, Conduct, and Governance—Two Models of the Corporation," *Creighton Law Review* 17 (1983): 1–19.

sentially a political institution responsible to a variety of constituencies, and in a democratic community the power of the corporation is legitimate only if its internal structure is democratic. Provision should be made for employees and other affected interests to participate indirectly or directly, including through representation on the board of directors. As there are multiple constituencies there must be multiple objectives, only one of which is that of making profits for shareholders. The role of management is to mediate among the various constituencies and objectives, giving weight to each, but not necessarily equal weight. There is an easy transition from recognizing the diversity of *interests* to accommodating the diversity of *demands*.

A different approach looks to the larger meaning of "politics." Rather than ask what groups have a claim, we ask what values should be protected and enhanced. This functional theory of corporate social responsibility shifts attention from the demands of constituencies to the requirements of institutional well-being and integrity.[56] Group claims would no longer be treated as irreducible and self-justifying, an approach which encourages political bargaining and compromise; instead, the mission of the corporation would be expanded to reflect its true role in the community. This expansion emphasizes the *substance* of corporate responsibility, that is, what is objectively required to sustain an effective work force, to do justice in the workplace, to care for the environment, and to meet changing economic and social needs. Responsibility runs to the social function, not to a constituency.[57]

This interpretation of corporate social responsibility is a summons to high politics, not low politics. Obligations are defined by a public philosophy, by a theory of the enterprise and of its place in the community, not by the raw play of power. Only with the aid of such a theory can we design institutions capable of fulfilling their social responsibilities in self-preserving ways. Only thus can we create a corporate conscience.

In recent years there has been a growing understanding that if moral competence is to be meaningful, it must be built into the social structure

56. Gunther Teubner, "Corporate Fiduciary Duties and Their Beneficiaries," in Klaus J. Hopt and Gunther Teubner, eds., *Corporate Governance and Directors' Liabilities: Legal, Economic and Sociological Analyses of Corporate Social Responsibility* (Berlin: de Gruyter, 1985): 149–77.

57. "Social groups are replaced by social functions. It no longer makes sense to search for legitimate group interests which have to be protected by [corporate social responsibility]. . . . Social groups, in this perspective, are not irrelevant. But they are reduced to an instrumental role insofar as they represent one of those societal interests, and are in a position to control the fiduciary duties which are, however, not owed to them directly but to social functions of other subsystems" (ibid., 164–65).

of the enterprise.[58] Thus understood, the corporate conscience is not elusive or indescribable, nor is it mainly a psychological phenomenon. A corporate conscience consists of specific arrangements for making accountability an integral part of corporate decision-making.

The main strategy is institutionalization. Fairness in industrial discipline; affirmative action to overcome discrimination and its effects; environmental protection; quality control; occupational safety: these and other aspirations cannot be achieved through rhetoric or through grudging conformity to external rules. They usually require specialized units capable of determining policy, monitoring practices, and establishing appropriate procedures.

Here the benign face of bureaucracy reappears. In Chapter 10 we noted that bureaucratic hierarchy is more than a formal chain of command. It is an arrangement of parts that have an integrity and continuity of their own. These parts are, in effect, internal interest groups. As sources of energy and centers of competence they may either subvert the enterprise or lend it life and strength. They serve the ends of policy insofar as they are effective guardians of particular standards or objectives. In this way values and policies are anchored in the group structure of the enterprise; in this way the corporate conscience is built up and made good.

▼   ▲   ▼   ▲   ▼

To describe the business corporation as a social institution is not to deny that it is primarily an engine of capitalist economic activity.[59] The question is what perspective, what vision, is brought to bear on that activity. This issue was highlighted in a comparative study of large companies in the insurance industry of the United States. The study identified systematic differences in management philosophy:

> Executives in *enterprise-oriented* corporations tend to take a narrow view of the firm as an autonomous economic entity. For them, the public interest is

58. See Christopher D. Stone, *Where the Law Ends: The Social Control of Corporate Behavior* (New York: Harper/Colophon, 1975); Eugene Bardach and Robert A. Kagan, *Going by the Book: The Problem of Regulatory Unreasonableness* (Philadelphia: Temple University Press, 1982), chaps. 8, 9; Serge Taylor, *Making Bureaucracies Think: The Environmental Impact Statement Strategy of Administrative Reform* (Stanford: Stanford University Press, 1984); Robert H. Miles, *Managing the Corporate Social Environment: A Grounded Theory* (Englewood Cliffs, N.J.: Prentice-Hall, 1987).

59. At issue is a *kind* of capitalism, not capitalism itself. For a contrast between major features of American capitalism and (roughly) German/Japanese capitalism, see Michel Albert, *Capitalisme Contre Capitalisme* (Paris: Editions du Seuil, 1991).

served best when the firm is able to maximize the pursuit of its economic self-interests, free of industry-specific intervention by the general public or its agents. This orientation causes these executives to devote considerable energy and organizational resources to the process of protecting and buffering traditional business policies and practices from external social and political contingencies.

In contrast, executives in *institution-oriented* corporations tend to adopt a broader view of their firm, which they perceive as a social as well as economic franchise. They believe that a large, complex corporation not only has a duty to adapt its business policies and practices to changes in society, but also that because of the scope and pervasiveness of its operations such a corporation can exert nontrivial influences on society. Recognition of these interdependencies between the large corporation and society causes institution-oriented executives to be more willing than their enterprise-oriented counterparts to expose the traditional business policies and practices of the firm to external social and political contingencies.[60]

These differences, it was found, have several correlates. For example, institution-oriented executives take a more collaborative, problem-solving approach to regulatory agencies; enterprise-oriented executives are more individualistic, that is, less concerned about the industry as a whole and more adversarial in their dealings with regulators. It was also found that institution-oriented companies tend to have strong internal organizations devoted to community relations, whereas such functions are at best weakly developed in the enterprise-oriented companies.

The practical significance of management's vision or philosophy is brought home by contemporary concern over the effectiveness of American business. An apparent loss of competitive vigor has received considerable attention in recent years. The decline, it is said, cannot be accounted for by external factors such as the international oil cartel or government regulation. Other countries have faced similar and even more severe constraints. The failure is one of management and leadership. Business success under modern conditions requires long-term perspectives, including sustained investment in technological innovation and patient preparation of markets, including foreign markets. But American management has produced a culture of shortsightedness.

The critics point to a relative decline in spending on research and development, especially in critical industries; to market-driven strategies, with excessive attention to imitative rather than innovative product designs; to recruitment of leaders from finance and law rather than on the basis of specific knowledge of, and commitment to, production and

60. Miles, *Managing the Corporate Social Environment,* 276.

technology; to a preoccupation with mergers and acquisitions; and to management doctrines that favor control and discourage initiative.[61] The basic outcome is a weakened commitment, not only to innovation, but to *any* distinctive competence. The institutional perspective I have outlined here is a voice of resistance to this culture of shortsightedness.

61. See, for example, Robert H. Hayes and William J. Abernathy, "Managing Our Way to Economic Decline," *Harvard Business Review* 58 (July 1980): 67–77. On the economic myopia of Anglo-American individualistic capitalism in contrast to the more communitarian, more institution-centered German/Japanese model, see, in addition to the work cited above, Lester Thurow, *Head to Head: The Coming Economic Battle among Japan, Europe, and America* (New York: William Morrow, 1992), chap. 2. In connection with the discussion of profit maximization above, pp. 347–50, see ibid., chap. 5.

PART FOUR

The Moral Community

THIRTEEN

In Search of Community

At many points in the preceding discussion an attentive reader will have readily discerned intimations of community. A communitarian perspective is, indeed, an irrepressible subtext of the argument thus far. Fellowship and moral well-being; core participation and the implicated self; the primacy of the particular in moral experience; authority as a function of the quality of consent; the transition from management to governance; institutional integrity, responsiveness, and responsibility: these and other topics have presumed or invoked a concept of community. But we have not yet explored the meaning of "community," nor have we dealt with the baggage it carries.

THE SOCIOLOGY OF COMMUNITY

Many writers (and readers) are troubled by the fact that the idea of community is so elusive. There appears to be no clear consensus as to its central meaning. Much the same may be said, of course, regarding many other key concepts in social science and philosophy, including the concepts of "morality," "the political," "law," "culture," and "rationality." In each case a working definition may serve the purposes of a particular argument or inquiry. Nevertheless, each term has rich connotations to which appeal may be made when some new line of inquiry is pursued. This process needs some discipline, but to try to stop it altogether would be futile and self-defeating.

A useful discipline is adherence to the rule that definitions in social theory should be weak, inclusive, and relatively uncontroversial. As I have noted in other contexts, it is in the formulation of theories, not definitions, that we properly argue about the dynamics and kinds of law, authority, socialization, or community. Hypotheses regarding rudimentary or elaborated states belong to the realm of theory. They should not depend for credibility on how a key term is defined. The point is not to eliminate controversy but to transfer it to a more appropriate place—a place where empirical investigation is relevant and helpful.

An appropriately weak, inclusive, and neutral definition of community is suggested, but not quite reached, by the following:

> Wherever the members of any group, small or large, live together in such a way that they share, not this or that particular interest, but the basic conditions of common life, we call that group a community. The mark of a community is that one's life may be lived wholly within it. One cannot live wholly within a business organization or a church; one can live wholly within a tribe or city. The basic criterion of community, then, is that all of one's social relationships may be found within it.[1]

This formulation properly points to *comprehensiveness* as the threshold criterion of community. It is too demanding, however, insofar as it insists that if a group is to be a community *all* of one's social relationships may be found within it. It would be better to say: "A group is a community to the extent that it encompasses a broad range of activities and interests, and to the extent that participation implicates whole persons rather than segmental interests or activities."[2] Thus understood, community can be treated as a variable aspect of group experience. Groups can be more or less full-blown communities, and they can approximate community in different ways.

It is not slipshod to speak of the European Economic Community, the Catholic community, the university community, the law school community, or the police as an occupational community. The main point here is that a framework of shared beliefs, interests, and commitments unites a set of *varied* groups and activities. Some are central, others peripheral, but all are connected by bonds that establish a common faith or fate, a personal identity, a sense of belonging, and a supportive

1. Robert M. MacIver and Charles H. Page, *Society: An Introductory Analysis* (New York: Rinehart, 1949), 8f.
2. The two elements of range and of significance for the person are not independent. If the person is implicated deeply, as in some churches and occupations, the range of activities encompassed by the group will tend to be extended. More aspects of life will be lived within the group.

structure of activities and relationships. The more pathways are provided for participation in diverse ways and touching multiple interests—for example, worshiping in Catholic churches, attending Catholic schools, contributing to Catholic charities, reading the Catholic press—the richer is the experience of community.

Treating community as a variable retains the threshold idea of comprehensiveness but does not commit us to a conventional criterion such as size or territoriality. Sociologists have often said that community necessarily presumes locality.[3] Most "community studies," taking that for granted, focus on a particular village, town, or neighborhood, where (more or less) complete rounds of life can be observed. This makes sense, as a practical matter, because common residence is a congenial condition—perhaps the most congenial condition—for forming and sustaining community life. But communities can be formed in other ways as well; for example, on the basis of concerted activity and shared belief. In the interests of coherent theory, we should avoid confusing a congenial condition or a highly probable correlate with an essential or defining feature.

Thinking of community as variable allows for the possibility that—as was discussed in Chapters 9 and 11—special-purpose institutions may become communities or at least quasi-communities. This form of community occurs most readily when purpose is not very rigidly or narrowly conceived, when leeway is allowed for controversy over ends and means, and when participation is an important part of the individual's life within the organization. Thus community is more likely to develop in military or police organizations, which encourage a shared lifestyle, than in, say, marginal business firms where employment is sporadic, personnel turnover is high, training is unimportant, and work is highly routine and specialized. In other words, *the emergence of community depends on the opportunity for, and the impulse toward, comprehensive interaction, commitment, and responsibility.* These are variable outcomes; they require congenial conditions; but they are not necessarily peripheral or unimportant, even within special-purpose organizations.

This argument leaves intact the analytical distinction between community and special-purpose organization. The "pure" organization is an instrument for mobilizing human energies in disciplined, goal-directed ways. A community, by contrast, has generic functions but no special

3. Ibid., 9–10. See also Leo F. Schnore, "Community: Theory and Research on Structure and Change," in Neil J. Smelser, ed., *Sociology: An Introduction,* 2d ed. (New York: John Wiley, 1973), 70ff.

purpose. This distinction is one of the hardiest and most useful in socio-logical theory.[4] The difference is often blurred in social reality, and we often want to move organizations *in the direction* of community, but the distinction remains a useful starting point for description and diagnosis.

Elements of Community

Although a *definition* of community is properly value-neutral, the *theory* we seek should be both normative and descriptive. We should be able to distinguish the better from the worse, not only according to some neutral criterion, such as "degree of social cohesion," but in the light of the best understanding we have of what makes for moral well-being. At the same time, we should pay close attention to the relevant descriptive sociology, that is, of the actual experience of living in communities. If it is to be effective as a guide to criticism and reconstruction, a normative model must build on that experience.

It has been said that community is a word that "seems never to be used unfavourably."[5] That is surely an exaggeration, for the experience of community has many detractors who emphasize its potential for oppression. Nevertheless, the generally favorable usage is easy to understand when we remember that community—like culture, friendship, socialization, family life—is a prima facie good thing. Typically, communities provide settings within which people grow and flourish and within which subgroups are nourished and protected. This establishes a presumption of moral worth. The presumption is rebuttable on a showing that a given community is too narrow or attenuated to provide an effective framework for common life, or that it is too rigid and stultifying to serve the needs of personal and institutional development or too insular or self-destructive in its dealings with other communities, or that it is otherwise inadequate from the standpoint of critical morality. The same logic applies to our appreciation of family, friendship, law, and culture.

Thus understood, a normative theory of community is at once affirmative and critical—affirmative in that it explores, identifies, and embraces the positive contributions of community to human flourishing; critical in that it asks of a particular community how far, in what ways,

---

4. Therefore it is surprising to read that "unlike all other terms of social organization (*state, nation, society,* etc.) it [community] seems never . . . to be given any positive opposing or distinguishing term" (Raymond Williams, *Keywords: A Vocabulary of Culture and Society* [New York: Oxford University Press, 1976], 66).

5. Ibid.

and with what effects it deviates from a standard. The standard may allow for moral plurality, that is, for different but roughly equal renderings of the good community, but it should have enough bite to distinguish the better from the worse, the genuine from the spurious.

Any theory we propose must take into account the key values at stake in the construction and nurture of a community. These constitute a complex set of interacting variables: historicity, identity, mutuality, plurality, autonomy, participation, and integration. Each has limited and primitive forms; each is the basis of a more elaborated ideal.

Historicity. The bonds of community are strongest when they are fashioned from strands of shared history and culture. They are weak and precarious when they must depend on very general interests or abstract ideas. Furthermore, the character of a community largely reflects the particularities of custom, language, and institutional life; a heritage of significant events and crises; and such historically determined attributes as size, geography, and demography.

Historicity has prima facie moral worth. Rootedness and belonging make for individual well-being as well as commitment to others, and a sense of history is needed for sound collective judgment as to means and ends. Communities, like persons, can do better, and be better, if they understand their own possibilities and limits. To reach that understanding, however, brute particularity must be transcended. The quest is for principles latent in the community's culture and history. Once formulated, such principles become resources for internal dialogue. As is more fully discussed in Chapter 14, they are instruments of reflective morality, that is, they are authoritative standpoints from which to criticize and change specific beliefs, norms, and practices. At the same time, the principles express a distinctive ethos and a special experience.

Identity. A shared history tends to produce a sense of community, and this sense is manifested in loyalty, piety, and a distinctive identity. Every effort to create a community fosters such feelings and perceptions. A formed identity is the natural product of socialization, a process that is carried out not only in families but in most other institutions as well. When socialization is effective there is always some identification of self with others, with locality, and with association. The outcomes of socialization are highly variable, however. The mere fact that an identity-forming process is at work does not tell us how effective it is, nor does it say what kind of self—conformist or independent, supine or resourceful—is being produced.

Of all the elements of community, the moral worth of a formed identity is the most problematic. (This is one reason to avoid the common error of equating a *sense* of community with community itself.) Fixed identities—local, religious, ethnic—are likely to generate demands for self-affirmation that all too often lead to insularity and withdrawal. This parochialism is a chief source of virulent antagonisms. Hence the formation of identities can be destructive of community. The gains in security and self-esteem must be balanced against the loss of more comprehensive, more inclusive, more integrative attitudes.

Mutuality. Community begins with, and is largely supported by, the experience of interdependence and reciprocity. These very practical conditions account for the voluntary and rational components of community. If people and groups do not need each other, if nothing is to be gained from reciprocity and cooperation, community is not likely to emerge or to endure. For this necessary condition to be sufficient, however, mutuality cannot be very narrowly focused. It must go beyond impersonal exchange, beyond coordination for limited goals. To be effective in forming community, mutuality must implicate persons and groups as *unities* and not only in respect to segmental activities or roles. In the context of community, mutuality contemplates continuing relationships and high stakes.

The modern contract is a classic expression of baseline or bare-bones mutuality; hence it is difficult to sustain community on contract principles alone. At least there must be a significant departure from the principle of *limited* obligation in favor of more diffuse and open-ended duties; and the realities of association may require *unequal* contributions rather than a carefully balanced reciprocity. A zealous regard for specifying obligations in advance tends to close relations rather than open them, undermines trust, and limits contributions. Indeed, wherever continuity and concerted effort are prized, the (modern) contract model loses force and relevance. As we move to association, and from association to community, mutuality reaches beyond exchange to create more enduring bonds of interdependence, caring, and commitment. There is a transition, we may say, from reciprocity to solidarity, and from there to fellowship.

Plurality. According to the pluralist and corporatist doctrines of Tocqueville, Lamennais, Gierke, and others, a community draws much of its vitality from "intermediate associations."[6] Such associations are

6. See Chapter 16, "Communal Democracy."

havens of protection and vehicles of meaningful participation. Through significant membership in corporate groups the individual's relation to the larger community can be extended and enriched. People lose the benefits of community when they are stripped of their group attachments and left naked before an impersonal or central authority. And the group structure of society generates countervailing forces to moderate the influence of any single power bloc.[7]

Thus understood, plurality is a normative idea. It does not refer to every dispersal of power and commitment, every proliferation of interests, groups, and authorities. A healthy differentiation of institutions and of personal, family, ethnic, locality, and occupational groups depends on the capacity of each to preserve its own well-being within a framework of legitimacy, and without fracturing or fragmenting the social order.[8]

Autonomy. Although pluralist thought has great merit, it also has a cardinal weakness: the assumption that individual well-being is effectively guaranteed by group autonomy and integrity. Pluralists have rightly emphasized that individuals need nurture, support, and group protection against external domination. But subsidiary groups can be oppressive, often more so than the state. Therefore pluralist theory must be modified as necessary to protect freedom *in* associations as well as freedom *of* association.

A concern for personal autonomy does not settle what freedoms are appropriate in the context at hand, nor does it assume that autonomy is equivalent to unconditional opportunity and choice. It does assume that the worth of community is measured by the contribution it makes to the flourishing of unique and responsible persons. As an attribute of selfhood and of self-affirmation, autonomy requires commitment as well as choice.

Participation. It is elementary that personal autonomy can be achieved only in and through social participation.[9] But what *kind* of participation? Some kinds encourage rationality and self-determination; others undermine them. Some are egalitarian; others demand a spirit of subordination. The most rudimentary (and important) forms of communal participation have to do with the basic continuities of life: procreation,

7. This pluralist aspect of community is emphasized in Robert A. Nisbet, *The Quest for Community* (New York: Oxford University Press, 1953).

8. When such pragmatists as William James and Roscoe Pound spoke of "giving effect to social interests," they took for granted that such interests stem from the natural, undistorted continuities of life and as such have prima facie legitimacy.

9. This postulate does not preclude physical isolation. People who choose to live alone, or prisoners in isolation, depend for mental health on prior socialization and on participation in a socially constructed symbolic world.

child-rearing, work, kinship, friendship. Participation in broader religious or political contexts builds on those continuities and tends to be distorted if they are weakened or absent. The mass mobilization of detached individuals is not a paradigm of communal participation. The lesson is that participation reflects and sustains community insofar as it entails multiple memberships and diverse commitments. The more compartmentalized, specialized, or single-minded the activity, the more limited is its contribution to the life of a community.

A flourishing community has high levels of participation: people are appropriately present, and expected to be present, on many different occasions and in many different roles and aspects. They are not *omni*present, however, nor are they asked to sacrifice their own most important concerns and connections. These are corollaries of what we earlier called "mediated" and "core" participation.

Integration. All the elements noted above require supportive institutions, norms, beliefs, and practices. These must exhibit enough coherence to sustain the foundations of a common life. We thus see the emergence of distinctively integrative political, legal, and cultural institutions. The quality of community depends, to a large extent, on the character of these institutions. How we perceive and construct the political and cultural order—whether as a tight system of integration and subordination or as a framework within which plurality and autonomy may flourish—becomes a central concern. There is, therefore, an intimate connection between democracy and community—a topic we explore in Chapter 16.

A fully realized community will have a rich and *balanced* mixture of all of these seven elements. We cannot ignore the givenness of received custom and decisive events, but the appeal to historicity must respect the other values, so far as they are affected. Similarly, the claims of plurality and autonomy must be balanced against those of mutuality and participation. In this normative theory, the moral quality of a community is measured by its ability to defend all the chief values at stake, to hold them in tension as necessary, and to encourage their refinement and elaboration.

It does not follow that any state of affairs less than a fully realized community is necessarily deficient from a moral point of view, any more than the morally best person must necessarily be the best-integrated or fully rounded. Different types of community—religious, political, occupational, institutional, international—will have different mixes of the main elements. A religious community may well give greater weight to historicity and mutuality than, say, an enterprise-based community will. And religious communities may differ among themselves in the weight they give to various forms and sources of fellowship. There is always room for debate as to the kind of community a group should be.

The Limits of Gemeinschaft

Our understanding of community owes much to, and is distorted by, the well-known polarities of *Gemeinschaft* and *Gesellschaft*. Building on the work of Gierke, Maine, Marx, and other nineteenth-century historians and social theorists, Ferdinand Tönnies (1855–1936) hit upon a striking way of characterizing the evolution of modern society.[10] His work does not trace that evolution, being mainly analytical rather than historical, a study of social types, not of sequences. Nevertheless, it has an important place among efforts to understand the transition from a kin-based world of organic unity to an exchange-based world of artificial association.

The transformation is familiar enough. It is, among other things, as Henry Sumner Maine put it, "the movement of the progressive societies . . . from Status to Contract."[11] But Tönnies's argument is more general than Maine's and is in some ways more profound. His theory speaks to differences far deeper and more pervasive than status or contract. They affect every aspect of everyday life, including how people think about authority, work, time, morality, and much else. The German word *Gemeinschaft* connotes moral unity, rootedness, intimacy, and kinship. Although usually translated simply as "community," it really refers to a *kind* of community, one that fully realizes values of historicity and mutuality, and does so even at considerable cost to personal mobility and autonomy.

In gemeinschaft, social practices and institutions are infused with intrinsic worth. Beliefs and institutions are "affirmed," not chosen or designed; they are valued for themselves, not for extraneous ends. As a result, people "remain essentially united in spite of all separating factors, whereas in the Gesellschaft they are essentially separated in spite of all uniting factors."[12] The gemeinschaft model closely fits what is

10. *Community and Society*, ed. C. P. Loomis (1887; reprint, New York: Harper, 1963).
11. Henry Sumner Maine, *Ancient Law* (1861; reprint, Boston: Beacon Press, 1963), 165.
12. Tönnies, *Community and Society*, 65.

often called a folk or traditional society; it resembles, too, an idealized feudal order.[13]

Tönnies thought he could discern within each of his two types a basic way of thinking, feeling, and acting. The more primordial form he called *Wesenwille*, translated as "natural" or "essential" will. *Wesenwille*, the basis of gemeinschaft, expresses a condition or state of being rather than a set purpose. It is motivation or conduct that emerges from growth and adaptation, that is, from the accumulation of experiences and commitments and from the formation of character; it reveals a person's authentic self, which must be a product of social history and social participation. A community based on "natural will" is person-centered. Its institutions recognize and uphold continuities of self and society. Emotion, preference, and rationality are governed by socially accepted criteria of intrinsic worth.

The alternative is *Kürwille*, the foundation of gesellschaft. *Kürwille* connotes, in Tönnies's usage, choice that is both rational and arbitrary. In gesellschaft, goals do not emerge from tradition or from the fabric of social life; they are not expressions of identity and self-conception. Rather, ends are forever posited anew, in response to changing circumstances and desires, by independent and rational actors. In this model the *choice* of ends is arbitrary, but their *pursuit* is governed by rational calculation. Thus gesellschaft breeds a positivist, utilitarian mentality. Within that framework neither ends nor means have intrinsic worth.

Strictly speaking, Tönnies's theory does not commit us to a particular historical model; it does not prejudge the form a community must take. Kinship, love, friendship, localism, and patriotism are particular manifestations of a more general imperative. There may be many ways of encouraging "natural will" without accepting the special constraints of a tradition-centered or folk society.

Nevertheless, the term gemeinschaft brings to mind a society warmed by intimacy and united by brotherhood. The imagery is seductive. There is a near-irresistible temptation to treat what was offered by Tönnies as an analytical device—an "ideal type"—as if it were the full embodiment of a moral vision. But there is more to community than intimacy and brotherhood, just as there is more to family life than love and

13. A study of medieval towns in Europe notes, however, that "the evidence does not tell us that medieval communes and guilds had a particularly holistic or collectivist mentality" (Antony Black, *Guilds and Civil Society in European Political Thought from the Twelfth Century to the Present* [London: Methuen, 1984], 65).

sharing. Gemeinschaft does not encompass the full range of variables that constitute community and affect its quality.

The selective focus of gemeinschaft is solidarity. Gemeinschaft prizes loyalty, commitment, self-acceptance—all the virtues and benefits of integrative participation in cohesive groups. The assumption is that such participation is beneficial, not only at the level of family and friendship, but also in the larger settings of community life. This crucial assumption leaves many questions unanswered, especially how far, and with what limitations, the primary-group model can serve as a foundation for the theory of community.[14]

The limits of gemeinschaft and of the primary-group model may be seen if we consider the difference between commune and community. An account of the hippie communes of the 1960s put it this way:

> Typically, communes were made up fairly uniformly of young people who identified with the hip subculture of drugs, rock and voluntary poverty. . . . By contrast, the community embraced a greater diversity of people, not just the hip and the young. Where communes left finances, work and decision to the fickle will of group consciousness, communities leaned more heavily on definite structures: work systems, treasurers, and corporations. Many were united around a single craft or art. . . . The physical, as well as emotional, distance was greater in a community than in a commune. Traditionally, a community was made up of separate houses rather than a large common dwelling.[15]

The quest of the commune is for communion rather than community. Communion is a psychic unity, whereas community embraces a range of activities and associations. Because it is narrowly based on psychic unity, the commune is an inherently unstable social form. If it desires more stability, the commune must become a community.

The lesson is that communities are characterized by structural differentiation as well as by shared consciousness. A natural community—even a highly organic community—cannot be completely homogeneous. As a framework for common life it must develop some division of labor, some system of authority, some proliferation of roles, groups, and institutions. These structures are sustained by ongoing, interdependent activities, not by symbolic experience alone. The basic fact is that participation in communities is mediated by participation in families, localities, personal networks, and institutions. This core participation,

14. For the primary-group model, see Chapter 7, "Segmental and Core Participation."
15. Robert Houriet, *Getting Back Together* (New York: Coward-McCann, 1971), 205f.

as we have called it, preserves the integrity and rationality of the participants. We do not think of participation in communities as irrational or self-destructive. On the contrary, without community, rationality is often precarious and may be undone.

Even participation in interest groups, which are normally governed by cool calculation of costs and benefits, may gain in rationality if it takes place within the framework of community. For conduct to be fully rational, the choice of ends as well as means should be subject to evaluation. The decision to join a group or make an investment may be unwise, not only if the project itself is dubious, but also if the decision to join or invest is capricious or opportunistic. The choice may not be governed by a defensible life-plan or by concern for broader and unintended effects. If reasoning about means and ends is to be effective, it requires an informing and restraining context.

Thus, the demands of community are not opposed to rational judgment and personal autonomy. On the contrary, any radical abridgment of these values signals the distortion or destruction of community. This follows from the idea that community is a framework within which ordinary social life goes forward. Normal life is lived concretely, in the light of practical needs and circumstances. A community cannot flourish if it does not foster and support the skills people need, including good sense in personal relationships. The rationality of basic skills is preserved even in highly integrated communities, such as the preliterate communities studied by anthropologists.

Nor will a community prosper if it tries to be completely homogeneous in thought and action. This was understood by Aristotle, who in his *Politics* criticized Plato for assuming " 'that the greater the unity of the state the better.' " He went on:

> Is it not obvious that a state may at length attain such a degree of unity as to be no longer a state?—since the nature of a state is to be a plurality, and in tending to greater unity, from being a state, it becomes a family, and from being a family, an individual; for the family may be said to be more one than the state, and the individual than the family. So that we ought not to attain this greatest unity even if we could, for it would be the destruction of the state. Again, a state is not made up only of so many men, but of different kinds of men; for similars do not constitute a state.[16]

In Aristotle's theory, the political community is the arena within which a common life is carried on and perfected. But perfection must take into

16. *Politics*, 1261a, trans. Benjamin Jowett, in Richard McKeon, ed., *The Basic Works of Aristotle* (New York: Random House, 1941).

account social reality, which includes the need for diversity, that is, for differentiated groups, roles, occupations, and functions. As a corollary, he wrote, "[T]he principle of reciprocity . . . is the salvation of states."[17] It may be said, indeed, that the integration of communities depends at least as much on interdependence—Durkheim's "organic solidarity"—as it does on symbolic cohesion or "mechanical solidarity."

Why this unity in diversity? Why is it correct to say, for example, that "*a certain degree of separateness of the parts* is necessary if the whole is to be considered a community"?[18] The answer lies in what it means to share a *common* life. A common life is not a *fused* life: in a fused life there would be no need for regulation or governance, no need to take account of individual differences, no need for adjustment, reciprocity, or cooperation. The tacit assumption here is that people and groups participate in any community, large or small, as individuated and self-regarding entities. They are independent as well as interdependent.

The distinctive function of community, then, is the reconciliation of partial with general perspectives. A community must recognize the legitimacy of egoism as a basic aspect of humanity and therefore as a necessary starting point for group life. If egoism did not persist there would be no need for community; if it had no moral and social worth, we might try to rid ourselves of it by repressive measures or by attempting to fashion a wholly altruistic self. But that is not the mission of community. Its true function is to regulate, discipline, and, especially, to channel self-regarding conduct, thereby binding it, so far as possible, to comprehensive interests and ideals.

What we prize in community is not unity of any sort, at any cost, but unity that preserves the integrity of persons, groups, and institutions. Thus understood, community is profoundly *federalist* in spirit and structure. It is a unity of unities. This principle has been implicit, and very often explicit, in much that has been said about morality and community.[19] Many social mechanisms—largely unconscious and adaptive—serve to strike a balance between integration and autonomy. Most important are appropriate methods of socialization, that is, ways of cultivating self-sufficiency and responsibility. Others are implicit in social

17. Ibid.
18. Joel Feinberg, *Harmless Wrongdoing* (New York: Oxford University Press, 1988), 104, my emphasis.
19. See the quotation from J. A. Hobson, below, p. 376; Chapter 16, on the theory of covenant; John Rawls on "The Idea of Social Union," in *A Theory of Justice* (Cambridge: Harvard University Press, 1971), 520ff.; and Amitai Etzioni's "I-We Paradigm," in Etzioni, *The Moral Dimension: Toward a New Economics* (New York: Free Press, 1988), chap. 1.

organization. In a well-wrought community, participation, as we have seen, is mediated by membership in subgroups and thereby sustains personal and group autonomy. This particularizing and decentering tendency is offset by another: the development of overlapping, crosscutting, "multiplex" relationships. A "multiplex" relationship serves "many interests."[20] The members of a family are the spouses, parents, children, siblings, and cousins; these same individuals may also be neighbors, farmers, property holders, religious communicants, clan members, and citizens. The greater the reach of the relationship—the more interests it touches—the greater is the cost of rupture. Thus mediated membership and multiple affiliation, working together, enhance solidarity at the same time that they preserve independence.

This line of argument suggests that it is as wrong to make a fetish of solidarity as it is to glorify unconditional independence. Each in its own way corrodes community. The first, in reaching for total integration, turns community into a parody of itself. The second offers an ethos too thin to sustain more than a minimal moral order. A genuinely communitarian doctrine—one rooted in the experience of common life—resists both extremes. It seeks theories and strategies that promise stable accommodation and conjoint fulfillment of all the values entailed by the ideal of community.

One such strategy looks to institutions as the chief agencies and most reliable safeguards of community. Institutions embody values and enhance integration, but they do so in ways that resist homogeneity and sustain differentiation. Strong communities are *institution-centered*. Their cohesion and moral competence derive from the strength and integrity of families, schools, parties, government agencies, voluntary associations, and law. When institutions are respected in all spheres of life, values of solidarity, duty, and restraint are vindicated. At the same time, a variety of perspectives, reflecting the variety of institutions, are appropriate and legitimate.

A focus on institutions turns attention away from the psychic cohesion so often associated with the idea of community. Instead of seeing community in the emergence of like-minded, undifferentiated individuals, we see it in a network of distinct but interdependent institutions. This does not eliminate the need for core values; indeed, if they are built into the premises and govern the operation of major institutions, core

20. Max Gluckman, *The Judicial Process Among the Barotse of Northern Rhodesia* (Glencoe, Ill.: Free Press, 1955), 19.

values are likely to be stronger and more effectively implemented than if they are manifested only in beliefs or feelings.

This perspective has special relevance for the place of community in modern mass society. We cannot be optimistic that community will flourish under conditions of high mobility and fragmented experience, where mutual commitments are weak, spans of attention are short, and gratifications are undeferred. These conditions undermine institutions. Their effects, however, can be resisted and contained. Even under conditions of mass society many institutions retain, and others develop, significant resources of continuity and strength. That is so because what they do has great practical worth, and because they become vested interests capable of generating loyalty and support. The contemplation of mass *populations* may drive us to despair. We may take some comfort from the relatively greater resilience of institutions.

There are echoes here of conservative doctrine, which treats institutions, not individuals, as constitutive of community. This is an important, if partial, truth. It need not follow, however, that institutions must be unresponsive or that, in their operation, only the status quo is protected. When the integrity of universities is respected, so too are academic freedom, creative expression, and the possibility of dangerous thoughts. The rule of law carries an inescapable message of restraint, but it also enlarges horizons and secures rights. That the insight is conservative need not lead us to prejudge whether a particular institution merits survival, renewal, expansion, or replacement.

LIBERALISM AND COMMUNITY

The multi-valued perspective outlined above demands a high tolerance for ambiguity. This has not been easy to come by, and as a result the quest for community has suffered frustration and confusion. There are communitarians of both left and right: anarchists, socialists, conservatives, and, more ambiguously, welfare liberals. Even the most ardent defenders of individual rights and freedoms do not deny the importance of community, for some purposes at least, and especially for consensus as to the worth of those rights and freedoms. Each doctrine tries to resolve (or escape) the irrepressible tension between social integration and personal autonomy; each highlights a different aspect of community or proposed road to community; each has embraced some values and slighted others. Who, then, speaks for community? Is there an authentic voice?

Communitarian Perspectives

The sharpest difference, as we might expect, is between conservative and anarchist interpretations. Conservatives find moral worth in the *historical* community, that is, in tradition, hierarchy, inheritance, and fixed status. These social anchors, properly set, are preconditions of personal integrity and therefore of genuine freedom. The keynote is security— personal, institutional, cultural. A well-ordered community provides reliable and comfortable avenues of social participation.

The anarchist vision, to some extent shared by Rousseau, Marx, and the American pragmatists, detaches the ideal community from the historical community. In this perspective, community is not decisively formed by history, particularity, and social structure. Rather, it arises from free communication, person-to-person interaction, and association based on mutual dependence and concern. The core values are liberation and fellowship; the main strategy is struggle against repressive control of any sort. Security is not a condition of liberty, as in the conservative view. Rather, it is a product of liberty.[21] Good order arises from reciprocity, trust, cooperation, and a shared understanding of the common good.

Although the contrast is stark, a revealing convergence can be seen. Anarchists and classical conservatives share a preference for decentralization and self-regulation. In both doctrines the favored unit of social organization is the small, intimate, person-centered community, where solidarity is most effective and most genuine; where persons are created and nurtured; where they become situated beings and implicated selves. For anarchists and conservatives alike, the individual person is the touchstone of worth; yet each rejects the idea that people can flourish by acting as separate individuals for wholly self-chosen ends.

Anarchist doctrine is radical and libertarian. However, it does not presume an atomistic or asocial conception of human agency and personality. The self is inescapably social: people depend on others for care and support, for, indeed, the very constitution of their selves. But they are also capable of independent growth and critical reflection. These capabilities, however, are not preformed; they depend on social participation.

21. According to Proudhon, liberty is "not the daughter but the *mother* of order" (P. J. Proudhon, *Proudhon's Solution of the Social Problem* [1848; reprint, New York: Vanguard, 1927], 45).

Both anarchism and conservatism are profoundly sociological in their premises and insights. Each finds intrinsic worth in the spontaneous and organic aspects of social life. For conservatism, social order is most genuine and most humane when it is the product of slow absorption and adaptation. For anarchism, a healthy social order emerges from the free interaction of human beings responding creatively to their situations and experiences. Neither perspective is congenial to an atomistic, contractual conception of social organization. In combination, they faithfully reflect the sociological image of persons-in-society.

Neither, however, taken by itself, is a reliable guide to the moral community. Conservatives are drawn to the gemeinschaft model. Their preference for structure and stability gives short shrift to individual opportunity and autonomy. And anarchists, although they want unity, see it as coming from wholly voluntary association. Driven by fear of domination, they recoil from all authority, in all institutions. They can neither embrace nor create viable systems of coordination and control.

Is liberalism a better guide? This question is more difficult, because liberalism is something more than an informing vision or a utopian ideal. Since the eighteenth century its doctrines have dominated Western thought and have been notably successful in the practical work of designing and managing political and economic systems. At the same time, the morality of liberalism has been much debated. Its perspectives have been vigorously criticized and reconstructed periodically. The recurrent quest is for a "new" liberalism, one that will bind the ideal of liberty to a more secure ethos of social responsibility.

Liberalism is an ideology of constrained liberation or, as we sometimes say, of ordered liberty. A social, political, or economic doctrine is liberal if (1) it seeks to free individuals, institutions, and practices from the restraints of custom, dogma, vested interest, and centralized authority; and (2) it holds that liberation must take place within a framework of orderly process, constitutional principle, and respect for social continuity. Taken together, these criteria distinguish what it means to be a liberal from what it means to be a conservative, a radical libertarian, a revolutionary, or a collectivist.

High on the agenda of all the great figures of the Enlightenment, whatever their differences, was the emancipation of human reason from ignorance, repression, and arbitrary convention. The economic liberalism of laissez-faire sought to release human energies from the fetters of a feudal and mercantilist past. Contemporary welfare liberalism seeks to liberate the disadvantaged from the stultifying effects of discrimination and economic hardship. The common thread has been, as Dewey said, the "liberation of individuals" for the "realization of their capacities."[22]

In the United States, the laissez-faire liberalism of Adam Smith has become today's political (but inauthentic) conservatism. Nevertheless, contemporary welfare liberalism builds on that earlier tradition. The core values of classical liberalism were autonomy and rationality. Individuals were to be free to pursue their life plans with minimal interference from the state or other institutions; personal conduct and economic enterprise was to be guided by a calculus of efficiency and effectiveness. It was presumed that rationality would follow naturally as autonomy was achieved.

These ideals still distinguish liberal from conservative sensibilities. Since the late nineteenth century, however, an important branch of liberalism has demanded a more stringent accounting of how these and related values are to be made good.[23] The new liberals have sought a richer meaning of autonomy and rationality, one more generous in spirit and more faithful to psychological and social reality. And they have brought to bear a lively awareness of changing historical contexts.

The distinctive program of contemporary liberalism is best revealed in its critique of *formal* notions of freedom, rationality, and justice. Modern welfare liberalism seeks *effective* freedom, *substantive* rationality, and *social* justice. This means, for example, that mere freedom from restraint is not an acceptable criterion of liberation. In itself such freedom may deny to most people the social support they need for genuine autonomy when they face psychological or economic dependency, and it may leave them without effective protection from the powerful and the greedy. Similarly, genuine rationality cannot be realized if it is limited to individual action for individuated goals; rational cooperation for collective goals is necessary if the underlying value, reasoned pursuit of human well-being, is to be achieved. And justice is illusory if it overlooks social conditions, such as inequality, or the interplay of private and public power, that distort legal outcomes.

This emphasis on substance—on concretely realized freedom, rationality, and justice—could be seen in many nineteenth-century criticisms of social conditions. It did not take long for people to realize that, in the words of Anatole France, "the law, in its majestic equality, forbids the rich as well as the poor to sleep under bridges, to beg in the streets, and

---

22. John Dewey, *Liberalism and Social Action* (New York: G. P. Putnam's, 1935), 56.
23. See Michael Freeden, *The New Liberalism: An Ideology of Social Reform* (Oxford: Clarendon Press, 1978); Harry K. Girvetz, *The Evolution of Liberalism* (New York: Collier, 1963); James T. Kloppenberg, *Uncertain Victory: Social Democracy and Progressivism in European and American Thought, 1870–1920* (New York: Oxford University Press, 1986).

to steal bread."[24] Some, like Karl Marx, drew radical conclusions and found liberalism itself flawed beyond repair. But others, such as John Stuart Mill, tried hard to reconcile libertarian ideals and collective action for the common good. This led him to break away from the Benthamite and laissez-faire doctrines he had embraced in his youth:

> While we repudiated with the greatest energy that tyranny of society over the individual which most Socialistic systems are supposed to involve, we yet looked forward to a time when society will no longer be divided into the idle and the industrious; when the rule that they who do not work shall not eat, will be applied not to paupers only, but impartially to all; when the division of the produce of labour, instead of depending, as in so great a degree it now does, on the accident of birth, will be made by concert on an acknowledged principle of justice; and when it will no longer be, or thought to be, impossible for human beings to exert themselves strenuously in procuring benefits which are not to be exclusively their own, but to be shared with the society they belong to. The social problem of the future we considered to be, how to unite the greatest individual liberty of action, with a common ownership in the raw material of the globe, and an equal participation of all in the benefits of combined labour.[25]

Mill was not a Marxist. Rather, he came to share some of the ideas of the earlier Utopian Socialists who feared a strong state and whose ideal was a cooperative commonwealth based on the voluntary association of workers.

The transformation of Mill's ideas from economic individualism to a mild form of socialism prefigured a broad movement of thought among English and American liberals in the late nineteenth and early twentieth centuries. In England, such influential writers as J. A. Hobson and L. T. Hobhouse insisted that liberalism (including the Liberal party) must look to the social foundations of welfare and liberty. They broadened the utilitarian perspective to include "social utility"; accepted the necessity of government intervention to enhance public welfare, especially the condition of the poor; demanded full economic opportunity and civic participation for all sectors of society; rejected a sharp division between public and private spheres of life; developed doctrines, such as "social property in capital," which justified regulation of private enterprise and recapture for the public of "unearned increments"; recognized that "freedom of contract" is illusory when the parties are radically unequal in social power; and emphasized the inseparability of ethics and politics, ethics

24. Words put into the mouth of a sardonic poet, who adds, "This equality is one of the benefits of the Revolution" (Anatole France, *The Red Lily,* trans. Winifred Stephens [London: John Lane, 1914], 95).
25. *Autobiography* (1873; reprint, New York: Columbia University Press, 1924), 162.

and economics. A recurrent theme was the need for a doctrine that would acknowledge the claims of community.

At the same time, these English liberals were keenly aware of the inevitable tension between individual and society. Like Mill, they were committed to "individuality" and therefore to resisting encroachments on personal choice and initiative. The great problem of liberal society, as they understood it, was to reconcile liberty and welfare. This would require, said Hobson,

> not a unity of mere fusion in which the individual virtually disappears, but a federal unity in which the rights and interests of the individual shall be conserved for him by the federation. The federal government, however, conserves these individual rights, not, as the individualist maintains, because it exists for no other purpose than to do so. It conserves them because it also recognises that an area of individual liberty is conducive to the health of the collective life. Its federal nature rests on a recognition alike of individual and social ends, or, speaking more accurately, of social ends that are directly attained by social action and of those that are realized in individuals.[26]

The well-being of individuals depends on the health of the collectivity; therefore society must be the unit of analysis, and the common good must be the focus of our striving. The common good in turn requires "an area of individual liberty."

This formula has served rather well, for almost a century, to express the commitments of welfare liberals and social democrats. As sponsors of regulated capitalism and the welfare state, they have curbed some economic liberties, redistributed income to some extent, and expanded the powers of government. They have also been chief advocates for civil rights and civil liberties. For the most part, therefore, welfare liberals have been faithful to Hobson's vision. They have shown that a new liberalism, though forsaking laissez-faire and reaching for social justice, can still maintain a strong allegiance to political liberty and personal autonomy. Nevertheless, serious questions are left unanswered.

Rights-centered Liberalism

The significance of the transition from classical to welfare liberalism has yet to be fully assimilated. As a result, the intellectual foundations of contemporary liberalism remain insecure. This unease takes two forms: uncertainty about individual *obligations,* as distinct from individual

26. J. A. Hobson, *Work and Wealth* (New York, 1914), 304, quoted in Freeden, *New Liberalism,* 110f.

rights; and a timorous reluctance to formulate and embrace positive conceptions of the common good.

The conflict between individual claims and collective life still vexes the liberal conscience. That is so in part because contemporary liberals remain faithful to the principle that basic liberties are at risk when social utility is taken as the sole criterion for judging morality and policy. The alternative is a political morality that "takes rights seriously" as a set of binding commitments.[27] At the same time, liberals resist the ethos of individualism.

Thus a centerpiece of John Rawls's *Theory of Justice* is the rank-ordering of basic principles. For this purpose he invokes two "priority rules."[28] The first is that "liberty can be restricted only for the sake of liberty," not to ameliorate inequality or disadvantage. Liberty cannot be sacrificed even to the pursuit of social justice. The second priority rule is that *social* justice—the mitigation of inequalities—must take precedence over efficiency and aggregate utility or welfare.

This rank-ordering is a way of taking rights seriously. Rights trump utilities, in Dworkin's phrase, not only as a matter of definition,[29] but in the ways they are institutionalized and in the relative weights they are given. The effect is to establish the priorities that must govern when the claims of community are asserted.

In keeping with the perspective of welfare liberalism, Rawls's "basic liberties" are mainly political and personal:

> The basic liberties of citizens are, roughly speaking, political liberty (the right to vote and to be eligible for public office) together with freedom of speech and assembly; liberty of conscience and freedom of thought; freedom of the person along with the right to hold (personal) property; and freedom from arbitrary arrest and seizure as defined by the concept of the rule of law.[30]

The list is rough indeed, but the perspective is clear. Freedom to amass wealth or to exercise unregulated private power is not part of this liberal canon. In much of economic life, liberty *can* be abridged to further ends other than liberty; control of pollution, restraint of monopoly, conservation of resources, and many other social objectives may take precedence over liberty of contract or the right to use one's property as one sees fit.

27. See Ronald Dworkin, *Taking Rights Seriously* (Cambridge: Harvard University Press, 1978).
28. Rawls, *Theory of Justice,* 302. See also Chapter 16, "Moral and Social Equality."
29. See p. 510 n.56.
30. Rawls, *Theory of Justice,* 61.

The strategy of rank-ordering is, of course, an essential aspect of constitutional democracy. The United States Constitution can be understood as, in part, an implicit set of priority rules. Freedom of speech and association, separation of church and state, due process, equal protection of the law: these injunctions limit what government can do in the interests of efficiency and welfare. Furthermore, the Bill of Rights does not protect all liberty, abstractly considered, but only those liberties that derive from our evolving understanding of what citizenship in a democracy requires; what abuses of power must be anticipated and checked; what kinds of strife are acceptable and which must be avoided; what forms of personal privacy and choice must be protected.

As constitutional history has shown, however, the idea that adherence to concepts of liberty and justice must limit what government can do in the public interest does not settle *which* liberties are basic or what justice requires. Does "liberty of conscience" include a woman's right to make her own conscientious decision to abort her fetus? Is affirmative action on behalf of minorities compatible with equality before the law? These and many similar questions are the stuff of social policy and the burden of much constitutional adjudication. They can be answered only by bringing to bear specific conceptions of individuality and the common good.

In formulating their vision of a just society, welfare liberals opt for community when property rights are at issue, but they shrink from community when political liberty and personal autonomy are in question. The rationale is clear. Investors and entrepreneurs are economic actors and as such do not ordinarily risk their integrity or well-being as persons or citizens. The restraints imposed by government are among the costs of doing business. Therefore government should be free to pursue collective goals without treating entrepreneurial liberty as sacrosanct. The rights of *personal* property, insofar as they refer to resources necessary for dignity and integrity, are more compelling.

The underlying idea is that any *utility* may freely be abridged in the interests of a greater utility. Any means that lacks intrinsic worth—the corporate form of organization, for example—must yield to a more efficient method or a more desirable objective. That principle cannot be applied, however, to political liberty, individual autonomy, and the claims of equality. These are not prized as means to other ends. Rather, they are valued for themselves as direct expressions and indispensable vehicles of personal fulfillment.

As a philosophy of liberation, liberalism is understandably preoccupied with individual, person-centered rights. This preoccupation has great merit, but it tends to create a rights-centered morality and a rights-centered politics. In the process rights are divorced from discipline and duty.[31] They become abstract, unsituated, and absolute. Claims of right—to freedom of expression or association, for example—are asserted without regard for context or for the multiple values that may be at stake. People forget that rights, in contrast to duties, "do not provide reasons for acting, at least not for the people who have them."[32] We may or may not invoke the rights we have or think we have, and that decision tells us much about character and civic virtue. There is a vital difference between invoking rights out of a sense of duty, as a form of responsible conduct, and doing so out of narrow self-interest.

Furthermore, in liberal thought and practice, it becomes hard to make the necessary distinctions among kinds of rights. The *logic* of liberalism accepts that rights are justified by their contribution to larger goods of freedom and welfare. The *ethos* of liberalism, however, gives rights a life of their own, detached from the assessment of conditions and consequences. A moral community must recognize baseline or "natural" rights, which derive from our understanding of what personhood requires. More specific rights, however, such as academic freedom, must be determined in the light of the ends they serve. Though they may be jealously guarded, and properly so, they must ultimately yield to the sovereignty of purpose. Moreover, a preoccupation with rights does not save us from the need to examine a community's commitments in order to decide what array of rights is appropriate and how far they should be indefeasible.

In a provocative and much-debated essay, Michael Sandel has argued that liberalism rests on a flawed conception of self and community.[33] It may well be that liberal thought, with its focus on autonomy and rights, has failed to appreciate the full significance of the proposition that selves

31. Abstractly considered, rights and duties are correlative: if one person has a right, someone else has a duty. But that does not mean they are nicely balanced in practice. Depending on the context, we can and do give greater weight to a sense of duty than to claims of right; we may differ in readiness to accept the one and assert the other.

32. Jeremy Waldron, "A Right to Do Wrong," *Ethics* 92 (October 1981): 28.

33. Criticizing Rawls's allegedly "individualistic" theory of community, Sandel writes: "To say that members of a society are bound by a sense of community is not simply to say that a great many of them profess communitarian sentiments and pursue communitarian aims, but rather that they conceive their identity . . . as defined to some extent by the community of which they are a part. For them, community describes not just what they *have* as fellow citizens but also what they *are*, not a relationship they choose (as in a voluntary association) but an attachment they discover, not merely an attribute but a constituent of their identity" (Michael Sandel, *Liberalism and the Limits of Justice* [Cambridge: Cambridge University Press, 1982], 150).

are constituted in the course of socialization and social interaction. Insofar as people are thought to be *radically* independent—constructing their own identities, choosing their own associates, negotiating their own obligations—the concepts of selfhood and obligation are surely impoverished. But liberal doctrine does not necessarily deny that selves are socially constituted or that deeply held convictions stem from communal involvements and attachments. The concept of a social self is wholly compatible with the recognition that people do make choices, including self-defining choices. Socialization may produce individuality as well as conformity; and the self thus created can actively choose (as well as be constituted by) a wide range of goals and values.

Liberal uncertainty about the claims of community does not stem, in any serious way, from abstract formulae about the boundaries of selfhood. Much more important is the history of liberal struggle to protect and extend civil liberties and civil rights. This experience has made liberals highly sensitive to the abridgment of rights, with the result that many have given relatively short shrift to the virtues of responsible conduct. If liberals are to take those virtues more seriously, a change in perspective is needed, including an increase in appreciation for the continuities of self and society. This may entail, as Sandel suggests, a rethinking of how selfhood is to understood and how it fits into liberal conceptions of morality and community. It does not, however, require a radical move from a wholly "unencumbered" to a wholly "encumbered" self.[34]

Liberal Neutralism

The liberal state, it is often said, is a neutral state; its "constitutive morality is a theory of equality that requires official neutrality amongst theories of what is valuable in life."[35] Government should not presume to say what sort of lives we ought to live, nor should it mold or constrain our preferences. It should only provide a framework for rational discourse and peaceful competition as it protects the capacity of all individ-

34. I do not read Sandel as requiring such a move. He speaks of identity as defined "to some extent" or "partly" by community attachments. These and other qualifications suggest that his point is to reconstruct liberal theory so as to enhance appreciation for the historicity of selfhood, including the givenness of attachments and the limits of choice—not to deny freedom or denigrate the importance of a critical standpoint. Indeed, such a standpoint is strengthened when it extends to reflection on identity and its sources rather than only on what a basically unproblematic self needs or desires. See Sandel's discussion of Charles Taylor's distinction between the "simple weigher" and the "strong evaluator" (ibid., 160); also Sandel, "The Procedural Republic and the Unencumbered Self," *Political Theory* 12 (February 1984): 81–95.

35. Ronald Dworkin, *A Matter of Principle* (Cambridge: Harvard University Press, 1985), 203.

uals to seek the good in their own way. In this view, the proper locus of moral choice is the autonomous person, not collective will or judgment.

The argument for neutrality is supported by a distinction between the right and the good. In this moral vocabulary, the good is a desired state of affairs, such as a particular way of life, set of virtues, or vision of happiness. There are many different such goods and many different conceptions of the good. The right, on the other hand, is a regulatory idea. Rightness refers to the moral principles, including principles of justice, that govern pursuit of the good. These ground rules do not prescribe specific goals, but they do rule some out, and they do say what means are legitimate. It is not right to lie or to break promises; it is right to be fair, to heed the voice of conscience, and to respect other people's needs and sensibilities. Whereas goods are plural and may be incommensurable, rightness is a sure and steady guide. The right is what all rational beings should agree to, just because they are rational; the good is inherently subject to diversity and contest.

This distinction has a long history and is useful for many purposes.[36] If, as we have said above, community is a framework within which plurality may flourish, then a contrast drawn between the right and the good seems apt and compelling. It justifies freedom for individuals and groups to choose their special identities and substantive goals while reaffirming the liberal commitment to *ordered* liberty. In this model of liberalism, community is not based on shared identity, shared purpose, or shared understanding of the common good; rather, it is constituted by the principles of right ordering that govern liberty and ennoble it as well.

The model is appealing, but it must ultimately fail as an account of liberal community. Contemporary welfare liberalism cannot adopt, as a *comprehensive* strategy, the separation of community from processes of goal-setting and self-definition. Ideals of caring and social justice— including care for children, health, families, the environment, aesthetic values, opportunity, and the well-being of future generations—are not merely regulatory or procedural. Insofar as they are achieved, they give shape to the community by setting goals, fixing priorities, and creating appropriate institutions.

The problem is that to determine the right requires some understanding of the good.[37] But for a liberal writer such as John Rawls, this is

---

36. For a survey see Abraham Edel, "Right and Good," in *Dictionary of the History of Ideas* (New York: Scribner's, 1973), 4:173–87.

37. "Thus, the right and the good are complementary, and the priority of right does not deny this" (John Rawls, "The Priority of Right and Ideas of the Good," *Philosophy and Public Affairs* 17 [Fall 1988]: 252).

explicitly a "thin" theory. The focus is on what Rawls calls "primary goods"—basic liberties, powers, and resources—which everyone may be said to need as conditions for pursuing an independently chosen way of life.[38] The appeal is to basic rationality; therefore "overlapping consensus" on what constitutes goods can be expected.

Thus understood, liberalism treats the political community as a framework within which autonomous choices can be made. The political quest for a distinctive *kind* of community is abandoned. We are not to seek, through politics and government, the kind of community that will best redeem the promise of fellowship or most closely approximate the potential for human growth, creativity, and responsibility. The liberal state can no more act to "advance human excellence . . . than it can act to advance Catholicism or Protestantism, or any other religion."[39]

In fact, despite this self-denying ordinance, the chief advocates of liberal neutrality have expressed strong and highly controversial views in favor of the responsibility of government for general welfare, including suggestions for programs to remedy social inequality, expand health care, and reconstruct public education. When viewed from the perspective of contemporary conservatives, the so-called thin theory of the good is undesirably thick. Much in the writings of John Rawls, Ronald Dworkin, Bruce Ackerman, and others argues for fundamental values—not only basic requirements of justice and citizenship but broader ideals of personal and social well-being.

For these liberals, the real sticking point is ideology or ideological thinking.[40] We are to avoid a choice among "comprehensive religious, philosophical or moral" doctrines, which include "conceptions of what is of value in human life, ideals of personal virtue and character, and the like," that "inform our nonpolitical conduct."[41] Here, as elsewhere, a sharp separation is made between the political and the nonpolitical. A "comprehensive" doctrine should be nonpolitical because it touches the self so closely and is a potential source of divisiveness. In this way Rawls reaffirms the historic posture of liberalism regarding struggles

38. As Rawls wrote not long ago: "[T]he basic list of primary goods (to which we may add if it prove necessary) has five headings: (i) basic rights and liberties, of which a list may also be given; (ii) freedom of movement and free choice of occupation against a background of diverse opportunities; (iii) powers and prerogatives of offices and positions of responsibility in the political and economic institutions of the basic structure; (iv) income and wealth; and finally, (v) the social bases of self-respect" (ibid., 257).

39. Ibid., 256.

40. See Chapter 14, "Ideology and Civility."

41. Rawls, "Priority of Right," 252.

over religious or philosophical doctrine, especially conflicts over religious orthodoxy. The most divisive issues should be removed from the political agenda.

This is not so easy to do. If the commitment to basic liberties and resources is more than half-hearted, it is likely to rest on a special conception of what personhood requires, not on one that every rational person would necessarily accept. How much and what kinds of freedom people require is not a narrowly technical or noncontroversial issue, to be disposed of with "and the like." Much more may be asked than can be accounted for by basic rationality. An appeal to "comprehensive" moral doctrine cannot be avoided; consensus cannot be taken for granted. The presuppositions of liberalism represent genuine moral choices, and their reaffirmation is a continuous act of moral choice, the more so as liberalism takes seriously the quest for social justice.

Consider, for example, the regulatory principle we call equality. Equality can be a very abstract and undemanding idea.[42] Equal justice may mean little more than the right to be treated as others are, however badly, within a category imposed by government and without the opportunity to question that classification. But the more attention we pay to *experienced* inequality, as it affects the whole person and many aspects of life, the more demanding the ideal becomes. The law looks more closely at the social reality of private bargains to prevent the strong from exploiting the weak; equal justice becomes more sensitive to practices that promote invidious discrimination. The transformed ideal is now an instrument of social policy, and as such strongly influences many aspects of government, business, and family life. Enhanced equality is then no longer simply a regulatory principle but a social goal. In this example, as in many others, a *value* becomes a *purpose* when making the value effective is our main concern. This goal requires something more than a generalized commitment to "basic liberties."

In the interests of consensus, liberals would like to draw a line between social utility and genuine moral choice. It would be convenient to say that spending money on public health and education does not presuppose any special conception of the good. These activities are assumed to be compatible with the neutral state. To sponsor them as aims of the political community and to enforce appropriate laws does not, it is thought, abridge personal autonomy or violate anyone's conscience.

Here, again, much depends on how far the values in play are elaborated. Public health and education *narrowly conceived* may indeed be

42. See Chapter 16, "Moral and Social Equality."

treated as utilities, and therefore as aspects of neutral, routine, municipal government. However, as we extend the meaning and enlarge the ambit of these programs, we find ourselves deeply implicated in specific moral choices. Education for basic skills may arguably be morally neutral, but not education for citizenship, for enlightenment, for social responsibility, for deferred gratification, for intellectual and aesthetic appreciation. Much the same distinction may be drawn in regard to defense policy, universal health care, and environmental protection. To face these and many other issues is an exercise in self-definition. The political community is led to ask: "What kind of a people do we believe we are?"

In some contexts, of course, the doctrine of liberal neutrality is highly important. Neutrality makes sense for a broad range of decisions, particularly in a community that celebrates private initiative and personal autonomy. A source of pride in American law is its special genius for releasing social energies by facilitating private agreements and associations. Here the neutral state is an appropriate model: only the rules of the game are enforced; people decide for themselves what arrangements to make and what goals to seek. In addition, many individual choices—vocational, marital, political, religious—are carefully insulated from officious intrusion and control. These choices have, for us, a special importance as aspects of freedom. Therefore liberal neutrality does express, with some fidelity, the premises of Western modernity.[43]

Nevertheless we must ask: Does the doctrine of neutrality, as an intellectual strategy, exaggerate the cultural trends of which it is a part? Does it thereby exacerbate the ills of modernity? Is this a case of overreaching, where a useful idea, detached from its proper contexts, is given an authority it should not have?

These questions are relevant because contemporary welfare liberalism—in many of its practices as well as in the writings of its most articulate spokesmen—clings to neutrality with respect to the good. This it does even as it strives for social justice and even as it defends the community's interests in enhancing the quality of life. This incoherence was tolerable so long as social utility—for example, guaranteeing a safe, convenient, and healthy city—raised no great questions of diversity in moral sensibility and choice, and so long as the basics of received morality and social discipline could be taken for granted. In the late twentieth century, however, the line between utility and morality has become ob-

43. In respect to some ideals and practices, such as impartiality in dispute-settlement and protection of basic human rights, the doctrine of neutrality may properly claim even more: it merits a respected place in the universal, cross-cultural theory of justice.

scured at many points. The quest for an environmental ethic, including preservation of species, has made this very clear, as have burgeoning issues in bioengineering and medical care. And no longer can we assume, as earlier generations did, that a stable cultural heritage, largely grounded in religion, is an inexhaustible resource, a permanent buffer, an ever-present mitigator of demands for liberation.

Our situation today calls for a more robust idea of community, one that gives greater weight to the claims of mutuality and fellowship. Liberalism's thin theory of community *weakens its capacity to speak with a clear voice* where the public interest demands discipline and duty as much as (and in a given context perhaps more than) freedom and self-realization.

The principle of neutrality is an obstacle to the reconciliation of liberal and communitarian perspectives. At bottom, the communitarian challenge is a demand for more extensive responsibility in every aspect of personal experience and social life. It calls for a doctrine that builds on the continuities of personal and social responsibility, personal and social integrity, individual and collective judgment. Such a doctrine is difficult to square with a restrictive view of what communal life entails and what judgments it may require.

An example of these difficulties can be found in Ronald Dworkin's effort to defend, on liberal grounds, government support for the arts. He accepts as an objective and collective judgment "that people are better off when the opportunities their culture provides are more complex and diverse, and that we should act as trustees for the future of the complexity of our own culture."[44] Therefore state support is justified:

> But art qualifies only on a certain premise: that state support is designed to protect structure rather than to promote any particular content for that structure at any particular time. So the ruling star of state subsidy should be this goal: it should look to the diversity and innovative quality of the culture as a whole rather than to (what public officials take to be) excellence in particular occasions of that culture.[45]

This argument is driven by a premise of official neutrality in aesthetic as well as moral choices. There may exist standards of excellence—even objective standards—but these are not to be defined or upheld by official authority. Diversity, innovation, and complexity are goods all may share and are therefore justifiable criteria, but no particular conception of good art should be adopted as an official standard. (I assume "complexity" is

44. Dworkin, *Matter of Principle*, 232.
45. Ibid., 233.

not a code-word for smuggled criteria of excellence.) Presumably even opportunities for criticism, debate, and reconstruction—governed by appropriate norms of representation and deliberation—are not enough to justify an authoritative collective judgment.

Is this what democracy requires? Is this any way to run a government? a university? an art museum? Some liberals think so, at least some of the time, and their belief is an important source of communitarian unease. A policy of official neutrality seems a perverse limitation on efforts to define the public interest or the common good.

Welfare liberals are understandably nervous about anything that smacks of gemeinschaft, which may threaten freedom of expression, privacy, and other aspects of personal autonomy. The dangers are real enough, but they do not necessarily entail a sweeping ordinance of self-denial. The principle of liberal neutrality imperils confidence in many public objectives whose implementation must limit personal choice. It is hard to justify sacrifice—a ban on gas-guzzling vehicles, a program of compulsory national service, a required course of study—when individual choice is held sacred.

The troubled ethos of welfare liberalism is a persistent, if largely implicit, concern in the chapters to follow. In discussions of civility, tradition, justice, and democracy an alternative vision of morality and community is suggested. That alternative is emphatically not a rejection of liberalism: it takes full account of that philosophy's great contribution to moral sensibility and institutional design.[46]

46. In other words, a communitarian liberal perspective builds on ideas and achievements already formed. Thus I agree that "the worthy challenge posed by the communitarian critics . . . is not to replace liberal justice, but to improve it" (Amy Gutmann, "Communitarian Critics of Liberalism," *Philosophy and Public Affairs* 14 [Summer 1985]: 322).

FOURTEEN

Civility and Piety

Two sources of moral integration compete for preeminence as foundations of community: civility and piety. Civility governs diversity, protects autonomy, and upholds toleration; piety expresses devotion and demands integration.[1] The norms of civility are impersonal, rational, and inclusive, whereas piety is personal, passionate, and particularist. The conflict between these very different aspirations generates troublesome issues of morality and community. Their reconciliation is a prime object of theory and policy. In this chapter some strategies of reconciliation are explored, with special attention to problems of critical morality, tradition, religion, and ideology.

Modern thought is not comfortable with the idea of piety. The democratic and secular person is likely to associate it with sanctimonious devotion to ritual and uncritical subordination to religious authority. But piety has a broader and more attractive connotation, perhaps best expressed by George Santayana: "Piety, in its nobler and Roman sense, may be said to mean man's reverent attachment to the sources of his being and the steadying of his life by that attachment."[2] This "nobler" idea treats piety as an aspect of human nature, a reflection of the need for coherence and attachment. The distinctive virtues of piety are humility and loyalty.

---

1. Compare this contrast with Durkheim's distinction between organic and mechanical solidarity. Organic solidarity generates rules of civility, whereas mechanical solidarity is based on a shared history and identity. See Chapter 5, "Marx and Durkheim."
2. *The Life of Reason* (1933; reprint, New York: Scribner's, 1954), 258.

John Dewey had a similar conception. He found "natural piety" in "human nature as a cooperating part of a larger whole."[3] Natural piety is an attitude of reverence and respect for human interdependence and for the continuities between humanity and nature. The root experience is a sense of connectedness or common mooring. Like Santayana, therefore, Dewey could think of piety as a pervasive human experience *and* as an enduring value.

Piety thus understood is not tied to any particular practice or belief. It does presume, however, something like a religious attitude. Such an attitude, as Dewey understood it, strives for "a working union of the ideal and the actual" at the same time that it takes into account human finitude and dependency.[4] To recognize an "enveloping world" beyond ourselves is to know that our achievements, however great, are not ours alone. "The essentially unreligious attitude," wrote Dewey, "attributes human achievement and purpose to man in isolation from the world of physical nature and his fellows."[5] In truth, "our successes are dependent on the cooperation of nature."[6]

Thus piety is an attribute of the implicated self. Among its connotations are those of "faithfulness to the duties owed to parents and relatives, superiors, etc. . . . affectionate loyalty and respect, esp. to parents."[7] These attachments have a claim to fidelity because they play a vital part in the formation of our selves. They are "sources of our being." In that sense, piety is ultimately an affirmation of self; a sign of psychological coherence; a foundation of self-respect.

In the life of piety, ideas are less important than feelings. But the feelings are not irrational:

> Piety is the spirit's acknowledgment of its incarnation. So, in filial and parental affection, which is piety in an elementary form, there is a moulding of will and emotion, a check to irresponsible initiative, in harmony with the facts of animal reproduction. . . . Piety is in a sense pathetic because it in-

3. *A Common Faith* (New Haven: Yale University Press, 1934), 25.
4. Ibid., 52.
5. Ibid., 25.
6. Dewey distanced himself from "militant atheism" as well as from "traditional supernaturalism." The two, he said, have something in common—an exclusive preoccupation with "man in isolation." Traditional religion "regards the drama of sin and redemption enacted within the isolated and lonely soul of man as the one thing of ultimate importance. Apart from man, nature is either accursed or negligible. Militant atheism is also affected by lack of natural piety. . . . The attitude taken is often that of man living in an indifferent and hostile world and issuing blasts of defiance" (ibid., 53). Compare Bertrand Russell's vision of man and nature, discussed in Chapter 1, "Naturalism in Ethics."
7. *Oxford English Dictionary*, s.v. "piety." A classic treatment of piety in these terms is Plato's *Euthyphro*.

volves subordination to physical accident and acceptance of finitude. But it is also noble and eminently fruitful because . . . it meets fate with simple sincerity and labours in accordance with the conditions imposed. It exercises the eminently sane function of calling thought home. . . . For reason and happiness are like other flowers—they wither when plucked.[8]

In other (less poetic) words, piety exhibits a healthy strain toward particularity and rootedness.

And yet the objects of piety are not *wholly* concrete. Relationships are idealized; memories are filtered; history is touched up. Images of family, institution, locality, and nation resist abstraction; they are densely symbolic; but they typically contain at least a rudimentary basis for criticism and judgment. If the ideal aspect is suppressed—if there is no critical standpoint—piety becomes morally suspect.

Love of country is a classic form of piety. It is a virtue, and a highly effective one at that, capable of creating a potent union of self and place, self and history. Patriotism extends the reach of fellowship, enlarges the meaning of self-interest, and reinforces morality by securing it to a particular heritage.[9] Like every other form of piety, however, it claims a core of unconditional devotion: "my child, my parent, right or wrong; my country right or wrong." The unconditional element in patriotism is necessary to its power; it is also a main source of moral failing. Therefore we are driven to invoke a higher patriotism, one that retains devotion but legitimates criticism.

Patriots must and do embrace, in some sense unconditionally, basic aspects of their community. But what aspects?

> The answer is: the nation conceived *as a project,* a project somehow or other brought to birth in the past and carried on so that a morally distinctive community was brought into being which embodied a claim to political autonomy. . . . What the patriot is committed to is a particular way of linking a past which has conferred a distinctive moral and political identity upon him or her with a future for the project which it is his or her . . . responsibility to bring into being. Only this allegiance is unconditional and allegiance to particular governments or forms of government or particular leaders will be entirely conditional upon their being devoted to furthering that project rather than frustrating or destroying it.[10]

8. Santayana, *Life of Reason,* 260f.
9. "What the morality of patriotism *at its best* provides is a clear account of and justification for the particular bonds and loyalties which form so much of the substance of the moral life" (Alasdair MacIntyre, *Is Patriotism a Virtue?* [The Lindley Lecture, The University of Kansas, 1984], 16, my emphasis).
10. Ibid., 13f.

Thus understood, patriotism is saved from idolatry, that is, from treating a limited, contingent reality as if it had an absolute claim to reverence and respect. In pledging allegiance to the nation "as a project" we identify ourselves with an idealized past, accept responsibility for failures as well as successes, and promise to care for the community's well-being. The commitment runs to *this* nation, not some other; therefore it remains particularized. As the meaning of patriotism is enlarged, however, critical distance is gained; a narrow parochialism is transcended.

Not only patriotism but every object of piety—friendship, kinship, parental love, institutional participation, religious faith—contemplates a relatively unconditional bond.[11] In this respect each differs from more routine, more interchangeable, more transitory experiences and relationships. As an expression of devotion to particular persons, institutions, communities, and beliefs, piety is a foundation for *sacrifice*. Furthermore, piety avoids gestures of alienation, rejection, or separation. This strategy of acceptance or inclusion—and a corresponding willingness to subordinate one's own proximate interests to another's, or to a higher good—is the benign face of piety.

But the same "unconditional" commitment—the same devotion to particularity—can be divisive, unjust, and destructive. Piety has corrupt forms that resist criticism, condemn apostasy, and create outcasts; that are self-righteous, intolerant, and unforgiving. This darker aspect of piety undercuts its moral worth. Therefore we need a complementary principle of order—the principle of civility.

▼   ▲   ▼   ▲   ▼

Like "piety," "civility" has an old-fashioned ring, and it too has suffered a radical constriction of meaning. Today "civility" means little more than politeness or courtesy.[12] In a broader and more ancient sense, however, civility is "behaviour befitting a citizen."[13] It is "the virtue of the citizen, of the man who shares responsibly in his own self-government, either as governor or as one of the governed."[14] To be civil is to be

---

11. Not every unconditional bond is equally compelling; each calls for a different quality of commitment, a different depth of attachment. Furthermore, on close inspection we can usually find one or more tacit reservations. Among these is the idea that the "unconditional" bond will be attenuated or dissolved if its moral basis is destroyed.

12. *American Heritage Dictionary*, s.v. "civility," offers only that meaning.

13. *Oxford English Dictionary*, s.v. "civility."

14. Edward Shils, *The Intellectuals and the Powers and Other Essays* (Chicago: University of Chicago Press, 1972), 60.

guided by the distinctive virtues of public life. These include, especially, moderation in pursuit of one's own interests, and concern for the common good. More particularly, civility signals the community's commitment to dialogue as the preferred means of social decision.

Thus civility presumes diversity, autonomy, and potential conflict. Whatever the context of public life—etiquette, justice, controversy—norms of civility are predicated on a regard for the integrity and independence of individuals and groups. Reconciliation is a keynote, and much attention is given to narrowing differences and encouraging communication. There is no question, however, of extinguishing interests or denying rights. In civility respect, not love, is the salient value.

Civility is not a morality of engagement, nor is it a call to passion or sacrifice. It is cool, not hot; detached, not involved. This is another way of saying that civility is a universalist ethic and as such must distance itself from the claims of particularism. As we noted in Chapter 7, a universalist ethic progressively extends the reach of a moral community by enlarging the circle of belonging and fellowship.

This critical social function of civility is distorted and frustrated by the characteristic forms of piety, which build on primordial ties of origin and kinship. Nevertheless, civility and piety are by no means wholly antagonistic. Respect is not love, but it strains toward love as it gains substance and subtlety. Rudimentary respect is formal, external, and rule-centered—founded in fear of disruption and lack of cooperation. The corresponding civility can be chilly indeed, as some connotations of "being civil" suggest. An important change occurs when respect is informed by genuine appreciation for the values at stake in communication and good order. Freedom, dialogue, and diversity are then prized for their intrinsic worth, not merely suffered as burdens to be dealt with by the forms of civility. As sensitivity to values increases, the line between civility and piety blurs.

In truly civil communication, for example, something more is required than self-restraint and taking turns. An effort must be made really to listen, that is, to understand and appreciate what someone else is saying.[15] As we do so we move from arm's-length "inter-action" to

15. Glenn Tinder sees an element of civility in what he calls "comprehensive communality": "This is perhaps a barbarous phrase, but it accurately denotes a certain way of relating oneself to mankind. To be comprehensively communal is, first of all, to be unreservedly attentive, not only to be attuned to man's voice wherever it can be heard, but to search out unvoiced experiences. Thus civility is manifest in Dr. Gachet's support for Cezanne and Van Gogh when they were unrecognized and maligned, in Dostoevsky's ability to enter into the minds of criminals, . . . in Abraham Lincoln's awareness that his

more engaged "interaction." We discover and create shared meanings; the content or substance of the discussion becomes more important than its form. The outcome is often a *particular* community of discourse and a *unique* social bond. A foundation is laid for affection and commitment. In this way piety fleshes out the bare bones of civility.

Furthermore, civil speech takes into account human frailties and sensibilities. Contempt is the enemy of communication; patience and empathy are its allies. Hence we reject as uncivil personal abuse, intellectual intimidation, and indifference to offense. On especially sensitive issues—religion, nationality, race, for example—civil communication treads lightly, with special regard for the sources of personal identity. When it is thus open to the claims of piety, civility shows a human face.

CRITICAL AND CONVENTIONAL MORALITY

A conspicuous feature of civility is the development of "critical" or "reflective" morality, based on reason and principle rather than passion and historicity. Piety, by contrast, is the realm of "conventional," "customary," or "positive" morality. The quality of community depends to a large extent on a proper mix of these ingredients.

By the conventional morality of a community is meant its historically given notions of right and wrong. Most of these beliefs are accepted unconsciously, as part of a world taken for granted, transmitted by socialization and reinforced by habit. Many are relatively superficial and easily changed. Others have deep psychological roots, and the prospect of change evokes strong emotional responses. These latter belong to what Freud called "superego morality." In either case, weak or strong, the beliefs and their associated practices may be justified and refined by reflection, but they are not founded on reflection.[16]

Such a morality has characteristic failings. It is often *incoherent,* in that it sends contradictory messages as to what is morally right; *naive,* in concealing the uncertain and problematic nature of moral judgment; *unrealistic,* in not adapting to new circumstances, including changes in

---

enemies in the South were human beings like the people in the North, fallible but in most cases doing what they thought was right. Such attentiveness expresses a concern for all human experience, an unwillingness that anything should remain unheard and unknown" (*Community: Reflections on a Tragic Ideal* [Baton Rouge: Louisiana State University Press, 1980], 187f.). This may go too far—not every experience is worthy of unreserved attention—but Tinder's conception of civility is close to that suggested in the text.

16. Hence Santayana called it "pre-rational" morality; see his *Life of Reason,* 442f.

attitudes or practice; and excessively *parochial,* in too closely identifying morality with the interests of a particular group or community. These and other limitations of conventional morality create genuine problems of choice and interpretation, problems that must be faced, in one way or another, by any society. Hence moral reflection is a natural and recurrent response to the inherent complexity of social life.

We should not identify customary morality with everything that is "received" or even "traditional." A received culture—the culture handed down—can include beliefs and institutions that spring from and are sustained by reflection and criticism. When Americans speak of "our traditions," many have in mind the special forms of American democracy, such as freedom of speech, federalism, or four-year terms for presidents. Understood in this broad sense, "tradition" can and does include much that is based on rational design and abstract principle.

We lose purchase on reality, however, and evade important issues, if we do not acknowledge the special connection between tradition and customary morality. Not every practice is a tradition. A practice becomes a tradition *when it takes on symbolic meaning* as part of the unique ethos of a group, an institution, or a community. In the making of tradition the most important element is shared historical experience. This particularity is expressed in narrative and legend, in sacred texts, in the creation of heroes, in ritual, monuments, holidays, architecture, hymns, and flags. The most compelling traditions are suffused with and supported by expressive symbolism. The more effective the symbolism, the more unconditional the loyalty it calls forth. Piety, not civility, is the guiding ideal, and that is precisely what makes tradition problematic from the standpoint of critical morality.

There is a sense in which every morality is critical, if only because each upholds standards of right conduct. The differences lie in the sources of those standards and in the attitudes taken toward those sources. Customary morality does not look beyond historicity and convenience. Critical morality postulates that any received code of conduct is subject to criticism and reconstruction in the light of reflection and inquiry.

Nevertheless, critical morality cannot be a rootless figment of the moral imagination. It is not made up out of whole cloth, nor is it the product of concocted schemes or premises. Properly understood, critical morality is (1) informed by historical and comparative study of moral experience; (2) anchored in the ethos of a particular culture; (3) responsive to the demand for justification; (4) enriched by dialogue; and (5) refined by a reasoned elaboration of concepts and principles. This is to say that critical morality is governed by all the dimensions of reason discussed in Chapter 2: experience, principle, prudence, dialogue, and order.

Thus understood, critical morality is continuous with customary morality. It requires assessment, evaluation, and an unending quest for principled justification, but there is no unbridgeable gap, no wall of separation. There is not even a prima facie case that any given product of reflection is necessarily superior to the adaptive outcomes of social life; if anything, the presumption goes the other way. Neither, however, is self-certifying. Custom must stand the test of reflection; reflection must yield to the verdict of experience.

The Moral Worth of Tradition

Critical morality must give due weight to the claims of tradition. This is so in part because the *pre*-judgments that form our minds are necessary starting points—and touchstones—for moral reflection.[17] We begin with, and come back to, the "intuitions" or "settled convictions" in which we have confidence.[18] This should not be understood as an individual experience. Rather, we take guidance from what a *representative* figure—the morally aware person—confidently believes is right or wrong. These historically determined premises are more than handy beginnings or rhetorical devices. They are indispensable for reflection because, in varying degrees, they are vehicles of congealed meaning and tacit understanding. Durkheim once said that "a society without prejudices would resemble an organism without reflexes."[19] He was not disparaging self-awareness but only reminding us that much social knowledge is tacit and subliminal.

My favorite example of the tacit knowledge in custom is Winston Churchill's explanation of why the chamber of the House of Commons is relatively small:

> [The chamber] should *not* be big enough to contain all its Members at once without overcrowding, and there should be no question of every Member having a separate seat reserved for him. The reason for this has long been a puzzle to uninstructed outsiders, and has frequently excited the curiosity and

17. In modern thought this has been most strongly emphasized by post-Kantian hermeneutic philosophers. For an influential contemporary treatment, see Hans-Georg Gadamer, *Truth and Method* (New York: Crossroads Press, 1975), 239ff.

18. See John Rawls on "reflective equilibrium": *A Theory of Justice* (Cambridge: Harvard University Press, 1971), 20f., 48ff.

19. Emile Durkheim (1886), quoted in Robert N. Bellah, ed., *Emile Durkheim on Morality and Society* (Chicago: University of Chicago Press, 1973), xxii.

even the criticism of new Members. Yet it is not so difficult to understand if you look at it from a practical point of view. If the House is big enough to contain all its Members, nine-tenths of its debates will be conducted in the depressing atmosphere of an almost empty or half-empty chamber. The essence of good House of Commons speaking is the conversational style, the facility for quick, informal interruptions and interchanges. Harangues from a rostrum would be a bad substitute. . . . But the conversational style requires a fairly small space, and there should be on great occasions a sense of crowd and urgency.[20]

"Logic," notes Churchill, "is a poor guide compared with custom."[21] His point is to show that custom has its reasons that logic may not know. The tacit knowledge of custom is often wiser than a scheme based on explicit theorizing, which may inadequately comprehend the subtle and multiple values at stake. Reflection, like tradition, has costs and weaknesses; it too is not self-justifying, nor does it necessarily improve the moral code it is criticizing. Reflection may be selective in its premises, mistaken in its logic, unsubtle in its characterization of a custom or idea. This is the truth behind Edmund Burke's rejection of speculative reason.

The fact that prejudgment can also be prejudicial in the modern sense of biased or bigoted, or be a reflex of ignorance, or shortsighted, underlines the need for criticism and reconstruction. But it does not cancel the claim of conventional morality to respectful and sympathetic examination. Critical morality, in other words, cannot be free-floating and self-contained. The attempt to judge without preconceptions, in a spirit of wholesale rejection, leads to sterility and irrelevance or to the arbitrary imposition of unworkable ideas.

It is an elementary lesson of social science that the human animal, if it is to grow and flourish, needs a framework of social support that must include moral guidance, symbolic expression, and a secure way of life. Hence we may say that, in principle, culture is a good thing. Within broad limits it does not matter what form a culture takes or what content it has. Any culture that is reasonably effective in forming personalities and transmitting a heritage is bound to contain elements out of which a more or less well-tempered moral order can be fashioned. This person-forming, life-enhancing work of culture is its main justification from the perspective of critical morality.

Because culture *is* a good thing, and because it is manifested in particularities of belief and practice, we reject ethnocentrism; we accept a

20. Winston Churchill, *Closing the Ring* (Boston: Houghton-Mifflin, 1951), 169.
21. Ibid.

prima facie obligation of cross-cultural respect and toleration. If such toleration is to be meaningful, however, it must extend to mores as well as to folkways. It is not enough to be tolerant of superficial variation, such as different ways of saying the same thing or exotic ways of eating dinner. We must also be tolerant of cultural premises (such as strong gender differences) and institutions (such as polygamy or theocracy) that we may consider wrong or offensive. We postulate the rough moral equivalence of many different ways of life, and this restrains a too easy application to other cultures of a critical morality we have developed for our own use and mainly out of our own experience.[22]

We should be careful to distinguish a generally positive attitude toward culture and tradition from the evaluation of specific institutions or practices. From the standpoint of critical morality no tradition is self-validating. Furthermore, *once we understand the role of tradition* in creating harmonious selves and societies, we can make that understanding a basis for assessment and revision of specific traditions. Although tradition in general has a presumption of moral worth, any given tradition may be impoverishing, destructive, divisive, even demonic. The same logic applies to family, friendship, and similar "good things." On the whole, abstractly considered, these are contexts within which virtue can flourish—but only if their positive potential is fulfilled and they are not, instead, crucibles of oppressive constraint, physical abuse, or emotional exploitation.[23]

As a philosophy of the present, American pragmatism is properly associated with criticism of tradition and openness to new experience. It should not be forgotten, however, that William James, John Dewey, and George Herbert Mead thought of truth-finding as a social process. "Far from asserting that the individual could make knowledge in his or her

---

22. This self-denying ordinance is to be set aside when it can be shown that the offensive practice (chattel slavery, racism, torture, genocide) is unacceptable from the standpoint of a universal morality as well as our own. Between innocent, morally neutral conventions or folkways and demonstrable violations of human rights lies a wide range of practices and beliefs that are morally problematic but understandable and tolerable in the light of the moral trade-offs every community must make. Appreciation of these trade-offs chastens the view that if we take our own norms seriously we *must* condemn the different norms of others. That may be true for some practices, such as genocide, but not for variations in, say, the extent to which egalitarian principles are accepted or sexual modesty is demanded. For another perspective, see Jeremy Waldron, "Particular Values and Critical Morality," *California Law Review* 77 (May 1989): 561–89. On cultural plurality and the limits of relativism see above, Chapter 4.

23. For a similar perspective, resting on a distinction between "intrinsic" and "functional" tradition, see William A. Galston, *Liberal Purposes: Goods, Virtues, and Diversity in the Liberal State* (Cambridge: Cambridge University Press, 1991), 280f.

own image, [James] was at pains to emphasize the power of socially possessed, traditional beliefs; he was, moreover, adamant about the obligation to integrate one's new experiences with the harvest of history."[24] In a characteristic phrase, James spoke of the "funded truths" gleaned from history, with which we are—and must be—in earnest dialogue.[25]

Moral reasoning and comparative study are indispensable, but what we learn is most pertinent and most compelling when it is applied reflexively, that is, to the understanding of our own moral identity. This self-engaged inquiry draws on intimate acquaintance with the nuances of conduct, the spirit as well as the letter of rules, the contexts of policy. Moralists speak in the accents of authenticity when, like Antigone, Jesus, and Martin Luther King, Jr., they find resources for criticism within a framework that is received, understood, and revered.

This argument echoes Hegel's critique of Kantian ethics.[26] Hegel rejected the idea that morality is a matter of rational choice made in the light of abstract or formal presuppositions such as the categorical imperative. Rather, moral redemption occurs in and through a historically given moral order. The content and texture of morality, not the form, are all-important, and these are determined by an ongoing collective life. In this view, moral principles are derivative, not constitutive; secondary, not primary.[27]

The Hegelian model does not deny—on the contrary, it proclaims—the need for critical morality to cure the limitations of conventional morality. The question is one of starting points. Hegel begins with the full concreteness of social practice and belief (Sittlichkeit) and from there moves to more general principles that purport to express the spiritual commitments or ethos of a people. These principles are often fiercely

---

24. David A. Hollinger, "William James and the Culture of Inquiry," *Michigan Quarterly Review* 20 (Summer 1981): 270.

25. William James, *Pragmatism: A New Name for Some Old Ways of Thinking* (1907; reprint, New York: Longmans, Green, 1948), 224, 233.

26. See Robert C. Solomon, *In the Spirit of Hegel* (New York: Oxford University Press, 1983), chap. 9; Charles Taylor, *Hegel and Modern Society* (Cambridge: Cambridge University Press, 1979), 72ff.

27. To say that principles are derivative does not mean they are unimportant as instruments of criticism and justification. However, allegedly constitutive principles may be wrong and even wrong-headed. What is primary, not derivative, is *the relevant moral experience,* such as a certain kind of family life or constitutional development. These experiences are to be accounted for, criticized, or justified. Any given set of principles may be inadequate, perhaps egregiously so. Hence we cannot accept as definitive a theorist's conclusion as to the constitutive principles of an institution or a doctrine. Such descriptions are always subject to error and debate. For a closely related argument, dealing with Ronald Dworkin's interpretation of liberalism, see Kenneth I. Winston, "Principles and Touchstones: The Dilemma of Dworkin's Liberalism," *Polity* 19 (1986): 42–55.

debated. Nevertheless, they are routinely appealed to as authoritative standpoints from which to criticize a given policy, practice, or belief. The elements of an ethos are not deductions from theoretical axioms. They are efforts to capture whatever internal coherence and latent message there may be in a moral order.

Hegel did not suppose that one ethos is as good as the next and that therefore only internal criticism is legitimate. He believed we could draw from the theory of community universal criteria of moral well-being, and he took the Athenian polis as a paradigm of moral achievement. But a morality is not worth much if it is not integral to a taken-for-granted world of cooperation and fellowship. Therefore critical morality must hold in tension the universal and the particular. It may reach for an ideal— Hebraic justice, Buddhist self-transcendence, Christian love, Greek civic participation—but the ideal must be grounded in and relevant to the historical experience of the community.

It could be argued that Hegel was addressing the *conditions* of morality rather than its *logic,* whereas Kant's main concern was the latter. But Hegel's critique goes to the heart of the Kantian view that distinctively moral conduct proceeds from a free and rational individual decision to embrace moral duty without regard to personal inclination or social consequence. For Hegel, morality springs, rather, from the continuities of individual and social life. To follow one's inclinations and assess social consequences, far from being alien to morality, is the best and most authentic way of being moral. This assumes, of course, that personal desires are at one with social norms and with the spirit underlying the norms, and that the consequences we care about have to do with *Bildung,* that is, the formation of character and culture.

A communitarian theory of morality has very practical significance for how we understand not only the *source* but also the *reach* of individual responsibility. Kantian doctrine is characteristically modern in tying moral responsibility to choice and intent. It is "free will" that defines to whom and for what we are responsible. In the more organic communitarian view, autonomous choice is only one criterion, and not always the most important. We are responsible for our *selves,* but the self as a biological and social formation is decisively affected by circumstances not chosen. Among these are memberships in family and community. A received identity has much to offer: inner coherence, security, self-esteem. Although people often detach themselves from their roots and try to send down new ones, the difficulties are great and the costs are high.

If unchosen belonging is a great advantage and is a critical part of self-hood, then the boundaries between individual and collective responsibility are indistinct. They cannot be neatly limited by the criteria of free choice and explicit intent. People who are nourished by a community and "accept" what they never dreamed of choosing cannot deny responsibility for their community's traditions and deeds. Contemporary Americans take pride in their political institutions and achievements; contemporary Germans are proud of their musical, literary, and scientific heritage. By the same token, however, Americans must take responsibility for the devastation of slavery, which extends to this generation and beyond; and Germans must take responsibility for the Nazi regime and the Holocaust. This does not settle what collective responsibility entails; there is an important difference between guilt and responsibility. But the principle cannot be dismissed as primitive or irrational or as simply a dangerous thought.

The great question is: Can critical morality be achieved in and through parochial achievements? Can people find their way to objective judgment while retaining and even deepening their special religious, national, or cultural identity? This has been a perennial challenge to moral sophistication. The appeal of a universal ethic—of civility—is forever countered by the persistent attraction of particular traditions and beliefs.

There is much to be gained, in strength and subtlety, from intimate acquaintance with a distinctive morality. The communicant experiences a tradition from within; draws self-confidence from a familiar idiom; learns from narrative and example; brings general principles to bear without rudely imposing an external ethic. The outcome is necessarily selective, as culture is selective. But if a people's uniqueness has something worthwhile to offer, its contribution will be most complete and most enduring if its agents are faithful to their origins. In an international assembly of scholars or judges or in an ecumenical gathering of religious leaders, we do not ask the participants to shed their distinctive identities. On the contrary, we hope to gain from their diversity.

From the standpoint of critical morality, however, parochial experience may not be taken as final or treated as an unqualified end in itself. A corollary commitment must be made to press the particular into the service of the general, that is, to draw from a special history a universal message. To do so is, inevitably, to create a basis for criticizing one's own heritage, not only from within but also in the light of other experiences and more comprehensive interests.

Two steps are necessary. The first, turning inward, examines the received culture to identify its moral premises. These serve as principles of criticism by means of which specific rules or practices can be assessed, revised, or rejected. Such principles, however, do not take us beyond culture-bound (though generalized) beliefs: for example, belief in the sanctity of heterosexual marriage or in the separation of church and state. The second step reaches for more universal judgments. We look to history and human nature for warranted conclusions about the conditions that make for personal and collective well-being.

The Enforcement of Morals

The interplay of critical and conventional morality is well displayed in common-law and constitutional adjudication. The judicial process—especially but not exclusively in appellate courts of the United States—may serve as a paradigm of the themes set out above. For the courts have a dual burden. They are responsible for a moral and legal heritage; they are also responsible for applying rules and doctrines to specific facts, which may mean doing justice in new or unforeseen circumstances. As they do so, they must articulate and reconstruct received law and custom; and they must bring to bear, inevitably if cautiously, a general understanding of social life, morality, and human nature. This theme is explored more fully in the next chapter. Here we consider some special legal issues, bearing on obscenity and homosexual conduct, that have helped to make clear what it means to both invoke and criticize a customary morality.

Issues of "law and morals" sharply reveal both the tension and the continuity between customary and critical morality. In question is the propriety of enforcing conventional views regarding deviant sexual conduct, sexually explicit communication, gambling, blasphemy, birth control, abortion, vagrancy, and drug abuse. Laws prohibiting or controlling these and similar activities are usually justified by reference to a serious harm, but the alleged harm often turns out to be difficult to identify, highly controversial, or only distantly related to the offending act. Because the victim is often either the very person who commits the offense or someone quite willing to cooperate in it, such as a prostitute, these crimes are sometimes called "victimless crimes."

Those who oppose the use of law to coerce virtue draw on a principle made famous by John Stuart Mill: "The only purpose for which power can be rightfully exercised over any member of a civilized community, against his will, is to prevent harm to others. His own good, either physical or moral, is not sufficient warrant. He cannot rightfully be compelled to do or forbear because, in the opinion of others, to do so would be wise, or even right."[28]

Mill's position is countered by the view that the cohesion and integrity of a social order depend on the continued assertion of a common morality.[29] The harm done by an offending pattern of conduct may be subtle and long-term; yet it may be of great significance to those who believe that their community's character and identity are at stake. And there may also be more immediate harm, in the form of environments perceived as degraded or of children exposed to destructive influences.

In the United States these matters raise constitutional issues of personal autonomy, abuse of power, and freedom of speech. A good example is the treatment of pornography. The courts have been torn between their commitment to freedom and their respect for what are taken to be widely shared and deeply held convictions about the limits of freedom.

During the first hundred and fifty years of the Republic, it was taken for granted that states and local communities could restrain "indecencies" of many kinds. The courts upheld broad legislative powers and wide official discretion. It seemed hardly necessary to define offenses that were distasteful to discuss and presumed to be self-evident to all right-thinking persons. In the late nineteenth century, however, American courts adopted the conception of obscenity formulated in an English case, *Regina v. Hicklin* (1868). The *Hicklin* test, as it came to be known, was whether "the matter charged" had a tendency "to deprave and corrupt those whose minds are open to such immoral influences, and into whose hands a publication of this sort may fall."[30] This broad standard said nothing about other merits "the matter" might have; made the susceptibilities of the most vulnerable elements of the population the criterion of what is harmful; and was read as allowing a publication to be banned on the basis of passages taken out of context rather than in consideration of the work as a whole. These criteria permitted local officials—and, through its postal laws, the federal government—to suppress distribution of literary works by James Joyce, D. H. Lawrence, Henry Miller, and William Faulkner, among many others.

28. *On Liberty* (1859), in *Utilitarianism, On Liberty, Considerations on Representative Government* (reprint, London: J. M. Dent, 1984), 78.

29. See, e.g., James Fitzjames Stephen, *Liberty, Equality, Fraternity* (New York: Holt, 1882), chap. 4; Patrick Devlin, *The Enforcement of Morals* (London: Oxford University Press, 1965).

30. Regina V. Hicklin, L.R. 3Q.B. 360, 368 (1868).

The later history of obscenity law, as made by the Supreme Court, has been an effort to revise and limit this sweeping grant of discretion *while retaining the core of conventional morality and upholding the propriety of legal enforcement.* Although the Court has greatly liberalized the restrictions on what may be said and depicted, it has not repudiated the idea that pornography is an evil that the police power of local communities may suppress. This compromise has earned the Court the contempt of libertarians and the anger of conservative moralists. For our purposes, however, it may be seen as an effort to reconcile conventional and critical morality.

In a series of troublesome cases that began in 1957, the Supreme Court attempted, in the interests of competing values, to narrow the definition of what is legally obscene. The Court sought to protect works of "redeeming social importance" or, in a later, more restrictive formulation, works of "serious literary, artistic, political, or scientific value" and to fulfill the society's obligation to be open to diverse perspectives and new lifestyles. Pornographic appeal to "prurient interest"—lewd thoughts and longings—is obscene and not protected by the First Amendment. But even if a work is not meritorious it cannot be banned merely because it has a prurient element or aspect. The work must be "patently offensive" to the "average person" according to "contemporary community standards," which may change and vary from one community to another; and the legislation must be specific in stating what acts or depictions are prohibited.[31]

These restrictions show the rudiments of critical morality and, at the same time, a deference to conventional morality. That deference is not easy to justify on the part of an institution committed to rational argument. Some say it "undermines the whole idea of rationality in legislation, substituting a notion of tradition that is a mask for ignorance and intolerance."[32] But responsible criticism should not too quickly disparage the moral worth of tradition or dismiss the implicit truths it may contain. The judicial opinions have indeed been short on moral argument; they have not gone very far to clarify just why obscenity should be restrained. It does not follow, however, that the evil of obscenity is unreal or unimportant. The want of a good theory cautions legal restraint, but it is not a reason to abandon responsibility.

31. Roth v. U.S., 354 U.S. 476 (1957); Stanley v. Georgia, 394 U.S. 557 (1969); Miller v. California, 413 U.S. 15 (1973); Paris Adult Theatre I v. Slaton, 413 U.S. 49 (1973).
32. David A. J. Richards, "Free Speech and Obscenity Law: Toward a Moral Theory of the First Amendment," *University of Pennsylvania Law Review* 123 (November 1974): 90.

It is not difficult to construct a plausible argument defending the tradition that exploitation of prurient interest should be discouraged by law. Most important, perhaps, is the idea that public life is degraded by uninhibited displays of raw impulse and emotion, especially when the effect is to celebrate or make commonplace various forms of brutality, indifference to suffering, or extremes of self-debasement. The restraint of public executions, cockfighting, and other events that have the effect of stimulating such feelings reflects this concern. A special anxiety is the competence of parents to be effective in socializing their children if they cannot count on the community to uphold their efforts to encourage self-discipline and defer gratification. Still another anxiety is the fear that values of love and intimacy will suffer as the tie between sex and personal commitment is weakened. Most specific, and for many most compelling, at least in the United States, is the argument that pornography degrades women.[33]

These ideas are worthy of respect because they resonate with much uncodified experience. Their logic has not been fully worked out, nor are they necessarily based on solid empirical evidence as to causes and effects. At bottom the obscenity decisions do not depend on scientific findings. Rather, the majority of the justices have deferred to conventional morality, insofar as it is expressed in local legislation, because they are persuaded it can have a rational, if unarticulated, basis and because they believe that, as a product of funded experience, it should be given the benefit of the doubt.[34] This shifts the burden of proof to those who deny the claims of conventional morality. It means the tradition cannot be overturned by a showing of *any* benefit of pornography, for example, as therapy. There must be convincing argument that more fundamental values, such as legitimate freedoms of expression or the integrity of the arts, are in jeopardy.

33. The feminist movement has highlighted this aspect of pornography. In response, Cass Sunstein has offered the following definition: "Regulable pornography must (a) be sexually explicit, (b) depict women as enjoying or deserving some form of physical abuse, and (c) have the purpose and effect of producing sexual arousal" ("Pornography and the First Amendment," *Duke Law Journal* 1986 [September 1986]: 592). Here a distinction is drawn between obscenity, which is a more general idea, referring to whatever is thought to be indecent, and pornography as "materials that treat women as prostitutes and that focus on the role of women in providing sexual pleasure to men" (ibid., 595). Although the impulse to draw such a distinction is understandable, and the etymology supports it, this seems an unwise restriction—even for legal purposes—of an idea that has come to mean "written, graphic, or other forms of communication intended to excite lascivious feelings" (*American Heritage Dictionary*, s.v. "pornography"). Pornography may also have other victims, including children of both sexes.

34. It may also be that "people are due respect and deference from the institutions that serve them even when their views are ill-founded or confused" (Kenneth I. Winston, personal communication, 2 June 1985).

▼   ▲   ▼   ▲   ▼

In the obscenity cases the claims of conventional morality are offset by a clear constitutional commitment to freedom of speech. That commitment is a resource for testing and restraining majority will (including attitudes long held, deeply felt, and widely shared) in the light of accepted principle. Here the courts help to fashion a critical morality by reaffirming a tradition—the First Amendment and its history—that is legally enshrined but socially vulnerable.

The judicial task is more difficult when constitutional protection of personal autonomy is sought on grounds less firmly supported by the explicit text of the Constitution. For example, the rights of homosexuals and the practice of abortion raise special issues of constitutional interpretation. In these matters, more general conceptions of morality and community are brought to bear. The judges who defend a right to choose abortion (or homosexual conduct) invoke a broad right of "privacy," which in turn includes rights of self-definition and freedom of intimate association. The arguments counterpose very different approaches to community, tradition, and critical morality. (We deal with the prohibition of homosexual conduct in the following section, and with abortion later in the chapter.)

The Hardwick Case

In 1986 the Supreme Court upheld as constitutional a Georgia statute that made sodomy a criminal offense punishable by imprisonment for one to twenty years.[35] The law was challenged by Michael Hardwick, whom the police found in his bedroom having sex with another man. (They had come to arrest him in connection with a different offense.) The local district attorney did not pursue the case, but Hardwick said the statute placed him in imminent danger of arrest. He claimed that under the federal constitution private homosexual conduct by consenting adults could not be prohibited; and his argument was sustained by a court of appeals.

To invalidate the statute, the Supreme Court would have had to find that a fundamental right was violated. The Court's majority failed to find in the Constitution any right that would protect homosexual sodomy from legislative prohibition. As Chief Justice Warren E. Burger

35. Bowers v. Hardwick, 478 U.S. 186 (1986).

said, in a brief concurring opinion, "To hold that the act of homosexual sodomy is somehow protected as a fundamental right would be to cast aside millennia of moral teaching."[36]

In a vigorous dissent Justice Harry A. Blackmun argued that a customary morality is not self-justifying: "I cannot agree that either the length of time a majority has held its convictions or the passions with which it defends them can withdraw legislation from this Court's scrutiny." The real issue, he insisted, "is the fundamental interest all individuals have in controlling the nature of their intimate associations with others."[37]

The opinions reveal important differences in the way community and tradition are perceived. The majority opinion is communitarian in its own way. Those justices give great weight to customary morality as the foundation of community and as the preserver of its identity. In the theory to which they implicitly adhere, a genuine community is a community of observance, where customary rules and practices matter more than abstract principles. A corollary is that the sense of community is best expressed in localist terms. Moral autonomy should be granted at the local level, where social life is most fully experienced and appreciated. At that level, moreover, political majorities have a prima facie right to uphold conventional morality and thereby to determine the culture of the community.[38]

This point of view should be distinguished from the argument that the enforcement of morals is justified by a general necessity to sustain a moral order. That in itself is no warrant for sustaining a *particular* moral code. But the real issue is: What is the moral claim of a community to uphold its view of what the moral order should be, and to do so by using the authority and coercion of government? This claim has special importance in the American federal system, which reserves to each of the fifty states broad powers of self-definition. In this case the Court decided that the issue of homosexual conduct should be left to the political process at the local level.

The dissenting justices have a very different view of community, tradition, and the rights of majorities. They find community and tradition in the American constitutional order. The Constitution itself is a prime source of tradition—a tradition that allows for change and growth, criticism and reconstruction. It consists of *premises and values,* not of particu-

36. Ibid., 197.
37. Ibid., 210.
38. They also have a right to *depart* from hitherto conventional morality.

lar rules and practices. To identify such a tradition we must locate implicit principles and guiding purposes. A strategy of generalization is required. In this perspective the moral order is not constituted by particularities of belief, observance, or connectedness. Rather, the community is defined by more general ideals, such as democracy, equality, and the rule of law—in a word, by civility. The relevant moral community is the nation as defined by the Constitution. The claims of localism are to that extent diminished.

In their reading of American constitutional history, the minority justices find an evolving consensus on the importance of personal autonomy: "Our cases long have recognized that the Constitution embodies a promise that a certain sphere of individual liberty will be kept largely beyond the reach of government."[39] They find, *in the reasons behind* the Court's protection of basic family rights, such as whether or whom to marry and whether to have children, a vindication of personal rather than institutional values:

> We protect those rights not because they contribute, in some direct and material way, to the general public welfare, but because they form so central a part of an individual's life. . . . And we protect the family because it contributes so powerfully to the happiness of individuals, not because of a preference for stereotypical households. . . . The Court has recognized . . . that "the ability independently to define one's identity that is central to any concept of liberty" cannot be truly exercised in a vacuum; we all depend on the "emotional enrichment of close ties with others."
>
> Only the most willful blindness could obscure the fact that sexual intimacy is "a sensitive, key relationship of human existence, central to family life, community welfare, and the development of human personality." . . . The fact that individuals define themselves in a significant way through their intimate sexual relationships with others suggests, in a nation as diverse as ours, that there may be many "right" ways of conducting those relationships, and that much of the richness of a relationship will come from the freedom an individual has to *choose* the form and nature of these intensely personal bonds.[40]

Thus a central tenet of the moral order, as laid out in this judicial doctrine, is a shared belief in personal autonomy and privacy, especially in the realm of "intimate association." This belief, the justices hold, is an authoritative tradition because it is anchored in the Constitution and because it makes sense in the light of moral and psychological theory. If the Court is asked, What kind of a people are we? What is our culture? the

---

39. Thornburgh v. American Coll. of Obst. & Gyn., 476 U.S. 747, 772 (1986), cited in Justice Blackmun's dissent.
40. Bowers v. Hardwick, 478 U.S. 186, 204f. (1986).

ready answer is: We care about people as individuals and we believe they should be free to form their own identities.

An underlying assumption is that the alternative life-style—the intimate association in question—is reasonably viable, healthy, and unthreatening.[41] The minority opinion does not rule out prohibition of incest, prostitution, or polygamy. Despite some sweeping pronouncements in the dissenting opinion, it is not the case that every intimate association is defensible, nor does every one represent so fundamental an interest as to merit constitutional protection. In the logic of the minority view, however, the burden of proof lies elsewhere. Those who seek prohibition must justify their claim that the practice is undeserving of constitutional protection; only then would toleration or prohibition become a legitimate matter of public policy, to be decided by the political process.

Both arguments appeal to diversity, plurality, and toleration. The majority justices say the states may decide for themselves whether homosexual sodomy is a crime. The dissenters argue that diversity must be protected *within* each state, on the basis of individual preference rather than community sanction. In the majority view, whoever has the most votes may decide what traditions should be upheld. The dissenters, by contrast, want openness to change so that new political realities may emerge. If an alternative lifestyle is suppressed within a state, it will not have a reasonable chance to gain support for political change.

In its quest for latent principles in our legal culture and in its appeal to moral and psychological theory, the liberal minority of the Court clearly spoke for critical morality. The majority opinion, in its blunt appeal to history, made no contribution to reasoned elaboration of fundamental law. It does not follow, however, that the minority argument is wholly convincing. Exception may well be taken, for example, to the assertions quoted above that "we protect the family because it contributes so powerfully to the happiness of individuals" and that "much of the richness of a relationship will come from the freedom an individual has to

41. It is instructive that the minority opinion finds support in the Court's earlier recognition that the state's interest in public education should give way to a competing claim by the Amish community in Wisconsin that extended public schooling threatened its way of life. In that case the Court said: "There can be no assumption that today's majority is 'right' and the Amish and others like them are 'wrong.' A way of life that is odd or even erratic but interferes with no rights or interests of others is not to be condemned because it is different" (Wisconsin v. Yoder, 406 U.S. 205, 223 [1972]). The Court should have said "*just* because it is different." There is an assumption that the Amish way of life is a morally defensible alternative, to be respected and tolerated, not merely endured. Furthermore, the Amish case speaks to *local* diversity and community *control*, not to individual choice.

choose the form and nature of these intensely personal bonds." A different understanding of family values and of what makes for rich personal relationships would convey a different message, even if it did not alter the legal conclusion.

Furthermore, the dissenting justices must rest, in part at least, on a finding of substantial support for the homosexual alternative or for toleration of it. A free society must present strong reasons for suppressing a minority. We therefore demand a showing of palpable harm: the liberty of thieves—no tiny minority—to pursue their occupation gets little sympathy. On questions of cultural identity, where specific harms are not shown, significant minorities should have a say in forming that identity. They should not be shut out by a mechanical and intractable majority. This principle is especially important when, as in the restraint of homosexual conduct and abortion, the political majority demands some major personal sacrifice.

But what if there is genuine consensus on, say, the wrongfulness of gambling, polygamy, suicide, or homosexual conduct? Does the individual's interest in freedom of choice overcome the community's interest in vindicating its beliefs—especially when a plausible case can be made for the merits of those beliefs?[42] That some people gamble, others commit suicide, or have multiple spouses, or engage in homosexual acts does not in itself call a consensus into question. Under such circumstances the law is properly administered with compassion, and with an eye to the possibility that fundamental rights are abridged. It seems wrong, however, to withdraw from democratic decision every expression of cultural identity that interferes with personal autonomy.

To be sure, a political majority may or may not faithfully register a social consensus. Any widespread challenge to a custom or belief will affect the deference we show toward majority will. When the enforcement of morals is at issue, it is important to know to what extent a political outcome represents the views of the community as a whole or is, instead, a device for imposing the will of one part upon another. This does not mean the majority is powerless to define the culture; it does mean that its claim to do so must be scrutinized and justified. Thus a prime focus of scrutiny is the *quality* of consensus. As Ronald Dworkin points out, "a conscientious legislator [or judge, we might add] who is told a moral consensus exists must test the credentials of that

---

42. For example, resistance to homosexual conduct may reflect the view that a basic feature of the human condition is the difference between males and females and that heterosexual union is important, not only for procreation, but also for fundamental reconciliation of a biologically divided humanity. The division is not absolute, of course; in American law it cannot justify inequality.

consensus."[43] Above all, we cannot accept as moral a consensus marred by bigotry and contempt. There must be a threshold standard of critical morality.

IDEOLOGY AND CIVILITY

A persistent threat to civility arises when piety takes the form of unconditional commitment to a creed or doctrine. This situation presents a major dilemma for public morality. Ideologies can be dangerous, even virulent, but they may also enhance personal, social, and moral well-being. Without vision, we are told, the people perish. But vision rests, in part at least, on intellectual coherence and the courage of conviction. Therefore much depends on the dynamics and functions of belief. We have to consider how ideas are *held,* that is, what their significance is for personal identity, motivation, perception, and judgment; and how they are *deployed* in social and intellectual life. Here, again, the quality of community is at stake.

Common speech, and social science as well, shows considerable ambivalence about the meaning of "ideology." The concept is often used pejoratively to denote a distasteful and morally suspect form of thought and persuasion, but it is also used in a neutral way, without prejudgments. To resolve this ambiguity it may be helpful to invoke once again the distinction between defining a term and elaborating a concept or theory.

An ideology may be defined as a relatively coherent doctrine that purports to identify a comprehensive moral and social truth. This value-neutral definition is weak and inclusive. The term is more specific, however, than "culture," "perspective," "outlook," or even *Weltanschauung.* Thus national consciousness is a cultural phenomenon, but nationalism is an ideology. Jewishness is a matter of tradition or ethnicity, but Zionism is an ideological doctrine that defines a social reality and asserts a moral imperative. An ideology is a kind of doctrine and is therefore more focused and self-conscious than a perspective or worldview.[44]

Thus understood, an ideology is a set of explicit and coherent beliefs about values and social reality. As a matter of definition the idea says nothing about distortion, exclusiveness, psychic coercion, or overreaching. When we speak of socialist, liberal, or conservative ideologies we

43. Ronald Dworkin, *Taking Rights Seriously* (Cambridge: Harvard University Press, 1978), 254.
44. Of course, the converse is not true: not all doctrine is ideological. Legal, medical, institutional, even theological doctrine may be narrowly focused and make no claim to the formulation of a comprehensive truth. Doctrine shades into ideology as it becomes comprehensive in its claims and relevance.

may be neutral in this way, referring only to the comprehensive character of their creeds and doctrines.

If this leaves us uneasy and dissatisfied it is because "ideology" has rich connotations that are not necessary aspects of the basic phenomenon. They are, however, in many cases and under the right conditions, highly probable associations. When we go beyond a minimal definition to consider what may be said, on the basis of theory and experience, *about* ideology, we discover some important correlates. Most important are those that speak to the functions, dynamics, and pathologies of ideological systems.

Ideologies are characteristically functional in that they articulate group perspectives and provide a basis for collective action. In other words, they are responses to social imperatives and they minister to the needs of group life. Many ideologies very explicitly claim to formulate interests and aspirations. For example, the ideology of women's liberation purports to speak for women, nationalist or ethnic ideologies for people who have a common history or language, Marxist socialism for the working class. Ideologies play an important part in efforts to raise the consciousness of such groups, that is, they encourage individuals to feel a sense of shared identity and fate.[45]

The dynamics of ideology are the adaptive mechanisms, the strategic perspectives, and the tactical gambits that make the ideology effective. For example, ideologies in action exhibit a strain toward internal coherence and orthodoxy, and this has a coercive effect on those who are true believers. They demand purity of thought and consistency of action. The muddle and compromise of social reality signals a "fallen" existence, one that may require correction through strenuous measures. Ideologists of both left and right are dissatisfied with the status quo; they insist that principles be rigorously realized in action; they are strong critics of hypocrisy.

The dynamics of ideology are not *inherently* pathological. The mere fact that a system of belief is socially integrative, or upholds group interests, or helps mobilize energies, or demands a principled way of life is neither harmful nor repugnant in itself. On the contrary, ideologies are

45. Some ideologies are defensive, that is, they rationalize or justify a social order. This is the central meaning of ideology in Marxist theory. Other ideologies are critical and future-oriented. In either case, when viewed from the standpoint of the group that adopts it, ideology has an integrative and self-justifying function. Any ideology that gains acceptance does so in part because of the contribution it makes to a group's cohesion and morale. It is always to some extent self-serving, shaped by the interests and dispositions of those who stand to benefit from its adoption.

often beneficial to society as a whole as well as to the groups for whom they speak. They make values explicit and draw out their consequences; they are important instruments of criticism and change. In recent decades, ideologies of feminism, environmental protection, and civil rights have done much to rouse and focus the conscience of the community. It is a mistake to deny the social benefit of a belief just because it invokes passionate adherence, serves group needs, or exhibits a strain toward orthodoxy.

Nevertheless, as ideologies harden, as they become more explicit and systematic, as their demand for commitment expands and intensifies, a destructive virus takes hold. Every ideology carries some risk of creating a closed world of communicants—impenetrable in conviction, mindless in obedience, fierce in hatred of heresy and opposition. Most ideologies are not so powerful or pressed so far, but it would be wrong to suppose that only the worst case is important. In fact, ideology may infect public morality in subtle ways, and these will vary in strength and significance.[46]

The pathology of ideology is sometimes called ideological thinking. Its hallmark is what Hannah Arendt called "the emancipation of thought from experience."[47] Here we must be careful to distinguish ideological thinking from routine and necessary abstraction. Every idea is an abridgment of reality; every idea simplifies and selects. But in science, for example, abstraction is tempered and restrained by empirical testing and self-correction; in poetry, abstraction is disciplined by a quest for immediacy and concreteness. Ideological thinking, by contrast, does not recognize the abridgment and does not struggle against it.

Ideologues make a headlong leap from thought to action.[48] They do not temper ideas in the light of social reality; they do not filter concepts through the fabric of social life; they do not reconstruct theories by considering alternative options, competing interests, or multiple values. Ideological thinking is a form of hubris—intellectual presumption— based on an excess of confidence in the power of abstractions and a want

46. Consider, for example, the creation of what we might call policy worlds in government. When policy-making becomes a highly technical exercise, there may easily be created an encapsulated world of arcane doctrine effectively insulated from moral reasoning. Defense analysis in the nuclear age is the most striking example of a policy world.

47. *The Origins of Totalitarianism* (New York: Harcourt Brace Jovanovich, 1973), 471.

48. An ideologue is one who engages in ideological thinking, not necessarily one who has helped to formulate the ideology or one who supports it in a general way. Thus people who call themselves Marxists are not necessarily ideologues, nor do they always accept the system as a whole or the political conclusions some have drawn from it.

of respect for the concreteness of social life. It is this concreteness Arendt had in mind when she called ideological thinking the "emancipation" of thought from experience.

The ideological style seeks a gratifying and stabilizing coherence. Yet the very effort to achieve that wholeness tends to reduce the complexity of social reality. The world must be simplified in the interests of consistency. Although ideologues often yearn for community, they are at the same time subversive of it. As they reach for their own truth, their own fellowship, their own moral identity, they undermine existing communities. Ideological orthodoxy is a breeder of factions. It hardens differences; demands purity and commitment; is forever reading people out of a group or community.

All this adds up to an assault on civility. Ideological thinking distorts communication and frustrates dialogue, not because such thinking is partisan or subjective, but because at bottom it stems from a want of respect. Without respect for the integrity of persons, events, institutions, and ideas no genuinely civil discourse can take place. And civil discourse is essential to the foundations of community. The destruction of community, then, is a major cost of ideological thinking.

IDEOLOGY AND ABORTION

A case in point is the controversy over abortion. Strong differences in belief and interest have been hardened and aggravated by ideological conflict. Fundamental questions of autonomy and responsibility are raised. Because the issues are so basic—and so personal—a moral chasm separates the "pro-choice" forces from their "pro-life" antagonists. The community is divided and, no less important, the values at stake are confused and distorted.

In the United States, the conflict has been most intense since the Supreme Court's 1973 decision in *Roe v. Wade*.[49] The majority of the Court found that a hitherto developed right of privacy was "broad enough to encompass a woman's decision whether or not to terminate her pregnancy." They continued:

> The detriment that the State would impose upon the pregnant woman *by denying this choice altogether* is apparent. Specific and direct harm medically diagnosable even in early pregnancy may be involved. Maternity, or additional

49. Roe v. Wade, 410 U.S. 113 (1973). In this highly controversial case the Court struck down a Texas statute that made abortion (except to save the life of the mother) a criminal offense punishable by two to five years in prison.

offspring, may force upon the woman a distressful life and future. Psychological harm may be imminent. Mental and physical health may be taxed by child care. There is also the distress, for all concerned, associated with the unwanted child, and there is the problem of bringing a child into a family already unable, psychologically and otherwise, to care for it. In other cases, as in this one, the additional difficulties and continuing stigma of unwed motherhood may be involved.[50]

The justices rejected an *absolute* right to abortion. The state, they said, has legitimate interests in maintaining medical standards, safeguarding health, and protecting potential life. Therefore "this right is not unqualified and must be considered against important state interests in regulation."[51] The question is, however, when the interests of the state can outweigh or constrain a woman's right to choose.

To balance these interests the Court looked for guidance to medicine and biology. Three stages of pregnancy were identified, divided for convenience into three-month periods or trimesters. During the *first* trimester, the state has no "compelling" interest. The decision is to be made by the pregnant woman in consultation with her physician. During the *second* trimester, the interests of the mother are still paramount, but now abortion threatens greater danger to her health; therefore the state may, if it chooses, "regulate the abortion procedure in ways that are reasonably related to maternal health." Only after six months, at the beginning of the *third* trimester, does the state's interest in "potential life" come into play. This is the point when the fetus is normally viable, that is, can live outside the womb. "For the stage subsequent to viability, the State in promoting its interest in the potentiality of human life may, if it chooses, regulate, and even proscribe, abortion except where it is necessary, in appropriate medical judgment, for the preservation of the life or health of the mother."[52]

50. Ibid., 153, my emphasis. Note that this line of reasoning looks to medical, psychological, and sociological evidence—not to history or consensus—for the discovery of a fundamental right. Compare Justice Rehnquist's dissent: he notes that "the asserted right to an abortion is not 'so rooted in the traditions and conscience of our people as to be ranked as fundamental.'. . . Even today, when society's views on abortion are changing, the very existence of the debate is evidence that the 'right' to an abortion is not so universally accepted as the appellant would have us believe" (ibid., 174). The majority opinion did, however, devote substantial discussion to the history of abortion law, concluding that criminal abortion laws are of "relatively recent vintage. . . . They are not of ancient or even of common-law origin. Instead, they derive from statutory changes effected, for the most part, in the latter half of the 19th century" (ibid., 129).
51. Ibid., 154.
52. Ibid., 164f. Later a problem would arise as to just when the fetus is viable, given advances in medical knowledge and technique. See William Webster v. Reproductive Health Services, 492 U.S. 490 (1989).

The Court's claim to have rejected an absolute right of abortion was technically correct but not entirely candid. As a practical matter it did create such a right during the first trimester; and during the second trimester the constraints relate only to the interests of the mother. From the standpoint of those who opposed abortion as a matter of principle, this was bitter medicine. It meant that *with respect to the vast majority of abortion decisions* there could be no regulation in the interests of "potential life." The Court offered no affirmation of that value as relevant to the early months of pregnancy. It saw no moral dilemmas. If there were any, they were to be faced by the woman alone.

Although the Court upheld the community's interest in "potential life," it narrowed the meaning of "life" by emphasizing a specific outcome—the birth of a human infant capable of surviving outside the mother, however dependent it might be on external care and nurture. This focus on parturition as a decisive moral and biological event has much justification. However, it does not exhaust the meaning of "potential life." More broadly understood, in a way that resonates with much ordinary experience, the phrase refers to the whole process of procreation.

A very convincing case can be made that women do indeed have a strong moral claim—and a constitutional right—to decide for themselves whether to go forward with an early-term pregnancy. The decision affects the woman's well-being in momentous ways, closing or opening options for paths of life that are, in themselves, morally acceptable. Whatever we may think of "privacy," a woman's *liberty* in this respect cannot be less important than, say, the constitutionally recognized right to send a child to private school, or the right to read pornographic material at home.

It does not follow, however, that countervailing values must be ignored. A right defined as fundamental necessarily limits majority will and governmental intrusion. But that does not mean regulation is prohibited. For example, First Amendment rights of speech and religious worship are subject to reasonable regulation in the interests of public order, education, privacy, reputation, and individual freedom from group oppression. In upholding, in the face of highly restrictive state legislation, a woman's right to choose, the *Roe* majority was, in my view, amply justified. Nevertheless, the Court could have done more to recognize the full range of values at stake. It could have pointed out that the protection of this fundamental liberty was a necessary but not welcome exercise, and that the community may properly be concerned about the fate of the developing as well as the viable fetus; hence some efforts to discourage abortion would be constitutionally acceptable, so long as this did not "unduly burden" the woman's decision.[53] Such a qualification might have helped defuse the controversy and have pointed the way to other, less punitive ways of vindicating the community's interest.

In proclaiming what amounted to an absolute right to early-term abortion, and in its apparent indifference to the fate of the fetus prior to viability, the Court seemed out of touch with the moral sensibilities of a great many people. It thereby angered those who opposed abortion and confused those for whom abortion was, at best, a difficult and even tragic choice. The majority justices did not speak to the concerns of these people; the decision deprived them of any significant voice in this major issue of social policy. Yet their sensibilities could not be dismissed as products of bigotry, ignorance, or the crude defense of vested interests. The differences over abortion were profoundly ideological, and the Court's posture offered little room for compromise or for a spirit of reconciliation.

The opponents of abortion were dismayed by the Court's "symbolic messages." Among these was a dramatic shift in what should be considered respectable opinion. A world taken for granted was rudely shaken:

> Accustomed as they were to thinking that theirs was the majority opinion, the pro-life people we interviewed saw in the Supreme Court's decision a way of thinking that seemed bizarre and unreal. Something they believed to be both fundamental and obvious—that the embryo was a human life as valuable as any (and perhaps more valuable than some because it was innocent, fragile, and unable to act on its own behalf)—was now defined as simply one opinion among several. What was worse, it was defined as an opinion belonging to the *private* sphere, more like a religious preference than a deeply held social belief, such as belief in the right to free speech. It was as if the Supreme Court had suddenly ruled that a belief in free speech was only one legitimate opinion among others, which could not therefore be given special protection by any state or federal agency.[54]

The effect was to galvanize action—and polarize opinion.

In the aftermath of *Roe v. Wade* two untenable extremes emerged. The pro-choice ideology celebrates autonomy, but it offers at best a limited

53. In her concurring opinion in the *Webster* case, Justice Sandra O'Connor argued that the Court had hitherto held "with fair consistency in the past: that, previability, 'a regulation imposed on a lawful abortion is not unconstitutional unless it unduly burdens the right to seek an abortion' " (William Webster v. Reproductive Health Services, 492 U.S. 490, 530 [1989]).

54. Kristin Luker, *Abortion and the Politics of Motherhood* (Berkeley: University of California Press, 1984), 140f.

vision of *responsible* choice. It is concerned, of course, with the well-being of women and the fate of unwanted children. In practice, however, will and convenience are allowed to govern the abortion decision. To say that a woman's body is hers to control, without taking other interests into account, oversimplifies the issues. The pro-choice slogans do not make sense of the Court's own ruling that third-trimester abortions may be restricted or even prohibited; and the slogans could lead to some commonly undesired outcomes, such as the claim that a woman may rightfully generate fetal tissue to be sold for use, say, in the treatment of Parkinson's disease. Pro-choice extremism limits the meaning of motherhood and denies respect for the emergent human being. It offers no basis for safeguarding the vulnerable continuities of biology and morality, procreation and commitment.

The anti-abortionist view has its own great failings, even when viewed as the voice of traditional morality. Although the sanctity of human life is a bedrock value, it is subtle in its claims, uncertain in its boundaries, forever troubled by conflicting interests. The pro-life activists seek to escape this complexity by espousing a simplified, rigid, and incompassionate doctrine. Driven by a hardened ideology, they embrace a highly unrealistic conception of maternal responsibility, and they greatly exaggerate the claims of emergent life.

It may be technically accurate to say that the life of a determinate human being begins at conception.[55] But this biological fact—abstracted from other biological facts, including that of the precarious and extremely rudimentary nature of the fertilized ovum or blastocyst, and abstracted from the process of procreation and nurture—does not settle any moral issue. Conception is an important event, but birth is far more important. The biological changes between conception and birth are accompanied by progressive transformations of meaning, attachment, and obligation. To overlook these differences is to impoverish moral judgment.

The statutes overturned in *Roe v. Wade* did not treat all abortion as homicide, to say nothing of murder. For example, a Georgia law allowed abortion when a licensed physician determined that, in his "best clinical judgment," the life or *health* of a pregnant woman would be seriously endangered; or the fetus would very likely be born with a grave,

---

55. However, the process of creating a unique biological organism is complex and extends beyond the moment of conception. Nor does the existence of an early-stage embryo guarantee the creation of a child. In the natural course of fertilization, most such embryos do not survive. To think of rudimentary embryos as children—a view urged by pro-life activists—is to accept that most children die before they have much chance to live.

permanent, and irremediable defect; or the pregnancy resulted from forcible or statutory rape (including incest). Similar provisions in other states were inconsistent with the view that the early-term fetus is a constitutionally protected person. Why should innocent persons be killed just because their conception resulted from, say, statutory rape? In pursuit of an iron logic, with its implications for the rights of the fetus, the anti-abortion movement has ignored the premises—and reached beyond the conclusions—of these "pro-life" statutes.

To some extent, the ideological conflict is exacerbated by an American preoccupation with individual rights.[56] This disposition is fostered by a constitutional system that allows broad opportunities for appeal to the courts. Such an appeal must be made on behalf of particular litigants who assert claims to specific rights. This procedure tends to set claimant against claimant, principle against principle, and to force a choice. Furthermore, the language of rights must have a subject—a bearer of rights—and this subject becomes the focus of attention. In the context of abortion the rights of the fetus are counterposed to the rights of the pregnant woman. Each is treated as a distinct entity, and their rights tend to be viewed as inalienable, absolute—and private.

The alternative is to treat the sanctity of human life, and related values bearing on procreation, as values belonging to the community as a whole. The strategy for upholding a community's values need not rely mainly on the allocation and balancing of individual rights. The maintenance of respect for developing life is a social policy whose implementation should be considered in the light of competing values, such as education and opportunity for women, population control, and resistance to conception by rape or incest. It should consider all the relevant realities, including the urgencies of sexuality, the various hardships entailed, and the resources available for a policy of unlimited concern for every stage of life. This perspective can take account of intrinsic ambiguities in the values themselves, establish priorities without negating any valid interest, and respond constructively to pervasive human frailty.

CIVILITY AND RELIGION

The First Amendment to the United States Constitution begins as follows: "Congress shall make no law respecting an establishment of

---

56. See Mary Ann Glendon, *Abortion and Divorce in Western Law* (Cambridge: Harvard University Press, 1987), 33ff.

religion, or prohibiting the free exercise thereof."[57] This dual command was a historic effort *to contain ideology and uphold civility while respecting the claims of religious piety.* The architects of the Republic were not enemies of religion. Some, such as George Washington and John Adams, were quite conservative on the subject and supported religious establishment at the local level. Most took for granted that "religion, morality, and knowledge" are "necessary to the good government and happiness of mankind."[58] But the new Congress decided to keep its distance. A variety of churches and sects were to flourish on their own, without the interference or sponsorship of government. A spirit of toleration would prevail.

What was being protected? What was feared and guarded against? For some leading spokesmen of the founding generation, religious liberty was a special kind of freedom of expression, readily coupled with rights of free speech and assembly.[59] James Madison wrote that the religion "of every man must be left to the conviction and conscience of every man. . . . This right is in its nature an unalienable right."[60] These children of the Enlightenment were mostly Protestants. They could readily accept, within the realm of religion, individual responsibility, voluntary association, and sectarian diversity. In proclaiming religious freedom they were affirming the sacredness and inviolability of conscience. And in their idiom conscience was intimately associated with religious belief.

At the same time, Madison and his colleagues in the First Congress (who wrote the Bill of Rights) were well aware of religious pluralism in the new nation. Although the country as a whole was mainly Christian and Protestant, no sect could claim predominance. Government author-

---

57. In a series of decisions beginning in 1925, the Supreme Court has held that this and most other provisions of the Bill of Rights apply to the states under the due-process clause of the Fourteenth Amendment, which was adopted after the Civil War.

58. This sentiment appears in the Northwest Ordinance, adopted in 1787 by the Congress of the Confederation and readopted by the First Congress in 1789. Article 3 of the Ordinance reads: "Religion, morality, and knowledge, being necessary to the good government and happiness of mankind, schools and the means of education shall forever be encouraged." Even skeptics about Christianity, such as Benjamin Franklin and Thomas Jefferson, could agree with this. For details, see A. James Reichley, *Religion in American Public Life* (Washington, D.C.: Brookings Institution, 1985), 93ff.

59. Thus the whole First Amendment reads: "Congress shall make no law respecting an establishment of religion, or prohibiting the free exercise thereof; or abridging the freedom of speech, or of the press; or the right of the people peaceably to assemble, and to petition the Government for a redress of grievances."

60. "Memorial and Remonstrance Against Religious Assessments," in Marvin Meyers, ed., *The Mind of the Founder: James Madison* (1785; reprint, Hanover, N.H.: University Press of New England, 1981), 7.

ity in matters of faith and worship had all too recently brought in its train oppression, corruption, and civil strife. The evil to be avoided was not religion as such, however, but sectarian dispute made dangerous by a demand for conformity enforced by law.

The adoption of the religion clauses in the Bill of Rights inspired no significant controversy, and for more than a century Madison's solution worked very well. Broad consensus existed on the value of religion; on Protestant Christianity as the mainstream; and on the legitimacy of religious diversity. Furthermore, the amendment had only a limited impact on the life of the people. It allowed each state to evolve toward religious liberty in its own way, at its own pace; and there were few federal programs that might raise questions about the connection between religion and government. By the twentieth century, however, the foundations of the consensus had been partially eroded. The country contained more—and more vocal—non-Christians, especially Jews; the Catholic presence was very much stronger; and there were more self-conscious agnostics and atheists. This deepened pluralism disturbed the early balance struck between civility and piety.

As constitutional history unfolded a latent conflict in the religion clauses became apparent.[61] The message of "no establishment" is separation of church and state. But the "free exercise" clause gives religion a privileged status, as entitled to special respect and accommodation. Moreover, free exercise extends to *practice* as well as belief—for example, to church organization, ritual, religious and religiously oriented education, and maintaining the Sabbath and other holy days. The Supreme Court has set limits, as when it denied nineteenth-century Mormons a constitutional right to polygamy, and when it has upheld laws against the use of illegal drugs in religious ritual. It has accepted, however, a broad range of practices as legitimate aspects of the free exercise of religion, notably the right of parents to send their children to parochial schools. In determining these rights and their limits, questions are raised as to how far government may burden or facilitate freedom of

61. This conflict has generated a large legal literature regarding how religion should be understood for constitutional purposes. "Free exercise" suggests an expansive view of religion, justifying wide latitude in religious identity and expression; but this runs up against the claims of secular policy, for example, as to acceptable holidays or medical care. "No establishment" calls for a more restrictive or strong conception of religion, to avoid encompassing such moral, social, and political doctrines as "secular humanism," or the premises of the Declaration of Independence, which may legitimately be supported and taught by secular government. For a general analysis, and an argument that religion should be understood differently in the two clauses, see David A. J. Richards, *Toleration and the Constitution* (New York: Oxford University Press, 1986), chap. 5.

worship.[62] The answers to these questions inevitably blur the line between church and state.

In 1947 Justice Hugo L. Black, speaking for a Supreme Court majority, offered this pithy, oft-quoted interpretation:

> The "establishment of religion" clause of the First Amendment means at least this: Neither a state nor the Federal Government can set up a church. Neither can pass laws which aid one religion, aid all religions, or prefer one religion to another. Neither can force nor influence a person to go to or to remain away from church against his will or force him to profess a belief or disbelief in any religion. No person can be punished for entertaining or professing religious beliefs or disbeliefs, for church attendance or non-attendance. No tax in any amount, large or small, can be levied to support any religious activities or institutions, whatever they may be called, or whatever form they may adopt to teach or practice religion. Neither a state nor the Federal government can, openly or secretly, participate in the affairs of any religious organizations and *vice versa*. In the words of Jefferson, the clause against establishment of religion by law was intended to erect "a wall of separation between church and State."[63]

Despite this ringing declaration, the majority decision *upheld* a New Jersey statute providing public funds for transportation of children to parochial schools: "The State contributes no money to the schools. It does not support them. Its legislation, as applied, does no more than provide a general program to help parents get their children, regardless of religion, safely to and from accredited schools."[64]

In subsequent cases, other Supreme Court majorities have stressed that "our prior holdings do not call for total separation between church and state. . . . Some relationship between government and religious organizations is inevitable."[65] Given the range of activities connected with religion, especially in education and medicine, and given the reach of government programs, religion is bound to experience both benefits and burdens. In modern society there is, and must be, a close nexus between government and other social institutions. Recognizing that fact, the Court has sought criteria for determining when a connection is *too* close. Thus in 1971 the Court formulated a "three-prong" test of con-

---

62. It has been considered a burden, for example, if people are denied unemployment compensation for quitting jobs when they require work on the Sabbath. Government facilitates free exercise by granting tax exemptions, allowing parochial schools to provide basic education, and by providing chaplains and chapels in the armed services.

63. Everson v. Board of Education, 330 U.S. 1, 15f. (1947).

64. Ibid., 18. In 1925 the Court had ruled that, under state compulsory education laws, parents have a right to send their children to religious rather than public schools if the schools provide adequate secular education.

65. Lemon v. Kurtzman, 403 U.S. 602, 614 (1971).

stitutionality: "First, the statute must have a secular legislative purpose; second, its principal or primary effect must be one that neither advances nor inhibits religion; finally, the statute must not foster an excessive government entanglement with religion."[66]

Each of these criteria leaves room for benefits to religion. A statute may have a secular purpose, such as support for education, health care, housing, or public holidays, yet it may significantly benefit church-related institutions and activities. (In some cases, such as granting tax exemptions for church property, the benefit is hardly incidental.) Similarly, a "principal or primary effect" does not preclude indirect or secondary effects; and a bar against "excessive" entanglements does not prohibit moderate or reasonable relationships.

The claims of piety, as expressed in religion, go beyond institutional connectedness. They have a constitutional basis in the "free exercise" clause. Government cannot be faithful to that principle and also be *indifferent* to religion or to the structure of opportunities on which it depends, let alone expressing open or latent hostility. Furthermore, responsible government cannot ignore the health of the moral order, if only because it has an elementary obligation to protect public safety. Government cannot forego the cultural and symbolic resources that sustain virtue and restrain vice. Insofar as religion contributes to moral ordering, it is likely to command from government at least benevolent neutrality. Like the family and like private education, most religious institutions as we know them have at least prima facie moral worth. Therefore accommodation of some sort must be accepted—and not only as a grudged necessity.

No clear consensus exists, either on the Supreme Court or in American public opinion, on just how to draw the line between government and religion. The justices disagree about what constitutes illegitimate "support" or "endorsement" of religion, and as to what government must do to insulate its own activities from religious influence. Debates continue over how much aid can be given to parochial schools; how much and what kinds of religious symbolism may be publicly displayed on government property; or what weight to give to traditional practices that associate government and religion, such as the employment of chaplains to offer prayers at legislative sessions.

The disagreements are important; they reflect genuine differences in emphasis and perspective. But they take place within a context of broad

66. Ibid., 612f.

agreement on some basic principles. There is a shared understanding that government (1) must have a secular purpose in order to justify any activity that directly or indirectly affects religion; (2) may not prefer one religion over another; and (3) may not pass judgment on theological issues, that is, on the ideas that inform faith and worship. These principles uphold the concept of a secular state, which is forbidden to impair religious freedom by preferring or imposing a specific doctrine. However, they do not necessarily bar institutional connections. And they are consistent both with advancing religion in various ways (for example, by encouraging religious affiliation or by accommodating a religiously oriented way of life),[67] and with inhibiting religion, by taxing church property or limiting practices (such as use of drugs) that are thought to be inconsistent with contemporary understandings of the common good.

This core consensus is not comfortable with the idea that there should be a "wall of separation" between church and state. That metaphor was used by Roger Williams in 1643 to protect "the garden of religion" from "the wilderness of the world,"[68] and by Thomas Jefferson in 1802 to protect government from religion. However, neither Williams in his time nor Jefferson in his was necessarily representative of religious or political opinion. Their special formulations need not be taken as gospel. In any case, no figure of speech, however compelling, can substitute for a carefully articulated principle; still less can it serve as a clearcut, unproblematic rule.[69] At best the metaphor is a symbolic spur to close scrutiny of questionable laws and practices.

The most difficult problems have to do with the rights of atheists and of minorities outside the mainstream. Any official endorsement of religion can be offensive to nonbelievers, who are thereby asked to associate themselves, however indirectly, with views they do not hold and may abhor. Furthermore, despite an ideal of neutrality, a government friendly to religion is most likely to acknowledge, in practice, the symbols and holidays of large and well-established groups rather than those of small sects or cults.

In a case involving public display of a Nativity scene at Christmas, Justice Sandra O'Connor tried to deal with this problem by saying that "the Establishment Clause prohibits government from making adher-

---

67. As in Wisconsin v. Yoder; see above, p. 407n.

68. Mark de Wolfe Howe, *The Garden and the Wilderness: Religion and Government in American Constitutional History* (Chicago: University of Chicago Press, 1965), 5f.

69. This echoes what Howe calls the unheeded admonition of Justice Stanley Reed that "a rule of law should not be drawn from a figure of speech" (ibid., 1).

ence to religion relevant in any way to a person's standing in the political community. . . . Endorsement sends a message to nonadherents that they are outsiders, not full members of the political community, and an accompanying message to adherents that they are insiders, favored members of the political community. Disapproval sends the opposite message."[70]

For Justice O'Connor, the issue is whether a *particular* religious belief has been endorsed. Instances of so-called ceremonial deism—legislative prayer, "In God We Trust," "One Nation under God," "God save the United States and this Honorable Court"—are constitutional because they have been sanitized, as it were, by long association with secular activities. "The question . . . is whether a reasonable observer would view such long-standing practices as a disapproval of their religious choices, in light of the fact that they serve a secular purpose rather than a sectarian one and have largely lost their religious significance over time."[71] The assumption is that no reasonable atheist should feel excluded by salutes to God that carry no special meaning. Such gestures may be undesirable, and even offensive to some, but they are not unconstitutional.

A rather different view was expressed by Justice Anthony Kennedy. Starting from the premise that "the Establishment Clause permits government some latitude in recognizing and accommodating the central role religion plays in our society," he rejected the idea that the "touchstone of an Establishment Clause violation is whether nonadherents would be made to feel like 'outsiders' by government recognition or accommodation of religion." This is an unworkable idea, he said, because minorities do and must suffer some sense of exclusion, and because it has the effect of consigning mainstream religion "to the status of least-favored faiths so as to avoid any possible risk of offending members of

70. Lynch v. Donnelly, 465 U.S. 668, 689 (1984). According to Justice O'Connor, this principle clarifies the "secular purpose" element of the *Lemon* test (see above, note 65): "The proper inquiry under the purpose prong of *Lemon* . . . is whether the government intends to convey a message of endorsement or disapproval of religion." In the case at hand O'Connor joined the majority, which found the display constitutional because, as was explained in her concurring opinion, "the evident purpose of including the crèche in the larger display was not promotion of the religious content of the crèche but celebration of the public holiday through its traditional symbols. Celebration of public holidays, which have cultural significance even if they also have religious aspects, is a legitimate secular purpose" (ibid., 691).

71. Allegheny County v. ACLU, 492 U.S. 573, 631 (1989). This was another Nativity-scene case. The Court found the display unconstitutional because of its prominence and because it was not placed in a context (other symbols, such as a Christmas tree or Santa Claus) that would offset its special religious significance.

minority religions."[72] Therefore he dissented from the judgment that a Nativity scene, standing alone, could not be displayed by a government agency as part of a celebration of Christmas.

Here again, as in the *Hardwick* decision discussed above, important differences emerge regarding community and tradition. One view, emphasizing civility, is prepared to forgo particularity and sacrifice localism. The other view, more sensitive to piety, is more willing to take risks in the interests of a richer public symbolism, and it allows more leeway for majority rule in local communities.[73]

▼   ▲   ▼   ▲   ▼

In seeking a balance between civility and piety, two aspects of religion should be distinguished. One refers to religion's social function, the other to its substance or content. Thus Emile Durkheim asked:

> What essential difference is there between an assembly of Christians celebrating the principal dates of the life of Christ, or of Jews remembering the exodus from Egypt or the promulgation of the decalogue, and a reunion of citizens commemorating the promulgation of a new moral or legal system or some great event in national life?[74]

Here we are invited to emphasize social effects or functions, and especially the work done by religion in promoting cohesion and morale. This function may be performed by a vague, inclusive, ecumenical symbolism. Any division between religion so conceived and so-called civil religion must be strained and artificial. Insofar as there is a "civil religion," it cannot but be "established."[75]

72. Ibid., 657, 670.
73. Justice Kennedy concluded his dissenting opinion by pointing out that he had his own doubts about the good sense of the Pittsburgh display: "To place these religious symbols in a common hallway or sidewalk, where they might be ignored or even insulted, must be distasteful to many who cherish their meaning. For these reasons, I might have voted against installation of these particular displays were I a local legislative official. . . . [But] the principles of the Establishment Clause and our Nation's historic traditions of diversity and pluralism allow communities to make reasonable judgments respecting the accommodation or acknowledgment of holidays with both cultural and religious aspects. No constitutional violation occurs when they do so by displaying a symbol of the holiday's religious origins" (ibid., 678f.).
74. *The Elementary Forms of the Religious Life* (1915; reprint, Glencoe, Ill.: Free Press, 1947), 427. Durkheim defined religion very broadly as "a unified system of beliefs and practices relative to sacred things" (ibid., 47).
75. Jean-Jacques Rousseau favored a "civil religion" with "simple dogmas," namely, "[t]he existence of a mighty, intelligent, and beneficent Divinity, possessed of foresight and providence, the life to come, the happiness of the just, the punishment of the wicked, the sanctity of the social contract and the laws: these are its positive dogmas. Its negative

The alternative is to take seriously the fears and aspirations of Madison and Jefferson. They worried about contention over distinctively religious *belief*; they sensed that Rousseau may have been right when he said that "one cannot live in peace with people one regards as damned"; they saw a special danger to community when government takes sides. In addition, they had a vision of conscience made good by freedom to seek, expound, or deny moral and religious truth. To make sense of this perspective, religion must be understood substantively, in terms that give a central place to the content and grounds of religious beliefs. Religious ideology need not contain a belief in God or an afterlife, as we know such beliefs in the West. But the historic religions have been notable in this, that at least some of the doctrines they embrace are inaccessible to ordinary criteria of rational discourse.

The functional interpretation makes its own contribution to public policy. The elements of a civil religion may be accepted and fostered without entanglement in theological or philosophical issues, but appealing only to the principles and symbolism of a secular order. Furthermore, a benign attitude toward religious institutions may be justified, in recognition of their secular value—so long as basic neutrality and secular purpose are preserved.

However, to deal effectively with the issue of divisiveness we need to recognize that religious doctrine characteristically looks to another realm—beyond nature, beyond social experience—for spiritual redemption or fulfillment. Redemption depends on fidelity to truths that have their own logic and symbolism. Religious doctrine is sacred, not only as a source of identity, not only as an affirmation of history, but as a manifestation of ultimate authority, allegiance, and concern. As such it is likely to claim *privileged truth*. But such a claim must be insulated from public debate regarding the common good. To be part of public debate, religious ideas must be adapted to the accessible language of morality and public policy.[76]

---

dogmas I confine to one, intolerance" (*The Social Contract and Discourses*, trans. G. D. H. Cole [1762; reprint, London: J. M. Dent, 1973], book 4, chap. 8, 307f.). More recently, Robert Bellah and others have tried to identify a more properly secular "civil" or "public" religion in America, made up of rituals and commemorations such as Independence Day and Memorial Day; such events as presidential inaugurations; and sacred texts, especially the Declaration of Independence, the Constitution, and the Gettysburg Address (Robert N. Bellah, *Beyond Belief: Essays on Religion in a Post-Traditional World* [New York: Harper & Row, 1970], chap. 9). For a critique of the concept of civil religion, see John F. Wilson, *Public Religion in American Culture* (Philadelphia: Temple University Press, 1979).

76. This does not preclude substantial and open *influence* of religious ideas on moral and political judgment. In the public realm of a pluralist and secular state, however, people

Thus understood, religious belief cannot be identified with political, economic, or social doctrines, or even with a systematic philosophy such as Aristotelianism, utilitarianism, or Hegelian philosophy. A distinctively religious dogma demands a leap of faith. Within a framework of faith the appeal to reason may be strong, as it is in Catholicism and other religions. But at the core is a mystery, which to the communicant makes sense but to outsiders is opaque and inaccessible. This has its psychological corollary. We freely criticize a person's political or metaphysical views, but we are loath to impugn beliefs that speak, in Tillich's terms, to matters of "ultimate concern."[77] Such beliefs are too closely bound up with a deep sense of personal identity and with that "integrity of man's moral and spiritual nature" we call liberty of conscience.

A strong conception of religion, one that makes doctrine and symbolism the core concerns, is compatible with a wide range of institutional and symbolic accommodations. So long as government keeps its distance from the thorny thicket of liturgy and dogma, it can pursue a policy of benevolent neutrality. Furthermore, a strong conception is required by the ideal of liberty of conscience. To respect that liberty is to respect the right to treat with high seriousness beliefs that are constitutive of personal identities. In the name of liberty of conscience we may ask exemption from certain political rules and policies.[78]

A corollary puts to rest the claim that secular humanism and other, similar perspectives, conservative or liberal, are in some sense religious doctrines whose establishment is forbidden and whose avowal must be

---

must appeal to one another in terms that can make sense to all. For an argument that personal religious belief has a legitimate place in public debate, on the ground that such beliefs are really indistinguishable from general value commitments, see Kent Greenawalt, *Religious Convictions and Political Choice* (New York: Oxford, 1988); that view is criticized in Kenneth I. Winston, "The Religious Convictions of Public Officials," *Canadian Journal of Law and Jurisprudence* 3 (January 1990): 129–43.

77. This idea is trivialized if it is interpreted as equivalent to "basic values." To have "ultimate concern," one must experience a spiritual awareness (and struggle) that goes beyond the embrace of values and even beyond belief. At stake is a person's relation to some ultimate source of judgment or affirmation. The quest is for a truth so profound and so personal that it defies expression in ordinary language. Paul Tillich emphasizes that "man's ultimate concern must be expressed symbolically, because symbolic language alone is able to express the ultimate" (*Dynamics of Faith* [New York: Harper Torchbooks, 1957], 41). Religious symbols (including rituals) speak to "first things," but they do so with reticence and in accents of mystery. A person who rejects traditional religious imagery, yet tries to articulate an "ultimate concern," is likely to be tongue-tied. I count myself among the tongue-tied.

78. As the Amish did when they insisted that schooling beyond the primary grades was incompatible with their religiously oriented way of life, and as pacifists do when they seek conscientious-objector status in wartime.

treated as a special liberty of conscience, distinct from freedom of expression. All such systematic perspectives contain an element of ideology and at least a strain toward piety; indeed, their presuppositions are sometimes hard to distinguish from religious articles of faith. But the ideas they contain are in principle subject to revision in the light of historical experience; they do not assert a privileged form of knowledge or insight; they do not look to a special source of authority.

We need not deny the convergence or overlap of religious and secular ideology. From the standpoint of both personal identity and social cohesion, secular ideology often serves as a surrogate for religion, and it may embrace a logic that is highly resistant to examination and correction. But there is a great difference in the appropriate *strategy of civility*. If an article of faith is religious, civility requires respectful insulation; if the belief is secular—however fundamental or comprehensive—it must be open to public argument and political decision.

FIFTEEN

Communitarian Justice

The promise of community is not a pledge of easy intimacy or innocent harmony. A communitarian ethos calls for integration, but also demands protection of diversity and reconciliation of interests. To meet this demand is the office of civility, which we discussed in the preceding chapter. The most important expression of civility is the virtue we call justice. Justice speaks civilly to the inevitable diversity of passions and interests. Differences are adjudicated, not erased; and discord is channeled into self-preserving paths. At the same time, justice takes account of the claims of piety. The commitments generated by a shared history and fate lend form and texture to the quest for justice.

I have called this chapter "communitarian justice" to underscore the continuities of law, justice, and community and to suggest that, if community is to flourish, a robust conception of justice is required. Communitarian justice, like all justice, is rooted in civility. Yet it reaches for a larger, more integrative ideal. It draws inspiration from the premise that "the law should take as its most central question what kind of community we should be."[1]

AN INTEGRATIVE VIRTUE

Justice is not the whole of morality. It has more to do with power, oppression, fairness, and equality than with love or altruism. Indeed, like

---

1. James Boyd White, *Heracles' Bow* (Madison: University of Wisconsin Press, 1985), 42. White also notes that "the current habit of regarding law as the instrument by which

morality itself, justice *begins* as a principle of restraint. It is at first mainly useful for curbing disorder and limiting the abuse of power. As Adam Smith pointed out, "[S]ociety flourishes and is happy" when the cooperation indispensable to human life is based on love and friendship. But though society can manage without affection, it cannot survive when hurt and injury are unrestrained:

> Beneficence, therefore, is less essential to the existence of society than justice. Society may subsist, though not in the most comfortable state, without beneficence; but the prevalence of injustice must utterly destroy it. . . . [Beneficence] is the ornament which embellishes, not the foundation which supports the building, and which it was, therefore, sufficient to recommend, but by no means necessary to impose. Justice, on the contrary, is the main pillar of the edifice.[2]

Mill had much the same idea in mind when he spoke of justice as "a name for certain classes of moral rules, which concern the essentials of human well-being more clearly, and are therefore of more absolute obligation, than any other rules for the guidance of life."[3]

A strong case can be made for moral realism in the theory of justice. To be realistic in this sense is to give special attention to the institutions and motivations we can *rely on* to mitigate oppression and win cooperation. This insight leads some writers to adopt a minimalist conception of justice. Thus Stuart Hampshire argues that justice is best conceived as a negative virtue: "One has to ask, in a Hobbesian spirit, what it prevents rather than what it engenders."[4] What it prevents is domination and ruinous discord. In this view, justice is about procedure, not substance:

> There is a basic concept of justice which has a constant connotation and core sense, from the earliest times until the present day; and it always refers to a regular and reasonable procedure of weighing claims and counter-claims, as in an arbitration or court of law. The procedure is designed to avoid destructive conflict. The just and rational procedure can be used both in arbitrating between competing interests and between competing moral claims.[5]

'we' effectuate 'our' policies and get what 'we' want is wholly inadequate. It is the true nature of law to constitute a 'we' and to establish a conversation by which that 'we' can determine what our 'wants' are and should be."

2. Adam Smith, *The Theory of Moral Sentiments* (1759; reprint, London: Bohn, 1853), 125.

3. John Stuart Mill, *Utilitarianism* (1863), in *Utilitarianism, On Liberty, Considerations on Representative Government* (reprint, London: J. M. Dent, 1984), 61f.

4. Stuart Hampshire, *Innocence and Experience* (Cambridge: Harvard University Press, 1989), 68.

5. Ibid., 63.

Taking justice as procedure, it is said, avoids arguments about conflicting ends or ideals; and it finds a solid footing in historical experience,
which speaks much more clearly about what must be prevented than
about the positive goods we can achieve.

A variant of this view is the Hobbesian claim that people seek justice,
and accept the demands of justice, because to do so serves their proximate interests. If they did not gain from the arrangement, they would
have no incentive to exercise the self-denial any notion of justice requires. On these premises, elaborate arguments have been constructed
to show how self-interest is served by embracing various principles of
justice.[6] In this way justice is made more secure, and more understandable as well.

This perspective makes a great deal of sense—so long as we have in
mind a threshold or baseline morality, and insofar as we postulate a fairly
narrow conception of what rational self-interest entails. The Hobbesian
model works best where survival (or some equivalent urgency) is at issue and where elementary cooperation is required. These conditions are
indeed very prevalent. Most activities and enterprises—including systems of justice—cannot survive without practical incentives and benefits. There must be a proximate gain, a "cash value."

It does not follow, however, that the promise of justice is necessarily
circumscribed by these motivations and urgencies. When we look beyond its rudimentary forms, we see that justice does more than enforce
minimal requirements of order and cooperation. *The process of doing justice stimulates moral and legal development.* To do justice, we must draw insight and justification from a larger context of moral experience and reflection. When we say that justice is part of morality, we do not mean
it is only a loosely coupled part. On the contrary, justice belongs to morality in an integral, organic way. It is nourished by and supportive of the
more general values that inform all moral experience.[7] Justice cannot be

6. Thus Rawls grounds his "difference principle," according to which inequalities
must be justified by the benefits they generate for the least advantaged, on a prudential calculation by persons in the "original position" who are called upon to formulate principles
of justice they would accept (see Chapter 16, "Moral and Social Equality"). However,
prudence-based theories tend to focus on negative justice—protection of basic interests
from domination and discord—because that is as much as the incentives will sustain.

7. This organic connection between justice and morality helps make sense of Aristotle's distinction between justice as "complete virtue" and justice "as a part of virtue."
The former is "the whole of excellence or virtue . . . in relation to our fellow men." The
latter has to do with specific principles of distribution, rectification, and the like (Aristotle, *Nichomachean Ethics,* trans. Martin Ostwald [Indianapolis: Bobbs-Merrill, 1985],
1129b25ff.). By first equating justice and morality, then distinguishing them as part and
whole, Aristotle recognizes their intimate connection. He thereby sets the stage for raising
expectations as to the moral worth of justice.

even moderately realized if there is no appreciation of personal dignity, trust, fidelity, caring, and rationality.

We have had occasion to notice, in another context, the continuities of procedure and substance.[8] The "regular and reasonable procedure of weighing claims and counter-claims" is not devoid of moral content. Adjudication as process has its own values, which include impartial judgment, respect for truth, and the opportunity for reasoned argument. Argument includes justification—appeal to pertinent norms and values—and justification is a prime source of moral development. The parties' claims of right characteristically invoke conceptions of the common good. Furthermore, although judges and mediators are properly neutral with respect to the interests of the *parties,* they may well be sensitive, in formulating rules, to larger values, including the well-being of an institution or a community.

Thus justice has a vital part to play, not only in the bare survival of moral systems, but in their flourishing as well. The struggle for justice has its own dynamic and reaches well beyond restraint of domination. Justice affirms the moral worth of individuals; sustains autonomy and self-respect; domesticates authority; and establishes a framework for moral discourse on public matters. Although justice *emerges* as a response to practical urgencies, it *eventuates,* under appropriate conditions, in ideas and practices that are subtler and more value-laden.

If we reduce justice to a negative virtue or to a way of achieving minimal cooperation, we lose a great deal of its resonance and promise. We fail to garner the psychological and intellectual benefits that come from receiving justice and doing justice. Most important, we miss the full contribution justice can make to the enrichment and enlargement of community.

As an integrative ideal and as a foundation of community, justice is necessarily contextual and historical. There is no one right model, nor can its meaning be captured by some single element, such as impartiality or procedural fairness, or by an abstract formula, such as giving to each his due. Like the concept of community, that of justice embraces a complex set of interacting variables. A theory of justice must be grounded in historical experience, that is, it should take its departure from principles that have received recurrent recognition. These include: *entitlement*—claims of right must be based on what has already been granted by law or custom; *justification*—when deprivations are imposed, reasons must be given or tacitly understood, and some form of consent

---

8. See Chapter 12, "Ends, Means, and Integrity."

is presumed; *equality*—at a minimum, like cases must be treated alike, and the intrinsic worth of every member must be recognized; *impartiality*—bias and self-interest must be excluded from rule-making and administration; *proportionality*—relevant differences must be considered when allocating benefits or burdens; *reciprocity*—a balance of giving and taking must be maintained, especially in determining mutual obligations; *rectification*—injured parties must be compensated for the losses they have suffered; *need*—allocations must be based on what people are thought to require for survival or for a minimally acceptable standard of existence; *desert*—comparative worth, merit, or blame must be weighed; and *participation*—every person must be recognized as a member of the community, especially in respect to basic rights and having a voice in decisions that affect vital interests.[9]

We can bring some order to this array by recognizing that some principles—entitlement, proportionality, need, desert—speak mainly to justice in the *distribution* of opportunities, benefits, and burdens. For many writers, this is the central meaning of justice.[10] Other principles, such as impartiality, bear on justice in *governance,* that is, on the way rules are made and implemented, especially where coercion is involved. Here procedural fairness and mitigation of arbitrariness are chief concerns. Still other principles—reciprocity, rectification, participation—make for justice in *social relations,* which includes the obligations and claims that arise from transactions, interdependence, injury, and group membership. In this relational or private justice, people are compensated for unjustified losses, and their legitimate expectations are vindicated. Finally, we may note that some principles—notably equality and justification—are pervasive. They are common threads in every kind of justice.[11]

9. This or any similar list could be extended or shortened, depending on the specific meaning we give to each element or principle.

10. According to David Miller, "[P]rinciples of justice are distributive principles. . . . Indeed, the most valuable general definition of justice is that which brings out its distributive character most plainly: justice is *suum cuique,* to each his due" (*Social Justice* [Oxford: Clarendon Press, 1976], 20). Dworkin, distinguishing justice from fairness, says that "justice is a matter of outcomes: a political decision causes injustice, however fair the procedures that produced it, when it denies people some resources, liberty, or opportunity that the best theories of justice entitle them to have" (Ronald Dworkin, *Law's Empire* [Cambridge: Harvard University Press, 1986], 180). Barry says that "the subject of justice is the distribution of rights and privileges, powers and opportunities, and the command over material resources" (Brian Barry, *Theories of Justice* [Berkeley: University of California Press, 1989], 292).

11. It does not follow from their being pervasive, however, that they exhaust the meaning of justice or that they are necessarily most important in any given context.

Principles of justice, like other moral principles, are both timeless and timebound. On the one hand, they are timeless, in that they reflect universal needs and aspirations, as well as universal problems of social organization. The claims they represent can be found, at least implicitly, in most, if not all, human communities. Ultimately they are warranted by our best understanding of what human well-being requires. No theory of justice can be adequate, no system of justice can be satisfactory, if it wholly neglects any of these principles. On the other hand, the principles are timebound, because the weight they are given varies markedly from one setting to another. Some cultures or epochs make entitlement the key to justice; others focus on merit or desert; still others lean toward need. It has been argued that a hierarchical society such as preindustrial England is drawn to entitlement; a market society to desert; the modern welfare state to need.[12]

Furthermore, within a given community, accepted principles of justice are often in conflict and require trade-offs. For example, where affirmative-action policies lead to preferential hiring of hitherto excluded minorities, justice as *merit* yields to justice as *participation* and *rectification*. But, in the same context, justice as *entitlement* may limit affirmative action, for example, when the courts give greater protection to the seniority rights of existing employees than to the claims of prospective employees.

Despite their variety and the different problems they address, principles of justice are governed by a common concern: the right ordering of interests and powers within a particular community. Each principle in its own way helps to chasten power or reconcile interests in the service of individual and collective well-being. Conflicts among the principles are inevitable, and no algorithm can be found for resolving them. Much room is left for controversy and accommodation, and for learning from experience what must be protected and what can be compromised. The integrative work of justice requires openness, patience, dialogue, and the balancing of values. It is not by nature swift and sure; it is never complete; and it is poorly served by sharp swords cutting Gordian knots.

Nevertheless, a communitarian theory of justice offers a basis for criticism and a program for enrichment. It asks of each principle how moral *responsibility* can be enhanced. We enrich the familiar forms of justice by infusing them with ideals of mutual trust, respect, reconciliation, and interdependence. This usually involves extending the reach of responsi-

12. Miller, *Social Justice*, chap. 8.

bility, or limiting claims, by taking account of unintended effects or by including interests not contemplated in an agreement or in an established mode of governance.

For example, individual claims to exclusive ownership and control of property are modified by recognizing the reserved rights of the community. Equality is tested by examining how far opportunity is equal in practice as well as in form. Blame takes account of whole persons and persons-in-context. Distributive justice is not necessarily tied to contributions or merit; and need must consider what people require, not only for survival, but for effective social participation. At every point, abstract criteria of justice are evaluated in the light of substantive outcomes.

Although justice is a moral and communitarian vision, we should recognize that it presumes egoism as well as benevolence, conflict as well as reconciliation. Justice defines the rights and responsibilities of ordinary people and ordinary officials in ordinary circumstances. It does not invoke the noblest human virtues—love, sympathy, courage, self-sacrifice; it is not a promise of moral perfection.[13] Communities that are viable as well as moral must show respect for the persistence of social division and the prevalence of human frailty. Therefore communitarian justice, however strongly it may be governed by a social ethic, can be no more than "an approximation of brotherhood under conditions of sin."[14]

FROM LAW TO JUSTICE

"For their laws," wrote Heraclitus, "people ought to fight as for their walls."[15] This ancient proverb reminds us that, in many societies, law is a mainstay of cultural identity. It is also the bridge between justice and community. Law pours content into abstract principles of justice; gives

13. Thus understood, justice has little in common with the utopian conception of a realm beyond egoism, a community so marked by harmony that rights become irrelevant. See Allen E. Buchanan, *Marx and Justice: The Radical Critique of Liberalism* (Totowa, N.J.: Rowman and Littlefield, 1982), chap. 4.

14. Reinhold Niebuhr, *The Nature and Destiny of Man* (1941; reprint, New York: Scribner's, 1949), 2:254.

15. Quoted by Werner Jaeger, with the following gloss: "The law is the spiritual wall that protects the life of the community. It cannot be safeguarded by fighting for the stone walls alone, which surround the city, if at the same time are overthrown the laws on which its internal structure rests. The law is the invisible foundation on which the members of a community stand. Through the law they are strong, because it forges together individuals, who in themselves are weak, into one unified *polis*" (Werner Jaeger, "Praise of Law," in Paul Sayre, ed., *Interpretations of Modern Legal Philosophy* [New York: Oxford University Press, 1947], 359).

them a distinctive configuration; binds them to a special ethos and a special history. This process is marked by an inescapable tension. Every legal order is to some extent a reflex of power and domination, yet every legal order has some commitment to principles of justice. How that tension is resolved is a key to the construction of moral communities.

Justice does not necessarily depend on law. A just settlement of disputes may be negotiated (or imposed) in informal ways through the exercise of parental or administrative discretion. Communication, compromise, mediation, bargaining, leadership, institutional design: these are the everyday methods by which just outcomes are sought and may be achieved. The virtues of openness, generosity, and wisdom are the foundations of just decision. Through them reconciliation is won; through them the sharp edge of power is blunted. These virtues are not, of course, unique to law; they may even be undermined by law.

Nevertheless, law and justice have a special affinity. Often language itself makes the link, as in the Latin *ius*, the German *Recht*, the French *droit*. Each connotes both law and justice. Other terms (*lex, Gesetz, loi*) refer to law more narrowly. In American life the association of law and justice is supported by considerable symbolism, some of which is writ in granite, as when we read on the frieze of the Supreme Court, "Equal Justice Under Law." The Constitution purports to "establish Justice"; our high courts are staffed by justices; the attorney general heads a Department of Justice.

The experienced connection between law and justice has generated sustained debate over many centuries. On one side are those who argue that law is inescapably part of morality; that a rule, doctrine, or procedure is legally defective if it does not serve the ends of justice; that legal obligation is a special form of moral obligation. This is the doctrine of the *natural law* tradition.[16]

On the other side are those who stress the distinction between what is legal and what is just. In this they draw upon a different strand of commonsense understanding, one that perceives law as a blend of power and convention. Law is the product of an accepted procedure such as a legislative act, a judicial decision, an executive order, or an administrative regulation. The moral worth of the procedure—its outcome for justice—is always open to question. Hence there is no intrinsic connection

---

16. Contemporary studies of that tradition include Heinrich Rommen, *The Natural Law* (St. Louis, Mo.: Herder, 1947); A. P. d'Entrèves, *Natural Law: An Introduction to Legal Philosophy* (London: Hutchinson University Library, 1951); John Finnis, *Natural Law and Natural Rights* (Oxford: Clarendon Press, 1980).

between law and morality, even if there is such a connection between justice and morality. And legal obligation is a political fact that may or may not be justified on moral grounds. These are tenets of *legal positivism.*[17]

The enduring character of this debate reflects the complexity of legal experience, which is not fully grasped by either perspective. This is not to deny, however, that there are genuine differences regarding the foundations of morality and the place of social institutions in a moral order. Natural-law theorists insist on the objectivity of ethics, though not necessarily of particular value judgments. Some at least are ethical naturalists in the sense discussed in Chapter 1. They also believe that the moral order is, at its best, an integrated system within which relatively autonomous practices and institutions are connected and sustained. Therefore they stress the *continuities* of institutional and moral life, including the continuities of legal and moral responsibility. In this view, the blurring of institutional boundaries is a necessary and desirable part of moral ordering.[18]

Like other forms of positivism (see Chapter 2, "Rationalism and Positivism"), the ethos of legal positivism is marked by a quest for clarity and determinacy. Our minds are only befuddled—institutions are only distracted—when important distinctions and boundaries are obscured. Intellectual, moral, and institutional integrity requires precision of thought and clarity of purpose. Furthermore, legal positivists, like other positivists, tend to be skeptical about the objectivity of moral choices. They would rather associate values with specific preferences, customs, or beliefs. They have been especially concerned to provide for social *order,* and to clarify and protect the distinctive functions of social institutions.

Positivism is not indifferent to legal values. On the contrary, from positivism we gain a steady focus on *clarity, certainty,* and institutional *autonomy.* These virtues serve the ends of justice. They uphold the expectations of citizens, limit the abuse of official discretion, and determine the reach of binding obligations. By insisting on a definite bound-

---

17. Legal positivism goes back at least to Thomas Hobbes in the seventeenth century and runs through Jeremy Bentham in the late eighteenth century, John Austin in the nineteenth century, and Hans Kelsen in the twentieth century. A new genre, largely stimulated by H. L. A. Hart, might be called neo-positivist. It includes Hart's *The Concept of Law* (Oxford: Clarendon Press, 1961); Joseph Raz, *The Concept of a Legal System,* 2d ed. (Oxford: Clarendon Press, 1980); and Neil MacCormick, *Legal Reasoning and Legal Theory* (Oxford: Clarendon Press, 1978). These works do much to temper traditional positivism. See, for example, Hart's discussion of "the minimum content of natural law," in *Concept of Law,* 189ff.

18. Blurred *boundaries* may nevertheless allow considerable institutional autonomy.

ary between the legal and the nonlegal, they sustain the independence of judges and the separation of law from politics. They thereby enhance, in some respects at least, the integrity of legal institutions.

To sustain these virtues, legal positivism, as its name suggests, gives pride of place to "positive" law, that is, to the conclusion reached by an authorized body, expressed in a determinate rule or judgment. The typical elements of positive law are statutes, judicial decisions, and administrative orders or regulations. The positivist sees this as the "core" of law or even as "real" law.[19] It has a clear stamp of authority and is the proximate source of legal obligation. To a large extent, then, positivism is faithful to legal experience and attentive to law-related values.

The truth in legal positivism is, however, a limited truth. The virtues of clarity, certainty, and institutional autonomy are contingent, not absolute. They do not always serve justice; indeed, they often get in its way.[20] Precise rules, clear concepts, and uniform administration are elements of *formal* justice, which equalizes parties, restrains partiality, and makes decisions predictable. These surely contribute to the mitigation of arbitrary rule. But legal "correctness" has its own costs. Like any other technology, it is vulnerable to the divorce of ends and means. When this occurs, legality degenerates into legalism. Substantive justice is undone when there is too great a commitment to upholding the autonomy and integrity of law. Rigid adherence to precedent and mechanical application of rules hamper the capacity of the legal system either to take new interests and circumstances into account or to remedy the effects of social inequality. Formal justice tends to serve the status quo. It therefore may be experienced as arbitrary by those whose interests are only dimly perceived or who are really outside the "system."

Legal Principles

A preoccupation with positive law impoverishes our understanding of the connection between law and justice. It is not accidental that the phrase "positive law" has retained its importance in the vocabulary of jurisprudence. The adjective is needed because the law embraces more

19. "Strictly speaking, every law properly so called is a *positive* law. For it is *put* or set by its individual or collective author, or it exists by the *position* or institution of its individual or collective author" (John Austin, *The Province of Jurisprudence Determined* [1832; reprint, New York: Noonday Press, 1954], 124).

20. Nor are they always effective in upholding social order. A flexible and responsive legal system may have more elements of uncertainty, but it may also be more capable of maintaining social continuity and stability, especially where relationships are ongoing rather than transitory and where, therefore, contingencies cannot readily be foreseen.

than positive law. Even a cursory look at the materials used in legal reasoning shows that a great deal more is included than determinate rules and precedents. Legal ideas, variously and unclearly labeled "principles," "concepts," "maxims," and "doctrines" have a vital place in authoritative decision.[21]

Of special interest are "those requirements of justice which lawyers term principles of legality."[22] These are the implicit standards Lon Fuller called "the morality of law."[23] To be effective—and just—law should be general rather than ad hoc; promulgated and open, not secret; mainly prospective; intelligible; realistic, in the sense of requiring only what can be performed; sufficiently constant through time to provide adequate guides to action; and effective as a governor of official conduct. Such criteria spell out the conditions that must be met if arbitrary decision-making is to be minimized.

These ideas are not "positive" law except in the older sense of being human rather than divine. They remain highly *in*determinate until they are embodied in specific rules or judgments. Yet they are closely woven into the fabric of legal thought, and they provide, as Roscoe Pound liked to say, authoritative starting-points for legal reasoning. They are an intellectual resource that combines, in uneasy and always changing proportions, the elements of an authoritative tradition with more general standards of rational inquiry.

Principles of law—tribunals should be impartial; no one should profit from his own wrongdoing; precedents should be respected; unreliable evidence should be circumscribed; a fiduciary owes duties of loyalty and good faith to a beneficiary—formulate legally recognized values rather than definite rights or obligations. Rules, by contrast, are meant to have determinate scope and application.[24] A rule is the product of reasoning that brings values to bear on a particular problem, such as

21. The variety of legal materials (and their variable authority) was emphasized by Roscoe Pound in a number of writings. See especially "Hierarchy of Sources and Forms in Different Systems of Law," *Tulane Law Review* 7 (June 1933): 475–87; also Graham Hughes, "Rules, Policy and Decision-Making," *Yale Law Review* 77 (January 1968): 411–39.

22. Hart, *Concept of Law*, 202.

23. Lon L. Fuller, *The Morality of Law* (New Haven: Yale University Press, 1969).

24. John Dewey had a related but somewhat different idea: "Now a genuine principle differs from a rule in two ways: (a) A principle evolves in connection with the course of experience, being a generalized statement of what sort of consequences and values tend to be realized in certain kinds of situations; a rule is taken as something ready-made and fixed. (b) A principle is primarily intellectual, a method and scheme for judging, and is practical secondarily because of what it discloses; a rule is primarily practical" (*Theory of the Moral Life* [1932; reprint, New York: Holt, Rinehart and Winston, 1960], 136). On Dewey's view, principles decay into rules as they become fixed and rigid: "Their origin in

what evidence is admissible in court. To formulate a rule that is workable and that reflects a desired policy, it is necessary to take account of relevant facts and to balance values. As Dworkin explains:

> A principle . . . states a reason that argues in one direction, but does not necessitate a particular decision. If a man has or is about to receive something as a direct result of something illegal he did to get it, then that is a reason which the law will take into account in deciding whether he should keep it. There may be other principles or policies arguing in the other direction—a policy of securing title, for example, or a principle limiting punishment to what the legislature has stipulated. If so, our principle may not prevail, but that does not mean it is not a principle of our legal system, because in the next case, when these contravening considerations are absent or less weighty, the principle may be decisive.[25]

Legal principles, it has been said, "are the meeting-point of rules and values."[26]

That law includes principles as well as rules is hardly a new or exotic idea. The point needs emphasis, however, because legal positivism—as an aspect of its quest for determinacy—tends to equate law with rules, or at least to treat rules as paradigmatic legal phenomena. Hence the critique of positivism in the writings of Lon Fuller, Ronald Dworkin, and others tends to shift attention from rules to principles, that is, from highly determinate to less determinate aspects of law.

Principles are important to naturalist jurisprudence because, in many cases, *they are points of transition from law to justice.* For example, the doctrine of *mens rea* (guilty mind) holds that a blameworthy state of mind is an essential element of a criminal offense.[27] The alleged offender must have had an appropriate intention (say, to steal or kill) or must have been willfully heedless of the harmful consequences of his acts. This principle limits the reach of the criminal law. Harms caused by accidents do not count as criminal unless the perpetrator was reckless or deliberately took an unjustifiable risk of harming others. And no one can be a

experience is forgotten and so is their proper use in further experience" (ibid.). It does not follow, of course, that all rules are products of such decay or have no independent justification.

25. Ronald Dworkin, *Taking Rights Seriously* (Cambridge: Harvard University Press, 1978), 26.

26. Neil MacCormick, "Law as Institutional Fact," *Law Quarterly Review* 90 (1974): 127. For extensive discussion of legal principles in a neo-positivist framework, see MacCormick, *Legal Reasoning,* chap. 7.

27. A few exceptions recognize "strict liability." For example, "the prevailing view on sex offenses with minors was (and continues to be in most jurisdictions) that strict liability applies to the age of the minor; no mistake, not even a wholly reasonable one, can be a defense" (Sanford H. Kadish and Stephen J. Schulhofer, *Criminal Law and Its Processes: Cases and Materials,* 5th ed. [Boston: Little, Brown, 1989], 301).

criminal who lacks the capacity to exercise judgment or to form the appropriate intent. In this way the law of crimes upholds concepts of voluntary action and personal responsibility.

The doctrine of *mens rea* is based in part on cultural and historical premises. A strong sense of personal responsibility is part of Western culture; perspectives emphasizing collective responsibility and the social determinants of conduct may be slighted. Still, *the principle is a window to justice.* Even on its own terms, as the ideal of a particular culture, it provides a standpoint from which to assess rules that would require punishment of children or the mentally ill or that would impose criminal sanctions without proof of criminal intent. Furthermore, refinement of the principle calls for moral argument, which invokes more general understandings of human conduct, motivation, and culpability.

Many legally recognized values—for example, that marriage implies monogamy or that a right to privacy should be recognized—must be understood as historically contingent. They reflect the moral sensibilities of a particular society or epoch. Although they function as principles of criticism and justification, we cannot say they necessarily reflect a view of the good that transcends historical and cultural limitations. They are not natural law in any strong meaning of that phrase.

We must be open, however, to the larger promise of a theory of justice. As Morris R. Cohen once said, a "science of justice or natural law" is a viable and even a necessary goal, despite the truth that questions of justice are relative to historical conditions:

> The objection ignores the difference between a substantive code and a science of principles, a distinction which ought to be as clear as that between the directions of the engineer to the builder and the science of mechanics. . . . Similarly, substantive rules such as those of property cannot be well drawn without taking into account specific agricultural or industrial conditions. But this does not deny—on the contrary it presupposes—the existence of a general rule or method for the determination of how far any property rule justly meets the demands of its time.[28]

In our quest for principles of justice we begin with historically given values. But when we are asked for *their* authority and must justify what we say, it is not enough to cite what Oliver Wendell Holmes called "can't helps."[29]

28. *Reason and Nature* (Glencoe, Ill.: Free Press, 1953), 411.
29. In a letter to William James (1907), Holmes wrote: "I have been in the habit of saying that all I mean by truth is what I can't help thinking. The assumption of the validity of the thinking process seems to mean no more than that: I am up against it—I have gone

The authority of a legal principle does not depend solely on moral argument or, indeed, on a theory of justice. A conventional element, a received touchstone of authority, is always involved.[30] Most principles are recognized and enforced on historical grounds. In any developed system, however, the authority of a principle is *reinforced* by persuasive moral argument and is *undermined* when the moral argument is weak or manifestly false. Official segregation by race was upheld by the Supreme Court for many years, under the doctrine of "separate but equal." That justification weakened as theories of racial superiority were refuted and as moral sensibility developed among leading elements of the community. By the end of World War II it was no longer respectable—intellectually or morally—to defend the subordination of blacks. That change was decisive for the Court's revision of its interpretation of what "equal protection of the laws" required.

In the process I have described, legal rules are open to change *from within the law,* that is, by appeal to principles that purport to have legal authority. Some of these principles, such as consistency, impartiality, and truth-finding, are solidly based on the elementary requirements of legal ordering; others invoke the moral vocabulary of a particular culture or time, including those ideas generally taken for granted in the society; still others appeal to the legal authority of knowledge, that is, to evidence and argument regarding relevant social, biological, and physical facts. In these ways the affinity between law and justice—always variable, always problematic—is established, enhanced, or renewed.

When we understand the texture of a legal system, we see what is sound in the connection between "law that is" and "law that ought to be." All law must meet some prescribed test of validity, but what counts as law includes, as Roscoe Pound put it, "authoritative precepts, developed and applied by an authoritative technique in the light of or on the background of authoritative ideals."[31] These precepts, techniques,

---

as far as I can go—just as when I like a glass of beer. But I have learned to surmise that my *can't helps* are not necessarily cosmic can't helps—that the universe may not be subject to my limitations; and philosophy generally seems to me to sin through arrogance. . . . I can't help preferring champagne to ditch water,—I doubt if the universe does" (Oliver Wendell Holmes, Jr., "Letter to William James," in Max Lerner, ed., *The Mind and Faith of Justice Holmes* [New York: Modern Library, 1943], 415). Holmes invoked "can't helps" again in "Natural Law" (1918), ibid., 395.

30. At an extreme, in a morally sensitive system of law the conventional element may be no more than an accepted practice of resolving controversies by offering relevant moral arguments. See Jules L. Coleman, "Negative and Positive Positivism," *Journal of Legal Studies* 3 (January 1982): 160.

31. Roscoe Pound, *Jurisprudence* (St. Paul, Minn.: West Publishing Co., 1959), 2:107.

and ideals are standpoints from which to criticize or justify specific rules. In other words, legally recognized standards exist to which appeal can be made for revision of what may have previously been taken as a settled rule of positive law. Therefore a considerable part of what the law *is* supplies criteria for deciding what the law *should be*. So long as we keep in mind the variety of legal materials, no paradox is involved.

What gives bite to the natural-law perspective is the following claim: The elaboration and refinement of principles and the criticism of rules in the light of principles are part of the legal process. They are *internal* resources for bringing logic and evidence to bear on law, and for moving law closer to justice. They are, in that sense, an appeal to "nature," that is, to knowledge regarding the conditions that affect the well-being of persons, institutions, and communities. Of course, what constitutes knowledge is necessarily open to inquiry and debate. Hence law is more uncertain and indefinite than traditional positivist doctrine could accept.

Reconciling Positivism and Natural Law

The contrasting perspectives of legal naturalism and legal positivism reflect genuine differences in sensibility and theory, but they are not irreconcilable. We may gain a more comprehensive understanding, while respecting the truth in both doctrines, if we keep in mind two important distinctions that we have previously invoked: (1) the difference between defining a term and developing a theory; and (2) the difference between analytical, logical, or "necessary" connections and empirical or probabilistic connections. The rights and wrongs of positivism and natural law are to a large extent revealed when these distinctions are understood.

As a matter of *definition*, we should be open to using the word "law" in a way that is general enough to embrace all legal experience, however various or rudimentary. We should identify law with the very practical functions that called it into being, and not only with the more complex or ideal states into which it may develop. In other words, we should be content with a weak definition of law.

Hence we can accept, as a starting point, the legal positivism of H. L. A. Hart. Hart argues that, in stepping "from the pre-legal to the legal world," a society develops special rules for curing the defects of a social order that is based only on informal or unofficial norms.[32] A regime of unofficial norms may be effective enough in governing the af-

---

32. Hart, *Concept of Law*, 91.

fairs of an informal group or small community, but as a system of governance it has a number of inherent limitations. Most important, it may lack any mechanism for resolving uncertainties as to the existence or scope of a norm. The special work of law—the task that is the common denominator of all legal systems—is to identify claims and obligations that merit official validation and enforcement.

Law thus understood may be quite rudimentary. It may consist of nothing more than the establishment of a public record of, say, land holdings or family privileges—a record that has a special claim to the community's respect as a guide to action. Whenever institutions arise to do this work we can speak of a legal order. Such institutions need not be specialized; they may be wholly integrated with religious ritual; there may be little or no apparatus of coercion. For them to constitute a legal order, it is essential only that what they say about rights and duties is accepted by the community as authoritative.[33]

This way of defining law is consistent with maintaining a distinction between law and justice. In this view law is institutional fact. It is a pattern of decision-making in which at least those members of a community who are in power govern their conduct in accordance with accepted rules. The rules may be unjust or repressive; they may uphold slavery, torture, class privilege, and the arbitrary power of a kin-group; but so long as deference is granted to rules that say who shall be king or who should have the right to extort confessions by torture, then the basic phenomenon of law exists.

We may agree with John Austin that "the existence of law is one thing; its merit or demerit is another."[34] It does not follow, however, that there is no *connection* between what law is and what it ought to be, or that the connection we find is accidental. It is important to preserve the distinction between law as an operative system and justice as a moral ideal. But clear distinctions are compatible with—indeed, they are important preconditions of—theories that trace connections and reveal dynamics. Law is not necessarily just, but it does promise justice. We must look to the theory of law and justice to understand why that promise exists and

---

33. "Acceptance" leaves many questions as to its scope and quality unanswered, but it does presume at least the rudiments of community. Hart speaks of "two minimum conditions necessary and sufficient for the existence of a legal system. On the one hand those rules of behaviour which are valid according to the system's ultimate criteria of validity must be generally obeyed and, on the other hand, its rules of recognition [rules for determining what is authoritative] . . . must be effectively accepted as common public standards of official behavior by its officials" (ibid., 113).

34. Austin, *Province of Jurisprudence*, 184.

under what conditions it may be fulfilled or abridged. The matter cannot be settled by definitional fiat.

Legal positivism is often associated with one key idea: there is no "necessary" connection between law and morality. The point is to emphasize that law can be and often is immoral and unjust.[35] This is so obvious that it may be difficult for the uninitiated to understand what the fuss is about. The problem is that the positivist formula is not so innocent as it appears. It is used to suggest that law and justice have *no* special connection at all. Natural-law theorists counter that law need not be understood as a mere datum of social power or convention. They see in legal experience the development of expectations and constraints, standards and aspirations, that push law in the direction of justice, even though the push may not go very far at any given time.

Both sides have failed to see that the connection between law and justice is variable and probabilistic, but not adventitious. There is *inclination* but not *necessity*. In their eagerness to stress the redemptive potential of law, natural-law theorists have been insufficiently sensitive to the ways law can be arbitrary and unjust. Positivists, for their part, have been only superficially empirical. While properly insisting on "law as fact" they have tended to ignore those aspects of legal experience that create a strain toward justice. It is not that law and justice *must* coincide in any specific case. Clearly they often do not. Rather, there are good grounds for believing that "the enterprise of subjecting conduct to the governance of rules" creates "the germ at least of justice."[36] Under proper conditions that germ will mature and flourish. If it does it will generate demands for and commitments to such values as respect for the person, self-restraint in the use of power, and reasoned justification.

The affinity of law and justice is neither necessary nor happenstance. It is not necessary because many contingencies and obstacles can intervene, notably the use of law as an instrument of domination. It is not happenstance because the quest for justice "under law" and through law

35. This argument is associated with a distinctive strategy of reform. Positivists such as Bentham and Hart prefer a strategy of *external* criticism. For that purpose they insist that the legal validity of a statute, judicial decision, or other official act should not be confounded with its moral worth. When these attributes are confounded, the legally valid decision may be taken as presumptively just, thereby weakening criticism of law. It is better, according to this view, to treat law as neutral and descriptive fact, without any intrinsic connection to justice and as no special resource in the quest for justice. Justice is a moral ideal, not a legal concept. It should be invoked by the political process, which is the appropriate mechanism for criticizing and changing law. The natural-law perspective prefers a strategy of *internal* criticism of existing law, invoking latent or implicit standards.

36. Fuller, *Morality of Law*, 106; Hart, *Concept of Law*, 202.

occurs for sound and recurrent reasons. Many human communities have discovered that legal rules and standards are effective devices for instituting fairness and correcting the abuse of power. This experience suggests that the moral worth of law has an underlying basis, a basis that must be sought in the nature of human personality and in the continuities of social organization.

Because all law is based in part on convention and political will it always contains an arbitrary element. For those who must obey it, the law is to some extent brute fact and brute command. But this arbitrary element, although necessary and inevitable, is repugnant to the sense of justice. A science of justice has the moral objective of *progressively reducing the amount of arbitrariness in positive law and its administration.* Arbitrariness is never eliminated entirely, but it is mitigated as knowledge is brought to bear and as a spirit of self-correction prevails.

A naturalist perspective does not shrink from recognizing wickedness done in the name of law; it readily accepts that rule by law, even when it meets some minimum conditions of, say, impartiality, "is unfortunately compatible with very great iniquity."[37] But it treats the values associated with law, and the potential of law for doing justice, as part of legal experience. It does not dismiss them as fantasy or banish them from inquiry.

A legal system cannot be effective unless it contains some degree of openness to the sense of justice. That is the germ of truth in the idea that immoral laws are invalid and impose no obligation. Such a proposition claims too much. It is true, however, that what is demonstrably unjust is legally suspect and may be challenged as invalid or at least as subject to close scrutiny and strict interpretation.

Affirmations of Community

The most important contribution of natural-law doctrine is its affirmation of community. The doctrine presumes that every legal order has an implicit constitution. Beyond the specifics of positive law are the *premises* of the legal order, to which appeal can be made in the name of justice and community. The premises create legitimate authority; they are the source of civic obligation. The duty of officials and citizens to obey the law is grounded on the implicit constitution, which in turn presumes community membership. At bottom, fidelity to law is fidelity to community.

37. Hart, *Concept of Law*, 202.

This does not tell us what *kind* of community is created or what its moral worth may be. A persistent problem for law and justice, as for critical morality generally, is the tension between particularized and generalized conceptions of community. We have encountered this issue before, in the discussion of obscenity, homosexuality, abortion, and religion. There we saw how the Supreme Court has wrestled with competing conceptions of community. One view emphasizes historicity and specificity; the other looks to constitutive principles. The former is drawn to piety, takes community and tradition as given and static, and resists a posture of criticism. The latter obeys a generalizing impulse and finds community in shared premises, in a process of self-scrutiny, and in the collective reconstruction of received norms.

These very different ways of integrating law and community result in profound differences in the reach and quality of justice. They suggest a distinction between *communities of observance* and *communities of principle*.[38] In a community of observance, law is a sacred guide to individual conduct and social practice. Fidelity to law means faithful fulfillment of detailed rules as to how to live a pious life. The most familiar examples of communities of observance are Judaism and Islam. The orthodox Jew or Muslim conforms every action to God's will, and the will of God is found in a book of law. Communion with God is achieved through obedience to his commands. The latter can be very specific indeed, governing diet, cleanliness, and family life as well as obligations of charity and ritual. The result is a culture sustained by "legal moralism," that is, by the use of law to enforce adherence to a prescriptive morality.

The alternative is a conception of law and society that looks to animating principles rather than conformity to rules.[39] Thus at an early stage Christianity broke from the Hebraic tradition by replacing faith in Torah with faith in Jesus. The central symbolism shifted from the tablets of Moses to the cross of Calvary. Jesus, it is said, came to fulfill the promise of Hebraic law, but also to transcend it. Saint Paul "worked out the doctrine that Jesus replaced the Law; that the Law had been necessary as a 'schoolmaster' before the arrival of Jesus; but that henceforth the

---

38. The phrase "community of observance" is from W. G. deBurgh, *The Legacy of the Ancient World* (1923; reprint, London: Penguin Books, 1961), 95.

39. Of course, Hebraic legal culture has principles as well as rules: "And what doth the Lord require of thee, but to do justly, and to love mercy, and to walk humbly with thy God" (Micah 6:8). However, "the orthodox Jew attaches so much importance to the forms because, the goal being clear . . . what matters on this earth is the way to the goal: and the Law, in his eyes, is the guidance that God has given him" (David Daube, "Two Jewish Prayers," *Rechtshistorisches Journal* 6 [1987]: 196). Thus law as prescribed conduct is in the foreground of consciousness; principle is in the background.

duty of man was to live, not under the Law, but in Jesus."[40] Redemption was to be found in acceptance of a central article of faith—belief in Jesus as human and divine, as Messiah and Son of God—rather than in following a sacred code of conduct. The effect was to highlight *general teachings*—the golden rule, the law of love, the sin of pride—that could be embraced by people of widely varying traditions and circumstances.

A community of principle is prefigured in the culture of ancient Greece. Werner Jaeger traces a development from law as the union of custom and divine commandment (*themis,* the gift of Zeus) to law codified as *nomos* and informed by a sense of justice or righteousness, or *dikē*.[41] *Nomos* and *dikē* have connotations of rationality and equality; they emerge, it appears, out of the struggle for justice and out of the process of doing justice:

> Dikē means the due share which each man can rightly claim; and then, the principle which guarantees that claim. . . . It is obvious how, during the struggles of a class which had always been compelled to receive justice as themis—that is, as an inevitable authority imposed on it from above—the word dikē became the battle-cry. Throughout these centuries we hear the call for dikē, growing constantly more widespread, more passionate, and more imperative.[42]

Although law as dikē retained the connotation of a divine or cosmic *order,* it seems to have lost the association with divine *command.*

The Greek conception of law became, in time, political rather than religious. To be governed by law was to be a responsible member of the political community. The guiding ideal was a kind of civility, not a pious deference to the will of God. At the same time,

> the Greek thought of the collective laws, the *nomoi,* of his polis as a moral and creative power. Our own conception of Law is so completely Roman that we find it hard to think of Law as a creative, formative agent, but this was the normal Greek conception. The Romans thought of Law at first in a purely practical way: it regulated relations between people and their affairs, and was itself a codification of practice. Not until Roman lawyers came under Greek influence did they begin to deduce from their laws general principles of Law, and to extend these in the light of philosophical principles. . . . [The *nomoi*] were designed not only to secure justice in the individual case but also to inculcate Justice: this is one reason why the young Athenian, during his

40. Daube, "Two Jewish Prayers," 196.

41. "Praise of Law," 374 n.39. Jaeger notes that originally *nomos* meant unwritten custom, but it later came to mean the written law. He also points out that "the law on which it [the polis] was founded was not a mere decree, but the *nomos,* which originally meant the sum total of that which was respected by all as living custom with regard to what is right or wrong" (ibid., 361). See also Werner Jaeger, *Paideia: The Ideals of Greek Culture,* 2d ed., trans. Gilbert Highet (Oxford: Clarendon Press, 1939), 1:chap. 6.

42. Jaeger, *Paideia,* 103.

two years with the colours, was instructed in the *nomoi*—which are the basic laws of the state, to be distinguished from specific enactments regulating such things as putting lights on motor-cars; these were only *psephismata* or "things voted."[43]

The legal experience of ancient Greece is notable as a quest for the ideal of justice and for principles of justice. These were inextricably joined, however, to the special history of Greek communities, and the *nomoi* inevitably stood as objects of reverence and sources of piety.

A COMMUNITARIAN LEGACY

The contribution of law to community and, through community, to justice can be discerned in a distinctive feature of the Anglo-American legal heritage—the common-law tradition. That tradition is worth a brief review, for it contains an implicit ideal of communitarian justice.[44]

In its simplest meaning, common law is judge-made law: law fashioned by judges in the course of deciding particular controversies. The alternative is law-making by legislatures or by decree. A more complex idea is the common-law *tradition,* the pattern of judicial prerogative and initiative that developed in England during the late Middle Ages and has remained ever since the core of legal culture in English-speaking countries.

We should take the idea of tradition seriously:

> A legal tradition, as the term implies, is not a set of rules of law about contracts, corporations, and crimes, although such rules will almost always be in some sense a reflection of that tradition. Rather it is a set of deeply rooted, historically conditioned attitudes about the nature of law, about the role of law in the society and the polity, about the proper organization and operation of the legal system, and about the way law is or should be made, applied, studied, perfected, and taught. The legal tradition relates the legal system to the culture of which it is a partial expression.[45]

43. H. D. F. Kitto, *The Greeks* (London: Penguin Books, 1951), 94.

44. This discussion draws on my essay "The Ethos of American Law," in Irving Kristol and Paul Weaver, eds., *The Americans: 1976* (Lexington, Mass.: Lexington Books, 1976). For historical and theoretical studies of the common-law tradition, see especially Gerald J. Postema, *Bentham and the Common Law Tradition* (Oxford: Clarendon Press, 1986); J. G. A. Pocock, *The Ancient Constitution and the Feudal Law* (Cambridge: Cambridge University Press, 1987); Melvin A. Eisenberg, *The Nature of the Common Law* (Cambridge: Harvard University Press, 1988); Guido Calabresi, *Ideals, Beliefs, Attitudes and the Law: Private Law Perspectives on a Public Law Problem* (Syracuse, N.Y.: Syracuse University Press, 1985).

45. John Henry Merryman, *The Civil Law Tradition* (Stanford: Stanford University Press, 1969), 2.

In the common-law tradition, judicial creativity has long been respected and even venerated, despite some occasional attacks and despite the claim that, in an important sense, the judges "discover" but do not "make" law.[46]

Here, indeed, is the paradox of the common-law tradition. It is centered on a primordial vision of law as *given*—if not by divine authority, then by history and practice—and yet as *adaptable* to changing needs and circumstances. On that understanding, common law is not made by judges or by any other sovereign power. Rather, it is an expression of community, a product of shared history and common life. To find the law one must know and acknowledge the community's institutions. The judges *speak* for the law but they are not its *architects*. What they say, including the precedents they establish, is only a corrigible indicator of what the law is in fact. For the judge, wrote William Blackstone, is "sworn to determine not according to his own private judgment, but according to the known laws and customs of the land; not delegated to pronounce a new law, but to maintain and expound the old one."[47] As Blackstone put it, the judges

> are the depositaries of the laws; the living oracles, who must decide in all cases of doubt, and who are bound by an oath to decide according to the law of the land. Their knowledge of that law is derived from experience and study . . . and from being long personally accustomed to the judicial decisions of their predecessors. And indeed these judicial decisions are the principal and most authoritative evidence, that can be given, of the existence of such a custom as shall form a part of the common law.[48]

Nevertheless, the task of the judges is inescapably creative. At a minimum they must choose among interpretations of experience to say which are truly binding for the case at hand.[49]

46. Elsewhere in Europe and Latin America a civil-law tradition prevails, largely influenced by the heritage from Rome and, especially in France, by the experience of the revolution, which was in part directed against the judicial system of the ancien régime. In civil-law systems, judicial creativity is at best a necessary fact of life, to be constrained as much as possible by legal codes and statutes. For an overview, see Merryman, *Civil Law Tradition;* also Bernard Rudden, "Courts and Codes in England, France and Soviet Russia," *Tulane Law Review* 48 (1974): 1010–28; Peter G. Stein, "Judge and Jurist in the Civil Law: An Historical Interpretation," *Louisiana Law Review* 46 (1985): 241–57.

47. *Commentaries on the Laws of England* (1765; reprint, San Francisco: Bancroft-Whitney Co., 1915), 1:117f.

48. Ibid., 116.

49. The paradox may be resolved, in part at least, if we keep in mind the distinction discussed above between positive law and its authoritative sources. The latter are more inchoate, more indeterminate—and more fundamental. What the judges decide is positive law for the parties and for others in the same circumstances; but what enters their decision is more general and diverse. Thus the common-law and natural-law (or naturalist)

In the view of its major apologists, especially Matthew Hale (1609–1676) and William Blackstone (1723–1780), the common law of England, as it had developed since the thirteenth century, was an exquisite combination of reason, custom, and experience. The judges, it was thought, spoke in the name of immemorial custom, which constituted the law of the land. In deciding which specific customs were binding and which might be ignored or changed, they perceived themselves as maintaining fidelity to shared experience and a common past. That past was taken to be a repository of good sense and social truth. The judges were to conserve and nurture a common reason while taking account of current practices, expectations, and necessities.

By the eighteenth century it was more or less settled that large areas of social life—in particular, commercial and property relations—would be governed by common law. In these "private" areas legislation was secondary and largely limited to confirming or amending common-law rules. In effect, the judges (and with them the lawyers and their clients) were delegated responsibility for managing private arrangements. The judges drew guidance from the claims of litigants, with little reference to royal or parliamentary will. They worked out policies and made law without guilt, because they did not suppose they were making political decisions. Their law was derived from custom and private ordering, which is to say, from the long-standing expectations and practical requirements of landholding, inheritance, trade, and industry.

This background suggests two corollary themes. First, the common law counterposes state and society. As they settle disputes and vindicate claims, the judges uphold a private sphere of life. The protection of individual and group rights, including modes of conduct hallowed by tradition, comes to define a legal order *that is independent of political authority.* When the judges invoke social experience and necessity, especially the security of transactions and of property interests, they implicitly postulate rights against the state. This experience feeds into and supports the common-law commitment to constitutional government.[50]

---

traditions converge. Both emphasize the need for inquiry, and especially for social knowledge, as part of the process by which law is determined; and common law, though mainly based on history and practice, must include criteria for choosing among historical facts, in the interests of justice and good sense as well as of authenticity.

50. For the American colonists, it has been said, this was the main significance of the English common law: "They conceived of the common law as being a limited set of essentially constitutional principles—principles of public or constitutional law" (George A. Billias, *Law and Authority in Colonial America* [Barre, Mass.: Barre Publishers, 1965], xiii).

Second, in the common-law tradition the authority of a rule is never completely settled. If experience is the book of law, then what is authoritative can only be understood in the light of changing circumstances. It follows that the authority of common law is fluid, variable, and problematic, with competing doctrines and alternative justifications bidding for respect. The common law, rooted in litigation, is an invitation to argument. The argument turns on what the law *is,* but it cannot ignore what the law *should be,* that is, what justice requires. Thus understood, the common-law tradition makes legal conclusions forever debatable.[51]

The common law is respected because it is presumed to be based on good-faith efforts by independent judges to make objective assessments of what the law is and, within limits, what it should be. The judges are expected to articulate a set of historically established principles of obligation, taking account of a wide range of legal materials, including legislation, judicial precedent, and social practice; to transform those principles into workable rules; to maintain the integrity of the legal process; and to obey the conclusions of legal reasoning rather than their personal inclination. This institutional morality is the key to their legitimacy.

The courts bolster their legitimacy by relying on a special mode of argument. In Sir Edward Coke's famous phrase, legal reason is "artificial reason."[52] It is so not only in being arcane and technical but, more important, because *it must start from premises that are authoritative and not merely sound.* A scientific assessment or moral judgment may draw on whatever ideas are helpful in reaching conclusions justified by fact and logic. A judicial conclusion must demonstrate continuity with what is already received and established.

Artificial reason is, then, the language of legal legitimacy. The continuing quest is for legal decision-making that is at once rational and

51. "Nor does the common law system admit the possibility of a court, however elevated, reaching a final, authoritative statement of what the law is in a general abstract sense. It is as if the system placed particular value upon dissension, obscurity, and the tentative character of judicial utterances" (A. W. B. Simpson, "The Common Law and Legal Theory," in A. W. B. Simpson, ed., *Oxford Essays in Jurisprudence,* 2d series [Oxford: Clarendon Press, 1973], 90).

52. In 1608, responding to a claim made by James I that as king he could decide legal cases using his own reason, Coke replied: "True it was, that God had endowed his Majesty with excellent science, and great endowments of nature; but his Majesty was not learned in the laws of his realm of England, and causes which concern the life, or inheritance, or goods of his subjects, are not to be decided by natural reason, but by the artificial reason and judgment of the law, which law is an act which requires long study and experience, before that a man can attain cognizance of it; and that the law was the golden metwant and measure to try the causes of his subjects; and which protected his Majesty in safety and peace" (quoted in Edward S. Corwin, "The 'Higher Law' Background of American Constitutional Law," *Harvard Law Review* 42 [1929]: 149f.).

traditional. The *received* law, including concepts and principles as well as definite rules, should be capable of reasoned elaboration. Conversely, the *emergent* law should be founded in propositions that define the historic commitments of the community.

In the common-law tradition the courts do indeed make law, but they do not make it out of whole cloth. Most legal scholars have long agreed that "judicial legislation" is an indispensable part of the legal process. But this does not tell us what is special about *judicial* legislation. Furthermore, "legislation" is not a proper synonym for "lawmaking." Legislation has a more focused meaning, connoting what legislatures do and the special institutional freedom they have. The United States Congress is bound by the Constitution but otherwise can freely register public sentiment and openly compromise political positions. A legislature may and often does build new policies on old ones, but its legitimacy does not depend on its doing so. Therefore it is misleading to say without qualification that common-law judges "legislate."[53]

In legal reasoning at its best we find a union of legitimacy and cognition. The law insists on received premises but (1) those premises are open to reconstruction as their logic is explored, and (2) in formulating legal rules the courts are to take account of social reality. Put another way, the common-law tradition commands inquiry. To find the operative law, judges must scrutinize the connection between legal abstractions and the practical workings of industry, government, or family life. The courts cannot know what is "informed consent" (in health law) or "abuse of power" (in the law of impeachment) or "detrimental reliance" (in contract law) without knowing how institutions work, how professional practice is organized, how people routinely carry on their business.

Implicit Law

The union of legitimacy and cognition in the judicial process can illuminate the interplay of critical and conventional morality, which we discussed at some length in the preceding chapter. These issues come to-together particularly in the quest for implicit law and in the justification of legal conclusions by appeal to moral and social theory.[54]

---

53. By the same logic, we should be wary of referring to administrative rule-making as legislation, since the rules made by administrative agencies, though they have the force of law, derive their authority from a legislative mandate and are supposed only to implement that mandate.

54. On implicit law, see Lon L. Fuller, *Anatomy of the Law* (New York: Praeger, 1968), 43ff.

When judges are called on to say what a statute requires or a precedent holds, their response is plainly interpretive. Courts are obliged to resolve ambiguities of meaning, and as they do so they reveal what, as they understand it, is implicit in the stated law. Meanings cannot be properly divorced from purpose and context; hence the study of meanings involves critical assessment of the reasons behind a rule and of the conditions that make a rule effective.

To find implicit law is to reveal a latent purpose, a value premise, or a factual assumption. The value premises of contract law, for example, are drawn from the accumulated body of rules and their operation. The apparent premises—consent as the ground of obligation; facilitation of exchange; good faith in negotiation and performance—are tested by legal experience, that is, by the way rules have developed and difficulties been resolved. At the same time, insofar as they are taken to be sound the premises are used to criticize existing rules and to guide the formation of new rules. In this way the implicit commitments of received law, appropriately generalized and clarified, become instruments of legal reform.

In the quest for implicit law the most important move is the *identification of values* that are fundamental to a sphere of life or to the community as a whole. When such values are made explicit they can serve as authoritative guides to interpretation. Thus, if the informing policy of contract law is to facilitate economic transactions, interpretation will tend to widen the kinds of promises considered legally binding; if the law upholds the family as an institution, doubts are likely to be resolved in favor of parental authority; if majority rule is taken as fundamental, it will be vindicated by insisting on one citizen, one vote; if personal autonomy is the mandate, maternal choice will be weighed more heavily than the community's interest in the life of an early-term fetus. These choices are seldom, if ever, *necessary* outcomes of judicial reasoning. Identification of values, though inescapable, is inherently controversial. The task places judges in the forefront of the effort to attain a central objective of critical morality: clarification of a community's moral commitments.[55]

The clarification of premises knows no near stopping-place. The more we demand by way of rational argument, the harder it is to remain within the bounds of a particular tradition or social setting. Consider, for example, the values at stake in the law of due process. These values include: *truth-finding*—in confrontations with government and in the

---

55. For discussion of how courts take account of "social propositions," including moral norms, see Eisenberg, *Nature of the Common Law*, chap. 4.

resolution of private disputes, every person has the right to such protection as the truth may give, within the limits prescribed by other
values such as the protection of privileged communications; *legitimacy*—legal process presumes a proper tribunal or officer acting within
a defined scope of authority and in accordance with accepted law; *fairness*—the case must be judged according to rational principles, without
caprice, prejudice, or disregard of consequences; *personal dignity*—some
minimum rights of personality are guaranteed, for example, forced confessions are forbidden; and *responsible governance*—government is to heed
affected interests as it pursues its own purposes. The underlying message is that arbitrary power is to be controlled and minimized.

The premises of due process, as of any other branch of law, are
normally presented as elements of a distinctive heritage. From the
viewpoint of the courts, this is necessary to their legitimacy. Note,
however, that the value premises do not specify particular procedures,
institutional forms, or even broad patterns or styles, such as partisan
advocacy within an adversary system. The right to be heard in one's
cause is implied, but not trial by jury or (arguably) a right against self-
incrimination. Particular procedures and desirable elements of fairness
are always arguable. In these discussions history, tradition, and circumstance loom large. That is so in part because we often have more confidence in a particular form or practice, rooted in experience, than in an
abstract statement of why the form exists or what values it upholds. Indeed, as Kenneth I. Winston has noted, "We often don't know what it
means to be committed to the value apart from the forms."[56]

It must be remembered, however, that the ends of justice, and many of
the means to those ends, are not bound to a particular history. Rather,
they derive from our general knowledge of human nature, society, law,
and government. They belong to the theory of political community, not
to the unique experience of a people.

To preserve their authority, judges emphasize continuity with the
past; therefore they tend to shun explicit moral theory. This strategy
works fairly well, up to a point. But insofar as they accept responsibility
for giving reasons and respond to demands for coherent analysis, they
cannot avoid constructing theories. This process may be relatively
straightforward, as when the court develops a theory of how certain accidents occur and draws inferences for, say, the liability of manufacturers
to consumers. Similarly, as experts in procedure, judges feel secure in

---

56. Personal communication, 9 August 1990.

theorizing about what constitutes good evidence (in the contexts they know) and how juries react to prejudicial information. American judges are comfortable with issues that require a theory of democracy, for example, as entailing protection of minorities from the tyranny of majorities. Like everyone else, judges are less sure of themselves, and less confident of their objectivity, when they must deal with abstract concepts of unsettled meaning and controversial import, such as the question of what a human person is or what constitutes invidious discrimination. Here judicial hesitation and restraint are very much in order. Ultimately, however, if the courts are to be both principled and responsive, they require theories of human nature and social life, theories without which moral argument cannot go forward.

CONSTITUTION AND COMMUNITY

The connection between common law and community comes into sharp and controversial focus in constitutional adjudication. Here judicial lawmaking raises grave questions of power and legitimacy. In ordinary common law, where no constitutional issues arise, the authority of the courts is subject to a decisive limitation: the legislature can overturn any common-law precedent, including any judicial interpretation of a statute. Here legislative supremacy prevails, at least in theory. A majority in Congress or a state legislature, with the approval of the president or a governor, can change the judge-made rule.

When a court interprets a constitution, however, its ruling can be reversed or modified only by the difficult and dangerous process of constitutional amendment, or by its own or a higher court's decision in a later case. In practice, therefore, on most constitutional issues the courts have the last word. In the United States, the authority to decide what the Constitution requires extends to "judicial review" of legislative and administrative actions, that is, to considering whether they may be held unconstitutional and therefore void.[57] In such matters the courts do not merely *supplement* the legislature, as in ordinary common law; they may also *override* the will of the majority as expressed by its agents.

This "anti-majoritarian" power has been firmly established in constitutional law since the early days of the Republic. Judicial review is not explicitly provided for in the Constitution. Rather, the power is implied

---

57. For the European experience, with an emphasis on "the expansion and legitimacy of judicial review," see Mauro Cappelletti, *The Judicial Process in Comparative Perspective* (Oxford: Clarendon Press, 1989), 117ff.

from certain key clauses, especially in Article VI, which states that "this Constitution, and the Laws of the United States made in Pursuance thereof . . . shall be the supreme Law of the Land," and from "the judicial Power of the United States" as set forth in Article III. The implication was recognized by Alexander Hamilton in *The Federalist*,[58] was debated in early Congresses, and was drawn authoritatively by the Supreme Court itself in *Marbury v. Madison* (1803) and in subsequent cases.

Although the Court purports to do no more than declare the meaning of the Constitution as it bears on the case at hand, that meaning is largely determined by a long history of interpretation. Constitutional law is not a direct application of the text of the Constitution. To find the *operative* law one looks instead to a gloss or extended commentary, which is found in the reported cases. The common-law principle of fidelity to precedent insures some continuity of interpretation. As a result, the law is reasonably predictable, at least for substantial periods and for many kinds of cases. That same fidelity, however, may lead the Court to pay more attention to the judicial gloss than to the text of the Constitution itself. Step by step, entering doors left open by preceding decisions, key terms and clauses are given new meanings. If this process goes very far, it may result in a perceived and troublesome discrepancy between the explicit text and what the judges have made of it.

The Constitution contains both highly abstract and very specific provisions. On the one hand, each state is allowed two senators, not "fair representation" in the Senate. On the other hand, the Constitution speaks of "liberty," "commerce," "property," "due process," "equal protection," "the executive power," and similar very general ideas. What these abstractions mean is hardly self-evident; yet they are clearly, even grandly, authoritative as starting points for legal reasoning. Abstract clauses may tempt the justices to elaborate correspondingly abstract principles, such as the idea, mentioned above in connection with the *Hardwick* case, that the Constitution protects "rights of intimate association," or the once-regnant notion that "freedom of contract" is fundamental to ordered liberty. The Court deals with "cases and controversies," as does ordinary common law, and this concreteness tends to limit

58. Alexander Hamilton, James Madison, and John Jay, *The Federalist* (1787; reprint, New York: Bantam Books, 1982), no. 78, 394: "By a limited constitution I understand one which contains certain specified exceptions to the legislative authority; such for instance as that it shall pass no bills of attainder, no *ex post facto* laws, and the like. Limitations of this kind can be preserved in practice no other way than through the medium of the courts of justices; whose duty it must be to declare all acts contrary to the manifest tenor of the constitution void."

the reach of any decision. Nevertheless, when the Court formulates a principle to justify its decision in a particular case, it must find an appropriate level of abstraction. If, whether through error or temptation, it finds the wrong level, the principle may become a loose cannon, an uncontrolled element in constitutional law.

As a higher form of statute, associated with the experience of a "founding," the Constitution introduces a significant ambiguity into the idea of democracy. A *contemporary* majority accepts subordination to an *ancestral* majority. The authority of the Constitution rests on a shared belief that the founders ably formulated the fundamental commitments of the political community. Its claim to legitimacy is based in part on the fact that the Constitution was adopted by a democratic process, though hardly one that would be acceptable today. The history is less important, however, than the tacit acceptance that has been granted by succeeding generations.

The generations of Americans alive today who accept the Constitution do so without debate and without voting. They are not asked to ratify its provisions, nor are they summoned periodically to revise it or to reassess its worth. Although they differ on many issues, most Americans have faith in the effectiveness and legitimacy of the fundamental law. They think of the Constitution as a vital part of the nation's identity. These beliefs have more to do with culture and socialization than with deliberate political choice. As shared understandings, they are vague and unstructured at many points, open to direction by legitimate authority. The loyalty they generate is generally taken for granted: it is tested only infrequently, cautiously, and indirectly.

This "foundational" or "constitutive" community needs a voice. A majority vote in Congress *may* be that voice, if it is sufficiently large or stable. Most often, though, legislative majorities are transient aggregations of political will. Presidents and executive agencies may also articulate the fundamental interests and aspirations of the community, including that of fidelity to the commands and premises of the Constitution. Indeed, any branch of government can make the community an object of moral and political concern—and every branch does so from time to time. In the American system, however, the Supreme Court has been given the leading role as defender of the Constitution and therefore as agent for the community that underpins it.

Taken as a whole, the Constitution is both majoritarian and antimajoritarian. It is majoritarian in that its principles guarantee the free formation of current majorities, who are empowered to decide who shall govern and, for the most part, what policies will prevail. But the majority is not sovereign. It can be formed only as the Constitution provides—not by "people power" in the streets, for example—and its representatives are bound, as Jefferson said, "by the chains of the Constitution." Judicial review is a way of implementing constitutional restrictions on majority rule.

The clearest and most compelling justification for judicial review is the need for coherence within a federal system. "I do not think the United States would come to an end," wrote Justice Holmes, "if we lost our power to declare an Act of Congress void. I do think the union would be imperiled if we could not make that declaration as to the laws of the several States."[59] With respect to the states, judicial review implements the supremacy clause and thereby vindicates national authority. Indeed, judicial assessment of the constitutionality of legislation deals mainly with the laws of the states.

But this political justification does not speak to the most controversial aspect of judicial review, which is not the practice itself but the way it is carried out. What principles may properly be drawn from the Constitution? How far may the Court go in finding *implicit* principles? How closely must it be governed—or can it be governed—by the explicit text? What theory of constitutional interpretation can be accepted as legitimate?

The Living Constitution

There is broad agreement that the Constitution must be, in some sense, a living constitution, framed for the ages, adaptable to new circumstances. Thus William H. Rehnquist, a conservative Justice (later Chief Justice) said:

> The framers of the Constitution wisely spoke in general language and left to succeeding generations the task of applying that language to the unceasingly changing environment in which they would live. Those who framed, adopted, and ratified the Civil War amendments to the Constitution likewise used what have been aptly described as "majestic generalities" in composing the fourteenth amendment. Merely because a particular activity may not have existed when the Constitution was adopted, or because the framers could not have conceived a particular method of transacting affairs, cannot mean that the general language in the Constitution may not be applied to

59. Oliver Wendell Holmes, Jr., speech, 15 February 1913, in Lerner, ed., *Mind and Faith of Justice Holmes*, 390.

such a course of conduct. Where the framers of the Constitution have used general language, they have given latitude to those who would later interpret the instrument to make that language applicable to cases that the framers might not have foreseen.[60]

Justice Rehnquist objected strongly, however, to a conception of the living Constitution that would substitute "some other set of values for those which may be derived from the language and intent of the framers." He used as an example the claim that conditions in a state prison were bad enough to offend the Constitution, and he rejected the view that "nonelected members of the federal judiciary" should be asked to serve as "the voice and conscience of contemporary society."[61]

Even a conservative view of the living (or responsive) Constitution must recognize that adaptation takes place, for the most part and legitimately, through a process of interpretation—that is, clarification, extension, and adaptation of meanings—rather than by multiplying amendments.[62] Furthermore, judicial interpretation generates more or less binding precedents that have the force of law, and these include principles that may guide future judicial lawmaking. Thus even "mere" interpretation, which Justice Rehnquist endorses, must entail judicial creativity.

The legitimacy of interpretation is unquestioned where the text of the Constitution is clear and specific, as, for example, in providing that the president "shall hold his Office during the Term of four Years"; where the justices can plausibly invoke the authority of the founders to establish the meaning of a phrase or the significance of a doctrine, such as "separation of powers"; and where a line of judicial precedents—interpreting, say, the meaning of "to regulate Commerce . . . among the several States"—has been well established. In these contexts the Court uses as touchstones the explicit text, the legislative history, and the principle of *stare decisis,* or respect for precedent. These same touchstones apply to the interpretation of ordinary statutes as well as a constitution. They are relevant and appropriate, but they do not bring into focus

60. William H. Rehnquist, "The Notion of a Living Constitution," *Texas Law Review* 54 (May 1976): 694.

61. Ibid., 695.

62. It should be noted that constitutional interpretation goes on in other branches of government as well, and among commentators, scholars, and the general public. The process is very often uncontroversial, as when eighteenth-century meanings must be expanded to include modern forms of commerce or military preparedness. The Constitution provides explicitly for "Armies" and "a Navy," but not for an air force. This particular transition is made easy by the explicit power granted to Congress to "provide for the common Defense," but that clause too requires interpretation.

Chief Justice Marshall's reminder: "We must never forget, that it is a *constitution* we are expounding."[63]

The really serious problems arise when the Court must interpret the larger meaning of the Constitution, that is, when answers must be sought to such questions as: What *kind* of government does the Constitution contemplate? What values does it protect? How can we relate the intent of the framers, including those who amended the Constitution, to the great transformations that have occurred in the size, composition, and distribution of the population, in economic organization, in the scope of federal responsibility, and in the diminished authority of the states?

As soon as we grant that the original understanding speaks to *principles* as well as specific rules or forms, the door is open to controversial interpretation. The eighteenth-century founders had a more limited notion of democracy than did the framers and ratifiers of the Fifteenth, Seventeenth, and Nineteenth Amendments.[64] Are the visions compatible? If not, then when we try to understand what the Constitution is about, whose vision should prevail?

To make sense of judicial review we must trace the interplay of constitution and community. Two connections are especially important. First, a constitution must be interpreted in the light of the community's history. This inquiry goes beyond making contemporary sense of old vocabularies. Far more important is the need to understand what changes have occurred in the basic realities, perspectives, and aspirations that underlie the Constitution. These include changes in the nature of the federal union, driven in part by the Civil War and its aftermath, and the enlarged promise of full citizenship.

Second, the Constitution cannot serve as a complete rendering of fundamental law. This is perhaps most clearly recognized in the language of the Ninth Amendment: "The enumeration in the Constitution, of certain rights, shall not be construed to deny or disparage others retained by the people." The amendment does not say what rights are retained; therefore it has not played a large role in constitutional law.[65]

63. McCulloch v. Maryland, 17 U.S. (4 Wheat.) 316, 407 (1819), emphasis in original.
64. The Fifteenth Amendment (1870) extended the right to vote to former slaves and to others who might be denied the right "on account of race, color, or previous condition of servitude." The Seventeenth Amendment (1913) provided for election of United States Senators by the people directly rather than by state legislatures. The Nineteenth Amendment (1920) extended to women the right to vote.
65. But see Laurence H. Tribe, *American Constitutional Law*, 2d ed. (Mineola, N.Y.: Foundation Press, 1988), 774ff.

Nevertheless, it reflects an implicit understanding that a written Constitution is necessarily an *abridgment* of the community's constitutional experience. It cannot spell out all the rights that are implicit in the history of the community's institutions or are "retained by the people," such as the right to travel or to choose a vocation. Nor can it specify all the powers of government. The founders did indeed strive to create a national government of limited, enumerated powers, and in the Bill of Rights they tried to protect what they took to be the most important and most vulnerable rights. They took for granted, however, much that did not seem vulnerable and that the common law protected.

It cannot be said that judicial review is a *necessary* component of constitutional government. The experience of England shows that fundamental liberties can be protected even though the courts do not exercise such power. It may well be that Congress and the state legislatures would act more responsibly, from a constitutional point of view, if they could not look to the courts to correct their mistakes and overreachings. But at least two conditions make the institution of judicial review—and a strong form of it—both probable and desirable: a *written* constitution and a *flourishing democracy*. The written Constitution, just because it is written, demands authoritative interpretation. Its abstract clauses, enshrined in a supreme statute, are an invitation to argument and litigation. Some device is called for to settle such arguments. Furthermore, the very flourishing of democracy, especially when traditions of legality and restraint are relatively weak or vulnerable, creates the need for a special institution to serve as an effective bulwark against majoritarian excess.

In interpreting the Constitution, the Court has a special obligation—greater and better-defined than the similar duty of legislators and executives—to speak for the community as a whole rather than for the majority or for a particular faction. To fulfill that obligation the Court must look first to the text itself, as a prime expression of the community's commitments and as the source of the Court's own legitimacy. The Court must also look beyond the text to the "law behind the law": history, tradition, and sound reasoning about what democracy and personal well-being require. Here again we see the importance of understanding that positive law—which in this context means the explicit text of the Constitution—cannot capture the whole of legally relevant experience.

The practice of judicial review builds a bridge between law and community. The bridge is constructed from strands of consensus, and especially from the moral and legal understandings that set limits to legislative and executive will. Some of these understandings are secure and unquestioned; others are elusive and emergent. The Court finds consensus and participates in its making, not by registering public opinion, but by deploying arguments about the meaning of the Constitution, including its meaning in contemporary life. A premise is that adherence to the Constitution commits the community to certain principles and that the commitment is binding even though, at any given time, public opinion might, say, reject or mutilate the Bill of Rights. Thus the Court has the task of recalling the community to its fundamental values and interests, that is, to its own foundations as a community.[66]

This difficult enterprise is, of course, subject to abuse. Insofar as the Court claims to speak for the community—a claim it cannot forgo—problems of accountability inevitably arise. The justices often err in their attempts to provide contextual readings of the Constitution. They occasionally engage in flights of speculative reasoning, paying inadequate attention to the interplay of critical and conventional morality. They may substitute personal preference regarding policy outcomes for good-faith interpretation of what the law requires. These failings are especially dangerous in a constitutional court, where great issues may turn on the choice of principles or starting points for reasoning.

The justices are constrained, however, by a jurisdiction restricted to cases and controversies; by the structure of the Court, which virtually insures dialogue and dissent;[67] by the political process, which governs their appointment; by their exposure to criticism from lawyers, legal scholars, political leaders, and the press; and by an institutional morality that imposes various forms of self-restraint, including respect for precedent and a preference for incremental rather than sweeping change. These modes of accountability do not guarantee purity or infallibility. Nor do

66. As is suggested in the discussion above, this task requires a theory of the American political community, and of the role of the Supreme Court in that community. Such theories are contestable; they reflect differences in political orientation; but they are far from irrelevant. Hence the president and the Senate have an obligation to inquire into the theories held, implicitly or explicitly, by prospective appointees to the Court.

67. "The United States Supreme Court is one collegial court, in which all the judges participate in all the decisions (unless a judge is disqualified from sitting in any particular case). But the House of Lords is not a collegial court; it is composed of about ten judges who are qualified to sit, rather than one single court. In practice the House of Lords sits in two panels, usually of five judges each. This difference is highly significant, because it reflects the English belief that it is largely immaterial which judges hear which appeals; the United States Supreme Court could not possibly sit in panels without a radical change in its functions" (P. S. Atiyah and Robert S. Summers, *Form and Substance in Anglo-American Law* [Oxford: Clarendon Press, 1987], 269). The "one collegial court" insures that differences among the justices will be aired, not suppressed.

they preclude controversy; on the contrary, they presuppose it. They are best understood, rather, as resources for self-correction.

RESPONSIVE LAW

Anglo-American common law has been a strong supplement to political democracy. The courts enhance democracy by strengthening and enlarging such political rights as voting, association, and speech. They also uphold such *non*political rights as rights of property, procreation, parental authority, marital privacy, travel, and personal security. These rights are derived in part from the Constitution but also from statutes and from principles of common law. In developing those principles and in adapting them to new realities, the courts begin with social usage. They confirm legitimate expectations, provide opportunities for the representation of interests, and exhibit a preference for law that is more emergent than imposed. Thus understood, the common-law tradition embodies a distinctively communitarian ideal: *the integration of law and society.* In what follows I argue that this integration is a key to social justice.

If a legal system is inefficient, or indifferent to social needs, it will deliver a cramped, selective, and impoverished justice. Legal ideas and institutions must be open to social knowledge and attentive to all legitimate interests. In short, justice requires a responsive legal order.[68] We have encountered the idea of responsiveness before, in connection with the discussion of institutional autonomy and integrity (see Chapter 12). There we distinguished responsiveness from opportunistic adaptation or capitulation to pressure. A responsive institution maintains its integrity while acknowledging the legitimacy of an appropriate range of claims and interests. Mere openness is not enough, however. A spirit of consultation must prevail and authority be subject to criticism and reconstruction, while the institution's basic commitments, and its capacity to function, are preserved and protected.

The desire for a responsive legal order has been implicit in much modern thought about law and society, including legal realism and sociological jurisprudence. These intellectual movements have studied law in context and law in action. They have explored the political, cultural, economic, sociological, and psychological realities that affect the quality of justice. They have argued, in various ways, that failure to take account of those conditions distorts reality, ascribes to the legal order an

---

68. See Philippe Nonet and Philip Selznick, *Law and Society in Transition: Toward Responsive Law* (New York: Harper/Colophon, 1978).

excessive dignity, insulates it from criticism, and offers society inadequate leverage for change. Without responsive law, the community is shortchanged and justice is at risk.

These criticisms take for granted the achievements, and the fundamental stability, of "the rule of law." The achievements include, most importantly, the independence of the judiciary; the idea that no official, however mighty, is above the law; and assurance that the law protects a substantial array of fundamental rights. This system of "autonomous" law—won at some cost in struggle and revolution—arises as a counter to "repressive" law.[69] Law is repressive when it legitimates domination by political, economic, religious, or other elites. In repressive law, protecting "the system" has first priority; the interests of the governed are given short shrift.

Institutional autonomy is, indeed, the chief bulwark of the rule of law. Judging, lawyering, fact-finding, rule-making: all require insulation from pressures that would corrupt them. The twentieth century has brought many reminders that legal autonomy *of some sort* is a necessary condition for justice. As the dictatorships of our time have shown, repressive law is hardly ancient history. In those regimes a primary victim has been the integrity of the legal process. High on the agenda in the struggle for freedom—in Eastern Europe, for example, or South Africa—is the building, or rebuilding, of legal institutions capable of resisting political manipulation. For those who suffer oppression, criticism of the rule of law as "bourgeois justice" or "liberal legalism" can only be perceived as naive or heartless, or both.

Nevertheless, the very stability of the rule of law, where that has been achieved, makes possible a still broader vision and a higher aspiration. Without disparaging (to say nothing of trashing) our legal heritage, we may well ask whether it fully meets the community's needs. Although a system that upholds basic rights is surely worthy of admiration, it does not justify complacent acceptance in the face of continuing deprivation and unfairness. So long as the system is basically secure, it is reasonable to accept some institutional risks in the interests of social justice.

Autonomous law tries to draw a sharp line between law and politics; it upholds a court-centered, rule-centered, rights-centered jurisprudence; and its main concern is with procedural fairness rather than substantive justice. Each of these attributes sustains the independence and legitimacy

---

69. For the concepts of "repressive," "autonomous," and "responsive" law, see Nonet and Selznick, *Law and Society in Transition*.

of the legal system. Each must be modified, as we shall see, in a regime of responsive law.

Responsiveness begins with *outreach and empowerment*. The capacity of law to deliver justice depends on the range of interests it acknowledges. All must have effective (as well as formal) access to the legal system, and the law must be open to new claims of right. In this century we have seen substantial movement in both directions. Labor and civil rights legislation; legal services for the poor; environmental and consumer protection: all have greatly expanded the reach of justice.

These changes have required political victories and landmark legislation. Courts have not been the only actors, or even the principal ones. They have, however, played a crucial role. The *Brown* decision of 1954, which struck down racial segregation in public schools, helped lay a foundation for the civil rights legislation of the 1960s. The Supreme Court has expanded other constitutional rights as well: for example, the right to counsel in criminal cases; freedom of the press; due-process rights for welfare recipients; student rights; greater equality for women. This work of the courts has blurred the line between judge-made law and political decision.

Social Advocacy

A limited reintegration of law and politics is a hallmark of responsive law. This is clearly displayed in the rise of social advocacy and public-interest litigation. Organizations such as the NAACP, the Sierra Club, and many others, both liberal and conservative, have looked to the courts for vindication. The use of litigation to influence public policy has become a prominent feature of the legal landscape.

Social advocacy draws heavily on the common-law tradition, which gives great weight to self-help and self-assertion: the judicial process is set in motion by partisan advocates who contribute decisively to the framing of issues and the interpretation of law. But the practice of social advocacy also *departs* from the tradition, in the direction of greater judicial control of the proceedings, judicial supervision of compliance, and a shift in focus from private ordering to government responsibility. Nevertheless, the tradition of self-assertion through appeal to the courts was an indispensable foundation for the rise of social advocacy.

Advocacy does not take law as given. Rather, the authority of a rule, as applied in the circumstances, is testable and problematic. Thus advocacy presumes and encourages searching criticism of received authority.

Especially in appellate advocacy, it is taken for granted that new law can be made on the basis of new facts and claims. This "open texture" of the common law, which includes common-law aspects of constitutional law, creates opportunities for litigation whose main object is to change the law or to restructure governmental agencies, rather than to win benefits for specific litigants.

Social advocates represent group interests—and appeal to the common good—by invoking norms that have some claim to legal authority. Therefore they choose forums that can be held responsible to those norms. Hence, the characteristic locale of social advocacy is the court or administrative agency rather than the legislature. The appeal is to legal entitlement, not political will. Nevertheless, politics is driven by the engine of justice. Liberalized rules of "standing"—eligibility to bring a case to court—open the door to lawsuits brought on behalf of the community to right a general wrong. When a legal starting point—an argument founded in a previously recognized principle, rule, or statute—is available, social advocacy becomes a supplement to voting, campaigning, debating, lobbying, and other modes of democratic political action.

In this "public law litigation" the role of the court shifts from resolving disputes among private individuals to vindicating legally established policies.[70] Among these policies have been desegregation of schools, consumer protection, environmental protection, occupational safety, voting rights, and prison reform. In public-law litigation the court is asked to consider whether a government (or institutional) practice conforms to constitutional standards, such as equal protection or due process, or to the requirements of a statute, such as the Clean Air Act.

The proceedings differ considerably from traditional private litigation, such as a suit for negligence or for breach of contract. Because they represent a broader interest, the parties are more indefinite; proper representation may be determined by the court as the case develops, in the light of what fairness may require.[71] The point of the lawsuit is to change the policy or practice, not to win damages for some wrongful conduct in the past. Moreover, the court is likely to remain involved in the case beyond the point of passing judgment as to whether, for ex-

70. Abram Chayes, "The Role of the Judge in Public Law Litigation," *Harvard Law Review* 89 (May 1976): 1381–86; and Abram Chayes, "The Supreme Court, 1981 Term," *Harvard Law Review* 96 (1982): 4–60.
71. In a school desegregation suit, for example, the court may have to decide which groups in a local community should participate in framing a consent decree. See Doris R. Fine, *When Leadership Fails* (New Brunswick, N.J.: Transaction Books, 1986), 135ff.

ample, a practice is wrongful. It may monitor future conduct.[72] As a result of these and other features of public-law litigation, "courts are inevitably cast in an affirmative, political—activist, if you must—role, a role that contrasts with the passive umpireship we are taught to expect."[73]

It should be emphasized that much of this development is due to major federal legislation rather than to judicial initiative or "imperialism." The legislation mandates affirmative government responsibilities, such as setting standards for clean water or occupational safety, and it is the duty of the courts to enforce such legislation when called on to do so. Although the character of the lawsuit changes, with the judge assuming a more active role, the fundamental nature of adjudication is not altered. The court is asked to apply received law to specific facts, and to do so in a disinterested way, hearing proofs and arguments in accordance with established procedures. Furthermore, public-law litigation does not *displace* the traditional kind, more typical of autonomous law. It is an *added* function, a supplementary way of implementing policies enacted by Congress or contained in the Constitution. This added function includes judicial response to claims based on the failure of legislators to act—for example, when constitutional norms are violated in the administration of schools, mental institutions, or prisons.[74]

Social advocacy cannot by itself build a high road to social justice. The great issues of opportunity and inequality must be met in directly political ways as well as through the courts. In the field of welfare law, for example, social advocacy has been fairly successful in protecting *already established* entitlements and in striking down obnoxious administrative regulations. These judgments touch closely on the expertise of

72. This expanded role is hardly unprecedented, especially in equity proceedings, such as bankruptcy, but it is not the representative mode of adjudication in autonomous law.

73. Chayes, "Supreme Court, 1981 Term," 4.

74. Among the problems raised by this new litigation is the possibility that in vindicating the rights of *some* people—say, the handicapped—courts will require expenditure of public funds without regard to fair and effective distribution of resources. For example, in the 1970s the cooperation of Massachusetts officials and a U.S. district court, responding to class-action suits by families of children in schools for the mentally handicapped led to a series of consent decrees mandating much-needed but expensive reforms. A prominent state legislator complained that the strategy of social advocacy, seeking reform through the courts, is "too myopic" and "one-dimensional" because it does not consider whether "if we give money to them [the mentally handicapped children], what does it mean to the kids who need mump shots?" Ultimately legislation was passed "that barred the state from signing decrees without the approval of the chairs of the House and Senate Ways and Means Committees" (Esther Scott, "Judge Tauro and Care of the Retarded in Massachusetts" [Case Program, John F. Kennedy School of Government, Harvard University, 1987], 9, 14).

the courts, and the remedies they offer do not significantly affect welfare budgets. Demands for enlarged distributive justice, that is, wider entitlements and higher benefits, have been less successful. Insofar as social advocacy becomes a permanent feature of the legal process, it will have to accept a defined role and limited aspirations.

These new forms of litigation and adjudication exemplify a creative interplay of law and politics. A wall of separation between these spheres has historically guaranteed legal legitimacy and promised legal integrity. These are no small benefits. But the wall has never been unbreached, even in the heyday of autonomous law. The well-organized and the affluent never supposed they would have no say in legal development. They worked for legal change, in their own interests, by appealing to courts as well as legislatures. As the molders of existing custom and practice and as the social class from which judges were drawn, they decisively influenced the path of the law.

Legal Pluralism

I suggested above that the capacity of law to deliver justice depends on the range of interests it recognizes and protects. This is the foundation of legal outreach and of its corollary, the reintegration of law and politics. A broader acknowledgment of interests necessarily expands the authority of government, including the courts. Otherwise, outreach would be futile and impotent. But the acknowledgment of interests is also a *limiting* principle and a principle of *respect*.

A responsive legal order is not set over society. Rather, it treats social interests as potential claims to intrinsic worth and therefore as objects of moral concern. Responsiveness demands conformity to social ideals, including principles of justice, but the premise is that "the center of gravity of legal development lies not in legislation, nor in juristic science, nor in judicial decision, but in society itself."[75] According to this sociological doctrine, which is sometimes called legal pluralism, legislatures and courts are only two among the diverse forms of legal order that regulate people's lives. The vitality of a social order comes from below, that is, from the necessities of cooperation in everyday life. This *indigenous* ordering can vary greatly in stringency and formality, from weak rules of acquaintanceship to the much stronger demands of employment,

75. Eugen Ehrlich, *Fundamental Principles of the Sociology of Law* (1913; reprint, Cambridge: Harvard University Press, 1936), xiv.

commerce, education, religion, and parental responsibility. Not all social order is law in any meaningful sense, but the rudiments of law may
be discerned whenever regulation is backed by the authority of employers, parents, or priests and whenever claims of right can be asserted.
As this "quasi-law" gathers strength and stability it is likely to determine the content of "official" law, that is, the law of the organized
political community.[76]

Like so many other ideas we have dealt with, legal pluralism is both
normative and descriptive. It is descriptive in that it calls attention to the
coexistence and interaction of different forms and sources of law within a
more or less unified legal order. Some examples are American federalism;
the interplay of European and indigenous legal systems in colonies or
former colonies; the emergence of "private government" in industry,
education, and religion. More generally, students of law and society are
interested in identifying a wide range of "semi-autonomous social
fields" capable of generating rules and winning compliance.[77] Legal
pluralism emphasizes the continuities between state law and the law or
quasi-law generated by the group structure of society. Law *in* society is
the preferred model, not law *and* society.

The normative import of legal pluralism is readily apparent. It posits
the moral worth of institutions close to the people, that is, based on
shared experience, reflecting shared sentiments, sustained by practical
needs. Such institutions have a prima facie claim to respect, forbearance,
and support. They are valued as extensions of personhood, as settings
within which social participation is most direct and most effective, and
as being accessible, understandable, and controllable. The interests they
protect are characteristically local or particularistic: intermediate associations of all kinds—neighborhoods, churches, schools, ethnic groups,
local government and business.

In all this, legal pluralism shares the moral posture of political
pluralism.[78] Law is more just when it springs from the character and

---

76. A somewhat stronger view, suggesting that "official" law is no more legal than
other forms, such as the law for the parties that emerges from a contract, is contained in
the following comment by Lon Fuller: "I mean the word *law* to be construed very
broadly. I intend it to include not only the legal systems of states and nations, but also the
smaller systems—at least 'law-like' in structure and function—to be found in labor
unions, professional associations, clubs, churches, and universities. . . . When the concept
of law is given this broad coverage, it becomes apparent that many of the central issues of
today are, in this extended sense, 'legal' in nature" (Lon L. Fuller, *The Principles of Social
Order*, ed. Kenneth I. Winston [Durham: Duke University Press, 1981], 212).

77. Sally Falk Moore, *Law as Process: An Anthropological Approach* (London: Routledge
& Kegan Paul, 1978), chap. 2.

78. Discussed in Chapter 16, "Communal Democracy."

condition of the people and when it is administered with due regard for the integrity of practices and the autonomy of groups. Thus responsiveness calls for respect as well as outreach: respect for ordinary people and their legitimate expectations; for the complex texture of social life; for the activities on which prosperity depends; for the actual and potential "living law" of private associations.

An example of this approach is responsive regulation of business. In its central meaning, regulation has to do with activities *that are valued by a community.* The idea is to uphold public standards or purposes without undue damage to activities we care about. Thus regulation is a particular kind of social control, one that provides protection as well as discipline.[79]

Responsive regulation is more problem-centered than rule-centered, more persuasive than coercive. As described by Eugene Bardach and Robert Kagan, for example, the "good inspector" tries to limit pollution or enhance occupational safety by techniques of dialogue, diagnosis, and institutional design.[80] Instead of "going by the book," with its emphasis on fixed rules, violations, and fines, responsive regulators take specific circumstances into account. They participate with business and other institutions in a cooperative effort to make law effective. This may involve forbearance to mitigate unreasonableness, or technical consultation to show how improvements may be made without undue cost, perhaps by bringing to bear the experience of other firms.[81] The ideal is to attain the maximum feasible *self*-regulation.[82]

As a great deal of experience has shown, both the regulators and the regulated lean toward informal cooperation. Such cooperation is often more cozy than constructive. Close association provides many opportunities for forms of mutual accommodation, which may include corruption. The alternative is not, however, legalistic and self-distancing en-

---

79. This excludes most of what goes on in the criminal justice system, except that the community may adopt a "regulatory" approach to certain activities, such as gambling, that are illegal but tolerated.

80. *Going by the Book: The Problem of Regulatory Unreasonableness* (Philadelphia: Temple University Press, 1982), chap. 5.

81. "Forbearance entails: (1) overlooking violations that pose no serious risk under the circumstances; (2) not enforcing regulatory requirements that would be especially costly or disruptive in relation to the additional degree of protection they would provide; (3) granting reasonable time to come into compliance and accepting measures that would provide substantial if not literal compliance; and (4) making allowance for good faith efforts on the part of the regulated enterprise" (ibid., 134).

82. See Joseph K. Rees, *Reforming the Workplace: A Study of Self-Regulation in Occupational Safety* (Philadelphia: University of Pennsylvania Press, 1988).

forcement. Going by the book is no guarantee that regulation will be honest, effective, or fair. In a responsive model, cooperation is visible, accountable, and subject to assessment in the light of such practical outcomes as accident rates or changes in company structure and policy.

Although responsive law deemphasizes coercion, it by no means rejects it. Responsive regulation is not the same as *de*regulation. Regulatory agencies must have authority, but the worth of what they do depends on how that authority is used. Rule-centered law tends to expend authority on securing conformity to rules, not on solving problems. Responsive law is less interested in rule-compliance than in mobilizing energies for the achievement of public purposes, and this requires respect for and deference to the needs of the enterprise.

Responsive law is a critical morality—part of the theory of justice. As such, however, it includes the principle of legal pluralism, which says that justice must take seriously the potential for self-regulation in social life. Therefore responsive law incorporates important aspects of conventional morality. But social norms and practices are not self-certifying. Responsive law criticizes and reconstructs group life even as it accepts a duty to defer.

Consider again what we have called private government. As an aspect of outreach, responsive law is sensitive to the interests of subordinate and dependent people, who may be subject to arbitrary and oppressive rule at work, in their unions, or at school. Therefore principles of fairness and due process are applied to these private settings as well as to public government. At the same time, responsive law takes full account of the differences among institutions, including the special kind of authority each may require.

Of special importance to legal pluralism is the fact that institutions have different internal moralities. Moreover, some internal moralities are more effective than others. Most families can be relied on to care for their children without external interference or goading. An internal morality is sustained by parental love and by feelings of solidarity among close relatives. The internal morality of business arises from the demands of rationality, including the utility of good relations among employees, customers, and suppliers. However, impoverished families and marginal firms are likely to have very weak internal moralities. These variations point to the limits of legal pluralism. The ideal depends on an underlying reality. Deference is unjustified if the institution in question has little or no potential for self-regulation.

Serving the Public Interest

The forms of responsiveness we have thus far discussed are essentially strategies of inclusion. Outreach expands the range of acknowledged interests; pluralism legitimates autonomous decision. These strategies do not, however, exhaust the meaning of responsiveness. They speak to *openness,* but responsiveness must include *competence* as well. A responsive legal order is more than a passive recipient of claims, more also than a friendly, nonintrusive facilitator of private transactions and associations. It must be an effective instrument for dealing with change and meeting social needs. This is the active, creative, purposive side of responsiveness.

It is necessary to distinguish between a genuinely instrumental or functional law and the *manipulation* of legal institutions. The latter occurs when, for example, political rulers tell "their" judges how specific cases should be decided, or when legislation is the creature of special interests. These characteristics of repressive law reflect a narrow, impoverished instrumentalism. This is very different from the form we associate with John Dewey's pragmatism, which regards ends as subject to revision in the light of all relevant values. Like Dewey's, the instrumentalism of responsive law is sensitive to the interplay of means and ends and is governed by the comprehensive interests of the community, not by self-serving commands or pressures.

For law to be responsive in that way, it must take seriously the idea of a public interest or common good. It must be prepared to consider how far rules, procedures, and doctrines meet the needs they were meant to serve. Just what those needs are and how they should be met is always an open question. Therefore legal institutions must be *instruments of inquiry* as well as of authority. And inquiry runs to the premises of law, not only to its implementation.

In the classic model of autonomous law—which includes Weber's conception of bureaucracy—the main preoccupation is with rules rather than principles. This creates familiar problems of rigidity and goal-displacement, which have their own consequences for doing justice. A less familiar consequence of rule-centeredness is that it generates passive and uncritical courts and bureaucracies. They recoil from an active role in reconstructing law. They eschew the task of revising rules, in the light of principles, to take account of changing contexts. They fail to grasp new opportunities to enhance the contribution of law to justice.

The basic move from traditional to responsive law entails a shift of emphasis from rules to principles. Instead of taking each rule as unproblematic, to be changed only by legislation, courts and other agencies look to the reasons behind the rule, that is, to the purposes, policies, and values it is supposed to achieve or fulfill. Thus responsive law puts into action the jurisprudential theory, discussed above (p. 439), that legal principles mediate the transition from law to justice.

For many years American courts took it to be a settled rule that, in the absence of an explicit agreement, employees could be dismissed for any reason or for no reason at all.[83] This notion of employment "at will" severely limited justice in the workplace. It left employees (except those covered by union contracts) vulnerable to the arbitrary authority of management. As we have seen, this rule has been seriously eroded. Many courts have looked beyond the form of employment to its substance. In contract law itself they have found principles, such as the idea that employers have an implied obligation of "good faith and fair dealing," that rebut a strong presumption of employment at will. These doctrinal developments have been responsive to multiple values, rather than to the single value of managerial control and discretion. They have taken account of the experience of collective bargaining; legislation regulating discrimination, safety, and other aspects of employment; and the widespread institutionalization of systematic personnel practices. As these considerations are brought to bear, a shift in social policy is discerned, and the authority of the rule is undermined. How far it will be applied, and with what limits, thus becomes a question to be decided on grounds of principle, policy, and social fact.

Any appeal to principle and policy is bound to be controversial. The issues are empirical as well as logical. Choices must always be made as to which principles are relevant, how narrowly or broadly they should be framed, and what priority any given principle should have. The social views of the judges, including how they understand their own role, will affect these decisions. The point is not to avoid controversy but to redirect and contain it. By engaging in supplementary rule-making while maintaining a distinctive institutional morality, the courts offer an alternative to open political controversy. The community can go forward without referring every issue to legislators and administrators; it can test the ripeness of an issue for more comprehensive solutions. In a common-law system controversy is channeled and to some extent

---

83. For background, see Chapter 11, "Private Government."

sublimated, but it is not eliminated. An opportunity is offered, however, to discern an emerging consensus and to give it some guidance.

The changes we have mentioned in the common law of employment have not occurred in a vacuum. The way was prepared by labor legislation, by changes in the organization of industry, and by greater public sensitivity to human rights and to the potential abuse of private power. The courts in turn prepare the way for new legislation on wrongful dismissal and other job rights. They do not act alone, nor can they accomplish major transformations without political support. In many areas, going it alone may have great costs. As was suggested above, when courts respond to the just claims of litigants, only one part of the community may benefit. Without the opportunity for compromise and trade-offs—a distinctively legislative function—the public interest in fair allocations and in controlling costs may well be ignored. This is an argument for legislative responsibility, not for judicial abdication.

Responsive law looks to the *partnership* of courts, legislatures, and executive agencies. This theme recalls one of Karl Llewellyn's favorite ideas—the "institution of Law-and-Government" or, as he sometimes said, "the going whole of Law-government." In his version of legal realism, which was a kind of sociological jurisprudence, Llewellyn stressed the continuities of decision-making and the interdependence of institutions. It is important, he said, to perceive law-and-government "as a *single* institution" made up of complementary and cooperative (as well as antagonistic) parts.[84]

In the contemporary situation, separation of spheres is no longer the key to political wisdom.[85] The community needs all the help it can get, from institutions capable of making up for one another's deficiencies. Without yielding the principle of checks and balances, of power taming power, the system must be open to new ways of infusing public policy with direction and commitment. For this we need cooperation and complementarity, not distance and division.

Blurred boundaries and overlapping functions are natural (if troublesome) offspring of moral decision. Concern for whole persons or for the comprehensive well-being of a group or community must take account of multiple values. Those values may be competing or complementary.

---

84. *Jurisprudence: Realism in Theory and Practice* (Chicago: University of Chicago Press, 1962), 174n. Llewellyn (1893–1962) was a leading figure in the legal realist movement of the 1930s and 1940s.

85. "We have gone far beyond Montesquieu. We have learned that danger of tyranny or injustice lurks in unchecked power, not in blended power" (Kenneth Culp Davis, *Administrative Law Text* [St. Paul, Minn.: West Publishing Co., 1959], 30).

In either case, the moral outcome is not likely to be unidimensional or single-minded. On the contrary, responsibility strains toward extension, not constriction; toward sharing, not exclusiveness. A good parent is a good teacher; a good school is a good parent. Each in its own way fulfills the function of the other.

Of course, institutional integration may be oppressive or counterproductive if functions are confused as well as overlapping. Then the integrity of judging, teaching, accounting, engineering, quality control, or parenting may be compromised. The answer, however, is not a retreat to insularity. Rather, we seek to clarify functions and study contexts in order to identify what *kinds* of autonomy and what *kinds* of integration are required or acceptable. We may discover that, in many contexts, the integrity of an activity requires interdependence and partnership as much as, or even more than, detachment or insulation.

If we find the reintegration of law and politics a threatening prospect, we may take some comfort from the distinction between "low politics" and "high politics." Low politics is power politics; it is the play of will, faction, interest, and domination. High politics is the realm of dialogue wherein the ends of group existence are defined. High politics is not divorced from self-interest; whether politics is low or high depends, rather, on how far self-interest is blended with a broader public interest that includes ideals of justice and citizenship.

It is proper that courts be insulated from power politics, but they have a legitimate part to play in the determination of public policy. Therefore they participate in "high politics." To be sure, courts maintain fidelity to law insofar as they build on received premises; therefore the policies developed by judges are not necessarily their own. Nor may judges legitimately act on behalf of special interests, though such interests often benefit from judicial conclusions. The responsibility of judges extends to justice as well as law. Justice requires critical examination of received law in the light of general principles and the circumstances at hand. In the common-law tradition this examination is legally required. Responsive law is a way of fulfilling the promise of that tradition.

▼   ▲   ▼   ▲   ▼

The concept of responsive law brings together the strands of theory we explored in earlier sections of this chapter: justice as an integrative and substantive ideal; the limits of legal positivism; the communitarian significance of the common-law tradition; constitution and community.

Throughout this discussion we have embraced a perspective of *critical affirmation*.[86] We have not celebrated positive law, for law as it is must be open to revision. We have, however, recognized the contribution of a legal heritage and have expressed confidence in ideals of justice latent in law and in the possibility of changing law from within, by opening its boundaries and by appeal to constitutive principles.

In the next chapter we continue the discussion of communitarian justice, with attention to such related issues as equality and civic participation. The focus shifts from legal theory to political theory, and, more broadly, to the social foundations of a moral community.

86. This perspective shares some elements with an intellectual movement (mainly among law professors) called critical legal studies. The latter, however, conflates criticism and deconstruction. It lacks a posture—and a supportive jurisprudence—of affirmation and reconstruction. See Roberto M. Unger, *The Critical Legal Studies Movement* (Cambridge: Harvard University Press, 1986).

SIXTEEN

Covenant and Commonwealth

How is the political community to be organized? What are its moral foundations? How does it relate, and how should it relate, to nonpolitical relationships and activities? Is politics a vital part of moral ordering, a vehicle of human flourishing, as Aristotle believed? Or is it better understood as a necessary evil, perhaps a sign of human corruption, as Saint Augustine took it to be?

In this concluding chapter we examine the moral premises of political democracy. These premises are communitarian, as we shall see. They are, however, by no means hostile to liberal ideals of moral equality, political participation, and personal autonomy. Rather, they highlight the community's interest in moral integration and social responsibility. The outcome is a perspective referred to earlier as communitarian liberalism.

As a framework for this discussion I invoke two old but not obsolete ideas: *covenant* and *commonwealth*. Each has both moral and political connotations. The theory of covenant is a theory of moral ordering; at the same time, it speaks to the nature of consent and the limits of political authority. A commonwealth is a "polity" or "body politic," but the concept connotes an integration of politics with economics and morals. Covenant is prepolitical, foundational, and consensual.[1] A commonwealth, on the other hand, is a going concern that must balance interests

1. On the political theory of covenant, see especially Daniel J. Elazar, "The Political Theory of Covenant: Biblical Origins and Modern Developments," *Publius* 10 (1980): 3–30; cf. other articles in the same issue of *Publius*.

and harmonize functions. Like piety and civility, which they partly parallel, covenant and commonwealth are complementary aspects of the moral community.

The idea of covenant comes to us from Hebraic and Christian (especially Calvinist) theology.[2] In biblical history, the interaction of God and humankind is marked by a series of covenants or treaties—with Adam, Noah, Abraham, Moses, David, and, in the Christian version, ultimately, through Christ, with all believers. God promises salvation, or at least his favor, on condition of faith and obedience. Sometimes the condition is only implicit: to Noah and Abraham, God speaks as though making a unilateral commitment, and, indeed, all God's promises are acts of divine grace. Nevertheless, a conditional element remains, and with it a conception of mutual obligation. As a result, although God's sovereignty is complete, the human perception of its *nature* is transformed.

Faith based on covenant might be called a constitutional faith. In so-called federal theology, the foundation of religious belief and commitment is a giving and receiving of promises.[3] The parties are not equal. They both act, however, as responsible agents whose word is their bond. Covenant creates expectations that the divine sovereign will act reasonably and without injustice. Bound by his word, God is no despot. For their part, the covenanted people accept subordination with dignity, as free persons entering a sacred compact; they are not debased, degraded, or enslaved.

The compact creates a *self-conscious* moral order. Most vividly at Sinai, the agreement with God is an agreement to uphold a code of responsible

2. See Delbert R. Hillers, *Covenant: The History of a Biblical Idea* (Baltimore: Johns Hopkins University Press, 1969). For a contemporary interpretation of the Jewish tradition, see Daniel Hartman, *A Living Covenant: The Innovative Spirit in Traditional Judaism* (New York: Free Press, 1985); on covenant in Puritan theology, Perry Miller, *The New England Mind: The Seventeenth Century* (1939; reprint, Cambridge: Harvard University Press, 1982), chaps. 13 and 14; and John Von Rohr, *The Covenant of Grace in Puritan Thought* (Atlanta, Ga.: Scholars Press, 1986), 17ff. According to Christian covenant theology, "God at the Creation entered into an agreement with Adam as the federal head of the race, promising to him and to his descendants eternal life on condition of his obedience to the Divine command that he should not eat of the fruit of the tree of the knowledge of good and evil. . . . Adam having failed to stand the test, God entered into a second agreement with Christ as the second Adam, on behalf of the elect, promising them forgiveness and eternal life in consideration of Christ's perfect obedience. . . . The covenant theology in its developed form is a scheme of doctrine in which the entire system of divinity is expressed in the terms of these two covenants, and man's assurance of salvation based upon the fact that he is included within the latter" (W. Adams Brown, "Covenant Theology," in *Encyclopedia of Religion and Ethics* [New York: Scribner's, 1912], 4:216).

3. In this context "federal" (from the Latin *foedus,* meaning treaty or alliance) and "covenant" are synonyms. To modern ears, however, "federal" carries a clearer connotation of reserved autonomy; it suggests a unity of unities.

conduct. God's commands are obeyed by fulfilling obligations to family and community; a social ethic is the linchpin of the covenant. The symbolism of a Supreme Deity gives morality a transcendent authority, protected from other claims and interests. And the commitment is personal as well as communal: "The league with God is directly with the smallest social units, and Israel is not a pyramid joined to the deity only at the top."[4]

This social ethic is something more than a natural, unconscious acceptance of social norms. (In that rudimentary sense, every community has a moral code.) Covenant presumes an act of faith and resolve, a self-defining commitment. It is a decision to embrace the pregnant premises of moral ordering. These include a sense of personal responsibility, an awareness of human frailty, and the aspiration to belong to a Kingdom of God, that is, to a community governed by moral ideals. This combination of faith, resolve, and idealism was the spiritual bridge from prophetic Judaism to covenantal Calvinism.

In modern usage "covenant," where it survives at all, is often no more than a fancy name for "contract." This attrition of meaning is unfortunate. The obligations of covenant ought to be seen as more comprehensive and more binding. As we have noted in another context, the modern commercial contract is marked by limited commitment. Terms and conditions are specified closely, and the cost of nonperformance is calculable. Furthermore, with some exceptions, the moral or legal obligation is not necessarily to *fulfill* the agreement, but only to make good losses that may be incurred in case of an unjustified breach. Covenant, on the other hand, suggests an indefeasible commitment and a continuing relationship. The bond is relatively unconditional, relatively indissoluble. Marriage is a classic example, as is the creation of a federal union such as the United States. The bond contemplates open-ended and diffuse obligations, implicates the whole person or group, and creates a salient status.[5]

4. Hillers, *Covenant*, 78. "Democratization of religious responsibility meant that covenant traditions were kept alive in the individual family. This is a feature so characteristic of modern Jewish life, and of Christianity as well, that it takes an effort to recall that in the ancient East much of religion was a matter for the state: the gods were the gods of the city, and specialists, the priests, saw to the 'care and feeding of the gods' and preserved the liturgy and mythology of the temple" (ibid., 80).

5. We should be careful to distinguish a covenantal promise from ordinary contractual promises. "The making of particular promises or contracts," it has been said, "presupposes the social institution of promising or contracts, and the obligation to keep promises cannot itself be founded on a promise" (Hanna Pitkin, "Obligation and Consent—II," *American Political Science Review* 60 [1966]: 46). That is, the obligation to honor "particular" promises reaches back beyond proximate consent to more fundamental commitments, which may include a covenantal promise.

In ordinary contracts consent is decisive and pervades the arrangement. The parties are bound only by terms they have accepted, implicitly or explicitly. Covenant is more ambiguous. The obligations of marriage, adoption, or citizenship of course contain vital elements of voluntarism and consent. But the covenantal promise is a beginning, not an end. The ensuing obligations are not fully specified in advance; instead, they derive from the nature and history of the relationship. Respect for parents, nurture of children, civic virtue: these duties and ideals are neither founded in consent nor created through negotiation.

Like the social contract of Locke or Rousseau, covenant may characterize an *emergent* association. There may be no fixed point of origin, no identifiable agreement. However, as in the case of marriage (but not common-law marriage), there may be an explicit agreement to form a covenantal bond. In either case the outcome is a commitment to foundational principles, that is, to beliefs and resolves that define the moral premises of a practice, association, or community.

Every genuine covenant restates and reaffirms the basic features of morality: deference to a source of judgment beyond autonomous will; constructive self-regard; concern for the well-being of others. At the same time, it establishes the principles of a *particular* way of life. Therefore any given covenant—even a covenant with God—is historically contingent. It may be more or less successful as a moral achievement, and it is always subject to deterioration or improvement. An operative covenant underpins the institutions and guides the development of a living community. It is not an abstract morality.

▼　　▲　　▼　　▲　　▼

The American Declaration of Independence is properly construed as a covenantal foundation for the United States Constitution. Abraham Lincoln spoke eloquently to this idea when, at Gettysburg in 1863, he invoked the memory of a new nation "brought forth upon this continent" "fourscore and seven years ago," that is, in *1776,* the year of the Declaration, not 1789, the year the Constitution went into effect. The revolutionary act of separation from Great Britain contained a ringing affirmation of moral and political principles. These were to be touchstones of constitutional *formation,* constitutional *validity,* and constitutional *growth.*

Lincoln's conception of a national covenant has been summarized by John Schaar:

We are a nation formed by a covenant, by dedication to a set of principles and by an exchange of promises to uphold and advance certain commitments among ourselves and throughout the world. Those principles and commitments are the core of American identity, the soul of the body politic. They make the American nation unique, and uniquely valuable, among and to the other nations. But the other side of the conception contains a warning very like the warnings spoken by the prophets to Israel: if we fail in our promises to each other, and lose the principles of the covenant, then we lose everything, for they are we.[6]

The nation, said Lincoln, "was conceived in liberty and dedicated to the proposition that all men are created equal," and the victorious Union army would preserve "government of the people, by the people, for the people."

The Declaration spoke of "unalienable Rights," which must limit the authority of government, whose "just Powers" derive "from the Consent of the Governed." These foundational principles left many questions unanswered. They did not list all the rights that are unalienable, saying only that *among these* "are Life, Liberty, and the Pursuit of Happiness." Nor was the meaning of these noble abstractions spelled out. They did not say how the consent of the governed is to be made good or how far democracy should extend. They did not even hint at the pitfalls that lay ahead, such as the inescapable tension between the authority necessary to govern and potential claims to limitless liberty; or the possibility that legislative majorities would run roughshod over the rights of minorities and individuals; or how the public interest was to be preserved when the quality of consent was marred by manipulation or flawed by poor judgment.

The Constitution was framed to deal with these issues. In creating a viable government it brought about a transition from covenant to commonwealth. The Constitution presumes a covenanted people bound to political ideals of liberty ("unalienable Rights") and democracy ("the Consent of the Governed"). But the framers had to transform those ideals into workable principles. They had to design institutions that would absorb the lessons of political experience and, especially, take account of human frailties. The Constitution creates a government that is open at

6. *Legitimacy and the Modern State* (New Brunswick, N.J.: Transaction Books, 1981), 291. "This makes it quite clear that we are dealing here with a conception very different from Rousseau's advocacy of a civil religion as the bond of political community. For Lincoln, the principles of the covenant set the standard by which the nation must judge itself: the nation is righteous and to be honored only insofar as it honors the covenant. For Rousseau, the civil religion is designed to induce the individual to venerate the nation itself" (ibid.).

one end to the moral covenant and at the other to the comprehensive and ever-changing requirements of social life.

The covenant is not static. It is responsive to the history of the community, which includes the experience of constitution-making. As constitutional challenges are met, underlying commitments are clarified and elaborated. The American covenant has reached beyond the eighteenth-century Declaration. Conceptions of liberty, equality, and democracy have been broadened and deepened to include more liberties (in the realm of free speech and marital privacy, for example) and more participation, especially by women and African-Americans. All this has been—and much remains—vigorously contested. The emergent covenant is forged in controversy—sometimes indeed, as in the Civil War, by soldiers in battle, or, as in the labor and civil rights struggles, by citizens in the streets.

MORAL AND SOCIAL EQUALITY

The "proposition" formulated by Jefferson and invoked by Lincoln, "that all men are created equal," is the chief covenantal premise of a moral community. As its biblical origins attest, this is not a distinctively liberal idea. Moral equality has been a centerpiece of much modern thought, religious as well as secular. In the dominant perspectives of modernity, the autonomous individual is seen as the touchstone of worth and the bearer of responsibility. Protestantism envisions a lonely quest for personal salvation; the social contract dear to the Enlightenment is an agreement among free, rational, and equal persons; utilitarian positivism embraces the motto "Everybody to count for one, nobody for more than one"; equal moral competence is a cornerstone of Kantian morality; and modern doctrines of subjectivism and relativism give everyone's preferences the same weight. Democracy as the sovereignty of public opinion is the political expression of this intellectual current. Jefferson entered about midstream, and the words flowed easily from his defiant pen.

The idea of covenant is helpful here. To be "dedicated to the proposition," as Lincoln put it, or to "hold these truths to be self-evident," in Jefferson's words, entails, inescapably, an element of resolve; a leap of faith; a self-defining commitment. This is not to say that the expression is arbitrary or merely emotive. The principle of moral equality is drawn from experience. In embracing it we take into account the evils that ensue when its message is rejected or ignored; the limits thereby put on what it means to be genuinely other-regarding; the vision thereby dimmed of human dignity and personhood. But the covenant is something more than an intellectual conclusion. It is a foundational *act,* a social decision, a venture in constitution-making.

As we effect the transition from covenant to commonwealth, from animating ideal to going concern, the principle becomes ambiguous and vulnerable. It is often hard to disentangle *moral* from *social* equality; indeed, a radical egalitarianism sees no difference between the two. They are indeed connected in important ways, but they are also distinct. Moral equality is a premise for *criticizing* inequalities of rank, opportunity, and resources. However it is also compatible with *supporting* inequalities, many of which have their own justification.

Moral equality is the postulate that all persons have the same intrinsic worth. They are unequal in talents, in contributions to social life, and in valid claims to rewards and resources. But everyone who is a person is presumptively entitled to recognition of that personhood. There is no question of saying that all people are or should be equal in all respects. Rather, persons are equal as moral actors and as objects of moral concern. In principle, as a starting point for moral reasoning, no individual's well-being is more worthy of consideration than any other's. The criteria of equality—the respects in which people are to be considered equal— derive from our understanding of what they need to sustain their dignity and integrity as persons.

The first premise of moral equality is that all people are of the same kind, by which we mean that they are alike in morally relevant ways. Here we draw on the root meaning of equality as identity or sameness. To say, as we sometimes do, that all people are "equally human" is formally redundant but metaphorically meaningful. The implication is that "being human" is a normative idea and not a merely descriptive classification. The norm of respect for all humans as persons is based on special facts about human nature, and those facts are not reducible to the biological definition of the species:

> That all men are human is, if a tautology, a useful one, serving as a reminder that those who belong anatomically to the species *homo sapiens,* and can speak a language, use tools, live in societies, can interbreed despite racial differences, etc. are also alike in certain other respects more likely to be forgotten. These respects are notably the capacity to feel pain, both from immediate physical causes and from various situations represented

in perception and thought; and the capacity to feel affection for others and the consequences of this, connected with frustration of this affection, loss of its objects, etc.[7]

Once we classify a creature as human, bearing in mind what Williams calls characteristics "likely to be forgotten," we grant to that animal presumptive personhood.

Although moral equality is a normative idea, it has a factual basis. Most important is the perception that all humans are roughly equal in moral competence and vulnerability. All normal persons have much the same capacity for moral choice *in respect to their personal lives.* We do not expect priests or moral philosophers to be significantly better than anyone else at making such choices. Despite differences in experience, education, character, and reflection, no moral elite exists. Furthermore, because we are all sinners, all in need of moral guidance, we think it right that everyone should "walk humbly in the sight of the Lord." Moral awareness deflates pride and rebukes pretense; it therefore has a leveling effect.

A corollary is that all humans are roughly equal in their capacity to become fully realized persons. Everyone can form a self; can invest that self with intrinsic worth; can make it the embodiment of personal and social continuity; can exhibit sustained concern for self-respect and self-determination; can reach out to others *for* sympathy and *in* sympathy. This is not to say that all people attain the same level of psychic and moral development or do so in the same way. But the differences are highly individualized, not systematic. They do not generate morally relevant *kinds* of persons.

These elements of human nature—the complex strands of moral capacity and vulnerability—define our "common humanity." They form the empirical foundation of other-regarding conduct, the attributes of the human being that evoke sympathy, appreciation, and fellowship; they tell us who is that "other" for whom we properly have concern.

Baseline Equality

The definition of what is vital to the status of person or citizen establishes a minimum equality of entitlement, or what we may call baseline equality. The equal claim to "life, liberty, and the pursuit of happiness"

7. Bernard Williams, "The Idea of Equality," in Peter Laslett and W. G. Runciman, eds., *Philosophy, Politics, and Society* (Oxford: Blackwell, 1967), 112.

implied by the Declaration is not a claim to equal prosperity, good fortune, or happiness. People do not have claims to an equally *good* life or to the fullness of any other value; an equal right to hold property is not a right to equal property. What is really at stake is access to the basic goods once called "natural rights": life itself and the conditions that make life possible, tolerable, and hopeful. As to basic goods all persons have the same claim and in that sense all are equal.

Baseline equality is contingent, not absolute. Its level is sensitive to changing expectations. This is perhaps best seen when we consider "equal justice under law" and "equal protection of the laws." In these phrases "equality," though rhetorical, is more than empty rhetoric. It is a mandate for *extending* legal protection to all persons, and especially to those hitherto disadvantaged or excluded. The legal effect is to enlarge the category of who is to be treated as a full citizen or, in the case of noncitizens, as one whose personhood is recognized and protected.

Whether it be an incident of full citizenship or a vindication of common humanity, the ideal of equality must be understood in an affirmative way. People are not treated as equally human if they are equally degraded or oppressed. As Jacobus tenBroek pointed out in his history of the equal protection clause, "[E]qual denial of protection, that is no protection at all, is . . . a denial of equal protection."[8] In other words, moral and legal equality are not purely formal notions; they are not expressions of equality abstractly considered. Behind the formal principle, which includes the norm of treating like cases alike, is a substantive concern for the fundamental interests of persons. If those interests are not protected there can be no moral equality.

In the United States, equal protection became an explicit constitutional principle as an aftermath of the Civil War. The immediate aim of the Fourteenth Amendment, including the equal protection clause, was to guarantee to former slaves and their descendants the rights of citizenship. But slavery is not mentioned in the core of the amendment (Section 1), which takes the high ground of abstract principle: "No State shall . . . deny to any person within its jurisdiction the equal protection of the laws."

That principle could be (and was) read as no more than a general restraint on arbitrary and unreasonable lawmaking by the states. Thus understood, the clause had the important but limited effect of codifying,

8. Jacobus tenBroek, *Equal Under Law* (New York: Collier, 1965), 237. See also William E. Nelson, *The Fourteenth Amendment: From Political Principle to Judicial Doctrine* (Cambridge: Harvard University Press, 1988).

reinforcing, and extending to hitherto excluded persons a principle already implicit in the American legal heritage: the concept of impartial justice, that is, the right to be treated as others are who are similarly situated. It prohibits favoritism and invidious discrimination and demands that the laws themselves, in classifying people and activities, should meet minimal standards of rationality.

These safeguards are vital aspects of justice, but they do not fully protect moral equality. For example, it was thought to be evenhanded justice when, in *Pace v. Alabama* (1886) the Supreme Court upheld a law forbidding sexual intercourse and marriage between whites and blacks, on the ground that the law applied equally to both races and to all members of each race; and when, in *Plessy v. Ferguson* (1896), it was decided that "separate but equal" public facilities met the standard of equal protection. Furthermore, understood in this way, the equal protection clause does not create or vindicate rights. Only if a right, such as the right to vote, marry, or pursue a common occupation, already exists, then in respect to that right everyone must be treated equally.[9]

This formal, policy-neutral perspective had a very practical significance. It limited how far the Court could go in overruling the policy choices of state legislatures. It avoided holding the states responsible for protecting a broad array of substantive rights. To do so would have greatly enlarged the power of the federal government. During most of the late nineteenth century, the majority of the Court refused to go down that road.

Nevertheless, latent in the concept of equal protection—and in the special history of the amendment—was a more substantive concern for rights that might be abridged by local governments. It was generally agreed that the Fourteenth Amendment, because of its peculiar origins, offered special protection to blacks. Therefore the courts could properly implement a public policy against oppressive racial discrimination by the states. This gave a stronger bite to the concept of equal protection: the courts could more readily ask whether there was justice in fact as well as in form, that is, whether there was substantive as well as formal justice.[10]

9. Of course, many rights are protected by the Constitution in other ways, but not, according to this view, by the equal protection clause.

10. Thus in 1886 the Court refused to uphold the conviction of a Chinese laundryman in San Francisco who had violated an ordinance purporting to regulate the safety of laundries. The ordinance required anyone operating a laundry in a wooden building to get a permit to do so. It was shown, however, that no Chinese person would be granted a permit and that the real purpose of the law was to force Chinese shopkeepers out of the laundry business. The Court condemned the law as one "applied and administered . . . with an evil eye and an unequal hand" (Yick Wo v. Hopkins, 118 U.S. 356, 374 [1886]).

In the mid-twentieth century, propelled by a deepened concern for civil rights, the Supreme Court took up in earnest the cause of substantive justice. This development had two main aspects: the identification of *fundamental interests;* and a corollary doctrine of *suspect classifications.* When fundamental interests are at stake or when people are classified in ways that, prima facie, deny them baseline respect, rules are subject to strict scrutiny. In such cases judicial deference to legislative will is not appropriate. When strict scrutiny is warranted, the presumption is that the legislation should be declared unconstitutional unless a compelling state interest can be shown.

Under the rubric of fundamental interests the Supreme Court has held that classifications are presumptively invalid if they inhibit the right to move freely from one state to another, say, by conditioning welfare benefits on a year's residence in the receiving state; if they abridge the right to vote, by a poll tax or by restricting the franchise for certain purposes to property owners; if the individual's vote is diluted by a legislative apportionment scheme that gives substantially more weight to voters in certain districts than in others; if a basic personal liberty, such as procreation, is invaded by a state law authorizing the sterilization of certain types of offenders; if access to justice, especially criminal justice, is restricted or denied on account of poverty. These protections are limited in various ways, depending on how far the fundamental interest is infringed and how valid and compelling the state's competing interest may be. But the doctrine of fundamental interests has established the idea that people have a claim to effective baseline equality, at least with respect to such rights as are explicitly or implicitly recognized in the Constitution. Therefore it is not enough for rulemakers to be rational; it is not enough that they be formally evenhanded. They may not run roughshod over interests deemed crucial to personal freedom and political participation.

The doctrine of suspect classification speaks specifically to the experience of subordination and oppression. A classification is suspect if it arises from and tends to perpetuate a system of domination, especially when the subordinate group is stigmatized as inherently inferior. Race, sex, illegitimacy, and alienage are categories that have sustained domination, disadvantage, exploitation, and worse.[11] In 1938, well before the advent of the Warren Court, Justice Harlan F. Stone suggested, in an often-cited footnote, that "more exacting judicial scrutiny" might be necessary where legislation restricts the political process or where "prejudice against

---

11. They have not, however, received equal recognition as such by the Supreme Court. For example, discrimination on the basis of sex may receive "heightened" rather than "strict" scrutiny.

discrete and insular minorities" undermines the competence of that process to protect minorities.[12] This brief remark helped lay the foundation for later development of the "strict scrutiny" doctrine. At the same time, it identified two main sources of relevant oppression: the tyranny of entrenched majorities,[13] and the stigmatizing effect of prejudice.

In applying the concept of equal protection, the Supreme Court has sought to learn from the traumatic history of racial discrimination: hence the concern for stigma, for vulnerable minorities, and for those, like women, who are not necessarily minorities but have been the victims of systematic domination. Categories such as race and sex are suspect because they have had a history of invidious use. For that reason it has become a familiar feature of American public policy to bar discrimination based on race, creed, color, sex, or national origin.

However, as the experience of affirmative action has shown, reliance on these abstract criteria—especially as direct instruments of judgment rather than as starting points for analysis—can be self-defeating. It was understandable that in 1896 Justice John Marshall Harlan, in his dissent from the decision in *Plessy v. Ferguson,* should have asserted that "our Constitution is color-blind" and does not "permit any public authority to know the race of those entitled to be protected in the enjoyment" of the civil rights common to all citizens.[14] This formula may have been appropriate in the context, but it was too absolute and too sweeping; it was not a realistic guide to a public policy seriously committed to overcoming the heritage of slavery.

In fact, Justice Harlan was well aware of the substantive evil to be addressed:

> What can more certainly arouse race hate, what more certainly create and perpetuate a feeling of distrust between these races, than state enactments, which, in fact, proceed on the ground that colored citizens are so inferior and degraded that they cannot be allowed to sit in public coaches occupied by white citizens? That, as all will admit, is the real meaning of such legislation as was enacted in Louisiana.[15]

Thus the problem was not race per se but racial classification for the purpose of treating blacks as "inferior and degraded." If the objective

12. United States v. Carolene Products Co., 304 U.S. 144 (1938).

13. More generally, the tyranny of an entrenched governing class, which may or may not represent a majority of the people, or may once have done so but now restricts the opportunity of minorities to become majorities, or otherwise abridges the rights of minorities.

14. Plessy v. Ferguson, 163 U.S. 537, 559, 554 (1896).

15. Ibid., 560.

was to *overcome* prejudice and *improve* the position of blacks, it did not follow that the Constitution must be color-blind. Even very weak forms of affirmative action, let alone preferential hiring or promotion, require public authorities to know the race of those entitled to legal protection. In time it was to become clear that the Constitution could not be read as requiring public agencies to be unaware of, and helpless to remedy, the most wounding reality of American life.

The constitutional doctrine of equal protection does not ignore or erase differences of talent, achievement, contribution, or good fortune. It is not a device for leveling gradations or for making society more homogeneous. *It is, however, a path to community.* Equal protection speaks above all to membership, and membership presumes that all who belong share a core identity. This identity is wholly compatible with rich diversity so long as that diversity does not undermine equality of membership. The most serious threat to such equality is division based on moral stigma. Whatever its source, whether it be a certain racial or ethnic origin or level of native intelligence, the effect of moral stigma is to rank some people as intrinsically less worthy than others. Vindication of moral equality, in the face of strong impulses toward moral hierarchy, is the primary mission of equal protection of the law.

The postulate of community generates expectations for effective or full membership. It is not enough to restrain or even to overcome the divisiveness of stigma. Nor is it enough to offer the individual a minimum of protection against the abuse of power. The dignity of membership carries with it a panoply of duties and rights, including rights of participation. What these are cannot be known in the abstract. There is no alternative to continuing examination of just what interests must be protected and what opportunities secured if the promise of community is to be redeemed. Furthermore, what people should expect in the way of protection and participation depends greatly on available resources. When resources are small and options limited, conceptions of personhood and citizenship are necessarily thin. With the enlargement of historical opportunity, the community can ask more of itself.[16]

16. The Warren Court made just such a reassessment of consciousness and competence. In its decisions regarding racial segregation the Court presumed that a transformation of moral sensibility was taking place that was spurred in part by new learning regarding the biology and sociology of race differences. Similarly, in its decisions regarding criminal defendants the Court was saying that the nation now had the resources and the institutional competence to provide lawyers for indigent defendants. It could thus flesh out the constitutional right to counsel in criminal cases.

Equal Treatment

The law of equal protection builds on an implicit distinction between equality of treatment and equality of consideration and respect.[17] For many purposes the law assigns the same benefits and burdens to very broad classes of people. This equal treatment pertains to voting, military service, basic education, family formation, and other rights, privileges, and responsibilities that are incidental to membership, necessary to effective participation, or indispensable to personal well-being. These are the "fundamental interests" the Supreme Court has, in its best moments, struggled to define. As to these interests equal *treatment* is required and justified because it fulfills the more basic value of respect for the individual as person or as citizen. Equalities of entitlement establish *what we can rely on* as warrants of common humanity or common citizenship.

Beyond this shifting baseline, however, there is no requirement that everyone be treated alike. On the contrary, equal treatment may run counter to equality of respect and consideration. Equality of concern means giving the same weight to every person's dignity and welfare. But to do so we must take account of different circumstances. A 30 percent tax on income may inconvenience the rich but really hurt the less affluent. As Dworkin points out, "[I]f I have two children, and one is dying from a disease that is making the other uncomfortable, I do not show equal concern if I flip a coin to decide which should have the remaining dose of a drug. This example shows that the right to treatment as an equal is fundamental and the right to equal treatment, derivative."[18]

Once a class of persons has been adequately defined, however, equal treatment may be the best way of assuring equality of respect and consideration. All taxpayers *of a certain kind,* as defined by their incomes, obligations, and activities, properly expect to have the same tax liabilities. More generally, the rule of law presumes that people and acts *can* be classified and that like cases *can* be identified for purposes of like treatment. Strictly speaking, no case is exactly like any other.[19] But the quest for classifications and, through them, for rules that make equal treatment

17. Ronald Dworkin has emphasized the distinction between "equal treatment" and "treatment as an equal." See his *Taking Rights Seriously* (Cambridge: Harvard University Press, 1978), 227.

18. Ibid.

19. See Kenneth I. Winston, "On Treating Like Cases Alike," *California Law Review* 62 (January 1974): 17f.,22f.

equivalent to treatment as an equal is a major part of legal inquiry. The refinement of rules, including rules defining exceptions, defenses, and excuses, reflects a demand for decision-making that is sensitive and circumstantial yet is, at the same time, committed to equal treatment for everyone who is "similarly situated." The objective is fairness based on moral equality, not consistency for its own sake. Clearly there is no *necessary* relation between fairness and equal treatment, but in many contexts—especially when we cannot nicely calibrate differences in impact, vulnerability, or need—a prima facie case for equal treatment is easy to make.

This background may explain why it is often said that equality needs no justification:

> The assumption is that equality needs no reasons, only inequality does so. . . . If I have a cake and there are ten persons among whom I wish to divide it, then if I give exactly one tenth to each, this will not, at any rate automatically, call for justification; whereas if I depart from this principle of equal division I am expected to produce a special reason. It is some sense of this, however latent, that makes equality an ideal which has never seemed intrinsically eccentric, even though extreme forms of it may not have been wholly acceptable to either political thinkers or ordinary men throughout recorded human history.[20]

But equality as equal treatment is often inappropriate. What is appropriate is moral equality or treatment as an equal. We cannot be genuinely other-regarding, whatever the circumstances, if we do not accept the idea that everyone has the same intrinsic worth. This is what underlies the view that "equality needs no reasons."

▼   ▲   ▼   ▲   ▼

Although it celebrates sameness and cuts across differences, the postulate of moral equality is more elevating than humbling. From its ancient beginnings it has been an expression of communion with humanity, of a shared sense of belonging to what Kant called "the kingdom of ends." In that kingdom every person is a peer, but not a lowly peer. The spokesmen for modernity wanted to raise people up, not level them down. They believed that a community of equals would be an assembly of the well-born.

But the modern temper has not been content with the Kantian ideal. The spirit of Rousseau and Marx is more prophetic and more critical; it

20. Isaiah Berlin, "Equality," *Proceedings of the Aristotelian Society* 56 (1956): 305.

demands that the ideal be realized not only in individual conduct but in social policy and practice. Every dimension of social life—politics, law, industry, education, medicine, family—is an arena within which moral equality may be achieved. As a result, the connection between moral and social equality becomes a central focus for inquiry and debate.

The covenantal premise of moral equality makes a difference for social policy in two basic ways. First, we may ask whether the ideal is *made good* in reality. Is equality of intrinsic worth fully recognized in fact— say, through effective equality of opportunity? Second, we may ask what the ideal *prohibits*. Moral equality is a principle of restraint. It limits the criteria legislators and administrators may use in choosing among individuals and groups; forecloses policies that dehumanize or degrade; and points to the risk that inequality may lead to domination and domination breed contempt. As we have seen, these perspectives have governed the development of constitutional doctrine in the law of equal protection.

The first of these, making good the ideal, is the more troublesome. Any systematic ranking of persons and any material differences in rewards are potential threats to moral equality. Yet we know that social hierarchy is a pervasive fact of human existence and that many inequalities are widely accepted and readily justified. It is perverse and unrealistic to demand that social inequalities be eradicated no matter what the cost to other values.

Equal Opportunity

In the ethos of classical liberalism, equality of opportunity is the key to reconciling moral and social equality. This is neither a claim to equality of condition nor a rejection of all socially derived inequality. The real target is the caste principle.[21] No one should be hampered, no door should be closed to anyone, because of a prejudice against that person's social origins. Whatever opportunities exist should be open to all without regard to social class or (as later extended) to race, creed, ethnicity, or gender. Thus equality of opportunity has the limited objective of overcoming prejudice while maintaining the legitimacy of differential rewards.

In its elementary form equality of opportunity does not contemplate removing or even mitigating *all* special advantages. A person born into

21. See Robert M. MacIver and Charles H. Page, *Society: An Introductory Analysis* (New York: Rinehart, 1949), 358.

affluence or "marrying well" or otherwise benefiting from special connections is certainly privileged, but not necessarily because society recognizes an intrinsic moral or social superiority. Nor is the principle violated when people have a run of good fortune. *It is not merit alone* that is vindicated when barriers of caste and stigma come down. The door is open to merit, but it is also ajar to luck, manipulation, aggressive competition, and natural talent.

The policy of affirmative action is wholly consistent with this classical conception of equality of opportunity. What is new is the effort to make opportunity *effective* by measures that take account of past or present invidious discrimination. The remedy may consist only in expending new resources on identifying, recruiting, and training people disadvantaged by discrimination; or it may benefit members of such a category regardless of whether they themselves have suffered discrimination, as a way of raising up the group as a whole; or it may go further, requiring public agencies and private enterprise to show evidence of good faith and hard work as gauged by actual accomplishment in recruitment. Such measures are controversial—and experienced as unjust—because they affect the routine expectations of people who are not disadvantaged by stigma. But whether the policy of affirmative action is weak or strong, soft or abrasive, the larger objective is the same: opportunity neat, unvexed by prejudice.

A broader view of equal opportunity looks to the removal of *all* disadvantages that might affect the competitive race and contemplates positive support for the development of individual potentialities. On this principle a modern opportunity-centered educational system allocates special resources for children of poor families and provides a variety of programs to encourage and sustain self-respect. Thus understood, equality of opportunity is not tied to ascription and stigma. It offers a larger vision in which every individual is free to become, and effectively able to become, a fully realized person. This could be the foundation of a comprehensive social morality—but not when it is coupled with a Darwinian ethos of competitive struggle or with a pitiless, unrelieved meritocracy.[22]

Meritocracy is threatening because of the latent conflict between equality of respect and full equality of opportunity. Talent and character are starkly revealed when everyone has the same chance to succeed. When achievement is a universal possibility, no one can take refuge

22. See Michael Young, *The Rise of the Meritocracy* (Baltimore: Penguin Books, 1961).

behind oppression and discrimination; no one can save self-esteem by claiming lack of opportunity. And it is but a step from the idea that a person's worth is bound up with achievement to the conclusion that some people are *inherently* more worthy than others. The "opportunity society" invites the return of moral inequality—and does so with an easy conscience.

The Least Advantaged

Equality of opportunity alone cannot fashion a moral order. The principle must be embedded in a larger context of social justice. A society committed to moral equality needs to offer something more than the opportunity to seek reward through merit. It must find ways of upholding the ultimate worth of persons without regard to differences of talent, effort, or character. This requires a more integral, more communitarian conception of how moral and social equality are related.

Using the idiom of contemporary philosophy and economics, John Rawls set forth such a conception in what he called the "difference principle."[23] Rawls did not argue for full social equality. On the contrary, he assumed that inequalities are inevitable and that they can be justified in many ways. The question remains, however, as to their *moral* justification. Inequalities may be good for prosperity, scholarship, art, family life, warfare, and much else; or inequality may be recognized as inescapable fact, whatever its utility. But these justifications do not speak to the moral issue. They do not bring other-regarding policy to the center of concern. They do not tell us how to make inequality part of the moral order.

Leaving aside refinements and qualifications, the difference principle asserts that social and economic inequalities may be necessary and desirable but that *their moral worth is to be judged by what they contribute to the welfare of the least advantaged.* This principle strongly echoes the Judeo-Christian association of righteousness with concern for the poor and powerless, for "the least of these my brethren" (Matthew 25:40). In the biblical view, it has been said, "the justice of a community is measured by its treatment of the powerless in society, most often described as the widow, the orphan, the poor and the stranger (non-Israelite) in the land."[24] In this tradition belief in the moral equality of the least advan-

---

23. *A Theory of Justice* (Cambridge: Harvard University Press, 1971), 62.
24. U.S. Catholic Bishops' Pastoral Letter, 1st draft, *Origins, NC Documentary Service* 14 (15 November 1984): 346.

taged establishes an obligation of assistance. Inequality as such is not the issue; it is not a question of requiring those who have more to help those who have less, *just because they have less*. The case is more desperate. The obligation runs to people who suffer or are degraded because they are impoverished; to people who are in danger of being excluded or forgotten as objects of moral concern.

Rawls's difference principle is both stronger and weaker than the biblical injunction. It is weaker in that it speaks to social arrangements rather than to personal responsibility; as a result, the sense of obligation may be more remote and more attenuated. It is stronger in that it offers a criterion for assessing systematic inequalities. To treat the poor and the wretched justly it is not enough to offer alms and kindness. They must belong to a community whose *institutions* serve their interests and offer them hope. Social justice may have its origin in personal compassion and responsibility, but it is not reducible to impulse and sentiment. The keynote is accountability.

For Rawls "all social values—liberty and opportunity, income and wealth, and the bases of self-respect—are to be distributed equally unless an unequal distribution of any, or all, of these values is to everyone's advantage."[25] This premise upholds equality as a fundamental value but also recognizes that other values, such as prosperity and security, are important to human well-being:

> Now since we are regarding citizens as free and equal moral persons (the priority of the first principle of equal liberty gives institutional expression to this), the obvious starting point is to suppose that all other social primary goods, and in particular income and wealth, should be equal: everyone should have an equal share. But society must take organizational requirements and economic efficiency into account. So it is unreasonable to stop at equal division. The basic structure should allow inequalities as long as these improve everyone's situation. . . . Because we start from equal shares, those who benefit least have, so to speak, a veto; and thus we arrive at the difference principle.[26]

In reaching for different values, moral equality cannot be compromised—but social equality is necessarily given up. The challenge is to preserve the former while sacrificing the latter. The difference principle purports to meet this challenge by insisting that inequalities be justified by their contribution to "the long-run expectations of the least fortunate

25. Rawls, *Theory of Justice*, 62. This "general conception of justice" is qualified in important ways, especially in that the difference principle must yield to the priority of liberty, at least in advanced industrial societies.
26. Ibid., 97.

group in society."[27] Only if we take account of the least fortunate can we be sure that inequalities will be "to everyone's advantage"; only thus will we extend equality of concern and respect to all.

In a weak form the difference principle, taken alone, might be compatible with a heavy burden of inequality and domination. If all we ask is that everyone gain *something* from a system of inequalities, the condition may be met all too easily. Most rulers claim they benefit everyone. That is part of their claim to legitimacy. Indeed, the least advantaged do often share in the glow of pomp and power, to say nothing of the minimum of security gained from a Hobbesian bargain. An ideal feudal system and trickle-down economics might fulfill the difference principle in this weak form.

But that is not what Rawls had in mind. The difference principle is not satisfied by *any* benefit. Rather, inequalities are to be arranged so that they are "to the *greatest* benefit of the least advantaged."[28] The force of this idea is to subject the system to close scrutiny. Inequality is morally justified if it does more than equality can do to improve the prospects of the least advantaged. A feasible alternative that does as well or better with less inequality should, however, be preferred.

The difference principle is founded in rationality and reciprocal advantage, not in sympathy and benevolence. In his basic argument Rawls imagined a social contract in which free, equal, and rational persons agree on the terms of their future cooperation. He posited an "original position" that includes a "veil of ignorance" that obscures from the parties their individual circumstances. Thus the bias that might come from such information is eliminated. In this hypothetical setting the parties are to choose principles of justice. As they are committed to rationality, they will necessarily choose the least bad or safest alternative. Anyone may end up highly vulnerable to loss of liberty or at the bottom of the economic ladder. Therefore everyone will want to insure against the worst alternative. The outcome will be a set of principles that protect the basic liberties of all and the interests of the least advantaged.

Thus the difference principle, subject to the priority of liberty, is the outcome of rational, self-interested calculation. It follows the logic of the

27. Ibid., 151.
28. Ibid., 302, my emphasis. See Rawls's "final statement of the two principles of justice for institutions": (1) "Each person is to have an equal right to the most extensive system of basic liberties compatible with a similar system of liberty for all"; (2) "Social and economic inequalities are arranged so that they are both: (a) to the greatest benefit of the least advantaged, consistent with the just savings principle, and (b) attached to offices and positions open to all under conditions of fair and equal opportunity" (ibid.).

maximin rule for choice under uncertainty: assume that every choice can have a worst outcome and opt for the one that is least threatening or least bad. According to Rawls, "[n]ot only do the parties protect their basic rights but they insure themselves against the worst eventualities."[29] Rawls made a special point of insisting that his argument is more cogent than classical utilitarianism because the latter presumes an unrealistic benevolence. The principle of aggregate utility, or the greatest good for the greatest number, does not insure that everyone benefits. Some must defer to the general good and thereby sacrifice their own prospects.

> It is evident then why utilitarians should stress the role of sympathy in moral learning and the central place of benevolence among the moral virtues. Their conception of justice is threatened with instability unless sympathy and benevolence can be widely and intensely cultivated. Looking at the question from the standpoint of the original position, the parties recognize that it would be highly unwise if not irrational to choose principles which may have consequences so extreme that they could not accept them in practice. They would reject the principle of utility and adopt the more realistic idea of designing the social order on a principle of reciprocal advantage.[30]

This is not to say that the difference principle lacks social utility. On the contrary, Rawls claimed that, because everyone benefits and therefore has a stake in the system, social stability is enhanced. "Since everyone's good is affirmed, all acquire inclinations to uphold the system. . . . Furthermore, the public recognition of the two principles gives greater support to men's self-respect and this in turn increases the effectiveness of social cooperation."[31]

The difference principle is justified by individual, self-regarding rationality, but this should not be understood as narrow selfishness. In the "original position" as Rawls presented it, the actors are governed by Kantian principles. Among these are respect for the moral autonomy of all participants, including the right of each to pursue the good in his own way; acceptance of rational principles of law-making, and particularly the categorical imperative; and the larger aim of seeking a harmony of human interests. Thus the original position presumes a fundamental morality. It is a morality that envisions, in the spirit of Kant and

29. Ibid., 176.
30. Ibid., 178. Rawls adds: "We need not suppose, of course, that persons never make substantial sacrifices for one another, since moved by affection and ties of sentiment they often do. But such actions are not demanded as a matter of justice by the basic structure of society."
31. Ibid., 177f.

his Protestant forebears, the lone individual in quest of the right, guided only by God or by abstract principles.

Nevertheless, the principle is a powerful expression of human solidarity. Within a theory of justice the abstract ideal of fraternity takes on a new and more specific meaning:

> In comparison with liberty and equality, the idea of fraternity . . . expresses no definite requirement. We have yet to find a principle of justice that matches the underlying idea. The difference principle, however, does seem to correspond to a natural meaning of fraternity: namely, to the idea of not wanting to have greater advantages unless this is to the benefit of others who are less well off.[32]

On this interpretation, what began as shrewd calculation—a hedge against unfavorable outcomes—generates an ethos of brotherhood and is a building block of community.[33]

The Egalitarian Temptation

Seen in its best light, the modern attack on social hierarchy puts moral equality foremost. Social equality is properly a means to that end, not an end in itself. When *invidious* distinctions are broken down, and when disabling disadvantages are repaired, human beings are made whole as objects of moral concern. They belong to a community that cares for all its members. This program has few critics. It is, after all, only a way of taking seriously a conception of human dignity that goes back to biblical and classical awareness.

But the committed egalitarian seeks more than moral equality. In what has come to be its central meaning egalitarianism is a call for comprehensive social equality. To be sure, few call for full equality of condition. But even moderate egalitarians resist inequalities based on differences in contribution, talent, character, and effort; grant only grudgingly the imperatives of social organization or the claims of other values; and find no solace in the random distribution of good fortune. Social inequalities are thought to be inherently evil regardless of whether

32. Ibid., 105.
33. Although Rawls's argument is ingenious and suggestive, it does not formulate a principle compelled by rationality. It might be equally persuasive to propose that social differences should always be constrained by a postulate of moral equality and that this requires both freedom from invidious discrimination and collective commitment to a social minimum, including the economic basis for effective participation in a political community. Everyone would be protected without being guaranteed gains proportionate to the gains of others.

they can be shown to be palpable threats to moral equality. We might call this the egalitarian temptation.

Historically there have been four main justifications for inequalities as contributing to the common good. It has been claimed that inequalities are essential for: (1) effective organization for prosperity, education, public safety, and similar social goals; (2) achievement of excellence and high standards, especially in the realm of "high culture"; (3) protection of freedom, including the freedom to become unequal in possessions and personal attainments; and (4) commitment to ascriptive unities, especially family membership, which depend on recognition of special benefits and privileges. None of these objectives can justify *unlimited* or *unrestrained* inequality. Each, however, has a strong claim to be recognized and supported—a claim that invokes practical as well as moral considerations, means as well as ends.

A major obstacle to clear thought on this subject is the egalitarian temptation to stigmatize as elitist any argument in support of hierarchy, leadership, or special distinction. The word "elite" does have unhappy connotations of insularity and arrogance, but some such idea, shorn of those connotations, is indispensable to social analysis. In the language of social science, elites are "functional, mainly occupational groups which have high status (for whatever reason) in a society."[34] In Harold Lasswell's pithy formula: "The few who get the most of any value are the *elite;* the rest are the rank and file."[35]

These definitions imply that elites are *multiple* and *contextual.*[36] A student orchestra is an elite group, but so is the football team; and neither may be highly regarded outside the school community. Indeed, every organization or community of any complexity can be usefully studied from the point of view of how leadership groups are formed, how they function, how they maintain themselves, and how they relate to the relevant nonelite: followers, constituents, spectators, the uneducated, the unskilled, the indifferent. And this can be done without any suggestion that members of the elite have special moral worth. On the contrary, there are elite spokesmen for odious ideologies, and there are elite thieves and assassins, who qualify as such simply because they are leaders or have special skills or commitment. Nor do elites necessarily coalesce

34. T. B. Bottomore, *Elites and Society* (London: Watts, 1964), 8.

35. Harold D. Lasswell, "World Politics and Personal Insecurity," in Harold D. Lasswell, Charles E. Merriam, and Thomas V. Smith, eds., *A Study of Power* (1934; reprint, Glencoe, Ill.: Free Press, 1950), 3.

36. This aspect is emphasized in Suzanne Keller, *Beyond the Ruling Class: Strategic Elites in Modern Society* (New York: Random House, 1963).

into an "establishment"; they may remain fragmented and highly vulnerable. The theory of elites is the study of these variable aspects of social organization. It is not in itself a social doctrine or prescription.

But a relevant doctrine is waiting in the wings. It is revealed when we focus on cultural, creative, or value-centered elites rather than on differential prestige, power, or wealth. The idea that elites may stand for excellence, or embody it, or have responsibility for it, draws on an important strand of ordinary language: the elite are "the best or most skilled members of a given social group" or "the choice flower (of society or any body or class of persons)."[37] Following this lead, we may say that the social function of value-centered elites is to elaborate, nurture, and defend particular skills, standards, and ideals. Insofar as this function is performed well, the community benefits. It is therefore in the community's interests to respect such elites and to grant them appropriate resources.

Dispraise of elitism looks only to the darker side of this social function. In fact, however, many of the values of a complex society are vitally dependent on the effective functioning of social elites. This may not be true of the most person-centered values, such as parental love, which are sustained by the satisfactions and urgencies of everyday life. But more impersonal values—intellectual, technical, aesthetic, legal, political—need special attention and support. They are characteristically subject to erosion and distortion, especially when exposed to short-run demands for payoff and gratification. By granting special privileges such as lifetime tenure to judges and professors or special awards to scientists, physicians, artists, athletes, and many other groups, we hope to encourage high levels of creativity and responsibility.

Democracy itself depends on the self-confidence and integrity of legal and political elites. Freedom of speech and association, equal protection of the laws, and other necessary ingredients of democracy are not self-sustaining. They require "eternal vigilance"—and that vigilance is mainly the work of committed elites. In our society these elites include the judiciary, other sectors of the legal profession, some executive agencies, and private organizations promoting constitutional principles, often in the course of defending their special interests. Democratic participation, too, can be sustained and effective only with the help of elite groups dedicated to mobilizing and channeling public opinion.

A preoccupation with social equality for its own sake can distort the quest for social justice. The real issue is not social equality but the cre-

---

37. *American Heritage Dictionary*, s.v. "elite;" *Oxford English Dictionary*, s.v. "elite."

ation of a community in which each person can flourish as a full human being. When people are pushed aside and left out—when a relatively powerless but substantial minority lives side by side with an affluent majority—the promise of community is unfulfilled. It is this condition, not inequality as such, that is morally offensive.

Social equality is not in itself an ennobling ideal. It is compatible with preference for a shared poverty in which everyone is equally miserable; it may also be an expression of envy. The drive for social equality, insofar as it is justified, must be tied to *other* values and must rest on a clear understanding of what *kind* of equality is at issue. What sort of equality is necessary if arbitrary power is to be restrained? if democratic participation is to be encouraged? if effective economic opportunity is to be guaranteed? if the number of stultified or degraded lives is to be minimized? Each of these questions calls for different answers. None demands more than the vindication of moral equality.

COMMUNAL DEMOCRACY

As an abstract idea, "consent of the governed" does not require democracy. There may be consent to a monarchy or to rule by a tyrant. However, the plebiscites that confirmed Hitler's rise to power were a parody of democracy, not its fulfillment. To forestall such a travesty, the Declaration of Independence couples "consent of the governed" with an affirmation of "unalienable rights." Within the terms of the Declaration, consent may legitimize a monarchy only if fundamental rights are protected.[38] Moreover, the founders of the Republic moved quickly to associate *consent* of the governed with *rule* by the people. The people's consent is necessary, not only to establish or confirm a regime, but also for the conduct of its affairs.

38. The Declaration says the people "may organize government on 'such principles' as they choose, and that they may choose 'any form of government' they deem appropriate *to secure these rights*. . . . And by 'any form of government' the Declaration emphatically includes—as any literate 18th-century reader would have understood—not only the democratic form of government, but also a mixed form, and the aristocratic and monarchic forms as well. That is why . . . the Declaration has to submit facts 'to a candid world' to prove the British king guilty of a 'long train of abuses.' . . . Thus the Declaration, accurately speaking, is neutral on the question of forms of government; any form is legitimate provided it secures equal freedom and is instituted by popular consent. But as to how to secure that freedom the Declaration, in its famous passage on the principles of government, is silent" (Martin Diamond, "The Declaration and the Constitution: Liberty, Democracy and the Founders," *The Public Interest* 41 [Fall 1975]: 49f., my emphasis). However, the early and virtually unanimous agreement that the newly independent states and the soon-to-be-established national government should be republican in form suggests that, in context, the Declaration as covenant went further than Diamond suggests. The signers may not all have agreed with Tom Paine that any king was illegitimate, but they did agree that, for America, kings were not wanted.

Democracy is the *self-preserving* consent of the governed. Self-preserving consent maintains the liberties and institutions of a free people. At a minimum this requires the familiar apparatus of democracy, especially freedom of speech and association, legitimate opposition, and regular elections. There must be legitimacy in depth, not merely a gross justification of the right to rule; and the people must be free to protect, and organized to protect, their vital interests. Consent must be revocable. Only then does consent become sovereignty; only then do the people's rulers become their servants.

As we consider the ingredients of self-preserving consent, the focus must shift from the people as an aggregate of individuals to the people as a functioning community. *The sovereignty of the people is established, confirmed, and exercised in and through community.* People act democratically, not as isolated or self-sufficient units, but as bearers of a common culture, including a political culture, and as interdependent participants in the group structure of society. Democracy flourishes when it is part of, and sustained by, an appropriate way of life.

When John Dewey distinguished "democracy as a social idea" from "political democracy as a system of government," he had something like this in mind.

> The idea [of democracy] remains barren and empty save as it is incarnated in human relationships. . . . To be realized it must affect all modes of human association, the family, the school, industry, religion. . . . Regarded as an idea, democracy is not an alternative to other principles of associated life. It is the idea of community life itself. . . . The clear consciousness of a communal life, in all its implications, constitutes the idea of democracy.[39]

In this view, democracy "is a name for a life of free and enriching communion" that "will have its consummation when free social inquiry is indissolubly wedded to the art of full and moving communication."[40] Democracy brings people together by perfecting communication and participation. As does the ethos of science, however, democracy also nurtures and sustains diversity and individuality.

In Dewey's ideal of communal democracy, "consent of the governed" should meet a high standard of deliberative intelligence; collective decision should be fully open to persuasion and argument; and the quality of political decisions depends on the extent to which

39. John Dewey, *The Public and Its Problems* (New York: Holt, 1927), 143, 148f.
40. Ibid., 184.

communal democracy has been attained.[41] This argument should not be construed as deprecating—or as indifferent to—the forms and procedures of political democracy. If the promise of democracy is to be realized fully, discussion and voting must be sensitive to, and enriched by, the experience of constructing what Dewey called the "Great Community." But elementary principles and rudimentary forms are indispensable bulwarks against regression to tyranny. No statement of a richer ideal can diminish the importance of baseline achievements.

In what follows we consider four principles of communal democracy: the protection and integration of minorities; the moral primacy of the community over the state; the responsibility of government for communal well-being; and the social basis of political participation.

The Protection and Integration of Minorities

Among the foundations of communal democracy is the integrity of decision-making by "the people as a whole." This means, above all, that democracy cannot be equated with majority rule:

> Since the Enlightenment political philosophers have debated the merits of two rival views about what democracy . . . really is. The first is a majoritarian conception: that a majority of voters should always have the power to do anything it thinks right or in its own interests. The second is communal: it insists that democracy is government of, by, and for not the majority but the people as a whole. The communal conception requires that each citizen have not only an equal part in government but an equal place in its concern and respect. Democracy, on that conception, is not undermined by but requires a system of individual rights guaranteeing the integrity of each person's basic interests and needs.[42]

The sovereignty of the people is not the same as the sovereignty of a majority. Majority rule is one way of expressing the will of the people, taken as a whole. It is not, however, the only way, nor is it a self-sufficient way.

For many important purposes, popular sovereignty seeks a stronger consensus than a bare majority can provide; it may demand, for example,

41. The phrase "communal democracy" is also used to characterize Dewey's conception in Mason Drukman, *Community and Purpose in America* (New York: McGraw-Hill, 1971), 324f.

42. Ronald Dworkin, "The Future of Abortion," *New York Review of Books* (28 September 1989): 51.

agreement by two-thirds of the voters or legislators. This requirement, as in the procedure for amending the United States Constitution or for overturning a presidential veto, greatly increases the power of minorities. This can be considered "undemocratic," however, only if we equate a majority with "the people."[43] The demand for consensus is a demand for *inclusion*. And the politics of inclusion are, in principle, a vindication of democracy.

Majority rule is not self-sufficient, because its legitimacy depends on the freedom of minorities to become majorities.[44] In a democracy the power of a majority can never be absolute or unrestrained, if only because the right of minorities to freedom of speech and association must be maintained. Properly understood, *democratic* majorities are freely formed expressions of revocable consent. (The majorities mobilized by authoritarian regimes do not meet that standard.) Therefore majority rule presupposes a limiting framework that says how majorities are formed and defines the extent of their powers.

The covenantal understanding is that the people-in-community are the safest repository of ultimate power. This does not say how the people shall rule; still less does it justify faith in the wisdom of particular majorities. Majority rule is a form of representation. It allows the community to go forward in a direction that roughly approximates the will of the people. Even under conditions of direct or "town meeting" democracy, the majority only represents—it need not reflect—the will of all who are assembled.

A "mechanical" majority—a faction large enough, cohesive enough, and enduring enough to shut out or negate minority views—threatens both community and democracy. The excluded minority suffers impotence and alienation; the unbridled majority is tempted to tyranny. Insofar as it resists compromise and scorns consensus, majoritarian democracy is anti-communitarian. It is also an impoverished rendering of the democratic ideal.

43. For example, a philosophical study of free speech includes the following statement: "Any distinct restraint on majority power, such as a principle of freedom of speech, is by its nature anti-democratic, anti-majoritarian" (Frederick Schauer, *Free Speech: A Philosophical Inquiry* [Cambridge: Cambridge University Press, 1982], 40). However, the author also notes that "equal participation by all the people in the process of government is even more fundamental to the ideal of self-government than is the idea of majority power" (ibid., 41).

44. On this and related issues, see Herbert McClosky, "The Fallacy of Absolute Majority Rule," *Journal of Politics* 11 (November 1949): 637–54.

The Moral Primacy of the Community over the State

In the 1980s, as the authority of European communism crumbled, voices were raised on behalf of "civil society."[45] The totalitarian systems had tried, with uneven success, to establish complete control over social life. In the attempt, they did much to destroy spontaneity, autonomy, and creativity at all levels and in all sectors of society. Among dissident intellectuals the response to this damage went beyond a call for democracy in *government*. They also wanted a free *society*. To achieve that end, they came to understand, a democratic government must be constrained by principles that affirm the primacy and preserve the integrity of nongovernmental interests, practices, and institutions.

The encounter with totalitarianism in the twentieth century has reaffirmed a doctrine that emerged with special clarity from the political struggles of the seventeenth and eighteenth centuries: the idea that the containment of despotism requires a counterposition of state and society. If freedom is to be protected, government must be seen as derivative and instrumental—as the agent of community, not its creator.

In his influential tract on *The Rights of Man* (1792), written in defense of the French Revolution, Thomas Paine gave full expression to this liberal demystification and depreciation of government. Social order, he argued,

> has its origin in the principles of society and the natural constitution of man. It existed prior to government, and would exist if the formality of government was abolished. The mutual dependence and reciprocal interest which man has upon man, and all the parts of a civilized community upon each other, create that great chain of connection which holds it together. The landholder, the farmer, the manufacturer, the merchant, the tradesman, and every occupation, prospers by the aid which each receives from the other, and from the whole. Common interest regulates their concerns, and forms their law; and the laws which common usage ordains, have a greater influence than the laws of government. . . . Government is no farther necessary than to supply the few cases to which society and civilization are not conveniently competent; and instances are not wanting to show, that everything which government can usefully add thereto, has been performed by the common consent of society, without government.[46]

45. Perhaps most clearly among Polish intellectuals connected with the Solidarity movement. See Z. A. Pelczynski, "Solidarity and 'The Return of Civil Society' in Poland, 1976–81," in John Keane, ed., *Civil Society and the State* (London: Verso, 1988), 361–80.
46. *The Thomas Paine Reader*, ed. Michael Foot and Isaac Kramnick (Great Britain: Penguin Books, 1987), 266f.

Governments are not divinely ordained. They are instituted for limited purposes, to meet social necessities. Accountable to those purposes, they may be removed for cause. The people reserve to themselves fundamental rights of self-preservation, including rights of property in their own persons, in their liberties, and in the products of their labor. When these or other basic interests are at stake, they maintain the right to resist and rebel.

All this was argued a century earlier by John Locke (1632–1704). As developed in his theory of an "original Compact," consent is the moral basis of political order. "Men being . . . by Nature, all free, equal and independent, no one can be put out of this Estate, and subjected to the Political Power of another, without his own *Consent*." A tacit assumption is that consent is rational and self-preserving. People give their consent to political authority

> by agreeing with other Men to joyn and unite into a Community, for their comfortable, safe, and peaceable living one amongst another, in a secure Enjoyment of their Properties, and a greater Security against any that are not of it.[47]

These ends of "Political Society" are not meant to be noble or inspiring. They are instrumental, not expressive; they speak to utility, not salvation. And utility is tested by the needs of the people, not of government.

This social-contract doctrine has strong overtones of individualism. A culture or an epoch is individualist insofar as it values autonomous and self-interested judgment, initiative, and achievement and insofar as it looks to agreement among individuals as the preferred basis of social organization. The idea of a social contract is indeed congenial to that outlook, for several reasons: it is easy to imagine a primordial or hypothetical occasion on which the people, *as separate individuals*, agreed on the need for government; the concept of reserved or "natural" rights is most readily associated with the claims and liberties of distinct individuals; and to the modern mind the idea of contract evokes wholesome connotations of voluntary association and responsible consent.

It is a serious mistake, however, to suppose that notions of limited government and reserved right require an ethos of individualism. Government may be thought of as the agent of a preexisting *community*, not of hitherto disassociated individuals. The community is composed of

47. *Two Treatises on Government* (1690; reprint, New York: New American Library, 1963), 374f.

many complex groups and relationships—economic, familial, religious, political—whose stability and vitality depend on the protection of fundamental rights. And these rights may be group-centered rather than individual-centered. From that standpoint, the idea that individuals act autonomously may seem odd, irrelevant, even blasphemous.

Nor is there anything individualist about protecting the basic liberties of *persons*. We have discussed above the important distinction between "person" and "individual" (see Chapter 8). Persons are concrete human entities, embedded in social contexts. They may or may not be thought of, or act, or be treated, as separate and independent agents; they may not be free to make and remake their social arrangements. Nevertheless, however deeply implicated they may be in the lives of others or in the requirements of institutional life, the well-being of persons depends on the security of "their Lives, Liberties and Estates, which I call by the general Name, *Property.*"[48] Whatever may be said of other aspects of his thought, *this* Lockean premise does not entail a radical individualism.

▼   ▲   ▼   ▲   ▼

In his theory of the "state of nature" Locke laid a foundation for the moral primacy of the community. In his view, community is logically (and often historically) prior to government. Locke's state of nature is not a Hobbesian state of war; rather, it is a morally governed order, "a State of Peace, Good Will, Mutual Assistance and Preservation," in which men live together "according to reason," in association with kin and neighbor, but "without a common Superior on Earth, with Authority to judge between them."[49] This *lack of a common authority* is the great inconvenience to be remedied by the founding of a unified commonwealth. The regime of law established by the commonwealth perfects community but does not create it.[50]

In this and other passages Locke treats "Civil Society," "Political Society," and even "Community" as synonyms. He did not have a clear way of distinguishing the inchoate underlying community, which embraces families, special-purpose associations, and recognized rights of property, from the organized political community. (Only the latter, not the former, can be the product of a social compact.) By the late eighteenth century, however, "civil society" came to be a way of referring

48. Locke, *Two Treatises on Government*, 95.
49. Ibid., 321.
50. Ibid., 368f.

"to the subtler, sometimes tacit interconnections of social life"[51]—in a word, to "society."

But why *civil* society? The revival of this usage in Eastern Europe owes much to the special idiom of Hegel and Marx.[52] There civil society is roughly equivalent to modern economic life; it is driven by self-interest, sustained by rights in property, and advanced by corporate organization.[53] Marx could dismiss this as *bourgeois* society and deny it moral worth. Hegel, by contrast, saw civil society as standing between the ethical consciousness of the family and that of the fully realized state.[54] In Hegel's conception, civil society is transcended when, in the ideal state, a sense of community is fully developed. But even then the values associated with civil society are maintained, not extinguished.[55] These values include individuality, universalism, rationality, and the rule of law. Hence the celebration of civil society—among intellectuals influenced by Marxism but distancing themselves from it—is a return to Hegel.

The idea of civil society is worth preserving, but we need not equate it with a market economy. It may well be that markets foster rationality, individuality, and legality, but these ideals can also have other causes and other homes. Under congenial conditions, with appropriate adaptations, they may extend to all social relations and groups. Furthermore, civil society, when contrasted to the state, must include a broad array of social

51. J. W. Burrow, *Whigs and Liberals* (Oxford: Clarendon Press, 1988), 26. This historian suggests an earlier provenance, "civil society" having "begun to be seen as a distinct category . . . in the seventeenth and eighteenth centuries." He adds that "Locke, in an age of revolution and threatened civil war, had distinguished civil society from political authority, in explaining how men might be without government yet not in a state of war, but this conception was unhistorical and unspecific. The relations of civil society, and its historical mutations, still remained to be picked out" (ibid.).

52. See Pelczynski, "Solidarity and 'Civil Society,' " 364.

53. The close connection between civil society and a market economy has been traced to medieval political thought. In medieval society there was, in addition to a guild mentality, "a set of practices and beliefs centered upon a market economy, social mobility, individual self-determination and private property." The latter "may best be characterized by Hegel's own term, 'civil society.' " In contrast, the ethos of the guild was based on fellowship and mutual aid. See Antony Black, *Guilds and Civil Society in European Political Thought from the Twelfth Century to the Present* (London: Methuen, 1984), 30ff.

54. G. W. F. Hegel, *Philosophy of Right* (1821; reprint, Oxford: Clarendon Press, 1952), 122ff.

55. For Hegel, "the modern state must be built around the free, rational individual. It must respect his freedom of conscience, freedom to select his profession, the security of his property and freedom of economic enterprise. It must allow for the dissemination of information and the formation of public opinion. It must be founded on the rule of law" (Charles Taylor, *Hegel* [Cambridge: Cambridge University Press, 1975], 450). Here Taylor stresses the "liberal" side of Hegel's theory, which is in tension with, and in part undermined by, the Hegelian quest for an ultimate *union* of state and society.

institutions, including private education, philanthropy, and much else that is not necessarily organized on market principles.

A striking feature of civil society is the interdependence of private and public morality, private and public institutions. Civil society is distinct from government and a brake on government; yet it is also sustained by law and even, in some respects, constituted by law. Private life is taken to be the chief source of order and well-being; yet civil society is a reservoir of reserved rights that are claims on public morality. Civil society includes the realm of kinship and custom; yet it is also the seedbed of critical morality. Every transition to civility brings with it an increment of public consciousness, that is, a sense of responsibility to standards that transcend private interests and parochial inclinations. This is the way a community is "civilized."

Earlier we noted that the common-law tradition tends to counterpose state and society. The judges defer to private ordering and postulate rights against the state. These rights, which can never be fully specified, are recognized as implicit in social order, not gifts of government. At the same time, since law is part of government, the counterposition of state and society cannot be absolute. The rule of law makes its own indispensable contribution to personal and group security by releasing private energies, facilitating private transactions, and stabilizing private associations. Hence the idea of civil society, which includes the rule of law or, at least, rudimentary versions of it, points to the *continuity* between state and society. Although these continuities are important, they do not negate the community's claim to moral primacy. That primacy can only be insured by an array of rights—personal as well as institutional.

Thus rights, far from being alien to communal democracy, are vital ingredients of it. They create an infrastructure for democracy. *But the determination of rights requires a communitarian sensibility.* The will of the community with respect to rights is discerned by examining its traditions, practices, and institutions, not necessarily by counting votes. Furthermore, in deciding what interests merit protection as rights, the courts look to the needs of historically situated persons and groups. They translate abstract or absolute rights into principles that take account of multiple values, constraining contexts, and historical opportunities.

This approach is consistent with recognizing "fundamental," "natural," "human," "moral," "baseline," "background," or "core" rights. All these terms have been used to denote *generic* rights, grounded in the human condition or guaranteed to all citizens or persons per se. Such rights do not stem from specific projects, relationships, or entitlements. Some needs, vulnerabilities, and threats are indeed omnipresent. They arise wherever human beings exist and interact; wherever, especially, power is exercised and authority is asserted. Every person has exigent needs for survival, self-respect, and the opportunity to flourish. These are routinely threatened by the community's own organization, including the structures of power it creates. Therefore we recognize, as applicable to every human situation, generic rights of life, liberty, and justice.

The context of community is crucial, however. To make any right effective it is necessary to consider competing interests and relevant conditions.[56] In conscripting soldiers, punishing criminals, educating children, or controlling traffic, the community may demand an involuntary sacrifice of life or liberty. If the liberty is "fundamental" (in American constitutional law, and elsewhere as well), special constraints are imposed on government, such as the need to show a "compelling governmental interest" and a "narrowly tailored" abridgment of the right. The more fundamental the right, the greater the constraint. Rights are not absolute, however, if only because, although they must be *stated* abstractly, they must be *applied* concretely.

To put it another way, the identification of fundamental rights is an aspect of constitution-making; and constitutions, whether tacitly accepted or explicitly adopted, must be interpreted. Interpretation brings to bear prudential judgment, which requires appreciation for the diverse interests and values at stake in the life of a community. Constitutional or common-law rights to life, liberty, and justice are authoritative *premises* for decision; they demand vindication; but their reach is not predetermined. There is room for the enlargement of rights as well as for their limitation.

The Responsibility of Government for Communal Well-being

Thus far we have considered two principles of communal democracy: the sovereignty of the people as a whole, understood as protecting minorities and transcending majority rule; and the moral primacy of the community vis-a-vis the state. We have also seen that the community, as

---

56. To be sure, a right is not meaningful if it may be overridden by any legislative goal or policy. As Dworkin says, "[R]ights trump utilities" (Dworkin, *Taking Rights Seriously*, xi). This is, however, a matter of definition. "It follows from the definition of a right that it cannot be outweighed by all social goals . . . but only by a goal of special urgency" (ibid., 92). The definition cannot tell us what rights exist or how they may be determined.

"civil society," relies on law to protect private interests. A third principle is more controversial: the responsibility of government for communal well-being. That is, we expect government to maintain in an optimal state the conditions that enhance the experience of community.

In a free society, it has been said, "the state does not administer the affairs of men. It administers justice among men who conduct their own affairs."[57] This classic formula by Walter Lippmann (1889–1974) is a plea for *limited* government, not *minimal* government. Much depends on how we perceive the reach of justice. To administer justice, is it enough to provide fair procedures for settling disputes and punishing crimes, within the framework of general rules drawn from social practice and custom? Or should justice consider substantive outcomes—especially how the weak fare against the strong? The more expansive our view of justice, the greater is the role of government and the more blurred is the boundary between state and society.

Even the strongest advocates of minimal government have recognized a role for government in providing for such public goods as defense, public safety, education, and sanitation. Modern conditions of urbanization and industrialization have greatly extended the need for collective action to sustain the infrastructures of civil society. In a free society that is also a complex and changing society, government cannot be limited to the administration of justice. The actions of people "who conduct their own affairs" have public consequences and depend on public support.

In the Western democracies, a serious, much-discussed challenge to limited government is the welfare state. The past century has seen a proliferation of programs for old age security, medical care, expanded education, housing, child care, unemployment compensation, and mitigation of poverty. These programs arise from inexorable pressures on the modern state to take responsibility for human misery and social inefficiency. The welfare state begins as a conservative strategy to forestall discontent.[58] At the outset only the most urgent demands are

---

57. Walter Lippmann, *An Inquiry into the Principles of the Good Society* (Boston: Little, Brown & Co., 1943), 267.

58. In 1881, Prince Otto von Bismarck, first chancellor of the newly unified German state, initiated a plan to protect workers against accident, sickness, and old age. This scheme of social insurance marked the symbolic beginning of the welfare state. "Bismarck's proposal was a decisive step away from poor-relief towards general transfers. It radically expanded the social responsibility and role of the state, and represented a new theory of social policy. While the goal of poor-relief had mainly been seen as the provision of minimum support for the most desolate of the needy, Bismarck's proposal was clearly understood to be not only about helping the poor but also (or perhaps rather) about helping

considered. When expectations rise, however, and democracy gains strength, much more is asked of government. The welfare state becomes the prime instrument of social democracy.

Social democracy is not necessarily *communal* democracy. Social democracy may or may not embrace concern for the vitality of community. It may be strongly individualist and statist. The programs of the welfare state are mainly designed to serve individual needs.[59] Guided by principles of equality and personal autonomy, they display only passing concern for the integrity and well-being of groups and institutions, that is, for the spontaneous arrangements of civil society. As government moves in to supplement (and replace) private ordering, the fabric of community is weakened. Kinship, religion, locality, employment, friendship, social networks, voluntary associations: all diminish in relative importance as resources for care and as centers of moral obligation.

Although the ideology of social democracy (or welfare liberalism) has often included affirmations of community, its operative ethos has been, in important ways, anti-communitarian. This slant stems mainly from the welfare liberal's commitment to rational organization and general rules—in a word, to bureaucracy. When liberalism becomes bureaucratic the spirit of liberation tends to suffocate. As Max Weber said, there is a "parcelling out of the soul," and not only among the bureaucrats themselves. Bureaucracy, if unrestrained, reduces clients to passive dependency and, when interests conflict, gives the benefit of the doubt to the system.

Like the market so prized by classical liberals, the welfare state easily becomes a bloodless repository of moral virtue. One grinds out exchanges; the other grinds out regulations. Insofar as a liberal regime fails to infuse administration with concern for the well-being of all partici-

---

society (*his* society, that is). Industrialization and the growth of the working class created tensions which the established order saw as threatening" (Stein Ringen, *The Possibility of Politics: A Study in the Political Economy of the Welfare State* [Oxford: Clarendon Press, 1987], 28f.).

59. This is partly due to administrative convenience. As one study of the fate of families in the Swedish welfare state put it, welfare bureaucracies "find it most efficient to treat the individual as the prime benefit unit. After all, families are endlessly fluctuating entities, whereas individuals are not; furthermore, not everyone lives with or even is part of a family anymore. In Sweden it is not families but individuals that have a national identification number, a number that is absolutely basic in the scheme of bureaucratic efficiency and control" (David Popenoe, *Disturbing the Nest: Family Change and Decline in Modern Societies* [New York: Aldine de Gruyter, 1988], 243). See also Alan Wolfe, *Whose Keeper? Social Science and Moral Obligation* (Berkeley: University of California Press, 1989), chap. 5.

pants and for all the interests at stake, it loses touch with what Lionel Trilling called "its great primal act of imagination."[60]

The alternative is not a rejection of government, let alone of rationality. Rather, it is for the architects of the welfare state to transform their vision of how governments fulfill their responsibilities. Two strategies are appropriate. If the government will pay more attention to communal values and civil society, it will more clearly perceive and more adequately protect the needs of individual persons. And if it will adopt postbureaucratic modes of organization, the welfare state can become more limited, more accountable, and more humane.

▼   ▲   ▼   ▲   ▼

The responsibility of government for civil society begins with responsibility for public safety, especially the security of persons, homes, and possessions. It matters a great deal, however, *how* law and order is maintained. If the police and other agencies are isolated from the community; if they are perceived as alien, oppressive, and insensitive; if they react to criminal conduct but are unresponsive to community needs, they will be neither effective nor humane. This is the message of much recent discussion of community policing.

Among criminologists and police officials, awareness is growing that something important was lost when patrol cars replaced foot patrol as the chief mode of policing in urban areas. The patrol car isolates police in their vehicles. They are sporadically *in* the community, but they are no longer *of* it. Reacting to calls relayed from headquarters, they mainly encounter episodes of trouble, victimization, and viciousness. They lose touch with ordinary life, and they do not receive all the different kinds of information that are relevant to public safety. Above all, the mission of the police is narrowed. As crime *fighters* they have a shortsighted view of what crime *control* may entail.

60. "So far as liberalism is active and positive, so far, that is, as it moves toward organization, it tends to select the emotions and qualities that are most susceptible of organization. . . . Its characteristic paradox appears again, and in another form, for in the very interests of its great primal act of imagination by which it establishes its essence and existence—in the interests, that is, of its vision of a general enlargement and freedom and rational direction of human life—it drifts toward a denial of the emotions and the imagination. And in the very interest of affirming its confidence in the power of the mind, it inclines to constrict and make mechanical its conception of the nature of mind" (Lionel Trilling, *The Liberal Imagination* [New York: Anchor Books, 1953], 8f.).

The alternative is a more intimate and reassuring presence. This requires foot patrol, local police stations, including "mini-stations," awareness of the neighborhood's people and problems, and involvement in community organization. "The central premise of community policing is that the public should play a more active and coordinated part in enhancing safety. . . . Community policing thus imposes a new responsibility on the police, namely, to devise appropriate ways of associating the public with law enforcement and the maintenance of order."[61] Responsive policing, like responsive regulation, requires outreach and respect.[62]

Community policing requires administrative restructuring to allow greater decentralization without loss of effective accountability and control. New criteria of police effectiveness would emphasize outcomes for public safety, including *experienced* safety, rather than arrest or crime-clearance rates. Explicit statements of policy regarding appropriate police conduct would cover modes of interaction in everyday settings as well as the more familiar issues of bribery, crowd control, and use of weapons. Policies and practices should be open to public criticism, and to reconstruction as necessary. Above all, leadership is needed to create and sustain an appropriate organizational culture. In these ways, the costs and dangers of responsiveness—including such matters as selective concern for the most cooperative sectors of the community—can be mitigated and contained.

As the example of public safety shows, a communitarian policy—a policy of responsiveness—softens the harsh contours of state power. In that context, and in many others, *communities are presumed to be viable.* The change occurs in government, not in the community. However, the viability of a community and its institutions cannot be taken for granted. It may be deeply divided along racial, ethnic, or ideological lines. However much diversity may be welcomed, government cannot remain indifferent or idle when social conflict becomes social torment.

Nor can it ignore needs that may arise for the repair or regeneration of social life. An important example is the fate of the modern family. Fam-

---

61. Jerome H. Skolnick and David H. Bayley, *Community Policing: Issues and Practices Around the World* (Washington: National Institute of Justice, 1988), 3. On the communal model of policing, see also James Q. Wilson, *Varieties of Police Behavior: The Management of Law and Order in Eight Communities* (Cambridge: Harvard University Press, 1968), 286.

62. Here outreach and respect run to the community, not to the criminal offenders. However, the community may be implicated in the offenses, in youth crimes and in other ways. Therefore respect for community may at times require forbearance in the handling of certain types of offenses. This has long been a (now highly controversial) police strategy in cases of wife-beating and child abuse.

ilies may be "here to stay,"[63] but a great many are under considerable stress. In part this stress results from very general conditions, such as changes in sexual mores, that have made family units precarious.[64] In addition, the large-scale movement of women into the labor force and the persistent poverty of many single-parent households have placed millions of American children at risk.[65]

If children are to grow and flourish—if they are to become disciplined and autonomous persons—they need to be raised by emotionally committed adults. For most children, these adults are the child's parents. Therefore the aim of public policy must be to supplement and strengthen parental responsibility. Programs for public assistance, day care, and early education of children are needed to help modern parents fulfill their responsibilities, not to supplant them. The administration of such programs should uphold parental authority.

Parental responsibility is a challenge to bureaucracy and therefore to the welfare state. The authority of parents is diminished if they are cut off from decisions affecting the child's health, recreation, and education. Ideally parents should have opportunities for both *choice* and *participation*. Choice presumes an array of alternatives, which runs against the orderly delivery of services by a conventional bureaucratic agency. Participation requires administrative openness, a spirit of consultation, and a relaxation of claims to professional expertise.

Proposals for choice look to market principles rather than bureaucratic principles. An example is the idea that parents of modest means, who cannot readily pay for the privilege, should nonetheless be able to choose the schools their children attend. Public funds would be allocated to each family in the form of scholarships or vouchers. This would expose public schools to competition (with private schools and among themselves) and presumably would generate a substantial increase in the number and variety of all schools. The assumption is that competition will improve the quality of education by eliminating bureaucratic obstacles to change and by creating incentives for plurality, innovation, and responsiveness. At the same time, parental responsibility would be enhanced.

63. Mary Jo Bane, *Here to Stay: American Families in the Twentieth Century* (New York: Basic Books, 1976).

64. The sociological debate over family "weakening" or "decline" is reviewed in Popenoe, *Disturbing the Nest*, part 1.

65. See Cheryl D. Hayes, John L. Palmer, and Martha I. Zaslow, eds., *Who Cares for America's Children? Child Care Policy for the 1990s* (Washington: National Academy Press, 1990), chap. 2.

These claims do not speak to the main causes of the crisis in public education in the United States. More fundamental are a vast increase in years of schooling; an excess of localism, which radically limits available resources; and a deep cultural resistance to the deferred gratification needed for scholastic achievement. Nevertheless, vested interest and bureaucratic rigidity undoubtedly contribute to the problem, especially in large urban school districts. It is easy to see why parental choice is a plausible and attractive strategy for overcoming these failures.[66]

We should recall, however, the point made earlier (p. 471) about self-regulation. The ideal, we said, depends on an underlying reality. If the conditions that make for internal morality are absent, we cannot rely on self-regulation. Similarly, we have to consider how realistic is the claim that parents of young children, especially poor parents, will routinely make sound choices that look to long-term educational benefits rather than to more immediate advantages, such as convenient location, and how realistic is the assumption that vouchers spent for tuition by individual parents will generate an array of good alternatives. Neither assumption is supported by evidence sufficient to justify a great deal of confidence in the market solution.[67]

Proposals for choice in elementary and secondary education are superficially communitarian, in that they appear to support parents and reject bureaucracies. In fact, however, the market model, in this context as in others, is anti-communitarian. It overlooks the principle that individual choice, to be fully rational, requires a supportive institutional context. For affluent parents, experienced in the ways of schooling and tied into networks of useful information, such a context is readily available. For others it is not. Furthermore, the market model is indifferent to education *as an instrument of the community,* invested with civic responsibilities as well as the education of individual children.

These cautions do not preclude extensive and hopeful experimentation. However, in such experiments it would be a mistake to pursue a fantasy of government without bureaucracy. Administrative controls and services of some sort will still be required. Any workable plan has to recognize that what parents prefer for their own children cannot wholly

66. See John E. Coons and Stephen D. Sugarman, *Education by Choice: The Case for Family Control* (Berkeley: University of California Press, 1978), and John E. Chubb and Terry M. Moe, *Politics, Markets, and American Schools* (Washington: Brookings Institution, 1990).

67. Nor is a market solution a necessary precondition for public support of parochial schools, assuming the constitutional problem of "no establishment" can be resolved. Whatever the merits of such support, it would be wrong for proponents to embrace a market model for that reason.

determine public policy. There must still be a system of *public* education, enlarged, indeed, under plans that include the participation of private schools. No such system can fail to take account of public concerns, including, among much else, the quality of basic education, teacher preparation, equality of opportunity, racial integration, care for the handicapped, education for civic responsibility.

The quasi-market created by such a plan must be a *regulated* market, heavily dependent on governmental protection and support. If, as expected, individual schools are given a great deal of autonomy, central administration may be smaller and less burdensome. But a governing agency will still be needed to establish and monitor minimal standards; regulate rates; bar discrimination; restrain arbitrary discipline and expulsion; provide for special educational needs, including the needs of a highly mobile student population; study and report on successes and failures; and see to it that the right to enroll in the school of one's choice is recognized in practice.

▼ ▲ ▼ ▲ ▼

In community policing and in parental choice in education, public policy is driven by the need for greater efficiency and effectiveness. An underlying theme in these examples, however, is the moral worth of diversity and particularity. The state moderates its impact on civil society, and therefore on individual persons, by respecting the integrity and enhancing the competence of private groups and institutions. Families, churches, colleges, unions, neighborhood organizations, and other voluntary associations are treated as "mediating structures" that stand between the individual and government, and as indispensable components of a flourishing community.[68] Such groups are primary objects of moral concern; they are also welcome resources for public policy.

This perspective reaffirms the truth in political pluralism. A fundamental tenet of that doctrine is the importance of *dispersed power* for safeguarding the liberties of a people. Ideally, power is dispersed when intermediate associations have effective autonomy. Historically, these were ancient and powerful institutions such as churches, the landed aristocracy, chartered towns and cities, and guilds. In a democratic age, new forms of association are needed. "If men are to remain civilized,"

68. See Peter L. Berger and Richard John Neuhaus, *To Empower People: The Role of Mediating Structures in Public Policy* (Washington: American Enterprise Institute, 1977).

wrote Tocqueville in 1840, "the art of associating together must grow and improve in the same ratio in which the equality of conditions is increased."[69]

This "art of associating together" is not an impersonal or manipulative art. It is not the creation of factions. Rather, the associations Tocqueville had in mind are those that have enduring worth, from the standpoint of communities as well as individuals. As such, they lend texture to the commonwealth, a texture that can sustain autonomous sources of social identity, train alternative leaders, curb precipitate action, and restrain the hand of government.

Thus understood, pluralism is an essential aspect of communal democracy. It stands opposed both to the view expressed by Thomas Hobbes that autonomous unities are "lesser Common-wealths in the bowels of the greater, like wormes in the entrayles of a naturall man,"[70] and to Jeremy Bentham's conception of a society as no more than an aggregate of individuals.[71] On the contrary, the quality of democracy depends on the vitality and diversity of group life.

Pluralist theory is by no means wholly satisfactory, however. Its deficiencies are revealed when we look more closely at two strands of the doctrine, which we may call participatory and oppositional. Participatory pluralism looks to *shared* power as well as dispersed power. Federalism is the keynote, and the federated unities are major social groups—religious, educational, economic, cultural, ethnic, political. In this view, the effective participants in the political community are associations, not individuals.[72]

This "functional" or "corporatist" conception of the political community is a potential threat to personhood and citizenship. As one self-critical pluralist put it, politics cannot be based on a divided self:

> My nature is not divisible into so many parts as a house into so many rooms. . . . The unit of society is the individual coming into being and functioning through groups of a more and more federated nature. . . . No one

69. Alexis de Tocqueville, *Democracy in America* (1840; reprint, New York: Alfred A. Knopf, 1956), 2:110.
70. *Leviathan* (1651; reprint, London: Pelican Books, 1968), 375.
71. See below, note 105 and accompanying text.
72. Therefore participatory pluralism is committed to a kind of corporatism. Some pluralist writers in the early twentieth century (such as guild and Fabian Socialists, and even Winston Churchill) proposed various schemes of "functional" representation. For example, they suggested an Industrial Parliament or an "alternative chamber," supplementing or replacing the House of Commons, composed of representatives of business, labor, and other major social interests. This presumed, of course, substantial organization of the represented interests.

group can enfold me, because of my multiple nature. This is the blow to the theory of occupational representation. But also no number of groups can enfold me. This is the reason why the individual must always be the unit of politics, as group organization must be its method. We *find* the individual through the group, we *use* him always as the true individual—the undivided one—who, living link of living group, is yet never embedded in the meshes but is forever free for every new possibility of a forever unfolding life.[73]

Insofar as pluralism depreciates or neglects the integrity and well-being of individual persons as organic unities, it fails as a foundation for communal democracy.

Furthermore, participatory pluralism tends to favor mainstream institutions and existing elites. This follows from the root idea that "the people's institutions" should be relied on, protected, and represented. Such institutions usually have a recognized place in the community's history. They are part of the established order. Thus participatory pluralism is drawn toward support of the status quo. Moreover, and in some ways more important, the experience of oppression *within* intermediate associations is played down or overlooked. The tendency is to assume that in checking the power of the centralized state and in furthering their own ends, associations necessarily serve the interests of their members. In fact, of course, many are highly undemocratic and unresponsive. Therefore principles of communal democracy must be applied to private government as well as to the state.

Oppositional pluralism is less federalist, less corporatist, more interested in the benefits of dispersing power among many different interest groups. This distinctively American—or liberal—pluralism rests its hopes on civil antagonism. It sees in group conflict a bulwark against Leviathan, a benign disorder framed only by quite general purposes and minimal restraints. The political community is thought to embrace a broad range of interests that are largely self-generating and self-sustaining. The government is properly responsive to those interests and seeks an equilibrium among them. The equilibrium, whatever it may be, defines the common good. There is no such thing as a transcending national or public interest.[74]

73. Mary P. Follett, *The New State: Group Organization the Solution of Popular Government* (New York: Longmans, Green & Co., 1923), 291–95. For Follett's contribution to the theory of authority, see above, Chapter 10, "Beyond Domination."

74. As Arthur F. Bentley (1870–1957), the father of American pluralist theory, put it, "[W]e shall never find a group interest of the society as a whole" (*The Process of Government* [1908; reprint, Cambridge: Belknap Press, 1967], 222). See also David B. Truman, *The Governmental Process: Political Interests and Public Opinion* (New York: Alfred

This reduction of the idea of a common good to the outcome of conflicting pressures is a chief limitation of pluralist doctrine, especially in its American version. Another limitation is that oppositional pluralism encourages a minimalist view of what freedom and democracy entail. A viable group structure of society may be perceived as necessary for maintaining the bare bones of liberty but may be expected to provide little more than a choice among competing leaders. There is no assurance that higher aspirations will be served. The idea of a common good remains remote; the participatory aspects of democracy are given short shrift; there is little prospect that membership in corporate groups will extend and enrich the individual's relation to the larger commonwealth. As a result, in oppositional pluralism the ideals that animated Tocqueville and his heirs may be unattained, forgotten, and displaced.

For the most part, the spokesmen for political pluralism—continental and English, as well as American—took cultural homogeneity for granted. They recognized that groups are important sources of personal identity, but the differences they contemplated did not run deep. They did not confront the special problems of cultural and racial diversity. Therefore political pluralism posed no serious challenge to liberal ideals of citizenship and legal equality. The criticism mentioned above, with respect to oppression within associations, could be accepted readily.

More serious difficulties arise when pluralism is based on cultural differentiation. At stake is the maintenance of a distinctive identity derived from history, language, ethnicity, or religion. Indigenous peoples in Canada and the United States; French Canadians; African-Americans; Hispanic-Americans; the Amish; and other ethnic and religious communities have all claimed rights of *cultural membership*. To implement those rights it is often necessary to uphold the integrity and authority of the group in respect to education, language, collectively owned property, and the governance of morals.

Communitarian pluralism respects minority cultures and affirms the value of cultural membership. It would provide considerable leeway to maintain group identity, as the United States Supreme Court did in the Amish case and in upholding the constitutional right of American families to send their children to parochial and other private schools. It

A. Knopf, 1951), 50f. In contrast, the participatory pluralism of the English writers presumed that, in sharing power, major social groups could work together to identify and pursue the common good. On the varieties of pluralism, see David Nicholls, *Three Varieties of Pluralism* (London: Macmillan, 1974).

would allow indigenous peoples to educate children in their own way, exclude nonmembers from their economic and cultural life, and maintain other forms of self-imposed segregation. It would take care to avoid coercive assimilation.[75]

Here again, however, the possibility of group oppression must be considered. It is one thing to support *opportunities* for cultural membership, including measures to strengthen such groups or at least limit their disintegration under the pressure of a mainstream culture. Insofar as membership is voluntary or is based on the consent that comes from routine socialization, the benefits of pluralism may well outweigh the potential costs. The case is different, however, when groups seek to *impose* their authority, especially by limiting opportunities for exit.[76] The comprehensive community—the unity of unities—has an overriding concern for the well-being of individual persons. That well-being is nurtured and sustained when rights of cultural membership are recognized and made meaningful, but it suffers when cultural membership is compelled.

Thus communal democracy, like community itself, is both particularist and universalist. The experience of community begins with the very concrete affinities of early life, especially families, peer groups, and, in many cases, supportive subcultures. Taken by themselves these affinities are isolating and parochial. To sustain community as a framework for the whole of life and for the flourishing of multiple groups, a transition must be made from piety to civility, and from bounded to inclusive altruism. Communal democracy with its moderated pluralism is the political expression of that transition.[77]

75. For an argument that recognizing cultural membership as a primary good is compatible with and even required by liberal principles, see Will Kymlicka, *Liberalism, Community and Culture* (Oxford: Clarendon Press, 1989).

76. According to a report in the *New York Times* (24 October 1990), Pueblo parents in New Mexico have been withdrawing their children from the elementary school on the San Felipe Indian Reservation in favor of a mainstream school six miles off the reservation. "One school has ties to the Pueblo Indian traditions . . . the other is part of the world outside. But despite a decade of efforts to improve the school for the Indian children at San Felipe, Indian parents are deserting it in droves. As a result, the Tribal Council—a sovereign government with broad rights to control its land and its members, according to the laws and treaties of the United States—is pressuring parents to keep their children on the reservation. The rebellious parents respond that they will send their children to any school they wish. . . . Council members have rebuked 'disobedient' and 'disloyal' parents, and they persuaded the reservation school to adopt a policy that makes transfer of a child's records difficult without approval of the tribal governor. . . . A Supreme Court ruling in the 1970's gave tribes broad authority to determine their own membership, but it is not clear if a tribal government has unlimited power to impose obligations on its members, like dictating what school their children must attend."

77. As George Santayana might have phrased it, the bonds of community, forged at the hearth, are tempered in the marketplace.

The Social Basis of Political Participation

We began this discussion by invoking John Dewey's conception of democracy-in-depth as affecting "all modes of human association" and creating "a life of free and enriching communion." In this view, democracy is communication, and communication is education. The consent of the governed is active, critical, and participatory. It is self-preserving, not only in guarding freedoms and advancing well-being, but also in creating responsible persons who can govern their own passions and transcend their private or parochial interests.

John Stuart Mill had a similar vision. In *Considerations on Representative Government,* he spoke of the salutary moral instruction

> afforded by the participation of the private citizen, if even rarely, in public functions. He is called upon, while so engaged, to weigh interests not his own. . . . He is made to feel himself one of the public, and whatever is for their benefit to be for his benefit. Where this school of public spirit does not exist . . . even private morality suffers. . . . From these accumulated considerations it is evident that the only government which can fully satisfy all the exigencies of the social state is one in which the whole people participate; that any participation, even in the smallest public function, is useful; that the participation should everywhere be as great as the general degree of improvement of the community will allow; and that nothing less can be ultimately desirable than the admission of all to a share in the sovereign power of the state.[78]

This is a major covenantal premise of communal democracy.

In the transition from covenant to commonwealth, the forms of participation must take account of human wants and limitations, including the practical need for representative government.[79] But the premise is not discarded. It has a vital part to play as a principle of criticism and as a guide to the improvement of democratic institutions.

If "the whole people" means, as we have suggested, "people-in-community," then *communal* democracy must be distinguished from *mass* democracy. Mass participation is unmediated, undeliberative, and unstable. Its level may be high or low, excited or casual. In any case, mass decisions are likely to be poor in quality and vulnerable to manipulation. In communal democracy, by contrast, people are tied into sta-

78. *Considerations on Representative Government* (1861), in *Utilitarianism, On Liberty, Considerations on Representative Government* (reprint, London: J. M. Dent, 1984), 233f.

79. Hence Mill concluded the passage just quoted as follows: "But since all cannot, in a community exceeding a single small town, participate personally in any but some very minor portions of the public business, it follows that the ideal type of a perfect government must be representative" (ibid., 234).

ble networks, understand their own interests, and are not very readily moved by transient appeals or superficial impulses. The American electorate is a mass some of the time and with respect to some issues, and is communal at other times and with respect to other issues. This variation accounts for many of the puzzles political scientists have encountered in analyzing voting and public opinion.

Benjamin Barber has noted that what he calls "strong" democracy

> is not government by "the people" or government by "the masses," because a people are not yet a citizenry and masses are only nominal freemen who do not in fact govern themselves. . . . Masses make noise, citizens deliberate; masses behave, citizens act; masses collide and intersect, citizens engage, share, and contribute. At the moment when "masses" start deliberating, acting, sharing, and contributing, they cease to be masses and become citizens. Only then do they "participate." . . . Indeed, from the perspective of strong democracy, the two terms *participation* and *community* are aspects of one single mode of social being: citizenship.[80]

Active, purposive, reflective citizenship is an alternative to undisciplined participation. Citizenship binds participation to public ends, creates obligations of duty and service, and presumes a framework within which dialogue and compromise may proceed. Thus civic participation is far more than the exercise of options by registered voters. It requires a public formed and regulated by the machinery of deliberation and by the experience of exercising responsible choice.

Therefore communal democracy is always a blend of direct and mediated participation. There is no substitute for an active, committed citizenry. The political process must be open to direct participation by individual citizens—not only that they may choose among parties or candidates but also that they may decide on major issues, including the shape of the process and the public agenda. At the same time, every form of direct participation must be mediated in some way. It must be filtered through a process that will take into account—and restrain—the potential degeneration of civic participation into mass participation. The former builds on community and enhances community; the latter distorts and subverts it.

This theory of citizenship is inadequate, however, insofar as it fails to recognize the continuities of civic and social participation. Consider the following comment:

80. Benjamin R. Barber, *Strong Democracy: Participatory Politics for a New Age* (Berkeley: University of California Press, 1984), 154f.

Far from positing community a priori, strong democratic theory understands the creation of community as one of the chief tasks of political activity
in the participatory mode. Far from positing historical identity as the condition of politics, it posits politics as the conditioner of given historical
identities—as the means by which men are emancipated from determinative
historical forces.[81]

The insight is important. Civic participation transcends the particularities of history, language, kinship, locality, and occupation. It creates
new identities and new solidarities. Furthermore, like justice, democracy
is an agent of civility. And civility, as we have seen, is a chief foundation
of community.

It does not follow, however, that political democracy is the sole creator of community, or that it can be effective without a nonpolitical infrastructure of association, interdependence, and moral education. A democracy is weak and volatile if citizens are badly divided, especially on
racial, ethnic, or religious grounds; or if many are incapable of participating, or are shut out from participating, in the rewards and obligations
of work, education, and family life. Citizenship cannot flourish—the
call to deliberation will not be heard—if the main sources of personal responsibility are attenuated or lost.

THE COVENANT OF REASON

Among the covenants that underpin a moral community is the common
faith John Dewey called "the method of intelligence."[82] By this he
meant a commitment to shared discovery—by rational inquiry, including learning from experience—of what it is good to have and right to
do. Without such a common faith, moral authority must rest on historicity and piety alone. There can be no secure appeal from conventional
to critical morality and no rational basis for reconciling opposing interests or transcending parochial perspectives.

Furthermore, democracy requires reflective morality. A regime of received or conventional morality depends for social unity on more or
less benign forms of domination, which includes socialization into accepted ways of thinking and feeling. A democracy cannot do without
socialization, but the preferred mode is participatory rather than repressive, and participatory socialization requires that reasons be given to justify authority. Although democracy is *open* to diverse perspectives, it is

81. Ibid., 133.
82. This was one of his favorite phrases; see, e.g., John Dewey, *Liberalism and Social
Action* (New York: G. P. Putnam's, 1935), 51.

formed by institutions of deliberation, inquiry, and responsible choice. The will of the people is disciplined by the requirements of communication, notably, mutual respect and rational discourse. Democracy is indeed the realm of freed intelligence, as Dewey said, but a truly free intelligence must also be authentic, that is, be governed by standards of intellectual integrity.

In contemporary philosophy and social theory, the notion of a common good, to be discovered by the "method of intelligence," meets considerable skepticism. Few would deny that deliberation has a place in political life, and almost everyone accepts the need for *some* objective standards of discourse and judgment. But strong currents of thought limit deliberation to the choice of means rather than ends. Many are skeptical as to the possibility of deciding, on rational grounds, what is good for a person or a community. Any conception of the common good, it is thought, must express a historically given unity or consensus.

To be sure, the covenant of reason, like any other covenant, presumes consensus, a *shared resolve* to prefer and perfect dialogue and deliberation. To this extent an element of historicity, of givenness and self-formation, is inevitable and indispensable. But the covenant of reason is peculiar in this, that it is reflexive and self-critical. No premise is excused from criticism, not even the commitment to rational inquiry, which may be less appropriate in some contexts than in others. And the chief significance of the covenant appears when the community must choose ends as well as means.

Resistance to the idea of a common good has three main sources. The most important is the subjectivism and relativism discussed above, in Chapters 3 and 4. In that view, although many moral covenants may be accepted, none has a rational foundation. No objective ground can be offered for principles of justice, including moral equality; for democracy; or for what we may take to be the welfare of the community. The act of acceptance is wholly contingent, nonrational, even arbitrary. The history of a culture is its own justification; nothing more is needed.

A different source of resistance and skepticism is the social theory of modern economics, which presumes a radical diversity of preferences and interests.[83] Because wants and needs differ, they cannot be aggregated or ranked in any rational way. Only a system of exchange or voting can produce a "right" outcome. When individuals and groups pursue their

---

83. And related fields of inquiry, such as public-choice and rational-choice theory. For critical reviews of economic doctrine, see Steven E. Rhoads, *The Economist's View of the World: Government, Markets, and Public Policy* (Cambridge: Cambridge University Press, 1985); Amitai Etzioni, *The Moral Dimension: Toward a New Economics* (New York: Free Press, 1988); and Wolfe, *Whose Keeper?* chaps. 1–3.

separate goals they can and do act rationally, but *communal* rationality is thought to be an idle dream or a dangerous fantasy.

A third source of resistance is the liberal fear that personal autonomy is endangered when the community uses its authority to endorse a particular conception of the good. People should be free to form and express their own moral identities, which are based on individual choices and commitments. The community should settle for a "thin" theory of the good, one that emphasizes procedure rather than substance, means rather than ends.

We have already given considerable attention to these issues. Indeed, the place of reason in moral experience has been a major theme of this book, and every chapter has spoken to some aspect of it. We will conclude by exploring briefly what sense can be made of the quest for a common good. In doing so, we shall respond to the criticisms indicated above and meet those criticisms with a strategy suggested by the title of this chapter—the interplay of covenant and commonwealth.

The covenants of reason, equality, and popular sovereignty are not self-certifying. Each must be shown to be justified by how it can contribute to the safety and flourishing of persons and communities. Each is chosen in the sobering light of known and rejected alternatives—with respect to reason, arbitrary or passion-driven decision; with respect to equality, invidious classification; and with respect to democracy, self-perpetuating oligarchy. Each is subject to failures of will, imagination, and intelligence; each may be marred by superficiality, complacency, or overreaching. Each must experience risks of corruption as the abstract ideal meets a living, changing, many-sided reality.

The *idea* of commonwealth, we have said, suggests moral, economic, and political integration. An *existing* commonwealth is, however, a going concern that must harmonize diverse interests and functions. The moral commonwealth cannot be wholly integrated; cannot be hostile to private, potentially divisive centers of power; cannot expect unqualified devotion to civic virtue. This want of purity is neither a conceptual flaw nor a second-best ideal. Rather, it is a wholly appropriate condition, given that we routinely expect and warmly endorse the multiplicity of interests in a flourishing community.

The quest for a common good takes place *within* and not *against* the experience of plurality. This positioning is the key to understanding how the covenant of reason meets the problems of commonwealth. In the following paragraphs we consider four challenges of diversity to reason.

Each tells us something about the limits and possibilities of social intelligence as a public virtue.

The Critique of Preferences

That people want different things and have different priorities is an obvious manifestation of social diversity. Much of this diversity, expressed as wants and preferences, is relatively immune from criticism. When the problem at hand is to meet the demands of a marketplace, we do not usually ask businessmen or economists to appraise the quality of consumers' preferences. To a large extent they must be taken as they are, on pain of business failure. Similarly, in a democratic election or referendum, what voters *want* is decisive. Their decision stands, whatever we (or they) may think about the quality of the election campaign, the choices available, or the responses of the voters. This respect for "revealed preference"—the decision to buy or vote in a certain way or to choose a particular spouse, vocation, church, or college—has both practical and moral dimensions.[84] Practically, it is a way of organizing society relatively efficiently, by relying on individual rationality and self-generated incentives; morally, it is an expression of regard for the autonomy, integrity, and good sense of ordinary people in ordinary situations.

According to John Stuart Mill, "the sole evidence it is possible to produce that anything is desirable, is that people do actually desire it."[85] This is surely an overstatement. Nevertheless, Mill was right to suggest that what people want, as revealed in their conduct, is very often the best indicator of what they need or should have—especially when their wants have to do with elementary conditions of survival and self-respect. And if a purported good is not sought—if it is irrelevant to basic human inclinations—we may well question its value.

It should be noted, however, that in the passage just quoted Mill preserves the distinction between the *desired* and the *desirable*. The former is evidence for the latter, but the evidence is not conclusive. What we want is always subject to criticism in the light of what is good for us. The focus then shifts from subjective to objective judgments, that is, from the expression of passion, interest, or inclination to the study of conditions

84. For an argument emphasizing the difference between *choice*, which has objective elements, and *preference*, which may be purely subjective, see James F. Reynolds and David C. Paris, "The Concept of 'Choice' and Arrow's Theorem," *Ethics* 89 (July 1979): 354–71.

85. John Stuart Mill, *Utilitarianism* (1863), in *Utilitarianism, On Liberty, Considerations on Representative Government* (reprint, London: J. M. Dent, 1984), 36.

and consequences. A reflective morality must always consider what the true interests of a person or group may be, and particularly what will make for enduring satisfaction and a flourishing existence. Such a judgment of course incorporates concern for subjective states and the quality of experience, including the emotions, desires, and satisfactions likely to be called forth, enhanced, or stifled. But a difference remains between what merely feels good or is believed to be good and what is adjudged good on the basis of sound theory and convincing evidence.

This critical function of reflective morality should be too obvious to mention. The matter is confused, however, by applying economic models, suitable for analyzing business decisions and some aspects of economic policy, to broader issues of social policy and moral judgment. As we have said, it is not always appropriate to look behind consumer preferences. But once we begin to consider how market decisions and the way markets are structured affect personal and communal well-being, preferences can no longer be taken as given. Some are self-destructive addictions; others are heedless of costs to the community. The critique of preferences is always an appeal to some larger good beyond immediate inclination or advantage. The larger good is often complex, subtle, and precarious, not readily captured by models that rely on highly simplified assumptions about what people want and how they think.[86]

The reconstruction of preferences is often frustrated, quite justifiably, by a preoccupation with rights. Many rights involve choice: of whom to elect, where to live, whether to procreate, what to buy, what information to receive. The protection of these and many other rights is a paramount function of the legal order. There is, in effect, a legal (even constitutional) limitation on the *enforcement* of reflective morality. With respect to many matters, in a free society people may choose as they please, whatever the quality of their preferences.

But the protection of rights can be a way of evading responsibility for informed judgment. A case in point is the fate of Nancy Cruzan, who suffered grave brain damage as a result of an automobile accident in 1983.[87] Fed by a tube implanted in her stomach, she remained in a "per-

86. For his own part, Mill did not shrink from subtle criteria of utility: "But there is no known Epicurean theory of life which does not assign to the pleasures of the intellect, of the feelings and imagination, and of the moral sentiments, a much higher value as pleasures than to those of mere sensation. . . . It is quite compatible with the principle of utility to recognize the fact, that some *kinds* of pleasure are more desirable and more valuable than others. It would be absurd that while, in estimating all other things, quality is considered as well as quantity, the estimation of pleasures should be supposed to depend on quantity alone" (ibid., 8).

87. See Cruzan v. Director, Missouri Dept. of Health, 110 S.Ct. 2841 (1990).

sistent vegetative state" for seven years. After she had been three years in that condition her parents tried to have the treatment stopped, but hospital officials refused. Lower courts agreed with the parents, but the Supreme Court of Missouri ruled that the termination of life-support must be based on "clear and convincing evidence" of the patient's own desire that such support be removed in case of radical and irreversible incompetence.

We need not take a position on the constitutional question before the Supreme Court.[88] From the standpoint of social policy, however, it is easy to see that the argument about Nancy Cruzan's preferences is out of touch with reality—especially the unquestioned futility of medical treatment. Everyone agreed Cruzan could not possibly regain consciousness, to say nothing of recovering. Hence all that could be preserved was a minimal level of biological existence. Under those conditions, a focus on previously expressed preferences, clear or unclear, can only distort the judgments that must be made by responsible relatives and officials.

It is one thing to take a patient's preferences into account out of respect for a life no longer viable. It is something else to assume that an expressed preference is beyond appraisal; that it would not be reconsidered in the light of actual circumstances; and that no weight should be given to the costs involved. Institutional safeguards are needed to protect a helpless patient's interest in possible recovery, however minimal. But such safeguards should not be confined to ascertaining or imputing preferences. The latter must, in the nature of the case, be uninformed by knowledge of specific circumstances; hence no truly informed consent is possible.

The Claims of Conscience

One source of diversity poses special problems for the sovereignty of reason in a moral commonwealth. This is the appeal to conscience. When we speak of "freedom of conscience as an indefeasible right,"[89]

---

88. The constitutional question was whether the State of Missouri infringed a fundamental right guaranteed by the Fourteenth Amendment by insisting on preserving Nancy Cruzan in her vegetative existence without "clear and convincing evidence" of her wishes. See the dissenting opinions of Justices Brennan and Stevens. The latter, especially, connects the "liberty" of the patient to her "best interests," thus calling for reasoned assessment rather than appeal to preference. See also Robin West, "The Supreme Court, 1989 Term—Foreword: Taking Freedom Seriously," *Harvard Law Review* 104 (1990): 98ff.

89. John Stuart Mill, *On Liberty* (1859), in *Utilitarianism, On Liberty, Considerations on Representative Government* (reprint, London: J. M. Dent, 1984), 76.

we have in mind something more specific than "the internal acknowledgment or recognition of the moral quality of one's motives or actions;
the sense of right and wrong as regards things for which one is
responsible."[90] At stake is personal *identity*, not *judgment*.[91] Liberty of
conscience does not mean freedom to construct an autonomous morality—a code of one's own—and call it sacred. Rather, we respect the right
of an individual or group to fashion a salient, self-defining principle
from some aspect of morality, such as a belief in pacifism, or from some
justification of morality, such as a religious doctrine. "Here I stand,"
said Martin Luther. "I can do no other." The bond between selfhood and
conscience makes sense of the connection between security of conscience and freedom of expression. Conscience yearns for moral witness,
often in and through religious affiliation.

An unspoken premise is that the *substance* of conscience—what is taken
to be right or wrong—meets reasonable standards of conventional and
critical morality. This does not preclude major differences in the content
of morality. Nevertheless, we do not recognize the liberty to decide, "as
a matter of conscience," that human rights are for one race only, or that
a good end justifies "any means necessary." The claim to be a legitimate
alternative conception of the good is not immune to the challenge of reflective morality. There should be reason to suppose that the alternatives
proposed are roughly equal in moral worth, or at least that they meet
some threshold standard.[92]

Beyond that point, however, the claims of conscience are insulated
from criticism and thus are excluded from the covenant of reason.
Deeply held convictions—for example, unique roads to salvation—are
very often difficult to articulate or are expressed in densely symbolic
ways. As we noted in another connection, they are not readily translated
into the more universal (and perhaps more arid) language of rational
discourse.[93] Furthermore, as we have also noted, civility ordains a reluctance to intrude on the precincts of piety. The principle of toleration sets
limits to the authority of reason.

Liberty of conscience is accepted as fundamental because it vindicates
an especially worthy form of individual and group autonomy. No celebration of casual or self-indulgent preference is intended. Rather, we de-

---

90. *Oxford English Dictionary*, s.v. "conscience."
91. But cf. Thomas Hobbes: "For a man's Conscience, and his Judgement is the same
thing; and as the Judgement, so also the Conscience may be erroneous" (*Leviathan*, 366).
92. See Chapter 14, n. 41, on the Supreme Court's implicit evaluation of the Amish
way of life.
93. See Chapter 14, n. 77.

fend the freedom of each individual to choose a path through the moral landscape and thus to achieve a certain kind of self-realization: one that binds the self to moral premises. By respecting this process we think moral competence will be enhanced; by treating it as precious we uphold a vital aspect of human dignity.

The risk, of course, is that toleration may abet evil and disarm the good. This danger is to a large extent avoided by safeguarding *belief* but limiting *conduct,* especially conduct that brings harm to others. The difficulty, however, is that belief is mainly protected by insuring freedom of *expression,* which blurs the line between belief and conduct. This is the lesson of much constitutional controversy regarding, for example, "demonstrative speech" (picketing, marching, flag-burning) and the dissemination of pornography. When the community assesses a form of expression for the harm it may cause, it may have to take into account the content of speech, especially if it contains a message of hate.[94] To this extent, the exclusion of conscience from the covenant of reason must be conditional and subject to close scrutiny.

These difficult decisions are not in themselves signs of moral disarray. They belong to normal problem-solving in a free society, which must balance values and accommodate interests. Moral confusion does occur, however, when we take the principle of toleration to mean that every claim of conscience must be treated as genuine or is entitled to equal respect. We should not confuse the fact that we sometimes need to grit our teeth in the face of evil, resisting the impulse to censor, with the idea that any conception of the good, whatever its impulse, form, or consequence, is a welcome contribution to diversity. When neo-Nazis demonstrate in hateful ways, it is not respectful tolerance that restrains us. It is a well-founded fear of slippery slopes. To protect ourselves from ourselves we need hard rules, especially rules that curb official coercion. But a claim to respect must find its warrant in something more than self-assertion.

94. In American constitutional law, speech in a public forum is subject to "time, place, and manner" rules, but ideally its *content* should not be regulated. This principle is subject to strain when the content of speech consists of "fighting words" or other incitements to riot or panic—that is, constitutes a direct threat to public safety or order—or of insults that amount to "intentional infliction of emotional distress." On the dilemmas confronting colleges seeking to restrain abusive speech directed against blacks, women, and homosexuals, see Thomas C. Grey, "Civil Rights vs. Civil Liberties: The Case of Discriminatory Verbal Harassment," *Social Philosophy and Policy* 8 (Spring 1991): 81–107. As Grey points out, even carefully limited restrictions, which protect all expressions of opinion but bar "personal vilification," are not likely to be content-neutral, since they regulate "only speech bearing on matters of race, gender, sexual orientation and the like, while neglecting other speech that might similarly provoke violence, or cause emotional distress" (ibid., 97).

Self-interest and Civic Virtue

A third source of troublesome diversity is the self-interested pursuit of private goals. In communal democracy that pursuit is protected. At the same time, self-interest is transcended both by binding it, in various ways, to the general good and by countering it with an ethos of civic virtue. Each sublimating strategy brings reflective morality to bear; each must appraise the interests pursued.

In Chapter 8 we explored the difference between unrefined and enlightened self-interest. There we argued, on the one hand, that enlarging selfhood to include social awareness changes the meaning of self-preservation. On the other hand, we stressed that a cruder self-interest is inescapable. People must and do give priority to the material conditions that affect their lives. This Hobbesian premise is especially important in the realm of political morality.

Counterposed to "passion," "interest" connotes cool calculation of worldly objectives. In the sixteenth century, interest referred to statecraft: *raison d'état,* not revenge, sentimental attachments, or other "disorderly appetites," should guide the prince.[95] In time the core meaning extended to private interests, and especially to economic advantage. These worldly concerns of course include prestige and influence, as well as wealth.

The main point is that interest (like Freud's "ego") is a powerful but *disciplined* motivator, a great source of constructive social energy. Under appropriate conditions of freedom, people can be relied on to defend their interests and take advantage of opportunities. This release of energies has substantial economic benefits and is a chief justification for capitalism. It is also important in politics, including the politics of moral progress. The drawbacks of capitalism are mitigated when workers advance their interests by joining unions or by demanding government regulation of industry to restrain exploitation. Similarly, the civil rights movement of the 1960s depended heavily on militant action—sit-ins and other demonstrations—by blacks in defense of their own interests.

There is much truth in Jeremy Bentham's hard-nosed comment:

> Every system of management which has disinterestedness, pretended or real, for its foundation, is rotten at the root, susceptible of a momentary prosperity at the outset, but sure to perish at the long run. That principle of action is most to be depended upon whose influence is most powerful, most con-

95. Albert O. Hirschman, *The Passions and the Interests: Political Arguments for Capitalism Before Its Triumph* (Princeton: Princeton University Press, 1977), 30ff.

stant, most uniform, most lasting and most general among mankind. Personal interest is that principle: a system of economy built on any other foundation is built upon a quicksand.[96]

As Bentham says, we cannot rely on disinterest or a sense of duty alone. Self-interest must play a part in any economy of incentives.

But self-interest takes different forms, some of which are more acceptable than others. Most obvious, and perhaps most fundamental, is the difference between short-run and long-run interests. When individuals and groups look beyond the short run, they must take account of a *range* of consequences, including their own needs for trust and cooperation. Hence concern for the long run often leads to moral improvement—a matter we considered in Chapter 12. Short-run thinking suggests a narrow rationality focused on definite and measurable gains. Long-run thinking, which imports more uncertainty, is better attuned to the requirements of reason.

We often distinguish, at least implicitly, between narrow and diffuse self-interest. The former is highly selective or single-minded. Some *particular* gain, such as reelection to office, a wage increase, or a profit margin, becomes the sole criterion of decision. This constricted vision is morally objectionable because it allows no room for the accommodation of interests. When we reject this single-mindedness, however, we do not necessarily repudiate a more comprehensive, more open-textured concern for the special interests of business or labor, teachers or students. We conceive those interests as fluid, complex, and open to reconstruction, not rigidly defined or narrowly construed. Self-interest, thus understood, is less likely to be the enemy of morality.

In a famous chapter of *Democracy in America,* Tocqueville tried to show "how the Americans combat individualism by the principle of self-interest rightly understood."[97] Self-interest, they hold, is an irresistible force, which cannot be overcome but can be directed:

> They therefore do not deny that every man may follow his own interest, but they endeavor to prove that it is the interest of every man to be virtuous. . . . The principle of self-interest rightly understood produces no great acts of self-sacrifice, but it suggests daily small acts of self-denial. By itself it cannot suffice to make a man virtuous; but it disciplines a number of persons in habits of regularity, temperance, moderation, foresight, self-command; and if it

96. "Tracts on Poor Laws and Pauper Management," in *The Works of Jeremy Bentham,* ed. John Bowing (1797; reprint, New York: Russell & Russell, 1962), 8:381. I am indebted for this reference to H. L. A. Hart, in Bhikhur Parekh, ed., *Jeremy Bentham: Ten Critical Essays* (London: Frank Cass, 1974).

97. Tocqueville, *Democracy in America,* 2:121.

does not lead men straight to virtue by the will, it gradually draws them in that direction by their habits. If the principle of interest rightly understood were to sway the whole moral world, extraordinary virtues would doubtless be more rare; but I think that gross depravity would then also be less common.[98]

In this view, self-interest is moderated by the practical requirements of work and cooperation. The virtues produced are virtues of self-discipline, not of nobility or self-sacrifice. They teach resistance to greed, dishonesty, and opportunism. They are, nevertheless, wholly compatible with profit-seeking and acquisitiveness.[99]

Tocqueville was tempted to idealize this emerging ethos. At least he gave it a friendly salute. He proffered the hope that American farmers and businessmen would show the world how to create a *decent* society, dull perhaps, perhaps lacking in grandeur, yet well adapted "to the wants of men of our time."[100] But he was wrong to suggest that self-interest "rightly understood" could be effective in combating individualism, that is, in curing the evils of raw or amoral self-interest.

The "bourgeois virtues" of thrift and fair dealing are real enough. When lost or attenuated, as in an era of fraud and manipulation, the moral order suffers. But those virtues do not insure that collective goods will be protected or achieved. The individualist logic of a market economy is not overcome by entrepreneurial probity, for the proximate interests of the enterprise must be paramount, and from a strictly economic point of view social responsibility is a luxury. Business leaders think they have a *duty*, in the interests of minimizing costs, to resist taxes. For the same reason, they often shortchange employees in matters of health and safety or pension benefits; and they avoid responsibility for social effects, such as pollution or waste of public resources.

The American founders tried to combine self-interest and civic virtue. They did not presume, however, "that man serves himself in serving his fellow creatures and that his private interest is to do good."[101] Without denying that possibility, they knew a commonwealth could not rely on it. Instead they sought a structural solution for the problem of "faction," which James Madison defined as "a number of citizens, whether

---

98. Ibid., 122f.
99. On the importance, in understanding Madisonian theory, of distinguishing between avarice and acquisitiveness, see Martin Diamond, "Ethics and Politics: The American Way," in Robert H. Horwitz, ed., *The Moral Foundations of the American Republic* (Charlottesville: University of Virginia Press, 1986), 99ff.
100. "Towards it, therefore, the minds of the moralists of our age should run; even should they judge it as incomplete, it must nevertheless be adopted as necessary" (Tocqueville, *Democracy in America*, 123).
101. Ibid., 121.

amounting to a majority or minority of the whole, who are united and actuated by some common impulse of passion, or of interest, adverse to the rights of other citizens, or to the permanent and aggregate interests of the community."[102] Although they intended to encourage the free play of interest, they recognized its potential for evil. In the new "extended republic" the variety of factions would counter each other. As a result, it would be "less probable that a majority of the whole will have a common motive to invade the rights of other citizens."[103] And the federal system would have the power to regulate private interests in the light of the common good.

In this Madisonian strategy, civic virtue is indispensable. Constitutional forms are not enough: "To suppose any form of government will secure liberty or happiness without any virtue in the people, is a chimerical idea."[104] People must be virtuous in accepting legislatively determined restraints; in being willing to pay taxes for collective goods; in selecting as representatives men of virtue and wisdom. Moreover, the system required civic virtue on the part of public officials, including judges and legislators. There could be no question, therefore, of depending solely on the benign effects of self-interested conduct.

Nevertheless, the main thrust of the Madisonian strategy is that power should check power, not only in government but in society as a whole. This principle remains a fundamental safeguard of liberty and security. It is no help, however, against the evil of a fragmented polity incapable of meeting its most urgent problems. Prescient as they were, neither Madison nor Tocqueville could foresee the need for strong institutions— within government, beyond legislative deliberation; outside it, beyond "special interests"—committed to defining and furthering the common good. Because of this weakness, and despite good intentions, Madisonian pluralism is in continuing tension with the covenant of reason.

Individual Interests and the Common Good

Even when we bring objective judgment to bear in assessing the claims of preference, conscience, and self-interest, we may still have difficulty accepting the idea of a *common* good. The same realism that moved Bentham to insist on the primacy of self-interest led him to say:

102. James Madison, in Alexander Hamilton, James Madison, and John Jay, *The Federalist* (1787; reprint, New York: Bantam Books, 1982), no. 10, 43.

103. Ibid., 48.

104. Madison, quoted in John P. Diggins, *The Lost Soul of American Politics: Virtue, Self-Interest, and the Foundations of Liberalism* (Chicago: University of Chicago Press, 1984), 68.

The community is a fictitious *body,* composed of the individual persons who
are considered as constituting as it were its *members.* The interest of the community is, what?—the sum of the interests of the several members who com-
pose it. It is in vain to talk of the interest of the community without understanding what is the interest of the individual.[105]

Here interests are taken to be objectively determined by a calculus
of pleasures and pains, but the locus of value is the individual. What
is good for the community cannot be determined apart from what is
good for the only units of society that have ontological reality. Without
that anchor, according to Bentham, social policy can be neither realistic
nor moral.

We may well agree that groups are composed of individual persons
and that the well-being of persons is the final criterion of morality and
utility. This does not, however, settle what constitutes well-being or
what it depends on. Personal well-being requires moral competence,
which includes loyalty, trust, and other group-centered virtues, and it
depends on group participation, nurture, and support. Therefore, from
the standpoint of the individual the community is hardly "a fictitious
body." Both the opportunities it offers and the constraints it imposes
have a vivid reality.[106]

Because personal well-being *is* the touchstone, the common good
tends to be identified with, as Bentham put it, "the sum of the interests
of the several members." This requires a criterion, such as purchasing
power or access to services, that can be summed or aggregated and
whose distribution can be studied. That measure then becomes a surrogate for happiness or well-being. Sometimes the common good is identified with a pattern of distribution; or the individual may be lost in a
measure of the common good that considers only total consumption or
income, without regard to how it is distributed. Either way, something
can be said about the nature of the system. We can know how much aggregate wealth there is, and how much is available for investment, and,
when distribution is considered, how much inequality exists.[107] Nevertheless, the focus is on *individuated* satisfactions, benefits, or rights.

105. Jeremy Bentham, *An Introduction to the Principles of Morals and Legislation* (1823;
reprint, Oxford: Blackwell, 1948), 126f.
106. All roles, relationships, practices, and institutions and all group characteristics
must ultimately be manifested in the activities and attributes of individuals. It does not
follow, however, that a system of roles is imaginary, that morale ceases to be a group attribute, or that "competitive strength" as an economic measure is a meaningless abstraction.
107. Among economists, the common good is often equated with allocative "efficiency" or "optimality," which is achieved when no one can be made better off without
making anyone worse off. This criterion may be objective, based on some theory of what

The alternative is to think of the common good as more profoundly systemic, not *reducible* to individual interests or attributes, yet *testable* by its contribution to personal well-being. The common good is served, for example, by institutions that provide collective goods, such as education or public safety. The strength or weakness of these institutions is a communal attribute, not an individual one. Furthermore, it is not necessarily in every individual's interest to support such institutions. They may be better off, as individuals, if they can avoid paying taxes for schools or other services they do not use but which are important for society as a whole.

Similarly, a major collective good is social integration. The appropriate level of integration varies according to context. Every unit of society requires a different formula for balancing freedom, order, and purpose. In arriving at such a formula, the well-being of individual persons need not be forgotten. When social integration is measured—for example, by some index of morale, such as a rate of absenteeism—the measure will take into account, at least indirectly, individual attitudes, behaviors, opportunities, and affiliations. And a *connection* is likely between personal and social integration. People can live more coherent lives and have more coherent personalities when they belong to coherent social worlds. But the common good is a state of the system, not an attribute of individuals.

▼   ▲   ▼   ▲   ▼

Collective goods are not necessarily more elusive or more controversial than individual goods. Much depends on whether we focus on *survival* or on *flourishing*. Whether we speak of individuals or groups, we can be surer of baseline needs than of higher aspirations or elaborated states. We know people should not be hungry and that children must be cared for. We may even be able to say how much and what kind of food is good for basic health. Similarly, we know communities should have safe streets and at least a modest level of prosperity. But when we can take survival-goods for granted and turn to the appraisal of personal life-styles or the community's choice of peace or war, conservation or

---

makes for desirable satisfactions, but it is more likely to be subjective: "Whatever else we mean by better or efficient, we certainly mean the following: one situation, one system, or one allocation is better than another if every individual feels it is better according to his own individual values" (Kenneth J. Arrow, *The Limits of Organization* [New York: W. W. Norton, 1974], 19).

growth, the criteria become apparently less objective and more open to debate. On that score, however, there is no distinction between individuals and collectivities.

It is tempting to limit the covenant of reason to the conditions of survival or of minimal well-being. The community would be neutral—would not apply "the method of intelligence"—where flourishing is at issue. We would leave such decisions to individual or group choice and to bargaining or voting, within a framework of general rules and protected rights. Such a perspective would vindicate Tocqueville's theory that democracy is good for avoiding misery and promoting comfort—but not for achieving noble objectives or a cultivated spirit.

This book has offered a different interpretation.

Name Index

Abernathy, William J., 354n
Ackerman, Bruce, 382
Ackrill, J. L., 149n
Acton, Lord John, 120
Adorno, T. W., 180n
Albert, Michel, 352n
Albrow, Martin, 273n
Arendt, Hannah, 11n, 138, 176–78, 411–12
Aristotle, 24, 38n, 326n, 368–69, 430n; on *eudaimonia,* 149; on prudence, 59–61, 209, 320n
Arrow, Kenneth, 537n
Atiyah, P. S., 462n
Austin, John, 50, 436n, 437n, 443

Bacon, Francis, 54
Bane, Mary Jo, 515n
Banfield, E. C., 338n
Barber, Benjamin R., 523–24
Bardach, Eugene, 352n, 470
Barnard, Chester I., 261, 277n, 287, 326n
Barnes, Barry, 105n
Barrett, William, 155n
Barry, Brian, 432n
Bayley, David H., 514n
Becker, Howard S., 129n
Bell, Daniel, 9n, 13n, 135n
Bellah, Robert, 238n, 425n
Bendix, Reinhard, 271n
Benedict, Ruth, 92, 112–13
Bennis, Warren G., 287n
Bentham, Jeremy, 50, 52–53, 436n, 444n; Marx's critique of, 135; on self-interest, 518, 532–33, 536

Bentley, Arthur F., 519n
Berger, Peter L., 517n
Berle, Adolph A., Jr., 246n, 346n
Berlin, Isaiah, 91n, 113n, 491n
Bernstein, Richard, 25n, 116n
Bettelheim, Bruno, 211n
Bidney, David, 93–94
Billias, George A., 450n
Bismarck, Prince Otto von, 511n
Black, Antony, 366n, 508n
Black, Justice Hugo L., 303n, 420
Blackmun, Justice Harry A., 298, 405
Blackstone, William, 449–50
Bloor, David, 105n
Blum, Lawrence A., 199n, 205n
Blumberg, Paul, 311n, 315n
Blumer, Herbert, 79n
Boas, Franz, 92, 100
Boisvert, Raymond, 25n, 31n
Bottomore, Tom, 271n, 499n
Brennan, Justice William, 293n, 529n
Brodbeck, May, 243n
Brooke, Christopher, 107n
Broom, Leonard, 190n, 232n, 267n
Brown, W. Adams, 478n
Buber, Martin, 70n, 71–72
Buchanan, Allen E., 434n
Burger, Chief Justice Warren E., 404–5
Burke, Edmund, 40–41, 57, 395
Burrow, J. W., 502n

Calabresi, Guido, 448n
Campbell, James, 31n
Cappelletti, Mauro, 455n

539

Subject Index

Philip Selznick is Professor Emeritus of Law and Sociology in the School of Law and the Department of Sociology at the University of California, Berkeley. He was the founding chair of the Center for the Study of Law and Society and of the Jurisprudence and Social Policy Program in the School of Law. His other books include *T.V.A. and the Grass Roots, Leadership in Administration; Law, Society, and Industrial Justice;* and, with P. Nonet, *Law and Society in Transition: Toward Responsive Law.*

Compositor: BookMasters, Inc.
Text: 10/13 Bembo
Display: Bembo
Printer and Binder: Maple-Vail Book Mfg. Group